Routledge Revivals

Santería Enthroned

Ever since its emergence in colonial-era Cuba, Afro-Cuban Santería (or Lucumí) has displayed a complex dynamic of continuity and change in its institutions, rituals, and iconography. Originally published in 2003 *Santería Enthroned* combines art, history, cultural anthropology, and ethnohistory to show how Africans and their descendants have developed novel forms of religious practice in the face of relentless oppression. Focusing on the royal throne as a potent metaphor in Santería belief and practice it shows how negotiations among ideologically competing interests have shaped the religion's symbols, rituals, and institutions from the nineteenth century to the present. Rich case studies of change in Cuba and the United States, including a New Jersey temple and South Carolina's Oyotunji Village, reveal patterns of innovation similar to those found among rival Yoruba kingdoms in Nigeria. Throughout, the book argues for a theoretical perspective on culture as a field of potential strategies and "usuable pasts" that actors draw upon to craft new forms and identities – a perspective that will be invaluable to all students of the African Diaspora.

Santería Enthroned

Art, Ritual, and Innovation in an Afro-Cuban Religion

By David H. Brown

Routledge
Taylor & Francis Group

First published in 2003
by The University of Chicago Press

This edition first published in 2019 by Routledge
2 Park Square, Milton Park, Abingdon, Oxon, OX14 4RN
and by Routledge
711 Third Avenue, New York, NY 10017

Routledge is an imprint of the Taylor & Francis Group, an informa business

Publisher's Note
The publisher has gone to great lengths to ensure the quality of this reprint but points out that some imperfections in the original copies may be apparent.

Disclaimer
The publisher has made every effort to trace copyright holders and welcomes correspondence from those they have been unable to contact.

A Library of Congress record exists under LCCN: 2002073564

ISBN 13: 978-0-367-32175-8 (hbk)
ISBN 13: 978-0-367-33219-8 (pbk)
ISBN 13: 978-0-429-31856-6 (ebk)

SANTERÍA ENTHRONED

SANTERÍA ENTHRONED

Art, Ritual, and Innovation in an Afro-Cuban Religion

DAVID H. BROWN

THE UNIVERSITY OF CHICAGO PRESS • CHICAGO AND LONDON

The University of Chicago Press, Chicago 60637
The University of Chicago Press, Ltd., London

Printed in the United States of America

12 11 10 09 08 07 2 3 4 5
ISBN: 0-226-07609-1 (cloth)
ISBN: 0-226-07610-5 (paper)

Library of Congress Cataloging-in-Publication Data
Brown, David H., Ph.D.
Santería enthroned : art, ritual, and innovation in an Afro-Cuban religion / David H. Brown.
p. cm.
Includes bibliographical references and index.
ISBN 0-226-07609-1 (alk. paper)—ISBN 0-226-07610-5 (pbk. : alk. paper)
1. Santeria—History. 2. Art and religion—Cuba—History. 3. Art and religion—United States—History. 4. Kings and rulers—Religious aspects—Santeria—History of doctrines. 5. Kings and rulers in art. I. Title.

BL2532.S3 B76 2003
299'.674—dc21

2002073564

This book is printed on acid-free paper.

To Morris, Sylvia, and Alan Brown,

and to

Melba Carillo, Theophus Smith, and Mestre João Oliveira dos Santos

The head carries the body, and only one king governs a town.

The king does not lie.

No king can be made a subject.

A king dies, a prince is crowned.

In the town of the blind, the one-eyed is king.

The wind said, "I'm unable to kill the king, but I can surely make his hat fly off."

When the wind blows, the mighty fall and the small are made great.

In the dark all cats are mulatto.

EIGHT PROVERBS FROM LUCUMÍ DIVINATION SIGNS

CONTENTS

ILLUSTRATIONS

Figures

Plates (*following page 244*)

PREFACE

This book emerges from an abiding interest in three topics, which sort out for me geographically widespread, multifaceted African Diaspora social and cultural expressions: the transformative power of ritual performance, the visual creativity of altar making and religious pageantry, and the brilliant innovations in religious practice and theology that Africans and their descendants have worked out in novel and harsh New World settings. Stepping back and considering those topics from a disciplinary perspective, I can rephrase this in terms of at least three fields I bring to "African Diaspora studies": American studies, anthropology and folklore, and art history. Each of those three fields is, of course, inter- or multidisciplinary in itself.

Graduate work in American studies provided me with the first space to contemplate the "newness" of the New World, its expanse of possibilities, and the struggles waged upon its soil. If the soil was not exactly new, "edenic" (Lewis 1955), "virgin land" (Smith 1950) to its original inhabitants, the cultural encounters it witnessed were "new," as were the harsh experiences of Native Americans and the Africans who arrived (see Mintz 1974a).[1] Upon my own first encounter with the creole cultures of the Caribbean and South America, as well as their presences in U.S. cities (i.e., the "Fourth World"), I could not but agree with Sidney Mintz that the "American" in American studies would have to be revised to include "the Americas"—indeed, to encompass huge regions of the Western Hemisphere (Mintz 1974a, 1). Native Americans were made foreigners in their own lands and were required to reconstruct themselves and their traditions, as the newest arrivals in this New World have been—including the eastern European immigrants who were my grandparents. The experience of African-Americans—defined as people of African biological and cultural descent in the Americas[2]—is both similar to and different from "immigrant" histories, as their ancestors were, in large part, forcibly brought as slaves. It is problematic to consider the history of the New World and, indeed, modernity, without considering the origins, history, and effects of the Atlantic slave trade, as well as the widespread influence of African-derived cultures. The historical, geographic, cultural, and political proportions of this point were first brought home to me in graduate seminars with David Brion Davis in 1982 and 1983 and in Robert Farris Thompson's courses on the Black Atlantic tradition (see also Mintz 1974a, chap. 1; Mintz and Price [1976] 1992, chap. 2) and were reinforced by later readings of Paul Gilroy's *Black Atlantic* (1993) and Peter Linebaugh and Marcus Rediker's *Many-Headed Hydra* (2000).

For centuries, people who have considered themselves Americans have been made almost foreigners and novices in parts of "their own" cities and cultural spaces (including the airwaves), as Henry James felt in his *American Scene* (1907), Robert Farris Thompson happily discovered in the 1950s at New York's mambo palace, the Palladium, and "Anglos" in Miami have lamented since at least the 1960s. As a fifteen-year-old in a New Jersey suburb in

1972, I had to revise everything I thought I knew about music and life when Muddy Waters's and B. B. King's blues belied the originality of rock 'n' roll and revealed the apartheid of the airwaves, which had filled my head since I got my first AM radio at age five. As a late baby boomer, a child of post–World War II mass culture, I was at least fortunate enough to have found Leroi Jones's *Blues People* (1963) in high school. Through the music—Muddy Waters, of course, and then Duke Ellington, Oscar Peterson, Charlie Parker, and Dizzy Gillespie, Miles Davis, John Coltrane, Sun Ra, Charles Mingus, the Art Ensemble of Chicago, and Anthony Braxton—I was led to American studies, where I originally wanted to research the social history of jazz. I belonged to the generations of American studies graduate students that had followed upon the "myth and symbol" investigations of nineteenth-century elite American texts and created an increasingly interdisciplinary field encompassing more and more areas of diverse American cultural experience. American studies, by the end of the 1960s "widen[ed] its boundaries to include black studies, popular culture studies, folklore studies, women's studies, ecology studies, film studies, material culture studies, ethnic studies, youth studies, Third World studies," and others (Wise 1979, 313; and see Lipsitz 1990). Thus, I researched black Southern folk thought in David Brion Davis's "American Intellectual History" seminar and was fascinated by Jean Christophe Agnew's innovative approaches to modern American cultural history—in which the ethnic, the popular, the commercial, the foreign, the gendered, the working-class, the black, and the altogether new proliferated and blended in the urban setting.

It was in the work of Robert Farris Thompson and John Szwed at Yale that I found a model that would connect my emerging American studies interests with the wider transatlantic African Diaspora world. Szwed and Thompson were members of a generation of American scholars who, in the wake of the Civil Rights movement, reclaimed the pioneering work of Melville Herskovits, which emphasized the resilience, tenaciousness, and diversity of black cultures. [3] They had researched and were encouraging young scholars to further investigate in the Caribbean and Latin America. Thompson offered a chart of the artistic and philosophical current from West Africa to the black Americas (Thompson 1983) and Szwed the theoretical and bibliographic means to approach the politicized question of creole cultures in the Caribbean via the fields of folklore and anthropology (see Szwed 1969; and Szwed and Abrahams 1978). But it was Barbara Kirshenblatt-Gimblett's call to folklorists in "The Future of Folklore Studies in America: The Urban Frontier" (1983), a title that would have pleased the founders of American studies, that provided me with the direction and questions I sought to develop. Kirshenblatt emphasized social heterogeneity, groups in conflict over urban "maps," innovation in response to a city's particular features, and "traditionalizing," as opposed to received notions of little enclaves of "traditions brought from elsewhere," which were doomed to homogenization with urban depersonalization (Kirshenblatt-Gimblett 1983, 181–82; see Brown 1999, 155–56).

My direction became clear with my first urban "fieldwork" forays into the Cubanized towns of New Jersey on the Hudson River, such as Union City and West New York. The Cuban influx there, and the building of bustling northeastern "Little Havanas" had paralleled in time, but were excluded from, my world in a sheltered New Jersey suburb no more than thirty minutes away. In the dislocations and revelations of this moment, I might say I tasted something of the postmodern texture of late-twentieth-century urban experience, in relation to which anthropology has had to put behind its enabling fiction of "remote areas" (Ardener 1987; see also Hymes 1969; Szwed and Whitten 1970) and wrap its mind around transnationalism, deterritorialization, and cultural hybridity (see Clifford 1988, 1994). It was Thompson who first suggested to me that I needed to travel neither to West Africa nor to the Caribbean to encounter African culture. And so it was: in Union City and West

New York I first documented Yoruba iconography in *botánicas* in November 1983. I had documented my first Santería *tambor de fundamento* (sacred drumming) in Elizabeth, New Jersey, the previous April at the invitation of master drummer Luis Bauzó, a Puerto Rican living in Brooklyn. He had learned the Afro-Cuban Lucumí tradition in New York City, in good measure from recordings. He had become the *olubatá* (master) of an important set of sacred drums constructed by the *babalawos* (diviners) of Templo Bonifacio Valdez, an institution dedicated to the practice of Ifá and Santería in Elizabeth, New Jersey. The connections gained there, among Cubans, Puerto Ricans, and African-Americans from the metropolitan area, expanded my work into Manhattan, the Bronx, Brooklyn, and Queens, as I was invited into their homes. Those connections eventually also led me to Havana (1986–2003) to document the family and religious background of several of the temple's members, to explore the various Afro-Cuban religions on the soil of their birth, and to begin the genealogical and ethnohistorical work that will be the basis of another book on the Ifá tradition in Cuba and the United States from 1830 to the present.

ACKNOWLEDGMENTS

Un solo palo no hace monte.
[One stick does not a forest make.]
—Afro-Cuban proverb

I have received invaluable moral and material support from numerous individuals and institutions during the researching and writing of this book, for which I am extremely grateful. A predoctoral grant from the Wenner Gren Foundation for Anthropological Research (1987) supported fieldwork in New Jersey, New York, and Miami. A Charlotte Newcombe Fellowship (Woodrow Wilson Fellowship Foundation) funded my dissertation writing (1997–98) and significant parts of the Ph.D. work appear, in revised form, in this book. A Smithsonian postdoctoral fellowship at the Center for Folklife Studies (1989) permitted theoretical refinements that contributed to the book manuscript. University Research Committee grants from Emory University (fall and summer 1992) provided me with course reductions to begin writing the book manuscript. I am very grateful to the American Council of Learned Societies (ACLS) for a postdoctoral fellowship to complete the first draft of the manuscript (1994–95). As the Rutgers Center for Historical Analysis Black Atlantic Project Senior Fellow for 1997–98, I was able to further develop theoretical and historical perspectives on the Black Atlantic. Finally, I am grateful to the W. E. B. Du Bois Institute for Afro-American Research of Harvard University for encouraging my continued investigation by having me as a nonresident fellow (1998–2003).

Special gratitude goes out to Dr. Francis and Mrs. Patricia Keneally for their generous subvention to support the publication of the color photographs.

I am grateful to my dissertation readers, Jean Christophe Agnew and John Szwed, and to my dissertation adviser, Robert Farris Thompson, who introduced me to the Black Atlantic world in his lectures and seminars at Yale University (1983–86). My research on Afro-Cuban religions had its genesis in Professor Thompson's spring 1983 graduate seminar entitled "Face of the Gods: Shrines and Altars of the Yoruba."

I remain indebted to many colleagues, friends, students, and assistants who responded generously with their feedback, resources, and moral support. I would like to thank (in alphabetical order) Roland Abiọdun, Michael Afolayan Oladejo, Andrew Apter, Brian Austin, Jacquelline Barnitz, Marc Bauerlein, Edna Bay, Julio Benítez, Jr., Herman Bennett, Ellie Berkowitz, Judith Bettelheim, George Brandon, Karen McCarthy Brown, Barbara Browning, Olivia Cadaval, Stefania Capone, Isabel Castellanos, Tom Concordia, Donald Cosentino, Pedro Cosme Baños, Joanne Crudgington, Clodimir da Silva, C. Daniel Dawson, Antonio de Armas, Gustavo de Armas, Lauren Derby, David Dorris, Henry Drewal, Christopher Dunn, Angela Economy, Brent Hayes Edwards, Robin Evanchuck, Arlys Evans, Antonio Eligio "Tonel" Fernández, Elizabeth Fenn, Ariel Fernández, Pilar Fernández, Ruddy Fernández, Ysamur Flores-Peña, Jacqueline Francis, Pamela Franco, Lisa Freiman, Phyllis Galembo, Henry Louis Gates, Jr., Judith Gleason, Salvador González Escalona, Marc Gottleib, Kenneth Haltman, Linda Henderson, E. Jane de Hohenstein, John Homiak, Marylin Houlberg, John Howett, Jean Howson, Alice Jarrard, Sidney Kasfir, Naomi Katz, Elliot Klein, Franklin Knight, Rebekka Kuntschik, Babatunde Lawal,

Cynthia Liesenfeld, Julie Levin Caro, María Teresa Linares, Natacha Lourdes López Grant, Rafael L. López Valdés, Tom Lyman, Ibrahim Mallerí, Kristin Mann, Morton Marks, Elizabeth Marzloff, James Lorand Matory, Elizabeth McAlister, Sara McPhee, James Meyer, Claudia Mola Fernández, Robin Moore, Beatriz Morales, Concepción Morales, Gerardo Mosquera, Joseph Murphy, Babatunde Nasiru, Ester Nicle, Robert Orsi, Luis Alberto Pedroso, Balentino Pérez, Clark Poling, Richard Powell, Richard Price, Jane Rehl, Elisha Renne, Natalia Revuelta Fernández, Cabelo Rolim, Norge Romero Cordiés, Zaidé Romero Cordiés, Lisa María Salb, Hédimo Santana, Michael P. Smith, Theophus Smith, Debra Spitulnik, Nicolas Spitzer, Jessica Taplin, Krista Thompson, Terri-Dawn Trosclair, Carmen Trujillo Pardo, Nong Tumsutipong, John Vlach, Derrick Williams, Jim Wafer, Patsy White, Katya Wilson, and Peter Wood.

I am grateful to the following people for their support in the preparation of the manuscript and illustrations and the production of this book: T. David Brent, Elizabeth Branch Dyson, Amy Collins, Perry Cartwright, Jennifer Gowins, Mike Brehm, Erik Carlson, Catherine Beebe, and Monica Holliday at the University of Chicago Press; Katherine Hagedorn and Grisel Lozano Garcini for their editorial and proofreading assistance; Isabel Castellanos, Executor of the Estate of Lydia Cabrera; and María Fernanda Ortiz Herrera, Representative of the Successors of Fernando Ortiz.

I would like to thank the following Cuban institutions: El Museo Polivalente de Regla, La Casa de África, El Museo de la Música, El Conjunto Folklórico Nacional de Cuba, El Grupo Afro-Cuba de Matanzas, El Museo Etnográfico de Guanabacoa, La Biblioteca Nacional, El Museo Nacional de Bellas Artes, La Parroquia de Regla, La Parróquia de Guanabacoa, El Cementerio de Regla, El Cementerio de Colón, Juego Eforitongó, Los Hijos de San Lázaro, La Comisión Organizadora de la Letra del Año, La Sociedad El Cristo, La Sociedad San Roque, La Sociedad Santa Bárbara, La Sociedad de San Antonio, El Cabildo Arará Sabalú Nonjó, El Cabildo de Santa Teresa, and El Cabildo de Fermina Gómez.

Still, neither my research nor writing could have been accomplished without the coauthors of this work, my most patient teachers and families of the Regla de Ocha, Ifá, Arará, Abakuá, and Palo: Perico Abasonga, Pedro Abreu, Roberto Almeida, María Eugenia Álvarez Pérez, Concha Angulo, Graciela Arandia, Francisco Aristola, Juan Arrencivia, Emilio Barreto, Luis Bauzó, Reinaldo Blayó (Ibae), Francisco "Lalo" Cabrera, Frank Cabrera Suarez, Olga Calvo Püig, Elpidio Cárdenas, Idalberto Cárdenas, Osvaldo Cárdenas Villamil, Melba Carillo, Luis Castillo, "Papo" Reinaldo Raimundo Chaguayceda, Rosario Chinique, Nelson and Pedro Collazo, Mercedes Cordiés, Radamés Corona, Candelaria Cruz, Lázaro Cuesta Valdés, Jorge Díaz, Alejandro Domínguez, Mercedes Durán, Manuel Erize, Ramón Esquivel Bolaños (Ibae), Eusebia Febles, Juanito Febles, Adolfo Fernández (Ibae), Raquel Fernández, Juan Gallo, Josefina García, Zoraida García, Eddy Guilarte, Cosme Guio (Ibae), Juan Gutiérrez Boza (Ibae), Ramiro Hernández Almirall (Ibae), Gilberto Herrera Rojas, Zenaida Justíz, Andrés Kolá, Lourdes López, Franky Malabé (Ibae), Lázaro Marqueti, Raymond Mazzero, Mercedes Melo González, Inocencia Mola, Fernando Zacaría Molina Puente (Ibae), William Muldro (Sim-El Fatunmishe), Ricardo Navarro, Nena's Botánica, Anna Ortiz, Salvador Ortiz, Jr., Ángel Padrón, Pedro Emilio Pérez Martín, Fernando Pichardo, Nydia Pichardo, Carmen Plá, Gualberta Püig, José Manuel Pulido, Librada Quesada Mazorra (Ibae), Miguel "Willie" Ramos, Rosamaría Roberts, Oscar Rodríguez, Pete Rodríguez (Ibae), Sandra Rodríguez, Gloria Rolando, Fredesvinda Rosell, Lázaro Ros, Antonio Sevilla, Chiqui Sevilla, Pablo Sevilla, María Sirgelina Martínez, Ernesto Valdés Janet, Hermes Valera Ramírez, Jesús Varona Puente, Margarita Ugarte (Ibae), Francisco Veitia, Ana Vidal, Roberto Villanueva, the Villalonga family, Alberto Villarreal, and Francisco "Minini" Zamora Chirino.

I am especially grateful to Michael Atwood Mason, Katherine Hagedorn, Stephan Palmié, Ernesto Pichardo, Andrew Apter, Judith Bettelheim, J. Lorand Matory, and Antonio Martín de Armas Arredondo, who remained steady and powerful interlocutors, critics, contributors of resources, and friends during the process of this work's research and writing.

INTRODUCTION

Interest groups coalesce, people teach, learn, innovate, and teach again, and culture becomes a concatenation of diverse efforts to construct it. Politicians, priests, and poets . . . do it differently. . . . Instead of commencing with a comprehensive concept [culture], we can move inductively, attentive to detail and disjunction, bit by bit working toward an unachievable completeness, learning how people, each of them individual, all of them social, use the resources within their command to create.
—Henry Glassie, "Tradition"

Poets can use what they haven't invented in order to invent what they want to invent.
—Kenneth Koch, "The Language of Poetry"

Big patterns are the yield of small acts.
—Henry Glassie, "Tradition"

In the early 1980s, I began exploring the *botánicas* of Hudson County, New Jersey, and the boroughs of New York for Yoruba religious iconography. The *botánica* is the principal retail outlet for Afro-Cuban religious images and ingredients. There were the thunder god's double ax and the iron god's deadly cutlass; here were the riverine goddesses' rounded fans, Orula's Ifá divination board, and Obatalá's flowing horsetail fly whisk. Over there were miniature *batá* drums, beads, and Babalú Ayé's healing broom. In abundance everywhere were masses of cowrie shells, fresh and dried sacred plants, and the indispensable ingredients of consecration: the four African "seeds" called *aché de santo*. Indeed, the very first *botánica* I visited in Union City, New Jersey, bore in its name the Yoruba-Atlantic keyword for spiritual power: *Papá Aché*, —"Daddy Aché." I woke up one morning in 1983 to an *I Love Lucy* episode featuring Desi Arnaz, a white Cuban musician from Oriente, chanting "Babalú-u-u-u!" as he beat his conga drum. I was trying hard to identify which iconography was "African" amid a welter of mass-produced objects and homemade assemblages including candles, flowers, oils, gourds, good-luck sprays, incense, little metal tools, cow horns, beaded baseball bats, dried flying bats, hunting traps, rococo soup tureens, rosaries, tourist machetes from Puerto Rico and maracas from Mexico, black plastic dolls in colorful skirts, iron cauldrons, conch shells, prayer cards, saint statues, Hawaiian hula skirts, neoclassical plaster columns, children's toys, cocoa butter, bows and arrows, cue balls, satin and lace dresses, burlap pants, leopard skins, horseshoes and railroad spikes, poster paints, bakers' caps, palm oil, buzzard feathers, and plants with names like *rompe zaragüey, siempre viva,* and *atinpolá*—from the Yoruba word *ètìpọn' ọlá*.[1] All together, in a single retail space, these eye-popping curiosities might resist identification and narratives of unity to the untrained eye, unless one were ethnocentric enough to consign them to the waste bin of urban kitsch. How should these objects be evaluated—as "very African," "a little

African," European—as in Herskovits's "Scale of the Intensity of New World Africanisms" ([1945] 1966, 53)?[2] Were they somehow the products of cultural "intermingling," "merging," "reblending," or "syncretism" (Herskovits 1941, 1958; see Baron 1994, 451–514); or would "creolization"—a concept I was beginning to grapple with in my readings of the Caribbean creolist literature of the 1970s and 1980s (e.g., Reisman 1970; Hymes 1971; Marks 1974; Abrahams 1983)—do better?

Subsequent visits to the "field" (1983–87), this time to the "house-temples" of New Jersey, New York, Miami, and Havana, brought me face-to-face, again and again, with what I was taught in Yale graduate seminars to read as *ojúbọ*—a Yoruba term for altar, which can also be translated as "face of the gods" or "face of worship" (Thompson 1983, 58; 1993; Drewal, Pemberton, and Abiodun 1989, 26). Still, in the face of this religion's voluptuous baroque splendor, it was difficult to be content with hard and fast analytical distinctions, such as "African" versus "non-African," which American scholars debated for nearly the whole of the twentieth century (e.g., Du Bois [1903] 1969; Herskovits [1925] 1992, 1941, 1966; Frazier 1934; Woodson [1936] 1968; Bascom 1950, 1952; Crowley 1956; Szwed 1969; Simpson 1978). In any case, the word *ojúbọ* never once fell from the lips of the Cuban and Puerto Rican priests I knew. Their *santos* (i.e., *orichas*) lived in porcelain soup tureens kept in *canastilleros*—multi-shelved cabinets surmounted by plaster saints, gilt candelabra, and spoked lamps modeled after the Holy Sacrament. Come festival time, the tureens, or *soperas*, received royal honors; they could be enthroned upon plaster Corinthian columns; draped with dazzling satin, lamé, chiffon, and lace, and presented with mounds of fruit and masses of flowers.

Clearly, I needed a more "local" set of terms. Just about every Sunday I found myself at a "Middle Day" celebration, in which initiates, gorgeously dressed in regal satin clothes and pasteboard crowns, appeared under grand canopied "thrones" (*tronos*) before "the people." These initiates, to whom visitors respectfully prostrated themselves, were introduced to me as new "kings," "queens," and "warriors." Royalty like this was nowhere to be found in the New Jersey suburb where I grew up, except if you read King Arthur, watched Ivanhoe on television, or fawned over Hyannisport's Camelot. Of course, you could find royalty of another order if you listened to the King, the Empress, the Duke, and the Count on old jazz LPs. Still, as I made my regular rounds through the 1980s, resplendent kings, queens, and warriors were everywhere being celebrated in the bedrooms, living rooms, and basements of Cuban and Puerto Rican New Jersey, New York, and Miami. "Thrones of the Orichas" was irresistible as the crowning figure for my writings that followed. *Canastillero* and *trono* became my *ojúbọ* (D. Brown 1989, chap. 7; 1993b).

One afternoon in early 1987, following a generous meal of *bistec* seasoned with *ajo, congrí, plátanos maduros, yuca con mojo, ensalada de aguacate,* and sweet, sweet *café cubano,* the New Jersey Yemayá priestess, sacred clothing designer, and popular singer Lourdes López set a conceptual challenge before me. With my naive comment that the style of her satin, puff-shouldered gowns for the female *orichas* looked "European," she was taken aback. López insisted that the designs were Cuban! Indeed, part of the gown was faithful to the specific *tradición* that her *madrina,* Hilda Herrera, had learned from her Ocha elders in Havana, who were members of the *rama Pimienta* (the "Pimienta" ritual lineage) of the feisty Aurora Lamar. The other part followed her *own* ideas. She was not European, so how could the gown be European? In fact, López herself had uttered neither "African" nor "European" in her prior explanations to me. So what was this self-conscious local blend of *tradición* and her *own* ideas? To her, it was not reducible to remote origins—Europe. And as such, it would resist the "violence" of trait diffusion analysis, of which Herskovits himself cautioned in 1945 ([1945] 1966, 54).

Still, other perspectives were added to the mix. The late Obatalá priest Ramón Esquivel Bolaños, who was born in Matanzas and studied interior design in Havana before his exodus from Cuba in 1980, was a partisan of European sources where the luxurious treatment of his *orichas* was concerned. One afternoon, he enthusiastically explained to me that, both in his altar making and home decor, he "favor[ed] Luis XV . . . in fact, all the Luises." By contrast, once again, Changó priest Ernesto Pichardo of Miami, a self-styled Yoruba purist, encouraged me to write a "scholar's corner" column for his Church of the Lukumí-Babalú Ayé's *Journal* (see Brown 1998). An authoritative article on the religion's arts, it would set the record straight to the *santeros* of Miami and the world: namely, that the *orichas'* thrones, fancy jackets, gowns, and crowns were "not the real thing at all, like it was in Africa."

In short, standing on divergent stylistic and iconographic grounds were a *mulata* clothing designer whose works were "Cuban," a *prieto* Cuban altar maker who believed his stylistic sources lay in the Bourbon Louis XV, and a *blanco* master of ceremonies, who wanted nothing but the West African "real thing." The nationalist Black American Yoruba movement, of course, had insisted upon this last point since the early 1960s, having purged their Cuban Lucumí-rooted religion of Catholic and colonial-era elements, preferring Yoruba cloth and statues to puff-shouldered gowns and plaster saints. There was not one approach to celebrating the gods; there were many.

THE LITERATURE ON AFRO-CUBAN LUCUMÍ RELIGION

The Afro-Cuban religion known variously as La Regla de Ocha, La Regla de Ifá, La Religión Lucumí, and La Santería ("The Religion") has been studied since the late nineteenth century in Cuba and the 1940s in the United States from diverse disciplinary perspectives and thematic bases. Its earliest scholarly study in Cuba's "republican era" (1902–59) was generated from within the fields of evolutionary anthropology, criminal ethnology, and legal medicine. Cuban scholars considered the troubling legacy of slavery and the African presence—seen as a veritable heart of darkness within the island's urban capitals—in relation to the shape and destiny of the modern Cuban nation. On the street, the police ferociously persecuted "atavistic" practices of African origin—Lucumí, Congo, Abakuá, Arará—from the mid-1870s until the mid 1920s (see Trujillo y Monagas 1882; Ortiz [1906] 1973; Castellanos 1916; Roche y Monteagudo 1908, [1908] 1925a; Helg 1995; Deschamps Chapeaux 1964; Chávez Álvarez 1991). Cuba's Afrocubanismo movement of noted writers and artists encouraged more benign and celebratory literary, folkloric, and artistic works on Afro-Cuban cultural themes from the 1920s through the 1950s. This impulse, as carried forward by Fernando Ortiz and his colleagues, students, followers, and critics has continued in earnest down thorough the present (see Carpentier [1933] 1979, [1946] 1984; Cabrera [1940] 1972, [1954] 1983, [1958] 1970; Lachatañeré 1938, 1942, 1961a, 1961b, 1961c; see also Blanc, Herzberg, and Sims 1992; and Kutzinski 1993). Ortiz's own work shifted over time from the invidious criminological approach he learned from Cesare Lombroso and Enrico Ferri to a more sympathetic, albeit still scientistic and now aestheticized, documentation of Afro-Cuban institutional history, festival, religious music, arts, and performance (e.g., Ortiz [1920] 1960, 1921, 1937a, 1937b, 1950, [1951] 1985, 1952–55; InterAmericas Society 1998, 81–181; Moore 1994; Mullen 1987). Cuban scholars since the "Triumph of the Revolution" (January 1959), led by Ortiz's students and followers, have continued to publish ethnographic, sociological, folkloric, literary, and ethnomusicological studies, as well as mount folkloric performances (Barnet 1961, [1966] 1980, 1983; León 1964, 1984; López Valdés 1985a, 1986, 1994; Martínez Furé 1979; González Huguet 1968; Gómez Abreu 1982; Bolívar Aróstegui 1990; Alén 1992).

The reigning approaches, following Ortiz, were the origin and history of Afro-Cuban practices and their "transculturation," which ostensibly celebrated Cuba's unique *mestizaje*, the mutual influence of diverse cultures in the formation of a wholesome Cuban national "stew" (*ajiaco*; see Mosquera 1996, 226). However, just as blood-based metaphors had crept into Herskovits's *cultural* diffusion studies of "retentions," "syncretisms," and "reinterpretations" in "New World Negro" groups (see Apter 1991), "transculturation" was, in good measure, a mildly transformed version of Cuban late-nineteenth-century racialized notions of sanitizing the nation of African atavisms and "uplifiting" Afro-Cubans on a hierarchical scale of civilization (see Fernández Carillo 1881; Ortiz 1906 [1973]; Martínez Furé 1979, 267; Mullen 1987; Hagedorn 2001, 173–74).[3]

Many Cuban ethnohistorians, fueled by the Revolution's official fight against "institutionalized racism," framed the predicament of African-derived cultures within the socialist lens of anti-imperialism and class struggle (see Hagedorn 2001, 138–41, 195; López Valdés 1985a). Correspondingly, others continued to emphasize the dissemination of Cuban national culture—which was seen as permeated with things Afro. Through scientific education, the sloughing off of superstition, and the public presentation of authentic "positive folklore" (e.g., Balea 1984; Martínez Furé 1979, 267), Cuba's identity as an "Afro-Latin" nation with inherent links to the African continent would strengthen under the 1970s policies of "Afrocastroism" (see Moore 1988, 139–322, especially 301–2).

Meanwhile, North American (and other) scholars approached the Afro-Cuban religions first from within Herskovits's notion of ethnohistory and cultural diffusion, particularly around the continuum of "African survivals" and New World "syncretisms" (Herskovits 1941, [1945] 1966). For example, his student William Bascom evaluated Santería ritual and Ifá divination for their African content (Bascom 1950, 1952) and would later, more broadly, define the Yoruba deity Ṣàngó as a phenomenon of transatlantic and pan-Afro-American diffusion (Bascom 1972; see also Simpson 1978; Courlander 1944). By the 1970s, following the Great Depression's intellectual emphasis on class and the post-World War II period's obsession with the "melting pot," the American academy became ripe for the disciplinary legitimization of positive and focused black culture study, spurred as it was by the Civil Rights and black cultural nationalist movements (see Szwed 1969).[4] Through the 1970s and early 1980s, Santería was becoming very visible in New York, Miami, and Puerto Rico. It was variously represented as a sign of ethnic diversity and as another heart of darkness smack in the middle of an otherwise wholesome American scene (Cicero 1980; Bearak and Jones 1978; "New York: Fifty-two 'sacrifice animals' are seized" 1983; and see García Cortéz 1971; Cintrón 1979). Though the great Machito, Mario Bauza, and Chano Pozo had voiced Afro-Cuban themes in their music from the 1930s to the 1950s, the 1970s New York *salsa* movement of a younger vanguard disseminated *lo afrocubano* and Santería to popular audiences as never before (see Marks 1974; Roberts [1979] 1985, 127–70; BMI 1976, 16–22).

Beginning in the mid 1970s, American and Cuban-American scholars produced a small avalanche of writings on Santería from within numerous fields: sociolinguistics (Castellanos 1977), ethnomusicology (Marks 1974; Friedman 1982; Castellanos 1983; Cornelius 1989; Hagedorn 1992, 2001), religious studies (Murphy 1981, 1988, 1994), anthropology (Dornbach 1977; Brandon 1983, 1990, 1993; Morales 1990), ethnohistory (Palmié 1991, 1993, 1995, 1996, 2002); ethnobotany (Marks 1987), neo-Marxist sociology (Gregory 1986), medical anthropology (Cros Sandoval 1979), urban fiction (Gleason 1975), Jungian psychoanalysis (Gleason 1987), social and immigrant psychology (Halifax and Weidman 1973), art history (Thompson 1983, 1993; Brown 1989, 1993b, 1996), and folklore and performance studies (M. Mason 1993, 1994, 2002; Flores-Peña and Evanchuck 1994). Lydia Cabrera, who left Cuba in 1960, continued publishing in exile (e.g., [1957] 1986, [1974] 1980, [1979] 1986, 1980). Puerto Rican investigators who encountered Santería on their island also published ethnographies (e.g., Sánchez 1978).

Added to the scholarly literature came a slew of uneven popular works (e.g., González Wippler 1982, 1989; Canizares 1993; Núñez 1992), a body of remarkable practitioner "manuals"—a genre that first emerged in Cuba and continued in the United States and Puerto Rico (Elizondo [1934?] n.d.; García Cortéz 1971, 1980; Rogers 1973; Canet 1973; Akoni 1975; Cortéz 1980; Ramos 1982a, 1982b, 1982c, 1982d; Ecún 1985, 1989; Castillo 1976)—and a rich quasi-academic literature in English by young priest-scholars, which has been directed to educating and advancing the Cuban-American and English-speaking practitioner communities (e.g., Pichardo 1989a, 1989b; Pichardo and Nieto 1984; J. Mason, 1985a, 1985b, 1992, 1994, 1996; Mason and Edwards 1981, Fatunmbi 1992).

The past twenty years have seen the legitimization of Afro-Cuban religion and culture in many public venues and forums, where funds were secured for multicultural programming in traditional museums (the New York Museum of Natural History and the National Museum of Natural History) and new kinds of cultural institutions (the Caribbean Cultural Center). Practitioners, scholars, and artists collaborated on exhibitions and conferences in which Santería arts and music were featured (e.g., Caribbean Cultural Center 1984; Boza 1986; López and Keiro 1987; see Moreno Vega 2000). Fine artists who became practitioners began to incorporate Santería and Yoruba images into a rich new mix of artistic expressions, inspired by multiculturalist debates on identity politics (e.g., Miralda and Mason 1985; Abramson and Rodríguez 1985; Lindsay 1992).[5] The year 1993 marked the protection of Santería by the "free exercise of religion" clause of the United States Constitution (see Palmié 1996; *Church of the Lukumi Babalu Aye, Inc. and Ernesto Pichardo, Petitioners, v. City of Hialeah,* 508 U.S. 520; 113 Sup. Ct. 2217).

In sum, early inscribed as a dark, contagious "infection" or "sore" on the Cuban body politic, as malign "witchcraft" (see Ortiz [1906] 1973, 20; 223; 230; Mullen 1987; Derby 1995), Santería eventually became an icon of Cuban national folk culture (see Hagedorn 2001). In the United States, Santería became a "mental healthcare system" for the shock of exile (Cros Sandoval 1979), a site of ideological struggle and antihegemonic praxis (Gregory 1986), a great crucible and repository of Black Atlantic artistic traditions (Thompson 1983, 1993; J. Mason 1994, 1996), and the protagonist and hero of a great constitutional battle over the "free exercise of religion" (*Church of the Lukumi Babalu Aye v. City of Hialeah;* Ellenberg 1987; Palmié [1988], [1990], 1996). With the debut recording of *A lo Cubano* (1999) by Cuba's hot new band, Orishas, Lucumí sound and motion have "recrossed" the Atlantic once again, and Santería has been reiterated as a potent marker in transnational Black Atlantic cultural currents (see Gilroy 1993). Orishas' initiated members live in Paris, their current DJ is an Algerian, and their work builds rap and scratch sounds over the internationally recognized Afro-Cuban *timba* and new *charanga* styles, which had voiced popular knowledge of Afro-Cuban religions (e.g., N. G. La Banda, Los Van Van, and David Calzado y La Charanga Habanera).[6]

APPROACHES TO AFRO-CUBAN CULTURE

In the preface to the 1992 reprinting of their pathbreaking 1976 essay *The Birth of African-American Culture,* Sidney Mintz and Richard Price honored me by quoting the opening paragraph of my 1989 doctoral dissertation as one example of the field's increasing "shift" to a focus on "*process* in the development of African-American cultures, of examining different kinds of blends and mixtures" (Mintz and Price [1976] 1992, x). More specifically, they were noting an apparent shift in the conceptual emphasis of what might be called the Thompson school of Black Atlantic studies, which, the writers imply, had formerly stressed pure African retentions but was now fully on board with an embrace of the idea of "'callaloo culture (a Caribbean culinary metaphor for mixture)" ([1976] 1992, x). " As they quoted me, "'The creative choices of self-conscious leaders and their dedicated constituencies have made possible the emergence, growth, and resilience of Afro-Cuban religions in Cuba and the United States despite relentless official efforts to coopt, control, and destroy them. The Afro-Cuban religions today owe their existence to a history of gains from hard-won struggles, not passive 'survivals,' where their resiliency is owed as much to innovative transformations wrought on New World soil as to the maintenance or preservation of "pure" African traditions.' *Mirabile dictu*" ([1976] 1992, x; the original is found in Brown 1989, 10). This passage still serves to encapsulate the thesis, at its most general, of the present work. However, it is worth qualifying the levels and kinds of processes I am taken to address, identifying the influences that have shaped this work, and clarifying some of the concepts I employ.

Clearly, Robert Farris Thompson's earliest scholarly treatments of Black Atlantic arts reveal a critical interest in the products *and* processes of "callaloo cultures." The clay "face vessels" of antebellum South Carolina blacks, for example, in Thompson's reading, resulted from the remarkable "blending of remembered ancestral and encountered alien modes." In this pioneering 1969 piece, "African Influence on the Art of the United States," he insisted that, because of the negotiation of African form and Western technique, "the phenomenon is more dynamic, historically, and consequently more interesting, as a subject for study than a mechanical carry-over" (Thompson [1969] 1983, 30–31, 41). Later, he would refer to such morphological and semantic negotiations as "creative[ly] reorganiz[ed]" and "creolized" forms (1983, 17–18). Thompson's use of traditional art historical methodology to document historical continuities with Africa were inarguably yoked to advocacy positions in the politicized debates within and without the academy as to the status of black Americans. Racists, skeptics, and rigid positivists continued to deny African continuities up through Thompson's 1969 article (Frazier 1934, 1939; Elkins [1959] 1963; see Szwed 1969 and Abrahams 1983). For Thompson, formalism, connoisseurship, and iconology could elicit new kinds of evidence within the discipline of art history and be marshaled to skirt narrow requirements for "documentary" proof of African historical connection (for formalism, see Podro 1982, 98–149; and Kubler 1962; for connoisseurship, see Offner 1950; for iconography and iconology, see Panofsky 1955; and Podro 1982, 178–208). In other words, formal and stylistic similarities could mark continuities that selective archives and positivist methodology might deny. A study of art—reinforced as well as possible at the time by reference to slave trade demographics—could "test" the "facile assumption of total disappearance of African custom in the United States" (Thompson [1969] 1983, 30). Thompson's 1969 article, which was patterned after the title, themes, and formalist approach of Richard Alan Waterman's important ethnomusicological piece, "African Influence on the Music of the Americas" (Waterman [1952] 1971), was integral to the revived struggle against the "myth of the Negro past" (see Herskovits 1941), which had lost steam until the Civil Rights and black consciousness era. It also emerged alongside debates in anthropology over how this field would have to be "reinvented" during a period of questioning the status quo, especially given anthropology's historical complicity in the colonial enterprise (see Hymes 1969) and the vestiges of racism and the denial of black cultural integrity in American social sciences (i.e., the "social pathology" school of black studies) since the 1930s (Szwed 1969). By the late 1950s, Herskovits's work had lost out to the social pathology school's fixation on the "Negro problem." Moreover, in the field of social anthropology, scholars had formulated positivist "standards for such research that virtually assured that no proof could be established" of African continuities (Szwed 1969, 167–68; M. G. Smith 1957).[7] Such documentary standards continued to be asserted through the mid-1970s. For example, Mintz and Price insisted that "comparative studies no longer can ignore the need to demonstrate historical connection (in the sense that historians and historically minded ethnologists would use the term)," though it must be said that these writers' intentions were not at all to deny continuity; on the contrary, they intended to encourage theoretical and historical subtlety in asking questions about the processes, levels, and specificity of such connections ([1976] 1992, 15).[8] Still, the insistence upon a new historicism in *An Anthropological Approach to the Afro-American Past* (Mintz and Price 1976) would remain a thorn in the side of Thompson's approach to the "Afro-

American past" for years (see Price and Price 1980; Karp and Arnoldi 1986). At the same time, it should be noted, the spirit of Thompson's works on African and Afro-Atlantic art forms were at one with the most important 1970s–1980s "slave community thesis" studies of strong and resilient African-derived black cultures, despite belated criticisms of these pioneer works by historians today.[9] These were inspired as much by Herskovits as by the powerful emphasis upon historical culture-study "from the bottom up" developed by historians of the working classes, ethnic groups, and women (e.g., E. P. Thompson 1964; Gutman 1976, 1977; see also Linebaugh and Rediker 2000). For post-1960s scholars of American slavery, Herskovits's work held out the idea of black cultural resilience and resistance through conservation and adaptation (e.g., Blassingame 1979; Levine 1977; Genovese 1976; Raboteau 1978; Thompson 1974, 1983; Thompson and Cornet 1981). Somewhat ironically, Sterling Stuckey's *Slave Culture: Nationalist Theory and the Foundations of Black America* (1987), which has empowered a new generation of positivist black historians (e.g., Gómez 1998, 1999), drew on core assumptions, data, and arguments of Thompson's 1983 *Flash of the Spirit.*[10]

If, in the estimation of Mintz and Price, my doctoral work represented a shift within the Thompson school to a more focused concern with "process" and "mixture," it is apparently because I attempted to ground my study of cultural forms (Lucumí ritual and iconography) in newly encountered New World and reconstituted African institutional formations (the *cabildos, sociedades,* and *casa-templos*), a central theoretical and methodological concern of their 1976 work (see Mintz and Price [1976] 1992, 14–22). I was interested as much in the "creolized" iconography and performances innovated within uniquely Cuban creole institutions, and island-wrought ethnic reformations, as in tracing Santería iconography directly to its West African "tribal origins." My use of the creole linguistic metaphor was intended to emphasize not merely, in the terms of Mintz and Price, the "cultural dimension" (the morphology and aesthetics of expression); it intended to address, to the greatest extent possible, given my training, the "'social' (or social-relational) dimension" as well. Creolization on the sociohistorical axis refers to the new "ways in which [forms] were used, by whom, and under what circumstances" (Mintz and Price [1976] 1992, 21). In other words, I tried to use the creole metaphor not merely as a buzzword for cultural "reblending" and "mingling," but, as Mintz and Price have put it, as a way to analyze the historical reconstitution and transformation of African-derived cultures in the Americas through the "creation" of new "social bonds" (Mintz and Price [1976] 1992, 43).

During the 1980s, I had worked with the critical distinction between the "social" and "cultural" dimensions of signifying practices in graduate seminars and teaching assistantships with Jean Christophe Agnew of Yale's American Studies Program, along with readings of M. G. Smith (1957) and Roger Bastide's *African Religions of Brazil,* which relied on "depth sociology," not Herskovits's "culturological" approach (Bastide [1960] 1978, xix–xxviii, 3, 13–18, 23, 109, 159; see also Palmié 1993). Regrettably, I was not introduced to Mintz and Price's seminal, but obscurely published, 1976 work until after I had completed my doctoral dissertation. With orientation from Joseph Murphy (1981) and George Brandon (1983), I drew from Bastide the hypothesis that Afro-Cuban religions had insinuated themselves into ("hid"), and then emerged from within, the multifarious "niches" or "new social frameworks" that Africans encountered and reworked in coastal urban settings, for example, the Brazilian and Cuban urban Catholic religious fraternities (*irmandades* and *cabildos,* respectively), and the calendrical festival cycle (see Brown 1989, 12–13, 35–64, 73–83, 103–13; Bastide [1960] 1978, 159–60, 58–77; 1972, 95).

Though much of this approach remains in the present work, I have elaborated my means of explanation through subsequent readings of Mintz and the Prices (Mintz 1974a; Mintz and Price [1976] 1992; Price and Price 1980), as well as through the works of, and formative discussions with, Stephan Palmié. In particular, I was influenced by his subtle and incisive revision of Mintz and Price's "rapid creolization" model and his application of the "ethnogenesis" concept to the urban Cuban case (see Palmié 1989, 1993; see my chaps. 1 and 2). Shrewdly applying the theses of Fredrik Barth, Mary Karasch, M. G. Smith, Mintz and Price, and others, Palmié showed that Afro-Cuban ethnic identities (the "nations") and their cultural practices were generated, redistilled, and "boundary marked"—in a word, *constructed*—through portable African and island-recreated "models of corporate aggregation." Afro-American "culture" was not superorganic, nor was it "autonomous" (in space and time, psychologically) as the thesis of a slave community had maintained (Rawick 1972; Blassingame 1979). Black cultures emerged and succeeded to the extent they could "manipulate" dominant institutions within the opportunities and constraints of specific local arenas. In other words, diverse Afro-American cultures were socially and historically articulated in very specific ways.[11]

Thus, a number of gestures I make in chapters 1, 2, and 3 are significantly indebted, if not also made in homage, to Roger Bastide, Sidney Mintz and Richard Price, Stephan Palmié, and important Caribbean creolists, such as Karl Reisman (1970), Morton Marks (1974), and Roger Abrahams (with John Szwed 1983). I owe the present work's concerns with the practical and interpretive dynamics of Afro-Cuban sociocultural "arenas" (see my chaps. 2 and 3) to discussions with Palmié, Andrew Apter, J. Lorand Matory, and James Wafer, along with readings of their works (Palmié 1989, [1990], 1991, 1993, 1994, 1995, 1996, 2000, 2002; Apter 1987, 1991, 1992; Matory 1986, 1988, 1991b, 1994; Wafer 1991). I owe the present work's concerns with practice, structure, expressive performance, context, agency, and history to my ongoing dialogue with Michael Atwood Mason (see his 1993, 1994, 1997, 2002), as well as my reading of Kris Hardin's important 1993 work, *The Aesthetics of Action* as well as Jean Comaroff's 1985 *Body of Power, Spirit of Resistance.* My engagement with Black Atlantic issues of communication, recrossing, the crystallization of new African diasporic "imaginaries" and narratives, and the shifting location of cultural authenticity (see chap. 2) I owe to readings of Paul Gilroy (1993), David Scott (1991), and Carlo Ginzburg (1980), as well as to formative discussions with my Rutgers colleagues Herman Bennett (2003) and Brent Hayes Edwards (2003).

Returning to the way in which the present work bridges the ethnohistorical concerns of Mintz and Price and the art historical concerns of Robert Farris Thompson, I should qualify the "levels" on which this book engages the issues of specific historical "process" and "culture building"—in a word, contextualization. Contextualization, taken as rigorous attention to historical *explanation,* is subject to limitation by my intensive concern with form history, a concern I owe not only to my art historical study under Thompson, but also to the art history emphasis of my graduate studies and my first university position in a department of art history. *Santería Enthroned* tracks the epochal transformations of three kinds of systems and their attendant meanings: institutional, ritual, and iconographic. For example, I trace transformations in the administrative institutions of Lucumí culture, including formalized systems of descent, ceremonies of accreditation, and problems of innovation, authority, and legitimation (chaps. 1 and 2), the building of Lucumí religious cosmology and divergent systems of initiation (chap. 3), and innovations in the iconography of "royalty" (chaps. 1, 4, and 5). In terms of historical narrative, I opted to emphasize a "vertical" thread of changing forms over time instead of grounding change in relation to thickly delineated historical and sociopolitical contexts. Though I situate changing forms in relation to the interests of relevant institutions, actors, and historiographical traditions of knowledge production (e.g., in chaps. 2, 3, 5), I do not intensively situate these changes within airtight frameworks of local and global sociohistorical *explanation,* an approach demanded by the chief exponents of the new "principled historical anthropology" (see Comaroff and Comaroff 1992, 18).[12] Some of my uses of "history" might be compared to those of art historian Michael Fried. Fried insists that his treatment of artworks is "historical" because of his highly *specific* treatment of art practices and their immediate critical context, for example, in the practice and critical reception of the nineteenth-century French realist painter Gustave Courbet. In this view, forms carry their own specific histories. That Fried's works do not cleave to the methods of historical explanation demanded by practitioners of the social history of art does not necessarily mean they are "ahistorical" and merely formalist and interpretive musings (see Fried 1990; Clark 1973, 1984).[13] In effect, Fried holds his ground in resistance to what Yves-Alain Bois (1990) identifies as the "theoretical blackmail" to conform to particular, invested disciplinary schemes and theoretical positions within the academy.

In short, social historians and historically minded ethnologists might search out works that attempt—with greater or lesser success—to contextualize changing aspects of Afro-Cuban culture in relation to Cuban political, social, and intellectual history (e.g., Saco [1832] 1946; Martínez-Alier [1974] 1989; Brandon 1993; Scott 1986; Fernández Robaina 1994; Helg 1995, 117–39; Palmié 1993, 1994, 1996, 2000, 2002; Moore 1986, 1988; Castellanos and Castellanos 1990, 1992; Moore 1994, 1997; Hagedorn 2001; Matory forthcoming). However, the kind of dialectical, comprehensive local and global historical account envisioned by the Comaroffs has, to my knowledge, yet to be written in this field. Apter, Matory, and Palmié are the scholars most likely to come close to the Comaroffs' program. In my view, we should work together within a multidisciplinary field of complementary interests and approaches. Historical anthropologists and social historians should continue doing what they do best. The net gain, I believe, is that my more "vertical" approach to institutional, ritual, and iconographic innovations in this study provides me the opportunity to focus closely upon organizations, objects, and performances; from specific archival, oral, and ethnographic data I can build detailed accounts of selected practices over time without having to pronounce on their multileveled historical causation. I tend to focus upon those historical references that are "cued" in particular contemporaneous texts and utterances. Such cues point the investigator toward a more selective contextualization, rather than to what folklorists Richard Bauman and Charles Briggs regard as "inclusive and falsely objective" sociohistorical contexts (Bauman and Briggs 1990, 69; and see Briggs 1988).

CHANGE, INNOVATION, REFORM, AND INVENTION

Before I finish outlining my uses of the term "history," I want to define how I chose, and intend to use, the terms "change" and "innovation." The latter appears in the subtitle of this book, and I use the former throughout my narrative, in addition to other terms, such as "revision," "transformation," and, especially, "reform." In my own discourse, I tend to use the term "change" in referring to shifts or transformations that are, shall we say, "structural," where I cannot identify particular agents or am unable or reluctant to digress into lengthy considerations of specific sets of social and historical conditions.

The use of the term "change," in the foregoing sense, can be vague. However, for better or worse, it draws upon a commonplace from the field of cultural anthropology, as put to use in diffusion studies of Africa and the Diaspora, most notably as one valence in the dynamic of "continuity and change" (Bascom and Herskovits 1959; see Price and Price 1980, chap. 8). Essentially, this phrase relies upon an idea of tradition as a relatively unchanging set of constraints, undergirded by norms and moral authority, which is "handed down" from past to present. It assumes that there were or are traditional societies and assumes the enabling modern ethnographic idea of synchronically describable "culture patterns." Such patterns can, however, shift or change, particularly given external (e.g., colonialist) influences and/or "modernization" (see Glassie 1995). In the tradition of New World Negro studies, "change" was laudable and necessary. For Herskovits, the process of "acculturation" meant "reintegration" of cultural elements, not dilution or loss. It provided for resilience and flexible adaptation—that is, change as based on "addition and synthesis to achieve congruence with older forms, rather than of subtraction and substitution, with their resulting fragmentation" (see Herskovits 1958, xxvii).

Recent scholars of Africa and the Diaspora have put the concepts of continuity and change to subtle and penetrating use, such as the Prices' rigorous microhistorical study of transformations in Suriname Maroon artistic styles from the early nineteenth century through the moment of their publication (Price and Price 1980), transformations owed as much to the internal dynamics of Maroon societies as to external influences. In the process, they incisively critique the attribution of stasis to so-called primitive societies. Kris Hardin grounds her study of continuity and change among the eastern Kono of Sierra Leone in the social theory of Anthony Giddens and the performance theory of communication of Indiana University folkloristics. For Hardin, instances of performance among reflective actors and audiences are highly invested with multiple interests; moments of performance, such as dance, make "social structure" or "structural principles"—otherwise analytical abstractions—"visible."[14] Reflective performers take on "responsibility" when they play with constraints, rules, and norms (the stuff of tradition) in front of evaluating audiences that can accept or reject a performer's innovations. Permanent change in, or a hardening of, social structure may result in and through performance (see Hardin 1993; Giddens 1979; Karp 1986; Bauman 1975).

Though I may, admittedly, finesse instances of apparent historical shifts through the use of "change," I try, where possible, to develop arguments in which I can use the term "innovation" in specific ways. I use "innovation" to mark instances of experimentation and revision with respect to received rules, norms, and traditions (or the perceived lack thereof), resulting in altered or entirely new practices. I like the term "innovation" because for me it carries connotations of self-conscious individual and group agency and choice within particular arenas of opportunities and constraints. In this sense, it also carries the assumption that actors are reflective and, therefore, are aware of such opportunities and constraints as particular channels of mobility (in class, race, gender, positionality) (see Hardin 1993; Giddens 1979; Karp 1986: Palmie 1993), the potential success of particular "tactics" (de Certeau 1984), and timely gaps in authority or control. Awareness of constraints might mean susceptibility to the force of the past, hierarchies of power and authority, unequal access to mobility and expression, potential opposition, and the possibilities of failure and loss of face and position.

"Innovation" has a long semantic history of challenges to the status quo within hierarchical and autocratic societies. From the Latin for "renew," "alter," and "make new," it has carried connotations of revolt (*Compact Edition of the Oxford English Dictionary* [hereafter, *Compact OED*], s.v. "innovation"). Individuals and groups can "renew," "alter," and "make new" practices and meanings—indeed, overthrow systems. On the other hand, of course, the state may innovate in order to shore up control and co-opt or crush opposition. I take the altering of the functions of the *cabildos* by enslaved groups to be innovations directed toward addressing African desocietalization in Cuba. These innovations led to permanent structural changes within the *cabildos* (see chapters 1 and 2). In response, the government innovated laws to co-opt, marginalize, and destroy black society and expression. With respect to Afro-Cuban religion, I use the term "innovation" in discussing conscious decisions by individuals and groups, such as Efuche Ña Rosalía, Obadimelli Octavio Samar, and the Society of Santa Barbára (1900) to restructure the "African" "head-and-foot" initiation in favor of the "modern" "pantheonized" Lucumí initiatory system, as well as to reconfigure the cowrie divination system on the model of Ifá. The *Pinaldo* ceremony, which grew out of Efuche's novel "confirmatory ritual" to legitimize priests with questionable credentials, was also an "innovation." The Society of Santa Bárbara formally reorganized a particularly Cuban religious hierarchy of priests in terms of putative rank and seniority, in particular, the hierachies of *babalawos* and *santeros* and men and women. I argue that such experimental, goal-oriented interventions were negotiated out of competing logics of tradition as interpreted by contemporaneous practitioners and tempered by pragmatism. They involved challenges to established authority and had to be instituted by means of rhetorical persuasion and personal authority building.

Still, in attempting to frame such innovations within an "experience-near" field of meaning (see Geertz 1983), I choose to emphasize a term used by practitioners themselves to describe the programs and actions of priests like Efuche and Obadimelli. In their stories, "reform" is used for this purpose. "Reform," in English usage, refers to "the amendment, or altering for the better, of some faulty state of things, [especially] of a repressive political institution or practice." As a verb, it means to "renew, restore, re-establish" (*Compact OED*, s.v. "reform"). Reform, therefore, implies value judgments along moral, ethical, political, or procedural lines, as well as the assumption that "correct" arrangements can be reestablished or restored. The apparent assumptions of Atandá and Añabí in reforming the *batá* drum practices they encountered in Havana would seem as good an example as any (see chap. 2). Ernesto Pichardo adds an essentialist component to Efuche's reform of the Lucumí religion: he believes that she, an African immigrant, led a movement to "purify" and standardize sets of heterogeneous and "incorrect" practices. Thus, reform can refer to an imagined return to a previous state, on a conservative axis. Still, like innovation, yet bearing connotations of a value-laden agenda, reform can involve incremental alteration or thoroughgoing transformation, including overturning extant practices or regimes of authority. In short, though I may use the term "innovation" in generally describing the accomplishments of particular historical actors and groups, I apply the term "reform" in specific cases to practitioners' historical consciousness and their modes of explanation.

In practice, movements to reform Lucumí ritual systems—whether or not they carried purist agendas—were highly selective, pragmatic, and experimental programs, which produced varied results, including developments not foreseen at their inception. Movements of reform and/or purification entail creativity, shrewdness, prudence, and rhetorical agility in their proposal and implementation. They generate resistance and attacks as much as assent; they succeed and fail. Cosmetic or "structural" change may result, and entrenched orthodoxies may harden, making further change more difficult.

In the idiom of Cuban practitioners, the term "invention" is never far from critical evaluations of "reform." The term "invention" is reserved, for the most part, for interventions that are, essentially, made up, without "logic" or reference to extant rules or customs, such as in the hierarchies of priesthood and the protocols of ceremony. Logic is found in common religious sense and in authorizing texts, such as the *odu* of Ifá. For example, *babalawos* and *oriatés* predictably demand from advocates of apparently novel practices: "Show me the *odu*"—meaning "Where is it written?" Here "invention" comes close to one Cuban connotation of *cambio*, "change," with an exclamation mark. The changing of practices can imply ignorance, if not also grave disrespect (*falta de respeto*). Baseless and unauthorized changes disrespect the priestly deceased, the *egun*, who delivered tradition, upon whose shoulders we stand, and to whom we must answer. For example, some Cuban practitioners have been known to exclaim, with regard to the modified rituals of the Black American Yoruba Movement (see Clarke 1997; and my chap. 5) or the neo-Africanist temples popping up in Havana, "They just go and *change* the religion!" "Change" in this context carries no neutral or descriptive meaning; it is negative. In cases in which the speaker wants to describe an instance in which practices are righted and corrected; in this case, "reform" would be the preferred term.

Clearly, one practitioner's reform is another's invention, and worse. The defenders of Efuche and Obadimelli praise, and remain in awe of, these towering figures in the oral history; their reforms were much needed and efficacious. In contrast, not a few *babalawos* interpret their reforms as "frauds" and "rip-offs" (*fraudes* and *plagias*). These are not, strictly speaking, merely illogical inventions, but willful and unauthorized appropriations, which carry degrees of disapprobation. Efuche's *Pinaldo* ceremony, the first beneficiary of which was Obadimelli, was a rip-off and fraud because, according to *babalawos*, it led to usurpation by *santeros* of the exclusive right of the *babalawo* to carry out ritual sacrifice of four-legged animals. Obadimelli, the first "modern" *oriaté*, is blamed for this. At the same time, the enhancing of the *dilogún* cowrie shell system in format and content by drawing from the Ifá corpus receives less disapprobation. Although, in some *ramas*, it superseded a very old tradition of *babalawos'* performing all divination in Ocha initiation (see chap. 3), *babalawos* generally respect competent shell diviners and may take pride in the fact that Ifá provided such a formative and formidable resource for the *dilogún*. In this case, plagiarism is taken positively as the highest form of flattery.

At the same time, some inventions, though they are controversial and dismissed in some quarters, may be redeemed to the extent that their logic can be demonstrated. For example, Miguel Febles Padrón "invented" a new divinity by the name of Ambita, a fierce manifestation of Osain who appears as a carved, magically charged figure comprising elements of the devil, a vampire, and a flying bat. While some *babalawos* dismiss Ambita as *mere* invention, others embrace him or, at least, concede that a logic underlies this composite divinity, which can be logically interpreted from Miguel Febles's personal *odu*, Odí Ká, and extrapolated from the widely accepted idea that the Devil does exist in Lucumí cosmology via a particular "road" of Echú, called Alosí.

While on the subject of definitions and approaches, and before turning to a discussion of chapter contents and organization, I should devote a word or two to the range of sources and historical materials collected and utilized in this work and how I have used them. My investigation relies upon significant archival data and upon published primary and secondary accounts to address aspects of nineteenth- and twentieth-century Afro-Cuban culture, religion, institutions, and aesthetic practices. I have used multimedia fieldwork documentation, including one-on-one interviews, to address contemporary ritual and aesthetic practices. And I heavily rely upon oral narrative, including genealogical recitation, in order to write about nineteenth- and early-twentieth-century Lucumí practitioners and their deeds, characters, and innovations, particularly in chapters 2 and 3. The last point deserves comment because the status and use of oral history have been, and continue to be, the subject of contentious debate among historians (see Cohen 1994).

I have chosen, taking into account the methodological risk, to treat some of the oral narratives I collected as relatively straightforward, using stories by contemporary informants to build a composite chronological, as well as thematic, account of late-nineteenth- and early-twentieth-century practitioners and the development of modern Lucumí ritual practices. In other words, I have utilized these stories for their empirical content (see Vansina 1985). Thus, in my historical accounts based on stories, I tend to suspend in-depth consideration of "the processes through which these stories develop," in particular, the "edges" of "our stories and of the stories being told to us from the past . . . work[ing] toward comprehending the forces emergent at these edges" (Cohen 1994, 21). As Renato Rosaldo puts it eloquently, "The process of reconstructing the past . . . requires a double vision that focuses at once on historians' modes of composition and their subjects' ways of conceiving the past" (Rosaldo quoted in Cohen 1994, 21 n. 34; see also Shryock 1997, 1–37). Methodologically, I tend to group, and periodize in terms of rough epochs, oral references to historical figures and events, pegging them, where possible, to more certain signposts as found in the archival materials. For example, I group oral accounts about the African *babalawo* Adechina Ño Remigio Herrera and his colleagues around several archivally verifiable dates, places, and events: his baptism, census appearance, marriage, and death, as well as his property holdings in Regla (chap. 2). I do this in order to hypothesize about when, with whom, and with what resources Adechina founded Regla's Cabildo of Yemayá and began initiating creole *babalawos*.

In order to write such an account, I have had to ignore many "edges." Clearly, the following kinds of self-reflexive questions deserve to be posed, but I reserve the right to consider them in my future writing. What were the social and performative contexts of different instances of "storytelling"? How did my status as an American, my apparent ethnicity, race, gender, and class, along with the particular questions I asked in interviews, stimulate, shape, or stifle the "tellers' narratives"? What resistances were offered to me and my questions and why? What was at stake for the "storytellers"? How did they conceive of the status of their material? How did they shade or hold back their material, and how and why did they stage their telling of it in particular ways? How did they conceive of themselves in relation to the material—for example, as historians in their own right protective of their turf, as heirs and protectors of a secret tradition, as potential entrepreneurs vis-à-vis "information" that could be packaged as a precious commodity? How did the processing of my field materials—the redaction of notes, transcription of tapes, and translations into English—as well as my theoretical, disciplinary, and ideological interests, transform their utterances and intentions, if at all—indeed, what affect did my textualization of fluid oral discourse have? In short, how do the politics, motives, and methods in and around the "multiple locations of historical knowledge" and its production (Cohen 1994, 4, 241–44) affect my fieldwork and the field I work in? How did they narrate and construct or reconstruct their "pasts" in relation to their present interests or the interests they perceived me to have? How has the history of Cuba's colonization, the painful experience of slavery, the neocolonial treatment of race, and the privation of Cuba's "special period" affect, if at all, their desire to share information with me? What were the "terms of exchange" that were necessary in order for me to get interviews and information? Through the most materialist of lenses, for example, it could be argued that my interests around this subject during the 1980s and 1990s had as much to do with "the conditions under which people are hired, given tenure, published, awarded grants, and feted" (see Rabinow 1986, 253–54) as the ostensible content of my fieldwork. In turn, my "informants"—whether I constructed them as disinterested friends, family, or mentors—had interests that had less to do with the content of their religions than with the tactics of control of resources, social position, and economic survival (see Rabinow 1977). It is not rare to encounter in any part of the world, for example, practitioners manipulating the "fieldwork relationship" to their advantage, where the fieldworker is an *extranjero* (foreigner or tourist), in order to *resolver* (resolve needs) within a society of chronic material deprivation (see Hagedorn 2001, 183–206; Rabinow 1977). In short, the edges of oral history production may have everything to do with issues of geopolitics and power.[15]

As indicated, in perhaps a riskier approach, I use orally collected stories in a highly speculative manner in order to reconstruct nineteenth- and early-twentieth-century innovations in ritual practice, for example, the advent of "confirmatory rituals" to relegitimate the initiations of arriving Africans (see chap. 2). I use such stories heuristically, in order to speculate about innovations in the past. In a slightly different academic domain, Yves-Alain Bois believes that theory can be used heuristically, if it seems appropriate to the project at hand, in order to open up questions; one can "store up" theory in order to apply it where it seems to work in this fashion, despite whatever anachronistic weight a particular theory carries (Bois 1990). In a sense, oral narratives about the past, whether or not they have empirical value, are somewhat like Bois's notion of "theories" or hypotheses. Conceived by contemporary motivated practitioner-*historians* (see Cohen 1994)—they may be profitably used by the tellers as well as scholars as speculative levers to open up, evaluate, and debate historical questions.

Though one should resist enchantment by highly presentist constructions of the past, it is evident that Lucumí historical consciousness—if one chooses to be attentive to indigenous conceptual frameworks (see Geertz 1983)—tends to blur otherwise rigid boundaries between the past and the present in the most practical ways. The ancestors, through genealogical linkages, gerontocratic authority structures, and the material presence of their living relics, exert powerful constraints on the thinking and behavior of the living. As John Mason aptly puts it, practitioners do not "worship . . . ancestor[s]. . . . [It] would better be labeled the carrying on of familial duties" (1985b, 2). "Familial duties" constitute "constraint"—in a word, "tradition"—and entail ethical and moral obligations in daily life. Thus, within the means and methods of contemporary practitioners' oral historical production, ongoing communication with, and serious veneration of, ancestors arguably saves such "theories" from charges of anachronism and presentism.

In sum, I use theoretically informed oral stories in order to derive hypotheses about agency, creativity, and inventiveness in early Lucumí practice, much as Mintz and Price use hypothetical cases to argue about the early creolization of Maroon culture in the forests of Suriname (see Mintz and Price [1976] 1992, 45–46). The point is to develop useful questions about the function and meaning of such confirmatory rituals in early practice. Equally important, as in the case of the variant "stories of Diaspora" related in chapter 2, the point is to demonstrate that the stories contemporary practitioners tell dynamically combine variant, complementary, and sometimes conflicting folk theories of Black Atlantic cultural transmission. To the extent that I can articulate my "mode of composition" at the "edges" of the oral history process, it has entailed "storing up" ethnohistorical "theories," such as the dynamic of creolization and ethnogenesis, as well as practitioner-historians' "theories," in order to organize and interpret orally transmitted materials about religious change. In my opinion, the conflict theory applied, and derived, by Apter in the African case and the ethnogenesis approach applied to the Cuban case by Palmié are not antithetical or anachronistic with respect to the oral narratives collected. Though my embrace of the ethnogenesis and creolization approaches in part serves to mount a counterargument to nationalist or essentialist narratives of strict African continuities, such theoretical tensions are already apparent in the highly variant, ideologically charged approaches to the past that have circulated among practitioners. In chapter 2, for example, I elicit variant "stories of Diaspora," some of which inscribe folk theories of continuity, and others, discontinuity, with Africa. I show how other stories detailing the origins and possession of ritual attributes are used as political ammunition to legitimize the authority of some present actors and delegitimize others. In chapter 3, for example, I demonstrate how variant, orally transmitted mythico-historical legends constituted, and still serve to reinforce, divergent ritual systems that are based on often controversial innovations.

ORGANIZATION AND ARGUMENTS OF THE PRESENT WORK

Chapter 1 looks closely at selected documents of Afro-Cuban institutional, performative, and iconographic practices in the nineteenth century in order to open up questions about the terms and meanings of innovation, and in order to mark a set of beginnings for a my narrative on the development of a modern religion popularly known as Santería. In order to do so, I unabashedly rely upon a creole, or island-born, beginning that many scholars before me have used in their narratives: the sociocultural setting of slavery during the late colonial period (see Mintz and Price [1976] 1992), including the institutions of the African "nations," their public performances, and their internal organization and objectives.[16] I rely upon several empirical and theoretical foundations, now commonplaces, that have been laid out by previous scholars of African Diaspora cultures in general and Yoruba-Atlantic religions in particular. All narratives have to "begin" somewhere, and I choose not to reinvent the wheel in order to tell the detailed story I want to tell about the emergence of a modern Lucumí religion (see chap. 2). Of indisputably West African origins, if that is where one chooses to begin (Herskovits 1941; Verger 1957; Thompson 1983, 1993), African Diaspora religions, nevertheless, owe much of their formative development to the social and cultural settings of urban, coastal regions of the Western Hemisphere, which provided unmatched possibilities for assembly, exchange, communication, and the regathering of resources and personnel in the oppressive context of the slave society. The religions arguably emerged out of neo-African "ethnic" formations, called "nations," and institutionalized "clubs" and mutual aid societies, called *cabildos, sociedades,* and *casas* (see Bastide [1960] 1978; Mintz and Price [1976] 1992; López Valdés 1985a, 1987, 1994; Palmié 1993). The Lucumí religion created by "the Yoruba in Cuba" (Bascom 1951) and their descendants finds some of its most forceful institutional beginnings at the end of the first third of the nineteenth century, when the loosening of Peninsular Spanish control on Cuban commerce and slaving, and an increase in the demand for African labor in western Cuban sugar production (1820–60), coincided with the fall of the Ọ̀yọ́ Empire (1835) and the massive selling off of Yoruba-speaking peoples from the Bight of Benín (see Curtin 1969, 31, 35, 40, 239–44, 247; Smith 1969, 51). The nations' religions in Cuba were creatively and selectively reorganized in settings of "encounter," in which African practices were conserved, as well as transformed, through processes of innovation and "culture building," entailing what some have called syncretism and creolization (see Herkovits 1958, [1945] 1966; Mintz and Price [1976] 1992; Murphy 1988). It is significant that such social and cultural transformations occurred in and through emergent kinds of expressive arts and performances, such as speech, dance, music, festivals, religious rituals, and art making (see Hardin 1993; Reisman 1970; Abrahams 1983; Abrahams and Szwed 1983; Castellanos 1990; Brown 1989, 1993a, 1993b; Thompson 1983, 1993; Nunley and Bettleheim 1988). The people and groups behind these arts and performances were historically conscious, aesthetically concerned, reflective agents of change (Hardin 1993; see also Price 1983, 1990; Price and Price 1980; Chernoff 1979; Mason 1997).

The figure of "royalty" appears again and again in my investigation of three areas of innovation in the nineteenth century: institutions (the *cabildos'* official hierarchies), performances (carnival processional and religious rituals), and iconography (the cluster of prestige signs that delineated neo-African kingship ceremonial; see Aimes 1905; Ortiz [1920] 1960, 1921; Cabrera [1954] 1983, 24, n. 1; [1974] 1980, 178–79). I begin with the rhetorically creative 1810 political speech of an African *cabildo* "king" (Monfundi Siliman) in order to tease out questions of multiple cultural identifications, new kinds of relationships among heterogeneous African nation members who were also slaves and subjects of the Spanish crown, and the historical awareness of African Diaspora agents. The document provides a set of "cues" or "frames" for "contextualiz[ing]" (see Briggs 1988, 14; Bauman and Briggs 1990, 66–69) several alternate trajectories of culture maintenance and building within Cuba's urban *barrios.* Briggs's notion that speakers' utterances contain selective historical references ("cues" or "frames") that are apprehended by certain audiences, guides, likewise, my opening to chapter 5. There, Calixta Morales (Oddedeí) provides an "experience-near" chronotope, a spatio-temporal metaphor, that frames and "contextualizes" a particular diasporic folk history and the imagined transatlantic community it implies ("the palace of the Obá Lucumí"). In chapter 1, as I show, Siliman's complex and complicated "kingship" entails the negotiation of multiple international and local constituencies and sites of power. Siliman, as a historical figure, mediates the three sides of the transatlantic triangle—Africa, the European continent, and the colony of Cuba. As a *cabildo* king under a kind of island "indirect rule," he must guide and discipline—in a word, manage—his African constituencies, as well as answer to the crown and the captain general of Cuba. This set of opportunities and constraints within a determinate arena crosscuts his agency, and involves responses that both perpetuate and resist the hierarchies and power relations of Cuban colonial society (see Comaroff 1985, 198; Apter 1991, esp. 245, 253–54).

Two cases of free Afro-Cuban creoles, the revolutionary José Antonio Aponte and the street "types" known as the *negros curros*, enlarge upon the terms and resources of cultural creativity and innovation in Havana's *barrios* during the nineteenth century. These figures are creole prisms of a sort, refracting and reflecting multiple currents of social and cultural influence. Aponte's visionary, epic program of black liberation is built up, mosaic-like, from strategic readings of dominant texts and historical events. Aponte modeled himself, in part, upon published images of the black kings and generals of Haiti's revolution, such as Henri Christophe. The *curros*, an astonishing kind of street aristocracy, intentionally used hybrid styles to distinguish themselves as free black people, to chart out and control their own public space, and to resist conventional identity assignments (see Hebdige 1979; Comaroff 1985).

My discussion of the *cabildos* and their carnivals provides a place to explore more directly how these colonial institutions—"niches" and "new social frameworks" in Bastide's terms—were sites of creative cultural work and resistance (Bastide [1960] 1978). These sites often revolved around dramatic public expressions of "indirection," "symbolic play," and "reprisal" (Reisman 1970). The *cabildos'* institutional structures, offices, performances, and iconographies were "remodeled" from remembered and encountered resources; the latter were forced upon and strategically manipulated by the African nations (see Reisman 1970; Herskovits 1941, 225), particularly the institutional structures and signs of *cabildo* monarchy and Catholic iconography. *Cabildo* monarchy both "revived" forms of African leadership and "imitated" and subverted forms of European kingship. *Cabildos* drew, as well, from the displays of colonial militias—including the Battalions of Pardos and Morenos (mulattoes and blacks) to which some of their members belonged—and the finery of the master class and Cuba's urban free people of color (Ortiz [1920] 1960, 1921). An exemplary case of "creolization" on its cultural as well as social axis (see above), *cabildo* royalty constituted a public festival lingua franca or template of shared performance style and iconography, which spanned in a single annual event the multifarious African nations. At the same time, along the cultural dimension of "ethnogenesis" (see Palmié 1993), each of the nations maintained and marked out for itself distinctive expressive practices.

Cabildo royal display was defined iconographically by European-style circular openwork crowns, fine cloth, dazzling jewelry, staffs and scepters, and canopied thrones and was deployed in public and semipublic performances of self-conscious decorum and order. *Cabildo* performances were built upon dramatic alternations or performative counterpoints, as when African masquerades and athletic dancing broke out in dance circles during scheduled or spontaneous pauses in processions. In short, "decorum" and "order" alternated dynamically with "wildness" and "noise" (see Marks 1974; Abrahams 1983; Kinser 1990).

Cabildo performances projected a divided address. The meanings of *cabildo* display ranged from socially safe, merely "slavish imitation" and catharsis in the minds of white observers (the conservative safety-valve theory of carnival) to more subversive displays of the social power and esteem of African kings within the fraught setting of "indirect rule" under the Spanish crown, the church, and the Cuban government (the theory of status reversal, symbolic inversion, and transformation; see Alonso 1990).

Fredrika Bremer's mid-nineteenth-century account of a Havana Lucumí *cabildo* concludes chapter 1. Within the Lucumí establishment, a religious performance, complete with drumming, dancing, and spirit possession, takes place. My reading of Bremer's account suggests the degree to which the *cabildos* could establish their more sacred and most subversive practices within controlled urban interior social space. It also delineates the differentiated inner workings of such a nineteenth-century African institution, particularly its dual hierarchy of administrative royalty and religious "royalty," that is, the priestly class. Third, it showcases important precedents for twentieth-century Lucumí practice.

All of the foregoing examples of borrowing and innovation in the nineteenth-century Cuban setting serve to reinforce and amplify the case made strongly by previous writers: "in the beginning," as it were, thoroughgoing transformation, as much as conservation, of West African social and cultural practices (on the slave ships, in New World colonies, and within West Africa itself over centuries) have characterized African Diaspora history (see, e.g., Mintz and Price [1976] 1992; Palmié 1993; Blier 1995; Cosentino 1995b; Polk 1995; Apter 1992; Akinjogbin 1972; Kopytoff 1987; Balandier 1968; Matory 1994, 1999, forthcoming; Gilroy 1993; Linebaugh and Rediker 2000).

In order to provide historical context for the emergence of twentieth-century Lucumí religion, I attach a coda to chapter 1, which outlines the transformations undergone by the *cabildos* in the setting of Cuban independence from Spain, Cuban nation building, the criminalization of the African religions, and the varying fortunes of Afro-Cubans themselves around the turn of the twentieth century.

Chapter 2 proposes that the "starting point" for twentieth-century Lucumí religion (La Regla de Ocha and La Regla de Ifá) was, in fact, a fluid, discontinuous, often fraught, "process," which revolved around contested institutional formations and performances authored by specific agents. Thus, I intend to nuance the now common idea that the nineteenth-century *cabildos* "incontestably form[ed] the starting point for the African *santaria* [sic] of Cuba" (Bastide 1972, 95). First, I identify three variant institutional trajectories, including a "transitional" form of *cabildo* or *sociedad* organization that bridged the *cabildos* of the colonial era (which ended in 1898) and the "houses" or "house-temples" of the American occupation periods and the so called republican era (1902–1959). Further I revise the idea of "*the* starting point" by eliciting ever more specific institutional formations—in particular, the religion's genealogical "branches" (*ramas*), "founder" figures (*fundadores*), and ritual descendants. In tracing the contemporaneous idiom and nomenclature used by contemporary practitioners to describe some of these institutions as well as profiling their seminal personnel, I argue for the elasticity of the ethnonym "Lucumí" over time. In doing so, I amplify the observations of previous writers, who argued that designations based upon putative ethnic identity during the era of the slave trade (e.g., the Lucumí "nation") became ethnically and racially heterogeneous religious denominations or "orders," La Regla, or La Religión Lucumí (see Murphy 1988, 33; Palmié 1993).

The identificatory markers of specific religious identity—branch and founder names—circulate with significant flux within contemporary memory and discourse. They are susceptible to manipulation, forgetting, and confusion, as well as recompiling (*recopilación*) through practitioners' private research and their interactions with ethnographers and historians. Religious identities can be constructed and reconstructed over time within what Shryock (1997) has called the "genealogical imagination." Genealogical reckoning is as much reinvented as it is, if at all, strictly preserved and handed down as a kind of "artifactual assemblage" (Handler and Linnekin 1984; see Clarke 1997). Discursively, "beginnings" and "origins," and, by extension, contemporary authority and sacred identity, thus remain contested (see Apter 1991; 1992, 13–34); putatively stable and legitimating origins regress or approach in time, shift from one founder figure to another, and are rhizomatic. That is, they can shift geographical "location" as they literally or imaginarily bounce back and forth across Atlantic space. For example, the "origin" of important religious objects (e.g., Olofin) and the authority gained by their possession have shifted back and forth across the water, from Africa to Cuba to Miami and back to Africa. The cultural value of these objects was transformed as well. Olofin began in nineteenth-century Cuba as a scarce, rarified symbolic object with a unique "aura," which derived from its location within a controlled religious hierarchy; it became, in many ways, a commodity fetish within a highly individualized religious marketplace in the 1950s (see Clarke 1997; Matory 1999, forthcoming; Gilroy 1993).

Utilizing oral history and archival data about specific

personages, I derive a series of hypotheses about the process of the Lucumí religion's formation in Cuba. The religion grew up around very small numbers of Africans and their early creole blood and ritual descendants particularly in the Havana Bay town of Regla; its emergence as a set of more or less systematic practices was relatively recent—as recent as the early years of the twentieth century; its formation, development, and dissemination were characterized by significant discontinuities; the ritual authority of the religion's African founders was not passively taken for granted, but had to be actively asserted and affirmed within local and regional networks of religious legitimation; the religion's founders and later exponents were historically self-conscious individuals who strategically positioned themselves socially, carefully selected, implemented, and disseminated the knowledge they possessed, and collaborated in setting up "commissions" of specialists and elders for this purpose. I derive these hypotheses mostly from stories that have circulated among practitioners in Havana and Matanzas.

Such "stories of Diaspora" and the Cuban experience that practitioners tell among themselves and to researchers turn on themes of continuity and discontinuity. The former themes emphasize direct genealogical and spiritual descent from West Africa, and the latter emphasize the creative work of particular historical actors—the religion's African and creole ancestors *on the island*—in revising and innovating according to local sets of conditions. In other words, what African figures carried to Cuba was selectively implemented and remade on the island. Many important ritual patterns of contemporary practice are the result of self-conscious "reform" movements from before the turn of the twentieth century, though many were inaugurated in the early republican era (beginning in 1902). I suggest that the credentialing problems of ritual identity, correctness, and authenticity were resolved through "confirmatory rituals," innovations (e.g., the "Knife" ceremony, or *Pinaldo*), developed by local and regional communities of Cuban Lucumí. The idea of confirmatory rituals, as local innovations, turns on its head a conventional linear notion of religious continuity.

The figure of "royalty" also underwent transformations in location, meaning, and morphology over time. By the early twentieth century, "Lucumí" *reyes* and *reinas* (kings and queens) would no longer be the hereditary or elected mortal *cabildo* rulers, who sat under canopied thrones. They would be manifested as at least two different kinds of roles: priests and *orichas*. They would be the revered de jure and de facto ritual specialists of Ocha and Ifá "houses": the *obás* and *oriatés*. They would also, not least, be the deities of the Lucumí pantheon themselves, the *orichas*. The principal, aesthetically marked site for the elaboration of royal iconography would not be carnival processions, but the festival shrines and garments of the *orichas*, the theme I take up and amplify in chapters 4 and 5.

Chapter 3 turns from the emergence of the Lucumí religion's "new social frameworks" (the *cabildos, casas,* and *ramas*) and their institutions of authority building (e.g., Olofin and *Pinaldo*) to the creation of its systematizing "modern" theological principles, initiatory practices, and rankings of ritual specialists. Building upon chapter 2's introduction of variant "stories of Diaspora," this chapter interrogates the "myths" and practices that have sustained and rationalized—discursively constituted—the Lucumí religion over time. How did forms of narrative production and practical innovation constitute a modern Lucumí religion? First, I reflect upon the metaphors scholars and practitioners have used to describe the collective Lucumí *orichas*, particularly the *orichas'* formation into a "pantheon" from West African, and other, religious resources transported from the Old World and encountered in the New. One dominant metaphor of process is that distinct heterogeneous regional resources were "fused" or "creolized" into one or more overarching New World systems. Another is that a single reified Yoruba "old structure" or "substratum" was reinstated or reconstituted in the New World.

Drawing upon revisionist scholarship on the Yoruba, I argue that the Cuban *orichas* are not only amenable, via analogy, to description as a pantheon (like those of the Egyptians, Greeks, and Romans), or as a "ladder of intercession" (like that of the Catholic God the Father, Christ the Son, Virgin Mary, and saints). I argue that these ostensibly foreign representations, in subtle ways, actually were formative in building the Lucumí *orichas* into a pantheon and ladder of intercession. In other words, borrowed "non-African" narratives may have helped recrystallize heterogeneous West African resources into a modern, theologically rationalized religion. Furthermore, over the course of more than one hundred and twenty years of narrative production about the Yoruba and Lucumí religions—by practitioners and scholars—it has become extremely difficult to tease apart ethnographic description and theological formulation. The narratives that ethnographers and practitioners tell, and have told, are mutually constituted in a kind of intertextual hall of mirrors. Both the Yoruba religion and its Cuban descendant can appear as a "great chain of being," with its controlling hierarchies. The creation narratives, dramatis personae, and hierarchical relations of matter and spirit within Catholic catechistic discourse, Cuban Lucumí *pataki*, and Black American Yoruba manifestos are seen to bear family resemblance. Theology and historiography seem to be inextricably intertwined and mutually defining. In one intriguing twist, Cuban *babalawos* do not merely draw upon the Egyptian cosmology as a convenient analogy with which to describe the theology of Ifá; some firmly believe that Ifá is the ancient Egyptian religion's literal descendant, which reflects late-nineteenth-century European ideas of world religious genealogy and the content of some Yoruba ethnographic writings and also resonates with centuries-old Ethiopianist discourse in the Americas ("Princes shall come out of Egypt"; see Raboteau 1983).

Amplifying the conclusions of chapter 2, I argue that the systematic *pantheonization* of the *orichas* and the *theologization* of the religion resulted, in part, from the strategic moves and authority-building of particular "reformers." Their authority building within and without the religion included their earnest attempts to create a resilient, "licit," "true," and progressive "modern" religion that could weather severe social dislocation, stigma, and persecution between the period of emancipation and the middle of the twentieth century.

Late-nineteenth- and early-twentieth-century "reformers" and "councils" of elders—just the kind of personnel that made up the famous Havana mutual aid society Cabildo Africano Lucumí (1900)—innovated in two crucial areas of religious practice: divination and initiation. The pantheonization of the *orichas* and the systematization of the religion's specialized bodies of esoteric knowledge were the result of self-conscious decision making and the rise of new kinds of specialists. I show that major innovations in initiation procedure took perhaps half a century to be implemented, a period that saw significant heterogeneity in practice. This century's most important innovation, the pantheonized modern initiation system, was not instituted fully in Matanzas until after World War II. What resulted, however, was not a thoroughgoing standardization; contest and debate over theory and practice produced divergences, leading to variant, "traditionalized" *oricha* "traditions." Such variations are reflected in differences in practice among regions and *ramas* and continue to be produced where shifts in alliances regularly occur between poles of orthodoxy and heterodoxy.

In a final set of case studies, I show that certain highly influential "myths of the Yoruba past" among practitioners and scholars have discursively produced divergent, ideologically motivated Lucumí religious systems. Drawing upon Andrew Apter's notion of "ritual field theory" among the Yoruba (Apter 1987; 1992, 33–34), I argue that two opposed ritual fields have constituted Lucumí theory, practice, and historical process: an "Ifá-centric" ritual field and an "Ocha-centric" ritual field. They are based in divergent cosmological models and structurings of ritual and oracular authority, particularly as they are embodied in the professions of the religion's two male ritual specialists and, often, antagonists: the *babalawo* and the *oriaté*. These two ritual fields may be seen as gendered. Structurally, La Regla de Ifá, with its male *babalawo* and his tutelary *oricha*, Orula, "feminizes" La Regla de Ocha (the collective *oricha* priests and their pantheon [see Matory 1986]); the *oriaté*, in turn, must decenter the *babalawo*'s authority in building his-story. The profession of *oriaté*, it turns out, developed from overlapping ritual roles, occupied variously by *babalawos* and heterogeneous *oricha* priests including roles played by women. Women were very powerful early in Havana and Matanzas but were marginalized after about 1935, when the last of these women had passed and the students of Obadimelli rose to prominence in Havana. As in the Yoruba case, advocates have rhetorically defended their positions by utilizing divergent origin stories, myth versions, and genealogical shape-shifting.

Ethnographic narratives of the Lucumí religion, in turn, have been shaped by divergent "myths" and practices—ritual fields—through their relative emphases on Ifá-centric versus Ocha-centric voices. This set of discussions culminates in the delineation of at least three different contemporary initiatory models, which vary according to the relative participation and authority granted to the *babalawo* and which are dominant or silent in the ethnography. If one were to depend, for example, on *babalawos'* historical explanations of these variations, one would believe that Ocha-centric versions were illegitimate breakaway practices contrary to *the* tradition; whereas, if one were to depend upon Ocha-centric voices, one would encounter *babalawos* as arrogant, macho, and even bumbling, interlopers within Ocha. In the rhetorical arenas of contemporary, as well as historical, practice, "traditions" can be dismissed as innovations, while innovations can be defended as "old traditions" (see also Wafer 1991, 56–57).

Chapter 4 closely examines Lucumí "royal" iconography, a theme I first address in the context of nineteenth-century festival practice. *Oricha* houses present their luxuriously dressed and crowned initiates (*iyawós*) under resplendent canopied thrones. Whereas chapter 3 traces ritual innovations leading to the modern Lucumí initiation (*asiento*), chapter 4 describes the cumulative result, as it were, of innovations in the *orichas'* sartorial appearance as publicly presented on the Middle Day festival. On the Middle Day, which follows the ritually intensive *asiento*, *oricha* kings, queens, or deified warriors appear in hybridized ensembles of consecration garments. Luxurious satin clothes and pasteboard crowns of apparently European style dovetail with recognizably Yoruba-derived beadwork, regalia, and painted head designs. This chapter's iconological descriptions and interpretations of the Middle Day's art media, drawing upon variant practitioner commentary and extant literature, lay the groundwork for chapter 5's art history of the same media in the context of a "creole" Cuban or Afro-Cuban cultural history.[17]

Chapter 4's close description throws into relief the marked aesthetic and symbolic distinctions between two groups of *orichas* who populate the differentiated landscape of the Cuban Lucumí imagination: the "royalty" of the "palace" and the itinerant "warriors" of the "bush" and the "street." The *orichas* Obatalá, Oyá, Ochún, Yemayá, Changó, and others are distinguished by luxurious thrones of prestige cloth, bejeweled pasteboard crowns, satin garments, domestic dance wands, such as fly whisks and fans, and a refined initiatory seat—an inverted mortar, called the *pilón*. The presence of the archetypal *oricha* warriors, Eleguá, Ogún, and Ochosi, in contrast, is elaborated by a cluster of natural, hard, and rustic attributes, which distinguishes them as mobile denizens of the street and the forest, zones that begin at the door to the house and extend further outside into uncharted territories beyond the "town." Appropriately, the warriors are initiated upon large stones or raw tree trunks; they are installed under lean-to-like thrones made of "leaves" and stand and sit upon a floor covered not with a worked straw mat but with *yerba fina* (grassy herbs). They wear farmers' brimmed straw hats and carry implements of work, war, and hunting. Differences within the Lucumí iconography of palace royalty and outdoor itinerants bear a family resemblance with distinctions made among the Yoruba, particularly between the cults of Sàngó and Ògún (Matory 1994, 6). Yet from an "experience-near" perspective

(Geertz 1983, 57), the Lucumí aesthetic and iconographic markers are built upon the terms of "local knowledge": for example, Cuban and Afro-Cuban historical and ecological distinctions between house and street, city and countryside, the island's urbanized west and its more rural center and east, and so on. Such distinctions also have occupied and organized the Cuban cultural imagination; they have formed opposed symbolic figures within Cuban arts, letters, and popular storytelling (see Landaluze 1881; Villaverde 1996; Barnet [1966] 1980; Elizondo [1934?] n.d., 19, and see Pérez 1988, 122–25; Williams 1973, chap. 25; Brown 1999, 194–98). At the same time, though particular clusters of attributes distinguish the warriors of the forest from the *orichas* of the palace, the initiations of all of them proceed according to a relatively standard and systematic modern ritual template. All undergo a similar *asiento* ritual of "putting the *oricha* on the head"; all appear under their Middle Day thrones as elegant ladies and gentlemen, the former wearing gowns and painted earrings, and the latter jackets and knickers along with painted mustaches and beards on their faces and representations of riding boots on their legs.

Integrally combined with attire that recalls European royalty and Cuban colonial aristocracy are elaborate beadwork objects and painted head markings, which appear to derive from the attributes of Yoruba shrine sculpture, possession priests, and kings. Yet, chapter 4's close description identifies a cluster of Afro-Cuban iconographic attributes that bears a family resemblance both to African iconographic models and to those of the colonial period: this is seen in the iconography of public ceremonial and African-derived religious ritual. *Cabildo* royalty led orderly public processions and ceremoniously observed semipublic African drumming events from throne seats within their establishments. At the same time, African-derived masquerades of rustic organic materials were danced in the same processions, while *oricha* priests became possessed in the drumming events. The aesthetic, performative, ecological, and institutional contexts of the modern Lucumí initiatory system resonate with similar distinctions observed in the colonial setting, a subject I amplify in chapter 5. Notably, the distinction between fierce, organic masquerades and refined *cabildo* royalty sheds light on the Lucumí initiatory distinctions between warriors and palace *orichas.* Whereas luxuriously dressed mortal kings and queens observed drummings from their canopied thrones in the old *cabildos,* the *orichas*—as luxuriously dressed kings and queens—came to receive similar honors from their own canopied thrones within the *casas de ocha* by the twentieth century.

For heuristic and descriptive purposes, chapter 4 depends upon a relatively synchronic picture of contemporary Lucumí iconography. Chapter 4 attempts to balance references to possible Yoruba iconographic sources of Lucumí ritual arts with references to more local Cuban sources. This reflects my intention, overall, to balance the Thompson (relatively more Africanist) and Mintz and Price (relatively more Creolist) approaches; that is to say, Thompson's master narrative begins with West African "traditional" cultures, which are tracked through their New World diffusion and "reorganization"; Mintz and Price's master narrative begins with the emergent "social bonds" of the slave ship and the New World plantations and forest outposts, from which "new" communities and cultures were "created" (Thompson 1983, 18; Mintz and Price [1976] 1992, 13–18).

Chapter 5 revisits the principal ritual media described in detail in chapter 4. It does so in order to launch an art history and cultural history of iconographic borrowing and hybridization in order to address the look and arrangements of contemporary Lucumí ritual arts. Local, or island, sources of borrowing are hypothesized as *cabildo* royalty, the icons and presentational devices of popular Catholic display, and the material culture of the Cuban aristocracy and bourgeoisie. In this way, chapter 5 brings the book's narrative full circle, as the book commenced with cycles of borrowing, or "appropriation"—a term of contemporary currency (see Atkins 1990, 42–43; Nelson 1996)—during the colonial period.

Thus, I sketch an art history, utilizing primary sources,

where possible, of the principal elements that came to constitute the Middle Day's iconography and media: the cloth hangings of the throne, the garments and crowns of the initiate, regalia and hand-held attributes, the soup tureen form, and the *canastillero*, or domestic altar for the *orichas*.

The leitmotif of chapter 5 derives from the figure enunciated by the elderly Ochosi priestess Calixta Morales in her mid-twentieth-century explanation to Lydia Cabrera of the Middle Day's significance: the "palace of the Lucumí King" (*To make a Santo is to make a king, and kariocha is a ceremony of kings, like those of the palace of the Oba Lucumí*). The metaphor of the king's palace is seen to organize the aesthetic guidelines and religious significance of the Middle Day's celebration. The palace is a beautifully adorned, enduring place of dignity, decorum, honor, etiquette, purity, spiritual power, and *communitas*, where enthroned *oricha* kings, queens, and deified warriors appear before and are recognized by "the people." "The palace of the Obá Lucumí" thus discursively functions as a chronotope, a spatiotemporal figure, which has animated and artistically organized religious art making and performance; it also anchors local narratives of the spiritual and aesthetic connections between Africa and the New World. In other contemporary terms, it is a principal narrative figure of the Lucumí "imagined community" in the larger African Diaspora (see Anderson 1983; Wafer and Santana 1990; Scott 1991; Gilroy 1993).

An important set of aesthetic conventions of Cuban, Cuban-American, and other Latino Lucumí practitioners for the representation of kings, queens, and warriors consists in what Ortiz identified as *adornos al gusto criollo* (adornments in the creole taste), which emerged in the last third of the nineteenth century among the "white" branches of Cuba's Afro-Cuban Abakuá society (Ortiz 1952–55, vol. 4, 5, 49–84). A similar class of lavish adornments appeared in late-nineteenth-century Ocha houses in which, for example, *mulata* mistresses of aristocratic white Cuban men underwent initiation (Cabrera [1974] 1980, 176). Such "adornments in the creole taste" appeared as marvelous hybrids of elements from European imports and Cuban material culture (cloth and porcelain), compounded with importations of West African trade goods (skins, horns, cloth, and cowries). The variant altar assemblages and ritual garments, which resulted, to an extent, from "consumer" choices, reflected processes of "creolization" and "re-Africanization."

In order to mark variant local criteria of iconographic change, the coda to chapter 5 briefly explores the Black American Yoruba Movement. It traces how, for African-American practitioners of the Lucumí religion in the United States, the *adornos al gusto criollo* were antithetical to nationalist concerns and purist links to the Mother Continent (Africa). For black Americans, the style of the Cuban palace of the Obá Lucumí evoked, among other things, the stage set of *The Three Musketeers* (Palmié 1995, 80). Still, the movement's Oyotunji Village, an invented South Carolina "Africa State," did not at all jettison the figure of royalty and the palace, but restaged it in the re-creation of an ethnographically researched neo-Yoruba kingdom. The thrones of the Cuban *orichas* became the thrones of the Yoruba-American *orishas* or *òrìsà*. The inhabitants of Oyotunji were "descendants of noble priests, devotees, kings and queens, who . . . [were] 'culturally imprisoned in racist white Amerika' and must reclaim their 'true selves' and lost nobility by embracing African traditions" (Clarke 1997, 124). The long-past mortal kings of the Yoruba town and the Cuban *cabildos* were revived in the institution of the village's highly esteemed paramount monarch, H.R.H. Oba Ofuntola Oseigeman Adelabu Adefunmi I. Oyotunji was a purist experiment: it "served as the focal point in the United States for the renaissance of traditional Yoruba art from earlier times" (J. Mason 1994, 244); it was, and remains, a brilliant, historically self-conscious innovation. The Oyotunji case reinforces chapter one's arguments about change and agency, illustrating just how swiftly a group can revise a historically entrenched and traditionally ingrained set of institutional, ritual, and iconographic practices and their attendant meanings (see also Mintz and Price [1976] 1992, 48–49).[18]

Part I

INSTITUTIONAL AND RITUAL INNOVATION

ONE

BLACK ROYALTY

New Social Frameworks and Remodeled Iconographies in Nineteenth-Century Havana

[The (African) *cabildo* king] wore very proper royal vestments of the Middle Ages, a red velvet tunic with a magnificent gilt paper crown. This black man, who was enormously tall and of a fine presence, gave his hand with solemnity to a black woman, who represented a queen. He walked with a deliberate and majestic step, never laughed and seemed to be deeply reflecting on the grandeur of his mission in this world.
—Leon Beauvallet, *Rachel and the New World: A Trip to the United States and Cuba* (1856)

European invented traditions offered Africans a series of clearly defined points of entry into the colonial world, though in almost all cases it was entry into the subordinate part of a man/master relationship. They began by socializing Africans into acceptance of one or other readily available European neo-traditional modes of conduct—the historical literature is full of Africans proud of having mastered the business of being a member of a regiment or having learned how to be an effective practitioner of the ritual of nineteenth-century Anglicanism. The process often ended [however] with serious challenges to the colonial power, often couched in terms of the socializing neo-traditions themselves.
—Terrence Ranger, "The Invention of Tradition in Colonial Africa"

Signs are never transparent and innovations are always partial. . . . [S]ubversive bricolages always perpetuate as they change.
—Jean Comaroff, *Body of Power, Spirit of Resistance*

On a Sunday afternoon in the summer of 1808, Monfundi Siliman, the Congo "king" of a Havana religious fraternity (*cabildo*), addressed a gathering of Africans concerning news brought by an arriving Spanish fleet. Napoleon Bonaparte's invading armies had been driven back by fierce Spanish resistance in southern Spain (Barcelona and Cádiz). Adamantly supporting the Spanish crown, King Siliman condemned the French as despicable, unbaptized dogs, among other things. Reminding his African listeners of what the French had done to "us" (blacks) in Saint Domingue, Siliman warned that Napoleon and his brother Joseph could invade Havana and perpetrate upon the audience what they were now doing to Spain.[1] "If you are Spanish, as I am," Siliman admonished his audience of members of diverse African "nations," "swear before the Island's Governor the defense of Havana to the death, to defend, together with the Spanish: Spain, God, Jesus Christ, The Church, and King Fernando VII." The blacks of Havana, he said, could join official militias, receive "flags, drums, rifles, and sabres, just like the whites," and would, ultimately, gain "money, horses, cultivated plots of land, houses and everything we want as free men." King Siliman's rousing proclamation concluded with a warning: "If you don't want to be free, you will be slaves, and you will not dance, sing, drum or have children" (Siliman n.d.).[2]

King Siliman's *Proclamation* illuminates the complexity of African identity, institutions, and expressive resources on the island of Cuba during the early nineteenth century. The esteemed royal head of a *cabildo* of the Congo "nation" (*nación*), Siliman was also a slave in the highly stratified Cuban colonial society. A historically conscious participant in a global struggle for the New World, Siliman officially identified himself as a passionate royal subject, the servant of a vast, divinely sanctioned chain of authority called the Bourbon Empire ("Spain, God, Jesus Christ, The Church, King Fernando VII," along with Cuba, its captain general, the City of Havana, and its African nations), which seemed threatened with extinction by Napoleon and his godless armies. Yet Siliman's unique vision of future freedom carefully balances a series of goods and rights on parity with "the whites" with specific markers of African cultural and social continuity: black flag-bearing regiments become Cuban yeomen whose communities "dance, sing, drum, [and] have children."

Siliman's relationship to his listeners and the composition of this audience were also complex. A Congo who probably spoke one or more western Central African ancestral and pidgin languages among his nation brethren, Siliman employed a version of the Afro-Cuban *bozal* creole[3] in this public setting as a bridge to his ethnically and linguistically diverse audience. Invoking the slavery-era ethnonyms of virtually all of Cuba's African nations, Siliman greeted his listeners as *Señores Congo, Luango, Carabaly, Lucumí, Arará, Macuá, Fanti, Mandinga, Mina, Brichi, Mondongo*, and *Intuanza*.[4] The members of these different nations were connected in Cuba not only by their competence in *bozal* language but by other "new social ties" as well (Mintz and Price [1976] 1992, 44). Thus, Siliman's opening literary salutation, which recalls the famous greeting of Shakespeare's Julius Caesar ("Friends, Romans, Countrymen"), registers both old and new identifications. "Palente, mingo, y crabela," he began, "tó ése unté quien vení de Guiné." [All of you who come from Guinea (Africa).] Despite their different origins on the continent of Africa (*Guiné*), they had become "relatives, friends, and countrymen/shipmates" through their experiences of the Middle Passage, the slave plantation, and bustling colonial cities like Havana.[5] Moreover, though he was the king of a particular Congo *cabildo* with authority over a determinate nation membership, Siliman seems to claim additional authority as elder at large, a kind of prime minister before this parliament of the nations. After greeting each group by name, Siliman blessed the assembly: "yó má negro que tó unté, etá bueno graciandio" [I am senior to all of you, we are good, thanks to God].[6]

In the early nineteenth century, King Siliman, and "those who came from Guiné," were Africans in Cuba but also were becoming *afrocubanos*. They were not only *in*, but also, in important ways, *of* a New World in the process of great change, and which they had a stake in defining for themselves. Following the successful Haitian Revolution, of which New World Africans were intimately aware (Scott 1986), they could be optimistic about future freedom and prosperity. This possibility, and Siliman's humane vision for Cuba's African nations under the banner of the empire, was, of course, easier to conceive from the point of view of the turn of the eighteenth century, with its Enlightenment-descended liberal Slave Code (*Código Negro*), than several decades later, with the Cuban sugar boom (1820–60), the spiraling and insatiable demand for new slave labor, an increasingly brutal industrialized sugar plantation regimen, the decrease in the possibility of self-purchase (*coartación*), the rising legal repression of African social and cultural activity following a series of slave insurrections (1810, 1812, 1826, 1830, 1837, 1840, 1841, 1844), and midcentury policies to end the "Africanization" of Cuba by "whitening" the island with the importation of European and Chinese laborers. Where, in 1810, Siliman could—at least with public sincerity—defend the crown, the Spanish, and the captain general against the French, many in the succeeding generations of Africans and Afro-Cubans would rebel against the captains general and the crown and fight the Spanish for Cuban independence in the revolutions of 1868–78 and 1895–98. Certainly, after "annexationist" sentiments among the Creole owning class (i.e., support for annexation to the U.S.) were renewed at midcentury in order to counter abolitionist discussion in Spain and maintain the slavery status quo, alliance to the crown would have seemed a better bargain, for a while. However, Afro-Cubans would soon confront the brutal fact that the independent nation they had fought twice to establish (the Republic was founded 1902) had dismissed their aspirations, instituted disenfranchisement, and ultimately mobilized violent state force to suppress Afro-Cuban organizing and advancement (see Pérez 1988, 72–100, 210–22; Helg 1995, 55–248; Fermoselle 1974).

CULTURAL TRANSFORMATION AND HAVANA'S *BARRIOS EXTRAMUROS*

The Afro-Cuban *barrios* of Havana, home to the "nation" residents whom Siliman had addressed, were great crucibles of social, cultural, and political transformation. Up through the period of emancipation (1880–86), Africans (*negros de nación*) and their island-born descendants (*criollos*) strongly identified with their respective nations' *cabildos*. The *cabildos* were social clubs and religious mutual aid societies of neo-African ethnic denomination. At the same time, the members of the heterogeneous nations took on significant aspects of a "creole" identity, as they shared myriad "ordinary and extraordinary experiences,"[7] and confronted in common many obstacles to their advancement and liberty. For example, they would share a class position and suffer a common stigma as slaves and, later, as working people of color. To communicate with each other, they spoke *bozal* and Spanish, as well as African languages within the *cabildos* and at home; they were typically baptized, held Catholic-style masses, and found allies against slavery in Catholic saints; and they responded to pressing social and political events and movements throughout the nineteenth century, including slave insurrections and the two Wars of Independence. These two trajectories of identity, the "neo-African" and the Afro-Cuban "creole,"[8] were complementary.

Responding to Mintz and Price's thesis of "early creolization" among "heterogeneous" African populations in the New World, Stephan Palmié draws on Cuban and Brazilian evidence (e.g., Bastide [1960] 1978) to pose an alternative thesis. In bustling urban coastal centers, such as Havana, Cuba, and Salvador, Bahia, Brazil, distinct African cultures were neither swiftly "creolized"—blended together—nor preserved in their pure preslavery state; they were reconstituted and redistilled as new, but not entirely unfamiliar, cultural formations through a process Palmié calls "ethnogenesis." In other words, discrete neo-African ethnic identities were recreated and reasserted in and through the framework of African "nation" institutions (*cabildos* in Cuba; *irmandades* in Brazil) and their annual cycles of feast day carnivals (see Palmié 1993). Mintz and Price were not necessarily wrong about "rapid creolization"; they merely overgeneralized their thesis from the Suriname Maroon case to other Diaspora centers, particularly urban coastal centers. Moreover, Mintz and Price's thesis remains an important corrective to Melville Herskovits's earlier notion that in remote Diaspora settings, such as Suriname's Maroon communities or Haiti's rural valleys, the "purest" African heritages were wholly preserved (Herskovits and Herskovits 1934; Herskovits [1937] 1975, [1945] 1966). Richard and Sally Price, for example, argue that the Maroons are, in fact, among the Diaspora's most creolized people (Mintz and Price [1976] 1992; Price and Price 1980), although scholars have documented numerous specific Mande, Dahomean, Yoruba, Akan, and Kongo bases of Maroon cultural forms (Herskovits and Herskovits 1934; Thompson 1993, 109–44).

Palmié's intellectual debt to Mintz and Price remains their forward-looking "culture building" perspective, rather than the more backward-looking "search for tribal origins" of Melville Herskovits (1941). The African nations in Cuba or Brazil were less direct and wholesale overseas extensions of Yoruba, Dahomean, Kongo-Angola, or Cross-River cultures—little "Africas in the Americas"—than new ethnic formations, which emerged within specific New World social arenas and political economies. On the ethnogenesis model, the differences between the nations—Lucumí, Arará, Congo, Carabalí, and so on—were owed as much to ongoing institutional and performative "boundary marking" strategies as to the conservation of essential African elements from their African source locales and regions—which were themselves highly dynamic and changed over time (Palmié 1993; Barth 1969; see also Smith 1957; Bastide [1960] 1978). For example, did Afro-Cuban creoles belong to Lucumí *cabildos* because of a transparent Yoruba ancestry? Or was an Afro-Cuban creole a "Lucumí" because of official membership in a Lucumí *cabildo*? This was an easier question to answer, perhaps, for African-born arrivals and freedmen who made it to cities and towns and could search out their "nation" brethren in the appropriate *cabildo*. It was a more difficult question for their descendants, who could be the products of ethnic intermarriages as the century came to a close. As the twentieth century approached, one could "become" Lucumí through initiation into the "Lucumí religion" (La Regla Lucumí or La Regla de Ocha). One could also become a *Tata Nkisi* (priest) of the Congo Cuban religion called Palo Monte or Mayombe, worship Arará deities of Ewe-Fon (Dahomean) origin, become an *obonekue* (member) of the Abakuá society, the sacred brotherhood of Old Calabar origin, as well as rise through the ranks of the Masons, rely on Rosacrucian geomancy, and take Communion in the Catholic Church.

Beyond the nineteenth-century palace-studded city of white merchants, planters, titled nobles, petit bourgeoisie, and house-slaves within Old Havana's fortress walls (the *intramuros*) were the *barrios extramuros* (neighborhoods outside-the-walls; fig. 1.1). The *extramuros* included large and growing African and Afro-Cuban free and slave populations. In 1827, for example, of Havana's total population of 112,000, 39,980 lived within the walls and 94,023 lived immediately outside the walls and in the various suburbs (Thomas 1971, 109), such as the small municipalities around and across the great bay, Guanabacoa and Regla. Over the course of the nineteenth century, the *extramuros* grew westward along the curving Gulf shoreline and south along the Bay of Havana, some neighborhoods bleeding into the bay's swampy low-lying border. Havana City *barrios*, such as the older Jesús María, Manglar, El Horcón, and Carraguao, and the newer San Lázaro and Colón, represented dynamic and diverse Afro-Cuban worlds outside the city walls, which were razed only in 1863.[9] The 1841 census showed that the City of Havana's nonwhite residents, who lived in the *extramuros*, constituted a majority of the total population of 388,073; among nonwhites, there were 188,929 slaves (48%) and 49,191 free colored (12.6%; see Kiple 1976, tables). On the island as a whole, the nonwhite population had already reached a high of 56% by the time of the 1827 census, causing the "Africanization" scare that led the Spanish authorities to encourage white working-class immigration from Europe; by 1861 the white population had resumed a majority status (61%; see Pérez 1988, 87).[10]

At the same time, many urban slaves and free people of color also lived in the *intramuros*. Numerous *cabildos* were located within the *intramuros* until 1792, when these institutions were banished to outside the walls. Moreover, many urban slaves lived in quarters in the mansion compounds of their masters within the *intramuros*. For example, the creole slaves who founded Cuba's first Abakuá lodge, Efik Buton (1836), belonged to Doña Josefa Aguilar y Díaz of the Belén neighborhood. For this reason, the Efik Buton members were called the "Belenistas" (Trujillo y Monagas 1882, 363–65; Rodríguez 1881). The Belenistas were considered to be well-heeled and powerful and could act with impunity under the protection of their powerful *amos* (masters).

The *barrios extramuros* were home to diverse Afro-Cuban groups and provoked fear and consternation among Havana's white citizens during the nineteenth and early twentieth centuries. In his early writings (see [1906] 1973), as he scientifically rationalized the progressive agenda of the modern Cuban nation, Fernando Ortiz—a visionary and man of his time—reflected a century or more of white

Figure 1.1.—*Bird's Eye View of Havana*, middle of nineteenth century, after the razing of the fortress walls. The Old City is still visible in its lozenge-shaped outline, and parts of the walls are visible at center left. The *extramuros* extend westward along the Atlantic coast (*middle left*), as well as south and southwest of the Old City.

anxiety and prejudice about urban black populations. The historical *barrios extramuros* were dangerous incubators of *la hampa cubana* (the Cuban underworld) and its *mala vida*, or socially unhygienic "bad life" of *delincuencia* (delinquency), earlier called "vagrancy" (see e.g., Saco [1832] 1946). *La hampa cubana* included in its orbit a range of black social "types" Ortiz delineated in numerous monographs and articles: the *negro esclavo* (slave), the *horro* (free), the *curro* (ostentatious street gypsy), the *brujo* (sorcerer), and the *ñáñigo* (secret society and gang member; see Ortiz [1906] 1973, ix, 7, 9; [1916] 1987; 1927; 1928; [1926–28] 1986; Brown 1993a; León and León 1986). From the point of view of later Cuban and North American ethnographic, historical, and Marxist studies, the *barrios extramuros* would, in contrast, be seen as the vital "strongholds" (*castizos baluartes*) of African traditions and resistance to colonial domination (see Cabrera [1954] 1983, 69, 24–26; [1970] 1983, 36–62; Ortiz 1950, [1951] 1985, 1952–55; Moore 1994, Franco 1977; Sosa Rodríguez 1982; López Valdés 1986; León 1984; Barnet 1983; Knight 1970; Szwed 1969; Abrahams 1983; Abrahams and Szwed 1983). I retain Ortiz's categories not necessarily to endorse them but to reflect long-held Cuban thinking, as well as usefully organize the following section.

Los Negros Esclavos

Arriving Africans joined two principal classes of *esclavos:* urban and domestic, on the one hand, and rural plantation slaves, on the other hand.[11] Arriving Africans who could not speak Spanish were called *bozales* (raw). The tag *negros de nación* referred to their birth in Africa. *Ladinos* were those who, though born in Africa, spoke Spanish or Portuguese and had been baptized. *Criollos* (creoles) were born in Cuba (see Knight 1970, 62). The nineteenth-century numbers of the urban and domestic *esclavos* were relatively small, and "more than 80% of those brought in between 1840 and 1860 . . . ended up working on the plantations of the interior," predominantly in sugar.[12] On the nineteenth-century sugar plantations, covering much of the western and central provinces of the island (Havana, Matanzas, Las Villas), field slaves lived in large, crowded, and guarded *barracones* and worked long hours in gang labor, especially during the *zafra* (harvest). Life was hard and short. Life expectancy averaged less than seven years from the time of arrival. Franklin Knight notes that the class of rural slaves lived a "world apart" from their urban counterparts (see Knight 1970, 60, 64–68; see also Pérez 1988, 98).[13] Urban slaves had the advantages of mobility, greater labor options, wider liberty in social and sexual conduct, access to certain legal protections (see Knight 1970, 560–61), and the organized presence of the African nations in the *cabildo* system. As a result, the institutions of urban centers, such as Havana and Matanzas, became strongholds of reemergent neo-African cultures.

Urban slaves, who worked for their masters as coachmen, carpenters, dressmakers, gardeners, musicians, domestics, and wet nurses, or were hired out by their masters (see Knight 1970, 60–61), worked alongside free people of color in many of the same skilled and semiskilled occupations. In the eighteenth and early nineteenth centuries, slaves hired out could keep part of their earnings, thus gaining opportunities to gather money for their *coartación*. Moreover, the African brotherhoods (*cabildos*) and other kinds of lodges dedicated much of their funds to buying their nation brethren out of slavery (see Bremer 1853, 2:381). In 1857, a free mulatto by the name of Andrés Facundo Cristo de los Dolores Petit, who had attained the high rank of *Isué* in Havana's Bakokó Efó lodge of the Abakuá society, "sold," some believe, the society's founding "secret to the whites" in order to buy his lodge brethren out of slavery (Cabrera [1958] 1970, 53). In the early to mid–nineteenth century, *cabildos* and Abakuá lodges greatly proliferated in the expanding *extramuros*, as did taverns and *bodegas*, neighborhood canteens that sold drinks as well as a variety of goods (see Trujillo y Monagas 1882, 363–65; Ortiz [1926–28] 1986, 17; Rodríguez Herrera 1958–59, 1:199; Landaluze 1881, 69). Beyond the fact that some urban slaves may have lived semi-independently in the *extramuros*, as well as *intramuros*, neighborhoods, these varied institutions of sociability and mutual aid permitted slaves and free blacks to mingle in a variety of activities and ways not possible for slaves on the plantations. That urban slaves could acquire cash, property, "dress . . . smartly . . . in the style of the whites," participate in urban attractions, have recourse to certain legal and extralegal protections (viz., the Belenistas), buy their own freedom, and even escape by melting into the urban environment, mitigated some of the harshness of the Cuban slave system. It also blurred, to an extent, the markers distinguishing slave and free status (Knight 1970, 60–62). That slaves could sartorially blur their objective status and partake of urban economic opportunities, not least, as small vendors and moneylenders (*prestamistas*) suggests the presence of a well-developed urban internal market system among them. This was likely linked to larger regional and transatlantic trade networks, in which a variety of raw and finished luxury items, as well as subsistence goods, must have circulated (e.g., island-made and imported luxury cloth, footware, domestic goods and housewares, and specialized foods).[14]

Los Negros Horros

The *barrios extramuros* also supported Havana's free people of color (*gente de color—los horros*), who had bought themselves out of slavery under the long-reigning policy in the Spanish possessions of *coartación* (see Ortiz [1916]

1987, 285–90; Marrero 1986, 13:163–66). The free African and Afro-Cuban creole population in Cuba was one of the largest historically anywhere in the colonial period, owing to this policy (see Thomas 1971, 35–36, 171–72; Pérez 1988, 62–64), though the possibilities for *coartación*, as indicated, diminished significantly during the nineteenth century.[15] Since the eighteenth century, free people of color had dominated the city's skilled and semiskilled trades—as carpenters, tailors, coachmen, drivers, masons, shipbuilders, stevedores, shoemakers, seamstresses, laundresses, domestics, and market women—"where they would always remain prominent or perhaps dominant even in the 20th century" (see Thomas 1971, 39, 169).[16] They were also priests, militia officers, physicians, attorneys, writers, poets, musicians, and artists, who often dressed "splendidly" and promenaded with their families in "a manner which denotes freedom and prosperity," as the Swedish traveler Fredrika Bremer observed in 1851 (quoted in Pérez 1988, 96). Though they were subject to official restrictions and discrimination in their access to institutions of government, higher learning, and the clergy, their "strategic place in the class-color-hierarchy of the colony" made them able to "undermine the racial assumptions of the colonial social order . . . [and] articulate the circumstances and grievances of the masses of people of color, especially slaves" (Pérez 1988, 96–97).

The case of the Cuban hero José Antonio Aponte, an early-nineteenth-century free creole of color who led a major "conspiracy" to liberate Cuba's slaves (1812),[17] illustrates the kinds of social and political directions members of this class could take and the wealth and diversity of cultural influences they could embrace in their creole self-fashioning. A first corporal in the Militia Battalion of Mixed Mulattos and Blacks—the militia to which Monfundi Siliman referred—Aponte was, like other skilled members of his class, a wood sculptor, painter, and master carpenter (Franco 1977, 119). Though Aponte's alleged Yoruba origin, Changó priesthood, Ogboni society membership, and Lucumí *cabildo* leadership remain unsubstantiated,[18] it is clear that he was a charismatic liaison between many of Havana's urban social and political groups, including the African *cabildos* and liberal white Freemasonry (Franco 1977, 8–13). Erudite and cosmopolitan—in truth, an early Black Atlantic artist-savant, as well as a revolutionary—Aponte was evidently conversant in the norms, languages, and histories of his African and creole constituencies. He was also a self-taught student of history, politics, and world cultures. The authorities found the interior of Aponte's small house on Havana's old Calle Jesus Pelegrino to be adorned with maps of Europe, Asia, and Africa, a white banner bearing the Catholic image of Nuestra Señora de los Remedios, the separatist revolutionary flag and shield,[19] copies of Spanish royal proclamations detailing the privileges of the members of the black and mulatto battalions, and numerous paintings, engravings, and saints' images. This last series of artworks included portraits of internationally famous revolutionary generals, such as George Washington, Toussaint-Louverture, and Henri Christophe—the new black king of Haiti, whose image Aponte was especially fond of showing to his colleagues (Franco 1977, 24–25, 17). As Julius Scott demonstrates, currents of communication around the Atlantic world at the turn of the eighteenth century connected and catalyzed revolutionary cultures and movements among African Diaspora peoples in different geographical centers (Scott 1986). Aponte's "small library" included Cuba's official almanac, novels (e.g., *Don Quixote*), and tomes on natural history, Spain's nobles and military, the city of Rome, Christian catechistic doctrine, world events, architecture, and philosophers, as well as the famous Renaissance Castilian grammatical text *Arte de Nebrija* (Franco 1963, 24; 1977, 132).[20]

Most outstanding among Aponte's possessions confiscated by the authorities was a dazzling seventy-two-page visual document, Aponte's own creation: his *Libro de Pinturas* (*Book of Paintings*). Beneath its laminated covers, its pages were colorfully drawn and painted by Aponte and his assistant, the professional artist José Trinidad Núñez.

The complex, collage-like work was a miracle of "hybridized" iconography, which paralleled and prefigured the kinds of "bricolaged" Old and New World forms that Africans and Afro-Cubans would forge in other domains (see below).[21] The *Libro de Pinturas* presented depictions of events and figures—particularly black figures—from the Bible, Greek mythology, folklore, world political, military, and ecclesiastical history, and current revolutionary events, as well as representations of Havana's architecture and cityscape, along with world geography. For example, pages 39 and 40 depicted the Roman and Greek mythological figures Venus, Cupid, Apollo, Hydra, Andromeda, Neptune, and the biblical event of Saint Michael the Archangel destroying Nebuchadnezzar's City of Babylon. The extremely complex page 44 included depictions of Egypt, the City of Alexander, the house of David, the mountains of Jerusalem, and an angel with a raised sword indicating the Temple of Solomon. It wove in visual narratives about the scorning of the nations that approached the gates of Jerusalem to receive the Queen of Sabá, blacks driving loaded camels, hunters with bows and arrows, elephants, a black man playing with a tiger, a woman and man tied to posts, and a black figure beating a white figure. The page ends with another narrative sequence about a Moorish king who killed an Abyssinian cardinal for preaching against the king's sinful living, only to be struck down himself in punishment by three lightning bolts from heaven (see Franco 1977, 137, 140, 141, 152–54). Many such pages, apparently painted in a realistic manner, meditated upon revolutionary heroes, themes of inhumanity and enslavement, miraculous religious happening, and justice, honor, redemption, and black destiny through a revisionist reading of dominant texts. Aponte's *modus operandi* and the work's apparent significance are not unlike Black North American Ethiopianist millennialist discourse, which situated the historical and spiritual trajectory of the "African race" in relation to a noble classical past, grave present struggles, and a future of promise and deliverance from injustice (see Raboteau 1983). The *Libro de Pinturas* was the apparent summation of this brilliant autodidact's cosmovision, if not also, as the authorities suspected, a cryptic blueprint for subversion and conspiracy (Franco 1977, 112–63, 24). The world of José Antonio Aponte, a revolutionary Renaissance man, was expansive, fueled by global influences that were employed, it appears, as much for his own intellectual, religious, and artistic edification as for the liberation of Cuba's slaves.

Los Negros Curros

A close look at Ortiz's third constituency of the *barrios extramuros, los negros curros,* shows how creative and unusual creole self-fashioning in the early nineteenth century could be, and particularly, how it could confound the colonial classifications of social order (see Ortiz [1926–28] 1986, 3–16). African-descended peoples were grouped into African and creole (*negros de nación* or *criollo*). Socially, they were distinguished by their condition of *horros* or *libertos,* free people of color (*gente de color*), or *esclavos* (slaves). Racial classification in official documents (e.g., baptism, marriage, death) marked one as either a *moreno* (black) or *pardo* (mixed). The *negros curros* were free Afro-Cubans. However, because of their particular origins and highly remarked-upon cultural peculiarities—duly noted in the nineteenth-century *costumbrista* literature (e.g., Landaluze 1881, 129–34)—they earned their own denomination: literally "the black showoffs" (see Brown 1993a). For Fernando Ortiz, who copiously cited contemporaneous accounts in his 1926 to 1928 serialized articles, the *curros* exemplified the *mala vida* and its associated varieties of *delincuencia* during the first half of the nineteenth century (see Ortiz [1906] 1973, ix, 7, 9; Ortiz [1926–28] 1986, 5–6, 189–91). Ortiz identified the *curros'* ultimate origins in the creole-speaking black underclass of Spain's southernmost Atlantic and Mediterranean port cities, such as Cádiz and Málaga. Now these *típos* would perpetuate their "roguishness" and "loutishness" (*picaresca, matonería*) in Havana (Ortiz 1953, 37–38). Though his account reflects the racist prejudice and the pseudoscientific criminological assumptions of the era, Ortiz astutely documented what recent writers would recognize as the *curros'* hybrid or bricolaged cultural style, and its intentional public use in assertive, parodic, and subversive fashion in order to "revise" and "reform" oppressed bodies (see Hebdige 1979; Comaroff 1985, 196–202; Apter 1992, 210–11). According to nineteenth-century accounts, the *negros curros* were loud, outrageously dressed men and women who hung out at local *bodegas* in the *barrios* Jesús María, Carraguao, and, especially, the low-lying, swampy Manglar by the shore of the bay (fig. 1.2). The *curros* were known for their flamboyant clothes and accessories, their outré hairstyle (*mancaperros,* which today we call dreadlocks), and their incomprehensible—to whites—pronunciation of the Spanish language. The men were known particularly for their filed teeth, drooping straw hats, flared linen shirts with high cuffs, striped bellbottom trousers, lowcut canvas shoes with gold buckles, and gold earrings. The women were known for their silk shawls, masses of gold jewelry, and loud wooden clogs (*chancletas*) (Ortiz 1927, 285–325; see also chaps. 3 and 4). The *curros* dramatically marked their early-nineteenth-century urban identity through dress, language, and the assertive occupation of public space (see Thomas 1971, 180).[22] As such, the *curros* presented themselves in a manner that defied easy ethnic or socio-institutional placement within the colonial society. They were neither members of determinate African nations, nor the free classes of tradespeople. Indeed, their nineteenth-century denomination, *curro,* was not grounded in empirical social categories, but based precisely on their manner of cultural performance—their expressive and subversive "showiness." Thus, the *negros curros* might be seen, in terms favorable to postmodern treatments of African Diaspora cultures, as Havana's nineteenth-century "Black Signifiers" or "Signifying Blacks" (see Gates 1988, 285–321). At the same time, however, the *curros,* arguably, remain ciphers in the historical accounts—projections of middle-class fantasy, fear, and moral condemnation. It is not entirely clear who they

Figure 1.2.—Víctor Patricio de Landaluze, *Los Curros,* 1881. Color lithograph, approximately 11 x 9 inches.

were beyond a host of startled and prejudiced contemporaneous representations of their alleged excesses and Ortiz's sociological typing. Indeed, observers' evaluations of these black men and women regularly conform to the stereotypes of sartorially outrageous blacks—minstrels, dandies, hustlers, and pimps—throughout the Diaspora and up through this country's 1970s "blaxploitation" films (see Gates 1990; Powell 2000; Hurston 1983, 53–54). Still, contemporaneous use of *curro* to name this group throws into relief the fact that identities, within and against the colonial constraints of race and class, were not born, but made, through everyday performances and textual representations of them. The *curros* fashioned themselves as the *chevaliers* and aristocrats of Barrio Manglar (Ortiz [1926–28] 1986, 23). But they were not the only aristocracy in town.

HAVANA'S MINIATURE MONARCHIES: THE *CABILDOS DE NACIÓN*

Africans and their creole descendants in Cuba, as well as diverse immigrant groups, created clubs, mutual aid societies, and religious fraternities as early as the sixteenth century, the first century of Cuba's colonization by the Spanish. The more formalized and officially regulated of these institutions were modeled on the traditional corporations that had organized Spanish society under Church and Crown since the thirteenth and fourteenth centuries (Ortiz 1921, 5–39).[23] Though the official religious fraternities associated with the Catholic Church were, strictly speaking, *cofradías,* these and the more informal social "clubs" were all called *cabildos* in Cuba. In a famous eighteenth-century example of the Roman Catholic Church's attempt at the "gentle" conversion of the African population, twenty-one African social "clubs" were incorporated as Catholic religious fraternities (i.e., *cofradías*) when the ambitious Bishop of Havana, Pedro Morell de Santa Cruz, instituted saintly devotions in each of them in 1755 (Marrero 1988, 14:172, 175, 282; see also Klein 1967, 100; Murphy 1988, 26–29; Brandon 1993, 69–74). Each *cabildo* undoubtedly mounted a *capilla* (shrine) to its patron *santo,* as the *cofradías* and *gremios* (guilds) in Seville had done in previous centuries, and would carry their patron out into the street in procession on feast days (Ortiz 1921, 12).

The institutions that Fernando Ortiz identified as *cabildos de nación* claimed African-born (i.e., *negros de nación*) slaves, as opposed to island born (*negros criollos*) membership. The *cabildos de nación* were headed by hereditary or elected rulers ("king" and "queen," sometimes "boss" [*capataz*] or "president"), were housed in their own establishments, and claimed an official Catholic patron saint. These *cabildos* provided in times of sickness and death, held masses for deceased members, collected funds to buy nation-brethren out of slavery, held regular dances and diversions on Sundays and feast days, and sponsored religious masses, processions, and dancing carnival groups (now called *comparsas*) around the annual cycle of Catholic festival days (see Ortiz [1920] 1960, passim; 1921, 5, 20; see also Arozarena 1961; Deschamps Chapeaux 1968).

State and church authorities intended the *cabildos* to be mechanisms of control from the top down along the lines of a divide-and-rule strategy, as Cuban historian Rafael L. López Valdés shows. In 1843, for example, the governor of Santiago de Cuba decreed "that the whites are prohibited from joining the gatherings of the blacks, that the black creoles do not join with the Africans and neither should the Africans or *bozales* [newly arrived] associate amongst themselves at will, as those of each nation will have their own exclusive *cabildo*. . . . A careful government should foment the principle of disunion, better through efficacious and indirect methods" (López Valdés 1987, 7).[24]

Whether or not the principle of "disunion" controlled the slave populations, it clearly had the effect of fomenting discrete ethnic identifications. In other words, particular ethnic identifications became institutionalized denominations within the *cabildo* system. Just as Roger Bastide demonstrates in the Brazilian case, the *cabildos* acted as "niches" or "new social frameworks" for the recreation of discrete neo-African social groupings (Bastide [1960] 1978, 159–60, 58–77; see also Mintz and Price [1976] 1992). As such, they also acted as "a hiding place" (Bastide [1960] 1978, 160) and as generative bases or "incubating cells" for the regathering of specialized bodies of knowledge and the intergenerational transmission of African-based religious cultures (Palmié 1993, 341; see chap. 2). Finally, as legalized religious societies under the banner of particular Catholic saints, these *cabildos* represented the historical drawing boards for the syncretic "double system" (Marks 1987, 227) of African and popular Catholic practices noted throughout the former Spanish, French, and Portuguese possessions in the New World (see Herskovits 1996; Bascom 1972; Bastide [1960] 1978, chap. 5; Thompson 1983, 18; Brandon 1993, 59–78, and table 3; see app. 5 of this book).

The term *cabildo,* literally "town council," derived from the nomenclature of Spanish ecclesiastical and municipal governance (i.e., *cabildo* is synonymous with *ayuntamiento;* Ortiz 1921, 11). In fact, it did describe a level of political and administrative jurisdiction, within limits circumscribed by the Cuban colonial government—headed by the island's captain general, who lived in a huge stone palace on Old Havana's Plaza de Armas. The *cabildos de nación* borrowed the titles of official state, church, and civic institutions, especially from the monarchy and the military, to describe their offices. *Cabildo* kings and, sometimes, presidents, were supported by a "court," consisting of a "queen" or two (second in rank), and lower-ranking officers, such as the *abanderado* (standard bearer) and the *mayor de plaza* (chief of ceremonies). These last two titles derived from formal hierarchy of the Spanish Cuban military and the battalions of *Pardos* and *Mulatos* (Ortiz 1921, 6).[25]

The *cabildos de nación* were, in effect, miniature neo-African monarchies of the urban Cuban *barrios extramuros.* The nineteenth-century historian Esteban Pichardo noted in his research in Cuban cities east of Havana that the *cabildos* were called "kingdoms" (*reinados*), as in much of Latin America during the same period (Pichardo cited in Ortiz 1921, 6; see also Bastide 1972, 97; McAlister 2002, 136–38). In Cuban cities, *cabildo* kings guided, disciplined, and inspired society members, who were their immediate subjects. In turn, *cabildo* kings were the "accredited ambassadors" representing their "nations" to the captain general of the Island. The *cabildo* "king" or "boss," Ortiz explains, "was the political link that legally united [his African constitutencies] to the society of the whites" (Ortiz 1921, 7). As a result, the global, hierarchical chain of command enunciated by Monfundi Siliman implied a principle of "indirect rule." The authority of the colonial government over the day-to-day management of massive and heterogeneous indigenous populations was mediated through an "indigenous" intermediary, the king. Undoubtedly, such indirect rule gave the king and his subjects a margin of room to move, as it were. Colonial Cuban power relations might usefully, then, be seen in Atlantic perspective. In other Atlantic colonial-era systems of indirect rule, such as the British Empire's government in Nigeria, power and authority over indigenous peoples were subject to forms of negotiation with local kings and chiefs.[26]

"FLAGS AND SABRES" MEET "DRUMMING, DANCING AND SINGING": HYBRIDIZED *CABILDO* PROCESSIONS AND PERFORMANCES

Sundays, saints' feast days, and momentous holy days witnessed grand street processions in which *cabildo* leaders and their entourages flamboyantly outfitted themselves in the garments of monarchy and military, while dancers donned plumed headdresses and African horned and vegetal masquerades (see plate 1).[27] Cuba's largest historical carnival took place on Epiphany, 6 January. Called "the Day of Kings" (*El Día de Reyes*), Epiphany marked the moment on the Catholic sacred calendar when the Three Magi, or Kings, traveled to present gifts to the baby Jesus. After 1792, when *cabildo* establishments were forcibly relocated to the *extramuros,*[28] carnival processions "came out" of their establishments and entered the fortress gates of Havana's *intramuros.* They marched through the business and residential thoroughfares of Mercaderes, Obispo, and O'Reilly Streets toward the central Plaza de Armas, the site of the palace of the captain general of the island. In the courtyard of the palace, as at other stops along the way, procession members performed dances, ritually demanded and received *aguinaldo* (money gratuities), and then returned home (see Brown 1993a, 54–55; and plate 1). *Cabildo* processions took over the main thoroughfares of the

Figure 1.3.—Pierre Toussaint Frédéric Miahle, *El Día de Reyes* (Day of Kings) carnival, Havana, 1838. Lithograph.

Old City's *intramuros* to such an extent that bourgeois families stayed inside. Genteel spectators watched and delivered *aguinaldo* from balconies or from behind barred windows (Ortiz [1920] 1960, 10–11; fig. 1.3, plate 1).

The ritualized exchange of *aguinaldo* exemplified the ways in which carnival could be an arena of contested meanings. For the giver of *aguinaldo*, the exchange could mean a condescending "tip" to an amusing black buffoon or beggar. For the receiver, *aguinaldo* could mean the power to extract tribute on a day in which status assignments became more fluid and reversible and the streets were temporarily owned by Havana's Africans. Moreover, the earning of money for one's own aesthetic enterprise—costume production and dance performance—one surmises, could revise the terms of the daily forcible extraction of slave labor (see Brown 1993a, 54–55; for other Caribbean islands, see Abrahams 1968; 1983, 100–105; McAlister 2002, 142–47).[29]

Carnival processions evinced both individual and collective performance rules. Though *aguinaldo* was individually demanded, the group as a whole presented, in sight, sound, and action, a force to be reckoned with. The group literally took over the street from curb to curb in a public space, where its collective identity and complex hierarchy were on display. The American physician J. G. F. Wurdemann described a dramatic Day of Kings procession in 1844 in the Havana Province town of Güines.

> [On] . . . *el día de los Reyes,* almost unlimited liberty was given to the negroes. Each tribe, having elected its king and queen, paraded the streets with a flag, having its name, and the words *viva Isabella,* with the arms of Spain, painted on it. Their majesties were dressed in the extreme of the fashion, and were very ceremoniously waited on by the ladies and gentlemen of the court, one of the ladies holding an umbrella over the head of the queen. They bore their honors with that dignity which the negro loves so much to assume, which they, moreover, preserved in the presence of the whites. The whole gang was under the command of a negro marshall, who, with a drawn sword, having a small piece of sugar-cane stuck on its point, was continually on the move to preserve order in the ranks. But the chief object in the group was an athletic negro, with a fantastic straw helmet, an immensely thick girdle of strips of palm-leaves around his waist, and other uncouth articles of dress. Whenever they stopped . . . this frightful figure would commence a devil's dance, which was the signal for all his court to join in a general fandango." (Wurdemann 1844, 83–84)

Wurdemann's description shows the nations' identifying flags (*banderas*) as rallying points for the public unfolding of multiple miniature monarchies. The historian Hubert Aimes, citing contemporaneous sources, wrote that on Sunday afternoons in Matanzas "flags on high staffs pointed out the places about town where the negroes gathered to indulge in their national dances" (Aimes 1905, 22). The *banderas,* in effect, colorfully remapped public urban space on the alternative political and cultural geography of the African nations.

Historically, *banderas* were time-honored markers of political units, institutions, and regions, as well as religious, mutual aid, and occupational societies in the Iberian-Atlantic world. Every banner would have its particular coat-of-arms, symbolism, and set of colors. The first and most common *bandera* flown in Cuba, of course, was the Spanish royal standard, which featured the figures of the castle and the lion and the preferred colors of red and yellow. As early as the time of Columbus, and through the centuries that followed, innumerable and diverse banners presided over all sorts of institutionalized events, particularly political and martial spectacles (see Roig de Leuchsenring 1950, 14–15). In Cuba, the form and iconography of the *banderas* of the *cabildos de nación* may have been influenced as much by the protocols of the Battalions of Mulattos and Blacks (Deschamps Chapeaux 1968, 50; Marrero 1986, 13:140–43)—which, as Siliman Monfundi noted, included such accessories as "flags, drums, rifles, and sabres"—as by the dominant institutional units of the state.[30] Similarly, Patrick Polk has demonstrated in the Haitian case, the banners (*drapo*) of the Vodou societies ultimately derive from the flags of the Napoleonic regimental tradition, which were taken up by the revolutionary forces of the emergent black nation in the early nineteenth century (Polk 1995).

Cabildo banderas featured specific information, such as the society's name, its founding date, its specific colors, the name and image of its Catholic patron saint, and perhaps other coats of arms—as in the Wurdemann example—embroidered or painted on decoratively fringed satin or silk panels. The *bandera* of each *cabildo de nación* was in the charge of a titled officer called the *abanderado* (standard bearer). An impressive *bandera* in the Fernando Ortiz ethnographic collection in Havana[31] features the society's name and founding date in gold embroidery: *LA SOCIEDAD DE SOCORROS MUTUOS NACION LUCUMI DE SANTA BARBARA, AÑO 1820* (the Mutual Aid Society of the Lucumí Nation of Santa Bárbara 1820). The red silk banner—red being the principal color of Santa Bárbara—probably also included the saint's image in its circular central field, the border of which is embellished with floral, and other organic decorative motifs (fig. 1.4).

Figure 1.4.—*Cabildo* banner of *La Sociedad de Socorros Mutuos Nación Lucumí de Santa Bárbara, Año 1820.* Silk, 43 x 30 inches. Fernando Ortiz Collection, La Casa de Africa, Havana. (Photograph by David H. Brown, 1992.)

Cuba's Lucumí *cabildos* frequently claimed Santa Bárbara as their official patron,[32] a saint whose function and iconography, particularly her association with fire and counterpointed red and white colors (figs. 4.10, 4.20, 5.21), were, and are, identified with the powerful Yoruba-Lucumí *oricha* of thunder, Changó. Therefore, the *bandera's* decorative organic motifs might be doubly read as the zigzag iconography of lightning associated with Changó.

The banners of the *cabildos de nación* played with the iconography of apical worldly and spiritual authority, particularly through their use of such representations as royal coats of arms, headgear, and the iconography of the societies' spiritual patrons. In doing so, they inscribed messages of both overt and covert allegiance. The *banderas* in the 1844 Wurdemann account seem straightforward enough. They combine the societies' (nations') names with graphic allegiance to the restored Spanish Bourbon empire of Isabella II (1830–68) by featuring Spain's coat of arms and the words "long live Isabella." Such expressions were consonant with Monfundi Siliman's declaration of fealty to King Ferdinand VII thirty-six years earlier. Yet, in practice, what kind of power, authority, and agency did these miniature monarchies and their kings imagine for themselves within the imperial chain of being that Monfundi articulated—the Christian God, Jesus, the church, the Spanish crown, Cuba's captain general, and the African nation? Who, in fact, ruled the *cabildos?* The double reference of many *banderas* to an African deity and a Catholic saint could, it appears, revise official allegiance to the church. The red *bandera* of the Sociedad de Socorros Mutuos Nación Lucumí de Santa Bárbara subtly heralded Lucumí identity and fealty to Changó. At the same time, as Roger Bastide suggests for the Brazilian case, the Catholic patron saints themselves were transvalued. The saints became the humanized "mystical kin," confidants, protectors, and liberators of the Africans. "In the end, the ultimate purpose of these fraternities became an earthly one rather than a heavenly one. They became a means through which slaves could gain their freedom. . . . [The Catholic religion] which was being used as a means of controlling [the black] and integrating him into a society that persecuted him [was transformed] into an instrument of ethnic solidarity and social justice" (Bastide [1960] 1978, 115–16, 114). In the very year of Wurdemann's account of black fealty to the Spanish queen, the Cuban government crushed the "Escalera" rebellion in Matanzas, hatched through *cabildo* organizations, and publicly executed its leaders in a brutal manner. Wurdemann's own account noted white "creole fear in the aftermath of La Escalera': 'All the horrors of San Domingo [Haiti] were to have been repeated [in Cuba]'" (Wurdemann quoted in Pérez 1988, 103).

It is thus not surprising that *cabildo banderas* could inscribe political messages during the public, liminal, and even potentially dangerous moment of carnival, when massive numbers of enslaved and minority populations filled the streets. In the first half of the nineteenth century, among blacks and the white Creole owning class, Santo Domingo was clearly not forgotten. For example, the apparently innocuous rivalry between two archetypal Cuban *cabildo* nations, the Congo and the Carabalí, in the eastern Cuban town of Bayamo in 1836 figured global political struggle through a battle of iconography: headgear. In eastern Cuba, Pedro Deschamps Chapeaux notes, *cabildo banderas* were influenced not only by the iconography of the black and mulatto militias—which were presumably loyal to the crown—but also by that of the Haitian Revolution. "This happened in 1836, in a dispute that occurred in Bayamo, Oriente, between the Congo and Carabalí *cabildos*. Organized under the patronage of San Blas and San Benedicto [respectively?], the *bandera* of the Congos flaunted a royal crown, proclaiming them devotees of the queen of Spain; the Carabalís substituted for the royal crown a hat of the model used by the principal chiefs of the Haitian government, and they said they were partisans of the captain general [of the island of Cuba]. The *bandera* was confiscated by the authorities, who saw in this dispute something more than the simple celebration of the patron saint of the *cabildo*" (Deschamps Chapeaux 1968, 50). Rivalries between religious societies throughout the Iberian-Atlantic Catholic world were commonplace, as were rivalries between the different ethnic nations in the colonial urban setting and throughout the African diaspora (Christian 1981, 118; Bastide [1960] 1978, 114; see also McAlister 2002). What did it mean for the Congos of Bayamo to side with the queen of Spain (Isabella II) against the captain general of the island of Cuba? If the Congos' imperial crown at all suggested royal disdain for mere island authority—the captain general—as well as their Carabalí rivals, the iconography of the Carabalí *bandera* was evidently seen as politically dangerous by the government. The Haitian military tricorne could stand for the slave system's overthrow—the Creole planter and merchant's worst nightmare (Pérez 1988, 103).[33]

Borrowed Royal Iconography and Creolization

Fernando Ortiz observed that the dress and accessories of *cabildo* processional in Cuba and throughout the Spanish possessions during the colonial period were "taken" and "borrowed" from Iberian and colonial institutions of monarchy and military, as well as from the material culture of the slaveholding class (Ortiz 1921, 6–9; [1920] 1960, 19). Throughout the African Diaspora in the colonial period, writers and observers consistently misunderstood the "artfulness" and signifying intent of black performances, conveniently seeing them as mere "imitation," a naive mimicking of white manners in order to enjoy prestige one day a year (see also Abrahams and Szwed 1983; Abrahams 1983, 13–18, 26; Piersen 1988, 117–28).

Cabildo kings typically came out on the Day of Kings in "long military coats, starched shirts, enormous ties, flamboyant double-peaked hats, gold braid and wide, loud sashes across the chest, decorations, swords on the belt, great staffs with silver points—a symbol of authority. . . . All of these adornments," noted Ortiz, "were taken principally from the Spanish army" (Ortiz 1921, 6–9; and see Ortiz [1920] 1960, 17–21; fig. 1.5, plate 1).[34] Alternatively, kings' costumes emphasized the monarchial attributes of crown, scepter, and prestige cloth (e.g., plate 1, *left*, and fig. 1.6). In towns outside of Havana proper, the nineteenth-century Cuban historian Esteban Pichardo observed, the rulers of African organizations were elevated on thrones and accompanied by grand entourages (Pichardo quoted in Ortiz 1921, 6). One impressive Havana *cabildo* ruler, as described in 1856 by the French writer Leon Beauvallet (1856), emerged on the Day of Kings in "a genuine costume of a king of the Middle Ages, a very proper red, close coat, velvet vest and a magnificent gilt paper crown This negro, who was enormously tall, and had a tolerably good-looking head, gave his hand gravely to a sort of feminine blackamoor who represented some queen or other. He

Figure 1.5.—*Capataz* or *rey* (boss or king) of *cabildo de nación* procession on the Day of Kings, with peaked hat, sash, silver-bulbed staff, and saber. (Courtesy María Fernanda Ortiz Herrera, Representante Sucesores de Fernando Ortiz.)

walked with a deliberate, majestic step, never laughed, and seemed to be reflecting deeply on the grandeur of his mission to this world" (Beauvallet quoted in Aimes 1905, 20–21; and Ortiz [1920] 1960, 17).[35]

The finery of *cabildo* queens included puff-shouldered, flowing gowns with petticoats, jewelry, and large umbrellas, as documented by the Spanish *costumbrista* painter, Víctor Patricio de Landaluze (1828–89) in his c. 1878 painting of the Day of Kings in Havana (fig. 1.7, plate 1).[36]

Figure 1.6.—Commercial calendar with cigar wrapper art (*marquilla cigarrera*) grotesquely representing Day of Kings "Crowned Devils," Havana, 1866. The caption reads, "The Crowned Devils will punish your sins." (From León 1984.)

Many of these aristocratic details of *cabildo* display were, in fact, imitations and borrowings from the most immediate source Afro-Cubans had available to them. For example, as Fernando Ortiz noted, the expensive silver-pointed hardwood staffs of the *cabildo* kings and the luxurious dresses and great parasols of the "Ethiopian ladies" of the court were often "loaned" (*prestaban*) to them by their masters (Ortiz [1920] 1960, 19). Still other hand-held staffs claimed non-African souces. Ortiz noted African-derived "idols" or "fetishes," which *cabildo* queens often carried, topped with small, dressed dolls, called *anaquillé* (Ortiz [1921] 1960, 40–41). Thus, in the center of a striking *carte de visite* from about 1860 of a Havana carnival group by the American photographer C. D. Fredricks (1823–94; fig. 1.7), a young woman stands serenely. Her simple but elegant puff-shouldered spreading white gown and tiara suggest her status as a member of the *cabildo*'s royalty.[37] Lacking only the group's king, the photograph documents the standard-bearer (*abanderado*) holding the society's flag on a pole, while three drummers sit astride their tubular Kongo *ngomo*-style drums (alt. *yuka, makuta;* see Ortiz 1952–55, 4:180–200).[38] Two of the

Figure 1.7.—C. D. Fredricks, *cabildo* carnival group, Havana, c. 1860. *Carte de visite* depicting standard-bearer, queen (with tiara, *center*), two dancers with plumed headgear, and three drummers. (Courtesy Schomburg Center for Research in Black Culture, New York Public Library.)

Figure 1.8.—Jean Baptiste Debret, *Coleta para a manutenção da Igreja do Rosario* [Collection for the maintenance of the Church of Our Lady of the Rosary (a church built by African nations in the Pelourinho section of Salvador, Bahía)], 1828.

drummers wear feathered spherical Congo wrist rattles, called *ensansi* or *maracas de muñeca*.[39] The two dancers wear plumed metabanded headdresses, bead necklaces, tight-fitting cloth tops, pleated skirts, and loose leggings.

The *carte de visite* nicely confirms the verisimilitude of Landaluze's 1878 depiction. Landaluze's queens wear puff-shouldered, petticoated gowns and tiaras, his drummers play *ngomo*-style drums, wear *maracas de muñeca,* and one dancer dons an identical costume of feathered crown, tight-fitting long-sleeved top and leggings, and a skirt. Landaluze does not fail to include a crucial detail: a finely dressed woman beneath the spreading umbrella holds an *anaquillé* in her right hand.

Elegantly dressed Afro-Cuban royalty, as documented by Wurdemann, Beauvallet, Landaluze, and Fredricks, were not alone in the Americas (see Koster 1817, 25–28; Debret [1834–39] 1940; Aimes 1905; Bastide [1960] 1978, chap. 5; Piersen 1988, 117–28; Hill 1972, 33–37). In Peru, Ortiz's research notes, black society queens emerged "in the dress style of the whites: covered with fine Spanish lace, a sash of precious stones, belt and scepter of gold, pendant earrings and necklace of pearls. . . . Each queen had her court of young slaves, in imitation of her aristocratic mistresses [female slavemasters], decked out luxuriously" (Ortiz 1921, 6–9). The African courts of the religious fraternities (*irmandades*) in Salvador, Bahia, Brazil, featured an equivalent cluster of royal attributes. The French artist Jean Baptiste Debret (1768–1848), visiting Salvador in 1828, depicted an enthroned king and queen, with their entourage, on the street beside what was probably a church (Debret [1834–39] 1940). The king and queen wear pointed and crucifix-topped double-arched crowns, respectively, along with crucifix necklaces and other jewelry. Seated on a heavy, thronelike chair, the king dons a mantle, an elaborate cape, and pantaloons with leggings and carries a figured scepter with a crown finial. The diminutive female attendant for the king's flowing cape and the sword-bearing male courtier wear feather-topped, turbanlike headgear (fig. 1.8). These double-arched and open crowns of multiple points, which are also documented in the Cuban case, derive from borrowings within the pan-European history of royal headgear. The open and/or arched crowns have their sources in the Roman diadem, the *fleurs-de-lis* of the Middle Ages, and subsequent modifications that produced double- and triple-arched crowns. The arched crown then appropriated ecclesiastical features (miters, crucifixes) beginning with the fourteenth-century rule of the Spanish Bourbon Charles IV. The divine authority of kings was signified precisely by the ecclesiastical regalia of the church.[40] These hybrid royal and ecclesiastical features of *cabildo* and *irmandade* crowns may have signified in similar ways for black kings and queens. As shown below, *cabildo* royalty were intimately tied to the divine sanction of their institution's spiritual patrons, the *orishas*. Such "borrowed" royal styles constituted, and continue to represent, an African Diaspora lingua franca of authority and elegance within the carnival framework of aesthetically marked public display.[41] Not surprisingly, such borrowings were a Black Atlantic phenomenon. Given the colonization and missionization of Nigeria in the second half of the nineteenth century, many beaded Yoruba kings' crowns drew their form and iconography from British royalty and the Anglican Church hierarchy (H. Drewal and Mason 1998, 70–77).[42]

Festival Theory and Creolization

Undoubtedly, elaborate courtly and military attributes created an impressive visual display, which was intended to win prestige in competition with other groups and to earn *aguinaldo* from charmed observers on carnival day. Yet such displays were also intended to underscore the participants' potent roles as duly constituted—hereditary or elected—year-round authorities. Despite their tone of condescension, the Wurdemann and Beauvallet accounts clearly show *cabildo* royal attributes as integral to a processional performance style of intentional and self-conscious formal "decorum" (Abrahams 1983, 17, 81–82, 90, 101–2, 155). This public display of formal decorum is an aspect of what Moore and Myerhoff term "secular ceremony" (1977, 3). Secular ceremony occupies the "ritual" end of the "play-ritual continuum" in the theorizing of festival performance. While play inverts the social order and leans toward license, ritual confirms the social order and is highly regulated. Play may rely on parody, irony, jokes, and clowning; its semantics may be open-ended, unorthodox, fragmented, and often highly individualized, enabling it to elude control and to transcend or subvert ideology. In contrast, ritual seriousness in public celebration, and its confirmatory and legitimizing symbols of flags, uniforms, and other attributes of authority, like crowns, scepters, sashes, medals, and so on—can reinforce and affirm a constituted social order if deployed by state power. Yet, when deployed by oppressed or marginalized groups, such authoritative symbols can represent not merely temporary expressions of "anti-structure" (Turner 1969; V. Turner 1977; Alonso 1990), but established and ongoing *alternative structures* of authority that publicly assert themselves during the carnival moment of "almost unlimited liberty." Though they "came out" (*salieron*) publicly only during Epiphany and selected feast days, black royalty, in fact, "ruled" throughout the year in their *cabildos*. Like Monfundi Siliman, they maintained great influence over large constituencies in the black *barrios*. In short, royal processions of stylized court and military dress "artfully" presented subversive models of power, authority, and collective solidarity (see Abrahams 1983, 26) in the face of the colonial social order. Such subversion and collective solidarity was achieved, not necessarily in the simple binary sense of "within the parameters of the masters' monopoly of power, but *separate* from the masters' institutions"; it was achieved, as Mary Karasch and Palmié astutely nuance the point, precisely by "manipulating elite institutions, to serve African goals" (see Palmié 1989, 8–9; 1992, 341; emphasis added; Mintz and Price 1993, 39; Karasch 1979, 138).[43] Manipulation was realized in and through what observers saw as "borrowing" and "imitation."

The specter of *cabildo* royalty may have provoked a certain anxiety in observers who could not reconcile conventional signs of high earthly authority (kingship) with the marching participants' racially and socially subordinate class status. In contemporaneous accounts, royal and military attributes and processional were regarded as mere imitations, as if the participants were impostors and buffoons playing at prestige and authority on their one day of the year to be king—their "only day . . . of freedom" (Ortiz [1920] 1960, 15). In other words, it was convenient for observers to confound, rather than critically differentiate, ritual and play (see Abrahams 1983, 26). The ambivalent rhetorical pattern in both the Wurdeman and Beauvallet accounts hedges an initial wonder at the impressive royal *cabildo* displays with condescending assumptions about black racial traits, character, and behavior, thereby attempting to contain meanings antithetical to operative stereotypes. Though Dr. Wurdemann intends to unmask black royal dignity as a pretense ("that dignity which the negro loves so much to assume"), he is compelled to note that such dignity (read critically as ritual seriousness) was "moreover, preserved in the presence of the whites" (Wurdemann 1844). The "mask" of solemnity and composure was stylized *and* real; indeed, it replaced the mask of the buffoon or grotesque that many observers expected of slavery's racialized others. Undoubtedly, the educated 1844 American physician and traveler was aware of early minstrelized representations of blacks in the United States (see McElroy 1990).[44] This public display of dignity of countenance and physical bearing by royally dressed Africans might be seen, in contemporary analytical terms, as the symbolic and practical "revision," or "reform" (see Comaroff 1985, 219–28; Apter 1992, 210–11), of the slave's body as the body of the king.

The ethnohistorical hypotheses of Fernando Ortiz and Hubert Aimes about the significance of *cabildo* kingship, ceremonial, and iconography were later echoed in the more theorized writings of 1970s American creolists. Ortiz and Aimes believed that the formal displays of black organizations in the Americas were "direct survivals" (Aimes 1905, 16) or "reviv[als]" (Ortiz [1920] 1960, 20) of "African" traditions of kingship. More recently, folklorists Roger Abrahams and John Szwed suggested that the apparently European-derived styles of black Caribbean performance, such as the use of ornamental Elizabethan high oratory in speechifying, courtly dances, and dress and the status order of British courtly hierarchy in carnival organization, were less "European" in their essence than "loan-translations" of foreign "prestige" forms. Loan translation, a concept borrowed from historical linguistics, may be seen to occur not only in language, but also in other expressive domains, such as music, iconography, and performance. In Szwed and Abrahams's elegant speculative argument about the formation of creole styles in the Caribbean, such borrowings acted as local "substitutions" for similar prestige varieties of public speech and acts that had existed in Africa (Abrahams and Szwed 1983, 36). "As with the majority of performance events introduced into Afro-American life from Europe," they write, "the focus and uses of the ceremony were changed along with some aspects of the pattern of performance, and these changes were in accord with the ethical and esthetic demands of a conceptual system shared by Africans and Afro-Americans" (1983, 36).[45]

In colonial and neocolonial Caribbean societies, sociolinguist Karl Reisman observes, people have historically borrowed new expressive forms as part of larger strategies of "reprisal" and "indirection"—the latter being a foundational concept that Reisman drew from Melville Herskovits. African values of "discretion, tact, and mature reserve," Herskovits believed, became resources in the "force[d] discretion" that was a "survival technique" during and after slavery in the Americas (Herskovits 1941, 158). Where black cultural systems—for example, creole speech—have been stigmatized and "denied," Reisman observes, people "'take on' forms from the immediate environment as a mask behind which, or through which, alternate meanings are conveyed. Or they may transform the meanings of forms which are forced on them." Such transformations—"maskings" and "transvaluations," respectively—produce "syncretisms [that] increase the area of conscious or unconscious double statement and the possibility of symbolic play" (Reisman 1970, 131). In producing syncretisms, creative agents "remodel" or "reshap[e] the forms of symbols to resemble as closely as possible *both the historical source and the forms current in the environment*" (131; emphasis added). Any "form that is retained [new or old] is likely to be one that can be interpreted in several ways, as related to a number of traditions" (132). In other words, syncretisms may not merely represent old wine in new bottles or new wine in old bottles—that is, masking or transvaluation, respectively. The historically situated performances of agents creatively change the shape of the bottles themselves into new, "creole" forms, which "resemble," but do not reduce to, their multifarious "sources." This family "resemblance" is symbolically ambiguous and aesthetically playful, as well as being strategically indirect, as in the trickster-like puns and metaphors that undergird "signifying" in black North American literary and popular discourse (see Gates 1988).

In Reisman's terms, Afro-Cuban organizations "took on" and "remodeled" the iconography, status rankings, and processional style of encountered colonial forms, including those of monarchy and military, as well as elements of the slaveholders' material culture. The unique institutions of *cabildo* kingship "resembled," but were not reducible to, their putatively African and European sources. These new institutions were "creole" not only because they were "island born" and locally elaborated over time, but also because they were shared and relatively standardized, like a lingua franca, among the quite heterogeneous African nations during the eighteenth and nineteenth centuries. Crowns, jewels, scepters, thrones, suits and gowns of fine cloth, *banderas*, ranked entourages, and so on—tokens of legitimation and empowerment—became the symbolic currency of public performance and reputation on the Day of Kings.

Thus, *cabildo* courts modeled their formal dress styles and processions not so much on "Europe," in any direct or essential sense, but on a variety of already elaborated, local sources, some of which had been compounded and revised over centuries. These included creolized contributions from the black carnival processions of Seville and the imported conventions of African kingship long modified by the use of European ceremonial.[46] One fundamental model of "kingship" must have come from the Three Kings or Magi of Epiphany themselves, who, in the New Testament, traveled to deliver gifts to the recently born Messiah. "Legend has it," Ortiz notes, that the Three Kings "were of royal lineage . . . [and they] were depicted in crowns and royal cloaks of velvet and ermine" (Ortiz [1920] 1960, 21; Bettelheim 1993, 20–22). Of the Three Kings, Balthazar, Gaspar, and Melchior, Melchior eventually came to be represented in art as *el rey negro* [black king] and was interpreted as such by minority populations in the Spanish domains as early as the fifteenth century (Ortiz [1920] 1960, 21; Deschamps Chapeaux 1968, 50–51). *Cabildo* members in Cuba were intimately familiar with the iconography of the Three Kings, and Melchior

Figure 1.9.—"Etiquette" or "court" ball of free people of color, nineteenth-century Havana. (From Levi Marrero, *Cuba, economía y sociedad* [Río Piedras, Puerto Rico: Editorial San Juan, 1986], 14:241.)

served as the preferred spiritual patron of some of Cuba's African nations, particularly the *cabildos* of the Congos Reales (Royal Congos; Ortiz [1920] 1960, 21; see Ortiz [1916] 1987, 45–46).

Still, the sources of the cluster of royal "attributes of European origin" of the Congo *cabildo* kings (such as dress coat and pants, a double-peaked hat or crown, a scepter, a saber, and a royal mantle) were overdetermined. European royal attributes of prestige had long been utilized by the Catholicized kings of the Congo (Ortiz [1920] 1960, 7). As early as 1491, King Nzinga a Knuwu of the Kongo capital, Mbanza Kongo, had accepted "brocade and velvet fabrics, lengths of satin, silk, and linen, [and] magnificent garments" from the Portuguese. Seventeenth-century drawings reveal that Congo kings owned intricately carved European-style wood thrones and circular, openwork pointed crowns as official "insignia of power" (see Balandier 1968, 45). Not only the Kongo-Angola groups, but many West African groups as well, who had also built much of their royal and martial iconography upon European imports—for example, thrones, banners, prestige cloth, and umbrellas—must have arrived in Cuba already familiar with iconographically hybridized royal displays (see Polk 1995, 331–34; Cosentino 1995, 248–50).

Other local sources of inspiration for carnival prestige iconography undoubtedly included the sartorial display and pomp not only of the Cuban colonial slaveholding classes, but also of the large urban class of *libertos* in Havana, both of which had their own proximate sources in a descending chain of imperial imitations. If the *cabildo* queens' dresses borrowed from the aristocratic opulence of their slavery mistresses, these latter "elegant Havanans" had themselves imitated "loyally . . . the fashions of Paris" by the middle of the nineteenth century if not before (Marrero 1988, 14:212). During the sugar boom (1820–60), Cuba's economically capitalist, but culturally aristocratic, white Creole owning class looked Europe-ward, particularly to France, and outmoded in the process the staid *Peninsulares* (the Spanish) around them who monopolized government and urban business.[47] The Creole planter elite bought nobility titles, built baroque and neoclassical style "sugar palaces" with "fountains, Renaissance ceilings, marble staircases, and baths," drove about town in elaborate *volantas* [coaches] with decked-out footmen, and put on lavish masked balls and theatrical productions—"elaborate costume occasions, attended by soldiers in full-dress, the civil guard and negro pages" (Thomas 1971, 142–48).[48] These upper-class Cuban Creole imitations and exaggerations, suggests Argeliers León, "came to us, copied at a distance, and so distended" (León 1984, 23).[49] If Cuba's *cabildos* at all imitated the island's upper class, they may also have looked to the class one step closer to them for sartorial and performative cues. The urban *libertos* (free people of color), as an observer noted, were "well situated economically as artisans, [and] were accustomed to celebrating high-toned balls, which would be called [*bailes*] *de etiqueta* or [*bailes*] *de corte* [etiquette balls or courtly balls]. There shone their best finery" (Marrero 1988, 14:241; compare plate 1 and fig. 1.9). As suggested by Argeliers León, the appearance of any cultural style was highly mediated. That colonial prestige styles were "copied"—copies of copies—is significant. The array of contexts for such imitations is equally significant. If the welter of prestige festival street dress was, in any way, directly copied in a descending chain of imitations, the "elaborate costume occasions" of the white creoles and the high-toned "court balls" of the *libertos* provided something more *copiable:* clusters of already stylized, highly legible sets of prestige signs, ripe for appropriation. These very sets or clusters of potent signs ultimately made up the neatly delineated stuff of dramatic "types," without which *costumbrista* literature and art, not to mention popular theater, could not work (see Moore 1997; Wilmeth and Wilmeth 1977; Cosentino 1995b).[50]

The Diablito: The "Fancy," the "Savage," and "Code Switching" in Afro-Cuban Procession Performance

Cabildo processions did not confine themselves to displays of royal opulence and formal decorum. They dynamically alternated varieties of expression along the ritual-play continuum. Sly expressions of humor, periodic "stops" of exuberant and raucous activity, and the display of African-derived visual and dance forms offered dramatic counterpoint to linear procession style and the signs of institutionalized royalty and military authority (see Marks 1974, 1982). In Dr. Wurdemann's 1844 account, that the "negro marshall" struggles to "preserve order in the ranks" hints that the linear procession form itself could barely restrain other varieties of performance and levels of meaning. Indeed, the quintessential dean of order himself doubles his performance repertoire by engaging in play. He carries "a drawn sword, having a small piece of sugar-cane stuck on its point." What emblem could better embody the bittersweetness of black carnival in the period's premier sugar-producing slave society than this precious detail? The entire Cuban "sugar palace," at its height between 1820 and 1860 (also the height of the illegal slave trade; Thomas 1971, 98, 137), revolved around that piece of cane, now sword pierced and held aloft by the formally dressed and officially empowered black *cabildo* officeholder, who was also a slave. Did his performance slyly comment on "cane" as the "signifying" slave songs of the antebellum United States "sang" upon "corn" (see Abrahams 1992)?[51] Was it the reminder of a current condition, a "bit" of which, in the "subjunctive mood" of carnival performance, could be nevertheless reflected upon, rotated 360 degrees for inspection, and subjected to transformation (see Turner 1982, 82–84; V. Turner 1977; Schechner 1985, 36–37; Bauman 1975)?[52]

In Day of Kings processions, the "switching" of performance rules (see Marks 1974) called for periodic stops, wherein circles (*corros*) formed in the middle of Havana's *intramuros* streets. Powerful drumming and athletic dancing commenced, and *aguinaldo* was earned from spectators (see Ortiz [1920] 1960, 9–10; Brown 1993a, 54–55; fig. 1.3, plate 1).[53] In the 1844 events witnessed by Wurdemann, the principal dancer of one such stop was a "fantastic . . . frightful figure" of "immense" proportions with "uncouth articles of dress," whose "devil's dance" initiated the apparent chaos of the "general fandango." "Devil's dance" appears to be a literal translation from the Spanish for dance performances (*baile de diablito*) by the masquerade figures called *diablitos* ("little devils"). The *diablitos* replaced the gowns, formal suits, and European-derived prestige materials of satin, velvet, lace, gold, and silver with African-style masquerades of earthy natural materials, such as raffia fringes (*empitadas*), animal horns (*cuernos*), and feathers (*plumas*) (fig. 1.3, plate 1).[54] Afro-Cuban carnival performance thus toggled between two contrasting codes. One revolved around formal processions of "flags, drums, and sabres, just like the whites" (as Monfundi Siliman had said); the other depended upon periodic breakouts of the distinct nations' African-style repertoires of vegetal masquerade, dance, song, and drum rhythms.[55]

Nineteenth-century observers apprehended the remarkable contrast of *cabildo* royalty and *diablito* as the contrast of the civilized and the "savage," of an amusing imitation of Europe and a dark, primitive Africa, of good and evil, of "order" and "disorder" (or "noise"; see Reisman 1970; Marks 1974). To these observers, the courtly and military displays were familiar, but humorous, reflections of colonial and Peninsular social hierarchies, as well as living documents of the Negro's supposed airs. In turn, the diverse horned and raffia African masquerades were delegated the "savage slot" (see Troulliot 1991). The positionality of African-style masquerade, characterized by its perceived grotesque features within the framework of an Iberian-descended calendrical feast, could not but identify them as *diablitos*, "little devils." "Surely," Fernando Ortiz explains, "upon having to name them, the whites found in the motley disguises, leaps and cabrioles, [and] horns and masquerades of the Africans, a certain analogy to the *diablitos*, or masks simulating the devil, which long ago accompanied the Catholic Corpus Christi processions in Cuba, as in Spain and other countries" (Ortiz [1920] 1960, 29).[56]

A close look at the two most important nineteenth-century depictions of Day of Kings festivities, by Pierre Toussaint Frédéric Miahle (1810–81) and Víctor Patricio de Landaluze (1830–89; fig. 1.3, plate 1), enrich the sense of Afro-Cuban carnival's group structure, hierarchy, distinct characters, and ethos. For purposes of this discussion, they clearly convey the sartorial and performative differences of *cabildo* royalty and *diablitos*. Landaluze and, though less so, Miahle carefully distinguish individual performative roles that are woven into the logic of the *cabildo* group's hierarchy and processional organization.[57] In the Landaluze work, two figures—an elegant captain or king with a coat and tails, sash, silver-topped staff, and top hat and a Carabalí *íreme* dancer in the conically hooded, tight-fitting, checked masquerade (*aformiremo*)—receive *aguinaldo* from genteel white observers, who are safely separated from the street space by balconies and barred windows (plate 1). Kneeling or gesturing *diablitos* occupy center stage: one with a horned headdress, bandoliers, wrist-rattles, and a raffia hoopskirt (called *la culona*); a similar though crownless figure kneels and courts the attention of a black woman in fancy dress; a third wears the plumed crown and closely fitting body suit of C. D. Fredricks's *cabildo* dancers (see above).

Landaluze uses the colorful umbrella to complete, as Miahle has done, a triangular composition. The umbrella, more important, frames two key figures in the hierarchy. Two elegantly outfitted women in white gowns and tiaras process beneath it, forming a subgroup behind the *diablitos.* In contrast to the active, interactive, and expansive gestures of the other street participants, these lighter-complexioned queens move in upright, sober fashion.[58] One carries in her right hand a defining accessory of black female participants: the *anaquillé,* a "doll" (*muñeco*) upon a short staff, which Ortiz took to be an "idol" and contemporary scholars know to reflect the handheld regalia of African royalty and religious leaders (Ortiz [1920] 1960, 40; see, e.g., Thompson 1970; M. Drewal 1986, 1989).

The representations of Landaluze were powerful in their realistic attention to distinctive Afro-Cuban cultural expression and institutional organization. Still, while Landaluze recognized the crucial performative distinctions between *cabildo* hierarchs and African dancers (*diablitos*) —and, therefore, a unique logic and set of values—the common contemporaneous genre of Afro-Cuban representations suppressed any such alternative reading of black society and expression. A Havana commercial calendar bearing the colorful and ubiquitous trade dress (*marquilla cigarrera*) of the booming tobacco industry emphasizes not Landaluze's sense of royal decorum (fig. 1.6); rather, it conjoins in a "general fandango" (Wurdemann's term) a crowned queen in spreading skirts with a male dancer wearing a plumed crown and pleated skirt. The image conflates what Landaluze intentionally separates. Employing the racist stereotyping of black physiognomy and gesture characteristic of the Cuban *marquilla cigarrera* and North American minstrel genres, the image renders the two participants as grotesques in ridiculous carnival abandon (see Kutzinski 1993, 47–80; McElroy 1990, xi–xlv, 26, 28–29, 36, 105). The elegant *cabildo* queen and dancer of C. D. Fredrick's 1860 *carte de visite* become not only "devils," but also feared bogeymen. The *marquilla*'s caption, "los diablos coronados castigarán tus pecados," warns, "the crowned devils will punish your sins." Performatively, within the logic of carnival exchange, this was one reason why spectators should deliver *aguinaldo* to them with haste. At the same time, the physiognomic distortions of the January 1866 *marquilla cigarrera* seek to complete, visually, the work that Wurdemann's literary condescension began. The *marquilla cigarrera* reduces the cultural integrity of *cabildo* performances to an isolated, humorous, and grotesque display for the pleasure of international consumers.

The nations' African masquerades might be interpreted as having "carnivalized" the ritual seriousness of orderly, linear royal processional. Their presence in the street *corros* (dance circles) introduced radically contrasting performance features, which fell toward the "play" end of continuum, including visual and gestural sets defined by M. M. Bakhtin as carnival's characteristic "grotesque" inversions and subversions.[59] Clearly, middle- and upper-class observers saw the African masquerades, their athletic dance steps, and the booming drum rhythms as a deliciously devilish, if also physically and morally repugnant and dangerous, disorder. Accounts typically report, for example, that Afro-Cuban street performances were "vulgar," "disgusting," "fearsome," and "noisy" (Ortiz [1920] 1960, 13 ff.). Yet *cabildo* processions and their *corros* were, on their own terms, highly "ordered," or "structured," performances (see Marks 1974). Each group's performances were marked by the visually, kinetically, and aurally identifiable traditions of particular nations. The Lucumíes, Congos, Ararás, Mandingas, and Carabalíes were immediately distinguishable by their clothing and markings. For example, the Ararás were known for their remarkable facial cicatrizations and necklaces of shells and animal teeth; the Mandingas stood out for their sartorial luxury: wide silk pants, short jackets, and turbans, all bordered with *marabout* (feather boa). *Ñáñigos* (Carabalí-derived Abakuá groups) were known for their peculiar plumed wooden emblems (*madero emplumado*). Most remarkable were the hooded *íremes,* who stalked, kneeled, and crawled in the angular feline movements of the Abakuá society's "leopard spirits" (see Ortiz [1920] 1960, 11–12, [1951] 1985, 444–46, 464–76; Thompson 1983, 36–39, 60–66).

During the stopped dance circles (*corros*), the solemn linear procession gave way not necessarily to "disorder," but to an alternate, or perhaps "deeper," order of African cultural display.[60] This came in the form of distinctive drum types, rhythms, and socioreligious dances of the nations' cultural repertoires. For the Carabalí *cabildos,* these included the Abakuá *íremes,* which emerged for the first time in 1836 and reflected the hooded "images" of the Old Calabar Ekpe, or Ngbe, societies; they included for the Lucumí *cabildos* masquerades that may have continued Yoruba Egungun and Gelede traditions (see Fernández Carillo 1881; Ortiz [1920] 1960, 31; [1951] 1985, 444–46, 450–76; Thompson 1983, 60–66; Leib and Romano 1984; Lawal 1996; *African Arts* 1978).

Beyond their distinct cultural features of putatively African derivation, Havana *cabildo* processions shared a common performative grammar or template. As the nineteenth-century accounts suggest, *cabildo* processions, including the more boisterous *ñáñigos,* shared time-honored conventions of differentiated roles within corporate hierarchies (e.g., flag-bearers, royalty, masters of ceremony, *diablitos,* drummers, and dancers), code switching between procession mode and *corro* mode, the principle of intergroup competition, the *matar la culebra* (kill the serpent) play, and the processional destination of the captain general's palace in the Plaza de Armas, with the objective of earning *aguinaldo,* not to mention having good fun (see Ortiz 1921; [1920] 1960, 10–20).

These two dimensions of *cabildo* procession, "national" distinctiveness within shared metaperformance rules, roughly parallel the axes of ethnogenesis and creolization (distinctive and shared sociocultural features, respectively). Year-round, and especially during carnival, the streets represented a dynamic cultural machine for emergent African Diaspora cultures. The streets preserved, recreated, and redisseminated African-derived cultural expressions among diverse subject populations. As Bastide writes, characteristically urban streets were "channels of communication . . . link[ing]" numerous institutions: the house, the church, the *cabildos,* and Africans otherwise separated by occupation, ownership, and geography. In ordinary and extraordinary experiences, "the street was the domain of the common people; whites merely passed through. The slaves used the street as a meeting place where they could linger and chat" (Bastide [1960] 1978, 118).[61] In the extraordinary space and time of carnival, as Morton Marks has written, an "'altered state of society'. . . is created as African performance rules emerge into the streets." Carnivals "break . . . the boundaries between private and public behavior created in part by the cultural dualities present in New World societies . . . by bringing private styles into the public domain, and by declaring social and cultural identities in the streets," with the potential for the participating constituencies to "shap[e] national popular cultures" (Marks 1974, 112–14; see also Abrahams and Szwed 1983, 49; see also McAlister 2002). Such an "altered state of society" provided license for alternative behaviors, performances, value sets, and conceptions of authority and allegiance. Though carnival provided liberty and license, police were ubiquitous, and ever vigilant against perceived disorder and potential insurrectional messages, as the Congo-Carabalí incident in Bayamo demonstrated (see Ortiz [1920] 1960, 12). In Havana, straying too far beyond official limits meant sure expulsion from the *intramuros.* The *muralla* of the fortress-like Old City, built to protect against outside attack, also functioned to prevent disorder in the capital's center—in other words, to protect it from inside attack.[62]

The very expectations of observers and middle-class readers—that carnival participants were buffoons and grotesques—provided a certain "cover" for socially assertive, contagious, and centrifugal tendencies within the colonial order (Reisman 1970, 129). *Cabildo* royal presentations were "safe" on the surface because their actors were just slaves; their performances were just entertaining—"slavish"—imitation. Wurdemann and Beauvallet could dismiss *cabildo* rulers as grandiose "kings for a day," but these figures, revered by their constituencies, reigned throughout the year within their *barrios* and domiciles. The African carnival participants of Wurdemann's 1844 procession in Güines could manipulate the space of negotiation and ambiguity created by "indirect rule" in order to give allegiance to Queen Isabella II, as well as their *cabildo* king and the nations's traditions.

The "fearsome," "horrible" *diablitos*, or "crowned little devils," were seen as dark, savage figures from beyond the pale of civilization (not unlike the teeming black *barrios extramuros* from the perspective of the *intramuros*), that is, Hell's representatives. Their role (*los diablitos coronados castigarán tus pecados*) was to present the specter of supernatural punishment for worldly indiscretions; yet, when assuaged with *aguinaldo*, they would presumably relieve Christians of their sins, and swiftly be gone. It seems that Christians historically have required primitive, dark, or grotesque mediators—fetishized embodiments of social contradiction and its "terrors"—in order to ritually "cure" themselves of their ills (see Taussig 1987; R. Ortiz 1989; F. Ortiz [1920] 1960, 34–43).[63] As Fernando Ortiz himself argues, the *diablitos* were none other than the sorcerers (*hechiceros, brujos*) of the African nations ([1920] 1960, 33). The dramatic climax of the Day of Kings consisted of a play called the "killing of the snake" (*matar la culebra*), which Ortiz hypothesized as a "rite of collective purification," not unlike the "expulsion of the devils" (e.g., "a monstrous Dragon") in the old Christian Corpus Christi festival of the European Continent and the colonies ([1920] 1960, 41–43) and the agonistic "Saint George and the Dragon" plays in pan-Anglophone Caribbean Twelfth Day Carnival (i.e., the Epiphany of the Catholics, January 6; Abrahams 1983, 13–18). African and European traditions of expelling maleficent forces (including the Spanish Inquisition's expulsion of *la cosa mala*), Ortiz hypothesized, apparently fed into the Day of Kings and cross-pollinated with similar African-derived public rituals in the formation of Cuban popular culture (Ortiz [1920] 1960, 25–28, 39). In sum, it is worth nuancing Morton Marks's fine formulation on the cultural dynamic of private ("indoor") and public ("outdoor") styles and value sets. Not only did the *cabildos'* "private" styles, when "outdoored," influence the emergence of national popular cultures (Marks 1974, 112–14) in politics, folklore, religion, music, dance, language, cuisine, and so on. If Mintz and Price are correct about the two-way "flow" of cultural materials ([1976] 1992, 23–37), then a Cuban official and popular culture must also have influenced the private styles of the *cabildos*. This is already demonstrated in the *cabildos'* official monarchial and military hierarchies, their role in indirect rule, their internal institutional structures, their Catholic devotions, their royal styles of dress, and so on. As the "outdooring" of elegant *cabildo* royalty and the grotesque *diablitos* were mutually entailed in building their respective meaning, so was the relationship between kings and African priests in a dual leadership hierarchy within these institutions.

ENTHRONED KINGS AND POSSESSED PRIESTS: ROYALTY, RELIGION, AND "THE LUCCOMÉES *CABILDO*" IN HAVANA'S *BARRIOS EXTRAMUROS*

On a Sunday afternoon in 1851,[64] the Swedish traveler Fredrika Bremer was escorted to a mysterious and exciting urban world just outside the walled *intramuros*. The festive tenor of the *barrio* she visited was the dramatic prelude to a powerful drumming and dancing event she later witnessed in "the Luccomées *cabildo*."[65]

> As these clubs generally meet in the afternoons and evenings of the Sunday, we set off in the afternoon to the street in which the *cabildos* are situated, for they occupy a whole street near one of the toll-gates of the city. The whole street swarmed with negroes, some decked out with ribbons and bells, some dancing, others standing in groups here and there. There prevailed a wild but not rude sort of lawlessness, and on all hands, near and afar off, was heard

> the gay, measured beat of the African drum. Round the gates of the different halls were collected groups of white people, most of them evidently sailors, who were endeavoring to get sight of what was passing inside; but a couple of negroes, stationed at each with sticks in their hands, kept the entrance closed with good-tempered determination, and did not allow the doors to open beyond half way. (Bremer 1853, 2:379)

Beyond the dramatic annual spectacle of *cabildo* carnival processions, the *barrios extramuros* specialized in public displays of African cultures in sight and sound on a weekly basis, specifically on the day of rest. The liveliness and color of this *barrio*'s streets, and the occurrence of drumming events on Sundays, reflect the tolerance permitted by the 1842 Bando de Buen Gobierno y Policía for slaves to engage in festivities on Sunday, as well as on saints' days and holidays. This "Proclamation of Good Government and Policing," enacted the same year as a very restrictive new slave code, reiterated elements of the 1792 regulations on *cabildos*, which had driven the *cabildos* outside the city walls, ostensibly because of the "raucous and disagreeable sound of the[ir musical] instruments" during their regular cycle of weekend and annual festivals (Ortiz 1921, 17; see also Ortiz [1916] 1987, 439–52).[66]

In Bremer's depiction, people engage in street dancing and socializing; some are garlanded unusually with "ribbons and bells," and the aural hallmark of Africanized cultural space in the Americas is ubiquitous: the "measured beat of the African drum." Yet the integrity of more guarded cultural and religious performances—a measure of the margin of liberty *cabildos* had to manage their own space and evolve their own cultural programs—could be controlled at the doors of these African "halls." Still, the cultural flavor of the *cabildos* remained of great interest to "groups of white people" gathered at their doors. These included European travel writers as well as sailors—whom recent scholarship has identified as the transmitters par excellence of Atlantic news, cultural currents, and exotic phenomena (see Scott 1986; Linebaugh and Rediker 2000).

"The Luccomée's *cabildo*" was the well-appointed Cabildo de Señora Santa Bárbara de la nación Lucumi Alagua (the Cabildo of Santa Bárbara of the Lucumí Alagua Nation).[67] Indeed, the *cabildo* was so well appointed that Bremer received a printed business card from the society's official master of ceremonies containing this information. A close reading of Bremer's 1853 account of the drumming reveals how an apparently well-established group of mid-nineteenth-century Lucumí had carved out a complex social and religious institution within Havana's urban colonial landscape. The account evidences a wealth of institutional, ritual, and artistic "remodeling," in Reisman's terms. It is thus worth quoting her rich description at length:

> Chairs were offered to us not far from the door; we were presented to the queen and the king of the assembly who made demonstrations of good-will, and we were then left to look about us in quiet. The room was tolerably large, and might contain about one hundred persons. On the wall just opposite to us was painted a crown, and a throne with a canopy over it. There stood the seats of the king and queen. The customary dancing was going forward in front of the seat. One woman danced alone, under a canopy supported by four people. Her dancing must have given great delight . . . for all kinds of handkerchiefs were hanging about her, and a hat, even, had been placed upon her head. The women danced on this occasion with each other, and the men with the men; some struck the doors and benches with sticks, others rattled gourds filled with stones, and the drums thundered with deafening power. They were apparently endeavoring to make as much noise as possible. While this was going on, a figure was seen advancing with a scarlet hat upon his head, and with a great number of glittering strings of beads round his neck, arms, and body, which was naked to the waist, from which hung scarlet skirts. This figure, before which the people parted to each

> side, approached me, bowing all the time, and as he did so the whole upper portion of his body seemed to move in snakelike folds. Still making these serpentine movements, he stood before me with extended hands, I being not at all certain whether he was inviting me to dance, or what was the meaning of his apparently friendly grimaces, and his great, black, outstretched hands. At length he uttered, with other words, "per la bonita!" and I comprehended that all his bowings and bedizenment were intended as a compliment to me, and I made my reply by shaking one of the black hands, and placing within it a silver coin, after which we exchanged friendly gestures, and my friend made a serpentine retreat, and began to dance on his own account, receiving great applause from the by-standers.
>
> The nation is regarded as rich, in consequence of the great prizes which it has won in the lottery, and this wealth it is said to apply to a good use—the purchasing the freedom of slaves of this tribe.
>
> These cabildoes are governed, as I have already said, by queens, one or two, who decide upon the amusements, give tone to the society, and determine its extension. They possess the right of electing a king, who manages the pecuniary affairs of the society, and who has under him a secretary and master of the ceremonies. The latter presented me with a small printed card, which gave admission to the "Cabildo de Señora Santa Barbara de la nacion Lucumi Alagua."
>
> After this, and when we had made a little offering to the treasury of the society, we took our departure, in order to visit other cabildoes. (Bremer 1853, 2:380–81)

The drumming event unfolds in the performance space before a painted crown and canopied throne, under which the *cabildo*'s elected royalty, the king and queen, sat. The Swedish traveler's straightforward mention of the throne, canopy, and crown suggests that they were, like the royal garments and accessories of the Day of Kings, derived from a conventional European iconography familiar to her. The Lucumí king and queen appear as hosts, overseers, and proud observers of the celebration. Their roles are clearly distinct from those of other participants of the identifiably African-style cultural activities proceeding before them. Beyond the king and queen, Bremer's account not only distinguishes a roster of additional administrative offices (more queens, a secretary, a master of the ceremonies); it also suggests a number of general and specialized performative roles, which resemble those of twentieth-century Lucumí religious practice. In addition to the various percussionists (members of a drum orchestra accompanied by others beating sticks and shaking gourds)[68] and the congregation of "by-standers" (presumably the nation's dues-paying membership and its guests), Bremer's account reveals people playing at least three other distinct performative roles during the event: two unusually adorned solo dancers, four individuals who elevate a "canopy" above the head of one of the soloists, and gender-separated groups of male and female dancers.

The two solo dancers, a woman and a man, are distinguished from the rest by their peculiar costumes, accessories, and the focused attention given them by all, including Bremer. The woman's adornments—"all kinds of handkerchiefs" and a "hat"—suggest markers of ritual transformation; indeed, she may be spiritually possessed by a deity. Four people elaborate the ritual setting for this soloist, whose presence under a canopy supported by attendants prefigures the ritual treatment of possessed priests and individuals undergoing spiritual cleansings in both the Bahian Candomblé Nagô and the Cuban Regla Lucumí traditions (see Carybé 1980, 89, 238; Brown 1989, 475).[69] The black male dancer—naked from the waist up, garlanded in "beads," and dressed in a "scarlet hat" and "scarlet skirts"—bears all the visual marks of the *oricha* Changó, undoubtedly the African counterpart of the *cabildo*'s official patron, Santa Bárbara (see Brown 1989, 474; Deschamps Chapeaux 1968, 50). The dancer's apparently flirtatious approach and provocative movements are consistent with aspects of Changó's character as it was manifested in Cuba (see Ortiz [1951] 1985, 333; Cabrera

[1954] 1983, 226; Bolívar Aróstegui 1990, 108, 111). In short, the two solo dancers may have been possession priests, individuals formally consecrated and prepared to be mounted by deities during drumming ceremonies. Bremer's description of women dancing with "each other" and men with each other registers not same-sex couples, but gender-separated "apart-dancing" (groups of women and groups of men), an African performance style that extends to religious ritual, including trance contexts (Thompson 1974, 30). Imaginably, these "apart-dancers" were also priests who formed the pool of potential "mounts" for deities.

Bremer's donations of money to the male dancer and the society's coffers not only suggest this international traveler's keen sense of cultural appropriateness, but also mark the difference between the *cabildo*'s religious and politico-administrative dimensions. Beyond Bremer's own interpretation of the first donation—perhaps it was a kind of *aguinaldo* for the apparently exotic and ingratiating black figure—the money represents a ritual tribute (*derecho*) to a priest possessed by a deity within Lucumí tradition. At the same time, Bremer was aware that the second donation would appropriately serve the society's administrative and mutual aid purposes, specifically, the buying of nation brethren out of slavery.

George Brandon cautiously suggests in his assessment of *cabildo* celebration that "it would be very surprising, indeed, given the intimate relationship which exists between music, dance, and religion in African cultures, if these dances did not turn into religious ceremonies at times, complete with spirit possession" (Brandon 1983, 79–80; see also Brandon 1993, 75–76). The performance details of the Lucumí Alagua event—drumming, apart-dancing, and color-coded cloth and accessories to mark the bodies of individual dancers, including one who fits Changó's Afro-Cuban profile—suggest that the event was in fact a "religious ceremony." Yet, the presence of an enthroned king and queen—over and above the drummers, priests, attendants, and master of ceremonies—distinguishes this old-style *cabildo de nación* and its Sunday celebration from twentieth-century Lucumí practice. Indeed, the Lucumí Alagua event recalls elements of Yoruba annual royal festivals, in which the activities of drummers, dancers, and priests proceed in relation to seated kings or local chiefs who observe the ritual activities from their thrones and palace verandas (see, e.g., Pemberton 1989; Pemberton and Afolayan 1996, 86, 100, 121, 143, plate 13; Smith 1969, 129; Apter 1992, 99–106, plates 1–10). Phases of the twentieth-century Lucumí drumming (*tambor*) also proceed before a canopied royal throne; yet this throne contains the deities themselves or newly consecrated priests, not elected or hereditary mortal kings and queens (see chaps. 4, 5).

Roger Bastide suggested that in the reconstitution of "African civilizations" in Brazil within such "new social frameworks" as the nations' religious fraternities, certain institutional and ideological distinctions were reinstated on a radically condensed scale (see Bastide [1960] 1978, 247–48). Based upon his readings of the nineteenth-century Cuban accounts against the background of available West African ethnography, Fernando Ortiz himself hypothesized that the costuming differences between the Day of Kings' *diablitos* and its kings reflected the institutional "division of the priestly and royal powers of the *cabildos*, as is common in the [African] peoples from where their associated members originated" (Ortiz 1921, 6).[70] Andrew Apter, in his recent description of Yoruba leadership patterns in Ayédé, Èkítí, shows the offices of "king" and "priest" as institutionally distinct. The king (*ọba*) "owns" the royal cults, but neither he nor his immediate ministers are normally priests (*aworo*) themselves. Likewise, Apter notes, "the cult and the quarter are distinct corporations, and . . . the former does not 'reduce' to the latter. The cult does not consist of the quarter, but performs its ritual *on behalf of* the quarter. The distinction is important because it underlies the *complementary* relationship between political and ritual domains" (Apter 1987, 84–85; 1992, 27). Such distinctions have formed part of a system of checks and balances between crown and town or cult at the kingdom level, and between chief (*ighare*) and cult priest in the next descending political unit, the quarter (Apter 1992, 83–84; see also Morton-Williams 1964). As Brandon astutely observes, "[t]he relation of the [Yoruba *òrìṣà*] cults to government and the communal infrastructure were severed when they were imported to Cuba so that orisha cults had both their top (connection with the major social and political systems) and their bottom (the infrastructure of communal life) cut away from them" (Brandon 1983, 525). Yet, these links, at the "top" and "bottom," were, as Bastide nicely demonstrates, reconstituted in a structurally faithful fashion within the institutional "niches" offered by the colonial society. Offically, the new "top," as Monfundi Siliman articulated the hierarchy, descended from the Bourbon king or queen, through the island's captain general, to *cabildo* royalty itself. Within the nations' *cabildos*, the *cabildo* politico-administrative hierarchy—*rey, reina, mayor de plaza, abanderado, tesorero* (treasurer), *secretario*, and so on—were formally distinguished from their religious counterparts, the priests, as well as from specialized corps of drummers, attendants, and dancers.[71] The politico-administrative hierarchy and body of the Lucumí nation's dues-paying membership were not "direct survivals" of African government and communal infrastructures but loan translations or remodelings as mediated by colonial social, administrative, and political categories—including the institutional forms of the *cabildo* or *cofradía* and *nación*, as Bastide's work shows. The old-style *cabildo de nación* was in one sense a miniature society within a society. It reproduced within its institutional structures on a condensed scale the linked hierarchical terms "nation," "government," and "religious cult." The *cabildos* were, in this sense, the "kingdoms" of the *barrios extramuros*, situated on a map of social and political geography peculiar to urban colonial Cuba. At the same time, the *cabildo de nación* "manipulated" more globally organized infrastructures in its internal constitution and relationships with the "top" and "bottom."

In the concentrated, yet heterogeneous, urban setting, numerous African nations or kingdoms "occup[ied] a whole street" in a single *barrio*, as Bremer observed in her 1851 visit. On a Sunday afternoon's walk, Bremer could encounter the Lucumí Alagua nation by exiting the *intramuros*, entering the guarded front doors of its premises, only to take her leave and "visit other cabildoes," where cultural forms from entirely different regions of Africa had been reconstituted and remodeled within the same institutional template of the *cabildo de nación*. These other *cabildos* also featured kings, queens, masters of ceremony, standard-bearers, treasurers, drummers, dancers, priests, and religious ceremonies. At the same time, their respective practices were distinguished by marked, local differences in performance style, including language, iconography, song types, drum rhythms, and names of deities. These practical manifestations of the sociocultural process described by Palmié as "ethnogenesis" (1993) are nicely summed up by a popular Cuban saying, "If you're not Congo, you're Carabalí" (Moore 1986).

CODA: STATE POWER AND THE TRANSFORMATION OF THE *CABILDOS* FROM EMANCIPATION THROUGH THE FIRST YEARS OF THE CUBAN REPUBLIC

The old-style *cabildos de nación* of slave membership disappeared or were transformed into different kinds of organizations with the radical social and political changes of the era of emancipation (1880s) through the first two decades of the twentieth century. New kinds of Afro-Cuban societies (*sociedades*), which blended institutional aspects of the old-style *cabildos de nación* with those of modern civic and religious organizations, were founded by ex-slaves and their descendants during this period, including many of the seminal creole "houses" (*casas*) of the Lucumí religion, which were called *sociedades* (societies) as well as *cabildos* (see chap. 2).

Severe government persecution of Afro-Cuban fraternal and religious organizations between 1875 and the early

1920s followed upon centuries of state and church attempts at legal and religious restrictions of *cabildos*. After 1792, the government began to restrict and suppress the *cabildos* and their celebratory public expressions, especially after it became apparent that their assemblies and performances had been staging grounds for subversive communication and insurrection during the infamous "conspiracies" of 1812 (Aponte) and 1844 (La Escalera) among others. With the 1884 ban on carnival processions—during the gradual "apprenticeship" (*patronato*) period following the 1880 conditional end to slavery—"the 6th of January of 1885 was the first silent Epiphany that Cuba had" (Ortiz 1921, 20–22). This ban, contained in one of the many "Proclamations of Good Government" of the nineteenth century, focused specifically on public celebration but left a margin of liberty for Afro-Cuban cultural practice within the *cabildos'* establishments. A "Disposition of the Civil Government" of January 7, 1885, for example, decreed that "the effect of said Proclamation should only circumscribe and limit the gatherings and processions of the *cabildos* through the public ways . . . [and] with regard to the gatherings that said *cabildos* are accustomed to carry out in their respective domiciles, they should continue the prevailing practice in the present" (Ortiz 1921, 20–22).

As historian Rebecca Scott argues, during the period of emancipation and apprenticeship (1880–86), the suppression of the *cabildos de nación* was meant to prevent consolidation of distinctive African-based group identities after the freeing of thousands of Africans and their inevitable arrival in the cities. Indeed, the *cabildos de nación* presented the specter of counterhegemonic ministates to the authorities (Scott 1985, 264–78). Whereas the original theory behind the organization of slave and creole populations into separate *cabildo* nations was based on the divide-and-rule strategy (López Valdés 1987, 6–7; see also Bastide [1960] 1978, 55),

> once emancipation had begun the significance of the *cabildo* changed. . . . *Cabildos* now appeared to be potentially separatist organizations in which free blacks could rule themselves, isolated from the dominant culture. With their structures of leadership and their ownership of property, they might become threateningly autonomous class, ethnic, or political institutions. The police inspector of Sagua la Grande, for example, denounced the form of the organization of the local *cabildo* Congo, whose constitution, he charged, resembled that of a state. . . . [Thus] the identification of former slaves with their African origins was now a threat, a countervailing loyalty that might prevent freedmen from feeling themselves to be Spaniards. Furthermore, both liberals and conservatives saw the extinction of African culture as necessary if freedmen were to be incorporated into society and become "worthy" of the rights that had recently been granted them. (Scott 1985, 266)

During this period, Scott observes, many such "ministates" were encouraged or forced to become civic-type organizations, some of which began to publish newspapers and manage social welfare and recreation programs. Afro-Cuban public culture on the model of the *cabildos de nación* was curbed, and the religions of African derivation were driven deep underground. In turn, the presence of distinctive Afro-Cuban cultural activity became increasingly suspect and fearsome in the context of Cuban nation-building ideologies; now, such "primitive" and "atavistic" African-based practices were considered "sores" (*llagas*) on the modern body politic from the standpoint of the Cuban "progressive" agenda (see Helg 1995; Ortiz [1906] 1973; Moore 1994; and below).

Scholars have identified the last two decades of the nineteenth century and the first decades of the twentieth century as the period in which independent "house-temples" (*casa-templos*) of Lucumí religion emerged from the socioinstitutional bases of the old style *cabildos de nación* (Murphy 1988, 33; Brandon 1993, 83). The great statesman, ethnologist, and theorist of the modern Cuban nation Fernando Ortiz was the first to recognize this historical transformation, but he saw its results as socially negative. According to Ortiz, the formerly wholesome mutual aid function of the *cabildo* and its vibrant public cultural activity gave way to savage underground fetishism.

> The government proposition, skillfully announced, of transforming the cabildos into modern organizations, failed totally. The government endeavored to attack the external and antiquated forms and was not careful to observe the persistence of the internal essence. The cabildo disappeared, with all the good characteristics it had: mutual support, security against sicknesses—the bases, ultimately, of a traditional and rigorous brotherhood; the noisy drum dances disappeared—inoffensive and so appreciated by the Africans; what remained in exchange, semiunderground [was] crude animist fetishism [*semioculto, el fetichismo animista selvático*] beneath a Catholic advocation and a constitution [*reglamento*] adapted to legal formula. And the authorities remained satisfied.
>
> How much better the opposite result would be! How much better it would be if today we had cabildos of mutual aid and public drum dances, and not sorcery temples [*templos brujos*], tolerated or clandestine!" (Ortiz 1921, 29–31)

After 1875, increasingly in the 1880s, and with an unprecedented ferocity between the first American occupation of the island (1899–1902) and the early 1920s, the government not only scrutinized but also attacked the "internal essence" of Afro-Cuban organizations. This took the direct form of state "persecution against *ñañiguismo* and other religious customs of African origin" (Ortiz 1952–55, 4:79), including violent police incursion into the "respective domiciles" of religious temples and the men's secret Abakuá society lodges. Black creole members of the Abakuá society had been arrested under Spanish colonial laws for illicit gathering—as *ñáñigos*—as early as 1839 (see Deschamps Chapeaux 1964). The decisive outlawing of the Abakuá society on 12 March 1875 commenced more than forty years of vigorous prosecution of *ñañiguismo* (a pejorative term for the Abakuá), which culminated in one of the twentieth century's most notorious desecrations of an Abakuá temple on 20 May 1914 in Havana's working-class *barrio* of Pogolotti in the municipality of Marianao. The public "revelation" and publication of the "secret" of these ostensibly dark, mafia-like criminal organizations, Police Inspector Rafael Roche y Monteagudo thought, would, logically, render them extinct (Roche y Monteagudo [1908] 1925a, 52, 74, 3–154).[72] However, despite much violence directed at the Abakuá, police success in extinguishing the Abakuá was, from the beginning, marginal. The Havana civil governor Don Carlos Rodríguez Batista's "suppression of the 'potencias' of *ñáñigos*," writes Ortiz, "was nothing more than the ostentatious simulation of a great police service. Rodríguez Batista had hardly stepped down as governor before the 'juegos,' supposedly disintegrated, [began] functioning anew, just as before" (Ortiz 1952–55, 4:81). For example, in 1889, under great duress upon their arrest, the leaders of Regla's major Abakuá lodges agreed to dismantle their organizations, turn over their "most sacred effects," and convince other lodges to do the same. They were freed for a short period in order to "destroy" their lodges. As Ortiz discovered through interviews and examination of numerous confiscated objects, many of those delivered up to the police were *falso* (false), suggesting that the contrite letter to a Havana newspaper explaining their actions was a dissimulation, a sly public performance of humiliation and contrition in order to survive (see Roche y Monteagudo 1908, 45; Ortiz 1952–55, 4:81).

Havana's Lucumí and Palo practitioners did not fare as well. From the end of the nineteenth century, the houses of Lucumí and Palo Monte priests—*los negros brujos* in Ortiz's classification of *la hampa cubana*—were the special targets of ferocious police raids intended to stamp out *brujería* (witchcraft). *Brujería* was perceived to be responsible for social "delinquency," in general, and the ritual murder of white children for their blood, in particular (see Helg 1995, 107–16; Ortiz [1906] 1973, 181–219; Castellanos 1916, 12–20, 47–49, 83–93; Roche y Monteagudo [1908] 1925a, 166–249). Through intensive reinvestigation, the state's cases against accused *brujos* have been entirely discredited; trumped up charges, rumor masquerading as evidence, racism, and public hysteria contributed to the brutal executions of innocent elderly African men by garrote (see Chávez Álvarez 1991; Helg 1995, 108–16; Palmié 2000; 2002, 210–33).

Given the state witch-hunts and yellow press vitriol, the *negros ñáñigos* and *negros brujos*, not to mention ordinary Afro-Cubans, became "icons of fear" in the tumultuous twenty-year period between emancipation (1886) and the first years of the new Republic. Not coincidentally, their persecution historically paralleled state repression of the Afro-Cuban Independent Party of Color, which culminated in the military massacre of three thousand protesters in eastern Cuba in the so-called race war of 1912. Socially and politically, the *brujería* persecutions justified the state's discrediting of the role Afro-Cubans played in the liberation of the nation from Spanish control in two wars of independence and the disenfranchisement of Afro-Cubans in the new Republic (Helg 1995, 107). Several accused *brujos*, however, managed to successfully challenge the state's campaign of religious persecution. In 1906, Julia Torres of Guanabacoa was accused of rape and denounced by an anonymous letter as "a healer and a witch using brujería, for which aim she was looking for a white girl to deflower . . . and collect her blood for her work" (Helg 1995, 131). This Lucumí priestess, very likely the same Julia Torres who served on the board of the important Havana Cabildo of Santa Bárbara (Changó Tedún; see Cabildo Africano Lucumí 1900), "cleared herself of the charges and recover[ed] some of her confiscated" sacred objects (Helg 1995, 131). The viciousness with which someone so honored for her leadership and spiritual authority within arguably the greatest Lucumí religious organization in Cuban history illustrates, as does the war against the Independent Party of Color, the extent of racist politics and white social hysteria during the "birth of a nation."

As sympathetic as the early Fernando Ortiz was to certain Afro-Cuban customs, such as "drum dances" and "mutual aid," his program of "criminal ethnology" both lent justification to state behavior and benefited in ethnographic data from police raids and confiscations of sacred objects (see Ortiz [1906] 1973). Following his salutary separation from criminal ethnology, Ortiz became an advocate of aspects of Afro-Cuban culture. Still, Ortiz, and the audience to whom he eventually presented a 1937 staged concert of Lucumí drummed music (see Ortiz 1937a; 1952–55, 4:235–38), were clearly more comfortable with aestheticized "Afro-Cuban culture" than with the religious rituals that were integral to that culture, including animal sacrifice. As photographer Jacob Riis and his progressive reformers sought to bring "light"—literally, in Riis's garishly flash-lit pictures—to the "dark," filthy, unsalutary immigrant tenements of New York's Lower East Side (Riis [1890] 1971), the early Ortiz and the vanguard of social hygienicists sought to sanitize Cuba's new republican space. Later, in gentler and more sympathetic fashion, he favored the "transculturation" or uplift of Afro-Cuban folk and their "folklore."

With the criminalization of Afro-Cuban organizations and their religious customs in the last third of the nineteenth century, the police were heroized as archangels fighting the hydras of *ñañiguismo* and *brujería* (see Trujillo y Monagas 1882; Roche y Monteagudo 1908, [1908] 1925).[73] Drawing on Italian sociologist Cesare Lombroso's medico-criminological model of biological "anomaly" and social hygiene, as well as the timely analogy of the yellow fever epidemic that plagued Cuba at the turn of the nineteenth century, Fernando Ortiz and others identified the houses of Afro-Cuban practitioners as "sores" and "centers of infection," which needed to be wiped out (see Ortiz [1906] 1973, 1–22, 223, 230; Mullen 1987; Castellanos 1916; Helg 1995, 96 ff.; Palmié 2000; 2002, 233–48).[74]

Ñañiguismo and *brujería* figured, as well in Cuban cultural fantasy as contagious forms of African primitive savagery that were undermining the fabric of the emerging Cuban nation. According to the late-nineteenth-century assistant of José Trujillo, one of Cuba's most tenacious and ruthless warriors against *ñañiguismo*, the "black race could ennoble itself only by consuming the white race." *Ñañiguismo*'s principal goal was to "drag down" into barbarism (*arrastrar*) Cuban whites of all classes, but particularly the Spanish-descended working class, whose baser instincts led them to put on the *ñáñigo* swagger in order to seduce black women (Fernández Carillo 1881; Roche y Monteagudo [1908] 1925b, 153–55). Thus, the specter more fearful to the authorities than the growth of *ñañiguismo* among Afro-Cubans between 1836 and the 1850s was the large-scale initiation of members of the non-black Cuban working-class into the Abakuá after 1863.[75] Though many "dissipated" wealthy youths and their "low-life" hangers-on were initiated during this period also, it seems that the greatest growth in nonblack initiations (including Filipinos and Chinese) is owed to the empowering function the Abakuá lodges offered to burgeoning dock labor during the period of intense proletarianization from the last third of the nineteenth century through the early 1940s (López Valdés 1985b). Indeed, beginning before the middle of the nineteenth century, the Cuban government sought white immigration from Europe to offset the specter of an African majority. This radically changed the demographics of the island: the white population increased by 86% in the middle decades of the century (1846–61).[76] In the cities, Louis Pérez writes, "[t]he increase of white workers augmented the ranks of the urban wage labor force, arguably one of the fastest growing sectors in Cuban society. . . . [I]t is clear that white workers were extending their control over urban jobs at the expense of free people of color," especially in Havana (Pérez 1988, 117). In addition to these sheer demographic changes, labor activism boomed, particularly in response to instabilities in the labor markets, especially for cigars. Cigar workers' unions were "mainly in the form of mutual aid societies, organized along national and racial lines, providing members accident, sickness, and death benefits" (Pérez 1988, 119). These kinds of organizations increased throughout the various labor sectors and regions, as did labor militancy. Threatened by this increasing power and a number of strikes, the government moved to suppress the expanding movement and, in general, began to shut down reformism as a whole in the second half of the 1860s. Repression increased throughout the island; military, over civilian, authority was reasserted. It is not surprising that, during the same period that "mutual aid societies . . . organized along national and racial lines" burgeoned, so did the "white" Abakuá lodges of the Akanarán Efó Ocobio Mukarará lineage founded by the *mulato* Andrés Facundo Cristo de los Dolores Petit. Therefore, *ñáñigo* persecution paralleled, and was in fact integral to, the state program of union busting and worker repression.

Ethnologists and criminologists, such as Ortiz and Dr. Israel Castellanos, the dean of Cuba's new forensic and identification technologies, went to great lengths to "scientifically" distinguish between *brujería* and *ñañiguismo* (see Castellanos 1916; Ortiz [1926–28] 1986, 3–35). *Ñañiguismo*, to Castellanos, was an atavistic, despotic, criminal organization like the Italian mafia, though *brujería* was not intentionally opposed to the law. Still, just as *ñañiguismo* sought to "consume" the white race and drag it down into barbarism (Fernández Carillo 1881), *brujería* (*witchcraft*) sought to consume the fecund womb of the nation by kidnapping and ritually killing its innocent white children, like "The Little Girl Zoila" and "The Little Girl Cecilia" (see Chávez Álvarez 1991). Popular misinformation and prejudice against the Afro-Cuban religions at the dawn of the Republic is reflected in Irene Wright's account of her visit to a Lucumí *cabildo* drum dance in the Havana suburb of El Cerro during the second American occupation (1906–9; see Wright 1910, 149–50). Wright confuses *ñañiguismo* and *brujería*, imagines miscegenation and sexual immorality at the root of Lucumí religious protocols, and inscribes ritual murder and violent street crime as central to the history of the *cabildos*. Though she was an American living in Cuba, who may have imported her own set of moral lenses, her account also reflects the opinions of Cuban state and church officials. Sex and immorality were never far from accounts of the African-descended religions. Wright's apparently puritanical suspicions were immediately raised when she observed the standard Yoruba-Lucumí etiquette of ritual salutation (*moforibale*, "I put my head to the ground"). A group of participants began to salute Wright's chaperone, a *mulato* priest of the *cabildo*, when they arrived at the house. "One pretty young girl, who might have 'passed for white' in her clean lawn dress with blue sash and neck ribbons he compelled by a glance to do as the rest,—to throw herself prone on the floor before him, and turn from hip to hip. We had no manner of knowing what immoralities lay behind many of the suggestive details we noticed," Wright reported (1910, 149–50). *Cabildo* history, and the Lucumí altars, rituals, and spirit possessions Wright witnessed, fared no better:

> Taken [at] its surface value, the performance we saw that afternoon was a demonstration of fanaticism and ignorance it would be hard to equal anywhere. It was the most astounding confusion of heathenish and Catholic worship one could imagine: they sang in barbarous tongue to Christian saints, and to them they sacrifice white cocks occasionally; in the dances, which must have originated about African campfires, they flaunt yellow as the color of Our Lady of Cobre, white for Mary of Mercies, purple and green for Saint Joseph, and red for their favorite saint, [the] protecting Barbara. . . . I asked police headquarters to tell me exactly what this *cabildo* was, and learned that it, and organizations like it, are all the law allowed, at that time, of the old ñanigo clans. It was, as it were, the threshold beyond which lie their nefarious mysteries and the trickery of witchcraft.
>
> The ñanigo clans were, I understand, a revival in Cuba of tribes that existed in Africa. . . . There was a time when on the "Day of Kings" their leaders were actually received in the palace of the governor-general; on that date their bands paraded the street and whites kept within closed doors. They had their jealousies, and members of rival clans killed and were killed in the public streets. One Spanish governor collected all their paraphernalia and boasted that he had persuaded them to disband. The police force of the American Government of Occupation declared that it had suppressed them. The spontaneity with which, during one carnival season not so long ago, certain groups of maskers appeared upon the streets, leads an observer to suspect that neither was successful. Later still, after two white children had been killed and cut up by "witch doctors" in the country, and the perpetrators of the crimes caught and convicted, the Provisional Administration grew critical of even such societies that we visited. I venture to say, however, that openly or secretly, they still exist, and if ever there is a negro uprising in Cuba they will play their prominent part. (Wright 1910, 149)

The "negro uprising" would not occur for two years after the 1910 publication of Wright's book, coming in the form of the 1912 Afro-Cuban rebellion against discrimination and disenfranchisement. Many Africans and their creole descendants had fought valiantly in the Second War of Independence (1895–98), as well as the first (1868–78), in order to better their lives, yet found themselves frustrated in the early years of the Republic by poor economic, social, and political prospects, including official disenfranchisement (Pérez 1988, 197, 210–12; Helg 1995, 98–106, 118–20). These conditions, and the intensified official racism brought by the two American military occupations (1899–1902 and 1906–9), were motivating factors in the 1912 rebellion in the east, which was brutally suppressed by the army (see Pérez 1988, 221–22; Helg 1995, 193–226; Fermoselle 1974).

The extent of Afro-Cuban religious practioners' participation in the rebellion and the decade or more of political organizing that preceded it is not clear. However, as suggested in the case of working-class organizing among whites and other immigrant groups and the exponential growth of the "white Abakuá," the early-twentieth-century witch-hunts against *brujería* were consistent with the oppressive social and political conditions leading up to the events of 1912, as indicated above (see Helg 1995, 106–16, 118–39). In any event, the emergence of the modern Lucumí religious societies between emancipation and the first decade of the new Republic did parallel the unprecedented vigor of Afro-Cuban social and political organizing (see Helg 1995, 124–30, 132–39, 141–59). Therefore, given the intensity of social restriction, political disenfranchisement, police brutality, and the fact that much of Cuba had been reduced to a wasteland by the Second War of Independence (see Pérez 1988, 189–91), the emergence of the Lucumí *casa-templos* represented quite a social and institutional achievement. Perhaps the greatest institutional achievement in Havana was the successful reorganization in 1900 of the Cabildo of Santa Bárbara, whose directors represented the most important Lucumí religious leaders of the day.

TWO

FROM *CABILDO DE NACIÓN* TO *CASA-TEMPLO*

The New Lucumí, Institutional Reform, and the Shifting Location of Cultural Authenticity

Adechina, when he was captured, swallowed his Ifá [divination palm nuts]; in the ship he defecated his Ifá and secretly guarded it. . . . Later, in order to continue [as a *babalawo*], Adechina washed his Ifá in the back of a bodega owned by Spaniards, together with Ño Carlos Adé Bí, who bought his liberty.
—*Babalawo* Hermes Valera Ramírez

In those days the Lùkùmí in Cuba enforced the rule of requiring newly arrived Lùkùmí, no matter what their claim to status was, to be reinitiated in the manner that had been redesigned to suit the conditions they found in Cuba. The second initiation set the stage for [Octavio Samar's] receiving the special name (i.e., Obadiméjì, "To Become King Twice").
—John Mason

Olofin is the highest attribute that one can have in the religion. He represents the Almighty Creator. Without him, *babalawos* cannot be initiated.
—Roberto Bolufer

Etymologies are seductive in part because of the ruse of origin—the implication that one can discover the roots of language use and transformation.
—Brent Hayes Edwards

CABILDO AS CRUCIBLE IN THE EMERGENCE OF TWENTIETH-CENTURY LUCUMÍ RELIGION

"The *cabildo* incontestably forms the starting point for the African *santaria* of Cuba," the French ethnologist Roger Bastide wrote in 1972 (Bastide 1972, 95). For Bastide, and the writers who applied some of his sociohistorical conclusions about northeastern Brazil to Afro-Cuban studies, the formation of the modern Afro-Cuban religions was similar to that of the Bahian Candomblés (Murphy 1988; Brandon 1993; Palmié 1993). Like the Candomblé temples, which, Bastide thought, emerged from the institutional "niche" or "new social framework" of the colonial-era religious brotherhoods (*irmandades;* Bastide [1960] 1978, chap. 2), the twentieth-century Afro-Cuban *casa-templos* grew out of the *cabildos de nación.* Still, scholars continue to debate the institutional origins of the modern Afro-Cuban *casa-templos.* For Fernando Ortiz, the early-twentieth-century Afro-Cuban "sorcery temples" (*templos brujos*) rose from the ashes of the *cabildos de nación* after the 1886 emancipation (Ortiz [1906] 1973, 68–72; 1921, 29–31). Locating this transformation slightly later, Joseph Murphy writes that "[a]fter Independence [1902], the *cabildos* were reformulated specifically as Afro-Cuban cult houses, called *reglas,* after the *reglamentos* or regulations of *cabildo* life" (1981, 210; 1988, 29–33).

In contrast, the Cuban anthropologist and historian Rafael L. López Valdés locates the origin of the modern *casa-templos* not entirely in the colonial *cabildos de nación,* but, in greater measure, in independent "house-temples" (*casa-templos*) of free Africans and creoles, which had been established in the nineteeth century, prior to the moment of emancipation. Despite the great numbers of Yoruba-speaking and related Bight of Benín peoples arriving in Havana and Matanzas from the end of the eighteenth century through 1865[1] and subsumed under the metaethnonym "Lucumí," López Valdés found that the Lucumí claimed proportionately few *cabildos de nación*. Only fourteen are listed in official records for all of Cuba across a couple of hundred years, from the seventeenth through the nineteenth centuries, and many of these were reorganizations of earlier institutions. In contrast, other nations just as populous (if not more so) as the Lucumí, such as the Congo and Carabalí, claimed scores of official *cabildos de nación*. Historical treatments of Afro-Cuban institutions, including Ortiz's own work, remain imprecise and confused, López Valdés argues, because the term *cabildo* was applied to heterogeneous African and creole organizations, from informal social "clubs" to the *cabildos de nación*—that is, registered organizations of slave membership linked to the church as official *cofradías* under a saint's patronage. Freed Lucumí, their creole sons and daughters, and their ritually initiated creole "godchildren," he speculates, were independently practicing their Yoruba-derived religion during the nineteenth century, if not earlier, and their "houses" were also called *cabildos*.

For López Valdés, this last class of *cabildos* formed the most significant starting point for modern Lucumí religious institutions—the *casas* of Havana and Matanzas. In short, these early *casas*, also called *cabildos*, not the *cabildos de nación*, should be the "new focus" of historical investigation where Lucumí religion is concerned (López Valdés 1994). Though Joseph Murphy takes Fernando Ortiz's narrower "old focus" on the *cabildos de nación* (Ortiz 1921) as his historical point of departure, he astutely anticipates López Valdés's hypotheses in identifying the economic resources, social status, and mobility of Havana's free urban *gente de color* of the colonial period as crucial in nurturing the emergence of twentieth-century Afro-Cuban cult life (Murphy 1981, 145–46; 1988, 29–33, 107).

Notwithstanding evidence of proportionately few colonial-era Lucumí *cabildos de nación*, a guiding ethnohistorical principle that joins the work of Bastide ([1960] 1978), Mintz and Price ([1976] 1992), and Palmié (1993) recognizes that large numbers of African arrivals do not enduring cultural influence make. Palmié usefully hypothesized that the *cabildos de nación* were important "incubating cells" of neo-African ethnic identities and religious resources (Palmié 1993, 341; see also Murphy 1988, 107). The Lucumí *cabildos de nación*, as my reading of Fredrika Bremer's 1853 drum dance account suggests (see chap. 1), harbored specialized personnel who, as mobile urban slaves, probably contributed their knowledge to extant or emergent independent house-*cabildos* during the nineteenth century. In turn, as Murphy notes, nation freedmen lent their resources to the protection and liberation of enslaved Africans (1988, 107). The treasury of Bremer's Lucumí *cabildo*, for example, was "appl[ied] to a good use—the purchasing the freedom of slaves of this tribe" (Bremer 1853, 2:381). Despite the divide-and-rule policy of official institutional separation of free and slave, and African and creole, *cabildos*, during the colonial period (see Deschamps Chapeaux 1968, 50; López Valdés 1987, 7), communication and mutual aid proceeded between all of these groups.

The reconstitution of Lucumí religious knowledge in an apparently pluralistic setting of exchange and intercommunication is exemplified in an oral history account collected by Fernando Ortiz in the 1930s and astutely used by Stephan Palmié to flesh out these processes (1993, 339–40). The important Lucumí institution of the sacred *batá* drums, including its specialized bodies of technical, herbal, and musical knowledge, and its corps of drummers "sworn" (*jurado*) into the cult of the drum spirit, *Añá*, arrived in Cuba not as an intact "tradition." A classic instance of "culture building," as Palmié demonstrates, the *batá* complex was recreated, disseminated through the urban *cabildo* networks of Havana, Regla, and Matanzas, and transmitted intergenerationally through descending ritual lineages of drummers.

> In Cuba the *batá* sounded for the first time in a Havana Lucumí *cabildo* named Alakisá on Egido Street. *Alakisá* means "slovenly" or "dirty" [*ripiao* or *basura*]. In the first third of the past century a Lucumí named Añabí arrived as a slave in Cuba, where he was known as Ño Juan el Cojo. It is said that in his homeland he was a *babalao, olosáin,* and *oni-ilú* [Ifá diviner, herbalist, and master of the *batá* drums]. Shortly after arriving in Cuba and being taken to work on a sugar plantation, a cart full of cane fractured his leg and he was transferred to a slave hospital in Regla. There, for the first time in Cuba, he heard with emotion the religious rhythms of the Lucumí music. There also he met an old slave, a Lucumí like himself, called Atandá, aka Ño Filomeno García, an *olúbatá* [master drummer] with whom Añabí had had dealings in Africa. Both of them went to the Alakisá and knew immediately that the drums being played there were not orthodox, they were profane [*judíos*], and that no set of consecrated *ilú* [*batá de fundamento*] existed in Cuba. In about 1830, the African *onilú* Añabí thus hooked up with Atandá, who had been an *agbéguí* or sculptor in Africa and who, in Cuba, had acquired a reputation for the religious sculptures he carved—they were remembered as being "very beautiful." Atandá also knew how to build drums, and the two friends constructed and consecrated a set of the hourglass-shaped *batá* drums. They "baptized" them with the name Añabí, which meant "born from Añá" (the drum spirit). Thus, they consecrated to Añá the first true set of sacred *batá* that existed in Cuba. . . . To Ño Filomeno García or Atandá and Ño Juan or Añabí is attributed the founding of a Lucumí *cabildo* in Regla, the Cabildo [of] Yemayá, along with the great African *babalao* Ño Remigio [Herrera, aka Adechina], father of the late octogenarian and popular *santera* Pepa, or Echubí, who, although blind, crippled, and almost an invalid, had continued directing the *cabildo* [until her death in 1947]. For this Regla *cabildo*, Añabí and Atandá made and consecrated a second set of *batá*, which they named Atandá. (Ortiz 1952–55, 4:315–16; my translation from the Spanish)

Figure 2.1.—Ño Remigio Herrera/Adechina (Obara Melli, c. 1811–27 January 1905), c. 1890. Note his Yoruba ethnic facial marks—three diagonal lines on each cheek. Museum of Regla.

Atandá and Añabí, evidently still enslaved during the period in which they constructed their first set of drums, took advantage of the margin of mobility and liberty the urban setting offered to make connections with each other, with the Alakisá *cabildo*, and with the Yoruba *babalawo* Ño Remigio Herrera/Adechina (fig. 2.1). Whether the Alakisá institution was a *cabildo de nación*, an unincorporated "club" of enslaved Lucumí, or an early house of free

Africans on the López Valdés model is uncertain. Still, the Alakisá (also Arakisá) were probably African born, for this nickname, meaning "slovenly" or "dirty," was given to the *viejos de nación* by the new generations of creole upstarts, according to Lydia Cabrera's sources ([1954] 1983, 25 n.1). In any event, it seems much more certain that the *cabildo* that Atandá, Añabí, and Ño Remigio Herrera/Adechina later founded was at first not a *cabildo de nación,* but a house-*cabildo* that claimed as its patrons a Lucumí *oricha,* Yemayá, and the preeminent local Catholic Virgin, La Virgen de Regla.

If Atandá was an "old slave" in the early 1830s, the revered Lucumí *babalawo* Ño Remigio Herrera/Adechina (Obara Melli) was still a recently arrived enslaved young man, perhaps in his late teens or early twenties in 1833, the year of his documented baptism. "Remigio Lucumí" was owned by the giant plantation of Don Miguel Antonio Herrera in Nueva Paz, eighty kilometers southeast of the city of Havana.[2] The Nueva Paz municipality was created in 1812, but its attractive, rich lowlands in the southeastern corner of the Havana province were settled as early as 1688 (Suchlicki 2001, 427). The Herrera family owned "thirteen mills and 24,000 acres, including the vast plantation proudly named *Sansom y Unión* (6,000 acres) at Nueva Paz" (Thomas 1971, 152–53, 138–39).

Perhaps it is so that the Cabildo of Yemayá was conceived and "founded" in Regla by Atandá and Añabí, together with Adechina, after the creation of the *batá* drums in the early 1830s. Remigio Lucumí could have encountered them on the streets of Regla or in the *cabildos* of Havana, for it is believed that he was a favored slave of his master, with unusual liberty and access to the urban setting.[3] Though it is not clear how he traveled to Havana, by the middle third of the nineteenth century the earlier (1838) Güines-to-Havana line had been connected well into Matanzas sugar mill country, running directly by Nueva Paz (see Thomas 1971, 122, 138–39). However, it is more likely that Ño Remigio Herrera/Adechina was already a free man, a stonemason (*albañil*), a significant Regla property owner, a protector of other Africans, and *padrino* to influential Spaniards when the Cabildo of Yemayá would have had the resources to become a functioning and expanding institution—perhaps as late as the 1860s or 1870s.[4]

Remigio Herrera/Adechina's Cabildo of Yemayá, or Cabildo of the Virgin of Regla, maintained by a free African and, after his death, by his creole daughter, bridged the era of the old-style *cabildos de nación* and the period of modern *casa-templos.* This *cabildo* functioned as a seminal Lucumí religious institution in Regla until the death of its *dueña,* Josefa Herrera ("Echubí Pepa") in 1947 (fig. 2.2, *center*). As such, this kind of organization represented one of at least three possible historical trajectories and institutional models of the many Lucumí *cabildos* or *sociedades* flourishing around the turn of the twentieth century. Some, such as the Cabildo of Yemayá, were apparently continuous in important ways with independent nineteenth-century houses-*cabildos* founded by freed Africans (Ño Remigio Herrera/Adechina and others). Others, such as many of the *cabildos* and *sociedades* Ortiz discovered in the 1909 Provincial Government of Havana Register of Associations, were "openly or covertly derived" from the old *cabildos de nación* (Ortiz 1921, 24–26). For example, the Cabildo Africano Lucumí, also known as the Sociedad de Socorros Mutuos bajo la advocación de Santa Bárbara, was "reorganized" and officially inscribed on 16 January 1891 by one Joaquín Cádiz (Ortiz 1921, 24, 26). Back in 1839, this *sociedad* had adopted the red and white *bandera* of Santa Bárbara, suggesting its status as a *cabildo de nación* or *cofradía.* Later, however, Joaquín Cádiz reinscribed the *cabildo* within the postemancipation legal framework documented by historian Rebecca Scott (see my chap. 1). It became a voluntary association with a constitution (*reglamento*), a hierarchy of officers, a program of "mutual aid in cases of sickness or death," and a dues-paying membership (see Ortiz 1921, 26; Scott 1985, 264–78). Finally, still other *cabildos* and *sociedades* were apparently newly founded by Africans or creoles in the decade or so after 1900—though they may have been based in earlier informal or family kinship groupings. For example, the Sociedad Lucumí Santa Rita de Casia y San Lázaro was founded in 1902 in the Havana municipality of El Cerro by the famous Lucumí priest "Papá" Silvestre Erice, considered "the last Lucumí pontiff" (*el último pontífice Lucumí*) upon his death at more than eighty years of age, about 1915 (Castellanos 1916, 38, 54, 56, 78; see also Roche y Monteagudo [1908] 1925a, 209–13).[5] Similarly, the three Lucumí *sociedades* of Palmira, Cienfuegos (formerly Las Villas Province), were inaugurated around the first decade of the twentieth century by African ex-slaves belonging to three families: Sevilla—or Iznaga—Fernández, and Entensa. The Lucumí Nicolás Iznaga, for example, was formerly enslaved by the wealthy Iznaga slaver and planter family of the city of Trinidad, on one of their ten mills on twelve thousand acres in and around the fertile environs of Cuba's south central Cienfuegos region (Thomas 1971, 119, 137, 147, 152). Upon his freedom, Nicolás changed his name from Iznaga to Sevilla and, later, in 1912, founded La Sociedad El Cristo along with other Africans from Palmira and Santiago de Cuba (see below).[6]

Despite their different historical trajectories, the Lucumí organizations documented by Fernando Ortiz, Rafael Roche y Monteagudo, Irene Wright, and Israel Castellanos bore important institutional features in common, many of which reproduced patterns of the nineteenth-century official *cabildos*.[7] For example, during the first years of this century, they claimed old African ex-slaves as founders, Catholic patrons, their corresponding iconographic *banderas* (banners), and saintly devotions enshrined in decorative *capillas* (altars), legalized *reglamentos* (constitutions), mutual aid functions, dual administrative and sacred hierarchies, dues-paying memberships, and double Catholic and Lucumí liturgical regimens and festival cycles. Thus, the Cabildo Africano Lucumí of 1900 celebrated the annual feast day of its Catholic patron, Santa Bárbara, on 4 December with a Catholic mass, a formal procession afterward, and a Lucumí drumming (*tambor*) for Changó (Ortiz 1921, 24). Likewise, Adechina's and Echubí's Cabildo of Yemayá was one of two principal Regla *cabildos* that organized the annual street processions and Lucumí drummings around the 7 September feast day of the Virgin of Regla, whose sacred images they maintained in Catholic domestic *capillas* (shrines; see chap. 5 and fig. 5.5). The "African *cabildo*" Irene Wright visited on the outskirts of El Cerro just before 1910 "was a social-religious organization licensed by the municipality under a name in which figured that of a Catholic saint" (Wright 1910, 149; fig. 5.10).

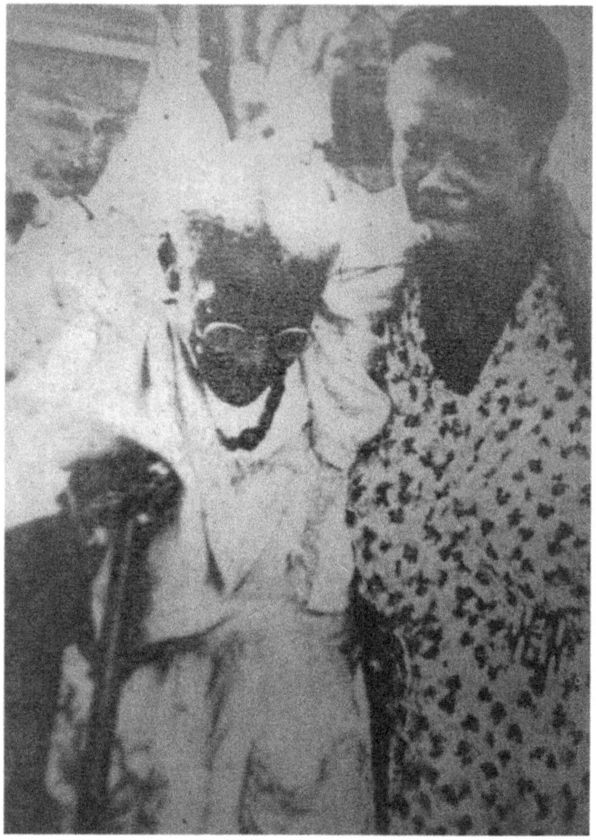

Figure 2.2.—Josefa Herrera, "Echu Bí Pepa," daughter of Adechina Ño Remigio Herrera, moving on crutches in the Virgin of Regla Procession, 7 September, probably early to mid-1940s. Museum of Regla.

The great similarities among the Wright (1910, 149–50), Roche y Monteagudo (1908, 79–83; [1908] 1925, 182–86), and Castellanos (1916, 38, 54, 56, 78) accounts suggest that the three observers all visited the same *cabildo*, the Sociedad Lucumí Santa Rita de Casia y San Lázaro of the Lucumí septagenarian "Papa" Silvestre Erice. The three documents together, complete with photographs of Silvestre and his richly adorned altar rooms, provide a stunning composite picture of this transitional institutional form, that is, a complex socioreligious institution that mirrored aspects of the nineteenth-century "old style" organizational patterns and prefigured the setup of modern Lucumí "house-temples" (*casa templos*). For example, organizations such as Erice's were established in houses that apparently doubled as private domiciles; they had begun to develop a racially heterogeneous membership; they featured multiple altars associated with an apparently systematized pantheon of deities that were indexed with Catholic saints and shared in their iconography; they had begun to elaborate the luxurious royal iconography and "creole taste" of the Lucumí *orichas* (see chaps. 4 and 5 and figs. 5.10 and 5.11). The drumming at Erice's *cabildo* was performed by a Lucumí *güiro* ensemble of drums and *chekeré* shakers; the interior rooms contained altars for Obatalá, Yemayá, Ochún, and Changó; the participants wore festival dress color coded to their particular tutelary *orichas* (e.g., the young girl's "clean lawn dress with blue sash and neck ribbons" for Yemayá or the Virgin of Regla); they sang in an "African dialect" (Lucumí); the drumming's spiritual guests of honor include the *orichas* Ochún and Changó, who possess their priests and dance. For example, "We were told," Wright reports, "that one song, movements to which simulated a snatching from above, was a prayer to Saint Barbara for blessings," a description that nicely describes Changó's most characteristic dance movement, which traces the path of lightning from heaven to earth (see Wright 1910, 149; and app. 1).

Just as freed Africans had established their house-*cabildos* independent of the nineteenth-century *cabildos de nación*, early-twentieth-century creole Lucumí priests would establish their own "house-temples" outside of the well-known early twentieth century *cabildos* or *sociedades*—whose annual festivals they undoubtedly attended and whose knowledge and resources they continued to depend upon. Still, where the early twentieth century *cabildos* were umbrella organizations connecting numerous emergent houses and ritual family lines, the typical twentieth-century "house" of Ocha has been composed of a single extended "ritual family" (*familia de santo*) directed by a single priestly elder who practices within a private domicile in more or less discreet or underground fashion. For example, the institution now remembered as the Cabildo of the Virgin of Regla/Yemayá of Josefa "Echubí Pepa" Herrera, the daughter of Adechina, was undoubtedly first housed in Adechina's own domicile at 31 San Ciprián (now Fresneda) in Regla's poor and black Third Barrio. The property that later supported the "house"-*cabildo* of his daughter (63 Perdomo [earlier named Morales]) was a vacant lot (*yermo*) in 1900 and remained so, it seems, until the first decades of the twentieth century.[8]

"KINGS FROM ACROSS THE SEA" AND KINGS AROUND THE BAY OF HAVANA: THE ELASTICITY OF "LUCUMÍ" IDENTITY

The changing institutional history of the Lucumí *cabildos* over the course of little more than forty years marks the transformation of the ethnonym "Lucumí." The early twentieth century transitional *cabildos* had become socioreligious societies of mixed composition, whose diverse members practiced what was emerging as the Regla Lucumí—the Lucumí *religion*. A Lucumí *cabildo*'s "identity," Murphy eloquently notes, "began to rest less on the ethnic descent of [its] members than on the spiritual path that [it] followed" (1981, 210; 1988, 33; see also Brandon 1993, 83; Palmié 1993). Irene Wright's account offers striking, albeit anecdotal, evidence of this crucial demographic shift in the practitioner base of the Lucumí *cabildos* in the period following emancipation (1880–86), the Second War of Independence (1895–98), the first occupation by the United States (1899–1902), and the establishment of the Republic (1902). When Wright visited the El Cerro *cabildo*, its leader was an "old man," an "African-born . . . surviving [ex-] slave" (Wright 1910, 147). Yet, by this time, the complexion of such a Lucumí society's membership had changed dramatically from that of the Cabildo de Señora Santa Bárbara de la Nación Lucumí Alagua described by Fredrika Bremer almost sixty years earlier. The American writer's escort, evidently a senior priest of the El Cerro *cabildo*, was "a mulatto, the leader of an orchestra well-known in Havana" (Wright 1910, 147). Upon his arrival at the house, this *mulato* Lucumí elder is ritually saluted by a "pretty young girl, who might have 'passed for white'" (149). If the "old African" leader represented the waning generation of *negros de nación*—these two other priests were, presumably, the creole children of mixed marriages who had entered the *cabildo* under initiatory criteria.

In a purely demographic sense, the Lucumí ethnic composition of the colonial-era old-style *cabildo de nación*—and the meaning of *Lucumí* as an ethnonym linked to birth on the continent of Africa—could not be sustained after Africans from determinate "nation" groupings ceased to enter Cuba in large numbers. Citing the 1899 census, historian Hugh Thomas notes that the numbers of African-born individuals in Cuba had dramatically decreased. In that year, no more than thirteen thousand African-born individuals were alive in all of Cuba (i.e., fewer than 1%) out of a total Cuban population of one and one-half million (Thomas 1971, 423). In that year, of the 1,784 African-born individuals living in Havana province (total population 424,811), only 836 lived in the city of Havana (total population 250,000; Thomas 1971, 429, 424). Of those creoles with direct African ancestry, over half (327,000) had been born since abolition in 1880, and perhaps only 70,000 of the total, fewer than 10%, were ex-slaves. The rest of these creole over-twenty-year-olds had always been free (Thomas 1971, 429).[9] It is true, and striking, that at the time of Lydia Cabrera's mid-twentieth-century research (1930–60), many practitioners of African descent continued to identify themselves with the specific regional Yoruba-Lucumí ethnonyms (e.g., Egua, Yesá, Ketu, Iyebu, Takuá) of their ancestors (Cabrera 1980, 2). If one follows Palmié (1993), however, these regionally marked identities were intensified, if not reinvented, through the process of "ethnogenesis" within the system of *cabildos*, the names of which were themselves historically marked by hyphenated compounds: Lucumí-Yesá, Lucumí-Oyó, Lucumí-Egua, and so on. Still, well before Cabrera's research, which began in 1930, the identifier "Lucumí" had increasingly gained the meaning of a specific religious "order" (*regla*) or "denomination" for Afro-Cubans and non-Afro-Cubans alike.

Equally striking, the full official name of Joaquín Cádiz's 1891 Cabildo Africano Lucumí, as reflected in the *reglamento* document of its later reincarnation (see Cabildo Africano Lucumí 1900), included an important qualifying tag: it was, more precisely, the Sociedad de Socorros Mutuos de Nación Lucumí hijos y descendientes—"Lucumí Nation children and descendants."[10] Joaquín Cádiz maintained the specific neo-African nation ethnonym (Nación Lucumí) in the society's name, which other early twentieth century *cabildos* had already replaced with an Afro-Cuban creole designation, such as the Mutual Aid Society of Persons of Color, Our Lady of Regla (Ortiz 1921, 23). In contrast, "children and descendants" registers the heterogeneity of its African-born, its creole, and, as I will show, its initiatory, Lucumí, membership, or "fictive kinship," as social anthropologists might say.

Two years after Joaquín Cádiz's 1891 reorganization, one José Cornelio Delgado petitioned to form society of nearly the same name; indeed, it was an apparent reincarnation of the earlier one, called the Sociedad de Socorros Mutuos de Nación Lucumí, sus hijos y descendientes, invocada a Santa Bárbara. Though it cannot be confirmed, perhaps it was that this new inscription was necessitated by the death of Joaquín Cádiz during the very period in which many African-born ex-slaves passed away. The society's new *reglamento,* published in 1900 during the first United States occupation of the island (1899–1902), presents two different, slightly overlapping, rosters of founders, directors, committee members, and lesser officers, including people now remembered as the most powerful and influential figures of the emerging Lucumí *reglas* of Ocha and Ifá in Cuba at the time. They were Africans and creoles; they were ethnically and racially diverse; they belonged to two different sub-*reglas* of priesthood within the Lucumí religion—La Regla de Ocha and La Regla de Ifá; they descended from different genealogical "branches" (*ramas*) of these two sub-*reglas;* they also practiced the Congo-Cuban Palomonte religion and belonged to the Abakuá society; and they were men and women. Thus, while *hijos y descendientes* could certainly refer to the blood "descendants" (*de sangre*) of two African-born Lucumí, like the child of Ño Remigio Herrera and his Lucumí second wife, Francisca Burlet (Josefa Herrera, "Echubí Pepa"), the identities of most of the roster's creole figures reveal that "children and descendants" referred significantly to "Lucumí" *ritual descent* (*de santo*). In other words, they were initiated in the Yoruba-Lucumí religion through formal ceremonies of consecration to the priesthood.

For example, of the thirty-one officers on the first roster, at least nine were already influential Havana creole *babalawos,* members of the male diviner fraternity called La Regla de Ifá; the others were prominent members of Havana's La Regla de Ocha community, consisting of the priests and priestesses of the *oricha* "pantheon" of deities (e.g., Eleguá, Ogún, Ochosi, Obatalá, Yemayá, Changó, and Ochún).[11] Strikingly, the organization's office of "honorary president" in 1900 was occupied by none other than the venerated Lucumí *babalawo* Ño Remigio Herrera/Adechina. Herrera's apparent figurehead role in 1900 and the absence in the roster of the society's 1891 reorganizer, Joaquín Cádiz, suggest the recent passing of Cádiz, as well as the unparalleled stature of Adechina in 1900 as one of the few—if not the only—surviving African-born *babalawos.* Ño Remigio Herrera, already an octogenarian, would pass away five years later, on 27 January 1905.[12] Still, among the society's *vocales* (speakers) was the ubiquitous old Lucumí, "Papá" Silvestre Erice, a septugenarian (see Castellanos 1916, 56–60, 75–78, fig. 15). Beyond these two Lucumí luminaries, at least six of the seven creole *babalawos* on the roster represented four of the five principal Ifá *ramas* (branches) in Havana (see below). For example, Eulogio Rodríguez (Tata Gaitán), Bernabé Menocal, and Esteban F. Quiñones were the Afro-Cuban creole ritual godchildren of three different African *babalawos* who had founded major Havana Ifá lineages. In turn, Luis Pacheco, a *mulato,* Bonifacio Valdés, a *blanco* of Spanish descent, and Pedro P. Pérez, a *mulato,* were the initiatory "grandchildren" or "great grandchildren" of another African founder, through the highly esteemed Esteban F. Quiñones.[13]

Among the women's leadership were founders of the most influential Lucumí *ramas* of the Regla de Ocha. According to the 1900 roster, Ña Caridad Argudín was the female "founder" (*fundadora*) of Cabildo Africano Lucumí itself; Ña Caridad was, moreover, the founder of the Lucumí root house (called Igoró or Aigoró; see Valdés Garriz [1995] 1997, 135),[14] which may have produced the sub-*rama* of the *cabildo*'s "second counselor," Apoto-Belén González and her famous descendants of the José Pata de Palo/Eshubí and Pimienta, and sub-*ramas.* Likewise, the *cabildo*'s "first counselor," Ña Margarita Armenteros, was the Lucumí founder of the "San José Ochenta lineage," which initiated, and worked closely with, the members of the Sotolongo family, Tiburcia and Eufemia—who appear among the "speakers" on the *cabildo*'s roster. The roster's Pilar Valdés may have been Ña Pilar, the partner of Gumersindo, the founder of "El Palenque," the old rural Lucumí village near what became the *barrio* of Pogolotti, Marianao, Havana (see Cabrera [1954] 1983, 25, n. 1).

In short, the Cabildo Africano Lucumí/Sociedad de Santa Bárbara of 1900 was a legally inscribed, voluntary institution with a patron saint, which was grounded in ever-"deeper" levels of a "hidden" sacred "center of gravity" (Bastide [1960] 1978, 160). The organization was a key, if not the key, institutional hub and cultural repository for the Lucumí religion in Havana, if not all of Cuba during this period. This status would be greatly reinforced by confirmation that the Cabildo Africano Lucumí/Sociedad de Santa Bárbara was none other than the twentieth-century reincarnation of the great Changó Tedún, the most widely remembered and important Lucumí *cabildo* in Cuba's history.[15] In any event, Cabildo Africano Lucumí, as suggested, claimed interlocking membership with other important Lucumí institutions: Adechina Remigio Herrera's Cabildo de la Virgen de Regla/Yemayá, Silvestre Erice's Sociedad de Protección Mutua Santa Rita de Casia y San Lázaro, known commonly as the Cabildo de Papá Silvestre, as well as Havana's principal Ifá houses of Tata Gaitán, Esteban Quiñones, Bonifacio Valdés, Pedro Pérez, and Bernabé Menocal, and the Ocha houses of Ña Caridad Argudín, Ña Margarita Armenteros, Ña Belén González, and, it seems, the great Palenque Lucumí village of Gumersindo and his "twin" Perfecto.

On the cultural front, Cabildo Africano Lucumí undoubtedly exerted tremendous influence and guidance with respect to Ocha and Ifá practice in Havana. The African godfathers of Tata Gaitán and Bernabé Menocal were close colleagues of Adechina, and these two men continued those fundamental connections in their collaborative ritual work after Adechina's death with Adechina's godchild, Bernardo Rojas Torres.[16] Ña Margarita Armenteros, as amplified below, worked closely with the famous Ña Rosalía-Efuche of El Cerro, who helped standardize Ocha initiation in Havana. Her systematizing of Ocha initiation must have been reinforced by the omnipresence and indisputable authority of the principal master of ceremonies for these houses, Timotea Albear Ayayi La Tuan (d. c. 1935), who may have been married to Bernabé Menocal and whose family members occupied positions on Africano Lucumí's board.

At the same time, it is evident that such interlocking membership between different houses also contributed an effect opposite to unity and uniformity—heterogeneity. For example, a reading of Fernando Ortiz's account of Havana's *batá* drum tradition and its variations suggests that the "substitute" *batá* tradition of Papá Sylvestre Erice's society—"orthodox [African] drums modified by 'white'" features—may have sought to become part of Cabildo Africano Lucumí's cultural repository. These latter drums, the *panderetas lucumís*, were "invented" by Fernando Guerra, Papá Sylvestre Erice's right-hand man and successor (Ortiz 1952–55, 4:332–35, 381–82).[17] According to Ortiz, Guerra and his orchestra were not authorized as *batá* drummers, and "hardly knew how to play, but with regard to their *panderetas*, they could put on [feign] a good show" (*dar el gatazo;* Ortiz 1952–55, 4:382; see Ortiz 1983, 267). Guerra apparently served as a cultural ambassador between numerous *cabildos* and *sociedades* themselves, and between the *cabildos* and the society at large, including Cuban academics and travel writers. The elegantly dressed, white-haired *mulato* Fernando Guerra corresponded with Fernando Ortiz (1952–55, 4:382–84)[18] and may have been the very same "mulatto, the leader of an orchestra well-known in Havana," who enabled the American Irene Wright to report on Papá Silvestre's *cabildo* drumming (Wright 1910, 147–49).

The institutional reach and diverse membership of the Sociedad de Santa Bárbara/Cabildo Africano Lucumí mark a crucial set of transformations in the history of the Lucumí, whom William Bascom (1951) identified as "the Yoruba in Cuba." During the slavery period, the prominent ethnonym "Lucumí" was elastic enough to encompass many West Africans who were not, strictly considered, the "Yoruba-speaking peoples" ethnographers and historians have recognized (see López Valdés 1986; see also Ellis 1894; Smith 1969; Bascom 1951, 1969b).[19] Redefined at least by the time of Cabildo Africano Lucumí's

1891 reorganization, during the the colony's postemancipation period, "Lucumí" could include "children and descendants," who might not have had African-born Yoruba parents or even grandparents. In turn, by the time of Cabildo Africano Lucumí's 1900 *reglamento,* if not before, "Lucumí" clearly included the racially heterogeneous members of a specific "ethnically" marked institution and religious denomination, the Regla Lucumí. While numerous Lucumí *negros de nación* belonging to *cabildos* during the slavery period wore ethnic facial cicatrizations identifying their Yoruba ethnic subgroup origins, as is evident in Adechina's late-nineteenth-century photographic portrait (see fig. 2.1), each of the directors of the Cabildo Africano Lucumí would carry a different kind of institutional identification badge, an oval medal of silver bearing the society's initials (Cabildo Africano Lucumí 1900, 6). Yet, these latter *naturales* (natives) of Cuba carried multiple levels of identity. They were the ritual descendants of specific Lucumí spiritual "families" (*familias*) or "branches" (*ramas*) through their consecration in initiation ceremonies. Official badges notwithstanding, all would carry in their heads and bodies the spiritual power (*aché*) of the *orichas* and/or of Ifá. Beneath their offices listed in the society's *reglamento,* their deeper marks of self-identification, belonging, and mutual recognition were constituted by affiliations with Lucumí *reglas, ramas,* and deities. Cabildo Women's First Counselor Ña Margarita Armenteros, a Lucumí (Yoruba) or first-generation creole, was a priestess of Oyá, whose sacred name was Ainá. Cabildo Mens' Speaker Bonifacio Valdés, a white creole of Spanish descent, was a priest of Obatalá and a *babalawo,* whose sacred sign was Obe Weñe and whose African title was Oluo Salakó.

Figure 2.3.—Eulogio Rodríguez Gaitán, "Tata Gaitán" (Ogunda Fún, 1861–1944), possibly 1900–1910s. Private collection, Guanabacoa.

Still, as the multiple identifications and affiliations of Eulogio Rodríguez Tata Gaitán suggest, the Cuban religious field was becoming increasingly heterogeneous and complex, and the denomination "Lucumí" would complement, if not compete with, other denominations. Born in 1861 in the Havana *barrio* of Jesús María to a comfortable creole family, Tata Gaitán, later of Guanabacoa (fig. 2.3), was a *tabaquero* by trade and is believed to have worked in Tampa, Florida, during the 1890s.[20] Recognized by his personal Ifá sign Ogunda Fún, he was the sole heir of the great Lucumí *babalawo* Olugueré Kó Kó and the only *babalawo* ever to be officially "crowned" as the *obá,* "king"—the master of ceremonies—of Cuba's Regla de Ifá.[21] As such, he was also recognized by the Cuban Ifá title Achadé. Tata was not only a priest of the Lucumí hunter-deity, Ochosi; he was also a powerful Tata Nkisi, a priest of the Regla de Congo or Palo Monte. During the late nineteenth century, Havana sources explain, "many *babalawos* had their *prendas* [Congo sacred cauldrons] in order to protect themselves."[22] Like many of his *tabaquero* colleagues and Ifá contemporaries in the late nineteenth and early twentieth centuries, Tata Gaitán was also a member (*obonekue*) of an Abakuá Society lodge.[23] Tata Gaitan's huge house and property, which he purchased in 1916, spanned more than a block in depth (51.50 meters). It contained stables for horses and coaches and an extensive *cuartería* (guest quarters) for the scores of *babalawo* colleagues, and Ocha, Ifá, and Palo godchildren, who traveled from as far as Palmira in Cuba's interior to undergo initiations and work the religion in Guanabacoa. Undoubtedly, Tata was multilingual: he not only spoke Spanish, but also utilized the Lucumí, Congo, and Abakuá Brícamo languages, as well as communicated in *bozal* with living African-born inhabitants or creoles and the spirits of the dead who would possess their mediums (see Cabrera [1979] 1986; Castellanos 1990). Not to be forgotten is that Eulogio Rodríguez Gaitán, a well-to-do member of Guanabacoa's elite, garnered significant power by playing a variety of roles in Guanabacoa's social life. He was the ritual "godfather" and financial supporter of local politicians, such as Guanabacoa's mayor; some say he initiated Cuba's dictator Gerardo Machado as a *babalawo.* He cared for the Parish of Guanabacoa's nuns, his neighbor's children, and street urchins; and, he acted as *tío político* (adoptive uncle) to a number of Guanabacoa's younger *babalawos.* In short, his house was a one-man mutual-aid society.[24] Thus, where the discrete nineteenth-century *cabildo* establishments on the same street separated the different African "nation" traditions (Lucumí, Congo, Carabalí) and their mutual aid functions, one twentieth-century Guanabacoa "house" would contain all of those traditions and services in the differentiated religious and social roles of a complex individual.

It is not surprising, as other important details of Cabildo Africano Lucumí's *reglamento* suggest, that the society's various "reorganizations" sought not only to define or redefine its administrative and social dimensions (for example, the responsibilities of the titleholdáers and the dues structure), but also the institutional and cultural "boundary markers" that constituted its identity as a highly visible representative of the Lucumí tradition (see Palmié 1993; and Barth 1969). Such markers gave concrete meaning and discipline to the concept of *regla*—literally "order," "rule." In the "African drum dances by the name of *Tambor*" (*bailes africanos con el nombre de Tambor*) that were held on festival days, according to the *reglamento,* "the use of other rhythms [*toques*] not of the African nation to which they belong are prohibited" (Cabildo Africano Lucumí 1900, 6). In other words, as Fernando Ortiz noted in his reading, the society's *reglamento* "prohibited . . . rhythms other than the Lucumí" (1921, 26). Were Joaquín Cádiz and the society's subsequent directors concerned that the Lucumí religious discipline might be diluted or *cruzado* (blended with features of other religions)? And, how, exactly, were Fernando Guerra's own "invented" *panderetas lucumís,* with their "white modifications" and drummers virtually incapable of playing *batá* rhythms on them, viewed by the more conservative members? In any event, the *reglamento*'s emphasis on the integrity of the society's drumming regimen exemplifies how crucial distinct cultural forms, preeminent among them a distinct corpus of drum *toques,* were to religious identity in an era of competing *reglas* that crosscut the Cuban creole population.[25]

New oral history research deepens the portrait of Cabildo Africano Lucumí and provides useful foundation for illuminating further its institutional connections and influence. My research among Havana *babalawos* reveals that the Joaquín Cádiz who reorganized Cabildo Africano Lucumí in 1891 was none other than the venerated African *babalawo* called Ifá Omí-Ogundá Teturá, believed to have arrived as a child in Havana during the middle of the nineteenth century. The name Ifá Omí is universally known among contemporary Cuban *babalawos* and appears in their ancestral *moyuba* prayers as Fa-Omí or Faomí among the generation of deceased African Ifá founders. Not a slave, two different Havana *babalawos* told me, Ifá Omí was a Yoruba "prince" traveling the world with Spanish traders or slavers. His surname, Cádiz, came from the southern Spanish homeport city of his ship.[26] One story relates that his arrival fulfilled the prediction of that year's annual Ifá divination sign, Odí Melli: a "king would come from across the sea" to assume the role of *obá* (king) of the Lucumí on the island of Cuba. Indeed, Cádiz's sacred Ifá name, Ifá-Omí, means "Ifá [of] Water." African Ifá elders already in Cuba, including *babalawo* Ifá Bí-Obeate Francisco Villalonga of Regla, according to one story, "discovered" Joaquín Cádiz on a Havana wharf one day when they heard this child-prince singing in Yoruba.[27] Whether or not any of these stories, narrated in greater or lesser detail by Havana *babalawos*, is literally true, it remains intriguing that Cádiz did occupy the highest *cabildo* leadership office, which, during the nineteenth century, was reserved for elected or hereditary royalty. Ño Remigio Herrera/Adechina, head of the 1900 Cabildo Africano Lucumí, though not remembered as African royalty by blood, nevertheless radiated such a powerful and regal presence that people of all stripes, upon encountering him in the street, would genuflect before him and kiss his hand out of respect and awe.[28] If Joaquín Cádiz was royalty by blood, Remigio Herrera was royalty by virtue of his seniority, history, and knowledge, most of which were produced on the island of Cuba.

Gone well before the time of Africano Lucumí's 1900 *reglamento* were the politically empowered "kings" and "queens" of the *cabildos de nación* who, crowned and elegantly dressed, led street processions and oversaw drumming celebrations from their canopied thrones. Following the deaths of great Lucumí founders of royal or quasi-royal status, such as Joaquín Cádiz and Ño Remigio Herrera (d. 1905), "Papá" Silvestre Erice (d. c. 1915) may indeed have been the "last Lucumí pontiff," who, according to his *cabildo* survivors, "would forever protect the earth with his mantle of precious stones and fringes of all colors (Castellanos 1916, 57).[29] Still, the sacred "center of gravity" (Bastide [1960] 1978, 160) of the transitional *cabildos* and the twentieth-century *casas* harbored two enduring forms of "royalty," which continue to characterize the *reglas* today. First, of course, is a form of royalty that manifested itself in the status and treatment of the deities whose spiritual presence formed this sacred "solid core" (Bastide [1960] 1978, 160) of the *cabildos* all along: the Lucumí *orichas.* The luminous and bejeweled trappings of the "kings" and "queens" of the old-style *cabildos*—European-style crowns, lavish garments of silk and satin, staffs, and canopied thrones—would remain with the *orichas* themselves as their semipublic festive cluster of altar and intiatory adornment (see chaps. 4 and 5). Second, the title of "king" (*obá*) continues to mark the ritual authority of the "masters of ceremonies" within the Regla Lucumí's two branches, Ocha and Ifá. As noted, formal "coronation" ceremonies existed among Cuba's Lucumí to install de jure *obás* within the Ifá hierarchy of *babalawos* and were performed on at least one occasion, perhaps as late as the 1920s. Cabildo Africano Lucumí's vice president, Eulogio Rodríguez Tata Gaitán, is considered to be the only *babalawo* to be formally invested as *obá* in Cuba.[30] Though these formal consecration ceremonies were never performed again, other twentieth-century *babalawos* of great *conocimiento* (knowledge) have acted as revered de facto *obás,* particularly Bernabé Menocal, the ritual godchild and inheritor of the Ifá genealogical "branch" of Joaquín Cádiz, as well as many of Menocal's equally powerful godchildren.[31] The royalty of Joaquín Cádiz thus begot the most important line of ritual royalty in Cuba. The "heads" of houses (*padrinos* and *madrinas*) within Ifá and Ocha have, since at least the early twentieth century, also depended upon the knowledge and experience of their expertly trained and, later, quasi-professionalized *obás* to direct their ceremonies. Within Ocha houses, *obá-oriatés* (king–"master of the divination mat" or "master of ceremonies") direct initiations. In a reconfigured way, the division of "administrative" and "ritual" roles characterizing the old-style *cabildos de nación* and the turn-of-the-nineteenth-century transitional *sociedades* endures in the structure of the twentieth-century Ocha and Ifá houses. The *padrino* or *madrina* runs the house on a day-to-day basis and claims ultimate responsibility for its doings; the *obá* conducts the house's regular initiation ceremonies.

FROM *CABILDO* TO *CASA* TO *RAMA*: THE SACRED "BRANCHES" OF OCHA AND IFÁ IN CUBA

The many *cabildos* and *casas* that bridged the nineteenth and twentieth centuries are fondly remembered by contemporary priests as the origins and strongholds of Cuban Lucumí culture and religion. They include Regla's two Cabildos of the Virgin of Regla/Yemayá (Josefa Herrera Echubí Pepa and Susana Cantero Omí Toké),[32] Havana's Changó Tedún (aka the Cabildo of Santa Bárbara), Marianao's El Palenque of the "Twins" Perfecto and Gumersindo (Cabrera [1954] 1983, 24–25),[33] and the Cabildo of Papá Silvestre. Matanzas's memorable Lucumí *cabildos* include the Cabildo of Fermina Gómez Torriente, the Cabildo Iyesá of the García family, and Cabildo Santa Teresa of the Cárdenas and Villamil families.[34] Matanzas Province's Arará *cabildos* (whose members descended from enslaved Fon, Mahi, Adja, Evhe, and other groups from the former Kingdom of Dahomey and present-day Togo), which, in some cases, formed ritual connections with the Lucumí of Matanzas, include the three Arará Dajomé-Magino *cabildos* of the Baró (town of Jovellanos), Zulueta (Perico), and Fernández (Agramonte) families (see Brice Sogbossi 1998, 41–58, 82–83; Vinueza 1986, 22–27, 37–50).[35] Another important still-functioning Arará *cabildo* in Matanzas is the Cabildo Arará Sabalú Nonjó in Matanzas City, founded in about 1880–95 as the Cabildo del Espíritu Santo (Holy Spirit). Its name, Sabalú, derives from Savalu, a Mahi town in the old Kingdom of Dahomey. The Cabildo Arará Sabalú, in turn, is the root of Havana's Arará practice established in the Guanabacoa house of *cabildo* status belonging to Pilar Fresneda (fig. 3.4), possibly the goddaughter of one of Arará Sabalú's founders, Flora Heredia.[36] Further into Cuba's interior, three Lucumí *sociedades* and one Congo *sociedad* continue to function today in the town of Palmira, Cienfuegos (see above).

Much emphasis in the historiography, perhaps too much, has focused upon the *cabildos* as the principal institutions of the Afro-Cuban religions' gestation and birth, as Rafael L. López Valdés pointed out. Given the overlapping leadership roles and institutional connections of Cabildo Africano Lucumí's membership, it is worth nuancing Roger Bastide's seminal formulation once again. A deeper "starting point" of the Lucumí religion lies not so much in the *cabildos* as in the revered personages who founded and led the religion's Ifá and Ocha "houses" (*casas* or *ilés*) and gave birth to their corresponding *ramas* ("branches"). A *casa* (*ilé* in Lucumí) refers not merely to the physical domicile of a priest, but to a ritual "family" of priests initiated by an elder of Ocha (*babaloricha* or *iyaloricha*) or Ifá (*babalawo*). *Rama* refers to the genealogical lineage or lineage tributary from which priests (and their houses) descend. *Casas* are the nodes, as it were, of the *ramas*, and these terms together constitute the sacred genealogical organizing principles of the Lucumí tradition. The *rama* is constituted by two levels of sacred reproduction and descent: the genealogically related, consecrated "heads" of initiated priests, and the genealogically related ritual "secrets" or *fundamentos* of the *orichas* that priests receive in their initiations, that is, sets of consecrated "stones" (*otán*), which reside in soup tureens and other receptacles, generally called *soperas* (see chaps. 4 and 5). Upon consecrating the "head" of an initiate, a ritual elder—the "owner" (*dueño*) of a "house"—becomes the "godparent" (*padrino* or *madrina*) of a new "godchild" (*ahijado* or *ahijada*). The new member of the house comes to have "brothers" and "sisters" (*hermanos* and *hermanas*) among the house's other initiated priests, both alive and deceased (*eguns*). The term "house" also can subsume collegial or "working" relationships with priests of other houses or *ramas* (see below).

The kinship relations of this sacred family (*familia de santo*) augment and complement the kinship relations of one's natural and baptismal families (*familia de sangre* and *familia de la iglesia*), utilizing the surrogate kinship terminology from the latter (*madrina* or *padrino* and *ahijado*).[37] In his writings, the Havana *obá-oriaté* Nicolás Angarica unified both levels of Lucumí sacred genealogy—priests and *orichas*—with a single metaphor, *la familia de soperas* (the family of *soperas*), which is synonymous with an expanded definition of the Lucumí concept of *fundamento*. *Fundamento* can refer both to the *orichas'* sacred stones and to the extended ritual family and genealogical lineage of the house, the *rama* or "branch" of Ocha (Angarica [1955?] n.d., 61; see Brandon 1983, 492–93; and see chap. 3).[38] In daily practice, a priest's genealogical descent and historical consciousness are instantiated in chants called *moyubas*, which "pay homage to" the *rama's egúns*—deceased founders, descendants, influential *obás*—a priest's deceased parents, grandparents, and selected relatives by blood, as well as the *rama's* living authorities (see Ramos 1982c; Mason [1985] 1993, 41–42). In short, the *ramas* and their *raíces* (root founders) constitute the most profound "starting point of the Cuban *santería*."

THE TRANSMISSION OF LUCUMÍ RELIGION INTO THE TWENTIETH CENTURY: FIVE AFRICAN NAMES AND IFÁ NARRATIVES OF ORIGIN AND AUTHENTICITY

Suggestive hypotheses about the genesis and development of the Lucumí religion emerge with the legendary names and events preserved in stories that contemporary priests tell about the history La Regla de Ocha and La Regla de Ifá. First, a small number of African and creole priests were responsible for founding and advancing the principal Lucumí *ramas* in Cuba. Second, in many cases, the houses of Lucumí *rama* founders and their immediate descendants did not begin to proliferate significantly until the late nineteenth or early twentieth century. Third, although practitioners ideally reckon their *ramas* as continuous and unbroken lines of spiritual descent from Africa, in practice, they recognize that the bodies of knowledge, spiritual resources, and ritual practices they received from their ancestors were not passively handed down, but were discontinuous, and actively created and recreated over time. Fourth, they also recognize that the ritual authority, correctness, and authenticity of Lucumí priests and their practices did not automatically emerge out of the Middle Passage but were actively made and remade in Cuba.

While caution is suggested at every turn in relying on all the details of oral histories as if they were wholly and precisely factual, the stories I collected in Havana and Matanzas conspire together to delineate a historical consciousness that includes a sense of dynamic process and conflict. For example, in the stories I heard, the most famous Lucumí founding figures used their cunning and intelligence during slavery to secure certain liberties and to position themselves socially and economically, cultivating influential allies in Cuban society. The *rama* founders and their immediate creole descendants often pooled their knowledge and economic resources with allies, and guarded secrets from rivals. Sometimes they sought to advance themselves entrepreneurially within and without the religion, and used "sorcery" (*brujería*) to defend themselves and neutralize their competitors. The systems of knowledge they transmitted to successive generations were not static bundles of tradition but were actively recompiled (*recopilado*), judiciously and selectively disseminated, and subjected to self-conscious programs of "reform." In addition, knowledge and practice were always debated and negotiated, in cases by "commissions" of elders, who gathered to formulate policies for the future (see chap. 3). At least by the middle of the twentieth century in Havana, and, perhaps later in Havana and the interior, relatively standardized "systems"[39] of knowledge and practice characterized the Lucumí religion, and critical variations continue to be maintained in the traditions of the individual *ramas*. Clearly, by 1900, authoritative and representative personnel and a hardy collective knowledge base for such "commissions" and systematizing movements were already firmly established in the Cabildo of Santa Bárbara/Africano Lucumí (see above and chaps. 3 and 4).

My genealogical field research finds that virtually all of Cuba's *babalawos*, living and dead, belong to five major genealogical *ramas*, which descend from five African founders. While the names of more than ten African-born *babalawos* are regularly invoked in the *moyubas* and stories of contemporary *babalawos*, five names stand out because they represent the generative *raíces* (roots) of the Ifá *ramas* on Cuban soil. That is to say, these five founders "left families" (*dejaron familias*), as *babalawos* say, by initiating and guiding creole godchildren who founded powerful and prolific Ifá houses. These five African-born Lucumís were Ño Carlos Adé Bí (Ojuani Boká, "Crown Gives Birth"), Ño Remigio Herrera Adechina (Obara Melli, "Crown Makes Fire"),[40] Joaquín Cádiz Ifá-Omí (Ogundá Teturá, "Ifá of Water"), Olugueré Kó Kó (Oyekún Melli), and Francisco Villalonga Ifá Bí (Obe Ate, "Ifá Gives Birth"). The legacies of other great African *babalawos*, such as Ño Juan el Cojo Añabí and Ño Filomeno García Atandá (Baba Elliobe), reside in the *batá* drum and Olokun ancestral masquerade traditions, but they are not cited by contemporary *babalawos* as the founders of Ifá lineages that continue down to the present. Others, such as Ño José Akón Kón (Oyekún Melli), who did not initiate anyone, are remembered as great teachers of Ifá.[41]

The five major Ifá *ramas* were, and are, centered in Havana, where the concentration of *babalawos* has always been strongest. Practitioners agree that religious authority in Matanzas was always centered primarily in the houses of the *iyalochas*, the female priests of the *orichas*, such as Ma Monserrate González, Fermina Gómez, and Felipa Calderón; some add that Matanzas was, and continues to be, "anti-*babalawo*."[42] Thus, while famous African *babalawos* lived, worked, and founded important *cabildos* in Matanzas (e.g., Ño Blas Cárdenas) and Palmira (e.g., Ta Vicente Goytizolo), virtually all twentieth-century *babalawos* from these areas descended from Havana *ramas*, particularly those of Adechina and Tata Gaitán. Ta Vicente Goytizolo, for example, reported to have been a nineteenth-century Congo *cabildo* king of Santiago de Cuba (see Castellanos 1916, 76), was initiated as a *babalawo* by Tata Gaitán, before the turn of the last century, and helped found the Sociedad El Cristo of Palmira's Sevilla Family.[43] Two Havana *babalawos* believe that Ño Blas Cárdenas, the nineteenth-century founder of Matanzas's Cabildo de Santa Teresa, was initiated together with Oluguеré Kó Kó in Africa and later played a role in training Oluguеré's heir, Tata Gaitán, in Ifá practice; recent research, however, finds that Ño Blas Cárdenas was initiated by Adechina on 3 December 1872. He is credited with founding the Cabildo of Saint Teresa in Matanzas in the early nineteenth century prior to becoming a *babalawo*.[44]

Notwithstanding the evidence of five genealogically distinct Ifá *ramas*, virtually all of the nineteenth- and early-twentieth-century *babalawos*, a relatively small group, regularly "worked together" in advancing Ifá in Havana.[45] Ifá's unity is this regard is substantiated mythologically and historically. Some *babalawos* believe, for instance, that Orula, the *babalawo*'s spiritual patron *orisha*, "really has only one house, while the *orishas* have many houses—there are many *orishas* but only one Orula" (see chap. 3). Upon sharing my research findings with the extremely knowledgeable Havana-made *babalawo* Oscarito Rodríguez, who is the current director of Cabildo Arará Sabalú Nonjó in Matanzas, he insisted that all *babalawos*, in fact, belong to "one *rama*." Despite their previous Ifá training in Africa, he explained, they were all "made" or "reconsecrated" in Cuba by Ño Carlos Adé Bí of Regla, who is considered by many to have been the earliest, and most elder, *babalawo*, among the generation of those born in Africa.

The Numbers Game

These findings reinforce, and are reinforced by, recent thinking in the field of African Diaspora studies. General explanations for the strength and prevalence of Cuba's Lucumí traditions, such as the massive numbers of Yorubas that arrived in Cuba until the late 1860s (see n. 1 above), are neither subtle nor specific enough to explain the transmission of the religions into the twentieth century. Numbers do not guarantee enduring cultural influence, and, more specifically, cultural influence does not guarantee religious persistence. Not all Yorubas entering Cuba were priests, and not all of those with the requisite priestly knowledge were able or willing to transmit what they knew to succeeding generations. As middle-aged and elder contemporary priests typically explain, many of their godparents were not willing to reveal their secrets, in good part, because of their fear of persecution,[46] as well as their conservative attitude about ritual knowledge. In a more tragic case, widely recognized among studious priests in Havana and Matanzas, the hermetic Arará of Matanzas's provincial towns "took their knowledge to the grave with them," and, for this reason, many Arará Dajomé-Magino traditions are extinct.[47] Moreover, the creation of a modern Lucumí religion has less to do with *when* the *ramas* were founded than when nineteenth-century individuals and groups were able to initiate and teach competent and effective descendants who could advance the religions in the twentieth century (see Bastide [1960] 1978, 160; Mintz and Price [1976] 1992, 19; Palmié 1993, 340).

Stories of Diaspora

Two kinds of diasporic story lines shape the historical consciousness of Lucumí practitioners. One is a story of linear continuity with an authentic origin or primordial spiritual ground: the *tierra* (homeland) of the Yoruba of West Africa or an ancestral personage (*egun*), for example, or a Lucumí or creole who founded a *rama* (branch) of the Lucumí religion in Cuba. The other is a story about agency, struggle, discontinuity, and heroic achievement. Its figures include the haloed African who was an ingenious and resourceful slave, the strong priestess who was a prolific initiator, *dueña* of a *cabildo* (owner of a founding religious house), and active reformer of religious practice, and the creole *babalawo* "big man" who shrewdly gathered resources and large constituences in his orbit (see Barber 1981).[48] The two stories are often intertwined to form a narrative dynamic of spiritual continuity and human creativity in the face of great social odds—foremost among them is the theme of slavery.

One powerful story of the first kind relates that, just prior to his capture by slave traders in Africa, the young Adechina "swallowed his Ifá" (*se tragó su Ifá*), which he carried in his stomach, defecated and guarded in the belly of the slaveship, and later reconsecrated in Cuba. "His Ifá" refers to the sacred nut kernels of the West African oil palm (Yoruba *ọ̀pẹ̀;* genus and species *Elaeis guineensis;* see Bascom 1969a, 26; 1952, 171). The nut kernels, called *ikín* in Cuba, constitute the essential *fundamentos* (i.e., *sacra*) and divination equipment of the *babalawos* of Ifá, who have the *oricha* Orunmila as their spiritual patron. This Ifá story about Adechina turns on a commonly invoked theme of Lucumí spiritual and practical continuity with West Africa, akin to the stories William Bascom recorded in Matanzas in the late 1940s. The most powerful *oricha* "stones" (*otán*)—the essential *fundamentos* of the Regla de Ocha—were "swallowed" by the slaves prior to their embarcation for the New World, he was told (Bascom 1950, 65). Still, these are not merely stories of passive cultural continuity. The clear-thinking, strategic response of swallowing the *fundamentos* in the nick of time required great resourcefulness and prescience on the part of these African ancestors. In turn, using the trope of procreation, the stories then transform the personages of Lucumí ancestors, such as Adechina, into the loving and committed progenitors of tradition. The original Lucumí *fundamentos*, the *ikín* and the *otán*, were re-gestated in the stomach of the slave in the belly of the slaveship; in turn, the body of the ancestor who conserved the precious *fundamentos* was the womb of sacred diasporic tradition. Still, these original *fundamentos* could only "grow" and have, as their "children" (Bascom 1950, 65), the *fundamentos* of the succeeding priestly generations with the active intervention of the tradition's midwives: its *padrinos* and *madrinas* (i.e., "godparents").

Thus, the second kind of story line foregrounds the theme that the rebirth of the Lucumí Ifá and Ocha traditions in Cuba required great resourcefulness, cooperation, and ritual "work" (i.e., performance) in the social setting of slavery and its aftermath. Ño Remigio Herrera Adechina and his elder African-born colleague, Ño Carlos Adé Bí, according to several Havana *babalawos*, were shrewd and ingenious individuals who negotiated unusual liberty for themselves as slaves and, using their various skills, won or bought their freedom from their masters. Ño Carlos Adé Bí gained his freedom after he impressed two Spanish guests of his master. Carlos divined for these two *españoles*, using a Yoruba-Lucumí Ifá divining chain (*opele*) improvised from vines and the circular skins of small oranges.[49] The guests, convinced of Carlos's "intelligence," had wagered that if he could divine about them accurately, they would purchase his freedom from his master, who was insensitive to the slave's special talents. Carlos's prediction proved accurate, and the Spaniards avoided a precipitous drop in their business fortunes.[50]

Stories about Adechina emphasize that he was a favored slave also recognized for his "intelligence." He was permitted access to the two important provincial capitals in western Cuba: Havana, approximately forty-five kilometers away from the plantation, and, Matanzas, thirty kilometers away. For example, as two Havana *babalawos* relate, Adechina was sent to Havana to conduct business for his master. In Regla, on the Bay of Havana, Adechina cultivated good "relations" with "Spanish" *bodega* owners and met Ño Carlos Adé Bí, possibly already a freedman. Shrewdly utilizing these precious early connections, Ño Carlos Adé Bí and Adechina took advantage of the safety of the *bodega*'s "back room" in order to ritually "wash" (*lavar*, i.e., reconsecrate) the African-born Ifá that Adechina had "swallowed." Two "new social ties" were formed, as a result. Notwithstanding the Ifá training Adechina had probably received in Africa, Ño Carlos Adé Bí became Adechina's "representative" *padrino* on Cuban soil,[51] and they formed cross-racial and cross-class relationships in order to secure the "back room" ritual space, at a moment when Lucumí sacred resources, personnel, and temples had not yet reached critical mass in Havana in the mid- to late 1830s (see below). These new relationships produced further results.

Ño Carlos Adé Bí, a "tough man, who had been the butler and personal confidant of a Spaniard," not only functioned as a ritual mentor for Adechina, but also had gathered the financial resources to "buy him out of slavery."[52] Adechina then began to navigate Cuban urban society with increasing force and success. Marriage documents reveal that Ño Remigio Herrera was, like generations of eighteenth-, nineteenth-, and twentieth-century people of color, a skilled artisan—a building mason, or *albañil*, a trade he may have learned in slavery. Following perhaps a decade or more in the City of Matanzas (c. 1840s–1850s), where he settled temporarily and began to build two or more families, he moved to Regla, probably in the early 1860s.[53] Documents indicate that Adechina had, in fact, developed significant relations among the town's elite. A Regla businessman, magistrate, pharmacist, and housewife witnessed, and acted as godparents for, his marriage to the Lucumí ex-slave from Matanzas Francisca Burlet on 26 October 1891. At least by 1881, when his name appears in the Regla census for the first time, Ño Remigio Herrera had become a property owner himself. By 1900, five years before his death, he could claim a large, valuable family home on a lot in Regla's Third Barrio, a sizable vacant property around the corner, and significant rental income. Attesting to his solid, independent economic position, his property deeds show the absence of a *hipotecario*, or cosignatory. Adechina's house was filled with children born to him and Francisca from the early 1860s on, children from his wife's previous marriage, and numerous boarders. Such resources apparently enabled him to develop the Cabildo of the Virgin of Regla/Yemayá and to maintain and advance strong ties with family and godchildren in Matanzas.[54] In sum, Adechina and Ño Carlos Adé Bí strategically positioned themselves—created the necessary social, economic, and institutional conditions—in order to "continue" as *babalawos,* found *cabildos,* and launch prolific *ramas.*

Adechina's stature and spiritually radiant character are reflected in his oval photographic portrait, possibly taken on the occasion of his marriage in 1891. In the only surviving photograph of an African-born *babalawo,* this white-haired sage with three Yoruba facial cicatrizations on each cheek presents himself in a formal Western suit and tie of the period (see fig. 2.1). This was an era in which Africans were rarely, if at all, immortalized in portraiture in Cuba; if represented or photographed at all during the nineteenth century, Africans mostly appeared as ciphers in the backgrounds of picturesque lithographed landscapes, in mug shots, and as "anthropological" specimens in criminological treatises.[55] In contrast, Ño Remigio Herrera's portrait suggests his intention to inscribe himself as an agent and a figure for posterity. The photograph is polyvocal; it claims a divided address. By having himself immortalized within the conventions of late-nineteenth-century photographic portraiture, he inserts himself into the public transcript, wherein the representation indexes his social status. The image was, in all likelihood, seen by an audience larger than his religious colleagues, godchildren, and family. Halftone versions of the same image were made, suggesting that Adechina's portrait was reproduced in the press (see Museum of Arts and Sciences 1988; Trujillo y Monagas 1882; Ortiz [1906] 1973, 135–38; Castellanos 1916; Scott 1985, plates; Cantero and Laplante [1857] 1984).[56] At the same time, from the moment of his death on 27 January 1905, Adechina Obara Melli would live on as a chief ancestral presence (*egun*) in the homes of his blood descendants and on the altars of his ritual descendants throughout the country (plate 2, left center); by the 1980s, the African presence in Regla would be symbolized by this portrait, which now hangs in the entrance of the Regla Museum.

The Problem of Olofin

The motifs of transatlantic "swallowed stones" and "swallowed Ifás" constitute diasporic *continuity* narratives, while the motifs of *cabildo* "reform" programs and secretly reconsecrated Ifás constitute diasporic *transformation* narratives. Clearly, Ño Carlos Adé Bí's reconsecration of Adechina's *ikín* enabled Adechina to "continue" as a diviner and healer. However, the *ikín* alone could not enable the intergenerational transmission of Ifá. That is, it could not spiritually authorize the "making" of new Ifás—the initiation of neophytes into *babalawos* and the confection of the "secrets" of Ifá's *oricha* interpreter, Orunmila. Enter the historical problem of Olofin, the preeminent *poder* or *fundamento* ("power") of La Regla de Ifá. Whereas the *ikín* palm nuts form the practical *fundamento* of a *babalawo*'s divining career, Olofin is nothing less than Ifá's meta-*fundamento* in its authorization of Ifá's reproduction through initiation. Without Olofin, there would be no "branches" (*ramas*) of Ifá. Theologically speaking, Olofin, meaning "Owner of the Law," is one of the three facets of the Lucumí God-Trinity (see below; and Díaz Fabelo 1960, 27–38; Pichardo and Nieto 1984, 35).[57] In practice, Olofin is materialized and enshrined in the form of a *lata cargada,* a spiritually "charged" and sealed cilindrical metal "can."[58]

According to the transformation/discontinuity cycle of diasporic narratives, the essential ingredients to confect Olofin were "missing" in Cuba. In order to fabricate Olofin (alternatively Odun) in Havana, one story relates, Adechina, Olugueré Kó Kó, Achadé, and other *babalawos* depended upon Adechina's alter ego, a Lucumí by the name of Salvador Montalvo. Montalvo, appropriately nicknamed "Odun," made at least one return voyage to his native kingdom of Ilé Ifẹ̀ in West Africa and secured the necessary ingredients of Olofin for Cuba's *babalawos.* Some believe that Adechina himself returned to Africa; still others believe that Olugueré returned, or tried to return, to Africa, but died in transit in Mexico.[59] Such Atlantic crossings and recrossings were not unknown during the period (see Sarracino 1988; Matory forthcoming), and often resulted in the reinstatement or "reform" of New World ritual traditions. For example, the African or creole *babalawo* known as Ño Ernesto Noriega returned to Cuba from a trip to Africa, carrying with him important sacred objects. These included a particular ancestor staff adorned with the nine bells and nine colors of the dead (*iguí égun*), which is credited with reestablishing this tradition in Cuba (Ortiz 1952–55, 2:299).[60]

According to the continuity cycle of diasporic narratives, Olofin's arrival in Cuba parallels the swallowing of stones and Ifás. Two writers believe that African *babalawos*, including Francisco Villalonga Ifá Bí, carried their Olofin secrets to Cuba on the slave ship in the nineteenth century (Bolívar Aróstegui 1990, 24; Canizares 1993, 50).[61] Though he did not mention the issue of Olofin to me, the late Feliberto O'Farril (Oche Melli), Cuba's late third most senior *babalawo*, proudly showed me the divining chain (*opele*) he believed Villalonga to have "tied around his waist" during the Middle Passage.[62] Ifá Bí's transatlantic *opele*, made of West African palm nut lobes, finds its practical opposite in the orange-peel-and-vine *opele* improvised by Ño Carlos Adé Bí on the Cuban plantation. The Olofin-bearing Francisco Villalonga Ifá Bí—the continuity figure of a one-way "diffusion" narrative from a West African origin—finds his opposite in "Salvador Montalvo-Odun," the transformation figure of a "two-way" transatlantic narrative. The former narrative coincides with the Herskovits diffusion school (Herskovits 1941); the latter narrative resonates with the Mintz and Price school (Mintz and Price [1976] 1992) and the recent Black Atlantic work of Paul Gilroy (1993). Two dramatic stories, one of direct continuity and reinstatement, one of discontinuity, Atlantic recrossing, and recreation, seek to explain Ifá's origins and "continuation" among the generation of Africans. The stories of Ifá's transmission into the twentieth century, through six generations of creoles, is equally dramatic.

The Extension of Ifá from the Lucumís to the Creoles

There were relatively few *babalawos* working in Havana between the 1880s and the first decades of the twentieth century, probably no more than 40 individuals, if that, out of a total Havana male population of color of around 50,000 and a total Havana population of between 420,000 and 450,000.[63] By 1948, according to William Bascom's estimation, only 200 *babalawos* practiced in Havana, when the city's population was approaching 1,000,000 (Bascom 1952, 171; Thomas 1971, 1095). A sixth of Cuba's 1953 population of 5.8 million lived in a Havana that had grown by leaps and bounds since the turn of the century; it was "a larger capital city in proportion to total inhabitants than any other in the world save . . . London and Vienna (Thomas 1971, 1096). My research suggests that in 1948, virtually all of Bascom's 200 "Havana" *babalawos* had been initiated as of the first two decades of the century, with the exception of the great old stalwart, Asunción Villalonga (Ogunda Masá), Ifá's then eldest luminary (initiated c. 1880).

Though Central and Old Havana have always been known for their *babalawos*, by 1948 the majority were ensconsed in the City of Havana's suburban municipalities and *repartos*, such as Guanabacoa and Regla, San Miguel del Padrón, Marianao, El Cerro, Párraga, Luyanó, Víbora, Lawton, and Mantilla. These suburbs, many outskirts of which remained *finca* ("farmland") as late as the 1950s and 1960s (e.g., Párraga), offered the possibility for *babalawos*, many of whom were workingmen or artisans, to purchase land and build or buy adequate houses to serve their ritual needs. Marianao, for example, grew "from a 'pretty little Cuban village' of a mere 5,000 . . . in 1899 to over 200,000 in 1958—the second biggest city in Cuba, if reckoned separately from Havana" (Thomas 1971, 1094). Between the 1930s and 1940s, it would become a *babalawo* stronghold, particularly its poor, mostly black, *barrio* of Pogolotti.[64] Still, the neoclassically colonnaded El Cerro, the earliest suburban escape from Old Havana (1890s), was one of the first municipalities after the older Guanabacoa and Regla to harbor the emerging cohorts of *babalawos*. In the wake of emancipation, the Old Havana bourgeoisie had fled to El Cerro, leaving their palaces and properties to be carved up into the infamous *solares* (tenements), which joined the teeming, dark underworld of Cuba's historical "other half" (*hampa cubana*) by the time of Fernando Ortiz's first published book ([1906] 1973). It will be remembered that Papá Silvestre Erice's *cabildo*, founded in 1902, was sought out on the "outskirts" of El Cerro by many a criminologist, ethnographer, and travel writer (see Wright 1910, 149–50; Castellanos 1916, 56; Roche y Monteagudo 1908, 79–83; [1908] 1925, 182–86). Outstanding in El Cerro was the Lucumí-dominated Barrio Atares, which became the home to some of the religion's most revered Lucumí and creole leaders, such as Efuche Ña Rosalía, Aurora Lamar (Obá Tolá), and her *babalawo* husband, José Ramón Gutiérrez. By the 1920s, the bourgeoisie were on the move once again, this time to the exclusive and soon-to-be art-deco-filled El Vedado section to the west. During this period, El Cerro also flourished as another great Ocha and Ifá stronghold. Thus, whereas the Africans and early creole *babalawos* had settled in the older colonial towns of Regla (Adechina, Atandá, Ifá Bí, Marcos García, Quintín García), Guanabacoa (Tata Gaitán, Valentín Cruz, Hilario Barbón), and San Miguel del Padrón (Secundino Crucet), El Cerro became home to numerous *babalawos* initiated in the late nineteenth and early twentieth centuries, particularly Ramón Febles, Bernardo Rojas, Gerardo de las Mercedes Valdés Montalvo, Francisco Febles del Pino, Enrique Santa Cruz, and their godchildren.[65]

Cuba's Ifá lineages expanded very slowly with the initiations of the first two generations of creoles between the late 1870s and 1902.[66] They began to expand with significant force between 1915 and 1920, a period of unprecedented economic prosperity (World War I produced the booming "Dance of the Millions" in 1920),[67] as these first two generations of creoles matured as *babalawos* and began to initiate prolifically. Each of the five Africans themselves had initiated no more than a handful of creole godchildren, between one and five. It was, in turn, the generation of creole godchildren, and in many cases, the generation of creole "grandchildren"—two generations from the Africans—who began to initiate great numbers of *babalawos*. For example, while Adechina initiated most of his five godchildren during the last quarter of the nineteenth century, such as Ño Blas Cárdenas and his colleague Atandá's oldest son, Marcos García, it was in 1902, three years before his death, that this great Lucumí initiated the creole who would dramatically extend the *rama:* Bernardo Rojas Torres of El Cerro and, later, Marianao. Similarly, the heirs of Ifá Omí Joaquín Cádiz and Oluguere Kó Kó, Bernabé Menocal and Tata Gaitán, respectively, were initiated in the last third of the nineteenth century and made scores of *babalawos*, who became famous and powerful in their own right. In the case of Ño Carlos Adé Bí, the great expansion of his lineage came only with the maturity of his Ifá "grandchildren," Pedro Pablo Pérez Rodríguez ("Periquito Pérez" [Obé Yono]) of Central Havana and Ramón Febles (Obetuará Lará) of El Cerro. Still, the most spectacular expansion of Adé Bí's lineage came only with his "great-grandchild," Gerardo de las Mercedes Valdés Montalvo ("Che Che" [Ojuani Alakentu]) of El Cerro, who was initiated in Ifá as a boy in 1910, and began prolifically initiating in the 1920s. As a counterexample, the powerful, but conservative and somewhat hermetic *rama* of Ifá-Bí Francisco Villalonga initiated comparatively few *babalawos* in its entire history until recently. Following the deaths of Ifá Bí's *babalawo* son and grandson (1953 and c. 1970, respectively), the Villalonga legacy grew exponentially in the hands of its powerful custodian, Ángel Padrón ("Bebo el Mokongo" [Baba Elliogbe]), only as of the 1960s and 1970s.[68]

Most or all of the African-born *babalawos* had passed away by the first years of the twentieth century. Most of the first generation creole *babalawos*, such as Ño Filomeno García Atandá's famous sons, Quintín (Otura Nico) and Marcos García (Baba Elliogbe),[69] as well as Valentín Cruz (Baba Elliogbe) and Esteban Quiñones (Ika Melli∫, died in the decade before World War I. With some interesting exceptions, the rest of this first generation of creoles, along with much of the second generation, died between the late 1920s and 1959.[70]

Though Ifá reproduced itself significantly before midcentury, my oral and archival research shows that its most radical expansion occurred only *after* Bascom's 1948 estimated census of two hundred *babalawos* in Havana. The explosion in *babalawos* began to occur with the passing of the powerful, conservative leaders of the prior two generations, particularly Ramón Febles (1939), Tata Gaitán (1944), Asunción Villalonga (1953), and Bernardo Rojas (1959). As amplified below, through their decisive control over the disemmination of Olofin, as well as the authorizing Ifá ceremony called *Wanaldo* (the Knife), they had exerted strict limits on the numbers of *babalawos* that could be initiated.[71] Between the 1950s and late 1970s, Havana's Ifá tradition not only grew exponentially, but also atomized into many "families" that achieved newfound independence from the elders and restrictions of their *ramas*.

Though intensive archival research into property and estate records would be required to substantiate causal connections between Ifá's institutional growth and particular social, economic, and political trends in Cuban history, oral research at least suggests the following.[72] The Lucumís Adechina, Ño Carlos Adé Bí, Olugueré Kó Kó, Ifá Omí, and some of their first creole godchildren initiated and schooled ethnically diverse creoles with critical combinations of personal shrewdness, property, social and political connections, and literacy, several of whom were of Spanish, Canary Island, and mixed descent. The Afro-Cuban creole Eulogio Rodríguez Gaitán was the son of an elegant, well-to-do Havana creole couple from Jesús María, Cristóbal Rodríguez and Mercedes Gaitán. By 1916, Tata Gaitán possessed the resources to purchase a mansion on vast property near Guanabacoa's town square, and in 1924, to purchase an expensive *panteón* (tomb) in Havana's Colón Cemetery.[73] As indicated, Tata Gaitán was a powerful *padrino* not only in several religions, but also in the larger social and political sphere. Similarly, the Afro-Cuban creole Bernabé Menocal cultivated social and ritual connections as *padrino* to the rich and members of the government.[74] A *criollo blanco* of Spanish descent, Bonifacio Valdés is remembered as a well-dressed, socially powerful *negociante* (businessman), whose pockets were always filled with gold coins.[75] The *pardo* Ramón Febles Molina, a prosperous maker of fine cabinets and funeral coaches, owned multiple houses and a vast workshop in El Cerro, raising there a large family. Following the historical pattern of mutual aid and sponsorship among religious compatriots, Febles supported *babalawos* of the preceding and succeeding generations. He maintained the old Lucumí Ño José Akón Kón and Febles's two esteemed Afro-Cuban creole godfathers, Esteban Fernández Quiñones and Valentín Cruz.[76] In turn, Febles financed the first Havana tailor shop, La Sastrería Moderna, of his younger friend and mentoree, Bernardo Rojas Torres, also from Güines. All of these relationships were realized and cultivated through ongoing forms of religious and social reciprocity and gestures of respect. For example, it is likely that Febles introduced Bernardo Rojas to the *babalawo* elders, which led to Rojas's own intiation.

Bernardo Rojas Torres (fig. 2.4), a *pardo* born out of wedlock in 1881, was initiated at age twenty-one by Ño Remigio Herrera/Adechina. For three years, *babalawos* relate, Rojas traveled daily, when he did not stay for long periods of time, from El Cerro to Adechina's Regla home across the bay to study with his master (who died on 27 January 1905). Just as Febles had "washed the feet" of Esteban Quiñones and Valentín Cruz, a standard gesture of respect toward the old Lucumís and creoles, so Rojas washed the feet and "cut the toenails" of Adechina.[77] In turn, the shrewd and prosperous Adechina, as he had undoubtedly advised the creoles Tata Gaitán, Bernabé Menocal, and Atandá's son Marcos, in effect, counseled Rojas to "go west, Young Man." The wise African knew a lot about the *oro* (gold) that was in the "west," in both senses of the term. Adechina's personal Ifá sign, Obara Melli, is the spir-

Figure 2.4.—Bernardo Rojas Torres (Irete Tendí, 1881–1959), c. 1910s–1920. Private collection, Havana.

itual origin of "commerce" and "wealth" in Ifá; there in Obara Melli are "born" "kingship," "riches," and the "jewels" of children.[78] One important ethical code of the *rama* he founded was that "in order to be a good *babalawo* one had to have a career; one should, and could, not, live off of being a *babalawo*" in order to avoid conflicts of interest between the spiritual vocation and self interest. One day, Adechina "read" Bernardo Rojas and said to him, "Anardo, the two things you creoles like most are money and alcohol. Take the first one and become a landlord. There you will find your progress" (*desenvolvimiento*).[79] This Rojas went on to do. On top of his tailor business, he bought and sold houses in El Cerro and Marianao. Eventually he ensconsed himself and his Ifá house in a grand colonnaded compound in Marianao, which surpassed even Tata Gaitán's Guanabacoa home. Undoubtedly, his business successes and power as a *babalawo* went hand in hand, as Adechina had predicted. Through the late 1950s, Rojas led Cuba's most expansive, well-organized Ifá *casa-templo*. His Marianao compound became known as *El Vaticano* (the Vatican) for his guidance, standardization, and domination of Havana Ifá practice.

In short, for this new *babalawo* cohort, which had begun to prosper financially and in the "jewels of children" (e.g., their Ifá godchildren), by the second decade of the twentieth century, their Ifá practices and careers as artisans and social *padrinos* were mutually reinforcing. In general terms, it is clear that the "Dance of the Millions" benefited many sectors of the island's population. In more precise economic terms, it appears that Ifá's growth benefited from a very specific historical conjuncture. Cuban creole tradesmen were, in fact, beleaguered by fierce competition from the new Spanish immigrants and other foreigners during the first two decades of the Cuban Republic (1902–12). Yet, by 1919, the Cuban creoles had made great advances over the foreigners (Pérez 1988, 203–4, 242). These Cubans included men like Febles, Tata Gaitán, Bernabé Menocal, and Bernardo Rojas. For example, Tata Gaitán was able to purchase his expensive home in 1916 and tomb in 1924. This period coincided with Febles's acquisition of more and more expensive homes and the birth of his nine children, and Rojas's first tailor shop.[80]

Knowledge and Organization

The extensive relationships the new *babalawos* developed with the surviving Africans and old creoles around the turn of the last century produced an enduring foundation and font for the dissemination of religious knowledge after the deaths of Ifá's founders. Given their resources and education, Febles, Rojas, and Pedro Pablo Pérez Rodríguez ("Periquito Pérez") were the first to begin collecting (*recopilando*), textualizing, and disseminating in the form of *libretas* ("notebooks") the Ifá oral tradition from the African and early creole elders, such as Adechina and Ño José Akón Kón.[81] In effect, they became the first "Ifá ethnographers," who documented and, as a result, transformed their own tradition. Given the foregoing, it is worth hypothesizing that the connection between the "color" of these men—*pardos* in nineteenth-century parlance, *mulatos* in twentieth-century parlance—their social mobility, and their education was critical to the "survival" and transmission of Ifá knowledge and the Regla de Ifá in general. It is possible, moreover, that Ifá's dominance in Havana, as opposed to Matanzas, is owed as much to Havana's demographics as to the dominance of women leaders and the "anti-*babalawo* attitude" in Matanzas.

The same social factors also provided the foundation for the institutional advances of Ifá and the growth of Ifá families. As in the preceding period of Cabildo Africano Lucumí, the role of organization, mutual support, and interlocking networks of social influence were crucial in Havana Ifá's growth between World War I and World War II. Bernardo Rojas's Ifá house, later called "the Vatican" when it was installed in the Marianao compound, brought together and trained *babalawos* from all five of Havana's principal *ramas* and created interlocking ritual relationships between them in the collective initiation of a large proportion of Ifás most reputed *babalawos* from about 1915 to 1959. As a result, Havana Ifá practice became highly codified under the "system of Bernardo Rojas."[82]

These organizing efforts and fortunes reached their peak during the nations' "Constitutional Period" (1940–53). Economically, this may have been aided by Cuba's turn out of the devastating effects of the depression; indeed, great economic advances were experienced during and after the Second World War (see Pérez 1988, 285). On the civic-religious voluntary association model of the earlier twentieth-century *sociedades,* Bernardo Rojas legally inscribed his Asociación Luz de San Francisco in 1936. Saint Francis is the Catholic counterpart of the Ifá diviner-*oricha* Orunmila.[83] The association featured a hierarchy of officers, gave church masses for San Francisco and Orunmila on their double 4 October feast day, and gathered the funds to realize the expensive and complicated annual Ifá "Reading of the Opening of the Year" on 1 January. Rojas's annual Ifá reading was attended by all of Cuba's *babalawos.* The association apparently grew in membership and expanded its resources and visibility through the 1940s and 1950s. The numerous church masses given by Rojas presented press photo opportunities in which Bernardo was pictured with one of his godchildren and political patrons, the senator "El Chino" Ayón. Rojas may have offered Ayón a reliable voting block, and one heavily documented mass, in fact, took place on the eve of Ayón's last election campaign in 1958.[84]

Following a similar pattern, the grandson of the Lucumí Atandá, Quintín Lecón Lombillo (aka Tín), inscribed his own Asociación de los Hijos de San Francisco de Asís slightly later. The ambitious Tín, frustrated in his attempts to persuade Rojas, then the second most senior *babalawo* in Cuba, to be the figurehead of his society, turned to Asunción Villalonga, Cuba's most senior Ifá authority. Tín, in an on-and-off fundraising effort with Rojas, gathered building funds for a grand social and educational center (El Edificio Social y Centro Escolar) in Regla. The site, at 47 Fresneda Street in Regla's Third Barrio, was appropriate; this traditionally black and heavily religious *barrio* had been the home of Adechina Ño Remigio Herrera, Ifá Bí Francisco Villalonga, Atandá Ño Filomeno García, and their important familial descendants, who worked the religion together, founded *cabildos,* and established seminal Lucumí traditions, such as the *batá* drums, Olokun masquerade, and Olofin. Not least in importance, Tín secured over forty thousand pesos from his powerful godchild, Carlos Prío Socarrás, Cuba's president from 1948 to 1952.[85] Like his predecessor, Ramón Grau San Martín, Prío, the last "reform" candidate of the Auténtico Party, presided over a "bloated," extremely corrupt, and "violent" adminstration, during which the term *gangsterismo*

Figure 2.5.—Cuban president Carlos Prío Socarrás (in office 1948–1952, *center left*) presenting reported forty-thousand-peso check to Quintín Lecón Lombillo (Otrupon Adakino), founder of La Asociación de los Hijos de San Francisco de Asís. Private collection, Havana.

was coined in Cuba (Pérez 1988, 284). Further research might discover that the history of Ifá's prosperity during this period was tied not only to social and political connections, but also to the patronage and cronyism economy of the Auténtico machine. A timely document, if not also a smoking gun, in this regard, may be the dramatic press photograph of Tín receiving a whopping check for, it is believed, forty thousand pesos from Prío in the Presidential Palace (fig. 2.5). As a result, Tín was able to lay the first stone of his dream Social and Scholarly Center on 23 June 1951 (fig. 2.6).[86] Though construction began on the soaring, art deco churchlike building, it was never completed,

Figure 2.6.—Quintín Lecón Lombillo (*standing, sixth from right*) and members of La Asociación de Los Hijos de San Francisco de Asís laying the first stone of their association building in Regla, 1951, including Asunción Villalonga (*fifth from right*), Feliberto O'Farrill (*fourth from right*), Aurelio Estrada, "Babel" (*fourth from left*), and Félix Pulido (*third from left*). Private collection, Havana.

for mysterious reasons, and remains a decaying hulk today.[87] Because of the reputed events surrounding this failed project and the confiscations that followed the Triumph of the Revolution at the apogee of Tín's fortunes in 1959, Tín became isolated from Havana's *babalaismo*. He died virtually alone in August 1999. Since he was isolated thus, *babalawos* were unaware of his death, and none of the indispensable Ifá funerary rites (*itutu*) were performed for him at the time. Tragically, Quintín Lecón Lombillo (Trupo Adakino), Cuba's most senior *babalawo* after the late 1980s, may be denied his place in the chants of Lucumí ancestor veneration (*moyuba*).[88]

The Politics of Olofin, the Reproduction of Ifá, and the Shifting Location of Cultural Authenticity

The social and religious factors that contributed to the growth of Ifá and the success of particular *babalawos* were reflected and shaped by what had become the enabling token of Ifá's reproduction: Olofin. Olofin would eventually become the Holy Grail, the crown of every rising *babalawo de movimento* ("mover and shaker"). Clearly, the heads of Cuba's great Ifá *ramas* are now remembered because they were charismatic founders and leaders, prolific initiators, great repositories of deep knowledge, and, in some cases, wealthy men. Yet, they could achieve this status, in no small measure, because they secured for themselves the singular token of Ifá's reproduction and the oracular key to the most far-reaching Ifá divination readings: the *fundamento* of Olofin (alternatively Olofi, Odun). Whether or not Olofin had existed in Yorubaland as just such an authorizing material shrine object is unclear. The term was documented in Yorubaland as early as 1848 as a lowercase noun, meaning "lawgiver" (Crowther 1848, 172).[89] It is merely mentioned in early-twentieth-century ethnography as one of many Egbado deities (Dennett [1910] 1968, 104). And, it is altogether absent in the important summative account of Bascom (1969b). However, in the influential work of E. Bolaji Idowu, Olofin is integral to the Yoruba High-God complex, as a "title added, or as an alternative, to Olódùmarè" (the "Supreme Being"). The name *Ọlọ́fin* means "ruler" and, according to Idowu, "appears to be as old as Olódùmarè," which, one assumes, is ancient (Idowu [1962] 1963, 36–37, 39).[90] In Cuba, Olofin not only became that member of the High-God "trinity" (Olodumare, Olorun, Olofin) with whom practitioners have had the most intimacy, but also was concretely materialized as La Regla de Ifá's supreme *fundamento*. As such, it became the metafoundation, ritual enabler, and spiritual horizon of La Regla de Ifá.[91]

It is not, perhaps, useful to debate here the "true" or "authentic" origin of "Olofin." However, it is, perhaps, more useful to interrogate the local claims and criteria of Olofin's authenticity and "true" origin at a given moment. For example, in the beliefs and actions of Cuba's *babalawos* over the course of, perhaps, 140 years, the operative "location" of Olofin's "authentic origin," depending upon the account, has shifted: from West Africa, to Cuba, to the United States, and to Africa once again (see Gilroy 1993, chap. 1; Shryock 1997, 11; and see below). Indeed, in terms of the most specific local criteria, Olofin's location is wherever an arguably legitimate shrine of Olofin is found: an unprepossessing room in Elizabeth, New Jersey; a great, pagoda-style house in Mantilla, Havana; or a bungalow in Miami's Little Havana. *Babalawos* have always debated the authenticity of this or that Olofin within the intra-Ifá politics of reputation and legitimacy; they also debate the origin of Olofin; some insist that it originated in Africa and others insist that it was created in Cuba.

Until the late 1940s or early 1950s, the *fundamento* of Olofin was rare. Its possession was highly restricted within the hierarchical Regla de Ifá. The living head of each major *rama* is believed to have possessed the *fundamento* of Olofin, which provided the spiritual means and authorization to initiate the priests of the Ifá diviner-*oricha* Orula. By the first decades of the twentieth century, there were probably no more than sixteen *olofistas*—legitimate possessors of Olofin according to dominant criteria—in Cuba.[92] The first Olofins confected in Cuba were, it is believed, collectively produced in the last third of the nineteenth century by Ifá's leading Africans, including Adechina, Olugueré, and Achadé. Olofin's first inheritors or recipients of newly "born" Olofins may have included Asunción Villalonga, Tata Gaitán, Esteban Fernández Quiñones, Marcos and Quintín García, Ramón Febles, Periquito Pérez, Bernabé Menocal, and Bernardo Rojas.[93]

The initiation of *babalawos* was limited and legitimated through control over the use and conferral of Olofin, as well as another crucial enabling key, the "Knife" of Ifá (*Wanaldo*, or *Cuchillo*). According to Ifá rules, a *babalawo* must first possess the Ifá Knife and the permission of his *rama* head in order to initiate others, that is, to start an Ifá "house."[94] In order to enable a specific initiation, the *babalawo* in question must "borrow" the *rama*'s Olofin if he has not already received it. Early creole *rama* heads and *olofistas*, such as Bernardo Rojas, and contemporary *babalawos*, such as Lázaro Cuesta Valdés (Iwori Bofún) have kept written ledgers of the *babalawos* "made" (initiated) with the *rama*'s Olofin. In order to officially "borrow" an Olofin, a *derecho* (money tribute) would be paid to the *rama* to spiritually enable its use. According to the protocol traditionalized in Havana, the *rama*'s Olofin was to be inherited by a deceased *olofista*'s eldest son, if he was a *ba-*

balawo, and, if not, by that *olofista*'s ritually eldest *babalawo* godchild. The identity and standing of the heir was supposed to be confirmed by Ifá divination during the *itutu* (funerary ritual) of the deceased and ratified by the surviving *rama* members' affirmation of the heir's good "moral character" (*la moral*). The legitimate heir was then "awarded" possession of the Olofin through special ceremonies of conferral (*la adjudicación*), and the heir was required to pay for a series of funerary ceremonies (*honras*) for the deceased. In practice, this process has been riven by intra-*rama* politics and interpersonal struggles for power.[95]

Legitimately in possession of an Olofin and the Knife, a *babalawo* would no longer have to borrow the *rama*'s Olofin in order to initiate a godchild. Though the loaning of Olofin should never be denied to a member of the *rama*, *rama* heads have often denied requests out of caprice, prejudice, or politics. Thus, the borrowing of Olofin could, sometimes, be a humiliating proposition, depending upon the reputation of the petitioner and the attitude of the *rama* head. In contrast, Olofin possession could enable its owner's complete independence from his Ifá *padrino* or *rama*, his ascension as the head of a new *rama* extension, and his patron status and reputation as a kind of local "big man."

The Lucumí and first two creole generations of *babalawos* stringently restricted the dissemination and use of Olofin. This was intended to maintain a traditional hierarchy of authority, to control initiation procedure and the dissemination of Ifá secrets, and, importantly, to ensure the character of *babalawos* as "real men"—that is, to ensure the exclusion of homosexual and "effeminate" men (*maricones* and *afeminados*) from La Regla de Ifá. Among the creoles, Bernardo Rojas was known to be one of the strictest in his control over the "extension" of Olofin.[96] However, around 1945, a powerful Havana *babalawo* by the name of Miguel Febles y Padrón began to change all that, over and above the "veto" of Bernardo Rojas,[97] who insisted that Olofin's liberal fabrication "was a profanation."[98] Cuba's maverick confector of Olofins would singlehandedly transform La Regla de Ifá, just as the era of Bernardo Rojas (d. 1959) was coming to an end.

The Era of Miguelito Febles

By the early 1940s, the sons of Ramón Febles Molina (c. 1845–1939), Francisco Febles del Pino (1908-c. 1975) and Miguel Febles y Padrón (1910–86; fig. 2.7), were learned *babalawos*, given the extraordinary education and experience in Ifá they had gained under their father's wing. Initiated as teenagers, they each had more than fifteen years in Ifá by the time of their eminent father's death in 1939.[99] The gentlemanly, sober, and upright Francisco ("Panchito") modeled himself on his father. He is remembered as "El Caballero de Ifá" (The Gentleman of Ifá). Bernardo Rojas and Tata Gaitán, but most often Panchito, were compelled to moderate the caprices of the ambitious, impetuous, and hard-drinking Miguelito. By the 1940s and 1950s, both brothers were much-called-upon *obás* who worked with all of Cuba's Ifá *ramas*. For several reasons, Miguelito would become the crucial bridge between the older, conservative generations of Ifá, which, by the mid-1940s, had mostly died out, and the growing Ifá families of the 1950s to the early 1980s. His increasing influence and, in turn, the proliferation of the Ifá *ramas* after the 1950s, are greatly explained by important developments around the problem of Olofin.

As a rising Havana *babalawo*, Miguelito Febles's first great strategic move was to wrest control of Olofin from his elder brother Panchito, who had rightly inherited it from their father, Ramón Febles, upon the latter's death in 1939.[100] Although Miguel *cogió* ("stole") the Olofin from its rightful heir, the genteel and diplomatic Panchito relented, it is said, and Miguel's Olofin was formally conferred upon him (*adjudicado*).[101] Miguel Febles became extremely powerful at the end of the 1940s, not only because of his searing knowledge of Ifá liturgy and his aggressive use of witchcraft (*brujería*) to control and subdue his rivals.[102] In addition, Miguel became the central, willing source, at a turning point in the island's Ifá history, of

Olofin. He gained for himself the power to select Olofin's recipients—most often those who could pay a premium price—and "block" the receiving of an Olofin from other sources, particularly those to whom he had already given an Olofin.[103]

From an analytical perspective, Olofin may be read as the embodiment of accumulated spiritual and social investments, a kind of fetish or storehouse of "symbolic capital." Olofin possession shaped, and was shaped by, traditionalized hierarchies of authority. Over the course of the twentieth century, Olofin became a kind of "commodity fetish" with a fluid "exchange value" in the hands of Miguel Febles (see Pietz 1996, 197–207; Bourdieu 1977, 171–83; Marx 1976, 138–39, 163–77; Taussig 1980). In contrast to other *babalawos*, whose careers revolved around attending to a diverse clientele, Miguel Febles "worked only for other *babalawos*"—in other words, as an *obá* and the provider of Ifá's *poderes* ("powers") to his colleagues. The owner of numerous houses, Miguel established a special "laboratory" for producing Olofins in an expensive, pagoda-styled house in the Havana municipality of Mantilla. Contemporary *babalawos* explain his peculiar career trajectory through an interpretation of his personal Ifá sign, Odí Ká. Odí Ká is the *odu* "where," one of its proverbs relates, "the spider is procreated in the cemetery" (*donde la araña se procreó en el cementerio*). The spider "eats cadavers," one Havana *babalawo* explained, "and Miguelito spent his whole life eating the blood of all the *babalawos* in Cuba who had capital."[104]

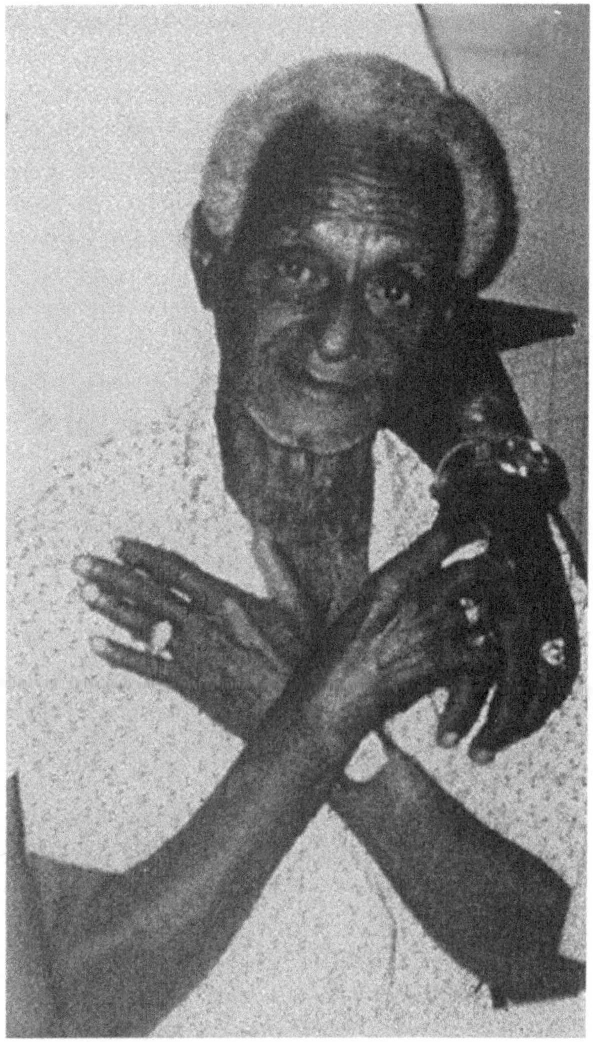

Figure 2.7.—Miguel Febles Padrón (Odí Ká, 1911–86), son of Ramón Febles Molina and América Padrón, 1982. Private collection, Havana.

Miguel embarked on this entrepreneurial Ifá career toward the end of the period in which the last of Havana's reigning conservative Ifá elders died (1936–59).[105] These years had as bookends the abrogation of the Platt Amendment (1934), leaving Cuba officially free of U.S. military intervention, and the end of Cuba's "Constitutional Period" (beginning in 1940). The period was steeped in political and business corruption, cronyism, gangsterism, and capitalism run amok; Havana became the premier tropical playground of the United States, in which prostitution and gambling reigned. It was also a volatile crucible of violent political struggle, state repression, coup attempts, a boom-and-bust economy, and working-class immiseration and illiteracy (see Pérez 1988, 276–312; Thomas 1971, 689–802). It was during this period, moreover, that the famous black secretary of the Communist Maritime Workers' Union, Aracelio Iglesias Díaz, also a *babalawo* and son of Changó, was killed in a Havana wharf dispute (Thomas 1971, 761). The apotheosis of Miguel Febles came during the last eight or more years of his life (1978–1986), following the deaths of his two immediate elders and principal moderating influences in his cohort, Panchito Febles (c. 1975) and Joaquín Salazar (1978). The 1980s, one of Febles's last students remarked, were the true "era of Miguel Febles."[106]

Miguel Febles's earliest Olofins went to several of his rising contemporaries of the 1940s, who became very powerful independent figures in Ifá. Febles then fabricated Olofins for his most esteemed godchildren.[107] Finally, for large sums of money, he mass-produced Olofins—more than eight hundred, it is believed—before his own unhappy demise in 1986 at the age of seventy-six, the result of a serious burn he received in a kitchen fire, which Changó, his tutelary *oricha*, had predicted years before.[108]

Therefore, the *babalawo* boom that followed William Bascom's estimated census of 1948 was not a chance event. Through his mass production of Olofins, Febles was single-handedly responsible for endowing with independence, power, and the potential for initiatory prolificacy most of Havana's major post–World War II *babalawo* "families," a set of liberties that his conservative predecessors and contemporaries Adechina, Olugueré, Tata Gaitán, Bernardo Rojas, Ramón Febles, Asunción Villalonga, Pedro Pablo Pérez, and others took care to limit during their lifetimes.[109]

Until about 1950, most Ifá initiations would turn out nearly the same score of top personnel, regardless of the *rama* in which they were conducted. By the 1980s, thousands of *babalawos* practiced in Havana and the United States, and many an Ifá *hombre de movimiento* had secured his own Olofin. In the process, Ifá *rama* organization became highly atomized, as each new Ifá *jefe de familia* (family chief) established his independent fiefdom. Though Febles's earliest Olofins empowered the important *babalawo* houses that expanded in influence from the 1940s to the 1960s, such as those of Juan Angulo of Párraga, Facundo Sevilla and Mario Fernández of Palmira, and Aurelio "Babel" Estrada of Regla, the men who received Febles's mass-produced Olofins from the 1960s to the early 1980s became the great *babalawo* factories of the Cuban Revolution.[110] By the mid-1990s, Elpidio Cárdenas (Otura Sá) of Central Havana had initiated more than one hundred *babalawos* over the previous thirty years. Havana *babalawos* estimate that between three and six thousand *babalawos* are at work in Cuba today.

Still, Febles's extraordinary Olofin legacy remains double-edged in the present. The frequently circulated rumor that the ever-tricky Miguelito sold many sealed Olofin "cans" that were actually *vacío* ("empty" and inefficacious), potentially destabilizes the authority of any *olofista* who bought one from him, as well as the legitimacy of the *babalawos* made in that *olofista*'s line. This great *jodedor*,[111] though he suffered Changó's wrathful punishment by fire, laughed his way to the grave. On his death bed in December 1986, he charged one of confidants to divulge to the mourners his last words: a reminder to them that they were all shameless sons of bitches (*descarados, sin vergüenzas, hijos de puta*). They were all cowards, who wouldn't "talk" about him when he was alive, out of fear, but would talk about him incessantly after his death.[112]

The religious meaning and value of Olofin and its possession shifted significantly from the early days of its reconstitution by the old Lucumí elders through the Era of Miguel Febles. Olofin began, around the last third of the nineteenth century, as the rare meta-*fundamento* of the hierarchical descent group, the *rama*. It was much like the single, foundational set of emblems, sacred drums and staffs, which authorizes the initiations of all the members of a single Abakuá lodge (*juego*) over time. The emblems belong to the *juego*, not the individuals occupying its offices (see Ortiz 1952–55. 4:1–85; Cabrera [1958] 1970). By the 1950s, in contrast, Olofin had become the aspiration, crown, and blue chip of every ambitious senior *babalawo*

(*Oluo*). At the time, the Central Havana *oriaté* Nicolás Angarica lamented that this modern phenomenon had rendered Ifá's controlled, African-derived title system a dead letter, and had caused a crisis of religious authority.[113] "Today we find ourselves in the position that, in order to open the year [with the annual Ifá reading], we have no idea who is going to direct us, *because all of the Olúos have Olofi*" (Angarica [1955?] n.d., 14, emphasis added). Thus, by 1955 Olofin had become relatively common; the "One" had become the "Many." What did it mean, for example, when multifarious Ifá houses employed their own Olofins to produce the ostensibly definitive Reading of the Year, and came up with divergent signs and predictions? The far reaching, universal predictions of the era of Adechina, Bernabé Menocal, Tata Gaitán, and Bernardo Rojas—a wholly unified tradition conducted at least until the 1959 death of Rojas, became limited to each *babalawo* "family." After Febles's death in 1986, his followers, under the leadership of Lázaro Cuesta, built a trans-family "Organizing Commission of the Reading of the Year," which has, over seventeen years, attracted four to eight hundred *babalawos* from within and without the country. Until 1 January 2000, more than five family heads independent of the "Comisión" took out their own readings; for 2000, two major groups took out readings that competed for recognition, the Comisión and the state-funded and directed Yoruba Cultural Association. The latter's reading is hotly contested by most *babalawos* because it emphasizes predictions that shine on the fortunes of the government and mutes predictions that are more difficult to swallow. The state utilizes the Association to coopt religious activity, earn hard currency from cultural tourism, and to project to the world its tolerance of religion.

Given its wide "reproduction," Olofin, from a Benjaminian perspective, might appear to have lost its status as a unique symbolic object, that is, to have lost its "aura" (Benjamin 1969), which was created and maintained by regulated scarcity and hierarchical rules of inheritance. In the transition, Olofin became something of a commodity fetish within an individualizing religious marketplace. That marketplace arguably exhibited certain monopolistic features mirroring aspects of Fulgencio Batista's crony-ridden dictatorship (1953–59; see Thomas 1971, 789–802, 996–1036). Ironically, this religious trend continued, and increased greatly, after the Triumph of the Revolution, despite, for example, years of the communist government's expropriations of "bourgeois" Cubans and the 1968 "intervention" to end any trace of private enterprise. During this period, the "authenticity" of Febles's Olofins would derive from the exclusivity of his Mantilla "laboratory" trademark, as it were, and his mafia-like ability, through fear and supernatural intimidation, to control their dissemination in the marketplace. During the 1980s, Febles became very rich by expanding his influence abroad, in the United States exile community and in Colombia, where his godchildren apparently included some drug dealers. Thus, the expropriation of the bourgeoisie and the Sovietization of the Cuban economy during the first twenty years of the Revolution encountered their underside in a secret ritual economy, which paralleled the rise of the Cuban privileged classes of military and party leaders and black marketeers. At the same time, the houses of Ifá, as well as Ocha, became, more than ever, crucial machines for the circulation of scarce resources and hard currency and the production of alternative forms of social power under the nose of the controlling state apparatus.

In an important sense, the operative location of Olofin's "authentic origin" shifted over the course of time. In the beginning, as it were, Africans in Cuba saw Olofin's ultimate source as "West Africa," from which nineteenth-century *babalawos* had embarked, and to which their agents are believed to have returned to reclaim Olofin's secrets. Then, a small Havana collective of Lucumí founders and later, a short roster of early creoles, became the *proximate* or local "origin" of this jealously guarded *fundamento*—for example, their Ifá houses in Regla, Guanabacoa, El Cerro, and Marianao. After the 1950s, the "origin" of Olofin, for all intents and purposes, became sited in the *fundamento* of Miguel Febles. *Fundamento* here refers not only to Febles's personal Olofin "can," but also to the operative location of his deep knowledge and social power. *Babalawos* traveled from all over just to get one. Yet, during the middle of the 1970s, Olofin's "authentic origin" would shift once again, through the rhetoric and practice of certain *babalawos*, not only to Miami, Florida, but also back to West Africa on the pendulum of transatlantic travel, on the crest of political exile, and within the ongoing recreation of "imagined communities" in the Diaspora (see Gilroy 1993, chap. 1; Clarke 1997; Anderson 1983).

The "Second Diaspora": Ifá and Olofin in the United States, 1950–1980

The migrations of Cubans to the United States, in small numbers after the mid-1940s, and in great numbers with the Triumph of the Revolution in 1959, took *babalawos* to New York, New Jersey, Miami, and Puerto Rico. The first *babalawo* to practice Ifá in the United States was an Afro-Cuban named Francisco "Pancho" Mora, who arrived in New York in 1946 or 1950, depending upon the account (Murphy 1988, 50; Caribbean Cultural Center 1984).[114] Yet the initiation of *babalawos* in the United States began, in fact, in Miami, and only around 1969 or 1970. The Northeast (New York and New Jersey) not only lacked a critical mass of *babalawos*, but also an Olofin. In Mora's case, the Olofin of his *rama* undoubtedly remained in the hands of his Havana godfather, Quintín Lecón Lombillo (aka Tín, aka Quintín García Lecón; figs. 2.5, *center right;* 2.6, *center*).[115] Tín neither gave out Olofins nor wanted his godchildren in Ifá to make other *babalawos*. For lack of an Olofin, Mora and his early New York colleague, Bebo Morales, who were in the United States at least by the 1950s, would have to have commuted to Cuba to find a willing Olofista to help them, in order to conduct initiations there prior to 1962, the year of the U.S. economic embargo against the Island. Returning to Cuba was the means by which the New York Cuban *iyaloricha* Mercedes Nobles and others initiated their American godchildren (Caribbean Cultural Center 1984). The "second Diaspora," like the first Diaspora, thus witnessed a critical discontinuity in the presence of Olofin. This problem would preoccupy Cuban-American *babalawos* for close to twenty years, would bring about great *discusiones* and *disgustos* (arguments and disaffection), and would cause irreparable divisions within and between the Cuban and Cuban-American *babalawo* houses. The problem of Ifá in the early exile period (1962–78) revolved almost exclusively around the possession of Olofin and the politics of its legitimacy.

Consistent with the demographics of exile,[116] the critical mass of Miami's first *babalawo* initiators and some of their new Ifá godchildren were white Cubans who had arrived in Miami prior to 1970, many before 1965. Depending upon the account, Olofin did not exist in the United States until 1965, 1969, or 1978. Indeed, this is the key point: the power and legitimacy of Ifá groups in the United States were gained and lost in the battle of claims and counterclaims with respect to the possession of Olofin. The first Cuban *babalawos* who initiated others into Ifá in the United States did so under the leadership of the *olofista* Carlos Ojeda (Osa Rete) of the Bernardo Rojas *rama*.[117] Though another Havana stalwart, José Miguel Campos Noroña (Irete Turá), apparently reached New York in 1965 with his own Febles-minted Olofin, New York remained an Ifá backwater, and Campos's older "brother" in Ifá, Ojeda, would carry the distinction of being the progenitor of *babalawos* in the United States (Cintrón 1979, 7).[118] Ojeda had received Olofin from Miguel Febles in Havana prior to his exit from the island. The explanatory account of the Ojeda group has remained that this Olofin was later spirited out of Cuba for him by a Trinidadian diplomatic contact. This enabling event is said to have occurred just months before the first initiations were to begin in late 1969. Five Cuban-born, Cuban-initiated *babalawo* exiles initiated at least five Cuban-born men in Miami at the beginning of 1970.[119] The Cuban-born Bobby Bolufer (Ogundá Leni) was one of the first two *ba-*

balawos made on U.S. soil, in Miami, and was initiated by the Cuban-born, Cuban-made, Diego Fontela (Obe Yono) of the Adé Bí lineage, through Bonifacio Valdés, Gerardo Valdés Montalvo, and Luciano Canto (Iwori Bobe)—Fontela's Havana godfather.

As social and ritual control had been exerted by powerful *rama* leaders in the past, the charismatic and godfather-like Ojeda (in the Mario Puzo sense), who had been a butcher (*carnicero*) in Havana, attempted the same in Miami; and he claimed the explicit blessing of Cuba's Ifá pope, Miguel Febles. Indeed, the ambitious Ojeda attempted to force all of Miami's *babalawos* to sign a contract giving him final word over Ifá activity in Miami. Partly in response to this new local throne of forceful and stringent authority, some of the very Miami *babalawos* who had initiated, or had been initiated, under the authority of Ojeda's Olofin now sought to gain their independence through receiving their own Olofins. Roberto Bolufer had left Cuba about as early as Pancho Mora (1946) and shuttled between homes in Puerto Rico and Havana for thirteen years before settling permanently on the former island in 1959. According to Miami accounts and Bolufer's own words, he and Diego Fontela traveled to Havana late in the 1970s to receive Olofin themselves—probably during the first opening to the island in 1978, when, during the Carter Administration's "dialogue" with Havana, the Cuban government permitted exiles to visit their relatives. The two claim to have received Olofins from Miguel Febles and Luciano Canto, who had forged a formidable allegiance, and were turning out dozens of new *babalawos*.[120] Almost immediately upon their return, the two began to initiate others in Miami and Puerto Rico. Fontela rose as a major contender in Miami, and Bolufer in Puerto Rico. By 1979, more than sixty *babalawos* had been initiated in Miami; Puerto Rico counted, including Bolufer, fourteen *babalawos* (Cintrón 1979, 7). With Miguel Campos in New York, a powerful mainland Ifá triangle took shape, which proceeded, nevertheless, under the vigilance, and often wrath, of the incomparable Miguel Febles.

An extraordinary and controversial set of events followed in the wake of the first Miami initiations in 1970. An insurgent group, led by one of the original Miami Ifá initiates, José Miguel Gómez Barberas ("Miguel Batea," [Otura Adakoy]), became frustrated in its attempt to obtain an Olofin (fig. 2.8, *right*). By 1975, Gómez reported in a flurry of correspondence with sympathetic Havana colleagues, that he had waited in vain for more than two years to receive from Miguel Febles crucial Ifá goods and services: an Olofin and the blessing to proceed with Ifá initiations.[121] Cubans know the signals their countrymen send, and Miguel Gómez knew that he had been "blocked" by Havana's pope and his minions in the United States. Hence, in lieu of receiving Olofin any other way, Gómez pursued a lead that had been brewing in Miami Ifá circles for several years. Moreover, it was one that had already been mined successfully by African-American Yoruba who, since at least 1971, had traveled to southwestern Nigeria for spiritual renewal (see Hunt 1979; Clarke 1997; Curry 1997).[122]

In a ten-day trip in September 1975 to southwestern Nigeria, Gómez secured the connection he sought in the town of Ọ̀ṣogbo, following visits to Ifẹ̀ and Ọ̀yọ́. As Gómez reminisced in a moving and quite circumspect 1989 letter to a Havana mentoree, "With the impossibility of going to Cuba, notwithstanding my relations since my youth with Miguelito Febles Padrón [IBAE, R.I.P] (a great loss)[,] and having the necessity of receiving Olofin, I directed myself to Nigeria[,] W. Africa." In Ọ̀ṣogbo, the great center of Ọ̀ṣun worship, Gómez received what was represented to him as Olofin, as well as other *òrìṣà* associated with Orunmila from *babalawo* Ifá Yemí Eleguibon (Ogbe Yono). Ifá Yemí was believed to be the *obá of Oshogbo,* as Gómez put it ("the highest Ifá official there").

Three years later, the resourceful Miguel Gómez hosted Ifá Yemí in Miami for forty-two days. There, utilizing Gómez's African-made Olofin, Ifá Yemí gave birth to three Olofins for three Cuban-American *babalawos* (fig. 2.8). The African connection was working, and Gómez

Figure 2.8.—José Miguel Gómez Barberas (*right*) with Yoruba *babalawo* Ifá Yemí Eleguibon (*center*) and Cuban-American *babalawos*, Miami, 1978. Private collection, Havana.

became, in effect, a transatlantic steward of this ongoing quest for the Holy Grail. Soon, he took three Miami Cubans to Nigeria to be initiated as *babalawos* in ceremonies unprecedented outside of the African-American pipeline, in which a group of Yoruba and Cuban-American *babalawos* worked together. In all, Gómez made five trips to West Africa.[123] Apparently, anticipating controversy and the religion's credentialing requirements (that is, that any ceremony be "witnessed" by *testigos*), Gómez heavily documented the Ọ̀ṣogbo trips, including photographs of the consecration ceremonies of three Cuban-American *babalawos* (fig. 2.9).[124] These would serve, presumably, as virtual *testigos* of the initiations, as well as mementos of the unprecedented journey.

Gómez's African trips and his relationship with Ifá Yemí revolved not merely around the "necessity" of receiving Olofin *outside* of Havana's legitimizing channels. Gómez had apprehended something more, and with it refigured his personal history and rewrote the history of Cuba's Ifá transatlantic tradition in a mode that recalls Alex Haley's *Roots*. Haley's Pulitzer Prize–winning book had spawned a "miniseries in 1977 with one of the largest television audiences ever" (Trescott 1992, 2). Through the Nigerian experience, Gómez could now represent himself as "the first Cuban that made physical contact with our ancestors in Oyo, Oshogbo, Ife, Republic of Nigeria, West Africa, the *Indefatigable spring of our Religious Origin, where our religion is practiced*" (emphasis added).[125] As the moving autobiographical narrative relates, Gómez was raised in the poor Barrio Príncipe near Cayo Hueso in Havana. At the age of ten, he came under the guidance of the venerated elder Afro-Cuban priests *babalawo* Secundino Crucet, Ayayi La Tuán Timotea Albear, and Tiburcia Sotolongo—his immediate neighbor, for whom he ran ritual errands. Drawing upon references from Ifá's oral history, Gómez, a white working-class Cuban, connected the dots to write for himself a remarkable, seemingly predestined, Black Atlantic spiritual genealogy. As Gómez confided to his dear Havana friend and mentoree, *babalawo* Radamés Corona, the great grandson of Tiburcia Sotolongo, Ifá Yemi Eleguibon's father and grandfather were not only great *obás* of Ifá in Ọ̀ṣogbo. In addition, his grandfather was none other than "the brother of *Atanda Faniyi,*" one of four enslaved Africans who, Gómez believed, established Cuba's Ifá tradition Cuba in the first place (Atandá, "*Anaí, Acaide* and *Oboola*").[126] In a stunning inscription of a prophecy realized, Gómez cast the birth of the three Miami Olofins along with his own African-made Olofin as as the "emulat[ion] of the case of the[se] 4 Babalawos that [arrived] in Havana" as slaves, and created the tradition.[127] Through typological inscription, Africa was reborn, again. Now, José Miguel Gómez Barberas's house had become a new sacred *tierra* [homeland], both a reflection of the *cabildos* of the first (African) Diaspora, and a fresh rebirth of the African homeland in a second Diaspora, in suburban Miami.

In sum, Gómez, separated by decree from Havana's religious resources and from the *babalawo* who claimed sole authority over Ifá practice in Miami (Ojeda), circumvented the Havana-Miami imperial network. He legiti-

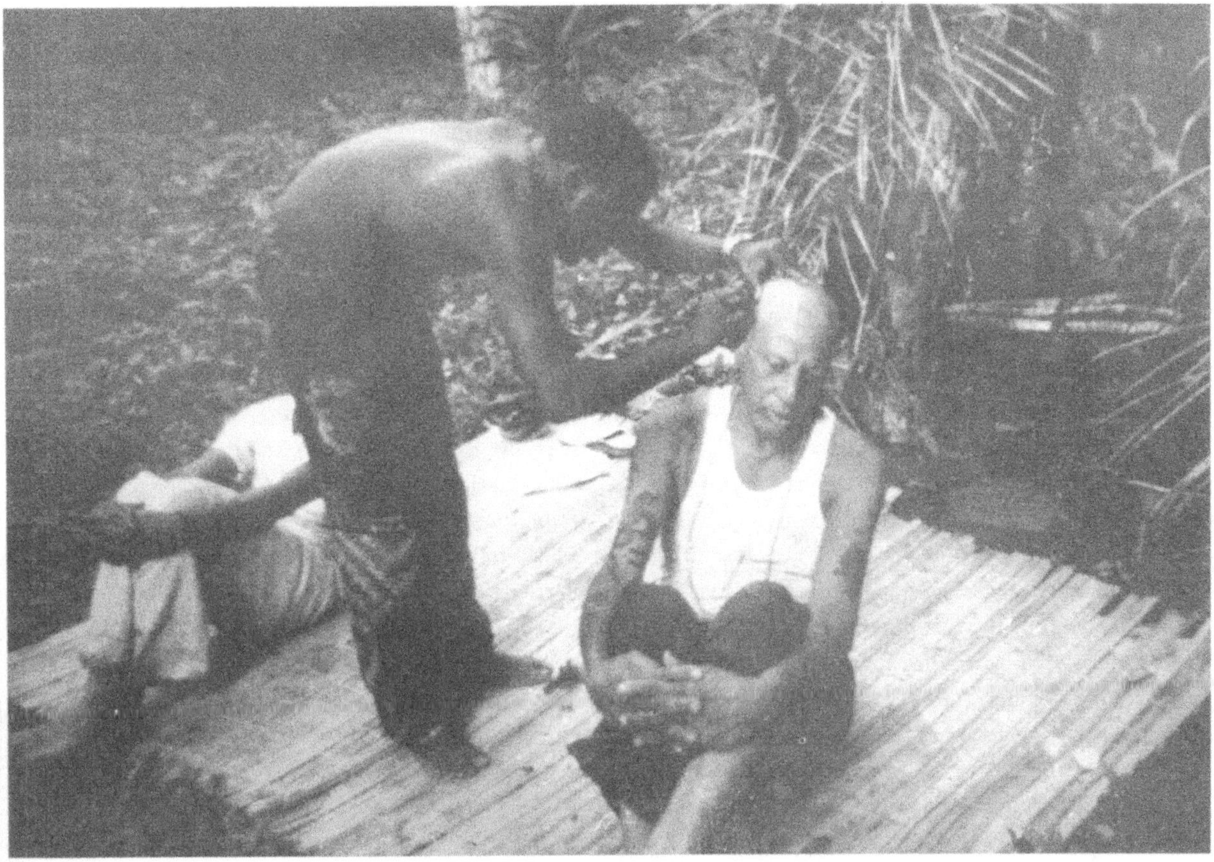

Figure 2.9.—Initiation of a Cuban-American as a *babalawo* in a bush grove in Ọ̀ṣogbo by the *babaláwo* Ifá Yemí Eleguibon, c. 1978. Private collection, Havana.

mated his own unique claim to authority by reyoking, in an explicit way, his Cuban and Cuban-American Ifá genealogy to its putative origin in West Africa. This practical and rhetorical move mirrored that of African-American nationalists in the Northeast, who had broken with their Cuban *padrinos* in New York in the early 1960s and rewired their *fundamentos* and genealogies to the transatlantic continuum (see my chap. 5; see also Clarke 1997, 131–44; Shryock 1997, 314, 320). Witness the rhetoric of Gómez's newly found authority: in addition to the African Olofins and Ifás the Gómez group acquired, they also returned with a set of sacred *batá* drums, documents of the experience relate. The drums came from "Osogbo, Nigeria, West Africa, *the sole place where the root, tradition, and practice of Ocha and Ifá are to be found*" (emphasis added). The Miami Cuban Ifá house of José Miguel Gómez Barberas, who was "born" with the authorization of Ojeda's Febles-made Olofin, leapfrogged its proximate Cuban origins and recast its identity as a direct African descent group. It became the Ọ̀ṣogbo-authorized house of "Omo Ordun Ifá Adakoy" (Olofin Owner Otura Adakoy).[128] Equally important, through newly asserted genealogical connections and a shrewd Black Atlantic rhetorical typology, Gómez reconfigured his house and *fundamento* as an essential, transhistorical descendant of the very Yoruba family whose important ancestor, Atandá, was shipped to Cuba in the nineteenth century.[129]

This group of white *babalawos*, with motives both similar to, and quite different from, the Black American Yoruba Movement of New York and their South Carolina Oyotunji Yoruba Village, established its authority and "completed the diasporic circle" (Omari 1991). They revised the modern Cuban creole terms of authority lodged in the island's lineages, particularly in the *fundamento* of Miguel Febles, by reinscribing a primordial and authentic African source (Clarke 1997). The difference between this group and the Black American Yoruba Movement was that these white Lucumí focused on a narrower transatlantic circle of identity formation—the office of the *awo* of Ifá (the *babalawo*). In contrast, the Black American Yoruba project had at its core racial and spiritual identity formation or reformation as New World Africans—specifically New World "Yoruba" (see Hunt 1979; Mason 1985b; Clarke 1997; Curry 1997; and see my chap. 5).

As Ifá politics have always proceeded, the status of not only the Ifá Yemí Olofins, but also all of those received during the opening to Cuba in the late 1970s, as well as Ojeda's itself—and by extension all the initiations conducted with them—has been debated and challenged. For many Havana *babalawos*, Cuba remains the authentic source of Olofin, as they assert that Olofin never legitimately "left" the island (see, e.g., Cabrera 1980, 178).[130] Many Cuban and Cuban-American *babalawos* remain dubious of the African connection. The Osogbo Olofins apparently became particularly controvertial because Ifá Yemí Eleguibon initiated women into Ifá, including a Jewish-American by the name of Patri Dhaifa, in New York on 22 January 1985 (González Wippler 1989, 110–20).

Not surprisingly, Miguel Febles, from nearly the moment that word of the African Olofins reached Havana, initiated an aggressive letter-writing campaign to reassert his authority to control, and speak for, "the" tradition. In doing so, he reiterated the authentic origin of Olofin and that tradition in Cuba. His explicit aim was to delegitimize Gómez's entire project, based on his reading of time-honored Lucumí principles. Gómez had transgressed, Febles argued, the very ground of "Our Religious Legacy" (*Nuestro Legado Religioso*) and its obligations, responsibilities, and requirements of "unity." Febles's philosophical and ethnohistorical articulation of the African Diaspora significantly diverged from that of Gómez. Employing the royal "we," Febles argued that the African practice and its system of authority was a "legacy" but had nothing to do with the legitimating "Ceremonies and Hierarchies" of *Cuban* practice (Febles stopped short of applying his critique to practitioners who were not Cuban, such as the Black American Yoruba movement). Febles, identifying himself as a "Cuban," unequivocally rejected "Africa" as a vehicle or token of religious legitimacy among Cuban and Cuban-American practitioners. In a series of letters and notarized documents worth quoting at length he argued:

> From [Africa] derives our Religious Legacy [*Legado Religioso*], Secrets, *Fundamentos*, and Ceremonies [*ritos*], of which we have absolute knowledge and control, [and which] for us is basic and proper . . . [,] to which we owe our obedience and respect, and which we defend with energy and loyalty.
>
> This is an unrenounceable responsibility of all.
>
> We reiterate that we have, for the Africans, principally the Yoruba, a great esteem through the painful ties of history, culture, and blood. But also we recognize that we Cubans, through our sound will[power] [*recta voluntad*], studies, and efforts, have in our Religion a possession of Universal Hierarchy, through our highest levels of knowledge, and through applied Ceremonies. In other countries, nevertheless, they have fallen into deterioration, stagnation, and corruption. . . .
>
> We maintain a clear and upright position . . . in defense of our Religious Legacy . . . when we reaffirm that we rec-

ognize solely as real and legitimate those Olofis and Santos received in Cuba or outside, carried out under Cuban Ceremonies and Hierarchies. Our attitude is honest and comprehensive when we *reaffirm that the Ifases made outside Cuba, by Cuban Babalawos that have received Olofin in Cuba, are recognized and legitimized by us. . . .* [He specifically mentioned as recognized Ojeda, Miguel Campos, Roberto Bolufer, and Diego Fontela, among others].[131]

We are advocates of preserving unity. Whatever difference arises ought to be corrected in an honest and fraternal way. . . . No one has the right to maintain a line of indiscipline, arbitrariness, anarchism, division, or distortion. . . . This is individualism and dishonesty.

We do not accept or permit that outside priests intervene in our affairs, in any form, pretext, or method.[132]

Implicitly, not only were contemporary African *babalawos* irrelevant, nothing more than agents of inappropriate "interventions" within the Our Cuban Religious Legacy, but also, to round out the charge, Febles argued that the specific Olofin and Ifá ceremonies conducted in Africa and Miami "showed a deficiency of talent . . . and a low standard." The African *obá* (Ifá Yemí), Febles contended, was a rank "beginner," and "discrepancies with regard to our *fundamentos* and ceremonies were detected."[133] Ifá Yemí was, in fact, a relative youth at the time, thirty-four years of age and with nine years in Ifá. In contrast, Miguel Febles was seventy-four years old and had fifty-two years in Ifá and at least thirty-five years as an *olofista*.[134] In Cuba, these criteria of seniority, knowledge, and accomplishments mattered greatly.

Of course, the earnest, though shrewd, Gómez countered Febles's argument not only by reasserting the "truth," correctness, and relevance of African origins, but also by arguing for the appropriateness of Ifá Yemí as Olofin's progenitor, precisely because Ifá Yemí's own family was the root of the very Africans who established the tradition in Cuba in the first place. Quite astutely, Gómez destabilized the absolutist notion of "Cuban Ceremonies and Hierarchies." Utilizing what, in fact, has become the rhizomatic and intertextual thematic of today's Black Atlantic scholars (e.g., Gilroy 1993; and see my chap. 3), Gómez asserted that crucial knowledge transmitted by Cuban *babalawos* derived not from within the Cuban Ifá tradition itself, but from data gleaned from beyond it: that is, from ethnographies. Gómez was not without his own form of proof. He revealed in a series of letters to *babalawo* Radamés Corona that he himself was directly responsible for introducing the famous Cuban *babalawos* Eulogio Rodríguez "Tata" Gaitán and Guillermo Castro—important elders and colleagues of Febles himself—to Fernando Ortiz at the University of Havana sometime in the 1930s. Tata Gaitán was apparently an "informant" of both Ortiz and Lydia Cabrera. Hence, if the great Gaitán and Castro learned from the oral history of their elders, they also "went to drink water at [the academy's] fountain" of knowledge, Gómez wrote: In other words, if they learned from the oral teachings of their African elders, they also completed their knowledge in fathoming Ortiz's library, which must have included all of the texts, African and New World, not to mention police-confiscated practitioner notebooks, that Ortiz had used to write his ethnographies, such as Bowen (1858), Binger (1892), A. B. Ellis (1894), Dennett ([1910] 1968), Crowther (1848), and Johnson (1921; see Ortiz [1906] 1973, 28–43; and my chap. 3).[135]

The Africans had carried their Ifás to Cuba and watched their families grow under the eye of Olofin—whether transported over the same shipbound route or recreated through Atlantic recrossing. Gómez complicates these heroic diaspora stories of Ifá's New World African presence not merely by recreating, through "emulation," the first Diaspora in Miami's second, predominantly white, Diaspora. A new, modernist, narrative, now centered around Gómez's own heroic intervention, argues that Ifá in Cuba could be completed only through ethnographic reading and *recopilación*. This element in the reconstitution of Ifá will be revisited in chapter 3.

THE TRANSMISSION OF LA REGLA DE OCHA INTO THE TWENTIETH CENTURY: IMAGINED COMMUNITIES OF RITUAL DESCENT, CONFIRMATORY INITIATIONS, AND THE CREOLE TERMS OF AUTHENTICITY

The names of the Lucumí *ramas*—the genealogical "branches" that link Cuba's religious "houses" past and present—do not refer directly to the official institutions of the old-style *cabildos*, which are supposed to have "form[ed] the starting point for the African [*santería*] of Cuba" (Bastide 1972, 95). Instead, most of the *rama* names refer directly or indirectly to La Regla de Ocha's individual Lucumí and early creole founders, often through African names, sacred signs, intriguing nicknames, local toponyms, historical ethnonyms, and allusions to idiosyncratic events. The "history" of this aspect of La Regla de Ocha depends upon a series of emblematic, sometimes cryptic, references, upon shifting memory, talk, and ongoing ritualizing in the formal veneration of ancestors. The work of ethnography, including priests' own investigations to illuminate their genealogies, aids and complicates the writing of such a history, as it strives to fix what is, by character, fluid and sometimes ambiguous.

That a number of the Lucumí Ocha founders played leading roles in early-twentieth-century *sociedades* and *cabildos* remains of great historical interest. Arguably, the *sociedades* and *cabildos* acted as legalized umbrella institutions for the emergence of the modern *casas de santo*. Key founders of these houses and their *ramas* worked together in such organizations as Cabildo Africano Lucumí, which claimed a history that dates at least to 1839, and perhaps to 1820 (Caridad Argudín, Margarita Armenteros, Belén González, and the Sotolongo and Albear families). Knowledgeable contemporary practitioners continue to speak about the importance of Cabildo Changó Tedún, though few know who founded or belonged to it. From the perspective of contemporary practitioners' historical consciousness, "the *cabildos*" remains simply a general reference point of the Lucumí past. More to the point, through their daily *moyuba* prayers, as well as ongoing talk, contemporary practitioners recognize and elaborate upon their spiritual identities with reference to the founders and bearers of their traditions. Thus, the following discussion focuses on the more specific category of experience-near genealogical reckoning, the *ramas*, or "branches," of the religion.

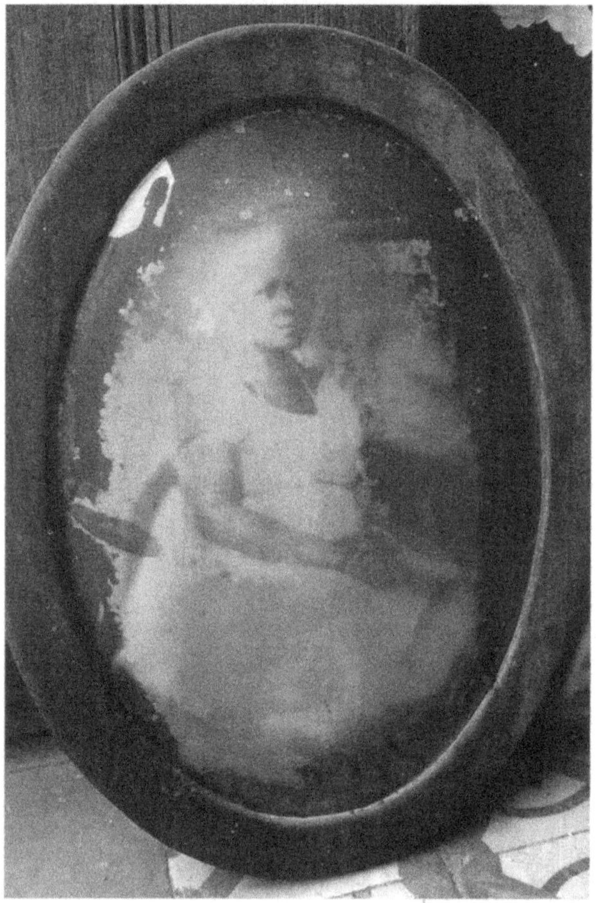

Figure 2.10.—Ma Monserrate González (Obá Teró), a core Matanzas Lucumí founder and the godmother of Fermina Gómez, photographed probably in the last third of nineteenth century. Private collection, Matanzas.

The Ramas

As George Brandon surmised years ago (1983, 502), the *ramas* of La Regla de Ocha in Cuba and the United States are traceable to a handful of *raíces* or *troncos* (roots or trunks), in pracititioners' historical consciousness. Late-twentieth-century priests cite seventeen principal *rama* names: Ma Monserrate, Ferminita, Los Ibeyi, Efuche, Ainá, Ña Margarita Armenteros, San José Ochenta, Igoró, Apoto, Culo Verde, José Pata de Palo, Aurora Lamar, Pimienta, Trapito, Obadimelli, Palmira, and Aratakuá. Other important *ramas* cited include Monserrate Asiñabí and Tía Julia Samá Abonse, also known as San Lorenzo de Samá. A number of these, and many more (e.g,, Adewá and Atí Keké), are redundant, or overlap, either through a strict reckoning of genealogy or in practice.[136] Some simply collapse into others, depending upon perspective. When redundancy and overlap are taken into account, and the names of the putatively African-born Lucumí founders are listed together, at least eleven seminal Lucumí are identifiable through the often cryptic genealogical citations, though contemporary priests still debate whether particular forebears were *de nación* or *criollos.* Those eleven are Efuche (Ña Rosalía, aka María Trujillo), Ainá (Ña Margarita Armenteros), Igoró (Ña Caridad Argudín), Apoto (Ña Belén González), Ma Monserrate (González), Francisca Entensa ("Palmira"), Obadimelli (Octavio Samar), José Pata de Palo (Urquiola), Los Ibeyi (the "Twins," Perfecto and Gumersindo), Monserrate Asiñabí, and Tía Julia Abonse.[137] They, their close Lucumí associates and/or creole godchildren in Havana, Matanzas, and Palmira, were responsible for founding and advancing Cuba's principal Ocha lineages (see also Mason 1996, 18–21, 26–28).

Ma Monserrate González and Ferminita

Ma Monserrate González (Obá Teró) is remembered as an influential Changó priestess of Matanzas and a Lucumí ex-slave (fig. 2.10).[138] According to John Mason's research, she was one of the two original sources of the *oricha*

Figure 2.11.—Fermina Gómez Torriente (Ochá Bí) of Matanzas, owner of the Cabildo of Fermina Gómez and Matanzas's Olokun drums. Private collection, Matanzas.

Olokun in Cuba, and was the priestess who gave Olokun to her creole protégé, Ferminita Gómez (Ocha Bí), also of Matanzas (fig. 2.11). The massive house of Ferminita Gómez, now crumbling, is still known as the "Cabildo of Ferminita Gómez." Its caretaker maintains there Ferminita's *fundamentos,* including Olokun's four goblet-shaped drums (see Mason 1992, 376; Cabrera [1974] 1980).[139] Depending upon the account or perspective, the *ramas* of "Ma Montserrate" and "Ferminita" are either genealogically related or distinct. Some say Ferminita was the daughter by blood and goddaughter in Ocha of Ma Monserrate; others emphasize their initiatory relationship alone. Still, eliciting the ritual genealogy of Ferminita is complicated by the fact that the responsibility for her initiation passed between two priests before it could be completed: from a Lucumí that Michael Mason's sources called Tomián Cordá-Isí to Ma Monserrate herself.[140]

Los Ibeyi (alternatively Los Papás Jimaguas, the "Twins")

According to Lydia Cabrera's elderly mid-twentieth-century informants, the "Twins" were two wealthy Lucumí, Perfecto and Gumersindo, who ruled an "African *barrio*" created around 1880 within the rural jurisdiction of Marianao. Called El Palenque (literally "runaway slave community"), it was home to numerous Lucumí and *criollos,* all "godchildren" of the Twins. In African-like compounds, the Twins kept multiple "wives," including Ña Pilar, Ña Chucha, and Ña Cecilia Pedroso. The Palenque conducted large annual *oricha* feasts for the community's two principal deities, Baloggué Ogún, the warrior, and Oricha Oko, the owner of the land, "just like it was done in Africa." Though dominated by Lucumí, El Palenque also produced "innumerable godchildren in Havana," including, many rich white women and men" (see n. 33 and Cabrera [1954] 1983, 25 n. 1). El Palenque was, thus, a great *mata*—"trunk," or authentic font—of Havana Lucumí practice; some say that several *ramas,* often considered to be distinct, in fact originated there.[141]

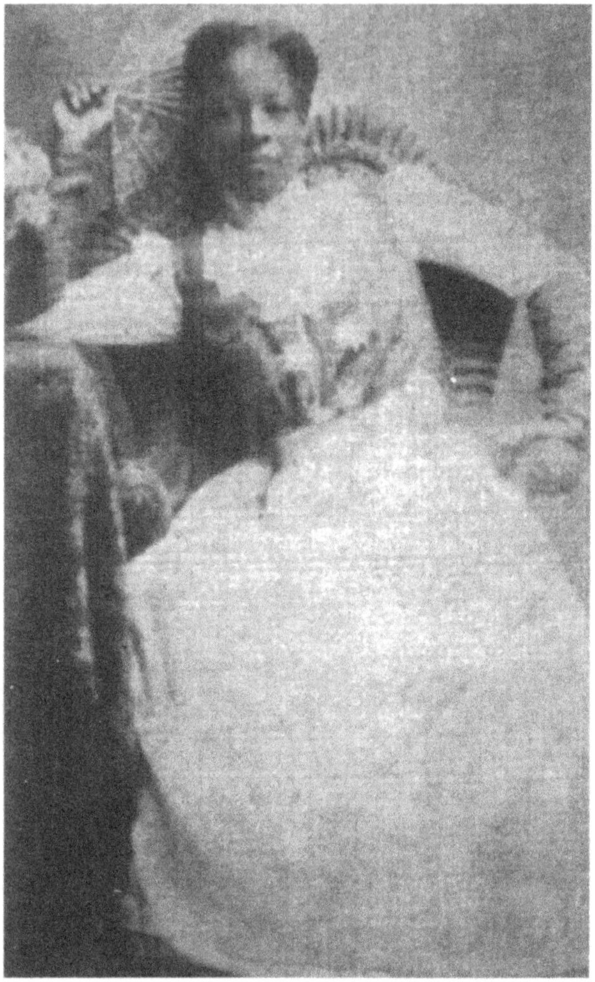

Figure 2.12.—Susana Cantero (Omí Toké), ritual granddaughter of African founder Efuche Ña Rosalía. Cantero founded one of two principal *cabildos* of the Virgin of Regla/Yemayá. Museum of Regla.

Palmira

The *campo* further east into Cuba's interior is responsible for the *rama* known by some as "Palmira." The rural town of Palmira consolidated numerous freed Africans who had worked the sugar mills and plantations of the fertile south-central region of Cuba around the colonial city of Trinidad. The *rama* Palmira actually refers to the specific lineages of at least two women, Francisca Entensa (alternatively, Estencel) and Guadalupe Estables,[142] daughters of Yoruba, who founded, or whose families founded, Palmira's Lucumí *sociedades* in the early Republican period. Francisca Entensa Pino, a priestess of Changó (Changó Gumí), founded Palmira's still-functioning Sociedad San Roque

(Eleguá) and died in 1959 at eighty-two years of age. Guadalupe Estables was the daughter of Sociedad El Cristo's founder, the Lucumí Nicolás Sevilla.[143]

Efuche

Efuche (alternatively, Fuche, Funche, Efushe) is known by Ernesto Pichardo's Miami house as a Yoruba priestess of Ochosi who arrived in Cuba as a free migrant worker in the late nineteenth century or the first years of the twentieth century. In contrast, Efuche's only surviving Ocha granddaughter, María Eugenia Álvarez Pérez (Ochún Niké) of El Cerro, insists that "Fuche came from Africa as a slave."[144] Consistent with the independent accounts of Michael Mason's Havana sources, the late *oriaté* Yrmino Valdés Garriz identifies Efuche by her Spanish honorific and first name, "Ña Rosalía" (Valdés Garriz 1997, 135).[145] Ña Rosalía Efuche, who lived in El Cerro, counted among her important early descendants the Changó priestess Luisa Arango (Changó Ladé) and the Obatalá priestess Andrea Trujillo (Igüín Yimí).[146] Andrea Trujillo, in turn, initiated the Regla Yemayá priestess Susana Cantero (Omí Toké; fig. 2.12), probably sometime after the latter's arrival in Havana from Cienfuegos in 1914. Cantero became very famous as the leader of one of the two principal *cabildos* of Yemayá/the Virgin of Regla (the other was Josefa Herrera-Echubí), which processed through the town's streets annually on 7 September, beginning in the year 1921 (see n. 32). Efuche is known by some as *la reformista de la religión* ("the reformer of the religion"), as she was responsible for instituting important structural innovations in the Lucumí and Arará *reglas* at the turn of the twentieth century or in the early Republican era (see below).

Figure 2.13.—Tiburcia Sotolongo (Ochún Migüá), goddaughter of Ña Margarita Armenteros of the San José number 80 *rama*. Modern painting after a late-nineteenth-century photograph. The painting is integral to an ancestor altar. Private collection, Havana.

Ña Margarita Armenteros (Ainá), or San José Ochenta

Oyá priestess Ña Margarita Armenteros (Ainá) was the First Counselor of Cabildo Africano Lucumí (Cabildo Africano Lucumí 1900). Many of her descendants venerate her together with her goddaughter, Ochún priestess Tiburcia Sotolongo (Ochún Migüá, fig. 2.13), and Tiburcia's own goddaughters, Hortencia Ferrer (Ochún Güere,

"Chenchita") and Margot Fundora Sotolongo (Ochún Letí),[147] all of Havana's Barrio Príncipe. Upon his initiation in Havana, researcher Michael Mason was instructed by his godparents that their house belongs to a *rama* called San José Ochenta. With considerable oral history research, Mason discovered that this *rama* name corresponds to the Havana address (80 San José Street) of the Ocha house run by Oyá priestess Ña Margarita Armenteros (Ainá). Moreover, a series of priests told him that Ña Margarita and Tiburcia Sotolongo worked closely together in this same San José house with El Cerro's Efuche and her two daughters, Atí Keké and Adewá (alternatively Adewaró, Adeguaró), whom some list as *rama* [heads] in their own right (Latin American News Agency 1996, 9). By the mid-1920s, Obadimelli was establishing himself in Havana and would soon serve steadily as the principal *oriaté* of the house.[148] Hence, though their *ramas* are distinct in terms of strict filial reckoning, there are good sociohistorical reasons to group Ña Margarita and Efuche as "one" *rama*, or as the coheads of one "house" that supported several interlocking *ramas* (see below).

Apoto, José Pata de Palo, Aurora Lamar, and Igoró

Apoto is remembered as an Ochún or Yemayá priestess, originally from Matanzas. Some cognoscenti believe that Apoto, also known as Ochún Laibó, was Ña Belén González, who, documents reveal, belonged to the Cabildo Africano Lucumí (Cabildo Africano Lucumí 1900; see Valdés Garriz 1997, 135). Apoto (pronounced AHpoto) is credited by Ernesto Pichardo, Miguel Ramos, and others with being the African root of the Matancero José "Pata de Palo" Urquiola (Echú Bí) and his goddaughter Aurora Lamar.[149] Stories told by Osvaldo Cárdenas Villamil suggest that Matancero José Pata de Palo (José "Wooden Leg"), a colorful figure, may also have been known as Ñó Córda-isí. Villamil tells of Ño Córda-Isí as a *criollo* (the "son of Lucumí slaves"), a priest of the trickster *oricha* Eleguá, who dramatically danced on his one leg when possessed during drumming celebrations, and the initiator of Ferminita Gómez.[150] Like many Ocha priests of the period from the turn of the twentieth century through the 1920s, José Pata de Palo's career bridged Matanzas and Havana. Havana was the home of José's equally famous and prolific Ocha goddaughter, Agayú priestess Aurora Lamar (Obá Tolá; fig. 2.14). Lamar is remembered as a shrewd and feisty character, whose larger-than-life stature has translated into fantastic claims for her initiatory prolificacy. Some like to say she initiated six hundred priests, and others, one thousand, including seven hundred priestesses of Yemayá! One hundred priests, total, is probably closer to the truth.[151]

Lending narrative color to the *rama* identifications of Urquiola and Lamar, a number of intriguing epithets for their lines circulate among practitioners, often without additional facts of their founder's Spanish or African names: Culo Verde ("Green Ass"), La Pimienta ("Hot Pepper"), and El Trapito ("The Little Rag").[152] As William Muldro recently discovered, the name Culo Verde, which is associated with, or substitutes for, José Pata de Palo as a *rama* designation, refers to a typical experience and westward migratory trajectory of Afro-Cubans. Born in Matanzas, José was considered by the Havana Ocha community to be a country bumpkin—a "green ass"—with questionable religious credentials when he first arrived in the big city, probably in the late nineteenth or early twentieth century.[153] Similarly, Lamar and/or her *rama* are known to some by such alternate names as La Pimienta, El Trapito, La China de Maximiliano, and La China of the Ten Cent [Plan]. The most common is La Pimienta ("The Hot Pepper"), which is substantiated partly by the story that the feisty and shrewd Aurora Lamar owned a brothel and initiated a number of prostitutes. "La China de Maximiliano" ("Maximiliano's China") registers the naming practices of children born with almond eyes, and also apparently refers to social details of her biography; it reflects the tatoo she wore on her leg—a reference to an erstwhile lover or exhusband, Maximiliano. "La China of the Ten Cent [Plan]" reiterates an epithet contemporaneous Santeros gave to

Figure 2.14.—Aurora Lamar (Obá Tolá), founder of the *Pimienta* (sub)*rama*, a descendant of José Pata de Palo Urquiola (Echú Bí), early twentieth century. Private collection, Miami.

her: for initiations, Lamar offered an "easy payment plan," in which godchildren could pay her in installments, receiving their *fundamentos* only when the payments were completed.[154] Some of these charming hagiographic terms are substantiated in fact. Aurora's husband, José Ramón Gutiérrez, was a dashing *chulo* and *prestamista* (pimp and loan shark, or *garrotero*, "strangler") in his youth, before he cleaned up his act when initiated as a *babalawo* by the upright Bernardo Rojas in 1923. For her part, Aurora Lamar was a notorious "madame" (*matrona de bordel*). Their huge El Cerro home, which became an important Ifá and Ocha house, featured a string of individual rooms (*cuartería*) in the back, which served as the brothel.[155] It is thus unsurprising that Aurora may have had a number of prostitutes as godchildren.

La Pimienta, Trapito, and Culo Verde, as well as La China de la Ten Cent [Plan], can be seen as mnemonic figures within oral tradition, laconic references that locate two founders, their experiences, and their *rama* relationships in narrative space and time. As Renato Rosaldo found in his research, Ilonglot oral history narratives often consisted of no more than cryptic lists of place-names, which gained significance in the context of oral performance and its "cues" to culturally prepared audience members (Rosaldo 1980; see also Briggs 1988; Bauman and Briggs 1990). Laconic or cryptic *rama* references also cue significances relative to the variant historical consciousness of Ocha practitioners.

Mercedes Melo González, an Ochún priestess, goddaughter and caretaker to the late José Ramón Gutiérrez, and inheritor of his large Barrio Atares house, poetically explains that "La Pimienta" ("The Hot Pepper") is a Spanish translation for the historically Lucumí-dominated neighborhood in which Aurora lived, Barrio [of the] Atares Hill. The Lucumí word *ataré* derives from the Yoruba term for malagueta, or alligator, pepper (*ataare*). Residents emphasized the Yoruba-Lucumí reference, while the *rama* preserved the creole Spanish name.[156] In this way, the significance of a locale in its social and religious dimensions is embedded in the name "La Pimienta." So are the ardent characteristics of Lamar's biography and practice (e.g., the madame, the lover of Maximiliano, the shrewd businesswoman and a priestess who wanted everything done quickly). Not least, Aurora Lamar was a priestess of Agayú, a fierce, "hot" *oricha*, who was born from the fiery magma at the center of the earth's core. Agayú's *aché* manifests itself as "The Volcano." Finally, "La China" and "La China of the Ten-Cent [Plan]" mark Cuba's inimitable naming practices, but the "Ten Cent," or "Easy Payment," plan also refers to Lamar's hybridized system of the exchange of goods and services within the

Lucumí initiatory tradition—a "layaway" plan for initiation, when, customarily, *all* of the initiation's funds are supposed to be placed before the initiator's tutelary *oricha* before anything else can be done. If Lamar's layaway plan was sensitive to the neighborhood's poor, it also indicates her vocation as a formidable female entrepreneur.

Similarly, the nickname given to José Pata de Palo, "Culo Verde" (Green Ass), is a direct cognate for the common Yoruba epithets *ará óké* and *ará oko*—in effect, "hillbilly"—which are given by urban Yoruba to rustic, often non-Muslimized or non-Christianized, people from the "bush."[157] "Culo Verde" thus refers in laconic, humorous fashion to the significances around José's migration between two key centers of Lucumí religious activity: Matanzas and Havana. Matanzas, further to the east, is considered closer to the *campo* of the interior, in contrast to the bustling, urbanized Havana. If the epithet registers a historical Havana social prejudice against eastern *guajiros* ("farmers"), more precisely it marks the operation of in-group and intergroup maps of regional difference and emergent hierarchies of prestige (e.g., a "Havana-centric" religious perspective). Moreover, it also refers to the rigorous, often politicized, process of evaluation, credentialing, and incorporation of "foreigners" within regional and local systems of Lucumí religious practice. José Pata de Palo had to "convert," as William Muldro found, to the Havana system of Ocha practice.[158]

Finally, "Trapito" emblematically marks the historical consciousness of local ritual innovation and "traditionalization." "Trapito," an idiosyncratic badge of Lamar's *rama*, or the sub-*rama* of one of her godchildren, refers to an incident in which the ceramic tureen (*sopera*) holding an *oricha*'s *fundamentos* broke as it was about to be "presented to an initiate's head" (see chaps. 3 and 4). Improvising, the attending priests wrapped the *oricha's* secrets in a piece of cloth (*un trapito*). Not inconceivably, the breaking of the tureen was interpreted as an oracular event, presenting a significant piece of otherworldly warning or knowledge and, thus, requiring this practice to be repeated. Presenting that *oricha*'s *fundamentos* to the head wrapped in cloth became a tradition in at least one branch of Lamar's line, and "Trapito" was added to the list of epithets for the *rama*.[159]

Depending upon perspective and relative knowledge—through oral transmission or active research—*rama* assignment of the same ancestor figures can vary greatly. Some contemporary practitioners mark "Culo Verde" and "Trapito" or "Pimienta" as distinct *ramas;* some emphasize one over the other, sometimes reversing themselves in another conversation on the same issue. When asking my godparents about the *rama* of our house, my *padrino*, a *babalawo* with a very good memory, first emphasized Aurora Lamar as the "root" of our *rama;* later, he added José Pata de Palo, locating him as our root. The latter emphasis came to the fore in a more general conversation in which he identified our *rama* as "from Matanzas" (i.e., the origin of José Pata de Palo). When asked the same question, my *madrina* reproduced this same pattern of enunciation.[160] Finally, when I asked my *padrino* if he had ever heard of Apoto Belén González, he said yes and acknowledged that she might have been José's initiator. However, he then suggested that Belén González herself might have been initiated by someone else, possibly the folks in El Palenque. In short, it may be that the enunciation of "Aurora Lamar" or "José Pata de Palo" carries contextual weight and can refer to more proximate or remote origins within Cuba itself, for example, a *rama* that developed in the Havana locale, even though it had its ultimate "roots" in Matanzas. These *rama* epithets are, of course, further debated. Some contemporary priests sharply distinguish Trapito and La Pimienta, suggesting that their practices differ significantly. In one case of distinction between these *ramas*, a Cuban-American priestess told me she was taught by her Cuban godmother that their line was Pimienta, not Trapito. Pimienta was the *rama* that relied on the services of *babalawos*, and Trapito eschewed *babalawos*. Another told me that Trapito, called Los Pañuelitos ("The Little Handkerchiefs," by some) has nothing to do with Aurora Lamar and applies to a different *rama* altogether. Ironically, my grandmother in Ocha, Berta Chacón (Ochá Linú), who is ninety-three years old and knew Aurora Lamar well, says she never heard of the terms "Culo Verde" and "Trapito" at all.

Rama designations and their relationships remain somewhat ambiguous and fluid. From the perspective of more remote origins—sometimes forgotten, sometimes remembered, sometimes contextually relevant, sometimes not—José Pata de Palo/Culo Verde is inclusive of Aurora Lamar/Trapito/Pimienta, and Apoto/Belén González is inclusive of both of them. Still, others turn these relationships on their head, chronologically. They claim that Culo Verde refers not necessarily, or exclusively, to José Pata de Palo, but to Echubí's "grandson" in Ocha, the famous *oriaté* Apolinar González (Ocha Weyé, "Polo"). Like José Pata de Palo, "Polo" himself relocated from Matanzas to Havana to work as an *oriaté*. There he was viewed as a "country bumpkin" or "green ass." Eventually he changed his style, unaccepted by Havana authorities, to conform with Havana methods."[161]

The case of Apoto and Echubí José's line is further complicated by recent oral history research. Natalia Bolívar, a Cuban investigator, and William Muldro—a New York priest researching his own *rama*, La Pimienta—now believe that the real or "principal" root of La Pimienta is two generations deeper than previously thought. They identify an Ochosi priestess, Ña Caridad, as the founder of a *rama* called Aigoró, reflecting Caridad's African name (which has the variants Igoró and Aiworó). In this reckoning, Aigoró intiated Apoto Belén González. In turn, Apoto initiated one "Luisa La China" (Ochún Miwá), who is credited with being José Pata de Palo's *madrina*.[162] At the same time, perhaps unsurprisingly, this narrative grants Belén González the status of "head of the Apoto *rama*." In this case, the definition of *rama* becomes fluid and can be used to designate the heads (*dueños*) of "houses" (*casas*) who, in some remarkable way, distinguish themselves, for example, through their initiatory prolificacy—that is, because they "left [great] families" (see above). Enter the term *raíz*, which comes to denote an ultimate "root" or "founder" on Cuban soil, while the *rama*, like a branch of a tree, can gain identity as it "grows," has "children," and even "walks" (Bascom 1950, 65). In any event, the association of Belén González and Ña Caridad is plausible, given the suggestion of their relationship provided by Cabildo Africano Lucumí *reglamento* (Cabildo Africano Lucumí 1900). Ña Caridad was, quite likely, this *cabildo*'s female "founder," Caridad Argudín, while Belén González was its Second Counsel. Seniority within the official *cabildos* and *sociedades* was probably not arbitrary, or based simply on merit, but also often reflected ritual seniority and African versus creole birth.[163]

In a slightly different case, *ramas* may collapse into one another, or assert themselves as distinct, depending upon what *kinds* of relationships practitioners believe define the *rama* unit. Formal genealogical relationships of connection may be balanced by collegial working relationships and location. For example, there may be good reason to consider that Ña Margarita (Ainá) and Efuche make up a single *rama*, called San Jose Ochenta. Ña Margarita, her goddaughter, Tiburcia Sotolongo (Ochún Miguá), Efuche Ña Rosalía, and her two daughters, Atí Keké and Adewá (aka Adeguaró), worked closely together in the house at 80 San José Street in Havana. At the same time, they undoubtedly formed interlocking ritual families. Just as the *ramas* of Bernardo Rojas (from Adechina) and Bernabé Menocal (from Ifá Omí) became interlocking as the two men served as "second godparents" (*oyubonas*) for each other's godchildren, it is likely that the members of San José Ochenta did the same. In the first sense, *rama* identification is expanded through intimate collegiality—not least because the members of the working group collectively "put forth their *aché*" in order to "make" a single "head" (i.e., intitiate). In the second sense, the *casa*, considered as relatively fluid, expands as an "extended family" that produces genealogically related sub-*ramas*. Notwithstanding, some contemporary Havana practitioners who descend from Ña Margarita Armenteros and Tiburcia Sotolongo have heard neither of Efuche nor of San José Ochenta.[164]

I have reserved discussion of the *ramas* of Obadimelli and Aratakuá for the end of this section because of their extreme complexity. The cases highlight the tenuousness of considering ritual genealogy as continuous and linear, and its oral transmission as orderly and transparent. Indeed, the very assumptions about the kinds of initiatory links hitherto assumed to constitute ritual descent require interrogation. Obadimelli (pronounced oba-di-MEji) was a famous and controversial Agayú priest by the name of Octavio Samar Rodríguez. Raised and trained in Matanzas sometime during the second half of the nineteenth century, he had relocated to Havana by the early to mid-1920s. He would establish himself in intimate working relationships with Havana's principal Ocha houses, including San José Ochenta and, undoubtedly, La Pimienta, Aurora Lamar.[165] Octavio Samar Obadimelli is remembered as one of the premier "architects" of the "modern" Cuban initiation ceremony and the tradition's first self-consciously "professionalized" male master of ceremonies (*obá-oriaté;* see below and chap. 3). His ascent and recognition in Havana apparently overlapped the end of the reign of Havana's two great female *oriatés,* Ayayi La Tuán Timotea Albear and Guillermina Castel.[166] As an *egun* (deceased member of a *rama*'s priestly line), Obadimelli is prominent in the *moyuba* prayers of many contemporary priests, not only because of his prestigious and formative role as *obá* to many *oricha* houses, but also because he is believed to have produced a *rama,* albeit small, of his own initiates. These include the Matanzas-born *oriaté* Nicolás Angarica, according to the latter's published testimony (Angarica [1955?] n.d., 8).[167] Obadimelli was the teacher of Havana's most recognized twentieth-century *oriatés,* including Pablo Liberato Valdés (Ewin Letí), Maximiliano Ordáz (Obá Yemí), Nicolás Angarica (Obá Tolá), and, undoubtedly, his own son, Lamberto Samá.

As argued in the case of Ifá, hagiographies and genealogies are often contested. Information transmitted by one teller is often partial and may be "completed" naively in the composite notes of the oral history investigator. Obadimelli's identity and status, as conveyed through one cycle of motivated stories, are relativized, and perhaps even challenged, when confronted with another set of stories. John Mason identifies Obadimelli as an African-born Yoruba Agayú priest (1992, 169), which is consistent with Mason's overriding interest in the African origins of Cuba's Lucumí. Pichardo and Ramos, who also seek to enunciate unequivocal narratives of a continuous Ocha past, credit Obadimelli with being the founder of a *rama* that came to bear his name.[168] Still another source identifies Obadimelli as the Ocha godson of an African, Tomián Ñó Córda Isí, which, technically, demotes Obadimelli to sub-*rama* status. If Ño Córda Isí was, in fact, José Pata de Palo, a "son of Lucumí," then Obadimelli is doubly demoted in geneological status and closeness to Africa: he was initiated by a creole (José Pata de Palo). Obadimelli's extraordinary status in one set of stories as the authentic African priest on Cuban soil is relativized by his complex and even contradictory translocal relations.

Obadimelli's *rama* genealogy is complicated, polyvalent, and historically discontinuous. First he was initiated into Ocha at least "twice" in different places by two different sets of godparents. Second, the very terms, means, and meanings of his "two initiations" were historically inchoate and discrepant, thus problematizing simple, presentist, definitions of the ideas of filial descent through initiation and the term *rama* itself.[169] While Octavio Samar's first initiation by Tomían Ño Korda Isí was, probably, the "head-and-foot" style that characterized Matanzas practice from the middle of the nineteenth century to before World War II, his "second initiation" was, apparently, unprecedented in kind and emergent in its very form. Indeed, it seems that his "second initiation" generated a provisional ritual model, which then launched and spread regionally an important innovation in twentieth-century Regla de Ocha. Apparently, his second initiation was not at all like the first—the "seating" of the *oricha* Agayú on his head. According to Michael Mason's discussions with Matancero *oriaté* Saúl Fernández, who now lives in Havana, upon Samar's arrival in Havana, he was made to undergo the "second initiation" by Efuche Ña Rosalía. Efuche was a top ritual authority in Havana, and she required the "second initiation" in order to legitimate Samar's ritual credentials. Michael Mason concludes from his discussions with Fernández that this second ceremony "spawned" what has become known as the *Pinaldo* (the Knife, see below).[170] This ceremony, unprecedented in Cuba, gave Obadimelli the honor of becoming "the first *Pinaldero* of Matanzas," Osvaldo Cárdenas Villamil reports. Through the ceremony, not only were Obadimelli's Havana religious credentials affirmed, but also his genealogy, in effect, was expanded and revised to prioritize a second set of godparents, Efuche being the principal. Not mere relocation from one city to the other, but reconsecration and the gaining of a *poder* (power) undergirded his new status as a practitioner in Havana. From the perspective of the present, should "Obadimelli" be considered a "Matanzas" or "Havana" *rama* or sub-*rama*? Does he represent one *rama* or two? Which "origin" takes precedence in any given reckoning? The answer would seem to be relative, and dependent upon the context, interests, and knowledge of the participants in any given discourse on the Ocha past.

The fluidity and ambiguity of *rama* linkages and ritual kinship are further exemplified in a different case that is no less intriguing. Ernesto Pichardo gives an account of his Ocha genealogy in the following way: His Cuban godfather, Changó priest Juvenal Ortega (Obá Dina), told him that their *rama* is "Palmira" (i.e., "Francisca Estencel"). However, in the same breath, Ortega continued, "In Cuba we count from Efuche, but our African line is Aratakuá." When asked by an inquisitive researcher how that could be so, Pichardo came up with an explanation of Ortega's claims: "Palmira," he said, refers to "Cuban geography"; Efuche was the root African initiator ("we count from Fuche") of a *rama* or sub-*rama* head, Francisca Estencel; and one or both of these women had an ethnic origin in the Aratakuá nation.[171]

Though it stretches the imagination, Ortega's narrative, rationalized on the spot by Pichardo, is not historically inconceivable. The *nación* Lucumí Takuá from the Tápà Nupe savannah region to the north of Ọ̀yọ́, was a significant contributor to Cuba's Lucumí priesthoods (Ortiz [1916] 1987, 56; Cabrera 1980, 2; López Valdés 1986, 72; Matory 1994, 292, 127).[172] This was particularly true in Matanzas, according to Osvaldo Cárdenas Villamil.[173] Second, since at least the 1840s and 1850s, and down through the present, Ocha priests and *babalawos* have traveled between, and created, geographically distant centers of Lucumí religious activity. For example, Havana's Tata Gaitán regularly traveled to Palmira between the 1880s and 1920s to initiate *babalawos*, and candidates from Palmira regularly traveled to Gaitán's house in Guanabacoa to be initiated there; this pattern has continued down to the present.[174] Efuche of Havana and Francisca Entensa of Palmira may also have traveled in this way. Indeed, such transregional travel was responsible for the initiation of Francisca Entensa's own younger contemporary from Palmira, "Ma Fea" Felicia Fernández, who inherited the Sociedad of Santa Bárbara from her mother, Ma Lugarda Fernández. Ma Fea (the mother of Tata Gaitán's Ifá godchild, Mario Férnandez), is believed to have been initiated by Josefa Herrera (Echubí) of Regla (Mason 1996, 27). Ma Fea's initiation could have taken place in Regla, Palmira, or Matanzas, since the great Felipa Calderón, the "Bishop" of Matanzas, participated in the ceremony.[175] It is therefore not inconceivable that Entensa's initiation proceeded in this fashion. Alternatively, as in the case of Obadimelli, many people during the era were initiated "twice," receiving, in the process, new godparents, and, consequently, alternate *rama* identifications: Entensa could have very well have been "reinitiated" by Efuche.

Still, such a positivist ethnohistorical approach, which seeks to "verify" oral transmissions and their attendant assumptions about identity, potentially narrows and flattens the kinds of strategic, creative, and even opportunistic diasporic identifications that practitioners imagine and construct for their own purposes (see Scott 1991). This "imaginary" and constructive work proceeds, in good measure, through ordinary and extraordinary social interaction and "performance"—what Erving Goffman called the "presentation of self in everyday life" (1959). Historically, local Lucumí ritual authorities looked askance at murky genealogical credentials. Reinitiations were conducted precisely to *reconstruct* the spiritual personhood and kinship of people they then got to incorporate into their growing houses and *ramas*—local, translocal, transhistorical, and diasporic sodalities that are the stuff of "actual" and "imagined" communities. Indeed, those same Lucumí ritual authorites had to narrate and "perform" their own competence and credentials *in order to* take on their positions of authority. Today, priests not able to recite their entire *rama* genealogy, which Michael Mason nicely sums up as a "genre of Lucumí performance," may be considered less than "competent," or even suspect. In our discussions, Mason and I have hypothesized that, on a day-to-day basis, some priests might not remember, or dwell on the question of remembering, their precise ancestral roots or the chronological order of their predecessors. In other contexts, for example, in which they face testy elders or must appear knowledgeable to precocious godchildren, they might feel pressed to rationalize a plausible genealogy that would not hold up to empirical scrutiny. Another, equally dramatic way ritual authorities and authority builders perform their competence and credentials, Michael Mason has astutely observed, is through the strategic parsing of the "contexts" of particular types of ritual work and narrative rationalization. For example, a priest with Matanzas and Havana experience and credentials recites one enabling ancestor veneration, rooted in Matanzas, when he performs a ceremony one way; he marshals an alternate, Havana-based list when he performs it the "Havana way."[176]

The foregoing cases demonstrate that *rama* identification can expand beyond strict genealogical connections, encompassing more informal, revised, improvised, or imagined linkages. They also demonstrate that various contextual reckonings of genealogical connections (more or less remote) can conjoin or disjoin, in surprising ways, regionally or locally distinct identifications. Obadimelli's "reinitiation" represented a personal and historical disjuncture between Havana and Matanzas systems. Juvenal Ortega's *rama* recitation unifies putatively distinct genealogical and regional idenfications. Likewise, in the cases of Efuche/San José Ochenta/Culo Verde/Trapito/Pimienta, and Ño Córda-Isí/Fermina/Ma Monserrate/Obadimelli, *ramas* may be unified or differentiated, depending upon perspective, specialized knowledge, or the speaker's agenda.

In this sense, *rama* can be a chronotope, a spatiotemporal figure that anchors the rhetorical construction of "imagined communities" of Lucumí historical and spiritual descent—one version of many African Diasporas (see Scott 1991; Wafer and Santana 1990). Recently, for example, an Ocha priest who is among the founders of the Black American Yoruba Movement sought to emphasize his African genealogy and identity through the citation of his *rama.* He said to me, "I am four generations from Ọ̀yọ́: Obadimelli initiated Fermina Gómez; Fermina Gómez initiated Christopher Oliana; and Christopher Oliana initiated me."[177] *Rama* might be thus taken by some to mean a verifiable, continuous genealogy from a single African founder down to the present. Or, it may refer to a more or less continuous, and masked, stratigraphy of linkages. Some of these linkages were instituted only because of situational innovations, not because of an essential, immutable, linear genealogy. *Rama*—as translated into nationalist or multiculturalist terms of "identity"—operates as a rubric and rhetoric of continuous spiritual descent (see Clarke 1997).

Reform, Reinitiation, and Confirmatory Rituals in La Regla de Ocha

Efuche of El Cerro is known by cognoscenti as *la reformista de la religión* ("the reformer of the religion"), as Ernesto Pichardo learned from his Miami Cuban elders.

"The reform movement was begun in Havana just after abolition, around 1886–96, by two ladies from Nigeria, free people who were priests of Ochosi [one was Efuche]. Their major complaint was that *oricha* worship was not what they knew to be its purest form. Then came Obadimelli who forwarded that reform. There was much variety then [that] is not recognized [now]."[178] The story of Efuche's "reform" is not unprecedented, for it resonates with a historical pattern, wherein entrenched local "traditions" confront the arrival of specialists. Their modifications may set new local standards, which are generalized regionally over time. Efuche's reform recalls Ortiz's narrative of Atandá and Añabí's correction of Havana's *batá* drum tradition, which affected drum practice in Matanzas and elsewhere (Ortiz 1952–55, 4:314 ff.). In Efuche's case, clearly some of her reform efforts were strategic modifications that were widely accepted, while others were taken by some groups as mere "inventions" that remain contested to this day.

The notion that Efuche arrived after abolition (1886) as a free migrant proposes a historical narrative of La Regla de Ocha characterized by temporal discontinuity and variation in practice. Efuche's intervention is believed to have occurred not during the pinnacle of Cuba's slave and sugar boom, the 1820s to the 1860s, but on the eve of the twentieth century, perhaps even in the first years of the Republic (beginning in 1902). Though the moment of Efuche's arrival is unverifiable, it nevertheless finds context in Irene Wright's discovery that between 1902 and 1907 ten "immigrants from Africa" were shown by the census to have arrived in Cuba (Wright 1910, 147). As recent African Diaspora research also shows, descendants of African ex-slaves who had been repatriated from Cuba to West Africa returned to the island at the beginning of the twentieth century (Sarracino 1988; see also Matory forthcoming on Brazil and Cuba).

The story of Efuche thus proposes quite recent origins for major developments in La Regla de Ocha, suggesting in place of a linear, passive diffusion of homogeneous ancient tradition a social process that required a series of "reform movements" to overcome "much variety" in the turn of the twentieth century's Havana Lucumí practices. Indeed, the time between Efuche's original "complaint" and the outcome of her "reform movement" in Pichardo's compact narrative must have seen moments of negotiation, and possibly outright struggle. This scenario thus begs not the simpler, ahistorical question of whether any given practice was actually "pure" or "impure," but the question of what criteria of purity animated the interactions of local interested groups. Pichardo's story does not assume the two Yoruba women's knowledge as "pure" in an absolute sense. They attempted to reinstate "what *they knew to be . . . pur[e].*"

One of at least three major innovations in Havana Lucumí practice instituted by Efuche Ña Rosalía is believed to be the *Pinaldo* ceremony, the consecrated Knife received by Ocha priests.[179] The way in which *Pinaldo* was applied, and the ceremony of "reinitiation" that Octavio Samar Rodríguez Obadimelli underwent in Matanzas (or Havana), turn a dominant narrative of diasporic religious transmission—the linear diffusion of knowledge from Africa to the Americas—on its head. Octavio Samar Rodríguez, a reformer in his own right, had to submit to a legitimizing or confirmatory ceremony early in his career. Arriving to the city of Matanzas—having been earlier initiated in Africa, one account relates (Mason 1992, 169), or in the Cuban *campo*, another story relates[180]—Samar was required to undergo a "second" initiation in order to confirm and legitimate his first initiation—which had not been "witnessed" by Matanzas or Havana religious authorities. The Lucumí praise name, Obadimelli, meaning "to become king [*obá*] twice," refers to his "double" (*méjì*) initiation (see Cabrera [1954] 1983, 228; Mason 1992, 169). John Mason explains: "In those days the Lùkùmí in Cuba enforced the rule of requiring newly arrived Lùkùmí, no matter what their claim to status was, to be *reinitiated in the manner that had been redesigned to suit the conditions they found in Cuba.* The second initiation set the stage for his receiving the special name" (Mason 1992, 169; emphasis added). The story Mason collected suggests not only that Old World resources were creatively and strategically reconfigured for New World "conditions," but also that built into the oral history itself is the principle that the working out of African traditions in the Diaspora is contingent upon the agency of historically situated, self-conscious actors and groups. Knowledge and credentials brought from Africa did not *necessarily* stand on their own, and religious knowledge does not exist in a vacuum. Newcomers had to be tested and incorporated by Lucumí and creole authorities within local, socioritual networks of authority, which were, along with the operative criteria that defined them, emergent. Osvaldo Cárdenas Villamil explains, for example, that no major ritual activity could proceed in the city of Matanzas without the approval of *la obispo* ("the bishop"), Felipa Calderón, a goddaughter of Ma Monserrate González. This powerful "bishop" of Matanzas was not African born, but the "first creole to be initiated to Ṣàngó by the Lùkùmí in Matanzas" (M. Mason 1996, 27).[181]

Ceremonies to confirm, legitimate, or otherwise accredit diverse individuals entering local systems suggest just how "creole"—that is, island born and rationalized—such systems were. Consonant with the overarching theme of this chapter, the foregoing examples illustrate that "authenticity," "legitimacy," "purity," and "correctness" revolved not necessarily around what was done in Africa, but around what was being redone in Cuba. The king made once never thought he would become the king made twice. And following his reinititation via the *Pinaldo*, there was no going back. Obadimelli thus legitimated, proceeded to institute "reforms" of his own, upon his move from Matanzas to Havana, which responded to grave challenges to his authority and authenticity. Obadimelli is praised by some Ocha priests, such as Angarica and John Mason, as the progenitor of the complete and correct initiation ceremonies for the *oricha* Agayú, which he carried to Havana from his native Matanzas (Angarica [1955?] n.d., 51; Mason 1992, 169), while others thoroughly reject the validity of his ceremonies for Agayú (see chap. 3). Moreover, Obadimelli is scorned by some Havana *babalawos* as the "inventor" of the "fraud" that confers upon the recipients of the *Pinaldo* the right to slaughter four-legged animals, a "tradition" that "usurped" the *babalawo*'s exclusive authority over this high level of sacrifice.[182]

Efuche herself, as noted, is credited with introducing into Havana practice an advanced initiatory ceremony called *Pinaldo*. Today, in the *Pinaldo* ritual, an Ocha priest receives the "knife" (*cuchillo*) of the *oricha* of iron, war, brute work, and killing, Ogún. *Pinaldo* grants the recipient Ogún's strong protection and, in some *ramas*, grants the spiritual authority and immunity to kill sacrificial animals with Ogún's knife.[183] Contemporary priests also regard the *Pinaldo* ceremony, consisting of a major sacrifice (*ebó*) to, and a comprehensive divination (*itá*) of, one's principal group of *orichas*, as "a confirmation" of one's original initiation.[184] One major reason why the ritual is "confirmatory," Ernesto Pichardo explains, is that this major sacrifice (*ebó*) is effected through the recognized priestly authority of *Pinaldo*'s conferring elder and is grounded, by extension, in the spiritual authority of that elder's extant *orichas*. "We do the feeding of the four-legged animals through my *orichas*, through the authority that is mine. . . . [T]he context of the ritual consists in this: because my *orichas* are valid, and you are going through this with me, your *orichas* are reconfirmed as valid." The oracular knowledge produced in the new *itá* of the *Pinaldo* deepens and confirms the recipient's spiritual trajectory. At the same time, the elder who delivers the *Pinaldo* may or may not be the original initiator (*padrino de santo*) of the recipient. If so, this original relationship is normally deepened and affirmed by the strong link of *Pinaldo*. If not, the *Pinaldo* elder may come to be regarded as the "new," "real" godparent of the recipient, while the *padrino de santo* becomes "an outsider." This shift in kinship relationships and social alliances takes on particular significance if the recipient's original godparent has died or been abandoned.[185]

Though it is risky to project backward the content and meaning of the contemporary *Pinaldo* ceremony, Pichardo's principle of "validity" suggests how *Pinaldo* may have been used as a confirmatory ritual within emerging versions of La Regla de Ocha. Individuals initiated previously by unknown or unrecognized people in the *campo*, in Africa, or even in unaccredited local houses, passed through *Pinaldo* as conferred by certain recognized elders.[186] As Havana *obá-oriaté* Saúl Fernández recently explained to researcher Michael Mason, people received *Pinaldo* as a way to "fix" and "confirm" (*arreglar* and *confirmar*) their *santos*, and it offered a ritual way to "save face" (*salvarse la cara*) with respect to their original, questionable initiations.[187] Efuche's *Pinaldo* ceremony was, in this sense, analogous to the reinitiation Obadimelli underwent in Matanzas or in Havana. Moreover, at the turn of the twentieth century or before, the recognized conferring priest, probably Efuche herself in many cases, became the "real" godparent of the new arrival. Thus, in addition to those people Efuche initiated for the "first time," as *madrina de santo*, it may be that the ranks of her influential *rama* were composed of godchildren reconfirmed through *Pinaldo*—which might account for Juvenal Ortega's complicated genealogical recitation (our *rama* is Palmira but "we count from Efuche"). According to Osvaldo Cárdenas Villamil, Matanzas's first *Pinaldo* holder (*pinaldero* or *tatachogún*) was none other than Obadimelli himself, who went to Havana in order to receive it.[188] If, as John Mason claims, Obadimelli arrived in Cuba already initiated and was reinitiated in Matanzas, only later receiving the *Pinaldo*, then he was, in effect, initiated "three times," the last by an African who is believed by some to have arrived in Cuba decades after his reported arrival in the nineteenth century (see Mason 1992, 169).[189]

The notion of Efuche's introduction of *Pinaldo* is interesting not merely because it accounts for the existence of one of the religion's key rank-conferring ritual passages. It begs the kind of question Mintz and Price raised more than twenty years ago in their speculations on the selection process underlying the formation of creole institutions ([1976] 1992, 42–60): what accounts for *Pinaldo*'s particular deployment against the background of the great knowledge Efuche presumably possessed? Were there elements of her knowledge that became irrelevant to, or structurally incompatible with, "the conditions [she] found in Cuba"? Otherwise the question and answer are rigged in advance: starting with what we find in the New World, we selectively construct and ossify West African history, as well as the history of Cuba's transatlantic cultural agents. Using formal similarities, as Herskovits tended to do, we might want to identify or verify the "tribal origins" of forms we find in Cuba, for example, *Pinaldo*, rather focus on the process of their selection and deployment on the island. Using Herskovits's concept of a tenacious "cultural focus" (see Herskovits [1945] 1966), for example, Herskovits's student William Bascom hypothesized not only that the "focus of Cuban Santería," the ritual complex of "stones, herbs, and blood," was extracted from "the wealth of institutional and ritual detail" of Yoruba society (Bascom 1950, 68) and implanted in Cuba as the core of Santería ritual. He also hypothesized that this focal Santería institution, "while it stands in clear relief in Cuba," might, upon further research, reveal "the real focus" of Yoruba religion itself, which was masked to ethnographers by all that West African institutional and ritual detail (1950, 68; see also Matory 1994, 223–24).[190] In other words, the discovery of a core Cuban practice is used to identify the very essence of Yoruba religion itself and posit an "origin" in West Africa. In a sense, Cuba gives birth to Africa historiographically. Clearly, Yoruba ritual does significantly revolve around envesseled stones that are washed in herbs and fed with blood (see Thompson 1993; Matory 1994; Apter 1992; Awolalu 1979). However, the contemporary institutional picture of highly codified, standardized sets of Afro-Cuban stones, cowrie shells, and iconographic attributes neatly contained in families of color-coded soup tureens, along with the meticulous classification systems of earthly formations ("stones"), flora ("herbs"), and fauna ("blood"), was painted *in Cuba* between the late nineteenth century and 1950, when Bascom wrote his seminal article (see chaps. 3, 4, 5).

The process of selection, innovation, and institutionalization creates creole products out of African resources through the negotiation of group interests and the social performances of charismatic actors (see Mintz and Price [1976] 1992; Palmié 1993). The correctness and effectiveness of a practice might very well depend upon the relative authority of its advocates and the expectations of an emergent community that accepts or resists a new "tradition." Efuche's *Pinaldo* was not self-authorizing simply because she brought it "from Africa." As argued, Efuche must have drawn upon tradition *as she knew it* from the particular local or regional milieu in which she was raised in Yorubaland. Thus, the question becomes, in effect, not what she *knew*, but how she persuaded people to see what *she* knew as correct, where local groups may have been invested in years of practicing the religion another way. This is precisely why the idea of Efuche's late arrival in Cuba is so interesting, whether or not she arrived in 1886 or 1907. In a sense, the "starting point of the Cuban *santería*" was not a place or institution—"the *cabildos*" or even "the *ramas*"—but the *process* of ongoing negotiation of interests among the emergent *ramas*.[191] For example, despite the great authority Lucumí founders, such as Efuche and Obadimelli, have held in the memories of practitioners, some of these founders' innovations were met with stiff resistance by founders in other quarters. According to Obadimelli's protégé, student, and historical defender, Nicolás Angarica, and more recently, John Mason, Obadimelli decisively enhanced initiatory practice in the cult of Agayú (Aganju) in Matanzas (Angarica [1955?] n.d., 49–51). He did so based upon "information about the ritual traditions and implements associated with Aganjù [he brought] from Yorubaland" (Mason 1992, 169–70). Later, Obadimelli carried these enhanced ritual methods and media to Havana, possibly around the turn of the last century (Angarica [1955?] n.d., 49–51; Mason 1992, 169–70). Though presumably of African provenance, the rituals were staunchly resisted by certain *ramas* invested in the initiatory paradigm for Agayú that had already been established as "traditional" in Havana. The new practice, initiating Agayú "directly," rather than through the "indirect" mediation of Changó, was so controversial and divisive that Angarica felt he had to continue in defense of Obadimelli's reform and his own credibility some fifty years later in his *oriaté* manual from about 1955 (Angarica [1955?] n.d., 49–51). Obadimelli's reform efforts succeeded in some *ramas* and failed in others. Thus, two principal forms of Agayú initiation persist today. Those who resist Obadimelli's method do so because they believe it could cause "madness" or "death" to befall the initiate. Defenders of Obadimelli's method and credibility point out the ignorance of their detractors.[192] The two methods continue to coexist, operating on different criteria of legitimacy that are rationalized more or less systematically within different *ramas*.

In short, the outcomes of "reform" movements entail multiple trajectories of institutional and cultural formation; they standardize heterogeneous practices, producing orthodoxies in the process; meanwhile, they also produce or harden multiple, alternate "traditions." As James Wafer shows for the Bahian Candomblé case, alternate traditions perceived as heterodox by elites or reformers are, in some cases, older, and thus more "traditional," than the putatively "pure" or "true" practices an Efuche or Obadimelli attempts to introduce (see Wafer 1991, 56–57). From this point of view, the institutions of reform, such as Efuche's *Pinaldo*, may be seen as "inventions," while the supposedly incorrect, corrupted, or "invented" practices of reform's targets are the traditional or traditionalized holdouts of established rear guards.

THREE

MYTHS OF THE YORUBA PAST AND INNOVATIONS OF THE LUCUMÍ PRESENT

The Narrative Production of Cosmology, Authority, and Ritual Variation

[Olofi (God)] . . . made the sky with the sun and the stars and the earth and the trees and all that live in it, and sent to the world man, who was naked and hungry. Olofi made all this. All is of Olofi. He made the world, the Santos, men, the animals, and later he said, 'you're on your own,' and *he left.* Olofi *retired. Olofi delegated his son,* Obatalá, his inheritor, as his stand-in. [Olofi] watches and Obatalá executes.
—Lucumí creation myth

Q. How many Gods are there?
A. There is only one true God.
Q. Where is God?
A. God is in heaven, in the earth, and everywhere: including within our heart.
Q. Who made the sky, the earth, and all things?
A. God, Our Lord, made the sky, the land, and all things.
Q. Who is God?
A. God is the Holy Sacramental Trinity.
Q. Which of three personages was made Man?
A. The second personage, which is the Son of God, was made man, and after he was made man he was called Jesus Christ.
—Nicolás Duque de Estrada, excerpt from "Explication of the Christian Doctrine Accommodated to the Capacity of the Newly Arrived Africans in Cuba"

There are ten basic components of Yoruba religious belief and practice:

1. The Yoruba believe that there is one God who created and controls the universe and all that is contained therein;
2. The Yoruba believe that there are forces of nature (or parts of God) who deal with the affairs of men on earth, and the governing of the universe in general;
3. The Yoruba believe that the spirit of man lives on after death and can reincarnate back into the world of men. . . .

10. The Yoruba believe that man can commune with God through the vehicle of tran[ce]-possession

—John Mason, *Black Gods: Orìṣa Studies in the New World*

True religion should be knowable, because we have the strict obligation to embrace it, and we cannot do that without knowing it. History affirms and proves that all beings, be they savage, barbarians, or civilized, in all times have believed in the existence of God. . . . Later, the truth of the existence of God is so incontrovertible, that it has been accepted by all peoples, and among them we find the peoples of the Yoruba of the continent of Africa—with a great devotion to God and the immortal beings, the Santos—for reasons indicated. The author of this book, intimately tied to the sentiments of the Lucumís and Ararás, and additionally by his [Lucumí] Religious Creed, is capable of revealing to the light of Civilization, without mystification, the truth of the Lucumí Religion of the Yoruba territory.
—Nicolás Angarica, *Manual de Orihaté: Religión Lucumí*

THE MIDDLE PASSAGE, "THE AFRICAN COSMOLOGY," AND THE THEOLOGIZING OF LUCUMÍ RELIGION

With good intentions, practitioners and scholars alike refer to the collective Cuban *orichas*, like their cousins in Brazilian Candomblé and Haitian Vodou, as a "pantheon" (e.g., Pichardo and Nieto 1984, 36; Ramos 1996, 60; Castellanos and Castellanos 1992, 18; Barnet 1997, 83; Deren [1951] 1970, 93–96). *Pantheon*, from the Greek (*pan* + *theos*), means "every god"—a council of the gods. The *panteón Lucumí* or *panteón Yorubá* consists of a hierarchical, extended family of archetypal spiritual beings, each of which controls a determinate domain within complex mythological, oracular, ritual, and social systems. In myriad writings and teachings, each *oricha* has come to be systematically identified with particular oracular coordinates, elements of the natural and social worlds, distinctive iconographic attributes and aesthetic preferences, proverbs and narrative legends, sacrificial formulas, flora and fauna, songs, drum rhythms, possession-dance styles, and so on (see Angarica [1955?] n.d.; Ortiz [1951] 1985; Cabrera [1954] 1983; Cros Sandoval 1975; Thompson 1983; Mason and Edwards 1981; Mason 1985a; Bolívar Aróstegui 1990; Brown 1996). As such, the *pantéon Lucumí* or "Olofi and his family" of *orichas*, are easily likened to "Zeus and his family" on Mount Olympus (Cabrera [1954] 1983, 77–78). At the same time, "Olofi and his family" have been likened to the Christian Trinity and its ladder of intercessors, including the Virgin Mary and the saints (Bastide [1960] 1978, 262; see Matory 1994, 224).[1]

This chapter explores how the "Lucumí Religion of the Yoruba territory" could be so amenable to comparison with these universalizing "non-African" models, and, indeed, whether the Lucumí religion was directly or indirectly shaped by these models. I hypothesize that the Afro-Cuban "Religious Creed," as Nicolás Angarica phrased it (see fourth epigraph), narratively and practically recrystallized at the hands of writers and "reformers" as a "modern," theologically rationalized twentieth-century religion. The question is less simple than whether the recreation of the Lucumí religion—putatively an "oral tradition"—relied upon popular Christian ideas, practices, or theological treatises. The question is more subtly related to how "modern" Lucumí religious knowlege and practice are heavily mediated and intertextual, a question ultimately about mutually entailed bases of knowledge production: Lucumí and popular Cuban "oral traditions," transatlantic late-nineteenth and early-twentieth-century ethnology, and the emergent genre of sophisticated "manuals" and private notebooks of self-conscious, "professionalizing," practitioners. As chapter 2 noted, for example, one *babalawo*'s claims to religious knowledge and authority included the assertion of his role as the bridge between the Cuban academy's erudite Fernando Ortiz and the religion's luminaries.

In order to explore these questions of emergent, highly innovative Lucumí theological conceptions and practices in the twentieth century, this chapter pursues the following themes: the ongoing reconstitution of "pantheons" in the "Yoruba-Atlantic complex" (see Matory 1994, 225 and Apter 1992); the mutually entailed production of religious theology, iconography, and historiography; the "slippage" and ambiguity in comparisons of "saints" and *orichas* (see also Apter 1991); the "pantheonization" of modern Lucumí cosmology as produced by trial-and-error ritual reform in initiation and divination; and, finally, the contest of centripetal systematization and centrifugal variation, in particular, how reform interests and professionalization produced variations in theory and practice.

Since the heyday of Melville Herskovits (1941) and his recuperation as a scholarly influence after 1969 (see Szwed 1969), compelling narratives of black cultural "continuity and change," "tenaciousness" and "creativity," around the tragic fulcrum of the Middle Passage, have informed most scholarly and popular accounts of the formation of the great New World Yoruba "pantheons" (Herskovits 1941; Mintz and Price [1976] 1992; Thompson 1983; Price and Price 1980; Verger 1957, 1993; Pichardo and Nieto 1984). As the story goes, in the Middle Passage, Yoruba-speaking peoples from ethnically and culturally diverse West African kingdoms carried the *òrìṣà* in their memories and bodies to the New World, where the deities regrouped on new soil but not in unpredictable arrangements (see Murphy 1988, 1994). In the same way that Herskovits applied a range of metaphors to flesh out the concept of "syncretism" first proposed by Raimundo Nina Rodrigues in Brazil (hybrid, consolidation, amalgam, mosaic, merging, mingling, reblending, interchange; see Baron 1994, pt. 2, 424–554; see also Bastide [1960] 1978, 19–23), scholars have tried out a range of heuristically useful metaphors to characterize the regrouping of the Yoruba *òrìṣà* into the pantheons of *orichas* in Cuba and *orixás* in Brazil: fusion, concentration, reconstitution, reorganization, reworking, joining, and creolization, as well as syncretism itself. "A remarkable fusion of *orisha* . . . took place in the New World," astutely writes Robert Farris Thompson, for example (1983, 17–18). In a process of local selection based on transatlantic patterns, each Diaspora center (e.g., Cuba, Brazil, Haiti, and Trinidad) distilled cognate rosters of the most prominent, regionally and institutionally "crosscutting" *òrìṣà*, especially those from Ọ̀yọ́, Ifẹ̀, and Ìjẹ̀ṣà, with contributions from Yoruba polities conquered by the Kingdom of Dahomey, such as Kétu, Sabẹ, and Dassa Zoumé.[2] In order to account for the results of this process, James Lorand Matory draws explicitly on the creole linguistic metaphor, suggesting that a selected pantheon of regional Yoruba deities, dominated by those from Ọ̀yọ́, emerged as the "'metalanguage' . . . or lingua franca" of the African Diaspora (Matory 1994, 226). A resulting creolized pantheon became the Ọ̀yọ́-inflected religious "mother tongue," to extend the metaphor, organizing the cosmology and ritual patterns of the Cuban Regla Lucumí and the Brazilian Candomblé Nagô.

As Pierre Verger (1957, 1993), Thompson (1983), Matory (1994), Mason (1992), and others have noted, many ethnically distinctive and geographically distributed West African gods encountered, reencountered, or were fused with one another in Cuba and Brazil. This process, in many ways, mirrored the fashion in which myriad deities had spread, changed, and regrouped in West Africa itself through the "socio-political 'bricolage'" of imperial expansion and wars, the migrations of refugee populations, and the rise of new northeastern Yoruba kingdoms and towns in the second half of the nineteenth century (Apter 1991, 36, 54–69, 1992, 36–39; see also Smith 1969; Blier 1995a, chap. 1). For example, as Verger notes in his discussion of the Bahian Candomblé pantheon against a dynamic background of Yoruba religious heterogeneity and "amalgamation," the deities Oríṣàálá (aka Ọ̀bàtálá) and Ògún—widely distributed and integrated among local pantheons in Yorubaland—reencountered one another in the pantheons of Brazil and Cuba. On the other hand, the riverine Ọṣun and Yẹmọja had been regionally exclusive in Yorubaland (the Ìjẹ̀ṣà vs. Ẹ̀gbá territories) but were "united" (*reunidos*) around the leading *orixa* of each Bahian *terriero*, "symbolizing the reassembly [*reagrupamento*] of those [people] dispersed by the slave trade" (Verger 1993, 17, 33; see also Bastide [1960] 1978, 62). The Cuban institutions witnessed a similar process. Each *casa-templo* would host and celebrate all of the *orichas*, which were ranked hierarchically: they would be theologically subject to the pantheon's arch-*oricha* Obatalá and, in practice, would submit to the authority of the "head *oricha*" of each *casa*'s spiritual "owner," be it the diviner Orunmila or another *oricha* of the pantheon.

In a slightly different kind of "ethnic" and "international" reassembly, the nineteenth-century reencounter in Matanzas, Cuba, of the Lucumí *orichas* with the *fodduces* (*voduns*) of the Arará nation followed upon centuries of religious exchanges between the Yoruba and Fon-related peoples around the western border regions of the Ọ̀yọ́ Empire and the expanding Dahomey kingdom, as a result of imperial conquest (Matory 1994, 8, 27, 128, 259 n. 5, 260 n. 8, 269 n. 4; Apter 1992, 15, 23–27; Smith 1969, 46–56).[3] In a dramatic case, for example, a mid-eighteenth-century Dahomean king imported the Yoruba Ifá divination system in order to centralize the kingdom's oracular authority by delegitimating and controlling the dangerously "centrifugal" and subersive tendencies of the country's multifarious *vodun* possession oracles with the power of Fá (see Zuesse 1979, 208; see also Herskovits 1938b, 2:202, 208).[4] It might be surmised that both the Dahomean Fá and the Yoruba Ifá went to Cuba, where Lucumí *babalawos* and Arará *bokonos* practiced versions of the Ifá oracle. In fact, the case is more complex. If independent, Dahomean-descended Fá diviners ever really did practice in Matanzas Province, today the Arará would not have such diviners at all but for their enabling reinitiation as Oluwó Popó Awó Bokonó by Havana's Yoruba-Lucumí *babalawos*. Presumably, of course, the "original" Dahomean Fá diviners, likewise, had to be initiated into the secrets of Ifá divination by Yoruba *babalawos*. This suggests, of course, how much this transatlantic process was not merely linear—characterized by distinct lines of African "origin" to distinct African-Cuban "traditions," or even "creolizations." Moreover, it was not merely discontinuous, being subject as it was to reconstitution based upon wholly "new" New World principles (Mintz and Price [1976] 1992). As J. Lorand Matory, Stephan Palmié, and others suggest, similar changes and exchanges historically occurred in a parallel manner, on both sides of an emergent and transforming "modern" Atlantic system (Palmié 1994, 2000; Matory 1993, 225–28; 1998; 1999; forthcoming; see also Gilroy 1993).[5]

In Matanzas, two great West African–derived thundergods, the Lucumí Changó (cognate of the Yoruba Sàngó) and the Arará Ebioso (the Fon Hẹvioso; see Verger 1957, 27–32, 305–11, 525–27, plates 45–65), would virtually confront one another from the doorways of their *cabildos*. At the same time, as in just the kind of intra-West African "fusions" in question, Ebioso and the other Arará *fodduces* were heavily shaped in Cuba by the identities and pantheon organization of the Lucumí *orichas* (see Cabrera [1954] 1983, 229; Galzagorry Madán 1983). The same phenomenon occurred in Brazil, as "Bahia's major ethnic groups reconstituted their own native beliefs and practices within the religious framework provided by the Yoruba" (Voeks 1997, 53–54).[6] Still, the Cuban Changó was not necessarily a one-to-one reflection of a single Ọ̀yọ́-Yoruba archetype. Changó, as did many of the Lucumí *orichas*, absorbed other regional Yoruba gods of similar identity. The Cuban Changó apparently absorbed the deity Aira, who is found in Ọ̀yọ́, as well in Kétu, Sábẹ, and Dassa Zoumé, towns in the Republic of Benín near the Yoruba border, and also the deity Jàkúta, also from Ọ̀yọ́. Jàkúta is likewise found in Abomey in the Republic of Benín. "Airá" and "Yakuta" became alternate praise names for Changó in Cuba (see Cabrera [1979] 1986, 40, 319; see also Verger 1993, 18; Herskovits 1938b, 164).[7] At the same time, Haiti offers a striking diasporic counterpoint to Changó's Cuban history. In Haiti, the Yoruba Ṣàngó, Ọ̀bàtálá, and Ọya-[Ì]yànsán were incorporated as hyphenate deities around the fulcrum of Ogou (Gu, or Ogun; e.g., Ogou-Yamsan, Ogou-(O)Batala, Ogou-Shango), who became the quintessential representative of the reconstituted Rada (Dahomean-Yoruba) pantheon (Brown 1991, 68, 71; Métraux [1959] 1972, plate 4; Thompson 1983, 163–64). In an entirely novel set of Cuban encounters, the condensed Lucumí and Arará pantheons would confront the new spatial proximity of the fierce ancestral spirit medicines (*minkisi*) of the western central African Kongo-Angola peoples, a phenomenon that mirrors the Haitian juxtaposition of the Yoruba and Dahomean gods and the Kongo-Angola ancestral spirits as two great pantheons, the "cool" Rada and "hot" Petwo, respectively. In Cuba, Lucumí and Palo constitute two putatively separate "religions," while in Haiti Rada and Petwo form two valences of one "religion," Vodou. Thus, in Haiti, the two pantheons are kept in separate rooms in the Vodou temple, and their celebrations are divided by temporal breaks (see Thompson 1983, 164; K.Brown 1991, 66–70; 1991, 100–101). In Cuba, the "fierce" congo spirit vessels (called *ngangas*, *nkisos*, or *prendas* within the Palo Monte religion), are segregated in locked rooms and closets sometimes directly adjacent to the Lucumí *orichas* (see D.Brown 1999). At the same time, these *ngangas* were, in syncretic (*cruzada*) houses, anthropomorphized and grouped after the model of the Lucumí pantheon and its iconography.[8]

As a result of this "creative reorganization of [West African] traditional religion" (Thompson 1983, 18), each Candomblé *terriero* and each Lucumí *casa de santo,* as Bastide observed, now "directed by a single priest, had to pay homage to each and every deity. Instead of specialized fraternities serving Ogun, Shangô, or Omolú [as in Africa], there was a single fraternity comprising daughters of all these gods. Thus all Africa [Yorubaland] was concentrated in the sect" (Bastide [1960] 1978, 62; see also Verger 1993, 33). Bastide's "concentration" of regional cosmologies materialized in the radical condensation of ritual space and ritual time—in miniaturized New World shrine arrangements, in the compressed sequences of sung invocation, and in the rearticulation of weekly and annual sacred festival cycles. Spatially, West African Yoruba kingdoms featured a stratified spectrum of shrines consistent with descending political units: shrines for kingdoms or "crowned towns, multilineage quarter-shrines, and lineage or family compound shrines (see Apter 1992, 35–69; 1995). These kingdom or town, quarter, and lineage shrine institutions each combined "clusters" of related, hierarchically organized deities and their priests. Historically, Yoruba cult institutions, especially the larger-unit kingdom or "crowned"-town cults, have elevated leading *òrìṣà* tied to the king's patrilineage over subordinate local *òrìṣà*. Cults of different towns within the same kingdoms, or quarters within towns, exhibit "alternate pantheons . . . positioning [select] *orisa* in relation to their dominant cults, and corresponding bases of political power." Such arrangements have changed over time with local and regional power struggles and royal successions (Apter 1987, 284; 1992, 61, 152–59).

In Brazil and Cuba, in contrast, shrines have been confined to private and sometimes collective domiciles, which were, and are, often cramped urban apartments. Except for the rarer examples of the spacious compounds of the Tula family in Placetas (Las Villas; see Gómez Abreu 1982) and the Sociedades of the Sevilla and Fernández families of Palmira (Cienfuegos), the Cuban Lucumí *oricha* pantheons have been confined to small single rooms, the *cuarto sagrado* or *igbodún* (sacred room), or multishelved cabinets called *canastilleros* (see Brown 1989, chap. 5; 1999). However, many Brazilian Candomblés were able to establish their condensed pantheons on sizable tracts of owned land in the nineteenth and early twentieth centuries, where the *orixás* occupy their own little "houses" (*casas*) around ecologically differentiated *terrieros* (sacred compounds).[9] Within a "telescop[ing] of ecology," observes Bastide, the "spatial sectors of the Yoruba homeland [were] concentrated in the restricted space of the Candomblé" ([1960] 1978, 249–50). Indeed, some of the large Bahian Candomblé *terrieros* conserve to this day in their sacred landscape architecture a miniaturized regional model of West African arrangements. At Ilê Axé Apô Afonja, built in 1910 in the neighborhood of São Gonçalo do Retiro (see Verger 1993, 30), when the priestesses go to Oxalá's (Obatalá) large white house, they say they are "going to Ifê," when they go to Xangô's red and white house, they say they are "going to Oyó," and when they go to Oxossi's blue and white house, they say they are "going to Kêtu."[10] The African origin of this particular Black Atlantic imagined community revolves not around a single mythic capital, but around a regionally differentiated "geography of sacred memory" (Cabrera [1958] 1970, 63–64; Sosa Rodríguez 1982, 452) of multiple capitals from which the Afro-Brazilian "nations" descended (Wafer and Santana 1990). A similar effect is produced in the practice of heterogeneous "religions" by Cuban priests: where, as mentioned, the Lucumí *oricha* and Congo *nganga* pantheons inhabit the same domicile, the segregated spaces designated to them are marked by contextually distinct spiritual energies, iconographies, ritual languages, gestures, and feelings (see Brown 1999). These same practitioners, who sacrifice and drum to the *orichas* and *ngangas,* may also go to church and Spiritist masses, where they kneel before the altar, say orations, light votive candles, and take Communion.

In sum, the ranked organization of the *orichas* in their

canastilleros within Cuban *casas de santo*, and the *orixás* in their "houses" within the Brazilian *terriero* compounds, concretize the New World "pantheons" in spatial and architectural terms, reinforcing the appropriateness of this metaphor from the Greek. Pantheon not only means "every god" but can also refer to "a temple consecrated to the gods" (*Compact OED*, s.v. "Pantheon") as in the Roman Pantheon, where statues of the gods filled niches around the interior of a huge domed space with an oculus open to the sky. Likewise, the New World pantheons are made concrete in condensed temporal format when all the deities are "called" in hierarchical sequences of sung, drummed, and chanted invocations—the *oro del santo* (Cuba) and the *xirê* or *oro* (Candomblé)—during single ritual events. In Cuba, between nineteen and twenty-six *orichas* may be invoked in an *oro* sequence, depending upon context (Ecún 1985, passim; Pichardo and Nieto 1984, 36; Mason 1992, 20–22; Angarica [1955?] n.d., 65).[11] Considered together, the "traditional" Nagô Candomblés of Salvador,[12] Bahia recognize up to twenty-four major *orixás*, augmented by their numerous avatars (see Verger 1993, 288–89; Carybé 1980, text pages; Omari 1984, 20–21; Voeks 1997, 55). However, fewer numbers may be invoked in particular ceremonies. The *xiré*, depending upon the orientation of the *terriero*, may invoke upwards of fifteen *orixás*. Such sequences, when drummed, may also make rhythmic references to the deities' "nations" or origin, such as Nagô, Kêtu, Ijexá, Gêge, and Angola (see e.g., Oxum 1997; and *Candomblé* n.d.).[13] Finally, in two larger temporal cycles, illustrating what Bastide described as "pouring African material into a Western mould," each day of the week is devoted to an *oricha* or *orixá* or cluster of them. The calendrical saints' days hence became the annual slots for celebrations honoring the *orichas* or *orixás*, replacing the regionally distinct annual festival cycles for local gods in Yoruba towns with a single, densely packed annual public festival cycle for the reconstituted New World pantheons (see app. 5; see also Mason and Edwards 1981; Mason 1985a; Cabrera [1974] 1980, chaps. 1 and 2; Ortiz [1920] 1960, 1921; Bastide 1972, 155; see Dennett [1910] 1968, 134–35).

"The Old Structure," the "African Cosmology," and the "African Substratum"

Despite the foregoing general emphases in the historiography upon the "creativity" of New World processes of change, as well as the historical heterogeneity and dynamism of West African religious history, the identities and relationships of the New World gods in many of these same accounts tend to follow, with minor changes, from prior patterns in a "traditional" Yoruba cosmology that is represented as relatively homogeneous. Some of the richest recent West African studies, for example, emphasize a regional diversity and specificity of cultural forms as functions of "the Yoruba World" and "Yoruba religious thought." This Yoruba world, or worldview, an ethnophilosophical notion, is, in turn, structured by "certain core principles" of cosmology, ritual, and iconography (e.g., Drewal, Pemberton, and Abiodun 1989, chap. 1, especially p. 26). Similarly, Roger Bastide, employing Halbwach's idea of "the social frameworks of collective memory," believed that, where the African nations were successfully reestablished in the New World, "the old structure," that is, "*the totality of the [Yoruba] liturgical drama . . . and the mythology which is linked to it*," could be "*reconstituted almost in full*" ([1960] 1978, 247; emphasis added). For Bastide, this successfully occurred in urban Cuba and Brazil, where the social "niches" of the religious brotherhoods—*cabildos* and *irmandades*, respectively—permitted the regathering of African sacred knowledge, "nation" personnel, and the entire Yoruba "liturgical cast" of deities.

The concepts of *the* Yoruba-wide "old structure" of ancient patterns, and, to some degree, the regionally defined "Oyo-inflected metalanguage," echo the idea of an enduring, transhistorical "African substratum," which creolists hotly debated from the 1950s through the 1970s in the wake of Herskovits's *Myth of the Negro Past* (Herskovits 1941; see DeCamp 1971, 18–21; Todd 1974, 38). For Herskovits, African-American culture change would always be guided by "powerfully pre-established patterns." New "additions and synthesis" would always "achieve congruence with older forms," particularly in relation to deep structural "grammatical configurations" from the West African heritage (Herskovits 1958, xxvii; [1945] 1966, 60). Was, and is, there an enduring African-based cultural "grammar" or "deep structure" beneath Diaspora cultures? For example, as the question was posed in the creole linguistic idiom, did the syntax of a single African language, or set of related regional West African languages, constitute the syntax of the Caribbean creoles; were the Caribbean creole grammars descended from an old Portuguese-based Atlantic trade pidgeon (monogenetic theory), or were their origins mostly "polygenetic," that is, descending from different sources independently? (see DeCamp 1971, 18–21; Todd 1974 31, 33–39).[14] Among the strongest supporters of the African substratum theory have been Alleyne (1971) and Asante (1990). Alleyne, like Herskovits, insisted on the "basic cultural uniformity of West Africa," such that in New World languages, the "syntax" or "deep structure . . . is African-derived and persists" (175–76, 179). Mintz and Price, among the vanguard of the creativity, or creolization, school, did insist on the importance of shared "abstract principles," "cognitive orientations," and "basic assumptions" among heterogeneous Africans in the formation of African-American cultures, particularly those principles that existed below the level of consciousness ([1976] 1992, 9–12). However, as outlined in my previous chapters, Mintz and Price also argued that these principles, orientations, and assumptions belonged to a heterogeneous pool of cultural "resources," which were selectively deployed within new socioinstitutional formations, in a word, in rapidly creolizing new communities (Mintz and Price [1976] 1992, 9–22, 42–53; Price 1972; Price and Price 1980, 194–216; see also Palmié 1993). As Mintz and Price postulated, whatever "deep structures" or "grammars" are observed in any given Diaspora center had to be *created* from such resources in the New World (Mintz and Price [1976] 1992, 18). Stephan Palmié, taking Mintz and Price as a point of departure, ingeniously argues that the structuring principles of West African corporate aggregations, such as the institutionally "cross-cutting" initiatory memberships of Yoruba *òrìṣà* cults and Cross River secret societies (e.g., Ekpe), represented one such resource, which could have formed the social glue for ethnogenerative neo-African associations in the New World. Yet new formations could emerge only as they articulated with specific socio-historical conditions as M. G. Smith emphasized (see Palmié 1993, 343–46; M. G. Smith 1957).

Returning to the question of the cosmological patterns of the Lucumí religion, does the *oricha* pantheon follow naturally from an overarching or regional Yoruba "old structure" or "substratum," which was "reconstituted almost in full" in the New World, or was it a novel construction based on some alternate, possibly borrowed, possibly heterogeneous, set of resources and "grammatical" principles? Did "Western" religious models in any way shape the narrative and practical production of diasporic Yoruba religions and participate in the crystallization of the *panteón Lucumí*? Some answers are suggested through a brief consideration of the "syncretism" debate.[15]

The idea of *the* old structure lends itself to a common structural-functional conceptualization of a dimension of New World religious creativity, the "syncretism" of African gods and Catholic saints. Virtually every writer since Raimundo Nina Rodrigues and Melville Herskovits has agreed that Africans and their descendants "worked out" a series of iconographic, functional, ecological, and temporal "parallels" between gods and saints, though the issue of belief—whether the saints merely "masked" the gods or were internalized along with the Catechism—has been enthusiastically debated.[16] My intention is not to engage the latter contentious issue directly here, but to interrogate received narratives about the generative organizing principles of the Lucumí pantheon. In the syncretic process among the Afro-Brazilian religions, Roger Bastide observed, there was the readily apparent "*structural parallel* between the Catholic theology of the saints' intercession with the Virgin Mary, the Virgin's intercession with Jesus, and the intercession of Jesus with God the Father and the African cosmology of the *orixás* as mediators between man and Olorun [Supreme God]" (Bastide [1960] 1978, 262; emphasis added).[17] In Cuba, as numerous scholars and practitioners have enunciated, under a single Supreme Being that identifies the Christian God Trinity with three Lucumí High Gods (Olodumare, Olorun, and Olofin), the *oricha* pantheon and the roster of local Catholic Virgins and saints came to form two "parallel," but functionally distinct, "paths" or "roads" (*caminos*)—the "road of the saints" and the "road of the *orichas*" (Bastide 1972, 156; Murphy 1988, 120–24; and Cabrera [1954] 1994, 367–68).

Predictably, the formalist notion of the "structural parallel" between the "Catholic theology" and the "African cosmology" reifies both sides of the equation as transhistorical givens.[18] As Apter (1991) shows, the legs of such syncretic parallels are conventionally inscribed in ethnographies as two synchronic systems or bodies of belief that are visually juxtaposed in synoptic maps, charts, or "tables of correspondences" (see Herskovits [1945] 1966, 1966; Bastide [1960] 1978, 264–67; Murphy 1988, 42–43; Brandon 1993, 77; Ramos 1996, 60–70; Lawal 1996a, 29–33; Deren [1951] 1970, 82–83). Mintz and Price, of course, argued over twenty-five years ago that cultures—in this case, "African" and "European"—did not encounter one another as transhistorical "bodies of belief"; whatever bodies of belief are observed in New World cultures were "built" over time in specific, fraught social arenas ([1976] 1992, 18; see also Palmié 1993). Apter, combining social theory and hermeneutics, argues that syncretisms are wrought in practice, diachronically, through agents' critical "revision" of dominant discourses, such as Catholicism (Apter 1991).[19] And, as one of Apter's mentors has insisted, the ongoing outcomes of practices are always implicated in the structures they have sought to revise. Because "signs are never transparent and innovations are always partial," Jean Comaroff writes, "subversive *bricolages* [or syncretisms] always perpetuate as they change"—that is, accommodate, as well as resist (Comaroff 1985, 198; see also Hebdige 1979, 103–5, 130). In other words, new arrangements could not always "achieve congruence with older forms." From the standpoint of the recent theories of practice, arguments for a cultural "changing same" are theoretically untenable, yet they continue to be resuscitated in the current debates over the concepts of "Diaspora" and the "Black Atlantic" (see Bourdieu 1977; Giddens 1979; Handler and Linnekin 1984; Gilroy 1993, 122; Clifford 1994, 321–22; Jones 1963, 153; Bell 1992, 87–88; Althusser and Balibar 1979, 21–22; see also Williams 1977, 123–27).[20]

Bastide's shrewd emphasis on syncretism as inventive cultural work, as a strategic form of resistance in its reinterpretation of colonial ideologies, and as a dynamic, locally variant "ongoing process" (Bastide [1960] 1978, 260–71), does not mask his more facile and romantic assumption of "the old structure", which could be fully reconstituted: *the* African cosmology. Still, during his mid-twentieth-century research, Bastide could not but observe incipient purist and nationalist forces among the Afro-Bahian Candomblés, which, beginning in the late nineteenth century, sought to "resist" and "counteract" the "syncretic" tendencies of the "creoles," that is, their supposed "assimilation" ([1960] 1978, 260). Thus, Bastide, writing in 1960, senses that "the old structure" may have emerged in Brazil as the ideological production of a "'back to Africa' movement" as much as anything else ([1960] 1978, 261).

As James Wafer argues more forcefully, the "African cosmology" was not the natural result of African arrangements and the slave trade, but was narratively created in Brazil by antisyncretic, orthodox constitutencies and their sympathetic ethnographic collaborators at the beginning of the twentieth century (Wafer 1991, 56–57; see also Stewart and Shaw 1994; and Palmié 1995). Together they "struggled to make Candomblé an 'official' religion, with a status on par with the Catholic Church. . . . [One] consequence has been a certain bias in anthropological studies of Candomblé—a tendency to write about it as an 'abstract corpus of beliefs deriving from Africa' [Frigerio 1983, 45], rather than a living social form embedded in the realities of contemporary Brazil." Paradoxically, Wafer concludes, "the re-Africanization movement, while aiming to counter white domination, has in some sense capitulated to it. In seeking the status of an 'official' religion for Candomblé, the re-Africanized *terrieros* have conformed themselves to the dominant culture's idea of what a religion should be—often with the assistance of anthropologists" (Wafer 1991, 56–57). The production of "the African cosmology" as an official theology equivalent to that of the dominant religion echoes elements of a story that began unfolding on the other side of the Atlantic in the middle of the nineteenth century in the putative source area of many African Diaspora religions.

Theology and Historiography

Following earlier observers of the "extreme diversity" of Yoruba cosmology, and "skeptical about certain overly structured [theogonic] concepts" (e.g., Verger 1993, 18), recent revisionist writers amplify the case that "Yoruba cosmology," often construed by observers as a homogeneous, overarching theological conception characterized by a hierarchical chain of being, was, indeed, invented in the middle of the nineteenth century by certain "Christian apologists"—including early ethnographers, missionaries, and converted Yoruba (see Matory 1994, 224; Apter 1992, 193–210).[21] As J. Lorand Matory eloquently argues, "The most widely cited among previous studies on the *orisa* (e.g., Ellis 1894; Morton-Williams 1964; Idowu [1962] 1963) have diagrammed . . . hierarchical 'pantheons' and chains of being, consciously highlighting the likeness of Yoruba theology to Christian and Greco-Roman formulations. . . . [M]odels systematized in this way represent not what is universal in Yoruba religion but the particular syntheses of Yoruba Christian apologists and interested assertions of the sort that particular kings and priesthoods make in order to enhance their own esteem in a competetive local context" (see Matory 1994, 224).

Much of the Cuban ethnography represents the Lucumí religion in terms that echo the overarching models of West African cosmologies. It is worth considering that New World ethnographies *derive* not necessarily from "Yoruba religion" as such, but, rather, from colonial era anthropological knowledge production.[22] For example, the Lucumí cosmology is typically depicted as a "hierarchy of being" (Brandon 1993, 77; see Matory 1994). Unsurprisingly, the Christian Yoruba thinker E. Bolaji Idowu's works, *Olodumare: God in Yoruba Belief* ([1962] 1963) and *African Traditional Religion* (1973) are often cited, and utilized analytically, in comparative treatments of the Lucumí religion (e.g., Murphy 1988, 132; J. Mason 1985a, [1985] 1993; Brandon 1993; Lawal 1996a; Castellanos and Castellanos 1992). For Idowu, Olodumare was and is the Yoruba Supreme Being and Creator, and the hierarchical pantheon of *òrìṣà* beneath him are his "ministers" (Idowu [1962] 1963, 57–106). In an important summative account, which reflects beliefs widely held among Cuban practitioners and scholars, the Lucumí hierarchy of being is comprised of a Creator, High God, or Supreme Being over a pantheon of *orichas*—who, like the Catholic saints, act as "intercessors" (Castellanos and Castellanos 1992, 21). Nuancing Idowu's model of Yoruba religion by following E. E. Evans-Pritchard's ethnography of the Nuer (Evans-Pritchard 1956), Castellanos and Castellanos characterize the Lucumí religion not simply as a "diffused monotheism" (Idowu 1973, 135–36).[23] Rather, they propose that the Lucumí case resonates more with Evans-Pritchard's perspective: "una religion teísta no tiene que ser monoteísta o politeísta. Puede ser las dos cosas a la vez" [a theist religion does not have to be monotheistic or polytheistic. It can be both things at the same time] (Castellanos and Castellanos 1992, 21, quoting Evans-Pritchard 1956, 316). Finally, applying a theological term typical of the West African historiography, the Castellanos and Castellanos account defines the Supreme Being Olodumare, as a *deus otiosus* (Spanish *Dios jubilado*, "retired" or "otiose" [see first epigraph above]; e.g., see Idowu's

[[1962] 1963, 140] review of Ellis 1894; Frobenius 1913; and Parrinder 1949).[24]

The foregoing analytical representations of the Lucumí religion remain useful to the extent that some are based on the very kinds of statements Lydia Cabrera's Afro-Cuban "old informants" offered to her in mid-twentieth-century interviews (cf. the first and second epigraphs), and on the religious treatises published by Cuban and Cuban-American Lucumí and Black American Yoruba priests since that time (see epigraphs and Angarica [1955?] n.d.; Pichardo and Nieto 1984, 36–37; Mason 1985a, 2–3). Indeed, such oral and written narratives on the Creation and its attendant hierarchies (Father and Son, Heaven and Earth), and the ranked *panteón* of intercessors, uncannily reproduce many of the terms and narrative patterns of late-eighteenth- and nineteenth-century catechistic doctrines used in Cuba to Catholicize *bozales* (newly arrived, "unseasoned" slaves) prior to their baptisms (see the second epigraph to this chapter). For example, God/Olofin, created the Heaven and the Earth, and sent his "son," Jesus Christ/Obatalá, to act as the otiose High God's "stand-in," a mediator between these two domains (see Apter 1991, 245, 253–54, on the analogous Haitian case, as well as K. Brown 1991, 6, 111).

E. Bolaji Idowu and many other writers on Yoruba religion were, as Matory (1994), Apter (1992), and Verger (1993, 35 n. 12) note, participants in the long historiographic tradition of "theogonic" or "theistic" representation of Yoruba religious practice, which began with Christianized Yoruba missionary-authors around 1845.[25] Twentieth-century writers on the Lucumí religion, in turn, are the inheritors (and the more or less critical interpreters) of the Africanist literature, the modern American ethnographic tradition since Herskovits, and more than three-quarters of a century of modern Afro-Cuban historiography, inaugurated with the first major ethnological publication by Fernando Ortiz ([1906] 1973, 28–115). A resourceful researcher, Ortiz availed himself of the works of A. B. Ellis (1883, 1894) and the Yoruba Anglican bishop Samuel Crowther (1848), among others, in his comparative analyses of Afro-Cuban *brujería* (i.e., Lucumí religion). Not to be outdone, the most widely circulated Lucumí practitioner manuals themselves quote and cite many of these same highly theologized late-nineteenth- and early-twentieth-century Africanist works (e.g., Ellis, Bishop James Johnson [1899], Dennett [[1910] 1968]; and Farrow [[1924] 1926).[26] Like the African and African Diaspora ethnographies, the many Lucumí practitioner *manuales* (manuals) and treatises also present neatly theologized accounts of the religion, complete with standardized pantheon lists and convenient "portraits" of the gods containing capsule descriptions of their mythology and symbolic attributes (e.g., Angarica [1955?] n.d.; Pichardo and Nieto 1984; J. Mason 1985, [1985] 1993; and see Verger 1993, 288–89; Cros Sandoval 1975; Thompson 1983; Lawal 1996a; Bolívar Aróstegui 1990; Ramos 1996; Barnet 1997, 89–96; see also Deren [1951] 1970, 82–83, 93–150). Pierre Verger himself, although insistent on the diversity of Yoruba and Yoruba-derived New World religious practices, codified the individual characters of the Candomblé *orixás* into pithy "archetypes" (*arquetipos;* Verger 1993, 288–89, and, e.g., 79–80). The most recent works by Cuban-American and Black American Yoruba practitioners are based on systematic research in the African and African Diaspora ethnography (e.g., J. Mason 1985a, 1992, 1994, 1996; Pichardo and Nieto 1984; Ramos 1996). One can only speculate how the *babalawos* Tata Gaitán and Guillermo Castro read what Ortiz made available to them when they "drank from the fountain" of the University of Havana library (see chap. 2).

Under the pen of some practitioners, as well as scholars, not only does the representation of the Lucumí hierarchy of being—its Supreme Being and *oricha* "pantheon"—recall or "parallel" the Catholic ladder of intercession and ancient religious paradigms, such as the Mount Olympus of the Greeks, but the Lucumí religion and its spiritual dramatis personae are cast, in influential twentieth-century writings, as the literal, historical descendants of ancient Egyptian cosmology, an idea about ultimate African origins that also lies at the heart of American Afrocentricity (e.g., Asante 1988; see Apter 1992, chap. 9; Lucas 1948;

Oduyoye 1971). To this day, not a few Cuban *babalawos*, whose Ifá manuals extensively cite and quote, for example, Wallis Budge's [Egyptian] *Book of the Dead* (1894, 1923), enthusiastically locate the origin of Yoruba and Lucumí religion in Egypt. The *babalawos* and their manuals heavily rely upon intricate Egyptian etymologies of Lucumí metaphysical terms and *oricha* names in their explication of their religion. The "irrefutable conclusion" of a widely circulated *babalawo* manual's anonymous author, for example, is that the Ifá divination system and its associated *orichas*, such as Orunmila and Odudúwa, originate in the ancient "cults of Osiris" and their "doctrines of the Aats de Sekhet-Aaru."[27]

It comes as no surprise that Joseph Campbell (1904–1987), the great popularizer of the idea of a universal world mythology, was enchanted with Maya Deren's description to him of the pantheon of Haitian Vodou gods (*loa*, or *lwa*), each with "his own drum beat, his own manner of behavior, his own costume, and his own domain of spiritual revelation—through all of which, as Maya talked, *I could readily recognize the motifs already familiar to me from the myths of the high religions, not only of antiquity, but also of the modern East and West*" (from Campbell's foreword to Deren [1951] 1970, ix; emphasis added).[28] In turn, the influence of Campbell's universalizing ideas on Deren, as she reveals in her preface, "sharpened my awareness of *that which man has in common, as expressed on the cosmic level of mythological concepts;* and it was his influence that inspired me to formulate, from the vast accumulation of my observations, the meaningful, metaphysical, structure of Haitian mythology" (Deren [1951] 1970, 12; emphasis added).[29] Here the "work" of ethnography—the active production of knowledge of human groups through writing—takes the "vast accumulation" of undoubtedly diverse practices "observed," and "formulate[s]" them into "the meaningful, metaphysical, structure of Haitian mythology." Anthropology constitutes its object (Fabian 1983).

Given the highly overdetermined character of the Black Atlantic discourse and historiography—a kind of intertextual and orally transmitted hall of mirrors—the lines between description and theological formulation, and between scholarly and popular narrativizations, remain blurred. Conjoined are myriad analytical tools, textual "readings," oral sayings and hearings, popular and scholarly sources and opinions, and creative rearticulations. As Carlo Ginzburg so brilliantly writes about the narrative production of the "cosmos of a sixteenth-century miller" (Menocchio) during his interrogations by the Inquisition, "a mass of composite elements, ancient and not so ancient came together in a new construction. An almost unrecognizeable fragment of a capital, or the half-obliterated outline of a pointed arch, might jut out from a wall: but the design of the edifice was his, Menocchio's. With an unselfconscious and open mind he made use of remnants of the thinking of others as he might stones and bricks. But the linguistic and conceptual tools that he tried to acquire were neither neutral nor innocent" (Ginzburg 1980, 61). Menocchio, in narrating his material and metaphysical world and its relations, drew on "terms infused with Christianity, neo-platonism, and scholastic philosophy" (61), directly through "schooling" and, indirectly, as they were already intermingled with generations of "traditions, myths, and aspirations handed down orally over generations" (117).

Clearly, neither Cabrera's "old informants" nor contemporary, erudite practitioners, are sixteenth-century millers. Some are highly educated and self-conscious writers and philosphers. Yet various "tools," terms, and concepts from the scholarly and popular domains continue to be combined in ongoing knowledge production of texts concerning the Yoruba-Lucumí religion. For example, New York *babalorisha* John Mason's cogent list of the "ten basic components of Yoruba belief and practice," written for English-speaking "New World Yoruba," functions both as a summative description of "Yoruba religion" and as a black nationalist countercatechism in relation to the texts historically used to convert slaves to Christianity (see the second and third epigraphs). Still, the list's subordinated structure and normativizing tone both resist and perpetuate hierarchies and terms used to represent the world's "greater" and "lesser" religious systems (as scholars in religious studies used to say). The theologized "ten components" seek to convert the reader to an uncolonized, pure, true, transhistorical Yoruba religious tradition. Yet, this religion aspires—through its very institutionalization and textualization—to be an official, legitimate participant in the American denominational landscape. Drawing from one of the world's putatively great religions, Mason writes: just as "the Ten Commandments guided the Israelites, the Yoruba are commanded by every aspect of nature—to look, to listen, to be quick, to be smart, or to be on guard" ([1985] 1993, 2–3). At the same time, as indicated, the "ten components" reproduce prior oral and textual sources and traditions, including the Yoruba-Lucumí creation myth, the Hebrew Bible,[30] and the Catholic Catechism (see also Moreno Vega 2000, 253, 264–66). As Apter, following Comaroff (1985), reminds us, the "ritual revision" of hegemonic discourses by subject peoples "also reproduces their grammar and syntax, which it reconstructs from below" (Apter 1991, 254). In the case of Haiti, for example, "[i]f Vodoun took possession of Catholic hierarchies through the very gods that possessed their devotees, it also reproduced the authoritative structure of God the Father and his saintly messengers, disseminating popular Catholicism throughout the countryside" (Apter 1991, 253).

Representations of the Lucumí Pantheon and the Hierarchy of Being

In Cuba, the Lucumí High God complex took the form of a Trinity comprising Olodumare, Olorun, and Olofin (see Pichardo and Nieto 1984, 28–33; Díaz Fabelo 1960, 28–33), who appear variously in the century and a half of Yoruba ethnography as alternate names for the Supreme God.[31] In Lucumí cosmology, the creation of the world was effected through the High God's materialization and extension as Odudúa and Obatalá—the former creating the earth, and the latter, human heads and bodies (see Pichardo and Nieto 1984, 36–37).[32] A great mediating link between spirit and matter, the sky and the world, Obatalá, the "son" and "stand-in" of Olofi (see the epigraph), could easily be seen, by some, to "parallel," and be figured by, the son of God, Jesus Christ, whose thematics Obatalá regularly utilizes in more "syncretic" houses, or on more "syncretic" occasions:[33] the goblet and Host (*Santísimo Sacramento;* see plate 10, center), the Virgin of the Immaculate Conception (plate 3), and the white dove that rises to heaven from Jesus' head in the baptism of Christ by John (fig. 3.1). The association of Obatalá and Christ, and their significance as mediators between God and the world, are underscored by

Figure 3.1.—Anonymous, *The Baptism of Christ.* Note the white dove at top center, mediating between heaven and Christ's head, which is being received by the hands of God. From a cut-out from an unidentifiable old commercial calendar hanging in the house of a Regla priest. Private collection, Regla, Havana.

the striking compositional representation of Obatalá in the popular Afro-Cuban painter Guzmán's work (fig. 3.2). Like Jesus in *Baptism of Christ* (fig. 3.1), Obatalá's head and body, forming an *axis mundi,* traverse and bridge the three ascending hierarchical zones of foreground, middle ground, and background—the sky. In *Baptism,* Christ's body, framed by foliage, as is Obatalá's, vertically traverses and bridges these three zones—including a middle ground that, as in Guzman's work, features ascending triangular forms (mountains and trees). Christ's body constructs two-thirds of an *axis mundi,* which is completed by the dove and the ray of God's grace.

In a meticulously organized scheme, each modern Lucumí *oricha* came to have a determinate functional domain of action, a unique set of highly readable iconographic attributes, and a corpus of hagiographic legends—all of which are analogous to the way the saints are represented. Indeed, the most self-consciously purist accounts of New World Yoruba religion, which seek to purge any reference to colonial and Catholic influence, nevertheless read like biographical dictionaries of the saints or primers on Greek mythology (e.g., Mason 1985a; cf. Coulson 1958; Farmer 1978).

The midcentury Afro-Cuban *obá-oriaté* Nicolás Angarica of Havana clearly rejected the iconography, legends, and patronage domains of the saints as primary reference points for understanding the *orichas.* Hence, Santa Bárbara's castle and burning tower, her violent death at the hands of her father, who was struck by lightning as a show of God's wrath, and her patronage of artillery were ideas "never conceived of by the Lucumí African believers." The "African Changó's true symbol," Angarica insists, is the thunderax (*oché*) rising from the center of Changó's head, which represents "war [*guerra*] on the head," in other words, "the problems [*problemas*], good or bad, that life creates" (Angarica [1955?] n.d., 52).[34] At the same time, Angarica formulated a clearly subordinated list of spiritual beings beneath the High God, which is organized along a vertical continuum, or chain of being. Each *oricha*'s seniority is based upon its relative "closeness" to the Creation and its principal elements (e.g., sky, earth, water) on the one hand, and the quotidian, material, human lifeworld, on the other hand. Ascendant is "Oloddumare," the "All-Powerful God" or Supreme Being. Next come the great "deities" (*deidades*)—meta-*orichas* that embody the elements of the Creation and have the most "intimate relation to Oloddumare." For Angarica, these include Olofin, Odúa, Olokun, Oricha Oko, Oke, Osain, Obatalá, and Naná-Burukú.[35] Then come those *orichas* "who are most tied to us human beings" in this world, including Eleguá (Echú), Ogún, Ochosi, Agayú, Changó, Ibeyi, Obba, Oyá, Yemayá, Ochún, and so on (12–62; esp. 37–38).[36] Angarica provides a densely narrativized portrait of each deity

Figure 3.2.—Guzmán, *Obbatala y Echu—Obbatala refrena a Echu por sus Travesuras* [Obatalá restrains Echú from his troublemaking], c. 1955. (From Angarica [1955?] n.d., 35.)

and details its relation to the signs (*letras,* or *odu*) of the *dilogún* divination system (12–65).

The charming illustrations in Angarica's book, drawn by the popular Cuban artist Guzmán, strengthen, at least iconographically, the *orichas'* universal ties to Greco-Roman types.[37] Guzman realistically renders Olodumare and the *orichas* as idyllic biblical figures of chiseled Caucasian features and classical proportions, gestures, and clothing (e.g., togas). Each carries a distinctive, highly readable attribute and occupies a determinate place in a hierarchical landscape of background, middle ground, and foreground zones. For example, Guzmán depicts Obatalá as a bearded old man who wears a toga and carries a shepherd's crook of that kind that would traditionally be associated with Jesus (fig. 3.2). Formally, Obatalá's figure is nearly centered and is framed with foliage. He stands as a powerful vertical axis that traverses the landscape's three zones. Thus, in this landscape's two-dimensional design, Obatalá's body, staff, and the white mountain in the background representing his *oricha* companion and support, Oke, bridge the domains of heaven and earth as an *axis mundi:* Obatalá's head is centered in the sky between the two white peaks of Oke and touches a cloud that rises to the firmament. In the lower foreground, well below the horizon, close to the earth, and framed not by the sky but by the earth's products, the trickster and forest dweller Echú sits upon a heavy, jagged stone and holds his distinctive staff: a crude hooked branch (*garabato*), not a graceful shepherd's crook. The pure and fatherly Obatalá, arch-*oricha* of the pantheon and the creator and "Owner of All Heads," "restrains" this very earthly trickster, Echu, "from his mischief" with a firm, but benign, extended hand.

It is worth offering the caveat that nothing in this discussion should be construed as a denial that central organizing principles of the Lucumí pantheon and Lucumí liturgy strongly reflect historical, mythological, and ritual patterns among the Yoruba-speaking groups. For example, the fundamental Lucumí idea of Obatalá as the "Owner of All Heads" encapsulates the geopolitical importance and mythical status of Ilé-Ifẹ̀ as the "spiritual head" of Yorubaland and the "cradle of the Yoruba" (see Apter 1992, chap. 1), as well as his key role as the spiritual potter who created the physical "vessel" that contains a human being's inner spiritual head or "destiny" (*orí;* see chap. 4). The role of the ubiquitous Èṣù (Ẹlẹ́gbá and Lẹgba) in Yoruba and Dahomean religion, as trickster, messenger, and guardian of the crossroads, decisively shapes the invocatory protocols of the Candomblé and Lucumí religions, where Exú/Echú is invoked and pacified first in order to "open the road" for all subsequent ritual undertakings. Given Obatalá's role as "Owner of All Heads" ("head" = *orí* = "destiny") and Echú's role as destiny's "guide" and potential obstacle on destiny's "path" through the world, these two *orichas* constitute the bookends of a fundamental Yoruba-Atlantic "philosophical conception" long ago articulated by Melville Herskovits: Echú is the "deification of Accident in a universe where predetermination is the rule" (1941, 71). As such, this conception embraces paradox and irony and also revises Christian notions of absolute good and evil, as Echú clearly resists strict assignment in Christianizing contexts to the category of the Devil (Herskovits 1941, 253; see also Wafer 1991, 14).[38]

Still, it is evident that the narratives and iconography utilized by practitioners and scholars to organize and represent the Lucumí cosmology are multiple and overdetermined: Yoruba, Egyptian, Greco-Roman, Judeo-Christian—with significant doses of the European-derived Kardecian vertical "spirit-matter continuum" (see Kardec n.d.; Brown 1999, 180–81; Harwood 1977, 40). Beyond the simpler issue of syncretic "parallels" between *orichas* and saints—virtually everyone agrees that Lucumí priests critically distinguish, and do not "confuse," the two categories of spirits (Bascom 1950; Bastide [1960] 1978, 272; Murphy 1988, 124)—it is not at all easy to tease apart the more subtly constructed practical and "theological unity" that is the Afro-Cuban popular religious worldview (Murphy 1988, 124). Given the historically two-way "flow" of cultural materials (Mintz and Price [1976] 1992, 23–37), it is, in some respects, "hard to distinguish Afro-Cuban religion from lower-class Catholicism" (Thomas 1971, 1124). Yet the very possibility that "non-African" deep structures, in addition to "the old African structure," shaped the narrative and visual production of diasporic religions remains controversial in a post-1970s ideological climate, in which it remains politically correct to insist that Africans covertly practiced essentially the "same" African religion in spite of colonial restrictions, that is, behind the mask, guise, facade, or veil of Catholicism (see Thompson 1983, 18; Mason and Edwards 1985, iv–v; Moreno Vega 2000, 2; see also Métraux [1959] 1972, 323–29; Bastide [1960] 1978, 261–62; Reisman 1970). In other words, as Paul Gilroy observes, in some quarters, the intellectual "embrace" of hybridity, "which modernity seems to promote . . . is less fashionable these days. Appeals to the notion of purity as the basis of racial solidarity are more popular" (1993, 188).

It is worth seeking a middle ground. Clearly the New World gods, saints, and pantheons do not conform to either-or formulations. Just as ambiguity and "slippage" (Apter 1991, 271) define the strategic "resemblance" of gods and saints—they both are and are not alike, thus challenging "the logic of Western thought, which is based on the principle of non-contradiction" (Bastide [1960] 1978, 271)—the New World pantheons are open to multiple interpretations. Angarica's vertical chain of being, which is iconographically represented as a conventional "Western" hierarchical landscape of heaven and earth, can also be interpreted by the Lucumí as a continuum of "the other world" and "this world" (Lucumí *orún* and *ayé;* Spanish *este mundo* and *el más allá, visible* and *invisible*—i.e., Yoruba *ọ̀run* and *ayé;* see Drewal, Pemberton, and Abiodun 1989, 14–16; Pichardo and Nieto 1984, 20–23). This semantic ambiguity between "Heaven/Earth" and "this world/the other world" has existed since the mid-nineteenth-century advent of Christianization in Yorubaland and the representation of Yoruba cosmology in missionaries' texts. It is no surprise that missionaries conveniently translated the biblical God in heaven as Ọlọ́run (*Dictionary of the Yoruba Language* [1913] 1979, 82).[39]

James Wafer astutely shows how the Candomblé cosmology can revise the Christian "orientational metaphors" of heaven as "up" and hell as "'down,' which results in the popular conception of a three-tiered universe, with the human world in the middle. . . . In Candomblé the various entities that populate the universe, and the 'places' they inhabit, are conceptualized as lying on a continuum between matter and spirit. The lowest place in this schema is the world of mortals, which is identified with 'matter.' All spirit entities occupy places that are metaphorically 'above' matter. These places are themselves hierarchically arranged, according to their degree of proximity to one pole or the other" (Wafer 1991, 14). An alternate reading of Angarica's illustration of Obatalá and Echú shows that, far from locating these two "spirits" in a remote "heaven," Guzmán grades them on just the kind of scheme Wafer identifies, with Obatalá higher and closer to Olodumare, and Echú lower and closer to the human lifeworld.[40] In the Lucumí conception, moreover, rankings along the spirit-matter continuum can be flexible and ambiguous. For example, Echú is, in fact, "everywhere and sees everything": he is a "warrior" of the highly "material" street and forest; he is also right up there as "God's secretary"; at the same time, he is not merely a "mischievous" *orisha* but is, in one road, Alosí, the Devil, who manifests himself in this world (Cabrera [1954] 1983, 88, 94; [1970] 1983, 51; Angarica [1955?] n.d., 35–37, 6). Obatalá, too, defies ontological confinement. Numerous relatively more "material" and more "spiritual" Obatalás, who are "younger" warrior types or "older" sage types, respectively, populate this continuum. Ayáguna, for example, fights wars, hangs around, chases women, and may drink heavily. So much for the mortification of the flesh. And, though many Lucumí rituals, such as the *nangaré,* actually address the sky and the sun in order to honor Olodumaré, Olorun, and Olofin (see Cabrera [1954] 1983, 468–70), in practice, "heaven" and the "other world" are just the other side of "this world"; they are two phenomenologically "heterogeneous," but not remote, dimensions of the same sacralized world (see Eliade [1957] 1959, 20–24). These contrasting dimensions "mirror" each other and are joined and mediated by the "crossroads" of ritual communication: divination, prayer, sacrifice, drumming, and spirit possession (see Deren [1951] 1970, 34–36).

It should also be clear that the *practice* of Lucumí religion tends to resist and revise any hierarchized theological scheme that presumes to describe it. For example, despite the scholarly and popular literature's ranked lists of *oricha* seniority, the authority relations between the deities and the hierarchical protocols of invocation can shift, depending upon socioritual context. Formally, the ranking *orisha* elder, Obatalá, is the "highest," and Ochún is the "smallest" or most junior. Yet, these relationships are fluid, since alternate *patakí* (legends) relativize and turn upside down, at least momentarily, any given hierarchy. In one important story, little Ochún, manifesting as the unprepossessing buzzard, saves the world from a scourge when all others have failed, demonstrating that "a junior can be . . . the elder among the elders" (Ecún 1986, 141). At another level, in the context of priestly seniority, despite mythological designations of Obatalá as "Owner of All Heads," or Orunmila as the "biggest" and "final word" among all the *orichas,* the tutelary *oricha* of any given Ocha house—whether it be Ochún, Changó, Yemayá, or any other—can assume authority over the priest's other *orichas* and those of the house's godchildren. Finally, the pantheon hierarchies of the multiple Lucumí *ramas* are fluid and have changed over time, not least because of intra- and intercult politics. This is a dynamic field of contestation similar to the one that Apter noted in Yoruba towns, which have manifested "alternate pantheons . . . positioning [select] *orisa* in relation to their dominant cults, and corresponding bases of political power" (Apter 1987, 284; see also Drewal, Pemberton, and Abiodun 1989, 15).

REFORM, AUTHORITY, AND THE LITERARY MARKETPLACE: NICOLÁS ANGARICA'S *MANUAL DEL ORIHATÉ*

In the end, revisionist critiques of ethnographic representations of Yoruba practice shaped by "Western"—Greco-Roman and Judeo-Christian—theological models do not discount the strategic usefulness of those "borrowed" models in the narrative production of religion in West Africa and the Diaspora. A closer reading of Nicolás Angarica's *Manual del Orihaté: Religión Lucumí* suggests as much. Building on the discussions of religious "reform," competition, authority, and authenticity in the previous chapter, I want to hypothesize that the theologization and systematization of Lucumí religion in Cuba were, in part, strategic moves in the authority building of particular reformers, as well as their earnest attempts to create a functional, resilient, "licit," "true," "modern" religion that could weather social dislocation, stigma, and persecution between the 1880s and the middle of the twentieth century (see Ortiz 1952–55, 4:79; Angarica [1955?] n.d., 9, 81; Helg 1995; Moore 1997; Chávez Álvarez 1991).

Nicolás Angarica's *Manual del Orihaté: Religión Lucumí* was intended not only as a specialized, esoteric manual for the "respectable and responsible profession" of *oriaté* ([1955?] n.d., 26). It was also a progressive manifesto intended to address the growing, translocal community of literate Ocha practitioners who were members of the larger reading public and who had not always been considered equal members of the Cuban nation (see Helg 1995; Fernández Robaina 1994). Angarica's writing of such a manual was a strategic intervention, for it intended to insert itself into the public transcript, as well as into the houses of *oricha* practitioners. The author's "great care that his definitions be exact and clear" for the purposes of "apprenticeship elevate [this work] to the category of ORIHATE'S MANUAL" (Angarica [1955?] n.d., 9). The manual, Angarica insisted, was "more than a scientific book." He wanted to "carry the spirit of his readers [with] a book that serves an educational end, knowing as I know the religious sentiment of my compatriots" (9). Born in 1901, the largely self-taught Angarica was raised by African-born Lucumís and Ararás on a sugar plantation in the small town of Perico, Matanzas (fig. 3.3). Taken out of school by his parents at age ten after two years of schooling, he worked as a "water carrier during the sugar harvest." Later he trained as a mason (*albañil*), and "dedicated himself to building large scale houses." At the same time, Angarica always struggled to "better the conditions of life" and, apparently to this end, became a delegate to the Municipal Assembly on behalf of several political parties in Matanzas, one of which he served as an executive officer (Angarica [1955?] n.d., 8).[41] Evidently a reflection of his diverse cultural, religious, and professional experiences as a kind of activist and organizer—what Angarica called his "struggle from different angles" (8)—the *Manual*'s approach weds a late nineteenth century progressive idea of reform, science, and education to the social, cultural, and spiritual advancement of the community of God-loving Lucumí practitioners.

That Angarica's reputation and actual contribution were, and are, debated suggests that the personal, religious, and political were not so separable for him.[42] Havana's field of *oriaté* was specialized and competitive around the time of his writing (c. 1955) and included such luminaries in great demand as Lamberto Samá, Maximiliano Ordáz, Liberato Valdés, Tomás Romero, and José Roche. Angarica's writing, therefore, may have intended to strategically insert the author himself, as a professional, erudite, modern Cuban, into the hearts and minds of Havana's *oricha* houses.

Figure 3.3.—Oriaté Nicolás Valentín Angarica (Obá Tolá), student and godchild of Obadimelli and author of *Manual del Orihaté*. Private collection, Havana.

Angarica clearly also intended his magnum opus to survive and compete in the larger literary marketplace of works on Afro-Cuban culture and religion.[43] Angarica wrote his *Manual* at the end of the thirty-year "Afrocubanist" literary period (mid-1920s to 1950s; see Kutzinski 1993, 134–62), which saw the publication of the last of Fernando Ortiz's ethnographies and the first of Lydia Cabrera's (Ortiz 1950, 1951, 1952–55; Cabrera [1954] 1983). Moreover, despite some improvement in the image of things Afro-Cuban during the period (Mullen 1987; Moore 1994; Hagedorn 2001; Blanc, Herzberg, and Sims 1992), Afro-Cuban religious activity was still largely regarded as *brujería* (witchcraft), a term used early by Ortiz ([1906] 1973), which the Afro-Cuban scholar Rómulo Lachatañeré publicly challenged, and sought to replace with *santería*, as early as the mid-1930s (see Lachatañeré 1938, 1942; Ortiz 1937b; Thomas 1971, 1124).[44] In 1953, even the most elegantly printed and painted vintage representations of Afro-Cuban figures by the fine artist Landaluze were still considered *cosas de negros* (n-word things) (Ortiz 1953). Angarica thus apparently needed to publicly define Lucumí practice, and that of its parent culture, the "Yoruba of Africa," in the most benign and universalist of terms, as "true religion[s]," having as their fundamental bases "the existence of God and the immortality of the Soul, like all other world religions" (Angarica [1955?] n.d., 9; see epigraph to this chapter).[45]

Still, the previous boom in Afro-Cubanist literary production may have hurt the cause more than it had helped. José Roque de la Nuez, a kind of crossover figure—both doctor and *santería* priest—argued in his lively prologue to Angarica's *Manual* that the marketplace was dominated by writers trying to make their literary reputations without caring whom they hurt by revealing religious secrets, doing so in a mostly a confused and pejorative manner. "The erroneous concepts acquired from the populace at large and from books written by opportunistic authors have caused the religion great damage in public opinion, causing the public to flee from it—believing it to be the repugnant religion of people of low social development [*baja cultura social*]" (Angarica [1955?] n.d., 3). Invoking the issue of cultural authenticity, Roque asked, "What knowledge could those modern writers have who were not *santeros?*" Roque marshalled as his principal example Lydia Cabrera's monumental work *El Monte*, which had been published in Havana just a year earlier (1954) than Angarica's manuscript was penned. Roque conceded that *El Monte* was a "literary jewel; but its knowledge of the Lucumí religion [was] confused [*mixtificado*], as much with regard to the ceremonies as the language" (3–4). In contrast, as Angarica asserted in his own foreword, given the author's "personal links to the Lucumís and Ararás, as well as his membership in the [Lucumí] Religious Creed, he could bring to the light of Civilization, without mystification, the truth of the Lucumí religion from the Yoruba territory" (9; see epigraph).

Angarica's status as a literate *oriaté*, who claimed descent from the great Obadimelli, his systematic, cleanly theologized presentation, and the "truth" of his information would, implicitly, revise the dominant opinion of the Lucumí religion as a product of *baja cultura social*—that is, of the savage, atavistic, and dark *hampa cubana* (Cuban bad life, underworld) in which Ortiz had earlier located Africanisms in thirty years of influential publications (see my chap. 1; Mullen 1987; Moore 1994). Angarica and Dr. Roque evidently intended to turn the tables: "true religion" and the "light of Civilization" were the symbolic opposites of *brujería* and the *hampa cubana*, respectively. The *Manual del Orihaté: Religión Lucumí* would effect such change by "dislodg[ing] other texts" from the literary arena (Said 1983 quoted in Bell 1992, 82). Readers should accept no imitations!

TWO GREAT INNOVATIONS: THE PANTHEONIZED "ARCHITECTURE" OF MODERN LUCUMÍ INITIATION AND THE COWRIE DIVINATION SYSTEM

Through discussion, debate, experimentation, and the advancing of self-conscious "reform" agendas, African and creole leaders worked to theologize and pantheonize the Lucumí religion and standardize the *orichas'* iconographic attributes, mythology, and associated liturgy. The "fusion" of selected Yoruba deities as the *panteón Lucumí* was historically related to intentional, systematic innovations particular leaders and groups wrought in the form and content of the Lucumí initiation ceremony, which came to be called the *asiento* or *kariocha.* Beginning at, or not very much before, the turn of the twentieth century, Lucumí and creole leaders in Havana and Matanzas began to enhance and standardize received, variant practices of initiation and divination (Ifá and *dilogún*) in order to create a flexible "modern" Regla de Ocha and Regla de Ifá.[46] The dissemination of these new systems took, perhaps, half a century. Significant time lags between Matanzas and Havana characterized this period, and significant variation and contestation among different cities and *ramas* remains today. These modern initiatory and divination systems were both the catalysts and corollaries of the "pantheonized" organization of Lucumí *orichas*, as well as the emerging professionalized role of the *oriaté.*

Echoing the observations of Roger Bastide on the presumed shape of precolonial West African arrangements, curator and Ocha priestess Marta Moreno pointed to central innovations in New World initiation practice in her catalog for one of the earliest exhibitions in New York on the Lucumí tradition: "the first slaves of Cuba and Brazil . . . decided that in order for the tradition to survive there, it was necessary to have initiates receive more than one Orisa [*orisha*] or two, as they had in Africa. . . . In Africa the initiate received one Orisa and became part of the family and community of that one Orisa. Therefore, [the town of] Osogbo is predominantly comprised of Ochun priests; Abeokuta predominantly Yemayá priestesses; Oyo predominantly Shango priests; Ife predominantly Obatalá priests, etc. In this structure an initiate of Obatala doesn't know the other divinities. In Cuba and Brazil the *Omo Orisas* [priests] are knowledgeable of all the Orisas and participate in rituals to all of the Orisas. Therefore the *terreiros* in Brazil vibrate with the presence of all the Orisas as they possess their children as do the *casa de santos* in Cuba and New York" (Caribbean Cultural Center 1984). Though this regionalized, one-town-one-deity model does not reflect more recent ethnographic studies documenting the "clustering" of *òrìṣà* within, and their migratory movement between, towns in West Africa (see Apter 1992, Matory 1994), Moreno touches upon the historical relationship between the fusion of New World deities and important innovations in Candomblé and Lucumí initiatory practices.

The idea of differences between the modern Cuban and prior West African models, particularly that Yoruba initiates received only "one Orisa or two," forms part of the historical consciousness of twentieth-century Lucumí priests. In his c. 1955 manuscript,[47] Nicolás Angarica explains that, in "Africa, when a person was initiated, all of the Orichas were not given to a person, [that is] nothing more than [the tutelary *oricha*] of the head [*la cabecera*, as well as] Elegguá, and Obatalá [were given]. . . . [N]o African brought to Cuba had more than the Ocha that he [had] made, and [of the] Ochas de Addimú [auxillary *orichas* they had]—many of these were fabricated here in Cuba" ([1955?] n.d., 78). Undoubtedly, Angarica developed this picture from the Lucumí who raised him and the luminary who taught him, Obadimelli. Africans arrived with their "head" *òrìsà* (*oricha cabecera*); the multiple *orichas* they might have been observed to own in Cuba were mostly acquired on the island, not received in their original African initiations. It is doubtful that all African initiates received Ọ̀bàtálá and Ẹlẹ́gbá along with their tutelary *òrìṣà*. Moreover, it remains unclear whether this practice was an African derivation at all, or an innovation among Cuba's Lucumí; yet it contains an undeniable logic. The tutelary *oricha cabecera*, whether it be Yemayá, Changó, Ochún, or any other, along with Eleguá and Obatalá, are basic to a Lucumí philosophical and initiatory conception: the *cabecera* gives equilibrium to the initiate's "head," a process that greatly concerns the head's creator, Obatalá. Yet without the warrior Eleguá's guidance and alliance on its "path" through the world (the "foot"), the head would confront insuperable obstacles or lose its way.

Angarica's emphasis upon the three figures—the *cabecera*, Obatalá, and Eleguá—thus supplies clues to the logic behind the modern initiatory system. In effect, Angarica spells out the principal building blocks of what, by 1955 in Havana and Matanzas, had fully developed out of the old "head-and-foot" system attributed to the Africans and had become the modern initiation's relatively standardized architecture: (1) Eleguá, (2) Obatalá, (3) a particular *oricha* Owner of the Head (*cabecera*), which is "made," and (4) a series of other *orichas* that could be "received" to fill out one's personal pantheon, such as Yemayá, Ochún, Changó, Obba, Agayú, and Inle.

The virtue of Marta Moreno's narrative is her gesture toward the agency and self-conscious decision-making of the founders of the Lucumí and Candomblé religions. The structurally similar pantheonizations of deities and initiatory patterns in Cuba and Brazil (see Murphy 1994; cf. Sarno 1978; and Gleason 1992) not only reflect similar West African cultural emphases and New World institutional patterns (see Bastide 1972), but also show, apparently, that similar kinds of "decisions" were made independently in those two centers. Still, the question remains whether these were the decisions of the "first slaves," in a kind of foundational, harmonious social contract, or the outcomes of a later, possibly contentious, series of "reform" movements and reactions. Oral evidence suggests the latter. That is, the decisive reconfiguration of Lucumí initiatory practice seems to have occurred not with the "first" small importations of Yoruba (i.e., sixteenth to mid–eighteenth centuries), but with the "last" surviving Yoruba (including free migrants) and their creole descendants around the turn of the twentieth century and later. Indeed, some of the innovations that define the "modern" initiation system were not implemented in Matanzas until after World War II (see below).

The Miami *obá-oriaté* Miguel Ramos relates that stories circulate among his religious elders, colleagues, and the Cubans he has interviewed on the island about "a meeting of the minds that took place in the early 1900s, where the idea of giving all the orichas [to initiates] was discussed." Luminaries such as Obadimelli (Octavio Samar) and Efuche (Ña Rosalía) are believed to have been among the participants.[48] Similarly, George Brandon speculates that local "councils" of priests and priestesses may have been formative in selecting, evaluating, and deploying heterogeneous West African resources and the planning and building of the Lucumí religion in Cuba, particularly in the "integrat[ing of] the separate cults of the Yoruba orisha into a single comprehensive structure which has itself evolved and changed over time" (Brandon 1993, 136–38).

Amplifying these hypotheses, Miguel Ramos believes that the innovations in initiation practice, particularly the principle of receiving multiple *orichas* in a single momentous ceremony, were geared to increase the resilience of the religion in conditions of social change.[49] The founders, Ramos says, felt that "some of the orichas were being lost, or running the risk of being lost; and to keep the tradition alive, [the religion] had to be altered."[50] The old Africans and their early creole descendants were dying off (see chap. 2), and, as some believe, the unifying effect of the turn-of-the-twentieth-century *cabildos* was receding. The religion was undergoing significant atomization with the proliferation of "houses" too numerous to count.[51] In short, under the modern system, all initiates would incur the responsibility of learning about, tending to, and transmitting the deep knowledge of a canonical set of interrelated *orichas*—a personal pantheon—whose interrelationships embodied the rankings and protocols of the pantheon as a whole.

Innovations in two major areas of practice came to characterize the modern Lucumí religion: initiation and divination. John Mason suggestively locates Efuche and Obadimelli at the center of innovations in these two areas, respectively. His sources, though lamentably unnamed, tend to corroborate what Ramos, Pichardo, Michael Mason, George Brandon, Marta Moreno, myself, and others have encountered in the oral history. Efuche, according to Mason, "introduced the presentation of more òrìṣà into the initiation ritual of priests" (Mason 1996, 18). Given "his mother's excellent training, [Obadiméjì] became one of the architects of the modern form of sixteen cowry divination and òrìṣà initiation rituals" (Mason 1992, 169). "Architects" is an apt characterization, for Efuche and Obadimelli were planners and system builders with an eye to the flexibility and longevity of the *oricha* religion.

Innovations I: Cowrie Divination

In Cuba, cowrie shell divination (*dilogún*) not only came to realize highly sophisticated interpretations based upon two throws of sixteen shells and their permutations, as opposed to simple combinations, but also "borrowed" Ifá's highly codified format of prayers, proverbs, taboos and advice, stories, and sacrifices.[52] It is worth hypothesizing that the theory and practice of the modern Lucumí religion, including the shape of the pantheon, the religion's ritual means and ends, and the status and reach of the *oriaté*, would be much impoverished and more dependent upon Orunmila's *babalawos* were it not for innovations in the *dilogún* system. Obadimelli was apparently at the forefront of *dilogún* innovation.

Since the early twentieth century, the Afro-Cuban cowrie system (*dilogún*), in most cases, has required that the diviner cast sixteen shells to the mat twice, consecutively, such that two figures or signs (*odu*/*letra*) "come out," depending upon whether the shells fall "mouth up" or "mouth down" (*boca arriba* or *boca abajo*). The resulting double sign, for example, Odí-Ché (7-5) or Obara-Melli (6-6), is further refined to determine the sign's valence (*iré* [+] or *osobo* [–]), the class of *iré* or *osobo*, and the spiritual source of the *iré* or *osobo* (*oricha, egun, orí* of the client, etc.). Ultimately, the diviner "marks," and later prepares, an *ebó*—a ritual resolution to the client's problem. A brief diasporic comparison and contrast is instructive in identifying principal innovations in the "modern" Afro-Cuban *dilogún* system.

Though regional variations may have existed, or exist, in Yorubaland, the particular sixteen-cowrie system (*mẹ́rìndílógún*) at least as documented by William Bascom (1980) appears to revolve around one "throw" of sixteen shells to the mat. The resulting figure is related to poetic "verses" recited by the diviner in order to frame the client's issues and seek their resolution. In the Brazilian Candomblé cowrie system (*jogo de buzios*), day-to-day readings may employ sixteen or fewer shells, which are cast once to produce a single figure. Depending on the diviner's orientation or compentence, information more apt to the precise content of the *odu* or more impressionistic and idiosyncratic may be conveyed to the client. According to the Italian ethnographer Stefanía Capone, two throws that produce a double-figure may be employed in the extensive divination session during the initiation of Candomblé priests, a practice comparable to the Afro-Cuban *itá*, which comes two days after the *asiento* ceremony (see my chap. 4; also see Wafer 1991, 114).[53] In two cases, the Afro-Cuban *dilogún* are thrown once to the mat: during an initiation, when the *orichas* are being "washed," and in the *itutu* funerary ceremony.[54] That one or two throws are employed in Cuba and Brazil does suggest, but does not confirm, variant African precedents for two contextually distinct divination formats that select between two options: one throw and two throws. Still, that the Cuban system has come to rely mostly on two throws points to significant modification and standardization in the pattern of Afro-Cuban *dilogún* use.

The enhancement of the *dilogún* was formative in the building and rationalization of the emerging Lucumí pantheon and liturgy. The *dilogún* system of *odu*, like that of Ifá, is a system for classifying, conserving, and interpreting knowledge, as well as transforming the human situation through the application of sacrificial formulas based in nature's *aché*. Like Ifá, it is a generative, metaorganizing grid, which groups, relates, and ranks the *orichas*, as well as worldly phenomena, within its signs and stories. It sets up protocols for which *orichas* one needs to "receive" and enunciates the proscriptions and prescriptions that initiates must follow in serving their stable of *orichas*. It comes as no surprise that the seniority protocols of the *orichas* in the pantheon are shaped by the positions they occupy within the ranked *odu* of the *dilogún* and Ifá systems. For example, the most senior *odu*, *Ellionle* (alternatively *Eyiobe*; Yoruba *èjì ogbè*), is the principal oracular domain of the Owner of All Heads, Obatalá, and claims as its defining proverb, "The head rules the body and only one king governs a town" (Elizondo [1934?] n.d., 9, 13, 39). Indeed, serious diviners of Ifá and *dilogún* rationalize all aspects of Lucumí theology and practice with reference to "where" a particular being, phenomenon, or issue is "born" (i.e., originates) in the system of *odu*, and cite chapter and verse to substantiate their arguments. Ideas and actions are baseless without their *lógica* or *por qué* (logic or reason), which are encountered in the proper interpretation of specific *odú*. Therefore, the flexibly hierarchical arrangements of the pantheon's *orichas*, their multilayered relationships with one another, and the kinds of appropriate human actions taken in relation to them belong not only to "tradition," in some general sense, but to a scientifically and mathematically organized system of knowledge. Clearly, reference to "the *odú*" depends as much upon ex post facto rationalization as upon execution of apriori principles. Thus, if not exactly a "blueprint" for the reorganization of

Lucumí religion, the *odú* provided indispensible generative schemes for its modern "architecture."

Innovations II: Initiation and the Presentation of Multiple Deities

The "African" or "premodern" initiatory model described by Nicolás Angarica is known by many practitioners as the "head-and-foot" system (*Cabeza y Pata; Pata y Cabeza;* or *Cabeza y Pié*).[55] Following their prior acquisition of Eleguá and his companion "Warriors" (Ogún, Ochosi, and Ósun) new priests emerged from their initiation ceremonies consecrated to a single tutelary *oricha* of the "head," the *oricha-cabecera*—for example, Obatalá, Yemayá, Changó, Ochún, or Ogún. The identity of the "head" was something predetermined, "chosen" in the other world before the human spirit embodied itself in the complicated and dangerous world. The Warriors "fought" for the "head," providing it with unmatched *firmeza* and *protección* (solidity and protection).

Evidently, in West Africa, as well as Cuba, at least two options have defined the relationship one could have with one's tutelary deity: it could be formally "mounted" on the head in a complex set of ceremonies for the priestood, in which the head is "shaved." Or, it could otherwise be inherited and maintained by devotees as the object of "worship," without such elaborate formal initiation ceremonies (see Bascom 1969b, 77–78). As Angarica's account notes, priests made in Africa or early on in Cuba in the head-and-foot model could acquire larger clusters of additional *orichas* in incremental fashion. That is, the original foundation of "head and foot" could be fortified by auxillary deities, some of which are now called *adimú-orichas*.[56] The resulting group could grow to be a sizable personal pantheon. Still, the head-and-foot system apparently produced smaller and highly variable personal pantheons among local Lucumí communities in Cuba. By contrast, the most widely recognized "modern" system entails the mounting of a single tutelary *oricha* on the head and the receiving of a standard group of four to five others all at once, in a single ceremony, following the earlier acquisition of the Warriors. Candomblé initiates receive critical groupings of perhaps three, and in some cases more, interrelated *orixás* in a single ceremony.[57]

THE "WARRIORS," THE "FOUR PILLARS," AND THE "HEAD": THE MODERN PANTHEON'S INITIATORY "PROTOCOLS"

It cannot be assumed that the contemporary, relatively standardized initiatory model encountered in Havana and the United States accurately represents the patterns instituted by a series of founder-reformers in the early twentieth century. Their efforts undoubtedly entailed trial and error, negotiation over time, and variant outcomes. Still, the following picture carries heuristic value in marking significant epochal differences between the head-and-foot system that "African[s] brought to Cuba" (Angarica [1955?] n.d., 78) and what their descendants innovated over perhaps a century or more.

The flexible modern initiatory system of multiple *orichas* revolves around three principal building blocks: (1) the "Warriors" (Eleguá, Ogún, Ochosi, and Ósun), (2) the "Four Pillars" or "Four Cardinal Points" of Ocha, and (3) the "head *oricha*" (*cabecera*) or "guardian angel" (*ángel de la guardia*). The Four Pillars or Four Cardinal Points—Obatalá, Ochún, Yemayá, and Changó[58]—are included in every modern initiation, and they are the principal referents of the four invocatory "colors" of Ocha: white, yellow, blue and red respectively (see Angarica [1955?] n.d., 72–73).[59] These four *orichas*, Cabrera writes, "are the primary *santos*, those most basic to religious life" [santos de entrada/santos de fundamento . . . a la vida religiosa] (Cabrera [1974] 1980, 130). With some qualification,[60] the tutelary *oricha* can be selected from among any of the Warriors, the Four Pillars, or a host of other *orichas*, such as Oyá, Agayú, Obba, Inle, Babalú Ayé (aka Asojuano and San Lázaro), Oricha Oko, Naná Burukú, Odúa, or Dadá. Virtually a "fifth" pillar, Oyá is a crucial and regular adjunct to the principal four. She is received by *iyawós* in every case, except by initiates of Changó and Yemayá.[61]

The major difference between the head-and-foot initiation and the modern system is that the former focused upon the most essential profile of an individual's destiny—the head and its protective "Warriors," while the latter added versatility in its elaboration of a priest's personal spiritual resources. Still, the head-and-foot initiation itself, however "African" it was, depended upon the innovative Lucumí consolidation of the unified Warrior phalanx from a range of West African hunter, warrior, herbalist, blacksmith, and diviner-deity types (see Thompson 1994). Second, the hallmark of the modern intiatory pattern would be the configuration of the Four Pillars as a comprehensive and versatile tool kit. In view of that, all Cuban initiates would receive Eleguá, Ogún, Ochosi, and Ósun together, either from a *babalawo* or an *oricha* priest. Eleguá "opens the way" and universally communicates with all other spiritual forces through his personal set of cowrie shells; Ogún eternally struggles to cut through fierce problems; Ochosi is a pathfinder, provider of sustenance, and first line of defense against unjust capture (e.g., by the law); the Ósun staff, in effect, a miniature shrine to one's spiritual head (*orí*), ensures mental stability and defends the *orí* against witchcraft and malevolent spirits of the dead (*egun*). In the full Lucumí initiation, the Warriors, received together in a prior initiatory step, along with the Four Pillars and the *cabecera*, are "washed" with herbal *osain* liquids, "presented to the head" of the initiate (with some exceptions), and "fed" sacrifices in one day of complex ceremonies called the *asiento* or *kariocha* (see chap. 4). The linear and hierarchical organization of multiple *orichas* on the floor of the initiation "room" (*cuarto de santo/igbodú*) is the practical result, and the vehicle, of this first-half-of-the-twentieth-century innovation (see fig. 4.1).

The configuration of *orichas* included in any given modern initiation is a variation on a series of codified and standardized "protocols."[62] The "line" of *oricha* vessels reflects the order of ritual work during the entire initiation. As a practical organizing principle, this order—with several exceptions—sequences the protocols in which the *orichas* are spiritually invoked, presented to the head, fed in the *matanza* (sacrifice), and interrogated in the *itá* with the cowrie shell *dilogún* oracle. The line's order draws its principal logic from the standard Lucumí sequence of called, sung, or drummed invocation, the *oro de santo* (alternatively *orú*), as well as the requirements of sacrificial protocol.[63] Like the drummed or sung *oro*, which methodically progresses through a ranked sequence of salutations to the deities in order, ultimately, to acknowledge, salute, and invoke a particular *oricha* of honor (see Mason 1992, 20), the line always begins with Eleguá, the spokesman (*vocero*), universal messenger, and "opener of the road," and culminates in the *oricha* of honor, the guardian angel-*cabecera* that is "seated on the head" or "put to the shoulder" of the initiate (see below). Ernesto Pichardo explains that, like a sung or drummed *oro*, the line's order concretely establishes the "appropriate context" and trajectory for the stated goal of the ritual undertaking. "The order reflects what you are trying to accomplish,"[64] which, in the case of the initiation, is calling down and then "mounting" on the head a particular *oricha*.

The sequence of *orichas* on the floor in any given initiation is a variation of the basic order utilized in the initiation of Eleguá: Eleguá *vocero* (plus the Warriors Ogún, Ochosi, and Ósun), Obatalá, Oyá, Ochún, Yemayá, Changó, and Eleguá *de cabecera* (Eleguá of the head). The little Eleguá *vocero* (with the Warriors) is presented to the seated initiate first,[65] is "fed" (sacrificed to) first, and "speaks" first through his cowrie shells in the Itá divination reading. The *cabecera* is put to the head last—when it is "mounted"—is fed last, and speaks last in the Itá. In the Itá, Michael Mason explains, "what Eleguá says sets the stage, and what the head says ends the conversation."[66] The compound *odu* signs that come out in the Itá for Eleguá and the *cabecera*, the foot and head, the first and last, respectively, are considered to be the most formative of the initiate's life and are the first ones that the initiate should learn and engage.

In initiations of the other *orichas*, the *oricha* determined to be the guardian angel is shifted from its position in that basic order and located at the end of the line as the *oricha* of honor. Thus, the line for the initiation of an Obatalá priest would be Eleguá (plus Warriors), Oyá, Ochún, Yemayá, Changó, and Obatalá. Oyá is included in initiations of Eleguá, Ogún, Ochosi, Obatalá, and Ochún, but not in initiations of Changó or Yemayá, as noted (see n. 61).[67] Beyond the case in which Agayú reigns as the guardian angel, he is received, as a standard matter, when priests of Changó are made and is received in some houses when Ochún is made. Agayú is added to support and protect his "younger brother," Changó (see Gleason 1992).[68]

A number of the *orichas* in the modern pantheon, although they may be selected as the guardian angel—the initiate is their "child"—cannot be mounted "directly" on the head, or are rarely, or no longer, done so for various reasons. For example, Olokun (the mystery of the bottom of the sea), Oricha Oko (the earth), and Odúa (Creator of the world, time, longevity, and life and death), are grand and powerful constitutent parts of the Creation; like Osain (owner of the *monte*), they are believed to be "too big" to be contained by the head of any single individual. For example, the famous *babalawo* Panchito Febles was a "child" of Olokun who received Yemayá, Valentín Cruz was a "child" of Odúa who made Obatalá, and Quintín García was a "child" of Dadá who made Changó.[69] At one time in Cuba, Dadá, Obba, Yewá, Osain, and Inle may have been mounted directly on the head; but initiated priests of such *orichas* and their requisite secrets apparently have not survived into the contemporary era in "direct" form.[70] For some of the foregoing *orichas*, and, especially for Babalú Ayé and Agayú, the style of initiation has varied greatly by region and *rama* and has been highly contested.[71]

The versatile modern matrix of the Four Pillars or Four Cardinal Points, a kind of metaphysical switchboard or universal joint, was apparently innovated in order to permit the initiations of the *orichas* that could not be mounted "directly" on the head. As indicated, this is highly contested ground, and some houses continue to criticize such "indirect" initiations as sheer "invention," as motivated by commerce or ignorance. Thus, the following discussion cannot necessarily be generalized to all practice. It represents observations made in the course of my research in Cuba and the United States. Examples of exceptions and contested practices are detailed below.

Representatives of four cosmological and practical metadomains, Obatalá, Ochún, Yemayá, and Changó, can act as mediators or channels to an outer tier of mythologically and oracularly related *orichas* indexed to them, which are called and mounted "indirectly." The indirect initiation procedure therefore requires a strategic modification in the initiation's invocatory protocols, specifically, the order of the *soperas* in the line on the floor and in the prayed and sung *oro* sequences used throughout the ceremonies. For example, Inle, known as the "Divine Doctor" (*el Médico Divino*), a kind of amphibious figure who combines elements of riverine and hunter-herbalist *orichas* (J. Mason 1994, 82–84), can be initiated "indirectly" via Yemayá, the "Mother of the Waters," who also embodies warrior qualities through her strong connections to Ogún. In short, one gets to Inle by going through Yemayá. The order of invocatory songs, the line of *soperas*, and, by extension, all the ritual operations of the *asiento* (consecration, presentation, sacrifice, and divination), rehearse the basic sequence of Yemayá's *oro*, with Inle pegged to the end yet preceded by his wife, Abatá, and his special guardian.[72]

In Spanish, this modified invocatory protocol is commonly articulated in the following way: "Yemayá is made *con oro para* Inle," although one often hears, "Inle is made *con oro para* Yemayá" (see Ecún 1985, 101; Sánchez 1978, 82).[73] The Spanish prepositional phrase, *con oro para*—"with *oro* for," or "toward"—registers the mediation of Yemayá and the redirection of her standard invocatory sequence (*oro*) as an organizing "context" and trajectory for Inle's indirect initiation. *Oro*—sung, chanted, drummed—is at the heart of spiritual communication and mediation with the spirit world. In the "mounting" ceremonies of the *asiento*, the mediating *oricha*'s *sopera* (Yemayá) will be "presented to the head" of the *iyawó*, while the *sopera* of the indirect *oricha* (Inle) will, in most cases, be "presented to the shoulder."[74]

In other cases, the rightful children of Odúa and Ósun, *orichas* linked to the Creator, the sky, the color white, and the *orí* (head or destiny), can "make" Obatalá *con oro para* Odúa or Ósun.[75] Children of Agayú, the fiery *oricha* of the volcano and the "brother" or "father" of Changó, as well as the children of Dadá, Changó's royal "sister," can make Changó *con oro para* Agayú and Dadá, respectively.[76] Children of Obba and Yewá, female *orichas* who owned rivers in Yorubaland, were objects of Changó's desire, and, ultimately, took refuge in the cemetery from Changó's procreative force, can make their benign riverine "sister"-*oricha* Ochún *con oro para* Obba or Yewá (see Mason 1992, 262–63; Ecún 1985, 233, 253; 1986, 114, 122–23). In Lucumí myth, Obba, having been deceived by Oyá and spurned by Changó, received support from her close sister, Ochún. Like Obba, Ecún writes, the virgin Yewá (*la doncella*) also "left to [Ochún the role of] her representative in the world; Ochún would be the only one qualified to mediate between her and her children in the kingdom of the living" (Ecún 1986, 123). Diviners try to substantiate these mediated relationships with reference to the *odus* of the *dilogún* system. Indeed, the principal basis of these mediated relationships resides in their overlapping cosmological categories and sites of oracular communication.[77]

Clearly, the transition between "premodern" and "modern" arrangements occurred over a significant period of time, a period that must have witnessed much heterogeneity in practice. It is likely that, through the first several decades of the twentieth century, priests specialized in the domains of their tutelary deities, initiating godchildren to their own head *orichas*, or a small subset of related ones. Within Havana itself much variation occurred during the same period even within and among *ramas* that worked intimately together. For example, a ninety-six-year-old Ochún priestess, María Eugenia Álvarez Pérez (Ochún Niké) of Barrio Atares in El Cerro, a granddaughter in Ocha of Efuche, recently related to me that she was initiated with the head-and-foot system in 1924, under the supervision of Havana's most recognized authorities, including Ramón Febles, Ayayi La Tuán Timotea Albear, Luisa Arango Changó Ladé, and Bernarda Padrón Ochún Miguá. Efuche, according to María Eugenia, had died some years before.[78] Six years earlier, on 25 April 1918, in Havana, Dolores Morales (Ochún Coyadé) was initiated in the modern form by Ña Margarita Armenteros's goddaughter, Margot Fundora Sotolongo (Ochún Letí). It is possible that Obadimelli performed the ceremony as *oriaté*, for he had worked closely with Fundora's mother, Tiburcia Sotolongo, and had directed Fundora's own initiation several years before. As "Papo" Reinaldo Raimundo Chaguayceda related from the initiation's notebook, which he has in his possession, "all of the *orichas* were given in the same order as they are today, and all of the signs of the Itá were double signs," indicating the modern form of cowrie divination as well.[79] Though these two *ramas* had been closely linked by working relationships for years, and though María Eugenia's godmother was a direct descendant of the modern intiation's innovator, Efuche, María went through the head-and-foot method six years *after* another initiate in the same city went through the modern form.

Though it remains speculative, it may be that, under the direction of the "reformer" Obadimelli, the 1918 initiation was carried out in the modern form, while the 1924 initiation, despite its occurrence in the Efuche line, was carried out under the direction of the elder queen of Havana's *oriatés*, La Tuán, and thus proceded according to older rules. Still, as Papo learned from Dolores Morales, his *oyubona*, whether one was initiated "head and foot" or with all of the *orichas* depended greatly upon factors of urgency, if not also economics. Dolores told him that "you could do head and foot, but only when no other remedy was available to solve the problem." In other words, in a pinch, it was easier, and cheaper, to perform the head-and-foot initiation as late as 1924 and receive the other *orichas* later when they were needed, or affordable.[80] Though La Tuán did not pass until

1935, by 1918 Obadimelli had conducted initiations for the *iyalochas* Ña Margarita, Tiburcia Sotolongo, and, perhaps, before her death, Efuche herself. By 1926, when Ña Margarita conducted her last initiation, "already Obadimelli had established his ritual family" and influence. With the death of La Tuán in 1935, Obadimelli, the "king made twice," ascended to the throne as the king of Havana's profession of *oriaté*.[81] Still, because of the closeness of the San José Ochenta group with Obadimelli and La Tuán up through the latter's death (Tiburcia Sotolongo apparently lived just doors away from La Tuán in Havana's Barrio Príncipe), it seems that different forms of initiation were being performed in the same houses, or neighborhoods, at the same time; the leading participants, though they may have harbored their own *criterios* (criteria), flexibly tolerated ritual variants, even if for no other reason than diplomacy, perhaps voicing their opinions when disrection permitted or when they could claim authority over a particular initiation.[82] Though speculative, it is conceivable that the transition from head-and-foot initiations to the modern initiation accelerated during this period (1918–35), and the new form began to dominate Havana practice from the mid-1930s forward. In the second half of the twentieth century, the modern system, for the most part, has become universal. Still, head-and-foot initiations continue to be performed throughout the country, particularly in Matanzas and further into the interior, such as in Palmira.[83]

Other initiatory patterns have changed historically and also remain contested between *ramas*. Within the constraints of certain rules of exogamy, most priests can initiate individuals into the cults of most of the principal *orichas* in direct, or indirect, fashion, though, as indicated, some "indirect" initiations remain controversial.[84] In most houses, especially in the United States, Changó priests cannot initiate the children of the goddess who seems to be his ideal lover: Ochún. The depth of passion between Changó and Ochún is so great that it can run as much to "hate" as to "love."[85] However, some *babalawos* in Cuba have now countered that they find no "logical basis" for this prohibition.[86] Indeed, in the first half of the twentieth century, it was fairly common for children of Ochún and Changó to initiate each other, as in the case of María Eugenia Álvarez Pérez of El Cerro, whose godmother, Luisa Arango (Changó Ladé), initiated her as a priestess of Ochún in 1924.[87] As Cubans often say, *las costumbres se hacen leyes*. In this case, the "customs [of one house or line] are made law."

What this provisional sketch of the history of Lucumí initiation, particularly the innovation of "indirect" initiations, suggests is how the "modern" system itself may have evolved and adapted over time, precisely as knowledge bases, practititioner specializations, and directing personnel changed. Where necessity was the mother of invention, the theory of indirect initiation and the codification of the subsets of *orichas* that each of the Four Pillars could mediate may have been innovated and refined over time in keeping with the receding of certain of those "indirect" *orichas'* cults in Cuba. At the same time, historical overlap continues down through the present. And controversy is never far from divergent practices.

Some historical innovations remain hotly contested mere "inventions" in the perspective of those who consider themselves the keepers of "tradition." In Havana and the United States among Regla Lucumí (*santería*) houses, the practice of initiating the "children" of San Lázaro/Babalú Ayé/Asojuano "indirectly" via Obatalá, Ochún, or Yemayá, or "receiving" San Lázaro as an auxilary *adimú-oricha*, is a common practice, though not without its own internal debates.[88] Yet it is ridiculed and rejected as a baseless invention among members of the Cabildo Arará Sabalú Nonjó of Matanzas, its descendants in Havana, and their intimate *babalawo* collaborators. They insist that "San Lázaro Lucumí"—as received or made indirectly—does not exist and was the "invention" of one Armando Zulueta of Perico, Matanzas.[89] The Sabalú assumption seems to be that the "roads" of San Lázaro Lucumí, which *santería* practitioners distinguish from the "roads" of San Lázaro Arará, were created for practical and commercial motives in order that *santeros* could initiate, give, and receive this *oricha*. In terms of Arará Sabalú institutional interests, not to mention principles of ritual correctness, the Lucumí laissez-faire exchange of San Lázaro usurps the exclusive authority of the Arará priest of San Lázaro, the Oluwó Popó, to "make" and "give" San Lázaro *Arará* to others. Cuba's *babalawos* rely upon the Oluwó Popó to "give" them San Lázaro Arará and to "feed" their San Lázaros. For example, the house of Havana's Oluó Popó Pedro Abreu of the Matanzas Arará Sabalú line conducts the indispensable ceremonies around San Lázaro Arará in preparation for Cuba's principal Ifá reading of the year (1 January), conducted in Havana.[90] *Santeros* in the line of Armando Zulueta, however, consider their San Lázaros entirely legitimate. *Babalawos* who reject the aforementioned protocols continue to fabricate and "give" San Lázaro Arará to their clienteles, particularly in Havana and the United States. The internationally recognized Church of the Lukumí Babalú Ayé is organized around the *fundamento* of a Babalú Ayé considered to descend from the Armando Zulueta line, which, in turn, gave birth to the Babalú Ayé of the Yoruba Oyotunji Village of Shelton, South Carolina (see chap. 5). The descendants of this San Lázaro consider it to represent a strong, legitimate tradition, and those "born" from it are regarded as powerful and efficacious. New research by one of these descendants (Michael Atwood Mason) does an end run around Arará Sabalú critiques by reemphasizing this Zulueta line as indisputably Arará. The founder of this Zulueta lineage, an ex-slave called Octavia Zulueta (Jundesi), was an Arará whose still extant San Lázaro is substantially the same as Armando Zulueta's and those that followed.

Figure 3.4.—Pilar Fresneda (Asonsiperaco), priestess of Asojuano/San Lázaro (Oluó Popó), ritually descended from the Cabildo Espíritu Santo Arará Sabalú of Matanzas. She established the principal Arará Sabalú house in Havana, in the municipality of Guanabacoa, early in the twentieth century. Along with her godchildren, she is credited with the strong presence of Asojuano Arará Sabalú in Havana today, particularly as her house served Havana's most famous *babalawos*. Private collection, Havana.

Despite certain standardizing decisions implemented by Lucumí and creole reformers, the pantheons of deities present in any given locale, *rama,* and house have been fluid. Between the late nineteenth and late twentieth centuries, vast changes and exchanges have occured in the composition of local "pantheons." Some deities and bodies of specialized knowledge circulated between regions were absorbed or sloughed off by particular groups, or were lost altogether. Some *orichas* and ritual practices moved eastward from Havana to Matanzas and the former Las Villas Province, and some have moved westward from Las Villas and Matanzas to Havana. For example, the Arará Sabalú *voduns* were established by San Lázaro priestess Oluwó Popó Pilar Fresneda (Asonsiperaco) in Guanabacoa (fig. 3.4) around the turn of the twentieth century. Fresneda, a daughter of an Arará ex-slave Ma Francisca Fresneda, was initiated by one of the Cabildo Arará Sabalú founders. Pilar Fresneda and her equally famous goddaughter, Oluwó Popó Taurina Montalvo (Enujere), were the original suppliers and maintainers of the Arará San Lázaros of Havana's *babalawos*. Pilar Fresneda was the mother of two of Havana's most recognized *babalawos*, Victor "Abuela" Rodríguez Fresneda and Bartolo Rodríguez Fresneda (the Ifá grandson of Adechina and a colleague of Bernardo Rojas), while Taurina married one of Bernardo Rojas's godchildren.[91] Thus, from a migratory perspective, the genesis of the Havana Arará Sabalú *rama* is found in Fresneda, Taurina, and their godchildren. Still, from the perspective of interinstitutional exchanges and pantheon building, the extending of the Havana Ifá pantheons to include San Lázaro Arará is owed to new kinds of working relationships between Havana's Oluwó Popós and its *babalawos*, particularly in the house of Bernardo Rojas. In turn, Havana's male Oluwó Popós supposedly reacquired tools of Ifá, enabling them to partly reconstitute the office of the Arará Awó Bokonó of the Fá System of Dahomey through initiations by Havana's *babalawos*. *Babalawos* of Ifá can confer upon male Oluwó Popós the right to divine with Orunmile's divining chain (*opele*). The Arará priest emerges from this ceremony with a new title: Oluwó Popó Awó Bokonó. Using the *opele*, this priest theoretically could read the will of the Arará *voduns*, which the orthodox Arará believe never owned cowrie shells and, thus, had to speak through Fá. In practice, however, *babalawos* perform this task, turning on their head practices earlier "reformed" by Efuche, who is credited with "giving the shells to the Arará." Efuche's move permitted at least some Arará houses to divine the will of the *voduns* with Lucumí cowrie shells. In this sense, Efuche's "reform" of Arará oracular practices was re-reformed by Havana's *babalawos*.

From Matanzas also migrated to Havana the "direct" method of initiating Agayú. It was the famous Matancero Obadimelli who introduced "Agayú direct" to Havana, and hence this fierce *oricha* became integral to pantheons of certain Havana houses that adopted Obadimelli's controversial ceremonies. In turn, Obadimelli's unprecedented receiving of Havana's *Pinaldo* was followed by the wide introduction of this ceremony—in part, a *fundamento* of the *oricha* Ogún—into the Matanzas pantheons. Though Ifá undoubtedly claimed some presence in Matanzas before the 1870s, Orunmila was introduced with great force into the pantheons of Matanzas and the central and eastern provinces by Adechina (e.g., his 1872 initiation of Matanzas's Ño Blas Cárdenas) and Tata Gaitán's initiation of more than ten *babalawos* from Palmira, Cienfuegos, Camagüey, and Santiago de Cuba between 1889 and the 1920s. In Tata's wake went Havana's Miguel Febles y Padrón, who delivered Olofin and Osain to the *babalawos* of Palmira and Cienfuegos. In a more dramatic case of invention, as well as migration, Miguel Febles created the fiery *oricha* called Ambita—part Osain, part Changó, and part Devil. Ambita was enthusiastically acquired by some Ifá groups, including groups in the provinces east of Havana, while it was rejected by others. From the east-to-west direction, in contrast, a famous Osain from Palmira is claimed to have been exported to Havana by the Sevilla family of the Sociedad El Cristo.[92] It is commonly believed that the *orichas* arrived in Cuba's eastern provincial capital, Santiago de Cuba, only in 1912, and possibly as late as the 1940s.[93] Indeed, it was none other than Havana's Aurora Lamar, supported by her *babalawo* husband, José Ramón Gutiérrez, who conducted the first initiations in Santiago de Cuba, probably between the 1920s and 1930s.

Certain *orichas* diminished in strength or type as older practitioners took their knowledge to the grave with them. A widely known Lucumí house of Naná Burukú is said to have flourished on the outskirts of the Matanzas Province town of Cárdenas at the turn of the twentieth century,[94] and Naná has always been central to the Matanzas and Havana Arará and Lucumí pantheons. Still, as early as the mid-1920s, the *babalawo* Ramón Febles Molina had to send his two young sons to the house of an aging specialist in the countryside, one Bamboché, in order to learn her deeper secrets, which, apparently, were being lost in Havana.[95] Today, in Havana and the United States, despite Arará Sabalú criticism, Naná Burukú is widely "received" within the Havana-descended Lucumí *regla.* Among the Arará Sabalú, Naná Burukú is the "grandmother" of San Lázaro and is "married" to Gueró (Dan Hwedó), the old Arará "serpent" *vodun.*[96] Yet the Lucumí equivalent of Gueró, the *oricha* Ochumaré, considered by some a "road" of Obatalá, has virtually disappeared from the Lucumí pantheon. Thus, one Cuban-initiated Puerto Rican–American *obá-oriaté* traveled recently to Brazil, where this deity's cult is actively practiced (Verger 1993, 206–11; Carybé 1980, 118–29). He claims to have received Ochumaré (Oxumarê) from a Candomblé priest in order to enhance his Miami house's pantheon.[97] Within Ifá practice, certain special *orichas* were jealously guarded as part of the pantheon of some individuals and groups (especially Olofin and Odúa), never to be acquired by some who are elders today. Like Naná Burukú, other *orichas,* such as Yewá, Obba, and Inle cannot be initiated "directly," perhaps because the knowledge of how to initiate them directly went to the grave with their last adepts. The most lamented case of "lost" knowledge, and hence lost deities and diminished pantheons, is that of the Arará Dajomé-Magino of Jovellanos, Perico, and Agramonte in Matanzas Province. With the recent death of Jovellanos's Maximiliano Baró Céspedes, the director of the San Manuel Society, many Magino traditions have collapsed. Havana and Matanzas priests lament that, because the Arará Dajomé-Magino were so hermetic and often did not educate their own children in the tradition, it has gone to the grave.

Beyond the issue of migrating, lost, invented, and recovered deities, and the historical ebb and flow of local pantheons, arises the simpler question of significant variation within local systems themselves. Although all of the Lucumí *orichas* are "sung to" in the invocatory *oro* of every house, the personal pantheons of *fundamentos* enshrined in those houses vary greatly in space and time. Some priests acquire over the course of their careers a full stable of deities, through the periodic "receiving" of auxiliary *orichas,* such as San Lázaro, the Ibeyi, Olokun, Obba, Inle, Odúa, and Dadá and rank-conferring *fundamentos,* such as *Pinaldo.* Others do not, and they operate on a reduced scale according to their needs. If they have to "make" or "give" an *oricha* they do not already "have," they either "receive" it as an auxiliary *oricha* from their godparent or have another priest stand in as the giver of that deity. The most active initiators tend to have the fullest personal pantheons, not only because they have "received" many auxiliaries in order to "give" them, but also because so much "giving" depletes one's personal *aché.* The "health" problems caused by this vicious cycle require one to "receive" additional *orichas* for spiritual "replenishment" (see Brown 1989, chap. 3). One New York priestess who made Obatalá in 1974 (with Oyá, Ochún, Yemayá, and Changó) received Olokun and the Ibeyi ("Twins") at that time. Yet, her intensive intitiatory work between 1981 and the present has required her to receive, as auxiliaries, the *Pinaldo,* one Lucumí and one Arará San Lázaro,[98] Oricha Oko, Agayú, Oggué, Inle, Obba, Ochanlá, the *fundamento* and shells of Ochosi, Yewá, Odúa, and a number of others. During this period she has intiated more than forty people and given many scores of her *orichas* as auxiliaries. Moreover, she "inherited" from deceased priests, and took on from invalided or wayward godchildren, numerous other *orichas* to care for. In the most concrete terms of space, spiritual expenditure, and day-to-day custodial effort, she maintains a huge personal pantheon, which embodies her spiritual autobiography as well as her ritual relationships with countless people. In contrast, less active priests live most of their lives in possession of the Warriors and the basic group of five or six *orichas* they received at the time of their original initiations.

One of the most dramatic examples of pantheon variation between houses or *ramas* is the case of Orunmila. Because of in-group restrictions, the *babalawos* of some Ifá *ramas,* such as the "Rama Marianao" of Bernardo Rojas, never received the auxiliary "powers" of Ifá (some call them *ori-ochas*), such as Odúa and Olofin. Others, who broke away from their restrictive *ramas* or were free within the rules of their houses and secured these and others, such as San Lázaro, Oricha Oko, Olokun, Oddé, Osain, Odúa, Orun, Ogboni, Ambita, and Olofin, have sizable pantheons. Still, the sharpest and most divisive line within the Lucumí religion, which boldly marks differences in local pantheons, revolves around the politics of Orunmila and the office of the *babalawo*. As a result of divergent "traditions" in different *ramas* and inter- and intracult politics, the *babalawo*, backed by his Orunmila, works with and supervises some houses but is excluded, with extreme prejudice, from others. As an *oricha*, Orunmila is universally respected. Yet his presence or absence in practical terms—where the institutional presence of *babalawos* varies—constitutes radically divergent pantheon arrangements, phenomenological domains, and authority rankings. Houses in which *babalawos* are not welcome pay homage to Orunmila, but neither the *babalawo* nor the *fundamento* of Orunmila is present. In houses in which *babalawos* and Orunmila's *fundamento* are present, not only the content of the pantheon is different. The hierarchical organization of these houses' collective pantheons is distinct. Orunmila "rules" these houses, literally from the top down. His *fundamento* is placed physically higher on shelves than all of the other *orichas*, including the "head" *orichas* of *santeros* who live in the house (wives, brothers, children, etc.). And he proscribes certain ritual activities, such as cowrie shell divination, under his roof. Such pantheon arrangements imply something of a distinct "cosmology" and conception of the cosmogony itself; in addition, family relations and ritual relations in the house tend to revolve around gender distinction: that is, they are strongly shaped by males—male *babalawos*.

Epochal and Regional Shifts in Initiation Practice: Matanzas and Havana

Recent interviews with Osvaldo Cárdenas Villamil, the director of Matanzas's Cabildo of Santa Teresa (plate 4, *center right*), nuances the historical picture sketched so far of the transition from a "premodern" to a "modern" Lucumí initiatory system. Cárdenas's narrative offers an enriched and specific sense of historical change and regional diversity. Cárdenas narrates the history of Matanzas Lucumí religion as a sequence of paradigmatic revolutions. Still, the three major periods in Matanzas's history of initiation practice he traces, covering the nineteenth century to the 1950s, are characterized by significant time lags, overlaps, and heterogeneity.

At least three dominant initiatory paradigms mark the historical periods he identifies: *santo parado*, *obé weo*, and *aberikiti*.[99] The earliest Lucumí priests of Matanzas in the nineteenth century, Cárdenas explains, were "believers" (*creyentes*) of particular *orichas* from their native West African regions, but the deities they followed were not always formally "crowned" or "seated" on their heads (*coronado* or *asentado;* see chap. 4). As Bascom observed with respect to Yoruba religion, different individuals could have different initiatory relationships to their deities. Some people were called to undergo intensive formal initiation ceremonies in which their heads were "shaved," while others more simply inherited the cults of family deities for "worship" (Bascom 1969b, 77–78). In Cuba, priests can inherit *orichas* from deceased ritual family or natural family members, can "receive" "washed" *orichas*, which have not been formally mounted on the head, or can go through the *asiento*, in which the head is shaved. In Matanzas, some priests during those early years had undergone such formal intensive initiation ceremonies—they were "shaved" and fully "crowned" ("seated") with a single *oricha*. Others were not. Of the latter group, a large percentage were considered to have *santo parado*. That is to say, they were followers and *montadores* of a particularly tutelary *oricha*. Yet, *santo parado*, according to Osvaldo Cárdenas Villamíl, refers to a *santo* (*oricha*) "at your side," but which has not been "crowned." Such folks were aware they could, or in some cases should, be crowned with *santo* but had not been because perhaps it was not a pressing necessity in their lives. In cases, full initiation was economically prohibitive or could cause social problems—for example, stigma and persecution. Cárdenas's grandfather, Juan Villamil, for example, had *santo parado*. A *montador*, he would become possessed by Ogún and perform "miracles" during drumming ceremonies. As well, during the daily round, he could become possessed by Ogún "at the drop of a hat" in the middle of a conversation.

During the same period, however, variations between individuals' initiatory status could also reflect marked differences in initiation models between the "nations" represented in Matanzas. Cárdenas believes, for example, that the members of the "Egguado" nation (Ẹ̀gbádò Yoruba) did not always "seat" their deities on the head, but presented initiates with a "washed" *oricha* (*lavado*)—a set of consecrated stones in a lidded vessel—following a purification of the head (*rogación de cabeza*) with a special herb called *diez del día* ("ten o'clock in the morning").

The next epochal phase Cárdenas traces was marked by the "earliest" (*primitivo*) standardized and widely disseminated method of formal coronation in Matanzas. Called *obé weo*, it involved the "seating" of a single *oricha* on the head after the initiate had received the Warriors (Eleguá, Ogún, Ochosi, and Ósun). Other, auxiliary, *orichas* could be received over the course of time in additional ceremonies. In Matanzas, according to Cárdenas, the Changó priestess Ma Monserrate González was central to the establishment of *obé weo*'s rituals for washing the head (*lavatorio de cabeza*) and seating it with a single *oricha* (*asiento*). This paradigm most resembles the old head-and-foot system discussed above.

It was not until after the Second World War, according to Cárdenas, that *obé weo* was "put behind us" and the "modern *pueblo de santo*" (modern community of *santo*) of Matanzas was born, although many priests who are still alive or have died very recently were initiated in the *obé weo* tradition. Among those was the late matriarch of the Cabildo of Santa Teresa, the Oyá priestess Tomasa Villamil, who was initiated 30 October 1944 (plate 4, *center left foreground*) and died in the late 1990s.[100] The modern initiatory system in Matanzas became known as *aberikiti*, Cárdenas explains. It may have resulted from the introduction and wide dissemination of the *Pinaldo* ceremony between 1944–51. *Pinaldo*, and other imported ceremonies, apparently revolutionized the initiatory system of ritual invocation, consecration, and sacrifice. Such additions during this period resulted in the receiving, during a single initiation, of multiple *orichas*, whose vessels would be arranged hierarchically in a *canastillero*, as had been done in Havana practice for close to a half century. Still, many variations in practice, as indicated, exist within Matanzas, as well as between Matanzas and Havana. While most priests, for example, answer the common question of what *oricha* they "made" with reference to their head owner and second "parent" *oricha* of the opposite gender (e.g., Obatalá with Oyá, Yemayá with Changó), Cárdenas himself says that he "has San Lázaro and Ogún," two male *orichas*. That Cárdenas has San Lázaro Lucumí naturally confounds the Arará Sabalú. At the same time, though he owns a host of other *orichas* common to personal Lucumí pantheons everywhere, he ranks and relates to them in mysterious ways that reflect historically and locally specific regimes of practice.[101] In particular, it is likely that Cárdenas locates at the forefront of his personal pantheon those two *orichas* who regularly possess him.

MYTHS OF THE YORUBA PAST: "THE LITURGICAL CAST" IN THE MIDDLE PASSAGE, "RITUAL FIELD THEORY," AND THE INVENTION OF THE *OBÁ-ORIATÉ*

As chapter 2 and the preceding discussions suggest, the reconstitution of Lucumí religious systems meant the "building" of not one, but two, *reglas*, La Regla de Ocha (the pantheon of *orichas* and their priests) and La Regla de Ifá (the diviner-*oricha* Orunmila and his *babalawos*), as well as a series of more or less intensive links between them. The strong social and rhetorical investments in these institutional arrangements, which have undergirded divergent ways of going about the religion, have also filtered into the historiography. As shown above, ethnographic accounts not only describe practices, but also reflect and endorse particular ideological agendas. Here I show ethnohistorical narratives of the African Diaspora to have such agendas in their subtexts.

Joseph Murphy offers a clean capsule narrative of diasporic cultural transmission, which reflects much popular and scholarly thinking about the seminal role of the Ifá oracle and the *babalawo* in the establishment of Lucumí religion in Cuba. "Knowledge of Yoruba culture and the cults to the *orisha* relied on the most centralized and portable repository of Yoruba history and culture: the *odu* of the Ifá oracle. These *odu* were deep in the memories of the *babaláwos* who, with princes and peasants, were carried in the holds of the ships of the Middle Passage. Santería was generated from these *odú* and the *babalawo* priesthood assumed authority in a condensed system of cult to the *orichas.* It is upon Ifá, then, that the ceremonial structure of Santería rests" (Murphy 1981, 227–28). Analogous to other Middle Passage stories of priests who swallowed their *orichas'* stones and carried them in the Middle Passage, this linear, diffusionist narrative of cultural transmission roots the religion's original stores of knowledge in the "memories" of a specific class of West African priests, Ifá's *babalawos.* The narrative culminates in a symbolic birth event, wherein the male *babalawo* plays *the* seminal, regenerative role. La Regla de Ocha is born from Ifá, and the *babalawo,* Ifá's interpreter, naturally becomes the ascendant authority in a "condensed system of cult to the *orichas.*"

The notion of the *babalawo* as progenitor and authority of the Lucumí religious system has much to recommend it. The Ifá corpus, with its comprehensively classifying grid of 256 *odu,* could certainly exemplify Bastide's "old African structure" and its total reconstitution in the New World. Like a mnemonic script, Ifá arguably served in the recovery of the all the "old actors," the reassembly of the "entire liturgical cast" (Bastide [1960] 1978, 247), and their respective dramatis personae: Olodumare, Olorún, Olofin, Odudúwa, Orunmila, the *oricha* pantheon, the *egun,* the *babalawos,* the *olorichas,* and so on. As Karin Barber observed of Ifá's totalizing reach and unifying role in Yoruba religion in West Africa: "The pantheon as a whole and the relationships between all these [spiritual] forces are mainly the concern of the *babaláwo,* the highly trained specialist Ifá priests, who master a great corpus of divination verses dealing with every aspect of the cosmology. Ordinary individuals [and other priests], though they consult Ifá constantly, have a more partial view of the cosmology determined by the particular powers and cults they are involved with" (Barber 1981, 729). That the West African *òrìṣà* priest maintains a "partial view of the cosmology" substantiates the Moreno-Bastide model of highly regionalized religious practice in Yorubaland: The Ọ̀bàtálá and Ṣàngó priest "do not know" the other deities (Caribbean Cultural Center 1984). But the *babalawo* does. According to this perspective, the *babalawo*'s "view of the cosmology" is not partial but *im*partial, total. It is worth noting that this may be true *within* particular regions or towns. However, with respect to "*the* [Yoruba] cosmology," if it can be said to exist at all, in practice, the horizon of particular Yoruba *babaláwos* must be "partial," precisely because *babaláwos* work in relation to local cosmologies. As Bascom notes, "[e]ach [regional] listing [of gods] reflects deities of importance locally, suggesting considerable regional variation in the Ifa verses because of their adaptation to local belief systems" (Bascom 1969a, 43). For example, during the period of Bascom's research, particular deities mentioned in the Ifá divination verses for the sign Ìwòrì Méjì in the Ọ̀yọ́ region (Ògun, Nana Burúkú, and Ṣọ̀npọ̀nọ̀n [Babalú-ayé]) did not appear in verses for the same sign in Ifẹ̀. Instead, Olóòórún and Ọ̀ṣùmàrè are mentioned in one Ìwòrì Méjì verse, Ọ̀rúnmìlà is central to another, and Èṣù dominant in another (Bascom 1969a, 43).[102]

In view of Bascom's findings, Karin Barber's description might describe Lucumí *babalawos* better than it does those of the Yoruba, who may be more narrowly specialized than their Cuban descendants.[103] The Cuban *babalawo*'s "generalist" orientation, in good measure, resulted from Lucumí historical developments—the pantheonizing of the *orichas*, the textualization of Ifá and standardization of the Ifá corpus, and a century of struggle over ritual domains between the *reglas*—not from the overseas transplantation of any original *babalawo*'s role. Though individual Cuban *babalawos* are known and praised for their particular specialties ("talents")—for example, making *ebó*, feeding Olofin, confecting Odúa, singing the *oro* of *egun*, working Osain, and so on—Cuban *babalawos* divine for clients in relation to a relatively standardized Lucumí pantheon and corpus of Ifá verses. This is true, not least, because all of the compiled private manuals they have studied since the early twentieth century are derived mostly from the same sources. Random comparisons between versions of "Dice Ifá" or "Tratado de Oduns de Ifá" texts, and between these texts and what any given *babalawo* is likely to summarize about a particular Ifá sign, bear this out.[104] The Cuban *babalawo*'s role assimilated and appropriated from other priestly West African and Lucumí groups such specialities as herbalism (Osain), ancestor ritual (Egungun and Olokun), and some Oro and Ogboni society functions, which, in West Africa, and early in Cuba, may have been located in other specific Lucumí priesthoods. Moreover, *babalawos* may have laid claim to many ritual functions within La Regla de Ocha's initiation practice.[105]

Ironically, Murphy's transatlantic historical narrative of Ocha's birth from Ifá, and the *babalawo*'s "natural" and presumably uncontested ascendance, is shaped by a central mythical assumption and official ideology of the Ifá cult itself and its *oricha*-interpreter, Orunmila. "Myths" and other kinds of stories, Richard Slotkin writes, are basic "hypotheses about the nature of reality," and can act as the organizing subtexts of historical narratives (see also White 1973). Myths present the "past" in terms of comprehensible images, they telescope time, and they iron out discontinuities. Myths carry the heavy ideological implications of interested groups. Thus, Slotkin insists that we ask, "Whose myth is it?" "Who does it serve?" (Slotkin 1985, 21–32).

In Yoruba and Lucumí mythology, Orunmila is praised as *ẹ̀lẹ́ri ìpín* (*elerí küín* in Cuba), meaning "witness at creation" or "witness of destiny." Powerful Yoruba myths locate Orunmila at the creation of the world at Ilé-Ifẹ̀, the "cradle of the Yoruba." As "witness at creation," Rowland Abiodun writes, Orunmila "has the unique advantage of knowing the destiny of everyone, including the other Oriṣa" (1975, 421–23; see also Lawal 1996a, 16).[106] Similarly, Oluo Hermes Valera Ramírez, a senior *babalawo* of Havana, eloquently identified his spiritual patron, Orunmila, in this way, "Orunmila, *elerí küín*, is the final testimony. Orunmila is the deity of Ifá as well as the deity of divination, the New Moon, the first and final of all things created and to be created. And only Olofin knows those that can be saved. Orunmila [which means "only Heaven knows who can be saved"] represents Wisdom and thus knows everything, past, present, and future. He carries out the responsibilities of the *adifá*, which means, 'the consultor of Ifá.'"[107] "Only heaven knows who can be saved" refers to Orunmila's knowledge, via his direct connection to Olofin, of the "destiny" of all beings. The statement's defining conceits of primordiality, ubiquity, and omniscience position Orunmila as continuous with, if not identical to, God (Olofin) himself, as well as "God's Secretary," Eleguá, who is "everywhere and sees everything."[108] Some *babalawos* have made even more grandiose claims for Orunmila's status. At an Ifá ceremonial meal in Marianao in the mid 1950s, the *babalawo* Bernardito Rojas posed to the seated group the mystery of "whether Eleguá is Orula or Orula is Eleguá." Bernardito's famous father, Bernardo Rojas Torres, responded from the head of the table with another mystery that surpassed the first: "We don't know if Orula is Olofin or Olofin is Orula."[109]

Claims to power and authority, rooted in the primacy of origins, particularly in the cosmogony itself, are encountered elsewhere in Yoruba society. Increasingly since the middle of the nineteenth century, Yoruba kings have legitimated their rule by tracing their geneological descent to Odudúwa, the Creator of the world at Ilé-Ifè (see Pemberton and Afolayan 1996, 2).[110] Such claims and their (fictive) genealogical rationalizations, Andrew Apter argues, have made up the discursive strategies of cult, kingship, and imperial politics. Apter shows that variant versions of Yoruba "origin myths" mediated the intense political struggles between competing Yoruba kingdoms during this period. The Yoruba historiography both reflected and shaped these struggles. For example, the renowned *History of the Yorubas* by Samuel Johnson (1921) draws generalizing historical conclusions from particular origin myths slanted to legitimate the imperial ascendance of the warrior Ọ̀yọ́ kingdom over the more ancient Ifẹ̀. Ọ̀yọ́-slanted "revisionist" origin myths rhetorically undermine Ifẹ̀'s own myths of its origin, in the beginning, at the "center of the world," for they propose that Ifẹ̀'s founder, Odudúwa, came from "somewhere in the east," for example, "Mecca," not from the sky.[111] In turn, the rising nineteenth-century rival kingdoms to Ọ̀yọ́ employed a diametrically opposed mythical strategy, an "Ifẹ̀-centric" strategy, by foregrounding myth versions relating their own "original" ties to Ifẹ̀, precisely in order to counter Ọ̀yọ́'s hegemonic moves against them. "The development of two ritual fields in response to Oyo conquest and expansion," Apter argues, "generated and preserved a divided repertoire of founding myths [and summative public festivals]; Oyo-centric rituals [undergirded by "mythical charters"] supported hegemonic claims which Ife-centric rituals implicitly opposed" (Apter 1987, 13, 18–19; 1992, 27, 31). Today, the "Ifẹ̀-centric" myths, based in highly selective texts from the Ifá divination corpus, continue to be used by certain African historians to generate narratives favorable to Ifẹ̀'s "true" cosmogonic origins and "explicitly antirevisionist 'history.'" The relative and debatable status of these narratives, of course, is repressed by Ifẹ̀'s meta truth claims to Ifá's "universality" and "homogeneity." In short, as Apter concludes, "Ifá's 'historical' claims are ideologically meaningful in their opposition to emerging Oyo-centrism. They may or may not be historically accurate." Still, just as in the case of similar claims to universality and homogeneity informing the Barber and Murphy accounts of Ifá, such myths "keep the *babaláwo* in business" (Apter 1992, 34). In other words, to more fully clarify a transatlantic parallelism, in Yorubaland, antirevisionist Ifẹ̀-centric myths opposed Ọ̀yọ́-centric myths as rhetorical tools that mediated imperial struggle; in Cuba, we might say, the "Ifá-centric" myths and rituals of Orunmila and his *babalawos* opposed the "Ocha-centric" myths and rituals of certain constituencies of La Regla de Ocha, the *oricha* pantheon, and its *olorichas, iyalochas, babalochas,* and *oriatés.*

Bearing in mind that selectively deployed origin myths and metaclaims to Ifá's universality and homogeneity sustain the truth claims of particular "histories," we can return to the Lucumí Orunmila. The origin myth of Orunmila as *ẹ̀lẹ́ri ìpín/elerí küín* functions as the subtext of Murphy's diasporic historical narrative. Just as Orunmila stood as "witness at creation" in West Africa, the Afro-Cuban Orunmila (aka Orula) and his *babalawos* stood as the supposed witnesses at the "birth" of the Lucumí religion on Cuban soil. Given the Yoruba *babalawo*'s assumed total "view of the cosmology," the *babalawo,* a man of prodigious "memory," would naturally be the original, comprehensive repository of Lucumí tradition. Because of this, he would, naturally, also become the ascendant religious authority in Cuba. As Roland Barthes wrote years ago, "Myth" turns "History into Nature" ([1957] 1972, 141), that is, particular ideologically charged events into transhistorical absolutes. Orunmila's status as *elerí küín,* and the Ifá conceits that the Ifá corpus is a historically continuous, uniform, homogeneous, universal, and comprehensive font of tradition, become, then, the rhetorical markers of the Cuban Ifá-centric "ritual field."

Ifá's official claims not only attempt to repress the "variant" myths and rituals of opposed "ritual fields"; they also serve to mask the historical problem of Ifá's own practical reconstitution in Cuba, particularly the claims of continuity and uniformity. For example, Yoruba *babalawos,* such as Ño Remigio Herrera Adechina, were born, and, presumably, initiated into Ifá, in West Africa. Yet Adechina arrived in Cuba as a teenager or preteenager—prime laboring age. Joaquín Cádiz Ifá Omí, stories say, also arrived as a child. Had either completely mastered the Ifá corpus and its liturgy prior to embarcation in the Bight of Benín? Undoubtedly of great innate capacities, they probably mastered, or at least "recompiled," the Ifá corpus and its liturgy in collaboration with other *babalawos* in Cuba, such as Ño Carlos Adé Bí. Immediately, the ground of the diasporic question is shifted from the imagined transfer of an original, complete, portable body of memorized knowledge to the recreation of the Ifá corpus and liturgy in Cuba, the very kinds of revisionist diasporic questions Mintz and Price posed in 1976 and Palmié pursued in his seminal 1993 article (see Mintz and Price [1976] 1992; Palmié 1993).

The slippages surrounding Ifá's official claims and Murphy's diasporic myth are glimpsed in the mundane concession every Cuban *babalawo* is willing to make. Lucumí and creole *babalawos* painstakingly reconstructed the Ifá corpus and liturgy, an extensive project of research, fieldwork, compilation (*recopilación*), and textualization, which was accelerated with the dissemination of standard manuals and the publishing of ethnographic works in the twentieth century (see Bascom 1952, 169–70; López Valdés 1985a, 87–88).[112] The many versions of Ifá *libretas* (notebooks) assembled in the first half of the twentieth century, copies of which are now universal among *babalawos*, derive in great part from the efforts of Ramón Febles, Bernardo Rojas, Pedro Pablo Pérez Rodríguez (the threesome that transcribed the oral teachings of African *babalawos* such as Ño José Akón Kón), Ramón Febles's son Miguel, and the mysterious and controversial compiler of Ifá texts, Pedro Arango, who was not himself a *babalawo*. At least one slightly abridged version of these *libretas* has been published (*Ifá en la Tierra de Ifá* [Castillo n.d.]) and has been available in Latino *barrio* religious stores (*botánicas*) in the United States for over twenty years. During the last few years, at least two "encyclopedias" of Ifá, numbering sixteen or more volumes, have been developed for sale to *babalawos* and libraries internationally (Ofún Yemiló 1997).[113]

One standard version, owned by most *babalawos*, contains around 450 pages, though elaborated and abridged anonymous versions also circulate. The first 370 pages contain, as in Castillo's text,[114] the systematically presented Ifá *odu*. Each *odu*'s text contains its corresponding principal prayers, proverbs, counselings, legends, and recipes for sacrificial formulas, *osain* medicines, and distinct Echús. The concluding section of around 80 pages, which is not included in the Castillo text, details secret Ifá ceremonies, such as the consecration of the *batá* drums. Ironically, this last section of ostensibly deeper knowledge also "recompiles"—with quotations, citations, and reproductions of tables and diagrams—Nigerian colonial-era Yoruba missionary ethnographies. Most notably, these manuals reproduce the chart of comparative *odu* names that R. Dennett himself recompiled from extant ethnographic sources (Dennett [1910] 1968, 149–50).[115] While it remains unverified, these ethnographic texts in English, probably quite difficult to procure and read for Spanish-speaking Cuban practitioners, were probably introduced to *babalawos*, if not also Pedro Arango, by the most resourceful and erudite Cuban scholar of the twentieth century, Fernando Ortiz, who had used many of these texts in his ethnographic works (Ortiz [1906] 1973). It will be remembered that Tata Gaitán and Guillermo Castro, according to Miami's José Miguel Gómez Barberas, "went to drink water at [Fernando Ortiz's] fountain" (chap. 2). The 1969 publication of William Bascom's *Ifa Divination* (1969a) has served similar purposes. A group of New Jersey *babalawos* privately translated this precious work into Spanish; however, they utilize it not as a "bible," but as one source among others for further *recopilación:* for recovering "lost" bits of information, and adding them to their own expanding stores of knowledge.[116]

The fluid, generative, and variant, rather than fixed, quality of the corpus is evident within the terms of Ifá's own narrative forms of knowledge production. Ifá could never be a static African survival. The West African Ifá corpus was historically built on divinatory precedent, a kind of "case law" principle, and the Afro-Cuban Ifá corpus is no different. Ifá speaks in Spanish of nuclear war, plane crashes, cancer, and AIDS, and its *babalawos* make predictions about the fortunes of the Cuban Revolution and its leader Fidel Castro. Not only are the *historias* of the *odu* saturated with the Cuban cultural experience, but also, as Rafael L. López Valdés argues, their original Yoruba "poetic form" has been shaped in Cuba by Spanish literary and popular narrative forms. At the same time, reflecting the dynamic of creolization and re-Africanization, "certain *babalawos* have consciously returned to the roots, motivated by the desire to find in the original Yoruba sources an enrichment and higher level of faithfulness from the religious point of view" (López Valdés 1985a, 87–88). Of course, such "recovery" projects are also innovative cultural work.

Finally, within the epistemological and performative terms of Ifá practice, the corpus resists textual containment and limitation; no single text could ever be "comprehensive." "Ifá"—a kind of spiritual map of the Creation, its evolution, and all possible human experience—cannot be apprehended and comprehended by a single knowing subject, as a whole, all at once. As *babalawos* themselves insist, Ifá knowledge is inherently distributed (*repartido*) and shared (*compartido*) among the consecrated mortal interpreters of Ifá, the *babalawos*. Any given text can represent, but not exhaust, what "Ifá says" (*dice Ifá*).[117] "Ifá" is, therefore, a discursive practice, a dynamic of collective performance, reciprocally built mastery, and the counterpoint of remembering and forgetting, which are constructed around the ladder of seniority within the institution of La Regla de Ifá. For example, in the complex divination sessions that require the presence of at least three *babalawos* (*bajón de orula*), the interpretation of any given Ifá *odu* figure is collective and unfolds diachronically. Interpretation begins with the most junior *babalawo* present and moves to the most senior. At large events, such as the annual Ifá "Reading of the Opening of the Year" on 1 January, several hundred *babalawos* may "speak" (*hablar*), in turn, according to their "years in Ifá." The reiteration and summary of basic details and stories by the juniors, who may not yet have the analytical and synthetic capacity of more mature *babalawos*, reminds elders of forgotten details and can inspire them to make connections and commentary at a higher level.[118] In short, a *babalawo*'s virtuosity is performed not by reading from the Ifá *libreta*, but by spinning out wise and logical interpretations from an *odu*'s multilayered contents.

Still, a grand textualist fallacy, as well as the rhetorical thrust of Murphy's Ifá-centric diasporic myth, reappear in the title of a recently published version of the Ifá corpus: *The Sacred Ifa Oracle: The First English Translation of the Complete Sacred Texts of Ifa—the Ancient African Religion Underlying Santeria, Candomblé, and Vodun* (Epega and Neimark 1995). Here Ifá "underlies" the three major diasporic condensed systems of cult that can claim Yoruba provenance in Cuba, Brazil, and Haiti. "Ifá" emerges as a "religion" in itself, and the three are its diasporic offspring. Moreover, the book's title foregrounds two familiar rhetorical claims of the cult of Ifá: comprehensiveness and primacy. Presumably, all that was necessary to produce this work was the "translation" of the extant "complete sacred texts." Our enchantment by Ifá's textualization in the twentieth century has made us forget that Ifá is still significantly an oral tradition, whose practice revolves, not least, around the virtuosity of improvisation (see Drewal 1992). Despite the work's systematic presentation of each *odu*, with its proverbs, prayers, legends, and a helpful "western observation" of its meaning, the Epega and Neimark text still functions in practice not as a "bible," but as one resource, among others, for reference and *recopilación*. It must be incorporated into any given *babalawo*'s performance of his competence in any local social and ritual setting.

Cuba's Ifá-Centric and Ocha-Centric Ritual Fields

With the insights of the conflict model that Apter applied to Yoruba kingdoms and religious ritual, we can understand that the *babalawo*'s official claims—the rhetorical markers and ammunition of the Cuban Ifá-centric "ritual field"—are historically meaningful within a determinate arena of contested authority and discursive struggle (see Apter 1992, 84–87; Lloyd 1968). This arena includes alternative ritual fields that relativize or reject—in a word, "revise"—the *babalawo*'s claims to ascendant authority. What I have in mind is an "Ocha-centric" ritual field that historically emerged alongside, and, in opposition to, its Ifá-centric counterpart, armed with its own rhetorical tools. Indeed, the two ritual fields were mutually constituted, that is, emerged in a battle of claims, counterclaims, reforms, and reversions. The "Ocha-centric" and "Ifá-centric" ritual fields are presented here as ideal forms for heuristic purposes. In practice, they constitute a continuum of numerous variations.

Though *babalawos* possessed great knowledge of Lucumí myth and ritual, they did not, and could not, do everything. *Babalawos* could not "make" (initiate) priests of the cults of the *orichas* of the Lucumí pantheon, and they could not divine with the *orichas'* own "mouths," the cowrie shells through which the *orichas* "speak" in oracular sessions called *itá*. The *orichas'* immediate custodians were to be found in another class of priesthood: the *babalorichas, iyalorichas,* and *olorichas* of La Regla de Ocha and their own master of ceremonies, the *obá-oriaté*. While the *babalawo* has been a respected figure appealed to by many Ocha practitioners, the idea that "the *babalawo* priesthood assumed authority in a condensed system of cult to the *orichas*" (Murphy 1981, 227–28) deemphasizes the institutional duality of the Lucumí religion and, most important, the overlapping and contested domains within it. La Regla de Ocha and La Regla de Ifá are historically distinct "systems of cult," which are vertically or horizontally linked—or not linked at all—depending upon the practices and politics of particular houses and their *ramas*.

As I argued above, the shape of any given historical and ethnographic picture, as in the case of Yoruba historiography, depends upon who authors it. In other words, whose myth is it? Not a few summative studies of Cuban Lucumí religion identify the *babalawo* as ascendant in the priestly "hierarchy of power and prestige," locating him at the apex of graphically represented initiatory pyramids (see e.g., Sánchez 1978, 33; Brandon 1983, 512; Pichardo and Nieto 1984, 32; Castellanos and Castellanos 1992, 84–85).[119] As it turns out, Murphy's account, which defines *babalawo* as the "high priest of santería" (1988, 175), revolves significantly around his formative fieldwork relationship with a prominent New York *babalawo* (Francisco "Pancho" Mora Ifá Morotí). Julio Sánchez's comprehensive ethnography of Lucumí religion in Puerto Rico (1978), which foregrounds Ifá-centric voices, was, according to Miguel Ramos, shaped by the religious system of the influential Cuban *babalawo* Roberto Bolufer, who had established Ifá on that island in the 1970s (see chap. 2; and Cintrón 1979). Lydia Cabrera's summative and normativizing accounts published in exile inscribe ritual models that revolve around the *babalawo*'s ascendance and supervision (Cabrera 1980, 181–84; [1974] 1980, 138, 148, 149, 158, 167). In contrast, her earlier, more open-textured ethnographic compilation, *El Monte* (Cabrera [1954] 1983), features diverse voices, myths, and statements collected from her "old informants" in Havana and Matanzas at midcentury, which can be taken to support a range of ideological positions.[120]

For example, in her exile works a conservative "*Olúo* [*babalawo* of rank] very interested in proceeding correctly without altering the tradition" informed Lydia Cabrera that the *babalawo* customarily held a series of prerogatives within Ocha initiation. These included the *babalawo*'s exclusive right to perform a number of ritual tasks, including the preparation of the Warriors, determining the *oricha* owner of the Ocha neophyte's head, conducting the initiation's crucial opening divination session and sacrifice (*la vista* and *ebó de entrada;* see chap. 4), consecrating its herbal *osain* infusions, and executing its intensive animal sacrifices (*la matanza*), among other things (see Cabrera 1980, 182–84, [1974] 1980, 149, 158).[121] Rationalized theologically from the Ifá-centric perspective, Orunmila is exclusively authorized by the High God, Olofin, to conduct these rituals. The *babalawo*'s prerogatives are concretely maintained through the exchange of traditional ritual tributes (*derechos*), marked sums of money for each task the *babalawo* carries out on behalf of Orunmila.[122] Where such tasks are denied the *babalawo*, Orunmila feels that he has been the object of a *falta de respeto* and a *negación de derecho*—a lack of "respect" and the denial of obligatory ritual payment. "But one must agree," Cabrera's conservative Oluo concedes, that "the old *babalawos* were a bit too despotic [*déspota*] and they wanted to dominate [*avasallar*] the *santeros*. The *santeros* thus went slipping out of their yoke." As a result, as the conservative Oluo argues, the *santeros* took over many of these key tasks in Ocha initiation and "usurped the (*derechos*)" collected by Orunmila's representatives (Cabrera 1980, 184). According to Teodoro Díaz Fabelo in his 1960 Ifá-centric ethnographic work, through sheer unscrupulousness and mercenary considerations, such *santeros* undermine Ifá's primordial standards of ritual correctness: "today, there are *babaloshas* and *iyaloshas* [in Cuba] who ignore the traditional rules [of using Orunmila] with secret motives: they do it in order to save the *derecho* to the *babalawo* and avoid his reprimand for the reckless way in which they conduct their rituals" (Díaz Fabelo 1960, 71).

The narratives of the conservative Oluo and Díaz Fabelo's ethnography implicitly situate the fulcrum of historical change around the opposed terms of tradition and modernity. Ancient "tradition" and original canons of ritual correctness have suffered because of mercantile considerations, though, as the Oluo concedes, the *santeros*, like abused serfs, had some reason to seek liberation from their feudal "yoke." Nevertheless, their historical message reproduces Murphy's myth: in the beginning was Orula, *elerí küín*, his *babalawos*, and a single, unified canon of ritual correctness, "respect," and tribute obligation. As they formalized their *regla* from the end of the nineteenth century through the first half of the twentieth century, *babalawos* would daily be confronted with the presence of a powerful class of professionalized ritual authority within the emerging modern Regla de Ocha: a capable male[123] master of ceremonies, who would sometimes be their ally and sometimes their rival: the *obá-oriaté*.

The Emergence of the Obá-Oriaté

The *obá-oriaté*, the "king" and "head of the mat" (i.e., of initiation and divination ceremonies), was crucial to the development of a modern Regla de Ocha.[124] A highly trained diviner of the enhanced *dilogún* cowrie shell oracle, the *obá-oriaté* (hereafter *oriaté*) is also called *italero*, after the cowrie divination readings (*itá*) he performs during initiations and major sacrifices (*ebó*). Apparently without precise African antecedents, the *oriaté*'s role was both the corollary and catalyst of the condensed Lucumí pantheon within La Regla de Ocha. Still, the *oriaté*'s bailiwick and authority were made, not given; they had to be established through rhetorical persuasion and practical struggle—not least through the publication of professionalized manuals, such as Angarica's *Manual del Orihaté: Religión Lucumí*.

First, prior to the relative standardization of the *oriaté*'s office and the modern form of initiation, it is likely that various priests specialized in the initiations of their own tutelary head *orichas*, or smaller, related groups of them—a reflection of more regionally differentiated "premodern" or "African" arrangements in Cuba.[125] Moreover, though recognized masters of ceremonies undoubtedly led initiations in Matanzas and Havana prior to Obadimelli's formalization of the *oriaté*'s role, the many specialized tasks of the locally and regionally variant forms of initiation were probably distributed among a number of skilled participants. In contrast, the professionalized *oriaté*'s knowledge and practical skills would come to represent a microcosm of the modern pantheon and its codified liturgy. With his godfather and teacher Obadimelli always at the forefront of his thinking, Nicolás Angarica insisted that the *oriaté* must "have knowledge of *everything* related to Ocha" ([1955?] n.d., 73, 113; emphasis added). Over and above even the most exceptional and prolific *madrina* or *padrino* of a *casa-templo*, the *oriaté* should play a leading and encompassing role: "The fact that your Madrina or

Padrino has marked down in their *libreta* [initiatory ledger] 50, 100, or 200 godchildren does not mean that this or that godparent has the vast knowledge of what is required to *administer a community*" (76; emphasis added). In general, the *oriaté* should be the "guide of the house, of its Madrina or Padrino, and the one directly responsible for the good and the bad that is realized" (76). Specifically, *oriatés* should be "the ultimate directors [*máximos dirigentes*] of our religion . . . because they make the Santo [initiation] and *direct all the ceremonies from beginning to end*" (112; emphasis added). Every house must "find a capable Oriaté to officiate in their rites of consecration, and if they don't, it is a profanation," Angarica admonished his readers (77).

Second, during the period of the *oriaté*'s emergence as a visible and widely respected figure in Havana (c. 1900–1940s), the many critical roles within the various phases of Ocha initiation—godfather of the Warriors (*padrino de guerreros*), diviner, herbalist (*osainista*), leader of invocatory songs (*akuón*), ritual "shaver" of the initiate's head (*afarí*), sacrificer of animals (*onichegún*), and so on—were apparently shared and contested among *babalawos*, the male and female godparent-heads of Ocha houses (*padrinos* and *madrinas*), and male and female *oriatés* (see Cabrera 1980, 184; [1957] 1986, 46, 32, 267; [1954] 1983, 88; [1974] 1980, 166–67). Though several of the revered early *oriatés* were women, such as Ayayi La Tuán Timotea Albear and Guillermina Castel (Angarica [1955?] n.d., 113), the professionalized *male oriaté* in the tradition of Obadimelli, Angarica's teacher, eventually came to control many (or all) of these tasks on the continuum between the Ifá- and Ocha-centric ritual fields. Cabrera's sources in *El Monte*, for example, suggest that both male and female *oricha* priests prepared the Ocha neophyte's Eleguá ([1954] 1983, 88); female priests like La Tuán in Havana and Ma Monserrate González in Matanzas, just as in the Brazilian Candomblé, washed and shaved heads (see Sarno 1978), and women, as well as men, sacrificed animals, including four-legged animals, with the knife (Gómez Abreu 1982).[126] Such decentralization and heterogeneity of Ocha practice apparently existed up through the time of Angarica's writing (c. 1955; Cabrera [1954] 1983, 88); otherwise, he would not have felt compelled to address these issues so emphatically in a normativizing and standardizing "manual."

The *oriaté*'s comprehensive knowledge of the pantheon and his associated ritual skills (shaver, singer, herbalist, sacrificer, diviner), and his "ultimate" "administrative" authority over houses of Ocha, make him rather like the Yoruba *babalawo* of Karin Barber's account and the Lucumí *babalawo* of Joseph Murphy's diasporic narrative. Where the knowledge and capacity of the Ocha *madrina* or *padrino* will be "partial" (see Barber 1981, 729), according to Angarica, that of the *oriaté* will encompass "everything related to Ocha." Moreover, the *oriaté*'s job description, the "direct[ion of] all the ceremonies from beginning to end," literally defines the *babalawo* out of the initiatory picture. Indeed, Angarica's *Manual* covers the entire range of Ocha practices without significant mention of the *babalawo*.[127] *Babalawos* simply do not appear in this institutional world, though, at the time of Angarica's writing, more than two hundred worked in Havana (Bascom 1952). Angarica's *Manual* delimited the domain of Ocha practice in a way that did not include the *babalawo*, and most examples of this genre, down to the present day, follow suit (see Ecún 1985).[128]

VARIANT INITIATORY MODELS OF OCHA INITIATION

Virtually every aspect of Lucumí initiatory practice has been debated among houses of Ocha and Ifá for more than 150 years. Very significant variation has always existed across any sample of houses, as much as twentieth-century ethnographers have attempted to describe, and even normativize, a model of Ocha initiation (see Sánchez 1978, 33; Cabrera [1974] 1980, 120–234; Murphy 1988, 92–113; Brandon 1983, 355–435; Castellanos and Castellanos 1992,

80–85). In practice, there is no single standardized initiatory scheme. The Lucumí "ritual system" is, in fact, a dynamic arena of motivated and competing ritual systems, or "ritual fields," which can be accounted for historically. Moreover, no few cases of idiosyncracy, incompetence point to and unscrupulousness point to a Pandora's box of divergent practices.[129]

A continuum of variant and competing "traditions"—that is, traditional*ized* sets of practices—emerged in Cuba in the twentieth century, based on years of debate, reorganization, and innovation. On one extreme was an "Ifá-centric" ritual field dominated by the *babalawo,* who "administers" an Ocha community under the umbrella of his own "house of Ifá." Here, Orunmila is the cosmological and practical "head." On the other extreme was an entirely "Ocha-centric" ritual field administrated and guided by the *obá-oriaté,* in addition to the *madrinas* and *padrinos* of the Lucumí religion's "houses of Ocha." Here, the *orichas* of these latter *babalorichas* and *iyalorichas,* under the administrative authority of the *oriaté,* are the leading heads. Along the continuum in between emerged a pragmatic and shifting set of fields that relied on the services of one, the other, or both, depending upon ritual context, necessity, and politics within and between *reglas, ramas,* and houses.

Within the Ifá-centric field, the receiving of the Warriors and the "Hand of Orula" (*mano de orula*) constitutes strict, hierarchical bonds of ritual kinship between a *babalawo* and his Ifá "godchildren" (*ahijados*). Upon receiving the Warriors, these "godchildren" are "in the *babalawo*'s house" and, therefore, subject to his Orula's supervision and final word in important matters. Acting on behalf of Orula, with the exclusive authorization of the High God, Olofin, the *babalawo* is, in this view, the religion's gatekeeper and principal religious authority. He is the new member's primary "godparent." The Echú of the *guerreros de babalawo* is clearly distinguished by Orunmila's green and yellow beads, which are embedded prominently around the blade and rooster feather protruding from the top of Echú's cement head (fig. 4.22, *center foreground*). Next received from the *babalawo* is the *mano de orula,* which consists of a green-and-yellow-beaded necklace and bracelet worn by the recipient around the neck and left hand, respectively, as well as a set of consecrated Ifá divination palm nut kernels (*ikín*), among other things, contained in a little *sopera.*[130] These two initiatory passages are spiritually and logically linked, some believe, for the *babalawo*'s Echú is, in effect, a "road," "adjunct," or "right hand" of Orula himself. Indeed, each *odu* of the Ifá divination system features its particular Echú, and the *babalawo* should fabricate and name an Echú according to divination signs related to his client-godchild's own destiny. This connection between Orula and Echú assumes a ritual protocol. In the strictest *babalawo* houses, no one other than a *babalawo* is permitted to "feed" this Echú, and its green and yellow beads should throw up a red flag to anyone (e.g., an *oriaté*) asked to do so. In other words, its presence indicates a *babalawo* rightfully waiting in the wings as the legitimate *padrino* of the initiate.[131] Depending upon the house, there is considerable wiggle room. In many cases, the *babalawo* understands that the initiate will be provided with an Eleguá—the Ocha counterpart, stand-in, or even substitute for Orunmila's Echú. In this way, this Eleguá, in harmony with the other *orichas* made and received in the initiation, can be washed, fed, presented to the head, and interrogated with the *dilogún* by the *oriaté* (see below).

In a *babalawo*'s house, his Ifá godchildren receive the *collares*—four to six color-coded *oricha* necklaces—from an Ocha priest or priestess, often the *babalawo*'s wife, who becomes their *padrino* or *madrina* "in *santo.*"[132] In strict houses, the *guerreros de babalawo* are received first, the *mano de orula* second, and the *collares* of Ocha third. A minor, but symbolically important, ceremony within the Ocha initiation throws into relief the *babalawo-padrino*'s primary role in Ifá-centric houses. Prior to the "shaving" ceremony conducted by the *oriaté,* the *babalawo* is ceded the role of "presenting the razor to the head" of the initiate (see Ecún 1985, 37), a form of blessing from Orula that symbolizes the transfer of the "head" of *his* Ifá godchild to the *padrino* or *madrina* of Ocha.[133]

In the Ochá-centric configuration, new members of the religion are linked to the *padrino* or *madrina* of an Ocha house through receiving the *collares*. Then, the *guerreros de santero* are received from their Ocha godparent or from an *oriaté*. In the last case, the recipient gains an additional *padrino*, who is not a *babalawo*, but a *santero*. This *oriaté-padrino* of the Warriors may be quite influential as one of the recipient's formative connections to the religion, and his influence may continue if he is important to the house—for example, if he works steadily as the house's "administrator" (see Brandon 1983, 366; M. Mason 1994). Within the Ifá-centric scenario, one can come to have as many as four concurrent *padrinos:* two (male) in La Regla de Ifá (*padrino* and *oyubona*) and two in La Regla de Ocha (Ocha *padrino* and *oyubona*). In contrast, in the Ocha-centric scenario, one can have three *padrinos*, including the *oriaté*, entirely within the domain of La Regla de Ocha.[134] In short, a person is either connected spiritually and socially *between* the two *reglas*, or connected entirely *within* La Regla de Ocha. The former configuration prepares and predicts one protocol and set of ritual expectations; the latter, another. The wires may or may not get crossed, depending upon the choices elders and godchildren make.

The ritual kinship links one has with Ifá predict, but do not ensure, that the ascendant authority of Orula will be carried forward with each succeeding generation within houses of Ocha. Ocha priests who "come from a house of a *babalawo*" are supposed to "use a *babalawo*" in the advancement of their own godchildren. Ocha priests who do not use *babalawos*, because their *rama* does not, or because they broke with a particular Ifá house, do not rely upon the *babalawo* for *guerreros*, divination readings, and other kinds of services. Ocha-centric priests often dismiss *babalawos* as arrogant interlopers in the field of Ocha. In contrast, *babalawos* and their Ocha defenders like to note that Ocha-centric priests reject the *babalawo*'s authority for purely personal or mercenary motives and, thus, deprive their godchildren of Orula's protection and wisdom, but "whenever they [themselves] have a big problem they run to the *babalawo* for help."[135] In many cases, out of preference or problems, godchildren shift alliances or find themselves in houses that have shifted alliances. Because *babalawos* often reject the Warriors made by *santeros*, as well numerous other powers they define as the "frauds" and "inventions" that "usurped" Orula's *derechos*,[136] they normally require new godchildren to receive the *guerreros de babalawo*, and sometimes even the *mano de orula*. Conversely, Ocha-centric houses require new godchildren who bring with them the *babalawo*'s Echú to receive a new one made by a *santero* (see also González Wippler 1989, 31, 168). Each side may regard the other's *guerreros* as a limited resource at best and a potentially "negative" and "dangerous" unknown at worst.[137] *Babalawos* who expect the *oriaté* or *padrino* to fabricate an Eleguá of Ocha for the initiation will feed Orula's Echú and Ocha's Eleguá in the same ceremony. *Padrinos* and *oriatés* who disparage, fear, or otherwise discount Orula's Echú simply put him aside, explaining, at best, that the Echú's presence in the "Ocha context" is inappropriate or irrelevant, adding that "your Echú understands this, because he should not be fed by an *oriaté*."[138] At worst, they may order the godchild to "get that fucking Echú out of here."

Ifá-Centric Rhetoric: There Are Many Orichas but Only One Orula: "Taking Out the Guardian Angel"

One of the greatest divergences between the protocols of Ifá-centric and Ocha-centric houses is found in the domain of divination, in particular, the relative oracular authority that is granted to the *babalawo*'s Ifá system versus the Ocha priest's cowrie system (*dilogún*). Ifá-centric houses regard Ifá divination as the firmest, truest, most definitive method for the revelation of an individual's destiny (*orí*), in particular, the momentous determination of the guardian angel, the *oricha* "owner of the head." Ocha-centric houses, in contrast, confidently employ an *oriaté*, or the *padrino/madrina,* who casts the *dilogún* to identify, or "take out" (*sacar*), the guardian angel, often followed by a confirmatory session with the *dilogún* of the initiating godparent's head *oricha* if needed.

Babalawos and *oriatés* who debate this issue rely on divergent interpretations of their divination systems and cosmologies and mobilize variant myths of origin to support their interpretations. Ifá-centric rhetoric predictably emphasizes Orula's cosmogonic primacy and unique spiritual insight, which derive from his position as "Witness at Creation," his closeness to Olofin and Odudúwa, (the creator-*oricha* who mediates heaven and earth, life and death), and his unmatched knowledge of the "destiny" (*orí*) of all beings—humans and *orichas.* A saying marshaled by several Ifa-centric priestesses of New Jersey's Temple Bonifacio Valdez explains their fidelity to Orula, and by extension, to the *babalawo:* "There are many *orichas* but only one Orula." In other words, though the *orichas* are normally subject to the calming, governing "head" of the Ocha pantheon's "father," Obatalá, they remain a multifarious, volatile, and self-interested bunch of characters who regularly quarrel among themselves—a cosmological dramatis personae that is mirrored by the *orichas'* idiosyncratic "representatives" on earth, the heterogeneous male and female priests of La Regla de Ocha. In contrast, Orula is known as unitary, disinterested, highly rational, controlled, and judicious. A saying similar to the first emphasizes the problematic sovereignty of so many *oricha* "houses": "The *orichas* have many houses (*ilés*) but Orula really only has one house"—meaning that all of Orula's *babalawos* are unified under one law and speak uniformly on Orula's behalf.

As is evident, the contest between Ifá-centric and Ocha-centric ritual fields is gendered. A crucial link in a great patriarchal chain of being, Orula mirrors the oneness of Olofin, who is gendered as male, and transmits Olofin's word down through the homosocial ritual fraternity of male "fathers of the secret," the *babalawos.* Ifá-centric priests and their *babalawos* thus believe that Orula was given ultimate authority by Olofin (God) to "settle disputes" among all the *orichas* and their "houses." Ifá-centric priests believe that Olofin, the lawgiver, accorded Orula the first, last, and most accurate "word" on the destiny (*orí*) of individuals. In contrast, they believe the *dilogún* system that Ocha priests utilize on behalf of the *orichas*—powerful and accurate though it is—reflects the timely and limited desires, outlook, and biases of the multifarious *orichas.* Orunmila's own name, as *babalawos* like to say, means "*Only* heaven knows who can be saved."[139]

In opposing Olofin, Orula, and the *babalawo* to the heterogeneous priests of the *oricha* pantheon, Ifá-centric rhetoric tends to "feminize" La Regla de Ocha. Ocha appears as a kind of fragmentary cult manqué, the principal oracle of which, the *dilogún,* never achieves authority in its own right, completeness, or spiritual reach. In the Ifá-centric myths mobilized to assert Orula's oracular primacy, Orula is the source of *all* divination and distributes a limited portion of his wisdom to two female *orichas,* Yemayá and Ochún, who, through synecdoche, stand for the *oricha* pantheon and La Regla de Ocha as a whole. Orula grants Yemayá and Ochún sets of cowrie shells, but he excludes them from the deepest secrets of Ifá. In the beginning, and forever after, Ifá's boundaries of authority, secrecy, and oracular competence are gendered with extreme prejudice. Unsurprisingly, the myths that most dramatically reinforce Orula's authority and the boundaries of his *regla* are those in which he either delegates limited powers to female *orichas* or guards secrets from them, particularly the *historias* from the *odu* Oche Melli, in which Orula catches Yemayá as she attempts to usurp his divination system and clients.[140] In this view, secrets "leak" from the "structurally female," heterogeneous cult vessel that is Ocha, which is composed of men and women, gays and lesbians, while the "structurally male," homosocial, and homophobic cult vessel of Ifá remains the paradigm of integrity: its *babalawos* are the impenetrable "fathers of the secret" (see Elizondo [1934?] n.d., 17–18; Matory 1986; 1994, 17, 18, 84, and chap. 5; 1988).[141]

Another related saying, "Orula doesn't make a *santo,* only another Orula" (in fact, a concise institutional description of key differences between the two *reglas*) is cited by Ifá-centric priests to explain Orula's impartiality, fairness, and disinterestedness in the determination of the guardian angel. The saying refers to the fact that Orula does not "give birth" to other *orichas,* only to a new generation of Orula's *fundamentos* and his representatives, the *babalawos.* In practice, this means that *babalawos* only initiate people—men—into La Regla de Ifá; they do not "make a *santo,*" that is, initiate people into the Ocha priesthoods. Therefore, the logic runs, Orula is immune to the jealousy and timely preoccupations of the other *orichas,* passions that might interfere with his fair and correct interpretations as to the needs of individuals. By extension, the *babalawo* has no *interés* (personal or financial self-interest) in the crowning of Ocha: he is disinterested in *which oricha* in particular is crowned on the head, and is concerned only that the "right" *oricha* is crowned, according to the initiate's destiny (*orí*). Orula might, in fact, determine that a person does not need Ocha initiation at all. In contrast, in this view, the *orichas* covet and quarrel over "ownership" of people's heads in their contentious *guerras de santo* ("wars between the *orichas*"). By extension, so do their representatives, the *iyalochas* and *babalochas,* in order to acquire godchildren, social reputation, and profit. Ifá-centric priests worry that, where *santeros* are not governed by Orula's judicious interpretation of Olofin's final word on destiny, incompetent, misguided, or unscrupulous, godparents might "put the wrong saint on the head" and destroy the initiate's life. They believe that such *santeros* exclude Orula's participation precisely in order to deprive their godchildren of useful independent information, to save money for themselves by witholding the *babalawo's derechos,* and to avoid divination results that potentially work against their financial interests. Priests of Yemayá, for example, who are barred from initiating the children of Oyá, might choose to do so anyway in order to make money.[142]

Of course, in practice, *babalawos* are not free of *interés* in so far as they may utilize their wives' reputations as *iyalochas* in order to acquire, in time, Ifá godchildren. Conversely, they aggressively recruit new members of the house through their initial delivery of the *guerreros* and *mano de orula,* and these first-level Ifá godchildren, through their subsequent Ocha initiations with the *babalawo's* wife, contribute resources, money, and reputation to the house. Among themselves, *babalawos* compete against one another for men to initiate into Ifá in order to increase their status as big men (i.e., through patronage, resource control, and reputation), and often do their best to control their *babalawo* godchildren's careers by strategically granting or denying the subsequent receiving of other enabling *poderes,* such as the Knife (*Wanaldo;* see chap. 2; see also Barber 1981; Apter 1992, 71–93).

Ocha-Centric Rhetoric: Primacy, "Equal Access," and "Responsibility"

Ocha-centric rhetoric seeks to undercut the notion of Orula's primacy, his oracular monopoly in relation to God, and the superiority of his Ifá divining equipment. As opposed to Ifá's centralizing and hierarchalizing of oracular authority, Ocha-centric models can be seen as relatively more decentralized, and even "centrifugal" (see Zuesse 1979, 208).[143] Ocha-centric logic grants cosmogonic primacy to *orichas other than* Orula and his Echús, particularly Eleguá of Ocha, Obatalá, and Changó. Miami *italero* Ernesto Pichardo shrewdly argues that Orunmila's role as "Witness at Creation" renders his positionality epiphenomenal: as a "witness," his knowledge is logically posterior, not anterior, to Creation events initiated and driven by more fundamental *oricha* agents.[144] Pichardo argues that the *dilogún,* as an oracular system, has "equal access" to "Ifá"—which he defines as "Total Knowledge"—no less than Ifá divination. For Pichardo, the cowries substitute equally well, in all circumstances, without fault or deficit, for Orula's equipment. Indeed, he argues, the Ifá and *dilogún* systems are wholly interchangeable and intertranslatable. Ifá merely uses a slightly modified nomenclature and a reordered system of figure seniorities for purposes of mystification.[145] In sum, Pichardo has argued, "there is no real difference between the cowries and Ifá. I can use cowrie divination as if I am using the *okuele* [Ifá divining chain]. I end up producing the same interpretation as the *babalawo*. . . . From a technical point of view, I'm not convinced that the *babalawo* has a superior [capacity] to [determine the guardian angel]. . . . It [depends upon] professional knowledge, not the position that they hold."[146] In this sense, Pichardo's progressive, revisionist perspective is meritocratic, not gerontocratic.

The logical lynchpin and principal conceit of the Ifá-centric perspective on oracular authority are found in the advice and warning that *babalawos* give their clients: "once you ask Orula to determine your guardian angel, you never again need to pose the question," for there is only "one Orula" and you will always get the same answer. Indeed, posing the question again, to Orula or to a cowrie diviner, would not only be a waste of time, it would also be a *falta de respeto* to Orula. Many *babalawos* are angered and insulted by clients who "shop around" for a comfortable divination result instead of submitting to Orula's final word, though some permit clients to approach other *babalawos*, presumably to check human, not Orula's, error.[147] Still, the "advice" that one should never ask Orula twice functions as a rhetorical device to maintain La Regla de Ifá as a closed, self-affirming system, to project Ifá as uniform and homogeneous, and to save face for Orula.

Ocha-centric houses, regardless of the ostensible "last word" Orula has given, often confirm the identity of a godchild's guardian angel with the cowrie shells of the head *oricha* of the godparent of the house.[148] Because it lodges potent, independent oracular authority in the multifarious head *orichas* that govern individual *casas de santo*, this practice turns on its head the Ifá-centric watchword, "There are many *orichas* but only one Orula." Ocha priests confidently employ the *dilogún* of Eleguá and/or those of their head *orichas* to determine and confirm the guardian angels of their prospective godchildren. They argue that the universal mediator, Eleguá, knows God, *orí*, the *orichas*, and the dead (*egun*) as well as anyone. Where the cowrie shells of initiating godparents' head *orichas* are used for this purpose, it is assumed that these head *orichas* are not vassals of Orula, but autonomous oracular agents who have rightful and ultimate authority—the "last word" and "responsibility"—to guide and determine the direction of Ocha houses, and the destiny of the individual "heads," that they "rule." The relative authority and priority that Ocha priests assign to Ifá versus cowrie shell divination can, therefore, significantly affect the shape of Ocha initiation, commonly called the *kariocha* ("to put the *oricha* on the head").

Self-conscious Ocha priests willing to engage *babalawos* in a rhetorical and institutional struggle over domains and authority thus produce counternarratives to attack and revise Orunmila's forcefully stated prerogatives. Debates of this sort take place in formal and informal meetings—at colloquiums, at dinners, and in houses where initiations are taking place. Private actions within the "room of *santo*" may quickly become known in tight local settings, such as Miami's Cuban Ocha community, where adversarial politics, incessant telephone and *cafetería* gossip, and conspiracy theories shape the discourse of the day.

Ernesto Pichardo rhetorically reclaims *orichas* and ceremonies from Ifá's "monopoly" by proposing earlier "origins" of those forms in the domains of West African priests. He reclaims authority over Eleguá, Ogún, Ochosi, Ósun, Odudúwa, Osain, Olokun, and the *egun* by asserting that these forms were "originally" in the hands of *oricha* priests but were, over time, captured and monopolized by Orunmila and his *babalawos*. "When we started talking to Yoruba people," Pichardo explains, the monopoly "blew up in the *babalawos'* faces. . . . 'We are the *babalawos*!' they say. They try to create an [invidious] distinction. . . . It's become a tradition [to them] for other motives." Pichardo thus radically relativizes the *babalawo*'s claims to historical legitimacy. "Once you take these things away from them . . . what do they have left? Nothing but Orunmila and Echú."[149]

Pichardo's shrewd argumentation recalls the Yoruba rhetorical strategy of "critical revision," as interpreted by Apter, in which protagonists on contested ritual and political terrains mobilize "deep knowledge" (*imọ jinlẹ̀*) in order to subvert hierarchical authority structures (Apter 1992, 7, 193–94, 31, 94–98, 210–11, 222–24; see also Lipsitz 1990). And, in appealing to African origins, Pichardo has used a form of argumentation perfected by the Black American Yoruba Movement in the 1970s and 1980s in order to propose a counternarrative to the authority claims of their strict white Cuban godparents (see Hunt 1979; Adefunmi I 1982; Mason 1985a). Still, Pichardo's counternarrative not only foregrounds his mastery of knowledge content. The real currency of Pichardo's rhetorical strategy, his symbolic capital, is the knowledge form: his rhetorical attacks contain historical information gleaned from scholarly research and interviews with Yoruba priests from West Africa. He and other learned priests, such as John Mason and Miguel Willie Ramos, have upped the ante of ritual debate within the religion by adopting forms of knowledge, argumentation, and presentation based in the apparatuses and resources of the academy. Their self-conscious scholarly works act not merely as neutral sources of information, but also as material demonstrations of their social and intellectual competence—in the Lucumí idiom, their *aché*—which have the potential to dislodge other entrenched ideological narratives (see, e.g., Pichardo and Nieto 1984; Pichardo 1989a, 1989b; J. Mason 1992, 1994, 1996; Flores-Peña and Evanchuck 1994; Epega and Neimark 1995; and see Bell 1992, 81–82).

Ritual Variation and the Kariocha of New Jersey's Templo Bonifacio Valdez

The Ifá-centric and Ocha-centric ritual fields are presented here as ideal types, which form the extremes of a continuum of variations in Lucumí ritual practice in Cuba and the United States.[150] The model of Ocha initiation advanced by Templo Bonifacio Valdez's founder, Luis Castillo, and practiced by the Ocha houses linked to him, his *babalawo* godchildren, and his close colleagues in Ifá, constitutes a site of significant variation within the Ifá-centric field itself. The temple's unusual model entails the extraordinary participation of Orula and *babalawos* in Ocha initiation. This model not only calls for the *babalawo*'s delivery of expected powers to his Ocha godchildren (i.e., the *guerreros* and the *mano de orula*), his performance of key divination readings such as "taking out the guardian angel," the *vista/ebó de entrada*, and his execution of the initiation's sacrifices (*matanza del asiento*). It is also founded on the comprehensive role of Ifá divination in organizing the Ocha initiation from the moment of its inception: indeed, it begins the steps of "making the Ocha" much further in advance than other houses. The sequence of several otherwise taken-for-granted initiatory steps, hitherto described in the literature as standard, is revised. Given oracular information determined far in advance of the neophyte's entrance into the room of initiation, the iconography of the Middle Day's throne and *ropa de santo* (see chap. 4) can diverge significantly from that of all other *ramas* of Ocha. The temple's unique initiatory model is entirely absent from the extant literature, where the conventional Ocha-centric or Ifá-centric models dominate.[151]

The temple's model revises the terminology of initiation used commonly by scholars and practitioners. Whereas the term *kariocha* ("to put the *ocha* on the head") has been used for generations to describe the *asiento*, the temple reserves the term exclusively for its own initiatory system.[152] Melba Carillo and other temple *santeros* refer to the standard Ifá-centric Ocha initiation procedure as the "regular *santo*." They consider this conventional Ifá-centric *santo* to be perfectly legitimate because it respects Orula and "uses" the *babalawo*'s services. Yet they are bound to use their *kariocha* because they belong to houses of Ocha in which the temple's *babalawos* have authority. The first Ochas made in the careers of the temple's founding Ocha priests were made with this revised *kariocha* model, and they cannot go back.

Three ideal scenarios describe the relationship (or the absence of one) between the two *reglas* in Ocha initiation practice on this revised continuum. The *kariocha* (the temple's model of extraordinary Ifá participation) and the Ocha-centric *santo* (which does not employ Ifá) lie on the extremes, and the "regular *santo*" (which uses the *babalawo* but not the temple's pecular *kariocha* model) lies in the middle. The "regular *santo*" may vary in its execution; for example, it may leave out minor ceremonies, such as "presenting the razor to the head" and the *babalawo*'s consecration of the *omiero* with his *aché*, which Cabrera's "conservative" *babalawo* informants insisted on to her (1980, 182–84). For economy of exposition, the "regular *santo*" and the "Ocha-centric" *santo* are reiterated in appendix 3. Suffice it to say that the Ocha-centric *santo* does not use the *babalawo* and substitutes the *oriaté*, or, in some cases, the *madrina, padrino,* or *oyubona* for tasks the *babalawo* would carry out in the "regular *santo*."

In the *kariocha* of Templo Bonifacio Valdez, Ocha initiates of *collares* receive the *guerreros* and the *mano de orula* from a temple *babalawo*, and their guardian angels are taken out in a *bajón de Orula*. The great divergence from the "regular *santo*" occurs with the following extraordinary ceremonies: Five to six months before the date of the *asiento*, a second *bajón de Orula* takes place. The *babalawos* divine the identity and specific road of the guardian angel—the initiate's primary "parent"—the road identities of the *orichas* Obatalá, Yemayá, and Ochún, as well as the identity of the second *oricha*-parent, an *oricha* that is of a gender opposite that of the primary parent. The hallmark of this unique model is that all of this information is divined *in advance* of the initiation's *itá* ceremony, that is, long prior to the *orichas*' "birth" in the *asiento*, as opposed to two days afterward in the *itá*, as is standard in the other two models. Moreover, during the second *bajón de Orula*, if Orula reveals that the initiate must receive auxilary *adimú-orichas*, these are prepared and received prior to the Day of the Asiento. The initiate the "goes into the room" with these additional protectors, instead of receiving them three months or more after the *asiento*, as is common in the other two models.

A temple priestess described to me the events surrounding the *kariocha* using the metaphors of the human reproductive cycle. Shortly after the second *bajón de Orula*, still months in advance of the *asiento* date, the *oricha fundamentos* of the initiate are "conceived" by the extant *orichas* of the sponsoring Ocha godparent in a series of secret procedures. The initiate's *oricha fundamentos*—that is, the sets of stones (*otán*)—remain in "gestation" with the godparent's *orichas* for many months until the date of the *asiento*, at which time the new *orichas* are "born." In contrast, while the *orichas* of the other two initiation models are also "born" in the *asiento* ceremony, they are not necessarily prepared in the same way ("conceived" and "gestated") during the preceding months. In the temple's *kariocha* model, two days after the *asiento*, the *oriaté* performs the *itá* ceremony. He omits the segment in which ordinarily he would "take out" the road identities of the *orichas*' Obatalá, Yemayá, and Ochún (and Eleguá or Ogún, if one of these is the guardian angel), as well as the identity of the second parent-*oricha*. For these identities were discovered by Orula prior to the *orichas*' "conception" months *before*, not two days *after* their "birth" in the *asiento*. The *oriaté* still gives a comprehensive reading of the new *iyawó*'s *orichas* and determines the initiate's *nombre de santo* and the identity of the second parent-*oricha*.[153]

The *kariocha*'s shift of divinatory responsibility from the *oriaté* to the *babalawo* is less significant in terms of labor than in terms of the oracular primacy and authority it grants Orula. The adjustments to the *kariocha*'s modified *itá* represent a subtraction of little more than five minutes of divination work from the standard *itá*. However, the *kariocha* institutes and affirms Orula's authority to divine the identity, and organize the initiatory configuration of, the *orichas* in advance of their ritual "birth" in the *asiento*. The temple's *kariocha* procedures, in effect, embody the cosmogonic role of Orula as *elerí küín* (witness at Creation): in the initiation's microcosm he is a "witness at conception," as it were. The logic of the *itá* in the "regular" and the Ocha-centric *santo* models, for the most part, assumes that the road identities of the *orichas* cannot be known until the *orichas* themselves speak through their own "mouths" (the *dilogún*), two days after their birth. However, depending upon the kind of work being done and the house involved, such oracular information about particular *orichas* is often taken out in advance.[154] The *kariocha* assumes Orula's ability to "know" the *orichas'* specific identities prior to the *orichas'* actual manifestation in this world.

The *oriaté*'s divination skills, as used in the "regular *santo*," are not seen as inferior in any way by the temple's members. While the *babalawos* consider the *dilogún* as unsuited to the task of taking out the guardian angel, they consider the shells perfectly adequate to the task of taking out the road or "path" identities of the *orichas* on the Day of Itá in the "regular *santo*." The *dilogún* are adequate to this task because after the *asiento* the *orichas* are no longer "competing" for the initiate's head; one *oricha* has been crowned irrevocably. "After the *ocha* is made, the *orichas* are no longer fighting. It is decided; it is done, final; all that is left is to determine the 'path,'" a temple *babalawo* explained. "We take out the saints beforehand because Orula tells us we have to. But even if the *babalawo* does this beforehand, the *itá* still has to be done, because the *babalawo* can't touch the shells. Those belong to the *santo*, and they have to be read by a priest of the *santo*."[155]

In other words, whether the the road identity of each *oricha* is "taken out" by Orula in the *kariocha* or by the *oriaté* in the regular *santo*, the *oriaté* still must extract and interpret the double *odu* figures from the *dilogún* of each *oricha*. These *odus* inscribe the cosmological "path" that fleshes out the identity of the newly consecrated *orichas* in very precise ways. The *oriaté*'s comprehensive interpretation of these *odus* communicates a crucial body of information—consisting of advice, predictions, obligations, prohibitions, and sacrifices—to the *iyawó*. The *iyawó*'s full embrace and implementation of this information is often of lifesaving significance, while the *iyawó*'s neglect of this information can result in tragedy and death. For this reason, as the *itá*'s information emerges through the *oriaté*'s interpretation of the *odus*, it is carefully recorded by a scribe in a *libreta* (notebook). The *itá* is "witnessed" by formally designated *testigos* ("witnesses"), who sign the *libreta*. The witnessed and signed *libreta* not only insures the authenticity and correctness of the initiation. It also stands as documentation in assigning culpability for ritual errors if later problems arise for the *iyawó*.

The metaphors of birth, marriage, parenthood, and *oricha* royalty or warriorhood, along with the related surrogate kinship themes of sponsorship and godparenthood (*apadrinación*), are common to the three initiatory models. One generation of *orichas* gives birth to another. New *oricha fundamentos* are born as "kings," "queens," and "warriors," and humans are "reborn" as *iyawós*—the *orichas' iyawós*—earthly representatives, potential possession mounts, verbally oracular mediums, and substitute "hands" for the conducting of cleansings. Yet, for the priests of Templo Bonifacio Valdez, the temple's *kariocha* model is believed by its advocates to follow more naturally the human reproductive cycle in the "conception," "gestation," and "birth" of the *orichas*. At the same time, the idiom used by priests and priestesses to declaim the virtues of the *kariocha* intriguingly draws upon modern scientific advances around human reproduction in order to highlight Orula's capacity as a diviner: for example, his discovery in advance of the "identity" of the *iyawó*'s *orichas* is likened to amniocentesis. If for some reason the initiation is canceled prior to the actual consecration day, the *asiento*, an *itutu* (funerary ceremony) must be performed for the gestating new *orichas*, which is likened by one priestess to an "abortion."[156]

Finally, the virtues of the *kariocha* model include possibilities for greater iconographic elaboration of the initiation's consecration garments and throne than the other models. If the *madrina* or *padrino* knows the road identities of Obatalá, Yemayá, and Ochún, then the *iyawó*'s consecration garments and throne cloth can be designed beforehand to express this specific level of *oricha* identity in particular configurations of colors and symbols. In contrast, houses using the other two initiatory models can represent these *orichas* only in their "normal" or metaarchetypal configurations of colors and symbols.

Many of those aware of the temple's *kariocha* model criticize it because of the theological and ritual problems it raises. One Havana *babalawo* insisted that it is "an error."[157] Ernesto Pichardo suggested that the model contains a "contradiction." For Pichardo, as well as the Havana *babalawo*, the road identity of an *oricha* cannot be known before the *oricha* is "born" in the *asiento* and is interrogated in the *itá*. It is an ontological impossibility. Only divination with the *dilogún* after orichas' materialization—their birth as specific "paths" (*caminos*)—can reveal their specific identities, which do not exist, as such, prior to that time.[158] At the same time, the temple's unwavering belief in Orula's primordial role as *elerí küín* would seem to save the *kariocha* from such a contradiction. For, as "witness at Creation . . . [Orula] has the unique advantage of knowing the destiny of everyone, including the other Orişa" prior to their arrival in the world during the Creation (Abiodun 1975, 421–23).

The temple's response to such criticism is that their *kariocha* is "older" and more "traditional" than the other models of initiation: Orula and his *babalawos* maintain secrets of African origin that have been lost to other *ramas*, particularly Ocha-centric *ramas*. It is, indeed, possible that aspects of the *kariocha* model derive from early Lucumí or Arará initiatory styles, which competed with the standardizing ritual forms and role professionalization of the *oriaté* and his enhanced cowrie shell system. For example, as indicated, the Arará Awó Bokónos *babalawos* of Havana have claimed exclusive historical authority to divine the will of the *voduns* with the Ifá system; the *babalawo*, not a priest using cowrie shells, conducts the initiation's *itá* in the Arará Sabalú branch in Havana. With respect to the Regla Lucumí field, José Miguel Gómez Barberas asserts that during his own Ocha initiation in 1929, directed by some of Havana's most recognized authorites, probably including Secundino Crucet Landa and La Tuán, *babalawos* entirely dominated the ceremonies from beginning to end, including the *itá*, which was performed "on the Tablero of Orula of the Babalawos" (see also Cabrera 1980, 184).[159] Though the historical source of the temple's *kariocha* practice is uncertain, its "secrets" are, some believe, based on papers that were transmitted from, or taken out of, Cuba in the late 1970s or in 1980 by priests of the Mariel exodus.[160]

That the *kariocha* is, in fact, "older" and more "traditional" than the two other models of initiation remains uncertain. The key point is that arguments cast in the idiom of primacy and traditionality rhetorically affirm the model's legitimacy and revise criticism by claiming to be grounded in unique, deep knowledge possessed and preserved by the cult of Orula. Arguments that serve to explain and defend "tradition" may, of course, be rationalizations of "traditionalized" arrangements, rationalizations that mask their status as part logical innovation based on recovered resources, part improvisation (see Schoemaker 1994; Kirshenblatt-Gimblett 1983; Drewal 1992). Still, *convincing claims* to legitimacy and historical precedence, as in the case of Olofin discussed in chapter 2, may be as important as the *veracity* of the claims in the success of competing groups within the fraught arena of relgious discourse.

CONCLUSION

Variant practices are not the stuff of immutable paradigms that remain constant through time. Variant practices, and apparently enduring paradigms, are produced over time, within dynamic settings of struggle and cooperation, innovation and rearguard reaction, social constraints and opportunities. Like innovations, variant practices are not passively produced. Whether based on innovations or splinter-group reactions to forms of domination, such practices are the result of agents' choices. The Lucumí

Figure 3.5.—Leaders and members of Ilé Tún Tún of Parraga, Havana (also known as Ilé Tum Tum and Ilé Títún), the re-Africanized Cuban Yoruba society of Fran Cabrera (Obeché, or Adebamiji; *middle row, third from right*) and Taiwo Abimbola (*middle row, third from left*), son of Yoruba *babalawo* and philosopher 'Wande Abimbola. Private collection, Havana.

"pantheon" was not passively produced by the aggregation of heterogeneous social groups, but was "pantheonized" though "reform" agendas and strategic choices by opinion leaders such as Efuche and Obadimelli, along with "councils" of Havana's reigning elders. The "modern" form of initiation, a turn-of-the-twentieth-century Havana innovation, played a formative role in the building and standardizing of the Lucumí pantheon. It was later standardized in Matanzas, following other initiation paradigms that had earlier been instituted by recognized leaders. Major variations, in the form of pantheonized "clusters" of deities, came through additions instituted through east-west exchanges between Havana, Matanzas, central Cuba, and Santiago de Cuba, spearheaded by particular priests, such as Tata Gaitán, Aurora Lamar, Miguel Febles, and, of course, Obadimelli. Such innovations took years to disemminate and standardize.

Reform movements, involving codification, institution organizing, authority building, credentialing, and personal and intergroup politics, produce variation as much as they intend standardization. Thus, Obadimelli's introduction of the "direct" method of initiating Agayú, Efuche's *Pinaldo*, and the way *Pinaldo* was apparently used to fortify the *oriaté*'s position as master of ceremonies produced reactions in the hardening of threatened old guards. Obadimelli was roundly criticized, and two models of Agayú initiation would compete with one another in Havana. Havana *babalawos* may, as a strategic response, have strengthened their opposition to the rising *oriaté* by increasing their versatility. Bernardo Rojas, for example, ruled that his godchildren should be initiated in Ocha before initiating in Ifá, so they could not be denied entrance into the room of Ocha by imperious *santeros*. Now, innovations instituted early in the twentieth century are subject to "reversion." The supposed African head-and-foot model has replaced the "modern" pantheonized initiatory model not only within the Black American Yoruba Movement in Oyotunji, South Carolina, but also in several Havana *babalawo* houses, given the newly emboldened positions some contemporary leaders have taken. One of the most notable recent movements is purist and antisyncretic. *Babalawo* Victor Betancourt, director of the Ifá Irán Lowó group of Havana Vieja, wears Rastafarian symbolism and recently reinstated the head-and-foot initiation style, thought to be of African provenance, among his Ifá godchildren. *Babalawo* Fran Cabrera's group, under the influence of Taiwo Abimbola (the Yoruba *babalawo* 'Wande Abimbola's son, who had been living in Cuba), founded "Ilé Tun Tun," a reborn Ilé Ifẹ̀ homeland on Cuban soil. Members wear African clothes and conform to the hierarchies and rituals believed to organize the Ifá order of the Ifẹ̀ kingdom (fig. 3.5).[161]

Orthodoxies or overbearing leaderships can cause disaffected factions to break off. Practices monopolized by *babalawos* for a good part of the twentieth century were and continue to be aggressively taken back by *oricha* priests. This has occured within a dynamic arena in which the Ifá-centric and Ocha-centric "ritual fields" are symbiotically related (they tug practices and ideas back and forth) and mutually constituted by boundary marking and constant one-upmanship. Individuals and groups may shift alliances back and forth between these variant practices, changing the strength of the consituencies involved. Thus, houses and individuals can move back and forth between using and not using *babalawos*, and this produces variants in models hitherto thought to be immutable.[162] It may take a splinter group years of resisting criticism and scorn before it is accepted, if at all. However, it knows it will, at least, be let alone. *Babalawos* and *santeros* in Havana and the United States today often state that they maintain their "own criteria" but do not criticize anyone (publicly). Given the atomization of "houses" and the decline of more or less activist local authorities, such as Bernardo Rojas, La Tuán, and Obadimelli in Havana and Ma Monserrate and Felipa Calderón in Matanzas, there is, as many put it, "nothing we can do." The case of Templo Bonifacio Valdez's unusual *kariocha* initiation shows how additional variations form along continua of practice, where it is often difficult to distinguish new groups whose innovations claim traditional status from established old guards, whose asserted original "traditions" are "traditionalized" innovations.

Part II

ICONOGRAPHIC INNOVATION

FOUR

ROYAL ICONOGRAPHY AND THE MODERN LUCUMÍ INITIATION

[A throne] means that a new king is being born. It is luxury. The *santo* is there receiving everything being done. Everybody comes to give *moforibale* to that *oricha.*
—*Iyaloricha* Melba Carillo

When they were dressing me with Changó's outfit, I was complaining that my *padrino* was painting me with a mustache. But he said, "remember, I have to transform you into Changó." They do everything they can to make you look like the deity, to make you look like a king, queen, or warrior.
—*Iyaloricha* Nydia Pichardo

YEMAYÁ: THE RADIANT PRESENCE OF A CROWNED QUEEN

It is Sunday, 8 September 1985, just after noontime in the front room of an unassuming frame house in need of some repairs in a quiet neighborhood several blocks from the old Route 1 in Elizabeth, New Jersey. The occasion is the festive "Middle Day" (Día del Medio) of the intensive first three days of Ocha's weeklong initiation period. The cleared twelve-by-fifteen-foot living room has given way to a commanding canopied throne installation resplendent with luminous satin in royal blue, immaculate white, and bold red. Shimmering metallic flecks on blazons of draped cloth and bright bands of silver trim on the initiate's consecration outfit catch and throw the light. The room radiates tranquility and a sense of slowed time but also harbors an edge of expectation and excitement. The initiate, a woman whom I will call Sara, wears a full-length flowing gown of rich royal blue satin. Its puff shoulders and broad escutcheon-like belt and the circular pasteboard crown seem to recall the splendor of eighteenth-century European monarchs. Thickly painted circular earrings and bold geometric markings around the circumference of her shaved head transform her face into an apparition. She is familiar to us, yet changed. She stands serenely and elegantly, though incongruously barefoot. She holds in her right hand an exquisite fan of a teardrop roundness, whose blue satin surface and raking silver trim echo the crown, gown, and belt. While her pasteboard crown's seven rising red parrot feathers seem to lift her effortlessly heavenward, the five heavy, multistrand bead sashes (*collares de mazo*) crisscrossing her chest challenge her earthly patience and balance. For she must "go to the floor" repeatedly to reciprocate the salutations (*moforibale*) of each priestly visitor who enters the increasingly crowded room to greet the "new queen." Visitors take their seats on low, crudely fashioned wood stools (*taburetes*) and gaze up at this royally dressed and enthroned *santo,* whom we recognize as Yemayá. In the Regla de Ocha idiom, Yemayá was "crowned" upon, and "rules," Sara's head. Yemayá is the majestic, embracing *oricha* of the sea and motherhood. She is a gentle nurturer, but also a demanding and fierce warrior. We make limited small talk with our friend, relative, or mother who yesterday became the *oricha*'s "bride." I have known her as Sara, but for a whole "year of white," she will be known and addressed only as *iyawó*, literally "junior wife" or "bride of the *secret*."

A close look at the Middle Day's objects and activities reveals many of the institutional, ritual, and iconographic innovations of the modern Regla de Ocha initiatory system, as well as significant variations across the religion's various *ramas*. The configuration of multiple *orichas* "made" and "received" by contemporary *iyawós* manifests the modern "pantheonized" initiatory model. The Middle Day celebrates the coronation of a "new *santo*," figured as a king, queen, or warrior (*rey*, *reina*, or *guerrero*), and its hybrid iconography condenses a cultural history of creole borrowings in dialogue with reworkings of Yoruba-derived patterns. The Middle Day's iconography of thrones, crowns, luxurious garments, and decorative porcelain vessels provides a powerful set of reference points for the ways the *orichas* have come to be visualized and experienced by Cuban and other Latino practitioners in the Caribbean and the United States.

THE CONSECRATION OF OCHA: A CAPSULE SUMMARY

The first full day of initiation, the "Day of the Asiento," involves the "birth" of two critically related earthly manifestations of the *orichas'* spiritual power (*aché*): a set of potent objects that will later be enshrined in the home, and the consecrated head (*orí*) of new priest. Both are "washed," "nourished," and "fortified" through the incorporation of the *orichas' aché*, which is drawn from elements of *la naturaleza* ("nature"), including fresh plants and the vital blood of sacrificial animals. *Asiento* refers to the Lucumí ritual technique of "seating" or "mounting" the *aché* of an *oricha* on the head (*orí*). The *orichas'* objects consist of their consecrated material "foundations" or "supports" (*fundamentos*)—sets of color-coded rounded stones (*otán*, or *piedras*)—which are accompanied by sets (*manos*, "hands") of cowrie divination shells called *dilogún* and miniature metal or wood icons (*herramientas*, "tools"). These stones, shells, and *herramientas* are contained within metal, wood, or ceramic vessels, generally called *soperas*.

The initiate—the "child" (*omó*) of a particular *oricha*—"makes Ocha" and becomes the earthly "representative" of that *oricha*, previously determined by divination to be the "guardian angel" or "owner of the head" (*angel de la guardia, dueño de la cabeza, cabecera*). On the Day of the Asiento, the *orichas'* objects and the initiate's head and body are consecrated with herbal infusions, called *osains*, concocted principally of fresh plants (*ewe*) and cool water, and "seasoned" with various activating (hot) and cooling (sweet or balmlike) ingredients. The *oricha cabecera* is then "mounted" on the head in a series of ceremonies. The *sopera* of the guardian angel is placed over the head, which is draped with four squares of cotton cloth in white, yellow, blue, and red. With a series of invocatory songs by the soloist *oriaté* and participant chorus that "call down" the *oricha*, the initiate may become possessed or spiritually "touched." Upon completion of the mounting ceremony (*montaje del santo*), the initiate becomes known as *iyawó*, the *oricha*'s "junior wife" (*iyá-awó*). The initiation procedure as a whole in the Lucumí ritual language is typically called the *kariocha*, literally "to put *ocha* on the head" (from *ka* [put], *orí* [head], and *ocha* [*oricha*]; see Cabrera [1957] 1986, 185; [1974] 1980, 128–73; Murphy 1988, 87; 1994, 92–104). The primary *oricha* "guardian angel" or *cabecera* is often referred to as one's "crown," an internalized spiritual presence that "rules" the head (*orí*) and authorizes, in turn, the priest's potential governance of a "house" of initiated "godchildren." These telescoping, hierarchical authority relations of *orichas*, individual heads and bodies, and the social body of the house are nicely encapsulated by a Lucumí divination proverb from the cowrie divination sign Eyionle: "The head rules the body and only one king governs a town" (Elizondo [1934?] n.d., 9, 39).[1] Following the "washing" and *montaje del santo* ceremonies, during which the *iyawó* has been blindfolded, the *iyawó* is permitted to "see" his or her throne, a beautiful cloth canopy that functions to symbolically evoke and instrumentally invoke ("call down"; see M. Drewal 1989) the *orichas* to take up residence with the *iyawó*. The throne becomes a kind of incubator for the *orichas'* collective *aché*. The canopied installation not only will serve as a royal seat and stage for the formal presentation of the initiate the next day, the Middle Day; it is also a spiritually protective space, a seclusion hut for a liminal initiate, and a symbolic birth site on the floor for the "newborn baby" of the house. Some *santeros* regard it as a kind of cell of "protective custody" and benign house arrest by the *orichas*. In fact, the throne's cloth and the white sheet and towel the *iyawó* uses for the week act as prophylactic and purifying *ebó* (sacrificial media). The *iyawó*'s white clothes for the week are stored in a large wicker basket (*canasta*), just as it was the Cuban custom to store the clothes of newborns in a basket. The *iyawó* lives in her "throne"-"house" for six days, in proximity to the line of *soperas* that contain the *orichas'* objects.

The *asiento* day is completed with the *matanza* (the killing), when the *orichas'* stones and shells "eat" the warm, *aché*-imbued blood of two- and four-legged animals symbolically appropriate to each deity. The *iyawó* is cleansed and fortified also by the *matanza*, as each of the animals sacrificed is touched to the cardinal points of the *iyawó*'s body. Thus identified through physical contiguity with these sacrificial animal messengers to the "other world," the *iyawó*'s death and rebirth is reenacted in objectified form; at the same time, the animals are sacrificial substitutes, which clean, and give their lives for the health, well-being, and salvation of the *iyawó*.

Following the Middle Day (often a Sunday), a special intensive divination reading called *itá* is conducted, in which the *iyawó*'s new *orichas* "speak" for the first time through their cowrie shells (*dilogún*). The *itá* identifies the spiritual coordinates (*odus*) and their associated bodies of "taboos" (*egües* or *ewaws*), guiding stories (*historias*), and protective sacrifices (*ebó*) that will serve to maintain the equilibrium of the *iyawó*'s consecrated head (*orí*), indicate auxiliary *orichas* to be received in the future, determine the particular "paths" or "roads" of the *iyawó*'s *orichas* (a number of *orichas* have different advocations), and identify the *iyawó*'s second "parent" *oricha* and Lucumí sacred name. The multivocal term for the human head, *orí*, also refers to the initiate's "destiny"; the *itá* inscribes the *iyawó*'s "past, present, and future"—that is, the "path" the *iyawó*'s head travels in this world, and what must be done to insure that this head's destiny is fulfilled (see Cabrera [1974] 1980, 179–224).

After five nights of sleeping and reposing beneath the throne's protective canopy, the *iyawó*'s consecrated *orí* is "presented to the sun" (often on a Thursday morning) in a brief ceremony conducted by the *padrino* or *madrina* and *oyubona* to advise Olorun that this is the last day of the initiation week's intensive process of the head's incorporation of *aché* substances through baths and special "African breakfasts." This is the last time the head will be colorfully painted with the head *oricha*'s special "signature" (*firma*). On the seventh day (often a Friday), after the sixth night under the throne, the *iyawó* emerges from seclusion and is reincorporated into the community on this "Day of the Plaza." In the morning, the *iyawó* is dressed in fine white clothes, shoes, and hat and is escorted to a "market" (*plaza*), a place of exchange, transition, and sociality. In Havana, this is typically the large market that stands at the intersection of Cuatro Caminos (Four Roads). In New York City, the market is often the Latino "La Marketa" in Spanish Harlem. Offerings at the four corners to Eleguá on a walk around the market are little *ebó* to protect the *iyawó* as he or she reenters the social world. Fruit that the newborn *iyawó* symbolically steals (but that is paid for by the accompanying *oyubona*) is carried back to the room in a wicker basket. The throne has been taken down—signaling the end of the weeklong period in which the *orichas' aché* is actively incorporated by the *iyawó;* the fruit is placed before the *iyawó*'s *orichas* in order to "refresh" them prior to a coconut divination that clears the way for their transition, along with their new owner, to the *iyawó*'s home, which will become a new "house of *ocha.*" For three months, the *orichas* repose on a mat, and the *iyawó* takes meals and sleeps (in some houses), likewise, on a mat. The *iyawó* is subject to many social and personal restrictions, such as going out unaccompanied by a *santero* and looking in the mirror. After a special *ebó* of the three months, the *orichas* themselves take up residence in a *canastillero,* a multishelved cabinet or armoire, often within their own sacred room (*cuarto de santo, igbodú*). At this time, the *iyawó* is "presented to the table," so that meals may be taken with adults, as well as "presented to the mirror." The *orichas* have become the true "owners" and "rulers" of the house (see Cabrera [1974] 1980, 225–28; Castellanos 1977, 85–99; Gleason 1992; González Huguet 1968; Brown 1999).

THRONE FORMS: ASIENTO, CUMPLEAÑOS, TAMBOR

Three principal *oricha*-throne variations, linked to three distinct events, share a basic form: an enclosure made of prestige cloth, such as satin, velvet, lace, chiffon, and lamé, or natural green leaves. Cloth thrones consist of a canopy overhead, a draped backdrop, and symmetrically parted and tied-back curtains in front. They may be actual curtains or the suggestion of them in swags of cloth stapled to the wall. Natural throne enclosures for the Warrior *orichas* are erected of leafy branches freshly cut from local trees. Throne enclosures may be formed in a corner, project straight out from a single wall, or span the entirety of one end of a room (figs. 4.1, 4.2, plate 7; plates 6, 8, 10; plate 9). With their parted drapes and valances, throne installations might recall miniature theatrical stages, curtained picture windows, or canopied beds; yet they are intended to realistically represent the dignified and lavish seats of "queens,". "kings," and deified "warriors."

The canopy, parted curtains, and backdrop of cloth thrones typically radiate the identifying colors of a single *oricha* of honor, a solid or counterpointed color pattern that approximates the coding of Lucumí *oricha* beadwork. Cloth and leafy thrones may be further adorned by square blazons of brocaded or sequined cloth with fancy borders, called *paños,* which are also color coded to the set of companion *orichas* received in the initiation.

While the *trono de asiento* contains and presents the richly dressed body of the *iyawó,* the initiatory mortar-like stool (*pilón*), and the straw floor mat, thrones built for "drummings" (*tambores*) and the *orichas'* annual "birthday" celebrations (*cumpleaños*) contain and present not the *iyawó,* but the *orichas* themselves (plates 5, 6, 7, 8, 9, 10, 11, fig. 5.31). The *orichas' soperas* are often elevated on pedestals, dressed with *paños,* and outfitted with the *orichas'* beaded attributes, including elaborate sashlike necklaces (*collares de mazo*) and dance wands. Some *orichas* (Oyá and Ochún) wear metal crowns, adorned with bracelets and miniature tools (see Brown 1993b, 1996, and below). The seated and festively dressed body of the *iyawó* under the *asiento* throne thus finds its direct analogue in the dressed *soperas* of the *orichas* under the drumming or birthday throne.

An *asiento* throne for the initiation of a priest of Obatalá, constructed for exhibition purposes at the Caribbean Cultural Center in New York in 1984 by Antonio Queiro (plate 5), was predominantly white, marking the central role of Obatalá as the *iyawó*'s guardian angel. The delicate, white parted curtains are sheer, light, and lacy while the background is quilted and soft—all textures appropriate to Obatalá, the venerable elder *oricha* of purity and calmness. Obatalá's central role is reiterated in the white cloth covering the *pilón.* In contrast, the *asiento* throne made for Sara's initiation by Ramón Esquivel,

Figure 4.1.—Drawing of initiation throne for Yemayá Mayelewo, New Jersey, 8 September 1985. (Drawing by David H. Brown.)

Templo Bonifacio Valdez's premier throne maker during the 1980s, announced the leading presence of Yemayá with its backdrop of alternating columns of royal blue and white, which radiated outward from a central red column (fig. 4.1). Each column was a discrete bolt of satin cloth stapled to the wall. The alternating colors approximated the counterpointed Lucumí bead pattern for this particular "road" of Yemayá, called Mayeleo: blue and white punctuated by red. Esquivel artfully utilized sheer, powder-blue chiffon curtains in order that their superimposition over the counterpointed background would conjure a range of blues, evoking the play of light, depth, and color variation that is characteristic of Yemayá's domain, the sea, particularly as it absorbs and reflects the firmament above. At the same time, the central red column encoded the hot, warrior-like characteristics of Sara's particular road of Yemayá.[2]

In the Queiro throne (plate 5), three artistically shaped

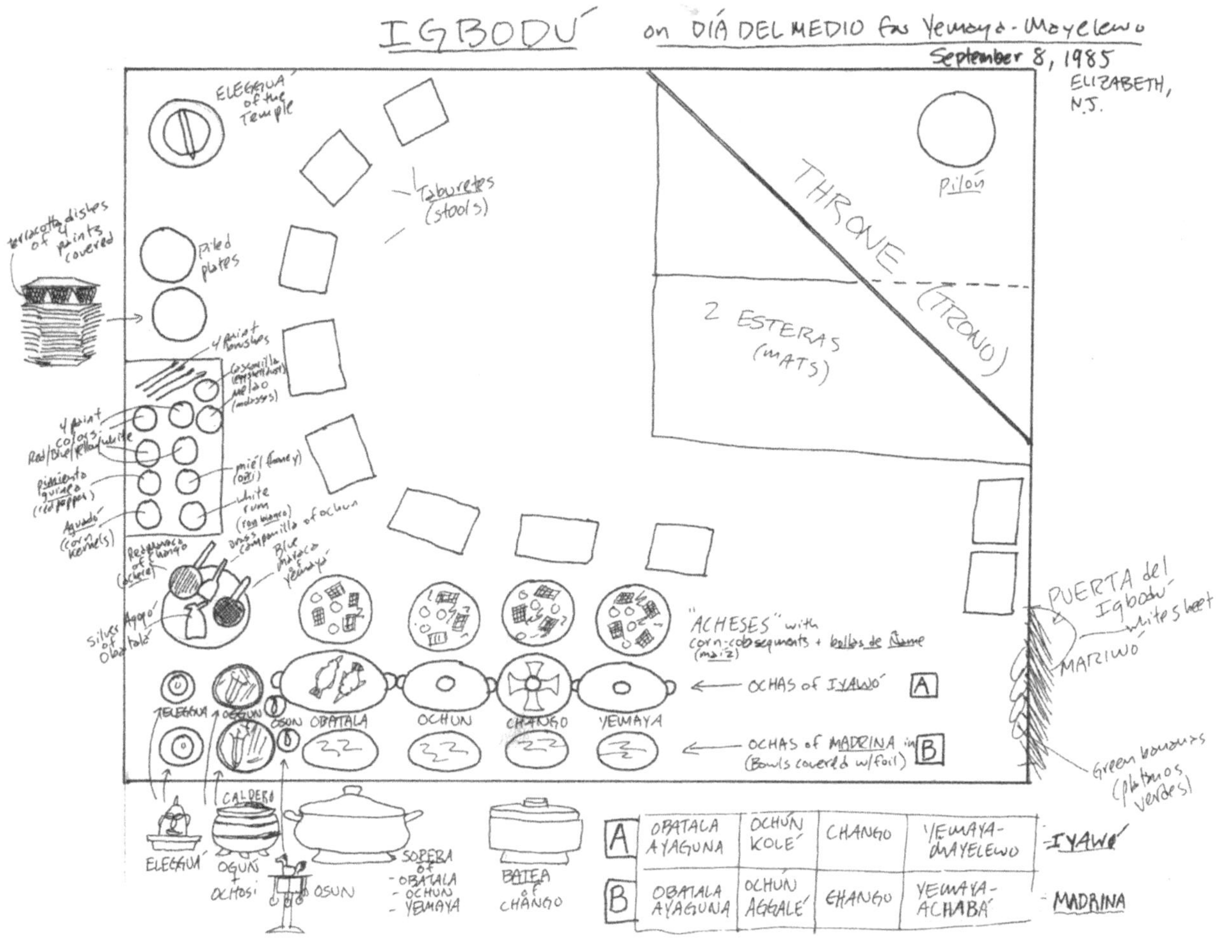

Figure 4.2.—Plan of the floor of the initiation room on the Día del Medio of Yemayá Mayelewo, New Jersey, 8 September 1985, showing position of throne and the two lines of *soperas*, as they were organized on the Día del Medio. (Drawing by David H. Brown.)

squares of cloth (*paños*) punctuate the curtained front, and one bisects the background. Together they represent the four fundamental or cardinal "colors" of Ocha, whose principal referents are the four standard *orichas* "received" by all *iyawós* in the modern initiatory system: Obatalá (white or silver), Ochún (yellow or gold), Yemayá (blue and white or silver), and Changó (red).[3] Queiro's throne symmetrically balances *paños* representating two intimately linked female *orichas*, Yemayá and Ochún, who are related to water and are regarded as "mother" and "daughter," or older and younger "sisters," respectively. Yemayá "owns" the oceans (*agua salada*), while Ochún is the owner of "sweet" inland waters (*agua dulce*), good fortune, and beauty—all things "sweet." Yemayá's blue and white *paño* recalls swirling seawater, and Ochún's, a yellow flower. The bold red diamond of Changó's *paño*, evoking this *oricha*'s falling thundercelts (*eduará*), commands rear center. Esquivel, in contrast, symmetrically balanced *paños* on either side (fig. 4.1), representing the harmonious mother-son pair, Yemayá and Changó, and placed Ochún's gold sequined *paño* inside over the *pilón*. These bold floating cloth forms hover about the canopy as a supporting liturgical cast to the guardian angel's lead.

The array of *paños* around the canopy bearing the dominant colors of the tutelary guardian angel not only reflects the modern initiatory configuration of multiple *orichas* made and received. It also registers an important aspect of the modern pantheon's formal hierarchy. The high central position of Obatalá's white *paño* in the Queiro Caribbean Cultural Center example reiterates Obatalá's role as the "owner" of the *iyawó*'s head. At the same time, like its silver, shieldlike counterpart in Esquivel's throne for Sara, it also announces Obatalá's status as the "(meta)-Owner of All Heads." The "father" and "king" of the Ocha pantheon, Obatalá is the mythological potter who created the physical head (*orí*), and who, along with his fecund royal wife Yemayá, in one cycle of legends, produced all of the other *orichas*. In the Esquivel example, the shieldlike silver *paño* also recalls the younger, warrior qualities, of some Obatalá "paths." In the Queiro example, Obatalá's *paño* is gathered in the middle to form symmetrical wings, which mirror those of the little decorative dove. The white dove (*ellelé*) is a sacrificial bird associated with the purity and celestiality of Obatalá and the head (*orí*) and symbolically mediates between heaven and earth. In the hybrid, or "syncretic," popular Cuban religious notion, the dove is linked to the Christian iconography of the soul, the Holy Spirit, the baptism of Christ by Saint John, and the themes of divine inspiration, ritual purity, and peace (fig. 3.1; see Apostolos-Cappadona 1994, 112–14).[4]

The throne's enclosure of cloth and *paños* reflects, but also revises and extends, the *asiento*'s themes of spiritual rebirth through iconography that projects the *orichas*' splendid royal presence. As pinned or stapled to the *asiento* throne, and as draped over the *orichas' soperas* in drumming or birthday thrones, the *paños* are, in effect, sumptuous, highly adorned versions of the four squares of cotton cloth (*paños*)—representing the "four directions of the canopy of heaven"—which are suspended over the *iyawó*'s head at the culmination of *montaje del santo* (see Gleason 1992; Murphy 1994, 99–100). Whereas this simple cotton cloth "canopy" of white, yellow, blue, and red squares serves to orient, invoke, and transmit the multiple forces of *aché* during the private *asiento* ceremony, the expensive and luminous throne canopy of cloth, with its luxurious *paños* in these same four colors, becomes a dazzling blazon, a banner (*bandera*) that heralds the *orichas*' immediate *public* presence in this world and proclaims their royal splendor, divine glory, and immense wealth on public festive occasions: the Día del Medio, the drumming, and the birthday.

THRONES FOR KINGS, QUEENS, AND WARRIORS

Iyawós who "make" Obatalá, Oyá, Ochún, Yemayá, and Changó[5] as their guardian angels are dressed and enthroned on the Middle Day with materials and iconographic details that express the "luxury" and aristocratic domesticity of crowned palace royalty. *Oricha* thrones employ prestige fabrics featuring the aesthetic qualities of luminosity, richness, or delicacy, such as satin, velvet, and lace and chiffon (plates 5, 7, 9, fig. 4.1). In contrast, initiates who make one of the three archetypal forest Warriors (*guerreros*), Eleguá, Ogún, or Ochosi, find themselves in markedly different thrones, which are constructed of "leaves" (*yerba;* fig. 4.3, plates 11, 12, 13, 14). Not palace dwellers, these three Warrior *orichas* are denizens of the marginal spaces between the "inside" and the "outside," the house and street, the town and bush, or the dangerous and unpredictable interzones of street and bush themselves. They are, Nydia Pichardo explains, "very much of

Figure 4.3. Warriors' leafy *trono del patio* (throne of the patio), New Jersey, 1985. (Photograph by David H. Brown.)

the street and very close to the lifeworld of us human beings. Changó, Yemayá, Obatalá, and Ochún are understood to be kings [and queens]; the other three are known as Warriors. Changó was a person [before he was deified] but he was a king; Eleguá, Ogún, and Ochosi are outdoor people, people *del monte, de afuera, de la calle* [of the forest, the outside, the street]. They are involved in the struggles of the street and our everyday lives. Ochosi is the *guerrero mago* [warrior magician]; Ogún is the *guerrero* who is ugly, savage, rough. Eleguá is the *guerrero travieso*, the warrior trickster. Ochosi deals with *la justicia* [police, or the law], Ogún with work and struggle. The other *orichas* are much more deified [*mas deificado/a*]."[6] "More deified" means more elevated and evolved on the spirit-matter continuum and suggests a common way of thinking about Lucumí cosmology as a vertical chain of being. This hierarchical ladder of "deification" locates more heavenly ("spiritual") creator *orichas*, such as the pure white Obatalá and Odudúwa, at the top, and the more "material" Warriors and scrappers, Eleguá and his companions at the bottom, with the other *orichas* on points in between (e.g., see my chap. 3 and Angarica [1955?] n.d., 35). The "closeness" of the three Warriors to the human lifeworld, a notion of proximity common to Spiritist thinking, locates them in the thick of "material" struggle: *la calle* (the street), hard labor (the plantation), violence (drunken brawls and revolution), and social unpredictability (precipitous changes, sudden attacks).[7] The distance between "more deified" and "less deified" also translates into Cuban cultural and ecological distinctions of controlled, tranquil domestic space, on the one hand, and the dangerous street, the shadowed forest, a countryside at the mercy of unpredictable weather conditions, and the arbitrary, exploitative, and violent slave plantation, on the other. The distance between the two markedly different zones is indicated in the aesthetic distinction between fine, luminous cloth and a natural thicket of "leaves" (*yerba*).[8] The three Warriors are intimates of Osain, the owner of the forest and its sacred plants (see Thompson 1994, 234–37), a set of relationships that finds exquisite expression in the Warrior's leafy thrones.[9] In Afro-Cuban religious culture, the *puerta de la calle* (door to the street) acts as the critical threshold between "inside" and "outside" spheres. It is not surprising, therefore, to find that, within priest's houses, Obatalá and the *orichas* are enshrined in elevated positions in decorative cabinets well into the house, while Eleguá and his companions live on the floor behind the front door (see Brown 1999).

The differentiated symbolic landscape marked by the contrasting iconographies of royalty and warriors strikingly resembles on a condensed scale, an Ọ̀yọ́-Yoruba mythico-historical distinction between the domain of the archetypal "king," Ṣàngó (Shango), and the domain of the archetypal itinerant warrior, hunter, and soldier, Ogún. J. Lorand Matory observes, "Rather than being an administrator, Ogun is a pathmaker. His purview extends not only to hunting but to all iron-related endeavors, such as warfare and road building. In Oyo territory, his contemporary priests are hunters and blacksmiths. Drivers as well sacrifice to him. Historically and mythically, he is far more closely associated with warriors and itinerant entrepreneurs than with kings. In the nineteenth century, his foremost clients were plebeian military commanders who displaced kings in the seat of power" (Matory 1994, 6; Apter 1992, 59; see also Barnes 1989b).

Still, while Yoruba origins explain something of the Warrior's distinctive iconography (see Thompson 1994), their more local historical reference points might be the Day of King's festival, in which blacks took over the streets in a fearsome annual eruption of "disorder," antislavery militancy, marronage, and two revolutions, the island's cultural geography of urbanized "west" and rural "east," and the contradictions of urbanization, in which the nation sought "progress" by criminalizing and demonizing Cuba's black presence.[10] For example, the contrast of *yerba*, animal horns, and raffia fiber (*mariwó*) to royal iconography finds historical precedent in the typologies of colonial-era street festivals, in which the "little devils" reigned. Fierce masquerades of animal and vegetal elements danced in athletic counterpoint to staid and decorous royal and military processional—which, nevertheless, evoked potent and autonomous black institutions. These aesthetic and performative contrasts are historically found throughout the Caribbean as the "wild" (alternatively "roots") versus the "fancy" aesthetic, wherein the former is explicitly agressive (see Bettelheim 1988; Kinser 1990, 151–94, 195–249). In the nineteenth century and before, rebels against slavery broke their chains and became *cimarrones*, lived in the forest, devised poisons with their herbalistic knowledge, and fought against the imperial and colonial oppressors in two Cuban wars of independence (see e.g., Barnet [1966] 1980; Helg 1995). During the "Ten Years War" (El Grito de Yara, 1868–78), the *campo* to the east evoked fear in the west. The economic crisis among *oriental* planters and the subsequent insurrections launched from within every sector of Oriente quickly spread into the huge Las Villas province just to the west. This, and the dramatic gains of the Afro-Cuban hero Antonio Maceo, with his ranks of poor whites and blacks, former slaves, and *cimarrones*, so scared the holders of western, slave-driven sugar wealth that Spain built a fortified *trocha* ("ditch") across the narrowest segment of the island in Camagüey, separating west from east. "To cross the *trocha*" would "set the stage for a war of the incendiary torch, a campaign of destruction of property and disruption of production. For military leaders the invasion of the west was linked directly to the abolition of slavery, and both were vital for Cuban success" (Pérez 1988, 123–24). During the early nineteenth century and before, the streets of colonial Havana were experienced as interzones not only of illicit, as well as licit, social, economic, racial, and sexual interchange, but also of disorder, violence, howling dogs, physical disease, and "social disease"—in the form of Afro-Cuban "sores" on the body politic (see, e.g., Ortiz [1926–28] 1986, 185–208; [1906] 1973). Cubans continue to make similar distinctions between the safe and clean *casa* and the dirty and dangerous *calle*, which is populated by shysters, drunks, toughs, and multifarious bad spiritual influences. If the initiatory "house" and "room of *santo*" are ritually made sacred, "set apart," in Mary Douglas's sense ([1966] 1985, 8), their iconography does not necessarily leave behind, but reproduces and intensifies, sets of distinctions inscribed by Cuban cultural history. Indeed, these cultural distinctions inform the spatio-performative protocols of the initiation process.

IN OBATALÁ'S HOUSE: THE TRANSFORMATION OF THE WARRIORS

Though *iyawós* of Eleguá, Ogún, and Ochosi are presented on the Día del Medio under their leafy thrones in the "sacred room" of the house (*igbodú, cuarto de santo*), each of these *orichas* also owns an additional throne of leaves constructed outside the house, called the *trono del patio* (throne of the *patio;* see fig. 4.3).[11] All of the ceremonies to "mount" these *orichas* are conducted in this patio space, which mediates between the house and the "forest" or "bush" (*monte* or *manigua*). The Warriors' *aché* is so hot, strong, and unpredictable that it may not be brought into the house until it is effectively restrained and "transformed" under the calming presence of Obatalá (see below and Angarica [1955?] n.d., 35–43; Mason 1985a; Brown 1999).[12]

The "making" of the three Warriors entails a complex sequence of outdoor ceremonies, which attract, seize, control, and transform these strong, potentially difficult characters. The sequence begins in a relatively remote, densely wooded site (a *monte*) just prior to the initiate's purification in the river (*río*) on the eve of the *asiento*. Special sacrifices and cleansings are performed in this natural, grove like environment. Eleguá and Ogún, for example, receive the hot blood of the *jutía* (nutria, bushrat), and the participants must then be rigorously cleansed of this zone's influences.[13] The *monte* and *río* are typically a wooded area and brook in a local park in New Jersey or the Bronx. In Havana, many houses have relied on the Martín Pérez River in the Reparto Mañana section of Guanabacoa, where a fenced-in *casa de santo* is adjacent to the water. Jehovah's Witnesses recently moved in and shut down access to this sacred forest and the river.

At the conclusion of the *monte* ceremonies for Eleguá and Ogún, a dramatic performance is required to "take the *oricha* out of the forest" (*sacarlo del monte*). Ideally, five priestesses (though it is often fewer) of Ochún, carrying plates of Spanish pumpkin (*calabaza*) doused with honey (*miel*), a neutralizing medium, lead the way for the initiate, who holds the objects of Eleguá or Ogún (Ecún 1985, 26, 54).[14] Still, "Echú" (the "negative" valence of the domestically restrained more "positive" figure called "Eleguá") can be so problematic that additional measures are required. The little cement figure of Eleguá (fig. 4.22) is tied to the initiate with rope to insure that this mischievous trickster in fact comes along (Ecún 1985, 25). The initiate is prompted to run to the river, and the participants strike him with freshly cut switches (*cujes*) to insure that problems are left behind, "because [Echú] is a very mischievous and rebellious boy" (Ecún 1985, 26). If all such pacifying measures are not taken so that "Echú does not enter the house . . . serious problems arise; for example, there could be discord between the participants; [Echú] could bring the police; [and] animals could die before the sacrifice [*matanza*]" (Ecún 1985, 55). In other words, in Obatalá's "house," decorum, order, and etiquette rule; the mischief of Echú, and the unrestrained behavior of other *orichas* of action, problems, and war, is undesirable and swiftly sanctioned in favor of the initiatory objectives at hand.

The Warriors' interior thrones bring the fresh green density and vibrancy of the *monte, la naturaleza,* into the house, though in carefully restrained form (plate 11). What is cultural, elegant, and domesticated for the other *orichas* is natural, rustic, and marginal for the Warriors. The Warriors' thrones recall the encampments of men on campaign. According to Obá Ecún, the thrones of Eleguá and Ogún should be hung with *mariwó* (palm fronds) and painted gourd containers (*güiros*)—the typical receptacles of Osain's magical-medicinal protective charms.[15] The *monte* motif is reiterated as the *jutía* bushrat, sacrificed to Echú or Ogún, is smoked and hung within the throne's branches. Ochosi's throne becomes a veritable hunter's den, with its displays of trophies and weapons—for example, the head and skin of the deer, a leopard skin, and a large bow and quiver of arrows (Ecún 1985, 25, 54, 78). Moreover, initiates of the Warriors do not sleep and sit upon straw mats, but must rely upon a hard floor spread with fine grasses (*yerba fina*). To the encampment theme, Eleguá's throne adds the topsy-turvy element of a child's playroom. Arrayed about the leaves are multifarious toys "and all sorts of candies this spoiled and childlike *oricha* enjoys" (Ecún 1985, 25; see plate 11). In the United States, the toys are typically the cheap and bountiful plastic kind, still in their colorful shrink-wrapped packaging from the revolving racks of discount stores: little guns, cars, and trucks, crayon sets, balls and jacks, miniature mechanical drawing boards, and so on. With its pine boughs, hanging gourds, airplane bottles of liquor, and colorful plastic toys, Eleguá's throne looks like cross between a lean-to and a massive Christmas tree. Commonly, and in great contrast to the other *orichas,* initiates of Eleguá and Ogún, dressed in their Middle Day best, are permitted to leave the throne and wander about the house. Throughout the afternoon, they serve *aguardiente,* strong rum, to visitors from little, painted clay jugs. At the Middle Day for the double initiation of Eleguá and Ogún in Guanabacoa recently, the two *iyawós* and their *oyubonas* left the house for the corner bar, purchased more bottles of *aguardiente,* and served all passersby as they processed merrily around the block. While the orderly house of Obatalá critically distinguishes between the inside and the outside, these irrepressible Warriors are permitted to breach the two domains.

ROPA DE SANTO: SACRED GARMENTS AND ACCESSORIES OF THE *ORICHAS*

On the Día del Medio, *iyawós* are dressed in the *orichas' trajes de gala,* their "best clothes." These outfits are called *ropa de santo* or *traje de medio* (sacred clothes or Middle Day suit). As in other forms of cloth work—thrones and *paños*—the colors and materials selected follow the iconographic requirements of the *orichas'* identifying colors and oracular numbers (see Brown 1996).[16] The preferred fabric is luminous, layered satin trimmed with metallic braid or sequins, and the intended aesthetic effects are resplendence, royalty, and luxury (see plates 12–16 and the first epigraph in this chapter). Even the rustic Warriors wear satin consecration garments, a sartorial concession they make to the decorum of Obatalá's house for the several hours they must spend inside on the Día del Medio (plates 12, 13, 14).

A 1980s *ropa de santo* ensemble for Eleguá produced by Cuban-born Yemayá priestess Lourdes López of West New York, New Jersey, features a red satin tunic with loose sleeves, black tubular cuffs, and a black close collar (plate 12). It is typical of the male *orichas'* jacket style. With its tubular collar and cuffs, and front that fastens at the side, it recalls seventeenth- and early-eighteenth-century military and cavalry tunics, as seen in aristocratic and royal portraits, such as those by the Cuban painter Vicente Escobar (1757–1834; see fig. 4.4).[17] The outfit's knickers, also typical of the male *orichas' ropa de santo,* are called *pantalones de bombacha.* They do recall the "Spanish breeches" of the sixteenth and seventeenth centuries, which were trimmed

Figure 4.4.—Vicente Escobar (1757–1854), *Retrato de Niño* [Portrait of a boy], Cuba, early nineteenth century. Oil on canvas. Note the tubular collar and sleeves and the style of the jacket, which is fastened down the side. (From Corporación Nacional del Turismo 1950.)

Figure 4.5.—Víctor Patricio de Landaluze, *Centinela Español*, Cuba, c. 1870s. Note the campaign hat with raised brim and the knickers (*bombachas*) tucked into tied gaiters (*polainas*). The "warrior's" gaiters are symbolically reproduced in the initiation room as the legs of initiates of Eleguá, Ogún, and Ochosi, and sometimes other orichas, such as Changó and Agayú, are painted with repeated hash marks (representing the laces of the gaiters). (Courtesy Museo Nacional de Bellas Artes, Havana.)

with ribbon and zigzag cuffs. Breeches, however, were open bottomed. Thus, in fact, the *bombachas* are closer to European "knickerbockers" (a term that originated in the United States) of the late eighteenth century and onwards. These are full, loose breeches gathered at the knee. Such knee-length loose pants were often combined with flaring, deep-cuffed boots (see Peacock 1991, 214–22) and could be seen in the seventeenth- and eighteenth-century European nobility's male riding wear, in the rugged outfits of musketeers, and in the uniforms Spanish colonial soldiers in Cuba. Víctor Patricio de Landaluze, for example, documented a Spanish sentinel in the countryside whose knickers were worn above high, cuffed leather boots, a combination suited to trekking, horseback riding, keeling, and taking aim with a rifle. The warriors's uniform is completed with a wide-brimmed, plumed hat (*sombrero*; figs. 4.5, 4.6, plates 12, 13, 14). The zigzag pattern of the jacket's waist, a playful, harlequin-like flourish for Eleguá, is echoed in the

Figure 4.6.—Spanish musketeer (*mosquetero*), c. seventeenth century. Note the high boots and knickers, as well as the plumed floppy hat. (From Ramón Garciá-Pelayo y Gross, *Pequeño Larousse Ilustrado*, 1984, 703. Courtesy Administration du Service Iconografique.)

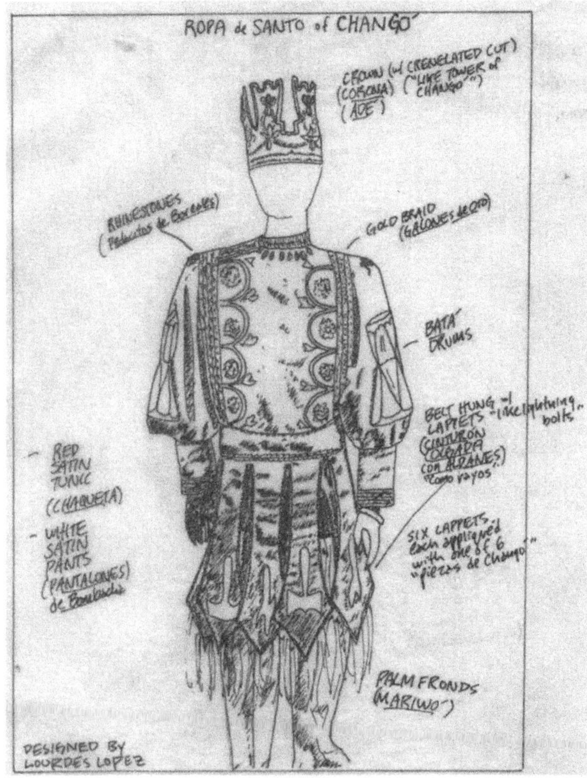

Figure 4.7.—*Ropa de santo* of Changó, by Lourdes López, 1984. Note appliqué patches of *batá* drums. (Drawing by David H. Brown.)

bombachas' cuffs, a feature also typical of the *bombachas* of the other male *orichas*. Each point of Eleguá's zigzags features a single cowrie shell. The jacket's sleeves and chest are adorned with emblem-like appliqués of black satin adorned with white military-like braid for a striking contrast, along with cowrie shells patterned in one of Eleguá's sacred numbers, three.[18] A final elegant touch is offered by the tapered and braided belt, tied to the side. López's designs for the female *orichas'* aristocratic gowns emphasize puff-shouldered, elbow-length sleeves, flowing, pleated skirts, and square, open collars that are decoratively bordered. On Yemayá's deep blue satin full-length gown, white and silver braids alternate around the square neckline and sleeves and on the broad belt. Ochún's gown is made of an expensive, honey-colored silk brocade with gold thread (plates 15, 16).

López's intricate iconographic appliqués manifest the *orichas'* character attributes, functional domains, animal avatars, and oracular numbers. The gown of Yemayá, owner of the sea, features rolling waves in silver lamé appliqué and other nautical iconography.[19] The double skirts of Ochún's gown part to reveal one of Ochún's avatars, the resplendent peacock (*pavo real*), complete with real feathers. Changó, the master of *batá* drumming and dancing, owns a jacket adorned with appliqués of double-headed *batá* drums at the shoulders. Each of the six-pointed lap-

Figure 4.8.—*Ropa de santo* of Obatalá, by Lourdes López, 1984. Note radiations of silver trimming from central snail shell, representing the Holy Sacrament. (Courtesy Caribbean Cultural Center and Lourdes López. Photograph by David H. Brown.)

Figure 4.9.—Jesuit monstrance on Abakuá altar. Antique cast brass, approximately 9 inches tall. It is a representation of the Holy Sacrament (*Santísimo Sacramento*), featuring the goblet and the circular paten, a disklike plate that supports the wafer of the Host turned vertically for observation by the flock. It bears baroque-style visually legible radiations of grace. (Photograph by David H. Brown.)

pets (*aldanes*), which descend like lightning bolts from his waist belt, bears an appliquéd thunderax (*oché-changó*). The lappets rise, fall, and swirl outward when Changó dances and somersaults, embodying the fury of the *trueno* (thunder; see fig. 4.7). Eight rays of sinuous silver braid radiate out from a large, round, opalescent snail shell on each puffy sleeve of Obatalá's jacket (fig. 4.8). The gentle, slow-moving snail (*babosa*), whose blood is white, is one of Obatalá's distinctive sacrifical animals; and one of Obatalá's sacred numbers is eight. At the same time, the

Figure 4.10.—Popular chromolithograph of Santa Bárbara with a goblet, a sword, and a crenellated castle tower as a crown.

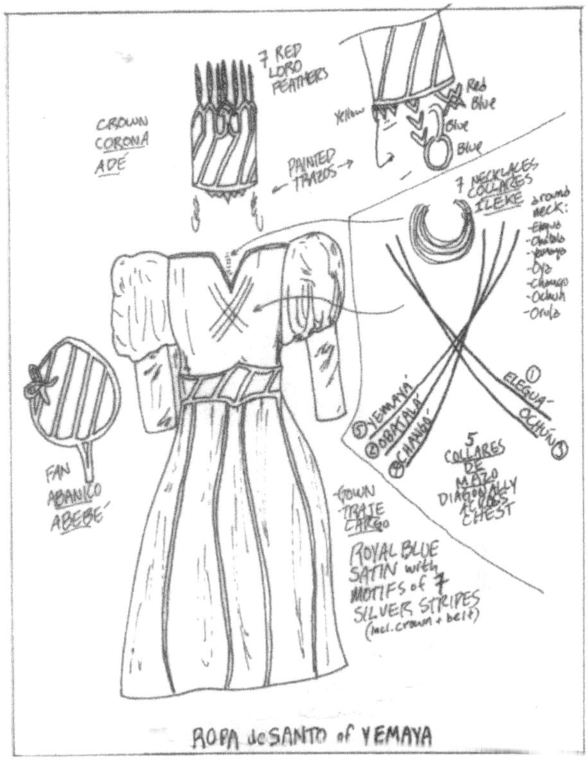

Figure 4.11.—*Ropa de santo* of Yemayá, by Dolores Pérez, including fan (*abanico*), crown with red tail feathers of African gray parrot (*pluma de loro,* or *ikodilé*). The schematic of the *collares de mazo* shows how the beadwork sashes were placed around the body. (Drawing by David Brown, 1988.)

design reproduces the baroque representation of the divine light of the Holy Sacrament (*Santísimo Sacramento*), which Obatalá borrows from the iconography of the Roman Catholic monstrance (or *ciborium;* figs. 4.9, 4.10, plate 10).

Headgear of Status: Crowns, Sombreros, and Ikodidé

Obatalá, Oyá, Ochún, Yemayá, Agayú, and Changó wear circular, open pasteboard crowns, which shimmer with metallic trim, sequins, rhinestones, metallic braid, and number-coded sets of cowrie shells. Lourdes López's Yemayá crown, for example, is encrusted with white plastic shells, opals, and sea horses. Changó's crown typically features the crenelations of the castle tower he shares with Santa Bárbara and constellations of cowrie shells (see plate 17, figs. 4.7, 4.10, 4.20). The number of points on each crown corresponds to the deity's sacred number-coded "signature": Obatalá's has eight points; Oyá's, nine points; Ochún's, five points; Yemayá's, seven points; Agayú's, nine points, and Changó's, six points (plates 15, 16, figs. 4.7, 4.8, 4.11, 4.12).

A bright red tail feather of the African gray parrot (Spanish *pluma de loro;* Lucumí *ikodidé*) is sewn or taped to each point of the non-Warrior *orichas'* pasteboard crowns—except those of Changó's initiates. These stout,

Figure 4.12.—Pasteboard crown of the "Middle Day" for Obatalá with eight *ikodidé*, designed by Lourdes López. Carton, satin, cowrie shells, sequins, and red tail feathers of African gray parrot). (Courtesy Lourdes López. Photograph by David H. Brown.)

sharp feathers stand upright like a circle of little flames (figs. 4.11, 4.12).[20] Some associate the *ikodidé* with the high status of their consecrated wearers, who are beneficiaries of *aché* from heaven (Thompson 1983, 18; J. Mason 1994, 214 n. 15). A Yoruba transatlantic motif, the feathers also turn up on the shaved and painted heads of Brazilian Candomblé initiates (see Carybé 1980, 29, 31, 37). In Yorubaland, red parrot feathers, as well as representations of encircling birds, are associated with the protective beaded conical crowns of legitimate kingship (Thompson 1970; Matory 1994, 54; see fig. 5.1). As well, the feathers "serve as signs of witchcraft" and "public disaffection"—the very forces that can lead to the downfall of crowned kings (Apter 1992, 109).

Curiously, though the *ikodidé* appears as a prominent motif in Lucumí praise songs about Changó's protection of the "heads" of the *orichas'* consecrated children,[21] it is conspicuously absent from his own Día del Medio iconography. Some believe that Changó does not need this powerful "symbol of prosperity, royalty, achievement, and good fortune" because he was "born, and died, a king" or was "born with a crown."[22] In other words, the inherent qualities and biography of the only *oricha* believed to have been a mortal ruler—the Fourth Alafin of Oyó—render the feather redundant.[23] Others emphasize the feather's explicit connection to problems of witchcraft and its corresponding antidotes. For *oriaté* Miguel Ramos, the red parrot feather is a sign of the initiate's protection against a "curse," to which Changó, "because of his truthfulness before God, remained immune. . . . The feather is placed on the head so Olorun [God] can recognize the initiate and exempt him from further sorrows." The children of Changó, who receive other kinds of protective measures, "are exempt from such evil machinations, or are not as affected by them."[24]

In contrast to the other *orichas'* royal crowns and acessories, the Warriors' headgear, as well as their side bags and handheld implements, combines references to occupations outside of political, community, and domestic boundaries: traveling and tracking, farming, guarding and killing, herbalism and witchcraft. The Warriors often wear common straw hats with wide brims, which protect the head against the elements, for example, the *sombrero de yarey*[25] of the *guajiros* (farmers) of Cuba's interior (plates 12, 13, fig. 4.13). Alternatively, they may wear wide-brimmed felt, leather, canvas, or satin-covered hats with plumes, which, in form, recall the headgear of flintlock-toting musketeers, Spanish-Cuban colonial soldiers, and the Child of Antioch with whom Eleguá is associated. This child Jesus figure is pictured in the countryside wearing a brimmed and plumed hat and carrying a staff fitted with a small gourd (plate 14, figs. 4.5, 4.6, 4.14). The gourd appropriately reproduces the natural ritual container of Osain, owner of the leaves, and the African Elegba's dance statuettes that feature small gourds (*àdo*) used for storing powdered medicine (*àṣẹ̀;* fig. 5.39; see Abraham 1946, 282;

Figure 4.13.—Víctor Patricio de Landaluze, *El Zapateo con Sombreros*, late nineteenth century. Oil on canvas, 13⅜ x 10⅝ inches. (Courtesy Museo Nacional de Bellas Artes, Havana.)

Figure 4.14.—Popular chromolithograph of the Child of Antioch (*El Niño de Atocha*). Note the wide-brimmed hat with plumes and the gourd on his staff.

Thompson [1971] 1976, chap. 4, figs. 6, 11, 14, 15; 1983, 28–29, 32; Carybé 1980, 47, 49). Open crowns are to the heavenward, diaphanous throne canopies of translucent cloth as closed straw hats are to leafy thrones, which, like forest cover, reproduce the shadowed spaces of the *monte adentro* (deep forest; see Brown 1989, 343–46).

As paragons of itinerancy and survival under fierce conditions, the Warriors carry rustic animal skin shoulder bags (*alforjas, carteras,* or *cartucheras*). The skin bags are physical embodiments of the sacrificial animals and ingredients used to feed and appease them. For example, those of Eleguá and Ogún are made of male goatskin and contain their favorite dried, toasted, and smoked provisions, as well as candy and cigars in the case of Eleguá (see plates 12, 13, 14). Ochosi's bag, as well as his cape and apron (*capa* and *delantalsillo*), may be made of the goatskin, or the skin of the deer (*venado*), a nondomesticated animal that underscores his role as a hunter of swift prey (plate 14).[26] As physical embodiments of movement, the shoulder bags are worn by the diviners, hunters, and warriors of Cuban Lucumí legends (*patakí*), who, Ernesto Pichardo notes, "carry their secrets with them while the other *orichas* keep their things in the houses."[27] Oddé, a special hunter-magician *oricha* received by *babalawos* carries a shoulder bag in his travels. A Lucumí divination legend utilizes Oddé's bag and remote forest grove as markers of deep secrets associated with danger, liminality, sacrificial killing, and the hunter's charge to provide spiritual sustenance to the *orichas* in the form of blood (see Elizondo [1934?] n.d., 47; see also Armstrong 1989).[28] In Lucumí, *odé* literally means "hunter," forms part of Ochosi's principal praise name (Odé Mata, the Hunter *oricha*), and identifies marginal zones "outside the house": "the street" and the "outskirts" (Cabrera [1970] 1983, 233–34; Abraham 1946, 449). Looking to Yoruba precedents, Miguel Ramos believes the *alforjas* to be "a recreation of the *apo* [*àpò*] or divination bags carried by Yoruba Ifá diviners" when they travel away from home to conduct oracular consultations (see, e.g., Bascom 1969a, 32 and plates 3, 4, 16; Drewal and Mason 1998, 230–35, 244).[29] Appropriately, *iyawós* of the Warriors are outfitted with their *alforjas* during the mounting ceremony under the exterior throne of leaves and, then, along with their *sombreros* and appropriate handheld weapons, make the trip indoors (see Ecún 1985, 39, 66). When they leave the throne for a barefoot afternoon stroll around the house or the block, they always don their *sombreros* and shoulder bags and take along their particular tools or weapons (*herramientas*).

Dance Wands: Tools of the Orichas' Spiritual Work

Next to the *orichas'* identifying colors, their handheld staffs and dance wands constitute their most basic and recognizable iconography. Royal fly whisks (Lucumí *iruké;* Spanish *rabo*) accompany the ensembles of Obatalá and Oyá (figs. 4.15, 4.16, 4.17); fans (Lucumí *abebé;* Spanish

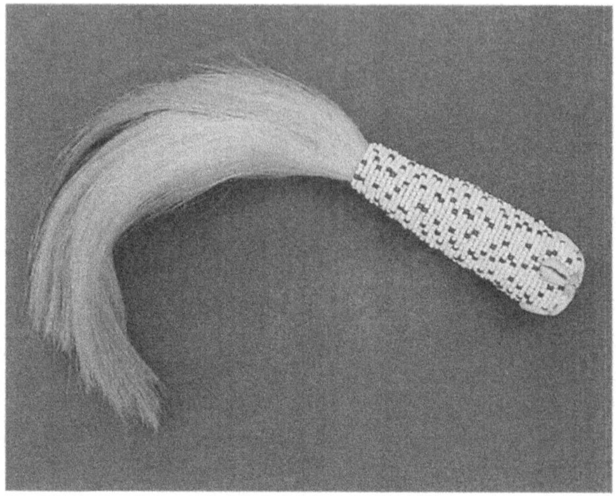

Figure 4.15.—Horsetail fly whisk of Obatalá (*rabo de caballo*, or *iruké*), designed by Pedro Abreu, Havana, 2001. (Photograph by David H. Brown.)

abanico) are carried by Yemayá and Ochún (figs. 4.18, 4.19); the thunderax (Lucumí *oché;* Spanish *hacha*) of "fire" and "problems" is held by Changó, or carried on his head (plate 17, fig. 4.20). Prototypes for these Lucumí staffs are found in the beaded or painted dance wands—fans, cutlasses, clubs, thunderaxes, fly whisks, and medicinal brooms—carried by priests in possession performances and displayed in shrines throughout Yorubaland (e.g., fig. 4.21), and a comparable repertoire of attributes is encountered in the Candomblés and Umbandas of Brazil (see Thompson 1983, 18–93; 1993, 145–282; Drewal, Pemberton, and Abiodum 1989, passim; Drewal and Mason 1998, passim; Omari 1984, plates 1, 3, pp.19–26, 33–39; Carybé 1980, passim; da Motta Lody n.d., passim; M. Drewal 1986, 1989).

Dance wands, when held and carried in a dance, become explicit embodiments of each *oricha*'s particular *aché*, in the sense of divinely given genius, vocation, and relationship to nature. As extensions of the hand, they serve to evoke, invoke, and activate the *orichas'* potential for trans-

Figure 4.16.—Oyá in the fierce whirlwind phase of her dance, with two fly whisks flailed in circular motion. Conjunto Folklórico Nacional de Cuba, 1986. (Photograph by David H. Brown.)

Figure 4.17.—Oyá with fly whisk atop her head. In this phase, she is a still, vigilant, and impassive warrior-queen and stands with arms akimbo—a crucible of potential energy. Conjunto Folklórico Nacional de Cuba, 1986. (Photograph by David H. Brown.)

Figure 4.18.—Semicircular fan of peacock feathers for Ochún, by Lourdes López, New Jersey, 1984. Approximately 15 inches across. (Courtesy Caribbean Cultural Center and Lourdes López. Photograph by David H. Brown.)

Figure 4.19.—Beaded fan for Ochún, by Ramón Febles Molina (Obetuanilara, c. 1845–1937), produced in Havana in the early twentieth century. Approximately 12 inches. Private collection, Havana. (Photograph by David H. Brown.)

formative action in the phenomenal world, that is, "work" (see M. Drewal 1989, 208, 223–29; Drewal, Pemberton, and Aliodum 1989, 16). Ogún's sharp, iron machete blade, for example, embodies his massive force and unhesitating swiftness in cutting through fierce problems, executing blood sacrifice, and causing injury through irrational violence, as well as creating technological solutions to human needs (see Barnes 1989b). The forceful texture of his dance movement repertoire demonstrates his agility, violence, and implacability (see Ortiz [1951] 1985, 304–6; Barnes 1989a; M. Drewal 1989).[30] Oyá's black fly whisk from the tail of a bull (*rabo de buey*) befits this queenly, erstwhile wife of Changó. At the same time, it is the sign of her storm patterns, her vigilance and judgment, her role as mistress of the dead, and her disposition as sentinel of the cemetery's threshold. She can be tempestuous, aggressive, stoic, or silently judgmental. In the climactic phases of her dance, Oyá's fly whisk (sometimes two, or a fly whisk and sword) traces the furious path of the whirlwind (*remolino;* see Ortiz [1951] 1985, 339–40); here, the fly whisk indexes sudden and calamitous transitions, including the passing of life (see Gleason 1987, 40, 44–45, 127; fig. 4.16). With her fly whisk held stoically over one shoulder, Oyá stands as a dignified and impassive warrior-queen at the cemetery gate as the dead are carried to their graves. With the fly whisk atop her head, arms akimbo, and eyes piercing, Oyá vigilantly stands in judgment (fig. 4.17).

Rounded fans (Lucumí *abebé;* Spanish *abanico*) mirror the fecund female bodies of Yemayá and Ochún, evoke cooling drops of water, and transmit refreshing, healing breezes (see Thompson 1983, 73–80).[31] The large, semicircular, whimsical fans of peacock or ostrich plumes that Lourdes López creates for these two female *orichas* (see fig. 4.18) are creole substitutions for the earlier Lucumí tradition of small, densely beaded, round and teardrop-shaped fans produced by the Lucumí in the nineteenth and early twentieth centuries (fig. 4.19; see Ortiz 1952–55, 2:300–301).

Changó carries a "thunderax," representing two bal-

Figure 4.20.—The "Alafin de Oyó" crown (Changó's crown), by the late Ramiro Hernández Almirall. Wood, cardboard, felt, beads, sequins, and rhinestones, approximately 10 inches high. From a special exhibition at the Museo Nacional de Bellas Artes, Havana, 1986. (Photograph by David H. Brown.)

Figure 4.21.—Ọyọ́ Yoruba shrine for Ṣàngó, with two mortars supporting thunderstones, three thunderaxes, rattle, horns, and *làbà* panels, Mẹ̀kọ, Nigeria, 1950. (Courtesy The Phoebe Anderson Hearst Museum of Anthropology and the Regents of the University of California.)

anced thundercelts (*eduará*). In a blend of male macho and meteorological fury, Changó mimes the spitting of fire through pursed lips, stomps about, grabs his balls, and performs athletic somersaults (see Ortiz [1951] 1985, 333). Customarily of cedar, a tall reddish tree, his thunderaxes (*oché*) range from straightforward cut-out-and-painted versions to voluptous, magnificently beaded, and cowrie-encrusted productions that weigh a couple of pounds (see plates 17, 9, *upper center*). When incorporated in dance, they bring his lightning *aché* down from the sky. As worn atop his crown, they signify "fire," or "problems," on the head, as well as his mythico-historical role as the "Alafin of Oyó" (fig. 4.20).[32]

In contrast to some of the more refined implements of palace royalty or aristocracy—for example, fly whisks and fans—the Warriors carry rustic implements of work,

Figure 4.22.—The Warriors—Eleguá (*embedded in shell, and in form of coconut*), Ogún (*iron pots, with Ochosi inside*), and Ósun (*staff, right*)—and the beaded, hooked staff of Eleguá. (Photograph by David H. Brown.)

herbalism, war, and hunting: a hooked staff (*garabato*) of *guayaba* wood for Eleguá, a bow and arrow (*arco y flecha*) and arrow-filled quiver for Ochosi, and, of course, the cutlass for Ogún (Lucumí *adá;* Spanish *machete;* plates 12, 13, 14, fig. 4.22). Eleguá's beaded hook permits this trickster and glutton to "trip up" unsuspecting travelers on his road and "grab whatever he wants" (plates 12, 18, fig. 4.22); Ogún's machete permits him to cut through fierce problems, though he sometimes kills in a spate of unrestrained violence (plate 13); Ochosi's bow and arrow permit him to skillfully reach his target from afar and provide sustenance to the world (plate 14). The Warriors' rustic and fierce iconography of war, hunting, and the countryside is made up of implements analogous to those carried by their forest counterparts in the "strong" Palo Monte religion (hooked staffs [*lungowa*], knives, machetes, and "charged" animal horns [*mpaka*]; fig. 4.23).

Although the basic iconography of these impressive dance wands is Yoruba-derived, it has been creatively reworked in the Cuban idiom. The red and black bead-wrapped hooked staff of the Afro-Cuban Eleguá (fig. 4.22) replaced the Yoruba Elegba's figurated phallic club (*ogo-elegba;* see Thompson 1983, 32). Fashioned in Cuba from his guava (*guayaba*) tree, the *garabato* was adapted from

Figure 4.23.—Congo-Cuban *nganga* (also known as *nkiso, prenda, caldero*) of Sarabanda (with warrior or forest attributes: hooked *lungoa*, knives and machetes) and *mpaka* (divination horns). Ethnographic Museum of Guanabacoa, Havana. (Photograph by David H. Brown.)

Figure 4.24.—Víctor Patricio de Landaluze, *La Mulata de Rumbo*, 1881. This fan-holding "*mulata* of the street" was a fixture of nineteenth- and early-twentieth-century Cuban arts and letters. She provided the model for and embodied the tensions of mixed Cuban identity. Lithograph. (From Landaluze 1881.)

the rural implement used by *campesinos* and herbalists for reaching, hooking, and pulling down foliage, herbs, and crops to be cut with a machete held in the opposite hand; this is one of concrete ways this male fraternity—Osain, Eleguá, and Ogún—may be seen to work together (Osain owns the plants, Eleguá grabs and holds just what he needs, and Ogún swiftly cuts).[33] Though Changó's principal icon is the thunderax, he also wields man-made weapons. His threatening whip-and-sword combination (*látigo* and *espada*) was standard equipment issued to Cuban plantation overseers (Thomas 1971, 114). The Lucumí appropriated these rural weapons of oppression, along with the machete of the brutal sugar cane economy, and transformed them into instruments of Afro-Cuban strength, liberation, and healing. From the urban environment, the Lucumí borrowed many of Ochún's feminine qualities and the style of her principal accoutrement from an extravagant colonial "Havana [,which] was known for its fans" (Thomas 1971, 145). Decorative fans were public attributes of two urban colonial female social types, the light-skinned demimondaine of the street (*mulata de rumbo;* see Landaluze 1881, 33; Kutzinski 1993, fig. 4.24) and the upper-class white bourgeois woman, "who had very little to do . . . and occupied [her] time managing [her] powdered eggshell cosmetic (*cascarilla*) and [her] fans" (Thomas 1971, 147).

"Beads Equal Money": The Collares de Mazo

On the Día del Medio, *iyawós* bear the weight of multiple bead sashes called *collares de mazo* (literally "bunched necklaces" or "bundle of bead strands"). They are slung diagonally across the chest in two directions like bandoliers, forming an X (fig. 4.11). Commonly, on the Día del Medio, the *iyawó* wears one *mazo* for each of the *orichas* "made" and "received" in the *asiento,* which may amount to five, six, or even seven.[34] Reflecting the methodical protocols of the initiation (see chap. 3), the *mazos* are placed over the *iyawó*'s body in the order in which the *orichas* are ritually addressed in all of the initiation's principal ceremonies, beginning with Eleguá, who opens the road, and culminating in the *oricha* of honor, the guardian angel.[35]

Painstakingly made by hand, the *collares de mazo* consist of multiple bead strands organized on the basis of an *oricha*'s signature number and pattern of counterpointed colors. The thick, sashlike circle of multiple strands is subdivided into segments by large, decorative fastening beads called *glorias.* Some Cuban *mazo* artists refer to the *glorias* as *casas* ("houses") and the multiple strands of beads between the *casas* as *caminos* ("paths").[36] Attached to the sash at each *gloria,* by tying or insertion, are multistranded tassles, called *moñas* (knots or ties). The *moñas* emanate from the sash circle like the tentacles of an octopus. One of them, the *moña principal* (principal knot), is the most worked and elaborate. The *moña principal* is formed when the two ends of the sash being worked are brought together and threaded through a large *gloria* (fig. 4.25, plate 18).[37] Obatalá-Ayáguna's *collar de mazo* is typically white punctuated by red (because Ayáguna is a "young" "warrior" related to Changó); Obatalá's signature number is eight and its multiples (sixteen, twenty-four, and thirty-two). An example produced by Melba Carillo of New York is composed of a sash of sixteen strands with eight main *glorias* and eight *moñas* (fig. 4.25).[38] Each *mazo* can weigh three or more pounds and may consist of more than twelve thousand glass, ceramic, metal, wood, and plastic beads.[39] Many *mazo* makers rely on plastic *glorias* for economy, in order to sell their work at reasonable prices ($70–$120); however, similar *mazos,* purchased from the same makers, are normally sold at inflated prices through *botánicas* at upwards of $175. Makers agree that plastic *glorias* are less aesthetically pleasing, and those with higher aesthetic standards and economic means prefer to use only glass, metal, enameled ceramic, and wood beads. *Mazos* can be further elaborated with beautiful and unusual glass, ceramic, or wooden *glorias,* other decorative fastening beads, crystal rosettes, cowries, semiprecious stones, and so on, which vary their texture, profile, reflectiveness, and weight. Such a decked-out *mazo* using the highest quality materials might cost $200 or more to make.[40]

New York *iyalocha* Melba Carillo understands the *mazos* she makes as formal descendants of the cowrie shell garlands and bandoliers worn by priests in West Africa, which she has seen in ethnographic photographs (e.g., Verger 1954, plate 131). For Miami *oriaté* Miguel Ramos, "beads equal money," and the *collares de mazo* "represent *iré ayé*—luck" in the form of money (see also Cabrera [1957] 1986, 170).[41] Indeed, the heavy, intricate *mazos,* dense treasure troves of brilliance, color contrast, and textural variation, embody and announce the *orichas'* wealth and power in a manner that does recall royal and ritual adornment in Yorubaland. There, resplendent art objects of beads and cowrie shells are the "prerogative" of kings, priests, and *òrìsà* (see Thompson 1970, 8; Bascom 1969b, 32; Drewal and Mason 1998). For example, the cowrie-

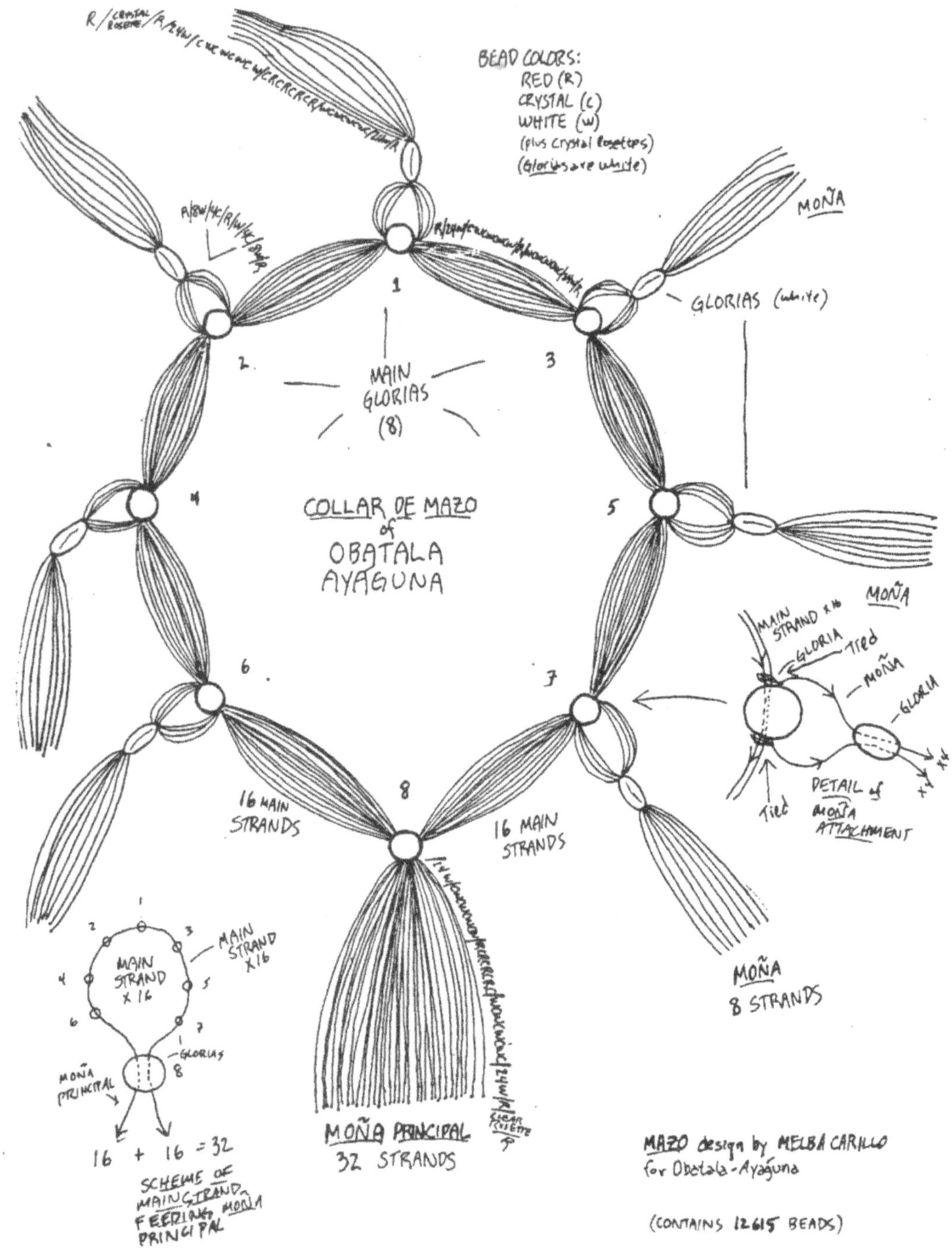

Figure 4.25.—*Collares de mazo* for Obatalá-Ayáguna, designed by Melba Carillo, New York, 1984. (Line drawing by David H. Brown.)

encrusted crowns of the royal diety Dàda (*baàyọ́nnì*) express "money on the head" (*olówó-orí;* Abraham 1946, 121); Elegba's prodigious garlands of cowries are signs of "wealth and fecundity"; the rich cowrie or beaded vests of Ibeji twin figures express "divine force," "command," the thunder god's power and royalty, and the great fortune and increase represented by twin birth (see Thompson 1993, 251–60; [1971] 1976, chap. 13, p. 4). Aesthetically, the additive accumulation of bead and cowrie strands, as with layers of expensive cloth, produces assemblages of density, intricacy, and weight; when worn, they produce the impression of larger physical girth, stature, and, by extension, well-being or authority (see Drewal, Pemberton, and Abiodum 1989, 91–92). Whether or not they are aware of specific historical precedents, such aesthetic and semantic effects are not lost on Cuban practitioners.

In Cuba, the beaded *mazos* are an integral component of the sumptuary preserve of the Lucumí *orichas* (i.e., the "prerogative of kings"), whose satins, brocades, bejeweled crowns, thrones, mortars, and handheld staffs of office are prestige possessions exclusive to them and are displayed only on the occasion of semipublic celebrations: the Día del Medio, drummings, and birthdays. Second, the *collares de mazo* mark boldly and bodily the claims of "ownership" that the *orichas* have made upon the "heads" of initiates. In their lives as objects, the *mazos* are activated as spiritual lassos by ritual elders, and by *orichas* when they possess their priests, to ensnare those "marked" for initiation, a dramatic move called *la prendición* (the "seizing" or "arrest"; see Cabrera [1974] 1980, 146–47).[42] The deployment of *mazos* in these preinitiatory settings, in which people are *prendido por el santo* (seized by the *santo*), prefigures the wearing of *mazos* on the Día del Medio, an aesthetically marked occasion on which *mazos* proudly proclaim the consecration of an *oricha*'s new child: a king, queen, or warrior. In this sense, the *mazos* mark the *orichas*' "weath" and "increase" in the form of their new "children"—their *iyawós*. When not encircling bodies, the *mazos* are draping or encircling the *orichas' soperas* in their permanent domestic shrines or on birthday and drumming thrones (plates 9, 17, 18, figs. 4.11, 4.22, 5.30*A*, 5.31; see Brown 1993b, 47; 1996, plates 1–4). Hence, the *mazos* mark and adorn two powerful containers of the *orichas' aché* in the phenomenal world: bodies and vessels. At festival time, both are "dressed" in prestige cloth, along with their special beadwork, and seated under the throne for formal presentation to "the people."

THE CEREMONIES THAT CHANGÓ "DESIGNED": INITIATORY SEATS FOR THE ARRIVAL OF KINGS, QUEENS, AND WARRIORS

Changó, the mythical Fourth "Alafin of Oyó," is the *oricha* most identified as the overseer and protector of the *kariocha,* as well as the provider of its means. "All initiation procedures practiced by the Lùkùmí in Cuba," John Mason writes, "are variations on the rituals performed when a priest of Ṣàngó [Changó] is initiated" (1992, 170). Changó, Miguel Ramos amplifies, "is believed to [have] designed the ceremonies of the initiation." Changó's presence is nowhere more apparent than in the object that serves as the *asiento*'s principal consecration stool, called *pilón* in Spanish and *odó* in Lucumí.[43] The *pilón* is a cilindrical-, hourglass-, or pedestal-shaped hollow mortar of cedar or mohogany, often adorned with low bas-relief, hand-painted, or burned-in surface designs. Once hewn by hand, like its morphological cousin, the Lucumí *batá* drum, the *pilón* is now typically turned on a lathe (cf. plate 19, fig. 4.21, plate 17; see Ortiz 1952–55, 3:115–18, 233).[44]

Changó's *pilón* is central to the cluster of royal iconography that elaborates the Lucumí initiation of the non-Warrior *orichas.* As Lydia Cabrera's midcentury Lucumí informants told her, the *pilón* is "the typical seat of honor [*sitial*] of the *asiento* ceremony of the god of fire Changó;" yet it could be "shared" with other *orichas.* "Yemayá, Ochún, Obatalá [may] sit on chairs [*sillas*]; [and] Elegua, Ogún, Ochosi [sic] . . . on stone," they added. However,

"Obatalá, Yemayá, and Ochún have the right to sit on the *pilón because they are kings and queens"* (Cabrera [1974] 1980, 162; emphasis added).[45] In other words, as Ernesto Pichardo explains, the mortar "extends" a principal sign of Changó's royal status—he was the "Fourth Alafin of Oyó"—to these other *orichas* and critically distinguishes their common "royal" or "palace" domain from the *monte* of the Warriors.[46]

In stark contrast to the lathe-turned mortar or upright chairs, Eleguá and Ogún require a large, often jagged, heavy stone (*piedra*), which is imported from the *monte* or, on occasion, the sea or river (Ecún 1985, 25, 54; see plate 18). Ochosi may require the raw trunk (*tronco*) of the almond tree (*almendra* or *almendro;* Ecún 1985, 78).[47] Eleguá, too, may utilize a trunk, but it should come from his own sacred tree, the *guayaba,* which is also the source for his hooked dance wand.[48] Stones and trunks are of a piece with the cluster of undomesticated aesthetic markers from *la naturaleza* that distinguishes the Warriors' initiations: leafy thrones, straw *sombreros,* animal skin bags, and rustic weapons and implements.

The Lucumí *pilón* (*odó* in Lucumí) is traceable to the shrines and initiation media of the Ọ̀yọ́-Yoruba royal cults. As J. Lorand Matory deftly shows, the mortar was and is central to the iconography of the Ọ̀yọ́ Empire, whose tutelary *òrìṣà* was Ṣàngó, the Fourth *aláàáfin* (see Matory 1994, 227; Smith 1969, 38–39; see fig. 4.21). Rejected by his subjects, one myth version relates, Ṣàngó abdicated his throne, hung himself from the *àyọn* tree, and was later deified by his remaining loyal followers as the fearsome *òrìṣà* of thunder and lightning (Abraham 1946, 621; Beier 1980; see also Drewal, Pemberton, and Abiodun 1989, 156, fig. 172). In the Ọ̀yọ́-North Kingdom of Igboho, Matory observed the *odó* in the royal shrines of Ṣàngó and Yẹmọja, whose claims to royalty derive from birth and marriage, which bridge two ancient Yoruba kingdoms. In one received genealogical reckoning, Yẹmọja is the daughter of Ọ̀bàtálá and Odùduwà (the Ifẹ̀ Kingdom); she is the wife of Ọ̀rọnyọ̀n (the founder of Ọ̀yọ́); and she is the mother of the principal Ọ̀yọ́ royal children, Sòngó, Dáda, and Ṣọ̀npọ̀nọ́n (see Abraham 1946, 680). The *odó* elevates the thunderstone-filled altar pots of Ṣàngó in Ọ̀yọ́ and Ọ̀yọ́-influenced areas and is used for the initiation of Ṣàngó's priests. As William Bascom noted in the caption of his well-known 1950 photograph of a Ṣàngó shrine in the town of Mẹ̀kọ, the "inverted mortar . . . decorated with a human face and a ram's head . . . serves as a stool when initiates are shaved" (Bascom 1969b, 86; fig. 4.21). The mortar is also integral to the choreography of public ritual performances: sitting or standing upon the mortar effects the invocation, spirit possession, and prophetic speech of Ṣàngó (see Thompson 1983, 86; Apter 1992, 106 and plate 6; Drewal 1986).

In Cuba, the Lucumí reinstituted the Yoruba Ṣàngó's mortar as a shrine pedestal and initiatory seat. Year-round, the mortar would continue to elevate Changó's wood vessel (*batea*) containing his thunderstones (*eduará*). As in Ọ̀yọ́-Yoruba practice, the mortar would be inverted as a ritual stool for his initiations. In the first half of the twentieth century, Fernando Ortiz found the *pilón* in use as an initiatory seat in the Lucumí consecration ceremonies for both Changó and Yemayá (1952-55 3:115–18). In Cuba, the *pilón* would also be used to elevate the shrine objects of Ọ̀yọ́-descended Lucumí *orichas:* Agayú (Changó's mythological "brother" or "father"), Dadá-Bañaní (Changó's "sister"), and, in some cases, Yemayá (Changó's mother). In time, as Cabrera's sources noted, Obatalá, Ochún, and Oyá would also sit upon the mortar in their initiations because they too, became "kings" and "queens" within the creole paradigm of Lucumí palace royalty (Cabrera [1974] 1980, 162).

Morphologically and semantically, the *pilón* overlaps with the figures of Changó's royal palm tree (*palma real, Roystonea regia,* family Palmaceae), the tallest, most regal tree on the Cuban landscape, whose top is regularly lopped off by lightning, the royal "castle" that serves as Changó's "lookout tower," which he shares with Santa Bárbara (Cabrera [1954] 1983, 221, 230), and the hourglass-shaped *batá* drums central to Lucumí possession ceremonies (plates 7, 17, 19). The royal palm, the mortar, and the burning tower can be seen as classic vertical *axes mundi,* lightning rods of Changó's powerfully hot, dangerous, energy—his *aché* (see Eliade [1957] 1959, 35–65; Thompson 1983, 84–97). Analogously, the *batá* drums produce his thunderous "celestial music," which incites the *orichas* to dance and "mount" their followers; Changó himself is known as the *rey del baile,* the "king of dance" (Ortiz 1952–55, 4:205; Ecún 1986, 94).

Changó's *pilón* is consecrated like other important *oricha* objects: it is herbally "washed" and fed blood sacrifices. When Changó's *pilón* is "shared" by, or "extended to," the other *orichas,* it is specially marked for the *oricha* who will sit upon it. "Whenever Shangó lends the *pilón,*" Miguel Ramos explains, "it has to be dressed with the colors of the Orisha being made [plate 5, fig. 4.1]; yet it always carries a red ribbon or something identifying Shango's ownership."[49] According to Ernesto Pichardo, Changó's ownership is also marked by his authorizing *firma,* a target-like red and white emblem, which is painted within the object's hollow interior. "Even though you're making another *oricha,*" Pichardo explains, "the Changó drawing [*firma*] remains inside."[50]

In the public Día del Medio (Middle Day) celebration, the *pilón* appears as an integral component of the larger assemblage, called the *trono del asiento.* Yet, as Lucumí priests have made clear, the *pilón* is itself is a "throne." For Cabrera's sources, the Spanish term *pilón* was synonymous with *trono.* It was also interchangeable with the Lucumí terms for mortar (*odó*), seat (*apotí*), and "throne of the king" (*ité obá;* [1974] 1980, 162–63; 1980, 184). Quoting her "old informants," Cabrera writes, the *orichas'* "'*apotí,* was no less than [their] throne! and was saturated with [their] power.' It is the symbol of the royalty and divine majesty of the Oricha" (Cabrera [1974] 1980, 163).[51] Up through the culmination of the *montaje del santo* ceremonies, the *pilón* stands independently of the cloth throne enclosure. Following the mounting ceremony, *iyawós* are seated on the mortar, eyes closed, directly facing the throne, and are then prompted to open their eyes to take in its grandeur. In effect, though the *iyawó* is not necessarily possessed, but clearly imbued with a radiant spiritual influence, the *oricha* of honor, materialized in the *iyawó*'s body, is given the opportunity to "see" the throne for the first time. Then *pilón* and *iyawó* are installed under the throne so the *matanza* can proceed.

The *pilón,* as a royal initiatory seat, produces the *montaje del santo*'s central "iconic" pose, and embodies the ritual principle of *asiento.*[52] At the same time, it is central in effecting the consecration of Ocha. At the culmination of the mounting ceremony, the godparent "holds the *santo* to the head" of the shorn, shaved, painted, and barefoot initiate, who is seated upon the inverted *pilón.* In the interpretation of Miguel Ramos, the ritual technique, dramatic effect, and meaning of the *montaje del santo* require the initiate to be *in a seated position.* "It is an enthroned position because the individual [who] is reborn arrives as a king/queen on his/her throne. The *pilón* is the throne as well as a communicating 'vessel' or 'vacuum' between the planes [spiritual and material]. The mortar is overturned because the precise purpose of initiation is 'turning over the life' of the individual and sealing the incarnated spirit within the body. . . . The [painted] *firma* on the floor [beneath the mortar, as well as on the head] call . . . the Orisha's ashé and presence. [They] seal . . . the incarnated spirit into the body with the insignia of his/her Orisha."[53] With the guardian angel's invocatory *firmas* and *aché* substances upon the head and underfoot, body and mortar become an integrated *axis mundi* and the initiate virtually hovers "between the planes."

Perhaps more important, as an orienting *axis mundi,* the *pilón* decisively purifies the initiate's body through Changó's connection between earthly fire and heavenly grace and Osain's healing plants. In a March 2002 interview in Havana, *babalawo* Antonio de Armas explained to me that the *pilón,* in its upright position—aperture upward—is about sacred nourishment: "like a goblet, one drinks from it, spiritually speaking." At the same time, he notes, the mortar historically was used to grind grain and, within the Lucumí and Arará religious context, sacred herbs. Indeed, Changó's mortar, in its initiatory use, would be inefficacious without Osain's herbally based "charge" (*carga*) contained within it, as well as the pounded herbal *machuquillo*—the *osu*—made from the *aché de santo* seeds and other secret ingredients. In effect, realizing the *kariocha* would be impossible without the critical relationship between Changó and Osain, which Lucumí legend represents as a pact (see Ecún 1986, 87–88). Thus, as de Armas explains, "when the *pilón* is turned over, the *osu* secret is placed on the floor beneath the mat on which it rests, as well as on the head. The *pilón* is also 'charged' [*cargado*] inside with an *osain*. The person making *ocha* will receive spirituality from *ilé gueré*, the depths of the earth [*la profundidad de la tierra*]. The *osu* beneath the mat acts to attract spiritual forces from the very center of the earth. They pass upward through the 'secret' of the mortar, which is the *carga*. This *osain* purifies these spiritual forces, as a kind of 'filter' that lives within the mortar, in order to prevent harmful forces from the earth from passing through the human body. Thus purified, it is said, the earth's spirituality 'passes through the anus and enters the body.'" Continuing upward, it enters the head, upon which the second *osu* has been placed, and is "reflected in the *eledá*"—a person's inner spiritual head. "The spirituality drawn from below is reflected [or radiated] above"; in other words, the *osu* that is below has its direct reflection in the *osu* of the head; it is a continuum. From here comes the relation or link between the *orichas* and Olofin "in heaven." The energy "rises from the head and arrives to Olofin, who then sends it downward, as the *oriaté*, in the *parada* stage of the initiation, is calling the *orichas* to come down." Under the view, supervision, and approbation of Olofin, the energy returns to the person sitting on the mortar, who is now "spiritually clean." Once again, via the *parada*, each *oricha* being called down continues purifying the *iyawó*. Everything that is negative is discharged from the body by the same route, the anus, only in reverse. The 'goblet'—that is, the turned-over *pilón*, mouth downward, functions as if it were vomiting or eliminating." Changó's mortar, in concert with Osain's powerful herbal knowledge—which gave the thunder god the power to spit fire and transform the world—is a veritable dynamo of purification and consecration.

Changó exerted a powerful influence over the modern Cuban Lucumí initiatory system as it was standardized over the course of the twentieth century. Beyond the mortar, his influence extended to a series of related objects and practices. These include, as mentioned, the sacred *batá* drums and the cowrie-encrusted, beaded, and fringed crown (*baàyọ́nnì*) of the Yoruba Ṣàngó's sibling, Dàda. In Yorubaland, the *batá* drums were evidently exclusive to Ṣàngó's cults; in Cuba, however, they would be used to praise, and "bring down" in possession, all of the *orichas*. They would also effect the authoritative completion of all *iyawós'* initiations in a ceremony called the "presentation to the drums."[54] Likewise, Yoruba Ṣàngó priests wore their exclusive cowrie-encrusted *baàyọ́nnì* crowns when they ritually excavated the deity's thunderstones from the remains of houses struck by lightning (Abraham 1946, 622; Thompson 1993, 246–51). In Cuba, this domical crown—formed by an inverted half calabash the diameter of the human head—would be built up of concentric rows of red and white beads alternated with rows of cowries. Along with twelve long beaded fringes (*esé*) around its circumference, the crown would also feature the braids (*trenzas*) of Dadá's hair, which represent her "wealth" (plate 9). In Cuba, the crown's owner would be Changó's "sister," called Dadá-Bañaní (see Brown 1989, chap. 7; 1993b, 48, 54; Thompson 1993, 249; see also Gleason 1987, 88–95).[55] However, as in the case of the *batá* drums and mortar, this dazzling object would no longer be exclusive to the thunder god's priests. It could be acquired by all priests, depending on their personal divination signs, as an auxiliary *oricha*. Popularly called the "crown of the saints" or the "crown of the *igüoros*" (Angarica [1955?] n.d., 45–46), Dadá's headgear is sometimes interpreted as the "crown" of a priestly career *en santo*. In the modern Lucumí system, Nicolás Angarica poetically explains, all the *orichas* "figure as pillars where [Dadá] plays the role of the roof" (Angarica [1955?] n.d., 49).[56]

It remains speculative whether this arguably Ọ̀yọ́-inflected liturgical complex (the Ṣàngó initiatory blueprint, the mortar, the *batá* drums, the Dadá crown) represents the strong demographic influence of the Ọ̀yọ́-Yoruba in the transatlantic slave trade, which fostered a diasporic ritual "metalanguage" or "lingua franca" (see Thompson 1983, 17; Matory 1994, 228). Or was the institution of this liturgical complex the result of the successful efforts of a limited number of authoritative priests to standardize what they regarded as an efficacious initiatory pattern from a larger pool of West African ritual resources (see Mintz and Price [1976] 1992, 46; Palmié 1993; and my chap. 2)? It is possible, for example, that for the Lucumí, the poignant model of Changó's mortal kingship, dramatic death, and momentous rebirth as an *oricha*, which is embodied in his "royal" iconography, was "creolized"—that is, "shared," "extended," and standardized through "reform" among emerging religious communities. The model clearly condenses key meanings of Lucumí *initiatory kingship:* living initiates undergo (symbolic) death, are purified and "reborn" as new kings and queens, and realize the capacity to transform themselves and others with the precious resource of their *orichas' aché*. Indeed, it is evident that this model of initiation bridged significant cleavages between *oricha* cults. For example, despite the symbolic, functional, ecological, and historical differences between the Yoruba cults of the hunter Ogún and king Ṣàngó in Yorubaland (Matory 1994, 6), the initiations of the Lucumí Warriors in Cuba would revolve around the same basic model as the non-Warriors. Though the rustic seats of the three Warriors, Eleguá, Ogún, and Ochosi, critically distinguish their symbolic and functional domains from Changó's elaborated mortar of the "royal palace," their initiations clearly proceed according to the same template: their *iyawós* are washed, shaved, painted, and mounted with the *oricha*'s *aché* in a seated position, with target-like *firmas* painted on their heads and beneath their feet.[57] They own "thrones," enjoy a Middle Day, receive oracular advice in the following day's *itá*, spend six nights on the floor, and complete their week with an excursion to the *plaza*. Though the narrower sense of "royalty enthroned" upon the imperial mortar is bracketed in their case, these *orichas* "arrive," nevertheless, as powerful "deified warriors," and they wear splendid satin *ropa de santo* and *collares de mazo* on the Día del Medio.[58] In short, the standard modern ritual template structures their initiations overall, while their peculiar Warrior sensibility is delineated through the symbolic and ecological distinctions of the *monte* ceremony and the realistic rustic iconography of their leafy thrones, stone or trunk seats, straw hats, staffs, and animal skin side bags.

ADORNING THE HEAD AND TRANSFORMING THE BODY: ROYAL REGALIA AND THE PROTOCOLS OF *ORICHA* KINGSHIP ON THE DÍA DEL MEDIO

All *iyawós* undergo the same basic protocol, with variations according to the particular *oricha* made. This section focuses on sartorial, artistic, and other expressive markers that constitute the outward presence of "kings," "queens," and "deified warriors" and index the sequence of transformations experienced by initiates. A series of clothing changes, physical modifications, and body adornments over the course of twenty-four hours registers a person's transformation from an uninitiated state (*aleyo*), to the highly liminal and symbolically dead condition of *abokú*—the period between the river and the *asiento*—to the living vessel of an *oricha*'s *aché:* the *iyawó*, the newborn condition that begins after the mounting of the *oricha* on the head and for a period of one year afterward.

On the eve of the initiation, often a Friday night, the *iyawó*-to-be is taken to the river just before dark in a set of "old clothes," which are cut off as part of an important purification; they are replaced with another set of old clothes, which can be of any color, though some houses suggest that white clothes mark the return from the river's cleansing ritual. Upon the return of the river party—the *abokú,* who arrives carrying upon the head a clay pot filled with river water and a river stone, is warmly welcomed into the house by the *padrino* or *madrina,* receives a feeding of the head (*rogación de cabeza*) with calming white substances (e.g., shredded coconut meat and cotton), and spends the night in preparation for the following morning's events (see Cabrera [1974] 1980, 140). Wearing the same clothes, the *abokú* passes the night on a floormat, marking a state of symbolic death, but outside the sacred room, which has been prepared with a throne and all the ingredients needed for the next day's *asiento.* The following day, the *abokú,* seated and facing the wall in *penitencia* ("penitence"), is "seized" with a white sheet in a minor ceremony often called "the second *prendición.*" Disoriented and, in effect, made formless, the *abokú* makes a ritualized entrance across the sheet-covered threshold of the "room of *santo,*" wherein, once again, the "old clothes" are cut off during an herbal "washing" (see Cabrera [1974] 1980, 158–59; Castellanos 1977, 88–90; Ecún 1985, 34; Gleason 1992). The *abokú* dons a new set of clothes.

The clothes worn by the *abokú* depend upon the tradition of the house and the *oricha* being made. Typically, the *abokú* is "shaved" in white clothes: often new pajama bottoms and a *camiseta de perro* (button-collared cotton short-sleeve shirt) for men, and a simple white dress for women. However, some houses dress initiates of the Warriors, as well as those of Babalú Ayé (Saint Lazarus), in a rustic outfit of *saco* (burlap). *Saco* is the material of common agricultural shipping bags of made of jute (*saco de yute;* see fig. 4.26).[59]

Figure 4.26.—Initiation suit (*traje del asiento*) for child Eleguá initiate, made of *saco* (burlap), Regla, c. 1940s. Museum of Regla. (Photograph by David H. Brown.)

The washing of the body and the cutting off of "old clothes" two times prepare the initiate for the decisive falling away of the old self, realized most dramatically as the hair is shaved and shorn from the head in clockwise fashion (Gleason 1992). The new, spotless white cotton clothes following the *asiento* and during the succeeding year (typically pajamas at night and informal whites during the day), are consistent with the required symbolic conditions for the nurture and care of this newly consecrated "head." White, which is the color of *orí,* embodies the purity of the creator and metaowner of this head, Obatalá, and is consistent with the spiritual protection and evolution of the *iyawó.* White clothes are also consonant with the *iyawó*'s regimen of spiritual hygiene and regulated program of behavior during the obligatory *yaworage,* or "year of white."[60]

Figure 4.27.—Lunch suit (*traje de almuerzo*) of gingham and white *pañuelo* (headtie) for Ochún, by Lourdes López. From the exhibition *Ritual Dress of Initiation*, 1987. (Courtesy Caribbean Cultural Center and Lourdes López. Photograph by David H. Brown.)

The kinds of clothes and clothing changes of the Día del Medio offer intriguing contrast to the white initiation garments and the daily white attire of the *yaworage*. Color is introduced in two principal changes of clothing, which refer to distinct roles the *iyawó* plays, corresponding to sequential phases of this full day's "coming out" ceremony. On the morning of the Día del Medio, following the first night on the mat under the throne, the *iyawó* is awakened, given an "African breakfast," changed out of the pajamas, and given a bath with a fortifying herbal concoction called *omiero*. Following the bath, the *iyawó* dresses in a colorful new outfit, called the *traje de almuerzo*, the "lunch suit."[61]

The *trajes de almuerzo* for most of the *orichas* employ gingham (*guinga*), a durable cotton cloth with a tight, checked pattern, which approximates the guardian angel's colors.[62] Cubans also refer to the cloth as *tela de cuadritos* (checked). With several exceptions, its pattern takes in at least one of an *oricha*'s dominant colors, plus white (figs. 4.27, 4.28). Although the *trajes de almuerzo* are stylistically restrained, they do receive little flourishes of adornment, such as rows of serpentine or zigzag braid, which may reiterate the *orichas'* signature color and number patterns.[63] In contrast to the other *orichas*, the Warriors often wear *trajes de almuerzo* consisting of a gingham shirt and knicker-like *bombachas* made of *saco de yute* (fig. 4.28).[64] The Warriors' use of *saco de yute* on the *asiento* and on the morning of the Middle Day may refer to their rustic ecological setting of the *campo* (countryside), as well as to hard labor, struggle, transportation, boundary crossing, and economic exchange—particularly between the country and the city and across water. *Saco de yute* is a multivocal attribute that bridges all the Afro-Cuban religions—Lucumí, Palo Monte, and Abakuá. Cloth from agricultural shipping sacks may have been utilized by Cuba's African plantation slaves, or *bozales*, to improvise their humble attire.[65]

The differences between the gingham *traje de almuerzo* and the *ropa de santo*—the *orichas'* regal satin garments—are functional, aesthetic, and experiential. They mark significant transitions in the day's activities.

Figure 4.28.—Lunch suit (*traje de almuerzo*) of gingham and burlap (*saco*) for Ogún, by Lourdes López. From the exhibition *Ritual Dress of Initiation*, 1987. (Courtesy Caribbean Cultural Center and Lourdes López. Photograph by David H. Brown.)

The *traje de almuerzo* is a natty, but aesthetically restrained, *oricha* dressing gown of sorts, which is worn during the preparations for the presentation ceremony in the afternoon. It is for taking a meal upon the mat on this momentous day: like a baby, the *iyawó* eats with a big spoon and an enameled tin cup, the handle of which is tied with a ribbon in the color of the guardian angel. The *iyawó* does not eat again until after six o'clock, when the precious satin *ropa de santo* is taken off and replaced by white cotton clothes. In Miguel Ramos's interpretation, the colorful *traje de almuerzo* provides the appropriate aesthetic setting for the repainting of the head with the *oricha*'s *firma*. Though the head is painted with this signature every morning for six days, the Día del Medio's signature is highly elaborated and decorative. In contrast, the *ropa de santo* of the afternoon is not for eating, painting, or sitting on the floor. It is made not of simple checked cotton, but of expensive satin and trimmings. As such, the *ropa de santo* marks the commencement of the public presentation of royalty. Whereas colonial-era Afro-Cubans may have worn the colorful *guinga* as presentable public attire, particularly on days off, only *cabildo* kings and queens donned expensive finery, on the aesthetically marked occasion of public festival presentation. Finally, the change from gingham to satin marks a shift between overlapping roles: *iyawó* as the consecrated newborn, who lives in seclusion upon the mat, and *iyawó* as the publicly celebrated and enthroned, new king, queen, or warrior.

From an experiential or phenomenological perspective, this change from the cotton *traje de almuerzo* to the satin *ropa de santo* marks transformations in the personhood of the *iyawó* (see Jackson 1986, 131; Mason 2002). Just as new *iyawós*, hitherto blindfolded, are permitted to "see" their thrones for the first time following the *montaje del santo*, they are permitted to "see" the *ropa de santo* only after their attendants have finished dressing them. When fully dressed—with royal clothes, crown, and dance wand—they are prompted to open their eyes. Of course, they can only look down, look above and to the side at draped satin, or look out at the people in the room. Still, they are physically constrained by the heavy *collares de mazo*, and visually constrained by a limited point of view. Seen by an "audience," they cannot (fully) "see themselves." Indeed, the absence of self-reflection—in a mirror, for example—discourages reversion of identification to the former "self" (is it "me" in these clothes?), leaving the elders and audience to *recognize* and constitute the object of their gaze as an *oricha* king, queen, or warrior. This is prime phenomenological terrain for the transformation of the personhood of the *iyawó* (see Mason 2002). Since the river, the initiate has remained something of an inchoate quantity, a kind of pre-ontological omelette, or "formless clay," whose formation, or reformation, and subjectivity are shaped by other agencies: the *orichas*, the elders, and now, a determinate audience (Lacan [1973] 1981, 29ff., 255–56). Using the grammatical idiom, James Wafer argues that the Candomblé initiation predicates the subject-initiate as the "logical patient" or object of the *oricha*'s "logical agency" (Wafer 1991, 101–4; see also Fernández [1974] 1986, 46–51; and Jackson 1989, 131). The Lucumí religious idiom reveals an analogous expression: "The head rules the body and only one king governs a town." Thus, the unveiling of the throne and the *ropa de santo* to the *iyawó* is, in fact, a "surprise" *for the santo* (*le sorprende al santo*), events that are marked by the formal erasure of the agency of the initiate's ego and the constituting of the "logical patient" as the "*oricha*'s representative on earth."

The *iyawó*'s changes of clothes on the Middle Day from white clothes, to checked gingham colors, to lavish satin with beaded and painted adornments, and back again to white clothes at the end of the presentation suggest a diasporic variant, albeit streamlined, of the Brazilian Candomblé's temporally extended "coming out ceremonies" (*saidas*). In a Bahian initiation documented by Gerardo Sarno in 1978, for example, the last of three major *saidas* consists of three consecutive clothing changes. In the last *saida*, the initiate appears first in white garments; second, in the deities' basic colors in understated cloth; and third and last, in the *orixás*' full regalia, including sumptuous cloth, along with brilliant metal crowns, and attributes, including dance wands (see Sarno 1978; Carybé 1980, 34–40; Omari 1984; and Murphy 1994, 62–65).

Orí Engalanado: "Decked Out" Royal "Heads"

The painting of the *iyawó*'s head on the morning of the Día del Medio both duplicates and revises the previous day's painted designs. More highly adorned, this day's designs are of a piece with the tone of festive celebration, royalty, and the evolution of the *iyawó* as a priest, the *oricha's* representative. The target-like, banded signature, painted each day, is called *firma* in Spanish and *osu* in Lucumí. *Osu* also refers to a mass of vital *aché*-imbued substances, which are placed upon the head, and work in concert with, the painted *osu* (see Cabrera [1970] 1983, 283; Mason 2002, 64). This transatlantic "*osu*-ball" (Yorubaland), "cone" (Brazil), or poultice-like mass (Lucumí *aché;* Spanish *machuquillo*), is a "nourishing" and "fortifying" medicine, which is absorbed by the *orí* in order that it embody the guardian angel and transform the life of the initiate.[66] The painted *osu* signature covers the head's calvarium with combinations of the four fundamental colors of Ocha: white, yellow, blue, and red. Each water-based color mixed from powdered tempera pigment and other ingredients occupies its own little terra-cotta dish and is painted with its own fine brush. Whereas the *oriaté* is responsible for most of the *firma* in the *asiento*, the *padrino, madrina, oyubona*, or *oyubona*'s assistant can paint the head on the morning of the Día del Medio and throughout the week.

The painting of the head in the *asiento*, as is the initiation as a whole, is a collective task, which has been contracted and authorized by the exchange of ritual tributes of money (Lucumí *achedín;* Spanish *derechos*).[67] The *oriaté* paints the *osu* on the calvarium, that is, the dome above the ears, but leaves untouched the central circle of the target-like *firma*. The initiate's face and neck are then dotted by brush with small spots in the same four colors by the participants who have been called to "work the *santo*"—the *levantados* (see Cabrera [1954] 1983, plates; fig. 4.29). In a determinate order, the two godparents, the *oyubona* and the *padrino* or *madrina*, complete the design. The *oyubona* paints special marks over the *firma*'s bands, and then the *padrino* or *madrina* fills in the center of the target-like form with the single color that represents the guardian angel being "made to" the *iyawó* (Ecún 1985, 39). These aesthetic variations and the corresponding artistic division of labor suggest the following principles: the concentrically banded *osu* is the unique invocatory "signature" (*firma*) of the *oricha* being made, while the myriad spots are in effect, the "signatures" of the *heads of* the individual priests "working" the initiation (see Mason 2002, 64). This division of labor also suggests the critical roles played by three groups of actors within a determinate protocol: first comes the *oriaté,* who directs the ceremony; next come the *levantados,* normally belonging to the house through kinship and loyal working relations, who put forth the critical mass of *aché* that makes the reproduction of this new *santo* possible; next comes the *oyubona,* the *iyawó*'s second godparent and nursemaid; finally comes the *padrino* or *madrina* who "makes *santo* to" the *iyawó.*[68] The sequential addition of paint, which culminates in the color of the head *oricha* being "made," provides a stunning example of Robert Plant Armstrong's concept of *syndesis* (accretion), an additive and intensifying process of ritual invocation. Syndesis "increases power through donation, enriching the item through prayer, sacrifice and tribute until presence is brought about." Realizing this *affecting presence* "is the process of bringing the work into the powers of being, of making the hidden visible, the latent manifest, the inaudible audible, the stilled dynamic" (Armstrong 1981, 13–17, 20).

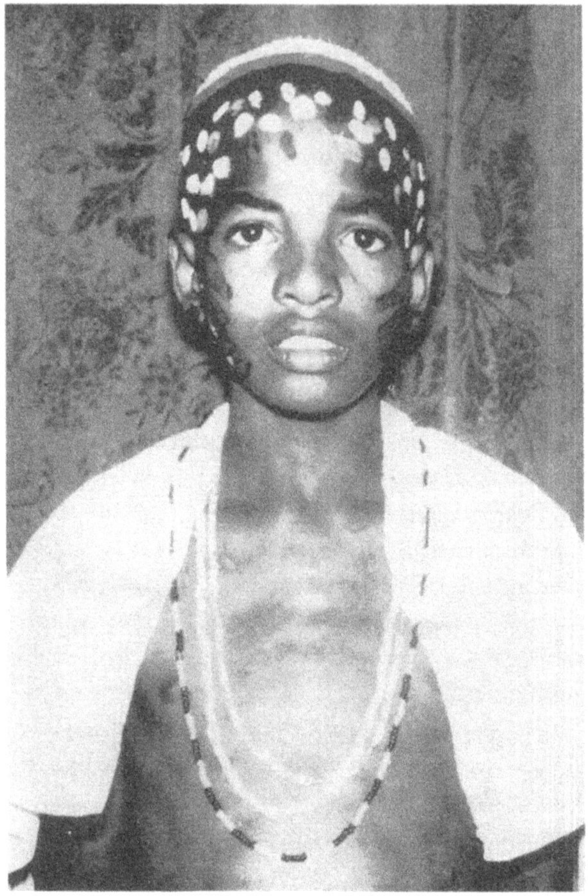

Figure 4.29.—Young Cuban *iyawó,* with the painted, target-like *osu,* the signature "spots," neo-Yoruba facial markings, *oricha* bead necklaces, and a protective white towel around his shoulders, photographed probably in Havana, mid-1940s–early 1950s. (From Cabrera [1954] 1983, plates. Courtesy the Estate of Lydia Cabrera.)

While *osu* refers, at one level, to "color" or "paint," the Lucumí called the *act of painting* the head *fi fi okán osú,* which Lydia Cabrera translates, perhaps too literally, as "putting heart [*okán*] in the paint" ([1970] 1983, 283; [1974] 1980, 162). The term *fi fi* seems to derive from the Yoruba expression for aesthetic elaboration, such as the incising of designs on a calabash or the decorative tatooing of the skin, as well as "scrupulous cleanliness" (Abraham 1946, 214–15; and see H. Drewal 1989; Drewal, Pemberton, and Abiodun 1989, 15).[69] Still, the concentrically banded component of the Lucumí *osu* seems to have no direct Yoruba or diasporic parallels, while the spots, lines, and geometric patterns on the face and head are well documented as transatlantic designs (cf. Cabrera [1954] 1983, plates; Drewal, Pemberton, and Abiodun 1989, 33; Matory 1994, 184; Carybé 1980, 26–29; Verger 1957, fig. 14; Drewal and Mason 1998, 65, 181).[70]

Diaspora scholars have interpreted these Yoruba transatlantic dotted markings as the "royal spots of the leopard." Indeed, the chants that accompany the painting of the *osu,* as glossed by George Brandon and others, convey that the painting of the *osu* transforms both the initiate and the participants into "kings" through its bold royal "leopard" symbolism (Brandon 1983, 398–99; Gleason 1992; Thompson 1993, 276). Though it is hardly clear that all Lucumí religious practitioners interpret the spotted designs in this way, the spots are consistent with the tone of the *asiento*'s "consecration," which many regard as a "coronation."[71] Most important, the spots are integral to the ontological transformation of the initiate. In fact, for the Yoruba, whether or not the spots refer to a specific referent, the artistic pattern called "*fínfín* (dots and dashes of intense color) . . . is a kind of sanctifying and sacred pointillism that conveys transformation and transcendance of worldly entities united with otherworldly forces. Symbolically, these dots and dashes are points of light and blessing" (Drewal and Mason 1998, 78–79).

Perhaps, after all, Cabrera's translation of *fi fi okán osu* may approach the broader sensibility of this spiritual and aesthetically marked ceremony of active transformation as effectively as the specific notion of royal leopard spots. Mixed with important ingredients of the *asiento* process, the *osu* beomes a spiritually activated medium, encompassing the semantic range of nourishment, vitality, rebirth, and kinship (see M. Mason 1994, 2002). *Okán* literally means "heart" and can refer to life force and the eternal labor of Ogún, which keeps the body functioning. "Heart" also refers to human feeling and positive collective sentiment, and sweet personal intention can be very important to efficacious spiritual work (Mason 2002, 106–7). The *fi fi okán osú,* the consummate prism, vehicle, and emblem for the *asiento,* is painted precisely in order to effect the invocation of an *oricha* and the head's embodiment of *aché,* which is completed by symbolic transactions of blood, herbs, and ritualized monetary tributes (*derechos*). Invocations—verbal, artistic, gestural—and exchanges of "blood and money," effect initiatory rebirth, and make for the acquisition of a new member of the ritual kinship grouping or *familia de santo* (Matory 1991a, 21–22, 28, 34–50; 1994, 191–93; see also Mason 1993; Wafer 1991, 21). Indeed, as Cabrera writes, "The members or godchildren of the same *ilé-Oricha* acquire [*contraer,* as in "contract to be married"] the equivalent of the members of a blood kinship group, with all the obligations that this implies" (Cabrera [1974] 1980, 129).

The foregoing associations of newly constituted identity and kinship are reinforced by another set of markings painted upon the face, which are patterned after Yoruba ethnic cicatrizations. These *ilá* (Lucumí), or *trazos* (Spanish), are painted on the initiate's cheeks in the color(s) of the head *oricha* (see Cabrera [1954] 1983, plates). For example, Changó's marks are red highlighted with white, Yemayá's are blue, Ochún's are yellow, and Obatalá's are white (fig. 4.29). In Yorubaland, facial marks (*ìlà*), which are cut into the skin with fine metal tools, identify individuals as members of particular regional or kingdom-based ethnic subgroups, formerly called "tribes" (Abraham 1946, 300–301; H. Drewal 1989; and fig. 4.30). Ethnic cicatrizations were ubiquitous among the members of Cuba's African "nations" during the slavery period; among the Cuban Lucumí groups, they were called *ilá, iláku,* or *ilá boyú* ("facial marks"; Cabrera [1957] 1986, 161). Cuba's Lucumí typically bore variations of three parallel vertical or oblique horizontal marks on each cheek (see Deschamps Chapeaux 1969, 67; and figs. 4.31, 2.1). In contrast, the surface-painted triple marks of the Lucumí religious initiation identify the *iyawó*'s face with a specific head *oricha.* In some houses, the marks, via their color and *oricha* association, may also refer to the putative original nation or kingdom of the *oricha* in question: for example, Obatalá came from Ifé, Ochún from Iyesá, and Changó from Oyó. According to *oriaté* Miguel Ramos, the *trazos* should further distinguish *iyawós* in relation to the gender of their head *orichas*: male *orichas* should get three repeated vertical marks, and female *orichas* are supposed to have three horizontal marks on each cheek.[72]

The Día del Medio's repainted dome of the head reproduces the concentrically banded signature and the *trazos*

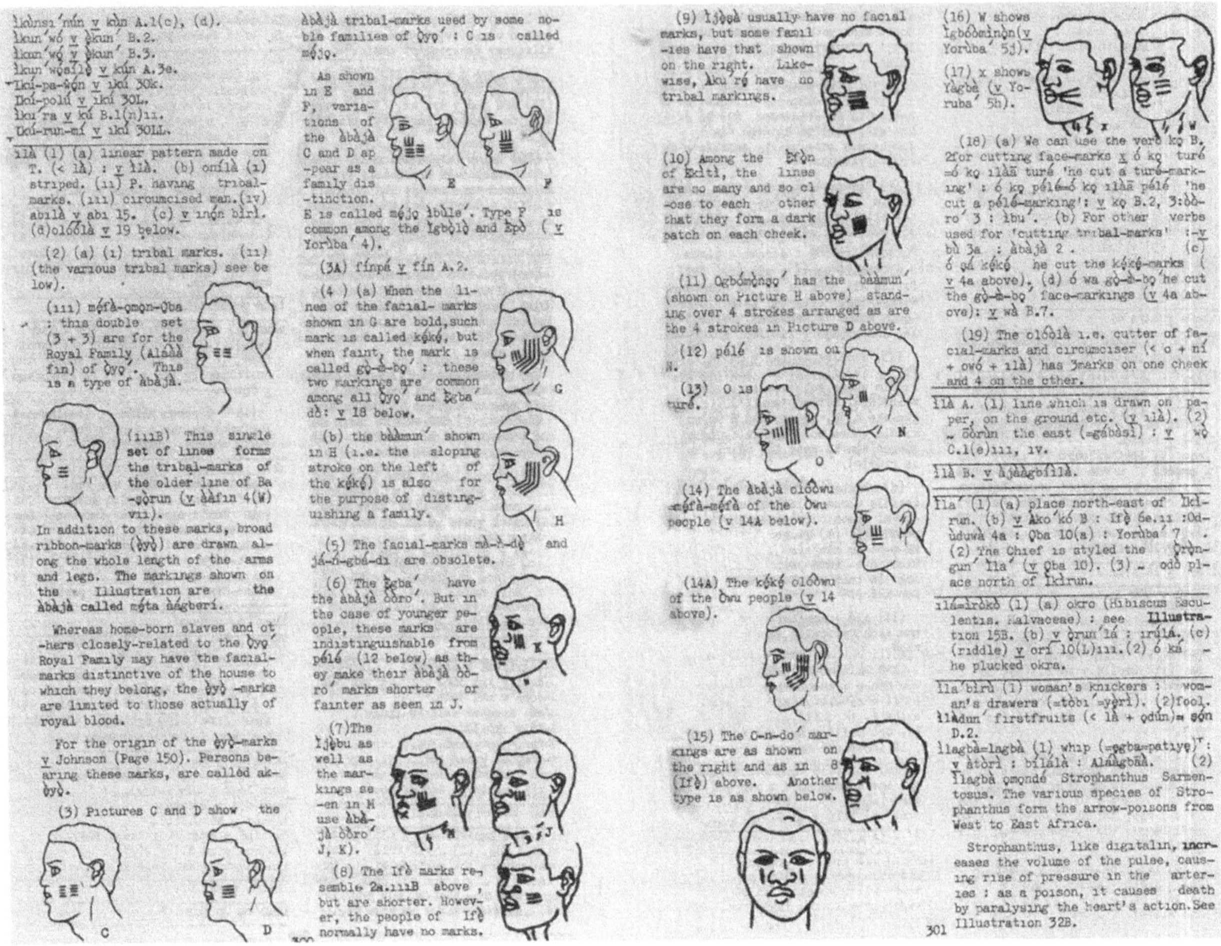

ìkìnsi'nún v kìn A.1(c), (d).
ìkun'wó v ẹ̀kun' B.2.
ìkun'wọ́ v ẹ̀kun' B.3.
ìkun'wọ́sílẹ̀ v kún A.3e.
Ìkí-pa-ẹ̀gọ́n v ìkí 30k.
Ìkí-polú v ìkí 30L.
ìkí'ra v kú B.1(n)ii.
Ìkí-run-mí v ìkí 30LL.

ìlà (1) (a) linear pattern made on T. (< là) : v ìlà. (b) onílà (i) striped. (ii) P. having tribal-marks. (iii) circumcised man.(iv) abílà v abi 15. (c) v inọ́n bìrì. (d)olóòlà v 19 below.

(2) (a) (i) tribal marks. (ii) (the various tribal marks) see below).

(iii) mẹ́fà-ọmọn-Ọba : this double set (3 + 3) are for the Royal Family (Aláàfin) of Ọ̀yọ́. This is a type of àbàjà.

(iiiB) This single set of lines forms the tribal-marks of the older line of Ba-ṣọ̀run (v àáfin 4(W) vii).

In addition to these marks, broad ribbon-marks (ẹ̀yọ̀) are drawn along the whole length of the arms and legs. The markings shown on the Illustration are the àbàjà called mẹ́ta ńàgbèrí.

Whereas home-born slaves and others closely-related to the Ọ̀yọ́ Royal Family may have the facial-marks distinctive of the house to which they belong, the ẹ̀yọ̀ -marks are limited to those actually of royal blood.

For the origin of the ẹ̀yọ̀-marks v Johnson (Page 150). Persons bearing these marks, are called akẹ̀yọ̀.

(3) Pictures C and D show the àbàjà tribal-marks used by some noble families of Ọ̀yọ́ : C is called mẹ́jọ.

As shown in E and F, variations of the àbàjà C and D appear as a family distinction.

E is called mẹ́jọ ìbùle'. Type F is common among the Ìgbọ̀lọ̀ and Ẹ̀pọ̀ (v Yorùbá' 4).

(3A) fínpá v fín A.2.

(4) (a) When the lines of the facial- marks shown in G are bold,such mark is called kẹ́kẹ́, but when faint, the mark is called gọ̀-ǹ-bọ' : these two markings are common among all Ọ̀yọ́ and Ẹ̀gbá dò: v 18 below.

(b) the bààmun' shown in H (i.e. the sloping stroke on the left of the kẹ́kẹ́) is also for the purpose of distinguishing a family.

(5) The facial-marks mà-ǹ-dẹ̀ and já-ǹ-gbá-di are obsolete.

(6) The Ẹ̀gbá' have the àbàjà òòro'. But in the case of younger people, these marks are indistinguishable from pélé (12 below) as they make their àbàjà òòro' marks shorter or fainter as seen in J.

(7)The Ìjẹ̀bu as well as the markings seen in M use àbàjà òòro' J, K).

(8) The Ifẹ̀ marks resemble 2a.iiiB above , but are shorter. However, the people of Ifẹ̀ normally have no marks.

(9) Ìjẹ̀ṣà usually have no facial marks, but some families have that shown on the right. Likewise, Àkú'rẹ́ have no tribal markings.

(10) Among the Ẹ̀fọ̀n of Èkìtì, the lines are so many and so close to each other that they form a dark patch on each cheek.

(11) Ogbómọ̀ṣọ́' has the bààmun' (shown on Picture H above) standing over 4 strokes arranged as are the 4 strokes in Picture D above.

(12) pélé is shown on N.

(13) O is turé.

(14) The àbàjà olóòwu mẹ́fà-mẹ́fà of the Òwu people (v 14A below).

(14A) The kẹ́kẹ́ olóòwu of the Òwu people (v 14 above).

(15) The O-n-do' markings are as shown on the right and as in 8 (Ifẹ̀) above. Another type is as shown below.

(16) W shows Ìgbóòmìnọ̀n(v Yorùbá' 5j).

(17) x shows Yàgbà (v Yorubá' 5h).

(18) (a) We can use the verb kọ B. 2for cutting face-marks x ó kọ turé =ó kọ ìlàà turé 'he cut a turé-marking' : ó kọ pélé=ó kọ ìlàà pélé 'he cut a pélé-marking': v kọ B.2, 3:òòro' 3 : ìbu'. (b) For other verbs used for 'cutting tribal-marks' :-v bù 3a : àbàjà 2 . (c) ó gá kẹ́kẹ́ he cut the kẹ́kẹ́-marks (v 4a above), (d) ó wa gọ̀-ǹ-bọ'he cut the gọ̀-ǹ-bọ' face-markings (v 4a above): v wà B.7.

(19) The olóòlà i.e. cutter of facial-marks and circumciser (< o + ní + owó + ìlà) has 3marks on one cheek and 4 on the other.

ìlà A. (1) line which is drawn on paper, on the ground etc. (v ìlà). (2) ~ òòrùn the east (=gábàsì) : v wọ̀ C.1(e)iii, iv.

ìlà B. v àjààgbílà.

Ìla' (1) (a) place north-east of Ìkìrun. (b) v Àko'kó B : Ifẹ̀ 6e.ii :Odùduwà 4a : Ọba 10(a) : Yorùbá' 7 . (2) The Chief is styled the Ọ̀rọ̀ngun' Ìla' (v Ọba 10). (3) ~ odò place north of Ìkìrun.

ìlá=ìrókò (1) (a) okro (Hibiscus Esculentis. Malvaceae) : see **Illustration** 15B. (b) v ọ̀rún'lá : irúlá. (c) (riddle) v orí 10(L)iii.(2) ó ká ~ he plucked okra.

Ìla'bìrù (1) woman's knickers : woman's drawers (=tòbi'=yẹ̀rì). (2)fool.

ìlàdun' firstfruits (< là + ọdún)= ṣọ́n D.2.

ìlagbà=lagbà (1) whip (=ẹgba=patiyẹ)' : v àtòrì : bílálà : Aláàgbàà. (2) Ìlagbà ọmọndé Strophanthus Sarmentosus. The various species of Strophanthus form the arrow-poisons from West to East Africa.

Strophanthus, like digitalin, **increases** the volume of the pulse, causing rise of pressure in the arteries : as a poison, it causes death by paralysing the heart's action.See Illustration 32B.

300 301

Figure 4.30.—Yoruba subgroup facial cicatrizations. Note marks for Ọ̀yọ́ (*2aiiiB, left center*), Ẹ̀gbá (*6*), Ifẹ̀ (*8*), Ogbómọ̀ṣọ́ (*11*), and Ìgbóòmìnàn (*16W, upper right*). (From Abraham 1946, 300–301.)

of the day before, but it omits the "spots." In the spirit of the day's festive tenor, the painter should, instead, "adorn the head as much as possible" (Ecún 1985, 45). Directly below, and around the perimeter of, the *firma,* on the forehead and nape of the neck, a series of bold geometric motifs are often painted. Miguel Ramos calls this set of festive designs *el peinado,* literally "the hairstyle" or coiffure. In some houses, these designs vary according to the gender of the *oricha* (not the gender of the priest). The design for male *orichas* in Ramos's practice, for example, consists of a row of repeated diamond or V-shapes just below the perimeter of the crown (VVVVVVV), while the design for female *orichas* consists of a scalloped pattern (UUUUU).[73] In contrast, the pattern the late Ramón Esquivel painted on Sara's head reversed the convention Ramos describes. It featured a tapered, pendant-like repetition of V-shapes in yellow, which was repeated on the nape of the neck in red and blue. Descending blue chevrons just forward of each ear completed the design (fig. 4.11). These geometric designs, particularly when they are combined with tiny decorative dots—that is, the dot-in-diamond motif—resemble the patterns painted upon Yoruba initiates' heads documented by Henry and Margaret Drewal (Drewal and Mason 1998, 23, 65). Whether or not all priests consider the gender of the *oricha* in the painting of these designs or the *trazos,* as Ramos does, it is clear that other prominently painted designs on the *iyawó*'s body more explicitly distinguish the *oricha*'s gender, such as earrings for female *orichas* and moustaches, beards, and sideburns for male *orichas.*

Though I have not heard the term *el peinado* used in other houses, it is worth pursuing one interpretive lead Ramos's usage suggests. Let us assume that the painted design does represent some sort of coiffure. First, given the foregrounding of the *oricha*'s subjectivity and attributes on the Middle Day, as opposed to the person of the initiate, a painted coiffure would logically not seek to reconstruct the lost hair of the person. In this sense, one would expect the *peinado* to belong to the integrated aesthetically marked ensemble of clothes and iconography appropriate to the particular *oricha* of honor. Like the other royal attributes—crown, regal clothes, scepter-like dance wand—the stylized and abstract *peinado* would seem to contribute to the decorous public representation of the new king, queen, or warrior *oricha.* In other words, the Middle Day represents, with significant realistic intention, just how the *oricha* should look as embodied by the *iyawó:* "beautiful," "elegant," "at its best," "decked out," in a word, *engalanado.*

Though the term *peinado* may not be universal among Regla de Ocha practitioners, the closest black Atlantic parallel of the design might be encountered in the elegant, geometric coiffures that are incised into the surfaces of wood and ceramic Yoruba shrine figures. Yoruba figurative shrine sculpture represents, in the astute observation of Margaret Drewal, "the union of the priest and deity in the [humanized] depiction of the former with the costumes, hairstyles, and paraphernalia identified with the latter" (M. Drewal 1989, 207; see also Matory 1994, 146–47; Apter 1992, 83). In the case of the Día del Medio presentation, the "union of the priest and the deity" comes not in the form of a shrine sculpture, but in the consecrated and aesthetically elaborated head and body of the

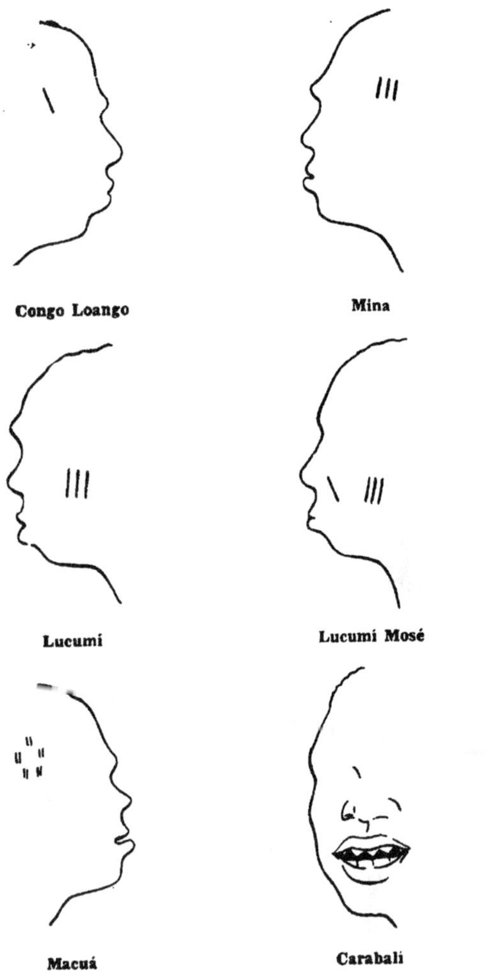

Figure 4.31.—Facial cicatrizations noted among Africans arriving in Cuba during the nineteenth century. Note Lucumí marks, *center left* and *center right;* compare figure 4.30. (From Deschamps Chapeaux 1969, 67.)

Figure 4.32.—The Ìyàwó Ọ̀ṣun of Ayédé, Èkìtì, Nigeria, with *irun àgògo* (bell) and cornrow hairstyle, characteristic of possession priests. (From Apter 1992, plate 7. Courtesy Dr. Andrew Apter.)

initiate, who is "transfigured" by the painted designs, *ropa de santo,* and other attributes *into* the *oricha* of honor (Flores-Peña and Evanchuck 1994, 14).

Worked, stylized, and beautifully sculpted hair remains integral to Yoruba social life and religion (Houlberg 1979, passim). In the religious domain, specific, named hairstyles are central to the priestly role as the "wife" of the deity, including the customary female bridal hairstyle known as *irun àgògo* (bell hairstyle; Drewal 1992, 182; see Apter 1992, plate 7; Houlberg 1979, 382–91; fig. 4.32). Such coiffures are integral to the cluster of aesthetically elaborated objects—cloth, beadwork, crowns—associated with royal and cultic titleholders. Indeed, hairstyles historically have both complemented and substituted for crowns. The African-American Yoruba have reclaimed this tradition, and Diaspora scholars have recently made the explicit connection between worked hair, priesthood, and public performance (Drewal and Mason 1989, 34, fig. 21). In Yorubaland, not only stylized coiffures, but also the natural texture of hair on newborn children are associated with royal status and wealth. For example, as indicated, the curly ringlets of hair associated with Yemọja's royal son, Dàda, are called *olówó-orí* ("head of money"; Abraham 1946, 121, 495). In Yoruba and Cuban Lucumí tradition, this particular deity's hair and head of royalty and wealth are ceremoniously represented with a special crown. Moreover, in La Regla de Ocha, actual black braids or plaits (*trenzas*) are often added to the Cuban Dadá's crown (plate 9; see Brown 1993b, 48, 54; Thompson 1993, 246–51, 301).

At this point, an alternative interpretation of the painted design is in order, which complements, rather than challenges, its identification by Ramos as a "hairstyle." Given Changó's intensive investment in the Lucumí initiation—as its "designer"—it may not be coincidental that the overall form of the *osu* and the geometric patterns below it strikingly recall Dadá's ceremonial "crown of the saints." Though cast in different media, both are based on the domelike form of the calvarium (the head's "crown"), are concentrically banded, and feature geometric, pendant-like fringes (see, e.g., Thompson 1993, plate 259). Thus, *obá* Ernesto Pichardo's creative explanation of the painted design below the *firma* may not be far from the mark. In his interpretation, the design reproduces the fringes of the Yoruba king's beaded crown (see Thompson 1970; Drewal, Pemberton, and Abiodun 1989, 33, 36; Pemberton and Afolayan 1996; Drewal and Mason 1998, 28–30, 55, 63, 145, 155–57, 203–6). The design "follows from the idea of the king and his headdress on a special occasion: the crowning of the king."[74] The painted geometric Lucumí designs, which are positioned, in fact, so that they appear to descend from the rim of the *iyawó*'s circular pasteboard crown, may indeed be a more ephemeral diasporic version of Yoruba and priestly crowns, as well as the crowns of the Candomblé. Intriguingly, just as the Brazilian Candomblé's circular, European-style metal crowns for some *orixás* feature straight or scalloped fringes of bead strands, the painted Lucumí design and pasteboard crown are visually integrated—a kind of composite of virtual and actual headgear. The pasteboard crown is itself of iconographic derivation similar to that of the Candomblé's European-derived models (see chap. 5; and Carybé 1980, 161, 163, 173, 175, 177, 179, 187, 20; Omari 1984, plates 2, 3; Galembo 1993, 148–49, 154, 164–67, 128).

The peculiar treatment of *iyawós* of the *orichas* Inle and Obba reinforces the hypothesis that Ramos's *peinado* is a stylized representation of hair appropriate to the decorous royal presentation of *orichas*.[75] In Lucumí practice, stylized, braided hair complements and reiterates other priestly, royal, and divine regalia, particularly cowries and beads in the representation of power and wealth. Initiates of Inle, it is reported, have only the very top of the head shaved, leaving hair around the circumference of the head. For the Día del Medio presentation, the hair must be worked into "braids" (*trenzas*), which are decorated with cowrie shells. This adornment thus combines the attributes of formal coiffure and crown of wealth (cowries). As another example of this phenomenon, Inle's coiffure makes Dadá's case more legible: the contiguity and identity of beaded fringe and plaited hair, which hang in parallel fashion (plate 9). Likewise, initiates of Obba, who have only the right side of their heads shaved, are formally presented with decorative ribbons worked into the braided hair on the left side of the head; this braided hair discreetly and decorously "hides" Obba's missing ear (see above). For the Yoruba case, Matory reports, "Cornrowing is associated generally with the neatness and decorousness of young adult village women, but in the politico-religious context it is associated with men's readiness for spirit possession. The only Oyo-Yoruba men who wear braids are possession priests" (Matory 1994, 146–47). Apter's documentation of similar possession priests in Ayede, Ekiti, shows the felicitous contiguity, as in the case of the Yoruba Dadà and Lucumí Dadá, of plaits and beaded fringe. The priestess called *Ìyáwó Ọ̀ṣun* of Ayédé, Èkìtì, in public ceremonial, wears both in a unified presentation: the *irun àgògo* "bell" coiffure and a bandlike crown with a beaded fringe (Apter 1992, plate 7; fig. 4.32). In the Lucumí tradition in Cuba, styled, braided, and decorated "hair" in the initiatory context, whether it is actual hair, as in the cases of Inle and Obba, or geometric, painted representations of hair—or a beaded fringe in the case of Dadá—is appropriate to the formal presentation of *orichas*, who claim the bodies and heads of *iyawós* as their mounts, representatives, and sacred workers in the phenomenal world. The apparently different interpretations of Ramos and Pichardo, therefore, complement, rather than compete with, one another: it is stylized hair; it is the fringe of a royal crown. Representations of "hair" or "fringe" are the logical culmination of a process that began twenty-four hours before, when the *iyawó*'s old hair was shaved away. Old hair is the mark of the *abokú*—the liminal novice undergoing symbolic death; the shaved head is the state of the *orí* in its consecration phase; finally, the *peinado*, or fringe, marks the *orí* as consecrated and "crowned" with the *orichas*' in its public celebratory phase.

Lucumí painted representations of "royal" heads on the Día del Medio encounter other kinds of painted adornments that are particular to Cuban cultural history. The curious mix throws into relief the hybridity of the day's royal and festive iconography. Female, and sometimes male, *iyawós* who make female *orichas*, such as Yemayá, Ochún, and Oyá, have a large circular earring painted on each side of the face just below the earlobe. In contrast, the faces of female *iyawós* who make male *orichas*, such as Eleguá, Ogún, Ochosi, Changó, and Agayú, as well as males making these same *orichas*, receive, instead of earrings, boldly painted mustaches (*bigotes*) and sometimes goatees and sideburns (*barbas* and *patillas*)—representations of hair associated socially with European and Latin American manliness, particularly from the seventeenth century forward. These, like the *trazos* and earrings, are painted in the *orichas*' signature colors. Thus, a female *iyawó* of Changó at Templo Bonifacio Valdez had her face painted with a red mustache and beard, which were outlined in white. Finally, *iyawós* who make the unambiguously male *orichas*, Eleguá, Ogún, Ochosi, Changó, and Agayú, also have parallel columns of hash marks painted on their bare legs (see, e.g., Brandon 1983, 405–6).[76] These leg markings represent *polainas* or *botas*—leggings, gaiters, or high boots—which descend from the zigzag cuffs of the knee-length *pantalones de bombachas* (knickers) down to the feet (see Ecún 1985, 45, 71, 96, 183, 203). These marks complete the logic of a sartorial ensemble that, like the outfits of seventeenth- and eighteenth-century courtiers and musketeers, and the nineteenth-century Spanish soldier as painted by Landaluze, combined knickers and tall boots or gaiters (figs. 4.5, 4.6). In contrast, the legs of female and male *iyawós* who make female *orichas* are covered with cloth. Of these, the female *iyawós* wear floor-length gowns and the male *iyawós* wear long pants (see, e.g., Flores-Peña and Evanchuck 1994, 48). Still, some houses paint the bare feet of the female *orichas* with sandal-like representations, the counterparts of male boots and gaiters. Thus, complementing the Yoruba-derived *oricha osu* signature, *peinado*, handheld royal or warrior attributes and beaded *mazos*, and facial *trazos*, are the gendered fashion marks of European and creole ladies, gentlemen, and soldiers.

The hybrid sartorial and iconographic presentation on the Middle Day finds something of a parallel in the conventions for dressing and painting the *iyawó*'s body. There is a curious double standard, which appears to reflect the sexual mores of Cuban, Cuban-American, and Latino society, rather than strict adherence to the logic of the *oricha*'s ownership of that body. The emphasis upon the subsuming of the initiate's gender by the *oricha*'s gender gives way, it seems, to the vanity of male initiates. Males and females who make the unequivocally male *orichas*[77] wear jackets and *bombachas* or long pants on the Día del Medio. Females who make female *orichas* wear long gowns. However, males who make female *orichas* do not wear dresses (see, e.g., Flores-Peña and Evanchuck 1994, 20). Their *ropa de santo* is an ensemble of a jacket and long pants, although *bombachas* are sometimes used. While the logic of the Día del Medio outfit revises the gender of female *iyawós* in favor of the gender of their male *orichas* (based, as it is, on male clothes), the gender representations of male *iyawós* remains constant, if only through a sartorial remedy. Male *iyawós* wear male clothes, regardless of their *orichas*' genders. Nydia Pichardo remembers that on her Día del Medio, "when they were dressing me with Changó's outfit, I complained that my *padrino* was painting me with a moustache. But he said, 'remember I have to transform you into Changó [*convertirte en Changó*].' They do everything they can to make you look like the deity, to make you look like a king, queen, or warrior."[78] When men make female *orichas*, their "heads" are represented through the appropriate iconography, such as the color of the *ropa de santo* and the details of the *osu*. However, they are spared gowns and painted earrings, though some houses paint earrings on males. In contrast, in Yorubaland, not only do male initiates wear the dresses of their female deities. In many places, the "wifely" status of the *aworo* (priest) translates into dresses or wraps and female hairstyles for *all* priests of *all* deities. For example, male priests of Ṣàngó in Ayédé, Èkìtì, wear the female bell hairstyle of cornrows surmounted by a bun as well as a gown (see Apter 1992, plate 7). In the Brazilian Candomblé, priests of both genders wear dresses, even for male *orixás*, though this apparently depends upon the *terriero* and the particular characteristics of the individual dancer, wherein the gender of the deity or the initiate may prevail.[79]

In any event, Yorubaland and Brazil evidence religious versions of transvestism and gender manipulation not normally found in the Cuban context (see Matory 1988; 1994, 171–215). Still, it remains quite common to encounter male priests of Ochún who are homosexuals and/or transvestites whom others expect to behave, on stage and off, with certain feminine characteristics. At the same time, though Cuban society has always defined gender narrowly and policed it rigorously (Lumsden 1996), it would be uncharacteristic and disappointing to many priests and visitors to the room if certain signature behaviors of female *orichas* were not manifested in their male *iyawós*, although too many such behaviors in the bodies of male initiates not known to be gay make people uncomfortable. At a 1992 Día del Medio in Havana, the members of the house carefully scrutinized the male *iyawó*'s behavior for telling manifestations of his head *oricha*, Ochún. The *iyawó*, in turn, played with Ochún's role and the visitor's expectations. Observers were charmed when he batted his eyelashes as the flirtatous Ochún is wont to do, but they were visibly relieved when he crossed his legs in a manner deemed not "too effeminate." Similarly, the initiation in Chicago of a macho, blonde-haired Mexican drug dealer as a priest of the domestic, long-suffering female *oricha* Obba provoked anxious and humorous responses in the *iyawó*'s visitors. Obba's *ropa de santo* was pink with gold trim. The right half of the initiate's head was shaved, because the hair on the left side must cover Obba's missing ear. This remaining hair was adorned with braids, pink ribbons, and bows. An *iyalocha* from New York noted with a chuckle, "Now here was this macho man with his big hulking body guards, all wearing cowboy boots. He had ribbons and bows and was sitting forward fanning himself with the *oricha*'s fan and making male gestures all at the same time."[80]

The Apotheosis of Kings, Queens, and Warriors: "Regalia" and the "Coronation"

The stroke of twelve o'clock noon decisively divided the Día de Medio's morning segment from the afternoon presentation in the houses I visited in the 1980s in New York and New Jersey, though some, particularly in Cuba, wait until two o'clock to begin the presentation. The noninitiated (*aleyos*) are permitted to enter the room only when the *iyawó* has been changed out of the *traje de almuerzo* and into the *ropa de santo*.[81] With the shaved head having been decoratively repainted in the morning, the *iyawó* is carefully dressed in the *ropa de santo* by the *oyubona*, and the *mazos* are placed over the body in crisscross position. In Melba Carillo's New York house, at twelve o'clock noon, the initiating godparent and/or *oyubona* places the pasteboard crown on the *iyawó*'s head. With its bold color, metallic braid, and circle of bright red parrot feathers, the crown frames the painted *orí* like a jewel within a gilt setting.

Though Melba Carillo often speaks of the previous day's *asiento* as a "coronation," she emphasizes the moment she must complete the dressing of the *iyawó* in the *ropa de santo* as a *coronación*. "I was taught that the *iyawó* had to be crowned by twelve o'clock; I know that at twelve o'clock I must crown this person."[82] Similarly, for Miami *oriaté* Miguel Ramos, the symbolic emphasis of the *asiento* is the "consecration" of the *orí*—its shaving, washing, and mounting—while the emphasis of the Día del Medio is the *orí*'s "coronation."

In Ramos's elaborate interpretation, the Día del Medio's "coronation" has three guiding themes: the *iyawó*'s *orí* is *engalanado*, *coronado*, and *confirmado* ("embellished," "crowned," and "confirmed"). Highly adorned with paint and surrounded with sumptuous satin and beaded accessories manifesting the *oricha*'s iconography, the *orí* appears as *engalanado*, "at its best." Second, the *ropa de santo*, pasteboard crown, sashlike *collares de mazo*, and beaded dance wand are not merely aesthetic signs of luxury and royalty. They are, more to the point, the *oricha*'s formal "regalia of coronation." Third, this coronation is a public conferral of authority and legitimation, in which this *santo*'s ascension to the throne is "witnessed" and "confirmed" by the community.[83] Seconding Ramos's interpretation, New York Obatalá priestess Marta Moreno Vega writes: "The *Diá del Medio* is the day the Santería community *publicly acknowledges* and celebrates the initiation of a new *iyawo*" (Moreno Vega 2000, 244; emphasis added). In these explanations by priests in New York and Miami, the Día del Medio's conventionalized cluster of attributes—throne, *osu*, crown, *ropa de santo*, *mazos*, and beaded dance wand—does not merely adorn something that has already been done; it is in itself central to a constitutive ceremonial of kingship. Though other priests emphasize additional or ostensibly more important moments of "witnessing" and "confirmation," such as the customary presentation of the painted *orí* to the sun (Olorun) on the morning of the sixth day, Ramos believes that the Día del Medio's "coronation" must commence at twelve o'clock noon precisely because the sun is at its apex. At that moment Olorun (God) witnesses the "assumption of status" of the new king, queen, or warrior.[84]

The dramatic visual tableau of the Día del Medio is formed by a proscenium-like throne of parted curtains, which reveals the highly adorned new *santo*. At this moment, the *iyawó* embodies the nascent *oricha* before "the people" for the first time. The *iyawó* is prompted to maintain decorum, including the appropriate sober bodily postures and facial gestures. With the dance wand in hand, the *iyawó* is told to sit uprightly upon the mortar, not to sit on the floor, to rise respectfully and face front when a priest enters the room, and, in general, to maintain a dignified and tranquil presence. If, within this ritual *habitus*, the seminal Lucumí principle, "The head rules the body and only one king governs a town," is internalized in the new self-concept of the initiate (M. Mason 1994; Bourdieu 1977, 78–86; Jackson 1986, 131), it is also objectified in the behavior of the visitors to the room, who actively participate in the afternoon's performance. In other words, the *orichas* "rule" not only the "head" of the *iyawó* and of those other priests, but those of all of the "houses" and followers of La Regla de Ocha, the "people." This is dramatically demonstrated in the gestures of respect and submission visitors to the room, from the most junior to the most elder, must perform before the throne. This visually dazzling and spiritually magnetic installation powerfully constitutes visitors as awestruck *spectator-supplicants*, beckoning and obliging them to perform gestures of deference. Before a throne, as priests learn through modeling the normative behavior and codes of approriateness of their elders, "everybody comes to give *moforibale* to the *oricha*" (see epigraph).

Each visitor's arrival in the room prompts the reiteration of a little performance by the *iyawó*. As the *iyawó* stands, the *orichas*' regalia are boldly and frontally displayed, the effect being to project the *oricha*'s spiritual radiance. Indeed, the makers of *ropa de santo* emphasize, for example, how important for visual impression is the front panel of male *oricha* jackets, which receives the most elaboration with cowries, reflective braid, and sequins. Female *iyawós*, with the help of their *oyubonas*, arrange and spread out their flowing skirts so the visitor can see the embroidered patterns within the multiple folds and pleats. The *collares de mazo*'s *moñas* are untangled, and the *moñas principales* are adjusted so that they fall elegantly to either side of the body. *Iyawós* are often prompted to raise and turn the dance wand so its designs are fully visible; Obatalá's *iyawós* may be encouraged to gesture with the royal fly whisk. Thus, the visitor is intended to be affected visually, emotionally, and spirtually moved by the *aché* of the new *santo*, as it is manifested in and through aesthetic means. The attention of attendants to the these divine, royal presences signifies both the *oricha*'s status and the active shaping of the newborn's self concept and bodily disposition as the *oricha*'s earthly representative (see Mason 2002). The *iyawó* waits for the visitor to offer a salutation and tribute of money (*derecho*),[85] and must be prepared to "go to the floor" if the visitor is an initiated priest. This may amount to going to the floor scores of times if the celebration is well attended. In the first movement of the salutation sequence, visiting initiated priests put their heads (*orí*) to the mat at the foot of the *iyawó* (give *moforibale*), in order to salute the *oricha* newly crowned on the *iyawó*'s head. In the *iyawó*'s reciprocation of the *moforibale* that follows, the *iyawó* not only salutes the *oricha* crowned on the head of the visiting priest, but also recognizes the seniority of the elder's *orí*—that is, extant heads are "older" in seniority than newly consecrated heads.[86] The elder (*mayor*) then "picks up" the *iyawó* in a gesture of blessing and support toward this new member of the religion (see Burgess-Polcyn 1986; M. Mason 1994).[87]

In sum, to the extent that the Día del Medio is a ceremony of "confirmation," it is, logically, incomplete without the assent of a determinate audience, which includes God, the ancestors, priests, and a larger community of relations. The *moforibale* gesture, rendered in a number of different contexts "to the feet of" a throne, an elder, an *oricha*, or an *iyawó*, constitutes and affirms social and ritual relations of authority and respect (M. Mason 1994).[88] The conscientious priests of La Regla de Ocha do not, it is clear, like to profane their consecrated heads by going to the floor and depositing tributes to a "crown" they do not recognize as *santo*, and they do not do so unless they are intentionally deceived.[89] Within the aesthetically marked frame of the afternoon's activites, these formal, positive gestures of respect thus complete the Día del Medio's performance cycle by enacting and demonstrating the community's recognition of the new king, queen, or warrior.

FIVE

"THE PALACE OF THE OBÁ LUCUMÍ" AND THE "CREOLE TASTE"

INNOVATIONS IN ICONOGRAPHY AND MEANING

To make a *santo* is to make a king, and *kariocha* is a ceremony of kings, like those of the palace of the Obá Lucumí.
—*Iyaloricha* Calixta Morales (Oddedeí), mid–twentieth century

[In my work] I favor the Luis XV style . . . in fact, all the Luises.
—*Babaloricha* and thronemaker Ramón Esquivel, 1987

In Spain, we went to a palace and saw a throne that was red. And I said, "Look! You could have an *iyawó* of Changó here." If you look at [our Santo] through the eyes of someone who is not a *santero,* you see a king of Europe of the seventeenth or eighteenth century, starting with the crown and [jacket] that is used by European royalty. And what kills me are the *pantalones bombachas,* very European; the use of satin—the color is very shiny; the use of precious stones; European fashion; the use of silver and gold also.
—*Iyaloricha* Nydia Pichardo, 1995

[The Santería gods] look like the Three Musketeers with the little knickers, knickerbockers coming up to here [pointing to his knee] and the little . . . almost like a beret to one side with a feather in it . . . ah, it's disgusting!
—Chief Ajamu

[W]e can no longer speak of tradition in terms of the approximate identity of some objective thing that changes while remaining the same. Instead, we must understand tradition as a symbolic process that both presupposes past symbolisms and creatively reinterprets them.
—Richard Handler and Jocelyn Linnekin, 1984

LYDIA CABRERA AND CALIXTA MORALES: "ROYAL HONORS" AND BORROWED ICONOGRAPHY

Early in her Havana fieldwork, Lydia Cabrera (1899–1991) accompanied two elder Afro-Cuban *iyalochas,* Yemayá priestess Teresa Muñoz (Omí Tomí) and Ochosi priestess Calixta Morales (Oddedeí), to an Ocha celebration, possibly in the black working-class *barrio* of Pogolotti in Marianao, the Havana suburb where Oddedeí lived. At this Día del Medio of a *mulata* who was being initiated as a priestess of Ochún, Omí Tomí and Oddedeí, Cabrera writes, "explained to me, without beating around the bush, everything I was seeing for the first time" ([1954] 1983, 27).[1] Perhaps it was during that auspicious moment that Oddedeí shared with Cabrera her thoughts on the origin and significance of Lucumí initiation: "To make a *santo* is to make a king, and *kariocha* is a ceremony of kings, like those of the palace of the Obá Lucumí" (Cabrera [1954] 1983, 24 n. 1). Accounting for the priests and priestesses who would have staffed such a house, Oddedeí told Cabrera, "the *babalao,* and the *mamalochas,* formed a court like the one *there*"—that is, in the palace of the Obá Lucumí (Cabrera [1954] 1983, 24 n. 1, emphasis added).[2] In later writings, Cabrera would summarize what she had learned. The Middle Day was observed, as explained "by some elders . . . for the simple reason 'that the *Orichas* were kings,' the evocation of the coronation of an *Obá* [king] in the ancestral homeland. Perhaps that they conserved the memory of their forebears—that divine treatment is accorded to the *Obá*—accounts for the 'reason that when one salutes someone who has made *Santo*, one is saluting a crowned king'" (Cabrera [1974] 1980, 178–79).

Though ethnographies of West Africa distinguish between the coronation rituals of West African divine kings and the initiation of cult priests (Matory 1986, 110–12; 1994, 178–215; Apter 1992, 84; Pemberton and Afolayan 1996, 79–93), Oddedeí invoked a powerful trope of royalty that, in fact, resonates across a series of related domains among the Yoruba themselves: those of gods, kings, ancestors, and priests. Many of the major Yoruba gods were "princes of the royal family" of Odùduwà, founder and first Ọ̀ọ̀ni of Ifẹ̀, princes "who traveled away from their home in all directions to found new kingdoms and dynasties" (Smith 1969, 19–20). Other *òrìṣà* were born from the union of Ifẹ̀'s Yẹmọja with Ọrọnyọ̀n, the founder of Ọ̀yọ́, such as the principal royal children, Sàngó, Dadà, and Ṣọ̀npọ̀nọ́n (Abraham 1946, 680). In Yorubaland, gods, kings, ancestors, and the priests of the royal cults each carry signs of royalty: valuable and intricately made attributes, such as beaded crowns, layers of expensive cloth, and ceremonial scepters, such as stylized swords, decorated staffs, and fly whisks (Thompson 1970; Apter 1992, 103–5, 157–58, and plates 1 and 2; Drewal, Pemberton, and Abiodun 1989, 31, 36; see also Drewal and Mason 1998, passim). In the public phases of their formal coronation ceremonies and annual festivals, "when, crowned and robed, [kings] took [their] place[s] in the throne room . . . or on its gabled veranda" of the king's palace compound (Smith 1969, 132; Apter 2002, 105; see fig. 5.1).

Oddedeí's "palace of the Obá Lucumí" might suggest itself as a straightforward ethnographic reference to West African royal palace compounds, for there was no "king's palace," as such, in Cuba—other than the magnificent colonial palace of the Spanish king's representative on the island, the captain general, which stands on the Plaza de Armas in Old Havana. Oddedeí's terminology depends, in fact, upon the "experience-near," "locally" significant nomenclature of Cuban social history: the *Lucumí* king (see Geertz 1983, 57). "Lucumí" was the metaethnonym that classified Yoruba-speaking subgroups and related Bight of Benín peoples during the era of the slave trade. It later became a common term defining the modern Afro-Cuban *regla* of the *orichas* descended from the "Lucumí nation," La Regla Lucumí (see chap. 2; Ortiz [1916] 1987, 50–51; López Valdés 1986). Therefore, *Obá Lucumí* may or may not refer to the Yoruba king known by the contemporary ethnographer of West Africa, and its historical signification thus becomes more ample. In this sense, Oddedeí's "palace of the Obá Lucumí" can be read as a powerful chronotope,[3] a spatiotemporal figure, which grounds and generates narratives of the imagined community of Lucumí in the Diaspora as much as it refers to the specific history and geography of the West African "source culture." For Oddedeí, the Regla Lucumí's "court" of "babalaos and mamalochas" was "just like the one *there*"—a deictic "there" that points to a more remote font of the *orichas'* powerful *aché*—Africa (also called Guinea)—a spiritual force embodied in the stones "swallowed" by Africans prior to their enslavement and the terrible Middle Passage, and made ever present in the local shrines and performances of Cuba's Lucumí (see chap. 2).

The Afro-Cuban palace of the Obá Lucumí, with its associations of spiritual origin and genealogy, ritual deep knowledge and royal protocol, recalls other diasporic chronotopes operative in Caribbean and South American diasporic narratives. The *Ginê* (Africa) of Haitian Vodouisants is the great ancestral site "beneath the water" (*anba dlo*)—local or imaginary bodies of water beneath the "earth"—from which the spirits (*lwa*) come when called, and to which the dead (*morte*) return (see Brown 1991, 30–33, 223, 282–86; 1995, 14–15; Métraux [1959] 1972, 28). The *Aruanda* (Luanda) of the Brazilian Candomblé Angola is the ancestral place in the "forest" from which the *caboclo*

Figure 5.1.—Oba Ademuwagun Adesida II, the Deji of Akure, on the throne in the courtyard of Akure Palace, 1959. Yoruba people, Nigeria. (Photograph by Eliot Elisofon. Image no. 2074, Eliot Elisofon Photographic Archives, National Museum of African Art, Washington, D.C.)

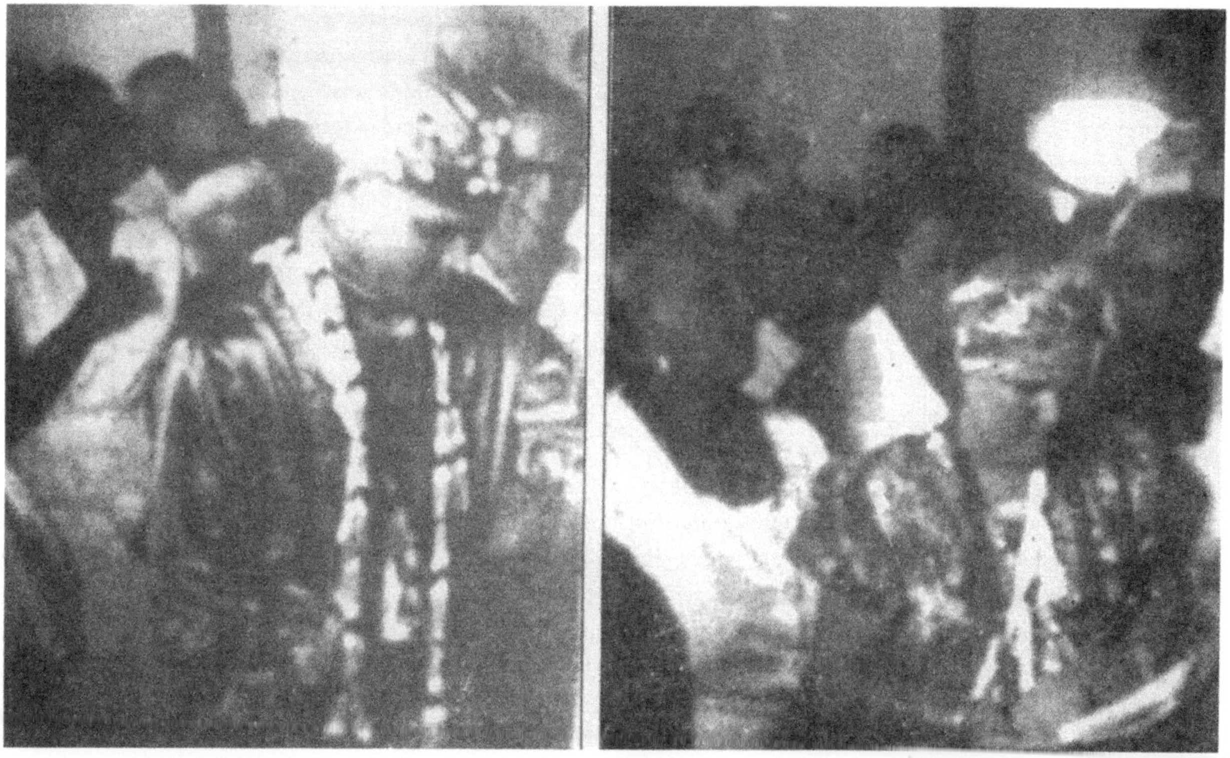

Figure 5.2.—Presentation of *iyawós* to the drums with *ropa de santo, collares de mazo,* and crowns, Havana (?), c. 1950. *Left,* Changó; *right,* Yemayá. (From Cabrera [1954] 1983, plates; photographs by J. Tarafa and J. Dobrony. Courtesy the Estate of Lydia Cabrera.)

spirits come, spirits whose iconography derives from the indigenous Amerindians of Brazil's interior as well as the nation's flag (Wafer and Santana 1990; see also Apter 1991, 235, 245; Marks 1974, 98–101).[4] And the "Angola" of the Afro-Brazilian *Capoeira de Angola* martial art refers as much to the *roda* (sparring circle) of the Capoeira "game" as it does to the Angola of western Central Africa itself. Finally, the Ifê, Oyô, and Kêtu of the Bahian Nagô Candomblés can refer as much to the individual shrine-houses of particular *orixás* on the grounds of the *terrieros* as they do to geographical points on the global map (see chap. 3).

Comparative ethnohistorical reference to the Yoruba source culture explains much about the contemporary patterns of Lucumí religion, music, and arts (e.g., Herskovits 1941, 61–85; 1930; Bascom 1952; Ortiz 1937a; Thompson 1983, 3–97; 1993, 145–282; J.Mason 1992, 1996; Drewal and Mason 1998). The Afro-Cuban *obá-oriaté* Nicolás Angarica was unequivocal about the "true" and "unmystified" source of his sacred practice and one of its important icons, the thunderax of Changó (*oché*): "the Lucumí religion from the Yoruba territory" ([1955?] n.d., 9). Still, reliance upon the putative Yoruba source culture cannot account, entirely, for striking features of Lucumí Middle Day ceremonial that Cabrera documented in the mid–twentieth century and Angarica and other *oriatés* encountered weekly during the same period in Havana. Photographs by Cabrera's collaborators, Tarafa and Dobrony, for example, document male and female *iyawós* dressed in regal satin *trajes de medio* and beaded *collares de mazo* (fig. 5.2). A jewel-encrusted tiara—essentially a wide, pointed, and tapered cloth band that is fastened from behind—complements the female *iyawó*'s brocaded gown, which features puff shoulders and a square neckline. A cowrie-encrusted satin crown, which recalls Napoleonic military headgear as much as Yoruba soft pillbox caps (*fìlà*), complements the male *iyawó*'s loose, eighteenth-century-style satin jacket, which is fastened on the left side of the chest.[5] Having just left undoubtedly elegant thrones,[6] the two *iyawós* move solemnly in procession in their "presentation to the drums," the *batá de fundamento*.

These midcentury *iyawós* are splendidly dressed *oricha* kings and queens, denizens of the Cuban elaboration of the palace of the Obá Lucumí. As described in detail in chapter 4, the principal artistic evocations of this "king's palace" are the canopied *trono*, the pasteboard or cloth *corona*, the satin *traje de medio*, the beaded *collares de mazo*, the handheld *atributo* (dance wand), the *pilón*, the painted *osu* and *peinado*, and, not least, the decorative porcelain or ceramic *soperas*. Clearly, not all of the gods that arrived in Cuba originated in Yoruba royal cults. Yet, as they were assigned their place and status in the modern Lucumí "pantheon," all of them, except the forest Warriors (*guerreros*), embraced the full complement of royal emblems, including signal attributes and ceremonies of the quintessential mythico-historical king, Changó, the "Fourth Alafin of Oyó." In the palace of the Obá Lucumí, lavishly evoked for the formal public presentation of the Middle Day, even the *guerreros* would wear satin *ropa de santo* and repose, however uncomfortably, under their special canopied thrones of leaves.

How did central elements of modern Lucumí initiatory iconography come to be elaborated in a system of objects and aesthetic preferences that appear to derive as much from European baroque, rococo, and neoclassical styles as from Yoruba kingship and cult ritual? How is it, for example, that a premier Afro-Cuban altar maker, the late Ramón Esquivel of Matanzas and Union City, New Jersey, "favor[ed] the Luis XV style" in his aesthetic elaboration of putatively Yoruba-derived deities? And, how is it that such aesthetic preferences have been widely regarded by most Cuban and Latino practitioners as appropriate, time honored, and "traditional"?

In order to attend to these questions, the following discussions revisit innovations in institutions, rituals, and artistic forms that I approached from different angles in the previous chapters (e.g., socio- and ethnohistorical, ethnographic). Taking as a point of departure the hypotheses of Lydia Cabrera and Fernando Ortiz about the historical relationship of *cabildos, casa templos*, and their "courtly reminders," this chapter seeks to sketch out an art history and "biography" (Kopytoff 1986) of the palace of the Obá Lucumí's principal formal markers: thrones, altars, their constitutent objects, and the *ropa de santo*. Each of these forms was developed over time in the context of emergent institutions and religious practices. In order to amplify the sense of how quickly innovations can take hold, the chapter closes with a capsule look at how new agents, equipped with an alternative take on the "Lucumí religion from the Yoruba territory," have sought to revise previous revisions and rewrite the institutional and spiritual history of the palace of the Obá Lucumí.

With a nod to the seminal writings of her brother-in-law, Fernando Ortiz ([1920] 1960, 1921), Lydia Cabrera suggested in a 1954 footnote that the colonial-era *cabildos* of the African nations carried on traditions of kingship that appeared to mirror those of Africa. In "the *Cabildos* the slaves . . . tried to revive in their celebrations the life-world of the absent country" (Cabrera quoting Ortiz [1921] in Cabrera [1954] 1983, 24 n. 1). Historian Hubert Aimes had posed this hypothesis in 1905, and Fernando Ortiz approvingly cited it in his seminal ethnohistorical work on the old Cuban Day of Kings festival (Aimes 1905, 16–18, 21; Ortiz [1920] 1960, 24). Attempting to connect the dots and make these historical insights significant to her mid-twentieth-century ethnographic work, Cabrera hypothesized that the "royal honors" rendered to *cabildo* kings and queens as late as the 1880s were, in turn, reflected in various "courtly reminders"—a certain "etiquette shown by junior priests toward their most distinguished elders"—which she observed in the modern Ocha houses of Havana and Matanzas in the 1930s, 1940s, and 1950s. All of "this is obvious," Cabrera writes, particularly in the gestures and symbolism of the *kariocha* and the Middle Day. It is precisely in support of this observation that Cabrera cites Oddedeí's "palace of the Obá Lucumí" narrative as corroboration ([1954] 1983, 24, n.1).

The octogenarians Oddedeí and Omí Tomí were undoubtedly taught by their African parents and kin about the origins of social and religious practices in West Africa. The memories of surviving African ex-slaves, and travel between Cuba and Lagos in the forty years around the turn of the twentieth century (see Sarracino 1988, chap. 2 and 52–53) meant that first- or secondhand knowledge of Yorubaland under colonial rule (beginning in 1860) could not have been scarce during the period of Omí Tomí and Oddedeí's youth and, even, early adulthood—Oddedeí was probably more than seventy years old when Cabrera first met her in 1930 (Intar Gallery 1984, 9, 14, 15). Moreover, by the time of Cabrera's intensive midcentury fieldwork (1942–58), a number of Lucumí religious practitioners had access to early West African ethnographic data via Fernando Ortiz[7] (see chap. 3). While Omí Tomí and Oddedeí did not know the West African palace of the Ọba firsthand, they clearly knew African-born Lucumí *cabildo* royalty, in addition to whatever white creole aristocracy they saw around them. Omí Tomí, who pridefully claimed part-Lucumí ancestry, as well as direct descent from an enslaved Mina Popó woman (from the Gold Coast), was a seamstress for "many old and opulent families in Havana," including for Lydia Cabrera's own grandmother and mother (Cabrera [1954] 1983, 24, 27). A priestess of Yemayá, Omí Tomí, was "known among the 'creme' of the colonial days in the festivals of the famous Cabildo 'Changó Terddún' and the old Ocha houses" of Havana (Cabrera [1954] 1983, 24–25, 47). The sartorial display of both white creole Cuban and Lucumí royalty could not have been lost on the highly skilled *costurera,* Omí Tomí. Oddedeí herself was an "aristocrat" of "pure Lucumí lineage" (*orilé̃ lucumí*). Her mother had been "rendered honors as *la reina* [queen] of the Cabildo of Santa Bárbara" in Havana—which was probably the old Cabildo "Changó Terddún" (Cabrera [1954] 1983, 27, 24). In the semiprivate *cabildo* drummings and public Day of Kings street processions—enacted as late as January 1884—Omí Tomí and Oddedeí must have seen not only Lucumí rituals for the *orichas,* but also the lavish royal and military vestments of *cabildo* kings and queens, elected and installed in ceremonies that were "revivals" of those from the "absent homeland." The palace of the Obá Lucumí had existed in Cuba after all.

The Ocha houses of the twentieth-century Regla Lucumí would not be ruled by mortal kings and queens who were elected annually and rendered honors as they sat enthroned before their nation's congregations during Sunday festive celebrations (see Bremer 1853, 2:380–81). Nevertheless, as in Yorubaland historically tropes of royalty are manifested across a number of domains within the Regla Lucumí. As indicated, the formal coronation of *obás* within La Regla de Ifá, and Lucumí religious titles such as *obá, obácolabá, obá-oriaté,* and *apetebí,* lend suggestive context to Oddedeí's remark that the "*babalawo* and *mamalocha* form a court."[8] Equally important, the principle that each *cabildo* claimed a beloved *santo* as its patron—a Catholic saint and a Lucumí *oricha*—continued as each modern house would be "ruled" by the tutelary *oricha* of its senior priest, a *babalocha, iyalocha,* or *babalawo.* Moreover, the old *cabildos'* annual elections of royal "rulers" continued symbolically in the annual 1 January "Ifá Divination of the Opening of the Year," in which a male and female *oricha* couple—in effect, a king and queen—are selected to "govern the year." The identity of a house's tutelary deity and the two annual rulers are marked by iconographically appropriate *banderas* (flags), a practice that recalls the identifying *banderas* of the *cabildos'* royal and military processions (fig. 1.4). In a similar way, moreover, Santería drumming ensembles in Cuba and the United States fly large fringed standards bearing the iconography and colors of their spiritual patrons over the performance spaces in which they provide the ritual music for dancing and spirit possession (see plate 4).[9] Finally, and not least, the *paños* and cloth of the *orichas'* royal *tronos* are themselves luminous *banderas*—the *orichas'* "colors"—that herald the gods' immediate spiritual presence. Formally presented *iyawós* and *orichas* do not appear without royal clothing, crowns, and regalia.

THE MULTIPLE LOCAL SOURCES OF LUCUMÍ ICONOGRAPHY

The local sources of the Lucumí *orichas'* cluster of attributes—throne, crown, *ropa de santo*, handheld staff, and *paño*—are multiple and overdetermined. It would be unwise to insist upon a single source. The elaboration of Lucumí religious display depended upon at least three fertile proximate sources: the *cabildos de nación*, the material culture of Cuba's social hierarchies, and popular Catholic iconography. First, the dress and accessories that graced *cabildo* kings and queens during formal festivals represent a potent set of historical prototypes for the modern ensemble of *oricha* royal attributes. The most suggestive published examples from the nineteenth century include the canopied throne and crown of Bremer's 1853 Cabildo Lucumí of Santa Bárbara (Bremer 1853, 2:380–81); the "magnificent gilt-paper crown" and the lavish red "genuine costume of a King of the Middle Ages" of Leon Beauvallet's 1856 *cabildo* monarch (quoted in Aimes 1905, 20–21); and the finery of the queens and ladies in waiting: petticoated gowns with puff shoulders and square necklines, jewelry, and openwork crowns or tiaras. These objects were richly documented by Víctor Patricio de Landaluze in the late 1870s and Charles DeForest Fredricks around 1860 (see plate 1, fig. 1.7). Still, as observed in chapter 1, *cabildo* royalty itself drew upon, and compounded, multiple and circular sources. The kinds of dress and accessories utilized by the old *cabildos* claimed long histories and were already "traditionalized" local expressions within the Afro-Cuban nations' repertoires when they were documented by mid-nineteenth-century observers.[10] They had drawn upon black and mulatto battalion military display, the history of which dated to the previous century, the time-honored religious iconography of the Three Kings, memories of African rulers dressed in European prestige garb, and Cuban sartorial markers of class distinction, which the planter-merchant class had already adopted from Europe and which functioned within the island's colonial social formation—not least as they had been appropriated by the "splendidly dressed" free people of color and urban slaves themselves at least by the turn of the nineteenth century (fig. 1.9).

Second, in an analogous but redirected form of appropriation, the priests of the emergent Regla Lucumí transposed expensive cloth and prestige ceramics from their locations as de facto sumptuary marks of class position to the matter-spirit hierarchy, where they came to signify the splendor, distinction, and wealth of the *orichas*. It would be surprising if Omí Tomí Teresa Muñoz, "seamstress to many old and opulent families in Havana," did not also produce luxury clothes from imported cloth not only for her white employers, but also for the Havana *cabildos* and houses in which she circulated. In a more well known African Diaspora parallel, the nineteenth-century Candomblé women of Salvador, Bahia, transposed the lavish, multilayered hoop-dress styles of their former slave mistresses—as well as the techniques of starching and ironing petticoats passed down through generations of female domestic slaves—from the axis of social class to the axis of human-divine relationships in their creation of the ritual finery of the *orixás* and their priestesses, the *iyalorixás* (Omari 1984, 33–34).

Third, the Lucumí *orichas* were iconographically elaborated as the status equivalents, if not the rivals, of revered local Catholic Virgins and saints. Is it possible to verify, for example, whether the *orichas'* openwork metal crowns of multiple arches or points were drawn from old *cabildo* royalty or from the ubiquitous local representations of the Virgins and saints of royal lineage, for whom such crowns are central iconographic elements? As worn by Catholic icons, crowns can signify "distinction, royalty, and victory." The Virgin Mary wears her crown as a descendant of the royal house of David, and because she is the "Queen of Heaven." The saints Elizabeth, Barbara, and Catherine wear their crowns to mark their royal lineages. When worn by martyrs, crowns signify "victory over human sinfulness and death" (Apostolos-Cappadona 1994, 90–91).[11] Crown-wearing Virgins and royal saints, of course, represent a large proportion of the Catholic figures associated with the principal *orichas;* indeed, all "Four Pillars" of the modern Lucumí tradition—Obatalá, Yemayá, Changó, and Ochún—are associated with Virgins or royal saints.[12] The *orichas'* crowns mark not only their royalty and high spiritual status. These "kings," "queens," and "warriors" also represent the sacred resources for the eternal protection of their "children" (the *oricha* priests) and their victory over human problems. This remains true today for Lucumí priests, while, for most modern peoples, subjecthood to royal rulers ended a century or more ago, and general popular interest in the theme of royalty is limited to the late Princess Diana and the Kennedy family; for example, in a country without historical royalty, Jacqueline Kennedy Onassis has been immortalized as "America's Queen" (Bradford 2000). The United States has long claimed its "warriors" in Daniel Boone, George Armstrong Custer, the Flying Leathernecks, and Delta Force. As commercial culture goes, it is unsurprising that Christian Dior recently introduced a stylized "warrior" into the world of fashion, complete with leather, fur, and tribal iconography (Christian Dior advertisement 2001). Of course, West Indians have long rallied behind Calypso royalty, such as "Lord" Kitchener (see Hill 1972, 64 and plates; Rohlehr 1990, 213–14, 408ff., 450ff., plates 39, 40, 47, 48);[13] jazzophiles continue to celebrate the "King" (Oliver), the "Duke," the "Count," the "Empress," the "Pres," and the "Judge" (see, e.g., Southern 1971, 379, 38492, 398);[14] and black New Orleanians have their "King of Zydeco," the late Clifton Chenier, and their beloved "King Zulu" (the 1949 king was Louis Armstrong), who rivals "Rex," the white king that embodies official Mardi Gras. Such royal titles within the musical sphere reflect an Afro-American tradition historically linked to colonial-era black institutions and societies, such as Trinidad's stick-fighting "yard bands" and "backyard tents," and black New Orleans's early African "nations" and later "social and pleasure clubs" (see Spitzer 1986, 373–76; Edmonson 1956; Kinser 1990, 46–47, 232–40; Hill 1972, 32–42; see also Piersen 1988). Lucumí priests and priestesses in Havana, New York, Miami, Chicago, Los Angeles, Shelton, North Carolina, Carolina and Santurce, Puerto Rico, Panama City, Caracas, and Mexico, D.F., who may attend "coronations" every weekend, speak of, and engage with, beloved *oricha* "kings," "queens," and "warriors" as central to their present lives (see Brown 1993b, 1996, 1999). These very same priests and priestesses, who go by their American or Spanish family and given names in the daily round, know themselves as the "children" and subjects of *oricha* royalty. They and their ancestors carry sacred Lucumí names that often refer to royalty, wealth, and virtuous qualities and are precious to their identities: Obadimelli ("king made twice"), Obá Tolá ("king that is wealth"), Obá Teró ("king that is cool water"), Obanyoko ("enthroned king"), Obá Bí ("king gives birth"), Eguín Koladé ("snail receives wealth"), Oñi L'adé ("honey is the crown"), Adé Kolá ("crown receives wealth"), and so on.

If Cuban Lucumí iconography borrowed from Roman Catholic prototypes, the latter were already overdetermined, locally elaborated versions of European baroque religious expressions. And, in many cases, *oricha* attributes did not so much *follow* from the saints' accessories; for particular adornments of some saints and *orichas* historically emerged in roughly parallel fashion and formed symbioses at the local level. For example, the site-specific nautical iconography of the Virgin of Regla, who presides over the Bay of Havana, its seafaring activities, and its storms, lent iconography to and historically paralleled the elaboration of the Virgin's counterpart, Yemayá. The Virgin of Regla,

Figure 5.3.—Iconography of the Virgin of Regla from her church interior. *Left,* coat-of-arms of Regla carved in relief on the Virgin's altar, with its key and fortifications; *right,* auxiliary Regla blazon with sea-tossed boat, maritime worker, and ship's wheel and anchor. (Photographs by David H. Brown.)

from which the seaport town derives its name, was proclaimed the patron of the bay in 1714. The key, ship's wheel, its anchor, and a rowboat formed elements of Regla's coats of arms with the Virgin's standard iconography, appearing in carved relief on her altar and in the silver crescent moon beneath her feet (fig. 5.3). In 1844, the American writer Dr. Wurdemann documented this Virgin's sanctuary as painted blue and filled with silver ex-votos that included nautical imagery, such as ships' anchors (Cabrera [1974] 1980, 111–16). In the minds of Regla's *santeros,* these insignia "colors" (blue and white with silver) and attributes of the black Virgin have always been shared with Yemayá: the key, the ship's wheel, the anchor, the boat, and the crescent moon, along with other appropriate symbols, became integral to Yemayá's metal *herramientas,* which go inside her *sopera* (fig. 5.4).[15] Though the Regla church might claim the Virgin's iconographic primacy, as well as co-opting formal aspects of Yemayá's worship (see below), Lucumí practitioners persist in asserting Yemayá's primacy and in "signifying" in relation to at least three visual and semantic domains (secular historical, Catholic, and Lucumí; see, e.g., Orsi 1985). The possibilities of such multiple signification represent not only a "struggle for posses-

Figure 5.4.—Examples of Yemayá's and Olokun's cast lead *herramientas:* sun, crescent moon, key, boat, life preserver, ship's wheel, mermaid, anchor, and propeller, Havana, 1998. (Photograph by David H. Brown.)

Figure 5.5.—Dressed statue of the Virgin of Regla from the Cabildo of the Virgin of Regla/Yemayá of Josefa Herrera (Echubí Pepa), with silk mantle (*manto*, or *pañuelo*), metallic floral appliqué, and tin crown, nineteenth century. Polychromed wood, cloth. Museum of Regla. (Photograph by David H. Brown.)

Figure 5.6.—Statue of the Caridad del Cobre from the Cabildo of the Virgin of Regla/Yemayá of Josefa Herrera (Echubí Pepa), nineteenth century, showing hand-embroidered satin mantle (*manto*, or *pañuelo*) in floral design and tin crown and halo. Polychromed wood and cloth. Museum of Regla. (Photograph by David H. Brown.)

sion of the sign" within hegemony (see Kelly and Kaplan 1990, 35; Comaroff 1985, 196; Hebdige 1979, 17), but also a pragmatic accord or accommodation over the sign.[16] Thus, for example, the important *capilla* (chapel, or altar) of the Virgin/Yemayá, located within the old *casa* of the Cárdenas family directly adjacent to the church, with its *oricha* altars behind the Virgin's *capilla*, complicates the teasing apart of causal influences.

Many shared adornments, such as the dazzling blue and silver brocaded mantles (*paños*), of the Virgin and Yemayá, as well as other Virgins and *orichas,* were apparently produced by the same hands, including those of the beloved Yemayá priestesses Panchita and Marcelina Cárdenas, the *camareras* whose photographs hang on either side of the Virgin's *capilla.* According to Regla museum museologist Luis Alberto Pedroso, the *paños* of the saint statues belonging to Adechina Ño Remigio Herrera's *cabildo* (e.g., figs. 5.5, 5.6) were produced by his daughter, priestess Josefa Herrera Echubí Pepa.[17] It is suggestive that the finely hand-embroidered and multicolored floral motifs upon the Caridad del Cobre's satin *manto,* produced early in the twentieth century for the *cabildo,* are remarkably similar to embroidery upon a satin *ropa de santo* dress for Ochún and a satin *paño* for Yemayá produced in Regla around the same time (see fig. 5.7). Such embroidery skills were undoubtedly widespread among Cuban women in general, and floral motifs were, and remain, quite common. Women's magazines sold in Cuba provided patterns and instructions for producing the same style of floral embroidery (fig. 5.26). Yet, while anyone could have produced adornments for secular dress and saint statues, it is likely that within *cabildos* and *casas* that owned saint statues, such as Josefa Herrera's Cabildo of the Virgin of Regla/Yemayá, priestesses with such skills would have produced *paños* for saints and *orichas* alike. As argued above, skillful seamstresses like Omí Tomí Teresa Muñoz, a contemporary of Josefa Herrera Echubí Pepa, as well as Calixta Morales Oddedeí, could undoubtedly have filled this role.

Figure 5.7.—*Ropa de santo* of Ochún, Regla, c. 1920s–1940s. Satin with hand-sewn floral embroidery in silk thread. Museum of Regla. (Photograph by David H. Brown.)

As Cabrera writes of this generation of women that included Omí Tomí, Oddedeí, and Josefa Herrera, "Those elderly black women who were instructed by Africans," many of whom worked as domestics, "also . . . knew the catechism by heart . . . were assiduous about the feasts of the church . . . the rosary, and book of the mass; they wouldn't pardon working on Sunday and made us pray the Padre Nuestro at night, even though we would be collapsed with sleep; they obliged us to kiss the holy bread every time it fell to the floor, and to cross ourselves each time we passed the front of the house of God—[which was also, to them] the *Ilé-Olofi* [House of Olofi]" (Cabrera [1947] 1994, 280). "Those old black women," of course, as Bascom noted in 1950, were never confused as to the identities and functions of saints and *orichas.* "The *santos,*" Oddedeí explained to Lydia Cabrera, "are the same here and in Africa. The same with different names. The only difference is that ours eat a lot and have to dance . . . those of yours, the whites, are assuaged with incense and oil . . . and they don't dance" (Cabrera [1947] 1994, 276; see also Murphy 1988,

Figure 5.8.—Echú figure, recovered from the Cabildo of the Virgin of Regla/Yemayá of Echubí after 1948, believed to have been carved by Ño Remigio Herrera/Adechina. Stone, cowrie shell, and paint, 10 inches high. Museum of Regla. (Photograph by David H. Brown.)

Figure 5.9.—Throne-canopy and chromolithographs of Virgins and saints over a cabinet (*canastillero*) of *orichas*, which are contained in plate-covered white bowls, in the house of María Andó de Cárdenas, Cuba, c. 1950. (From Cabrera [1954] 1983. Courtesy the Estate of Lydia Cabrera.)

116–25). Still, both *orichas* and *santos* deserved lavish adornment, which manifested itself in a kind of sartorial lingua franca, as satin and metallic *paños*, miniature metal crowns, and a concise body of attendant iconography.

As many scholars have noted, the *santos* of the Catholic church were by no means remote and foreign presences to the African nations and to the Lucumí houses. By the middle of the eighteenth century, at least, the Cuban saints and Virgins were as much—to borrow from the contemporary African American idiom—"in the house," as in the church. They were and are influential popular figures. As noted in chapter 1, in 1755, Havana bishop Morell de Santa Cruz instituted devotions in twenty-one African *cabildos* (Marrero 1988, 14:172, 175, 282). When José Antonio Aponte's *cabildo* was searched by the authorities following his arrest for "conspiracy" in 1812, it was found to contain diverse images and statues of Catholic saints, including Our Lady of Remedies (Franco 1977, 24–25, 8–17). Throughout the African

Diaspora during the colonial era, Christ, the Virgin, and the saints, such as Our Lord of the Good End, Our Lady of the Rosary, Saint Benedict the Moor in Salvador, Bahia, and Saint James the Elder (Sin Jak Maje/Ogou) in Haiti were embraced as the "mystic kin" and powerful liberators of Africans, and the "syncretized" manifestations of the African gods themselves (see, e.g., Cosentino 1995b; Bastide [1960] 1978, 115–16; Cabrera [1954] 1994). In Havana, the religious objects recovered from the virtually abandoned Cabildo of Yemayá/the Virgin of Regla at 63 Perdomo Street, following the 1947 death of its leader, Echubí Pepa, included not only African-style mortars for grinding herbs, seeds, and "powders" and a hand-hewn stone Eleguá, probably made by Adechina (fig. 5.8), but also a set of four exquisitely carved, hand-painted, and luxuriously dressed *santitos* (figs. 5.5, 5.6). Typical of the finely carved and meticulously cared-for wood statues of the Cuban colonial era, these were the principal saints associated with the Four Pillars of the Lucumí pantheon: the Virgin of Mercy (La Virgen de las Mercedes, associated with Obatalá), the Virgin of Regla (La Virgen de Regla, associated with Yemayá), the Virgin of El Cobre (La Caridad del Cobre, associated with Ochún), and Saint Barbara (Santa Bárbara, associated with Changó). Now exhibited in the Museum of Regla's branch galleries adjacent to the Regla church itself, they are beautifully crowned and haloed in gold and lavishly dressed in hand-embroidered or painted *paños*. Each is enshrined in its own miniature painted wood-and-glass shrine display (*capilla*). These saints of the *cabildo* were undoubtedly the images carried in procession by the institution's members on the saints' feast days (see, e.g., Cabrera [1974] 1980, 17). Though the presence of these saint statues may indicate formal, and not always substantive, adoration for every practitioner, images of saints appear universally in Cuban and Cuban-American *casas de santo*, occupying the front rooms of homes, adorning walls, surmounting *oricha* festival thrones, and standing atop *oricha* cabinets (see plates 3, 8, 20, 27, figs. 5.9, 5.10, and see Murphy 1988, 108–12; Brandon 1993, 166–72).

Figure 5.10.—*Capilla* (altar) throne for Santa Bárbara and Changó, with *pabellón* (valance) of red silk damask, at the Sociedad Santa Rita y San Lázaro of Silvestre Erice, El Cerro. "A kind of dossal or curtain [*dosel* or *colgadura*] of [white] fine point embroidery covered the altar," Roche writes. "The dossal [was] surmounted by a canopy-like hanging [*pabellón*] or valance [*bambalinas*] of red silk damask, a unique ornamentation that showed some artfulness" (Roche y Monteagudo 1908, 83; [1908] 1925a, 182).

"CHEAP HANGINGS," THE "ROBES OF THE SAINTS," AND "SOUP TUREENS": CATHOLICISM AND POPULAR CULTURE IN LUCUMÍ ICONOGRAPHY, 1910–1950

The early-twentieth-century accounts of Fernando Ortiz ([1906] 1973, 32–179), Irene Wright (1910, 149–50), and Rafael Roche y Monteagudo (1908, 83; [1908] 1925a, 159–252) register a thoroughgoing hybridized Lucumí *oricha* iconography as firmly established by the first years of the Cuban nation (founded 1902). The altars documented by these writers, in *cabildos* led by "old Africans," reveal the integrated presence of Lucumí and Catholic iconography, as well as adopted objects of Cuban popular culture. During the Lucumí gourd shaker and drum ensemble (*güiro*) event that Irene Wright attended in the El Cerro "African *cabildo*," she was "shown altars . . . in an adjoining room." "One was to Our Lady of Mercy, one to Saint Joseph, and one to Saint Barbara, at the base of whose shrine was an iron image of a black jockey such as used to stand, before good taste made them scarce, on sidewalks before houses in the North as hitching posts. These altars were decorated with cheap hangings and tawdry trinkets, which had, probably, their secret meanings. In another room, in which also was a bed elaborately trimmed with yellow satin and ribbon, was an altar to the Virgin of Cobre. There were dishes of food before it, in the process of being blessed, I gathered, and there was a covered soup tureen we were given to understand held a holy secret" (Wright 1910, 148–49). Though described in a condescending tone, the "cheap hangings and tawdry trinkets" of the first room surely refer to thronelike canopies and drapes, *paños*, and Lucumí beadwork (see figs. 5.10, 5.11). The altar of the second room is clearly a specially prepared throne room to honor Ochún, in which a *plaza* of dishes of blessed food surrounding this *oricha*'s *sopera*-enclosed *fundamento* ("holy secret") is arranged on the floor before a lavishly adorned bed.

If Wright's descriptions are accurate, these intricate assemblages included the adapted and/or customized products of secular material culture, as Saint Barbara's altar features an iron "black jockey" figure; at minimum Wright may have used a pejorative American reference familiar to her in order describe the carving of a nonacademic, or "self-taught," sculptor. The "covered soup tureen" was, in fact, a central feature of the middle-class china dinner service (*vajilla*), which was commercially available via European export beginning in the early nineteenth century (see below). Most intriguingly, the apparently lavish altar for Ochún is cast in the distinctively creole style of this deity of love, fortune, and femininity. One of Ochún's important local cultural referents is the well-known nineteenth-century social "type," the fan-wielding *mulata* or *mulata de rumbo*, a ubiquitous fixture in high arts and letters, popular culture, and commercial imagery from the 1830s onward (fig. 4.24). The *mulata* has been a central trope through which Cuba has struggled over its claimed *mestizaje* national identity and its attendant anxieties about social crossings of race and class and miscegenation (see Kutzinski 1993, chaps. 1, 3; Landaluze 1881, 33–40; Cabrera [1954] 1983, 37; Thomas 1971, 1118). The multifaceted Lucumí Ochún, in the most general terms, is associated with sweetness, love, fortune, healing, and kinship, as well as witchcraft. In some "paths" she can manifest herself as a highly sexualized denizen of the demimonde, the street, the boudoir, and the brothel.[18] An enduring set of representations within the modern Lucumí iconography of Ochún is a bed, lavishly decorated with yellow or gold satin and lace. The late Afro-Cuban throne artist Juan Boza drew upon this tradition as recently as 1986, in the form of a trompe l'oeil gold-lace-and-satin bed-throne for Ochún and Obba, whose tureens and *plaza* sit in the same position as those observed by Irene Wright around 1910: on the floor at the footboard (Boza 1986; plate 6).[19]

Wright's El Cerro "African *cabildo*" of 1910 was apparently not only very well known among practitioners; it was also, as noted, a frequent stop on the turn-of-the-twentieth-century travel, ethnography, criminology, and journalism circuit in Havana; descriptions of its contents and events were written, and photographs of its altars were published in at least one well-known book, which was reprinted a number of times (Roche y Monteagudo 1908, [1908] 1925a). The "altars" of Wright's account turn out, it seems, to be the very same examples Rafael Roche y Monteagudo described and photographed just before 1908 in El Cerro's Sociedad Santa Rita y San Lázaro, which Israel Castellanos identified as the "witchcraft" organization par excellence of Papá Silvestre Erice (see Roche y Monteagudo 1908, 83; [1908] 1925a, 182–86; Castellanos 1916, 38, 54, 56, 78).[20] It was thus no coincidence that Wright found herself with Papá Silvestre Erice, for her "guide," a "Havana . . . orchestra . . . leader," "a mulatto [and an] officer in the organization" was very likely Fernando Guerra, a *mulato*, a priest of and heir to Papá Silvestre's *cabildo*. Guerra was the leader of a newfangled *batá de pandereta* drum orchestra, an insistent correspondent of Fernando Ortiz, an eccentric early republican *hombre de movimiento*, and a liason between a number of institutions and notable individuals in Havana (Ortiz 1952–55, 4:381–85; Palmie 2002, 249–52, 254, 256–59). In short, the visibility and accessibility of this *cabildo* across social domains suggest that its hybrid iconography was not anomalous at the time; it may very well have been representative—a showcase—of a significant trend in modern Lucumí arts, the audience for which was multiple.

Figure 5.11.—Lucumí *chekeré* gourd shakers and *capilla*, or throne, for La Virgen de La Caridad del Cobre and Ochún at the Sociedad Santa Rita y San Lázaro of Silvestre Erice, El Cerro. (From Roche y Monteagudo 1908, 79.)

In Roche y Monteagudo's extensive and more careful documentation, Wright's "cheap hangings" and "tawdry trinkets" materialize as elegant throne-altar installations set into the corners of complex shrine rooms. Even the hard-boiled, merciless warrior against Afro-Cuban *brujería* Rafael Roche y Monteagudo was touched by the altars' aesthetic virtuosity. "A kind of dossal or curtain [*dosel* or *colgadura*] of [white] fine-point embroidery covered the altar," Roche writes. "The dossal [was] surmounted by a canopy-like hanging [*pabellón*] or valance [*bambalinas*] of red silk damask, a unique ornamentatíon that showed some artfulness" (fig. 5.10; see Roche y Monteagudo 1908, 83; [1908] 1925a, 182). *Pabellón* can refer to the canopy of a bed, altar, or throne, as well as to a processional banner (*bandera;* see Ortiz 1921, 16); and *bambalinas* can refer to the hanging valance of a theatrical proscenium or window frame (García-Pelayo y Gross 1983, 504,

91). The *cabildo*'s altar table elevates a carved wood statue of Santa Bárbara, dressed in red and white cloth, another of San Cristóbal, a set of animal horns (*cuernos*), a *sopera* adorned with plantains and okra, and a set of "helpers" (though Changó is not known to use a *sopera*). Two decorative metal candelabra with tall white candles frame the central figure of Santa Bárbara, San Cristóbal, and the white *sopera.*

In short, the altar presents, around the fulcrum of Santa Bárbara, a classic Lucumí configuration of Changó, his elder brother Agayú (San Cristóbal), the horns (*cuernos*) of the *oricha* Oggué, Changó's everpresent companion, two of Changó's favorite food offerings, and, it appears, his divine children—the Ibeyi twins in the form of San Cosmian and San Damian. Another altar, adjacent to a wall hung with the Lucumí gourd shakers (*chekeré*) Irene Wright must have seen played at the *cabildo*'s drumming event, distinguishes itself with parted satin curtains trimmed in lace, a short pleated valance, and a horizontally striped altar skirt (*frontal*). A *sopera* for the Virgin of Charity (Ochún) is surrounded with a fringed Canary Island shawl (*chal canario*) and calabashes of honey (fig. 5.11). Certain "roads" of Ochún receive just such a shawl, and it is a regular gift rendered to this *oricha.* One of the standing iron "black jockey" sculptures does, in fact, resemble carved and cast figurative trade signs collected as American folk art in the 1920s and 1930s (see, e.g., Hartigan 1991, 16). The *cabildo*'s altar assemblages, albeit jarring to outside observers, ingeniously combined furnishings that would otherwise work within any Cuban middle-class interior—damask, satin, fine-point embroidery, candelabra, carved saint statues—with Lucumí-specific iconography and sacrificial ingredients.

Figure 5.12.—Víctor Patricio de Landaluze, *El Místico del Ángel,* n.d. (From Corporación Nacional del Turismo 1950, cover.)

Symmetrically parted curtains, a fringed canopy or valance, and/or a cloth-covered and elevated table supporting icons and vessels are, and have been, common elements of church and domestic popular Catholic altar organization. In Cuba, Víctor Patricio de Landaluze documented, for example, a nineteenth-century Afro-Cuban coachman (*calesero*) praying before a fine-lace-covered altar table with a satin *frontal* in a church side chapel (fig. 5.12). Fernando Ortiz provided two turn-of-the-twentieth-century illustrations of domestic altar tables, more and less elaborate, in the homes of suspected Afro-Cuban practitioners (*brujos;* fig. 5.13). These examples share the rectangular table, seminal Roman Catholic iconography (crucifixes or saints), and fine white cloth; however, the Afro-Cuban domestic examples in Ortiz's work display, as well, open vessels and Afro-Cuban iconography, such as the bow and arrow of Ochosi (fig.

Figure 5.13.—Domestic table altars documented by Fernando Ortiz in the early twentieth century. (From Ortiz [1906] 1973, 64, 63. Courtesy María Fernanda Ortiz Herrera, Representante Sucesores de Fernando Ortiz.)

5.13, *top*).[21] At the same time, it is clear that elevated *òrìṣà* vessels, framed by a proscenium and valance-like "hangings," have characterized Yoruba shrines for centuries (fig. 5.37; see Brown 1993b, 58; Pemberton 1975, 20-22).

In the Roman Catholic context, a pure white linen cloth, covering the top of the altar table and extending down the sides, symbolizes the shroud of Jesus. Since the fourteenth century, the Host has been prominently displayed atop the altar for adoration and meditation in the form of a gold monstrance (Apostolos-Cappadona 1994, 22, 244; see figs. 5.12, 4.9). In the Afro-Cuban context, similar cloth may also have stood for spiritual purity and framed a religious intentionality thoroughly concerned with the workings of the High God (Lucumí *Olodumaré*, Congo *Nzambi*, or Abakuá *Abasí*), and it may have referred as well, depending upon the particular interests of the practitioners, to the God and saints of the church.

Beyond the elements of the table, cloth, statues, and *frontal*, such dramatic framing devices as valances and parted curtains are found, as well, in churches, on domestic altars, and in the formal compositions of two-dimensional representations of Christ, the Virgin, and the saints, as well as secular nobility. These are encountered throughout the Catholic world and include highly elaborate baroque representations of religious themes found in Spain's New World colonies, such as Cuzco, Peru (Apostolos-Cappadona 1994, 49, 331; Fane 1996, 115, 122, 127, 219, 220, 225; Feduchi 1969, 285; Damian 1995, figs. 20, 22, 24, 25, 27, 30, 34, 35; figs. 5.14, 5.15). The valance of the Virgin's *baldachino* (canopy) and parted curtains are directly comparable in design intention to those of Papá Erice's hybrid thrones, as well as innumerable contemporary examples (compare figs. 5.14 and 5.15 with 4.1, 5.9, 5.10, 5.11, 5.36, and plates 5–10).

In Roman Catholic church interior furnishings historically, a fine silk brocade canopy—(*baldachino* or baldachin)[22]—"was positioned over altars, chancels, tombs, and statues, thereby implying the spiritual significance or power of whatever or whoever was beneath it. In the Roman Catholic tradition, the *baldachino* was the canopy under which the Blessed Sacrament [or the image of Mary] was carried in liturgical procession" (Apostolos-Cappadona 1994, 48–49; see also Fane 1996, 225; Damian

Figure 5.14.—Anonymous, school of Cuzco, *Virgin of Cocharcas under the Baldachino*, 1767. Oil on canvas, 56¾ x 42¼ inches. Banco de Crédito del Peru, Lima.

Figure 5.15.—Anonymous, school of Cuzco, *Virgin of Bethlehem with a Needle and Thread*, eighteenth century. Oil on canvas, 40½ x 30 inches. Ronna Hope Katizin Collection, Fort Lauderdale, Fla. (Courtesy Carol Damian.)

Figure 5.16.—View of the throne room (*salón de trono*) of Carlos III of Spain, in the eighteenth-century style of Louis XV, Palacio de la Granja. Red silk brocade, gilt throne. (Feduchi [1965], 205, plate 87.)

1995, fig. 27; fig. 5.14). According to Renaissance art historian John Howett of Emory University, the representation of the child Jesus seated upon the lap of the crowned, cloth-draped, and enthroned Mary mirrors the hierarchical organization of the church altar itself, on which the Host is mounted and displayed (see also Apostolos-Cappadona 1994, 232–33).[23]

Among the Spanish Bourbons, the baldachin, and related dramatic devices of procenium-like framing and lavish cloth adornment, bridged several forms of royal domestic furnishing: thrones, altars, beds, grand portals, and window treatments. Spanish Bourbon royalty utilized the baldachin form, combined with representations of the royal crown, in their thrones in order to mark their high status as divine rulers (see Feduchi [1965], 205, plate 87).[24] For example, the throne of Carlos III (1716–88, crowned 1759) in Spain's Granja Palace featured a luxurious tapestried and fringed canopy; both the dossal and the rococo throne seat feature detailed royal crowns. With its baldachin and crown, the throne has already become a hybrid form: altar and royal seat (fig. 5.16).

The baldachin form, lavish cloth, and Roman Catholic iconography also figured into the domestic furnishings of Spanish royalty and nobility. These folks rested comfort-

Figure 5.17.—Royal bedroom with circular-canopied bed and crucifix ("bed altar").

Figure 5.18.—Altar and mirror in royal bedroom of Isabel II (1830–68) of Spain, in eighteenth-century style, which she revived with the Bourbon Restoration. (Feduchi [1965], 285, plate 189.)

ably in beds adorned with baldachins and crucifixes (fig. 5.17). Their bedrooms, such as that of Spain's Isabel II (1830–1904), also featured personal altars lavishly framed, and draped with the cloth of the Virgin Mary, as well as window treatments and mirrors that followed similar principles of presentation. Isabel II, with the restoration of the Bourbon monarchy, revived her preferred Louis XV style of the eighteenth century (fig. 5.18). The stylistic and semantic kinship of these eighteenth- and nineteenth-century royal furnishings—thrones, altars, and beds—becomes all the more legible in view of charming representations of the baby Jesus from the same period in his own canopied bed altar (see Feduchi [1965], 285, plate 189; 1969, 222–33, 302, 311). Ironically, the baby Jesus' bed is no longer a simple manger of straw, but a sumptuous *baldachino*. Here, divine beings and sacred objects are elevated, framed, and surrounded with sumptuous materials marking them with transcendent status; kings and nobility appropriate these metonyms to their grandiose programs of self-presentation.

Indeed, scholars have interpreted such interior furnishings as "theatrical" devices of baroque "spectacle"—the performative props of spiritual elevation, personal aggrandizement, and political maneuver through architecture, furnishings, framing, and adornment (Jarrard 1993). Whether seated under the baldachin, reclining in bed,[25] kneeling before an altar, gazing into a mirror, or looking out the window, the subject is visually and phenomenologically set apart and staged as a figure of special grace and status. Queen Isabel II could kneel before the Virgin Mary—framed within an altar; in the same space she could stand and gaze into a mirror framed and scaled to match the proportions of the altar itself; reflected thus, she would appear as the featured object of appreciation. Of course, as elevated and framed by the royal throne, she could take on spectacular semidivine proportions and be the recipient of the solicitous and awe-inspired gaze of her subjects; her status would be affirmed through performances of words, gestures, and gifts.

Similar forms appeared in the palaces of Cuba's Spanish nobility and, most prominently, within the palace of the captain general of the island. There, in the nineteenth century, a throne was constructed in anticipation of the Spanish crown's visit, which never, in fact, occurred (fig. 5.19). The throne's low-relief red circular baldachin frames a dossal featuring a painting of the queen mother and her seated child, with a crown upon a table just within reach; this provides the dramatic backdrop to the elevated throne seat. Baldachin and seat are surmounted by gold openwork crowns. Thus, the painting and throne are mutually reinforcing, as the former predicts the presence in Cuba of the king, seated on the latter. The child is probably Don Carlos, who became Charles III in 1759.[26]

In Cuba, as in Spain, domestic furnishings for windows and interior portals were stylistically continuous with throne adornment, utilizing expensive treatments of drapes, valances, and swags (fig. 5.20). Given other borrowings from Spanish and Cuban colonial material culture, for example, the sartorial display of *cabildo* royalty (see chap. 1), it is not surprising that Afro-Cuban Lucumí *tronos* "took on" and "remodeled" similar features (see Reisman 1970). The "throne with a canopy over it," the

Figure 5.19.—Throne for the Spanish crown in the Palace of the Captain General, Plaza de Armas, Havana. (Photograph by David Brown, 1994.)

"seats" of the *cabildo*'s royalty, and the "crown" upon the wall, described so casually by Fredrika Bremer in 1853, strongly resonate with the form and sensibility of the thrones of Carlos III in Spain and Cuba (see app. 1; figs. 5.16, 5.19). In turn, with their canopies, valances, dossals, and curtains, the thrones of the *orichas* could become elevating and framing devices for the presentation of "kings," "queens," and deified "warriors." They became special altars for a kind of sacred "spectacle" writ small: the elevation of the *orichas'* lavishly dressed *fundamentos* (plates 6, 7, 8, 9, 10, figs. 5.10, 5.11,). If these thrones served as dramatic portals to the other world and theatricalized sites of hierophany (visible manifestations of divinity), they also served the symbolic and practical needs of "making" kings, queens, and warriors. They would become beds for *iyawós* during the weeklong initiation period (plate 5, figs. 4.1, 4.2). If the throne's straw mat condenses traditional Yoruba codes of respect, designating a space of spiritual radiance, protection, and prohibition, it also mediates between the lowly and humble straw of the newborn's manger and the throne of kinship.

The popular Afro-Cuban throne-altar form of dazzling cloth, canopy, symmetrically parted curtains, valance, and dossal, with the added features of the straw mat, *soperas,* beadwork, food offerings (*plaza*), and, sometimes, saint icons and candelabra, had become a widely employed hybrid form of *oricha-santo* shrine presentation and iconography at least by the turn of the twentieth century, if not much earlier. If the ultimate "source" of the throne-altar form might be traced to the Palace of the Captain General and the houses of Havana's nobility, it is likely, as Bastide argued in his Afro-Brazilian study, that the black religious fraternities represented more direct, fertile ground for the alchemy of the "two Catholicisms," which generated new forms (see Bastide [1960] 1978, 109–25). For example, the saintly devotions instituted in Havana *cabildos* by Morell de Santa Cruz in the middle of the eighteenth century could not have escaped individualized elaboration along the lines of multiple currents of iconographic and decorative traditions. Though these altars remain undocumented, their arguable heirs in the transitional *cabildos* and *sociedades* of the turn of the twentieth century are instructive. In Papá Silvestre Erice's Santa Bárbara throne (fig. 5.10), the white parted curtains and red satin fringed *pabellón* not merely reproduce the framing devices of do-

Figure 5.20.—Valance-adorned portal in the Palace of the Captain General, Plaza de Armas, Havana. (Photograph by David Brown.)

mestic Catholic altars. The *pabellón* exemplifies a brilliant hybrid elaboration: along with the curtains, the display, of course, manifests the counterpointed colors of Changó and Santa Bárbara—red and white. More profoundly, the *pabellón* itself reproduces, in its outline, the Lucumí Changó's double thunderax. The axe-shaped red blazon of cloth, Changó's *bandera,* would become an enduring feature of his twentieth-century thrones, as seen in a New

Jersey drumming throne Ramón Esquivel built for Changó in April 1983 (see plate 7, *center;* see also Brown 1993b, 46–47; 1996, 105–15).

Lydia Cabrera astutely noted that such dramatic displays impressed themselves upon the popular Cuban religious imagination "so vividly, with their realistic images and all the theatricality of the sanctuary and its liturgy [,which] must have been so moving in [their] extraordinary emotionality" (Cabrera [1954] 1994). As elements of baroque-influenced display were creatively incorporated into Afro-Cuban and domestic popular Catholic altar presentation, the outcomes shared more than mere morphology with their putative local sources. As Cabrera suggests, certain dramatic forms of altar display were emotionally moving and, undoubtedly spiritually affecting. They were chosen and employed, albeit on a smaller scale, to adorn the *ochas* and *santitos* in peoples' humble homes precisely for that reason.

Figure 5.21.—Popular chromolithograph of Santa Bárbara, a crowned "royal saint," with belted and seamless chaste white robe with close collar. Attributes include a wafer and sacramental cup, a sword, and a burning castle.

Robes of the Saints: Models for the Ropas de Santo?

At the El Cerro drumming observed by Irene Wright, two dancing "performers" were possessed by their "saints" (Ochún and Changó), and were changed out of their street clothes into elaborate costumes. Having taken in the *cabildo*'s altar rooms, Wright "returned to the dancing in time to see one apt performer throw a fit. The 'saint' had entered into her. Immediately other women unbound her hair and removed her shoes. They hustled her into the other room and returned her clad in *a garment which seemed to imitate the robes [that] altar images of the Virgin and saints wear.* She wore gold and brass bracelets which jingled as she danced forth. She proceeded to salute all present by throwing her arms about the shoulders of men and women alike (Wright 1910, 149; emphasis added)."[27] Notwithstanding critical differences of detail between the clothes of the Lucumí *orichas* and those of the "Virgin and Catholic saints," a comparison of the two kinds of sacred garments is instructive. Immediately, Wright's usage in English—"robes" of the saints—evokes the Spanish term for the *orichas'* own satin garments, the *ropa de santo* (robes, or clothes, of saint), which, in turn, is a direct Spanish loan translation of the Yoruba-Lucumí *achó-oricha* (cloth or clothes of the *oricha*).[28] The "robes of the saints"—in the icons of the Virgin, in particular—are multilayered ensembles, consisting of a floor-length seamless

Figure 5.22.—Popular chromolithograph of San Cristóbal (Saint Christopher), "the Ferryman," with seamless belted robe.

white robe, sometimes with raised floral embroidery or brocade, and often accompanied by a vertical rectangular brocaded apron. The sobriety of the robe comes with its comprehensive coverage, particularly its close collar. Such robes are often belted, as in the case of Santa Bárbara and San Cristóbal, and are signs of virginity, chastity, or service (see figs. 5.21, 5.22).[29] Some of the Virgin's robes represented in the chromolithographs and statues that have been popular among Cubans are, in fact, more elaborate floor-length gowns of lace, brocade, or embroidered fabric, though none of the most common Cuban examples competes with the lavish, colorful, brocaded robes and gowns of the saints and Virgins of the eighteenth-century Peruvian Cuzco school (see Damian 1995; figs. 5.14, 5.15).

In Cuban Catholic representations, the most highly embellished garment of the Virgin Mary and female saints is the luminous satin or silk mantle (*manto, pañuelo, paño*), the sparkling surface adornment of which is produced in brocade, embroidery, handpainting, or metal repoussé floral appliqués. Typically cast in the personage's dominant color—red for Saint Bárbara, blue and white for the Virgin of Regla, yellow for Our Lady of Charity of Cobre, white for the Virgin of Mercy—the mantle drapes the shoulders, often the head, and flows down about the entire body. Parted to show the white robe or gown underneath, the *manto* can recall the revelatory effect of altar curtains. A gold or silver openwork crown—pointed or arched—along with a circular halo, sit atop the *manto,* or sometimes atop a lace *mantilla* draped over the icon's head (see plate 8, figs. 5.5, 5.6).[30] The *manto* contributes to the saint's visual spectacle during public processions. As documented by Tarafa perhaps in the 1940s, the capacious *manto* of the Virgin of Regla, trimmed with a silver sawtooth border, spreads outward to embrace the participants of the annual 7 September street procession (fig. 5.23).[31] During the year, the Virgin of Regla's sea-blue *manto,* adorned with a silver fringe and silver relief appliqués of flowers, leaves, and urns, is displayed in an *armario vitrina* or *canastillero* (glass armoire) in the chapel behind the main altar of her church (see Brown 1993b; and fig. 5.24).[32]

In contrast to the clothes of Virgins and saints, the *ropas de santo* for female *orichas,* as described at length in the previous chapter, consist of puff-shouldered, belted, full-length gowns with open, round, square, or V-cut necklines (plates 15, 16). The *orichas* do not wear halos, although their luminous clothes, like the saint's robes and *mantos,* are meant to radiate spiritual energy. Still, the *orichas' ropas de santo* are far from sober and "chaste" garments that express "virginity"—not least because the *orichas* engage in sexual activity throughout the Lucumí legends, called *patakí.*[33] In addition, the *orichas* are known for their exuberant physicality and sensuality in dance. As Oddedeí noted laconically, the Catholic *santos* simply "don't dance"

Figure 5.23.—Annual 7 September "double" feast day of the Virgin of Regla and Yemayá, c. 1950. The Virgin wears a lavish *manto* appropriate to the public festival. (From Cabrera [1954] 1983. Courtesy the Estate of Lydia Cabrera.)

(Cabrera [1947] 1994, 276). In contrast, not only do the female *orichas* dance, but their full, pleated skirts are specifically constructed as active and meaningful elements of dance performance as well. Ochún raises and roils her skirts to act coquettishly, to suggest the river's fluid movement, and to transmit the powers of healing and witchcraft. Yemayá waves her skirt to produce forceful breezes that can heal as well as destroy. As she spins, the skirt whirls outward to evoke whirling currents that clear whatever is in their path—a movement cycle known as the *agolona* (open the road). Similarly, Oyá's moving skirts evoke the whirlwhind's fury and the forces of swift change (fig. 4.16).

In some respects—color, fabric choice, adornment, layering, brilliance—the female *orichas'* clothes do recall the robes of the saints. However, in other respects, they appear to have different historical prototypes: for example, the finery of the colonial era's *cabildo* queens, who wore more revealing square necklines, skirts of a more fecund fullness provided by petticoats, and puff shoulders. These features produce a sense of the wearer's living, sexualized, and procreative body through fullness and revelation of skin, whereas the Virgins and saints project a slim, sometimes diaphanous body profile, which deemphasizes the wearer's worldliness. Still, the clearest similarity between all three historical garment types is encountered in surface adornment and fabric. The *orichas' ropas de santo* share with

Figure 5.24.—Mantle (*manto*, or *paño*) of the Virgin of Regla, Regla, 1989. Satin with silver (metal) repoussé floral appliqué. (Photograph by David H. Brown.)

the robes of the saints, not to mention the clothing of the *cabildo* queens, the unmistakable mark of richness. Bridging the "road" of the saints and the "road" of the *orichas* is a sartorial lingua franca of highly worked prestige materials and adornments, particularly expensive cloth with raised organic motifs (i.e., in brocade, damask, embroidery, or appliqué). Moreover, they share a saturated baroque color palette incorporated within a methodical system of color coding. Finally, they share a highly readable iconographic system, which includes handheld and other attributes, such as the sword, goblet, and crenelated tower of Santa Bárbara/Changó, the anchor, key, and ship of the Virgin of Regla/Yemayá, and bright metal crowns. These metonymic attributes evoke the saints' hagiography and the *orichas patakí* legends (see figs. 4.10, 4.20, plate 17; figs. 5.3, 5.4).

Hence, Irene Wright could observe that the "same symbolism in color and ornament" that *cabildo* practitioners "flaunted" in their dances in honor of their "favorite saints . . . each of whom has an African name," was also "recognize[d]" by the "local Catholic church" (1910, 150). Such color-coded cloth dedicated to saint and *oricha*, particularly as used intentionally in the day-to-day dress of female priestesses, Roche y Monteagudo noted, served as "ex-votos or promises, dedicating the colors as offerings for favors received: to recuperate health, for the obtaining of some object, or the realization of desires or aspirations" (1908, 68; [1908] 1925a, 169). These "colors" typically took, and take, the form of the checked gingham *tela de cuadritos* of the initiation's lunch suit (fig. 4.27). As museologist Concepción Morales found in her research among elder Regla priestesses, the *traje de almuerzo*, in effect, becomes an *ebó*, a healing sacrifice: it "can be used as daily attire, although many *iyawós* prefer to put them away, and wear them on days on which they feel depressed, sick, or sad."[34] For example, one regularly observes women and men in Havana's Church of Saint Lazarus wearing the burlap clothes of this old mendicant biblical parable and his Lucumí parallel, Babalú Ayé.[35] Spending many hours sitting in the Church of the Virgin of Regla, I observed women placing ex-votos at the Virgin's feet, including folded bolts of blue satin cloth. On the occasion of church processions, women and men wear the colors common to the saint/*oricha* of honor, and on 7 September the women carry female dolls (*muñecas*, formerly called *anaquillé*) wearing the same signature colors of the Virgin of Regla/Yemayá (plate 21).[36] These same color patterns are worn for Lucumí drummings: priests wear checked gingham or solid cotton and the *orichas* wear satin. Where the capacious mantles of the Virgin and female saints evoke the potential for spiritual succor, the cloth of the *orichas*, in the form of *paños* and parts of the *ropa de santo* ensemble, are put into action during drummings to bless and "cleanse" participants (fig. 5.25).[37]

Ocha priestesses continue to draw on a time-honored repertoire of luxurious styles of adorment for their *ropas de santo*, including the *mantos* and crowns of the saints and Virgins. For example, Lourdes López, a Cuban-born singer and Yemayá priestess living in Noth Bergen, New Jersey, designs puff-shoulder, belted satin and brocade gowns for the female *orichas*, which feature a square, open neckline and, often, double, pleated skirts (plates 15, 16). The square neckline is a "tradition" of her house, López says, which is insisted upon by her godmother, a respected elder Cuban-born *santera* who lives in the Bronx, *iyaloricha* Hilda Herrera. López follows, and improvises around, this traditional constraint of the square neckline by tapering or zigzagging its border and adding repeated parallel rows of decorative metallic braid. In contrast, she feels "freer" to experiment with the form of the skirts, which have no codified rules.

López's *ropas de santo* for Yemayá and Ochún, produced in the early 1980s reiterate aspects of the mid-twentieth-century photographic documents by Tarafa and Dubrony, as well as the festive dress of colonial-era *cabildo* queens and free blacks (plates 1, 15, 16, figs. 1.9, 5.2). The square neckline and full, multiple skirts recall both precedents; and the options of smooth satin or allover brocade,

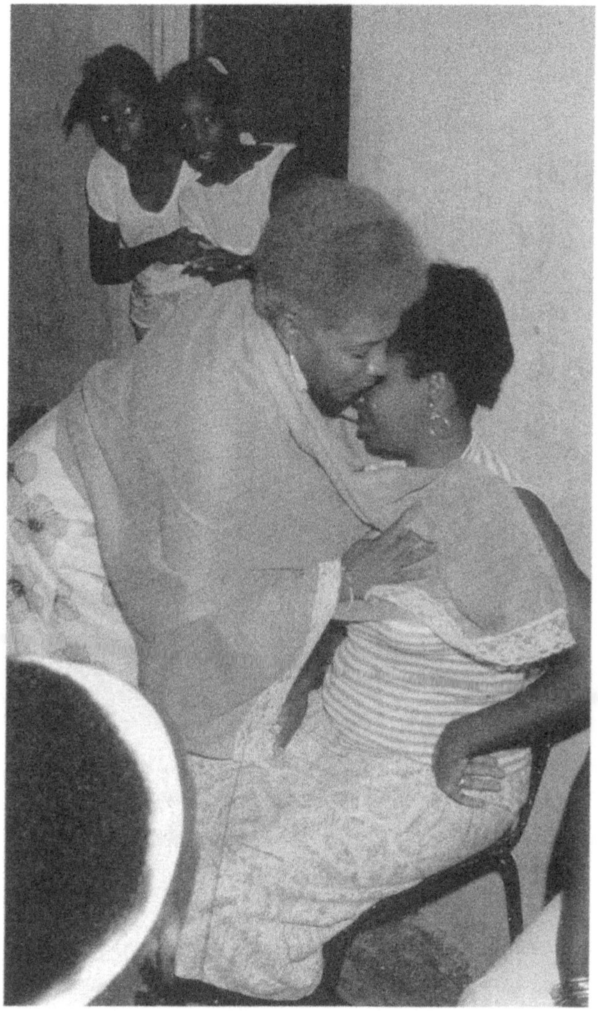

Figure 5.25.—Ochún blessing and "cleaning" a participant with her *paño* at a "Violin" ceremony for Ochún, at the Cabildo of Saint Teresa, Matanzas, 29 July 1989. (Photograph by David H. Brown.)

as seen in her gowns for Yemayá and Ochún, respectively, recall the contrast between the *ropas de santo* of the two *iyawós* photographed by Tarafa and Dubrony (fig. 5.2). At the same time, López has used the *mantos* and crowns of her saints *como modelo* (as a model) for aspects of the *orichas' ropas de santo.* Atop López's large *oricha* cabinet (*canastillero*) stands a large cast of Catholic *santitos* associated with the principal Lucumí *orichas.* Of plaster, they are brightly painted and elaborately dressed and reach up to one and a half feet in height. López pointed out to me the statue of the Virgin of Mercy (La Virgen de las Mercedes) and compared its gilt white crown to the one she had recently made for Obatalá, the significant differences being Obatalá's particular iconography (fig. 4.8). Therefore, though ethnographers imagine remote Roman Catholic or European precedents in her designs that are not explicit in her own explanations, with her saints atop the *canastillero,* López does not have to go far to find a model.

Still, the stylistic repertoires of *ropa de santo* designers move beyond saints, *cabildo* finery, and the particular traditions of their houses. Contemporary designs are potentially expansive and are limited only by the imaginations and resources of the makers. For example, priestess Nydia Pichardo noted to me that an appropriate model for imitation and revision could be a particularly beautiful wedding dress she observed in the window of a Miami bridal store. Given such commercial sources, Pichardo noted, "many of the women *iyawós* of Obatalá look like brides, especially when their gowns begin to use tubular sleeves that fall below the elbow" (see fig. 4.11). Indeed, she continued, "if you really want to research the sources of the *ropa de santo,* go to the local fabric store and look through the pattern books for women's dresses."[38] By the twentieth century, and probably much earlier, diverse models of formal apparel styles, as well as interior decor, were available to Cuban women in family and women's magazines, as well as pattern books circulated throughout Latin America.[39] For example, the Mexican magazine *La Familia,* sold in Cuba during the first half of the twentieth century, offered examples of puff-shouldered, belted, and pleated women's dresses, decorative adornment, and fancy domestic furnishings, such as cotton, silk, satin, and lace bedclothes and window treatments that were elaborately trimmed, embroidered, and appliquéd with floral patterns (fig. 5.26).

Figure 5.26.—Women's dress and adornment styles, as shown in the magazine *La Familia*, 1943. Note the puff sleeves, tubular arms, pleated skirts, and hand-embroidered floral designs.

Figure 5.27.—*Negrito*, probably Paquito Rodríguez, 1920s–1930s. Note the blackface and exaggerated *guarachero*-style ruffled sleeves. Centro Urdilio Urfé/Museo de La Música. (From Moore 1997, 148.)

It remains to be discovered whether the highly stylized presentation of *orichas* on the Día del Medio was not also historically influenced by a range of popular media, such as the Cuban vernacular theater tradition (*teatro vernáculo*, or *teatro bufo*) or twentieth-century movies and *novelas*. The vernacular theater employed, as did nineteenth-century *costumbrista* art, casts of distinctive "types," whose characteristics were immediately discernible through highly legible attributes in physiology, costume, facial expression, iconography, music, and dance (see Moore 1997; Cosentino 1995a, 39–42; Wilmeth and Wilmeth 1977; figs. 5.27, 5.28, 4.5, 4.13, 4.24, plate 1).[40] Framed by compact theatrical proscenium arches and curtains, *oricha* kings, queens, and warriors appear as a hyperstylized dramatis personae of courtly ladies with flowing gowns and large earrings and natty gentlemen with *pantalones de bombachas*, courtly jackets, riding boots, and distinguished mustaches and beards. Each presents a distinctive set of colors and handheld attributes (plates 12, 13, 14, 15, figs. 4.7, 4.8, 4.11, 4.12, 4.15, 4.16, 4.17, 4.18, 4.19, 4.20, 4.22). One notable example of direct imitation of the vernacular theater and stage rumba tradition is exemplified by the work of Rigoberto Rodríguez Duque, a fa-

Figure 5.28.—Cover for sheet music of "¡Ay! Mama Inés," by Eliseo Grenet, late 1920s. Note the vernacular theater costuming in the eighteenth-century style for the male actors to the center-left and far left: loose sleeves with tubular cuffs, a braided panel *(far left)* across the jacket's front that is fastened on the side, and knickerbockers (*bombachas*). Museo Nacional de la Música. (From Moore 1997, 151.)

mous twentieth-century Havana *santero.* He clearly drew on a popular figure from Cuba's blackface vernacular comic theater, nightclub, and carnival circuit traditions (1812–1930s) in his conceptualization of Changó: his sculpture of the thunder god atop a decorative wood vessel appears as the stereotyped *negrito,* with white eyes, red lips, jet-black skin, and the puffy-sleeved red and white *guarachero* costume of the *teatro bufo* and early cabaret rumba traditions (cf. plate 17 and fig. 5.27; and see Moore 1997, 45–61, 148, 153). Another suggestive example, which resonates with the highly stylized male *ropa de santo,* is found in the eighteenth-century costume style of a male character in a 1920s vernacular theater production, immortalized on the cover for the sheet music of "¡Ay! Mamá Inés," by Eliseo Grenet (Moore 1997, 151). The character's jacket features loose sleeves with tubular cuffs, a braided panel across the jacket's front, which appears to be fastened on the side, and knickerbockers (*bombachas;* fig. 5.28, *far left;* see also *center left*). Finally, though large circular earrings, which appear as painted representations on the heads of female *orichas,* formed part of the ensemble of historical black "types" (*negras curras,* portrayed in fig. 1.2, and *cabildo* queens; see chap. 1), this highly visible attribute of black female display was standardized in stereotyped blackface female characters of the vernacular theater, for example, the *negra conga* (Moore 1997, 120).

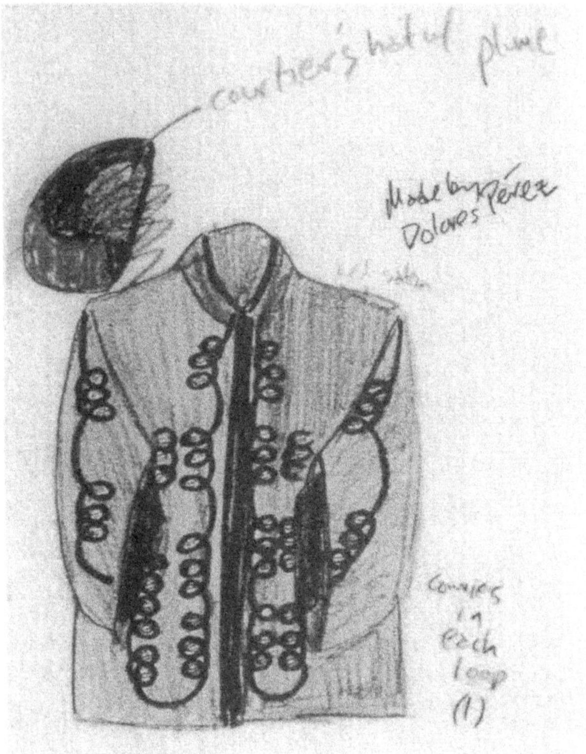

Figure 5.29.—Chinese-style *ropa de santo* of Eleguá, with floppy brimmed and plumed musketeer's hat, designed by Dolores Pérez for Melba Carillo, New York, 1988. (Drawing by David H. Brown.)

In the contemporary setting, a range of stylized colonial costumes is regularly seen in the ongoing Cuban *telenovelas*, broadcast on the island at 4:30 P.M. and 9:30 P.M. One recent story, called "The Captivity of the King," depicted all forms of slave, street, military, and noble attire. Some contemporary designers have looked to more exotic, foreign, sources. The well-known California *ropa de santo* maker Dolóres Pérez, considered it appropriate to design a red and black jacket for Eleguá based on a Chinese style, which was used for a 1985 New Jersey initiation. However, instead of relying on Chinese domical headgear consistent with the suit's historical style, she created an Afro-Cuban–Chinese–European hybrid ensemble, featuring a floppy, plumed courtier and musketeer's *sombrero* covered in red and black satin (fig. 5.29; see also Flores-Peña and Evanchuck 1994, 23–24).

THE MANY ROLES OF CLOTH: *PAÑOS*, "THRONESCAPES," AND THE APOTHEOSIS OF THE HYBRIDIZED ALTAR ASSEMBLAGE

While lavish *ropas de santo* dress the *orichas'* living altars (their *iyawós* and priests) on formal occasions of presentation and possession, the equally lavish *paños* of expensive fabrics "dress" the *orichas'* altar installations. *Paños* cover the *orichas' soperas* and adorn the canopies, backdrops, and parted curtains of thrones. Typically forty-five-inch squares of fancy fabric, such as silk, satin, velvet, lamé, sequin, chiffon, and lace—often combinations of these—are sewn atop other layers to produce a double or triple thickness of cloth. The squares are then trimmed with shimmering metallic borders of braid or sequins, and often additionally adorned with appliqué emblems (e.g., *batá* drums or a rooster for Changó, peacocks for Ochún, and anchors and ships' wheels for Yemayá) and patterns of cowrie shells consistent with the *orichas'* iconographic requirements (see Brown 1996). Fabric colors, patterns, combinations of cloth, appliqués, and trimming materials are appropriately coded to each of the *orichas'* sacred colors; additional adornments, such as cowries, are organized according to the signature numbers of the *orichas* (three for Eleguá; eight for Obatalá; nine for Oyá; five for Ochún; seven for Yemayá; six for Changó; see plate 12, figs. 4.7, 4.8). In the many Cuban and Cuban-American houses I have visited,[41] the preferred *paños* are brocaded or faux-brocade fabrics with floral motifs in silver and gold metallic thread (or metallic "print"). *Paños* should be *brilloso* (lustrous, shining), so they reflect light and, thus, radiate the *orichas' gracia* or *aché*, indexing their "wealth" and status (plates 5, 6, 7). Still, some houses prefer a more subdued aesthetic, for example, utilizing *paños* in fine silk but free of flashy metallic trimmings. Impoverished Cuban houses rely on whatever cloth they find available on the island or can obtain from abroad (plate 10). African-American and African-inspired Cuban houses may combine silks and satins with Yoruba cloth or eschew non-African cloth altogether (fig. 5.48).

Beneath spreading throne canopies and parted curtains, the *orichas* pose elegantly, like an assembled opera cast at curtain call or, more aptly, like royalty sitting in state. For drummings (*tambores*) and the anniversaries of priests' initiations (Spanish *cumpleaños*, i.e., "birthday"), the *orichas* to occupy the throne may be elevated on a table, pedestal, or milk crate or placed on the floor.[42] With several exceptions, their *soperas* are draped with their own *paños*, atop which are placed their *collares de mazo*, metal crown (in the case of Ochún, Oyá, and sometimes Yemayá), beaded dance wands, and other attributes. The aesthetic density of decorative embellishment in the *paños'* brocaded cloth, and the additive accretion of beaded and metal attributes, throws each *oricha* into striking relief against the luminous satin surface of the throne's canopy and background (plates 7, 8, 9).

An apparent proximate Cuban source for the *orichas' paños* is encountered in the *mantos* (alternatively *paños*) worn by local Virgins and saints. However, the draping of sacred statues and vessels with cloth in West Africa is also amply documented (see Verger 1954, plate 119; Thompson 1993, 163, 267, 274, 275; fig. 5.30, *A, C, D*). Therefore, the iconographic "sources" and functions of the Lucumí *paño* tradition may be overdetermined rather than owed to a single antecendent. As indicated, the saints' *mantos* are objects of prestige for dramatic display; they also evoke the ability of saints and Virgins to embrace, protect, and bless the fold. The *orichas' paños* can play similar visual and physical roles; however, the meaning and function of *paños* and throne are extensive and complex. Though in one phase of their "biographies," as it were, they are objects of prestigious display, *paños* are also often pulled from their thrones during drummings and birthdays by possessed priests—they are activated—in order to bless and "clean" members of the congregation (fig. 5.25). Cloth's associations of loving embrace, spiritual protection, and cleansing are reiterated in Lucumí *ebós*, in which they are integral to human-divine cycles of gift exchange (see Brown 1996, 117–21). Perhaps the most apt example comes in the form of the cloth throne enclosure itself. The Afro-Cuban throne form, particularly the *asiento* throne (plate 5), is a "container" of cloth (Gleason 1992, 85–89). The throne insulates and separates newly born *iyawós* from the unwanted influences of spirits of the dead (*eguns* or *muertos*) and the many *aleyos* (uninitiated) who come to visit. When *iyawós* temporarily leave the throne's precinct for their daily ritual bath or to go to the bathroom, a mobile canopy of cloth provides continued spiritual protection: the *iyawó's* white sheet or white towel (see fig. 4.29), which is suspended over the newly consecrated head.[43] Only when the *iyawó* reenters the throne's cloth-enclosed precinct may the sheet or towel be removed. The one white sheet, used as a towel after the *iyawó's* daily bath and as nightly bedding, along with one white towel, used as a bib during meals and a pillow at night, serve the entire week without being washed. They are absorbent media to protect and clean the *iyawó's* body literally and figuratively. That is, they are *ebós* that work during the week to absorb any and all negative spiritual influences. When the *iyawó* completes the initiation week—which some refer to as (spiritually) "protective custody"—the throne, which has served as a prophylactic *ebó* in and of itself, is taken down.[44] The historically enduring gesture of cloth suspended over priestly bodies, which effects protection and healing, is encountered also in powerful *ebós* conducted during drummings and other ceremonies. There, *orichas* possessing their priests may direct the participants to assemble under a suspended sheet and process through the performance space (see Brown 1989, 475–76). Fredrika Bremer documented an early example of this ritual pattern (1853, 2:380–81), which is found throughout the African Diaspora (see, e.g., Carybé 1980, 88, 239, 241).

Figure 5.30.—*Top left, sopera* of Ochún covered with *paño,* topped with brass crown and *mazos; bottom left, iyawó* of Ochún as presented to the drums with crown, *paño* on head, *mazos,* double skirts, and peacock avatar; *top right,* statue of La Caridad del Cobre with crown, halo, *paño,* and double skirts; *bottom right,* cloth-covered wood shrine figures of Yẹmọja, Ìbàdàn, Nigeria. (Drawn from a photograph by Pierre Verger, 1954. Drawings by David H. Brown.)

Plate 1.—Víctor Patricio de Landaluze, *El Día de Reyes*, c. 1878.
Oil on canvas, approximately 12 x 21 inches.
(Courtesy Museo Nacional de Bellas Artes, Havana.)

Plate 2.—Ño Remigio Herrera's photograph on the ancestor altar (*bóveda*) of the Society of Saint Barbara, Palmira, Cienfuegos (*left center*). Note also Tata Gaitán (*upper left*), Secundino Crucet (*lower left*), Bernardo Rojas (*upper right*), Ramón Hugues (*center right*), Mario Fernández (*lower center*), and Ma Lugarda Fernández, founder (*upper center*).
(Photograph by David H. Brown.)

Plate 3.—Throne celebrating the feast day of San Manuel/Odúa and the Obatalá Yekú-Yekú of Ramón Esquivel, Union City, New Jersey, 1 January 1987. The quilted satin *paño* for Obatalá features a realistic figure in relief of the crowned Virgin Mercedes. Built into and behind this table-throne is the leftover 17 December festival throne for the house's celebration of San Lázaro/Babalú Ayé. (Photograph by David H. Brown.)

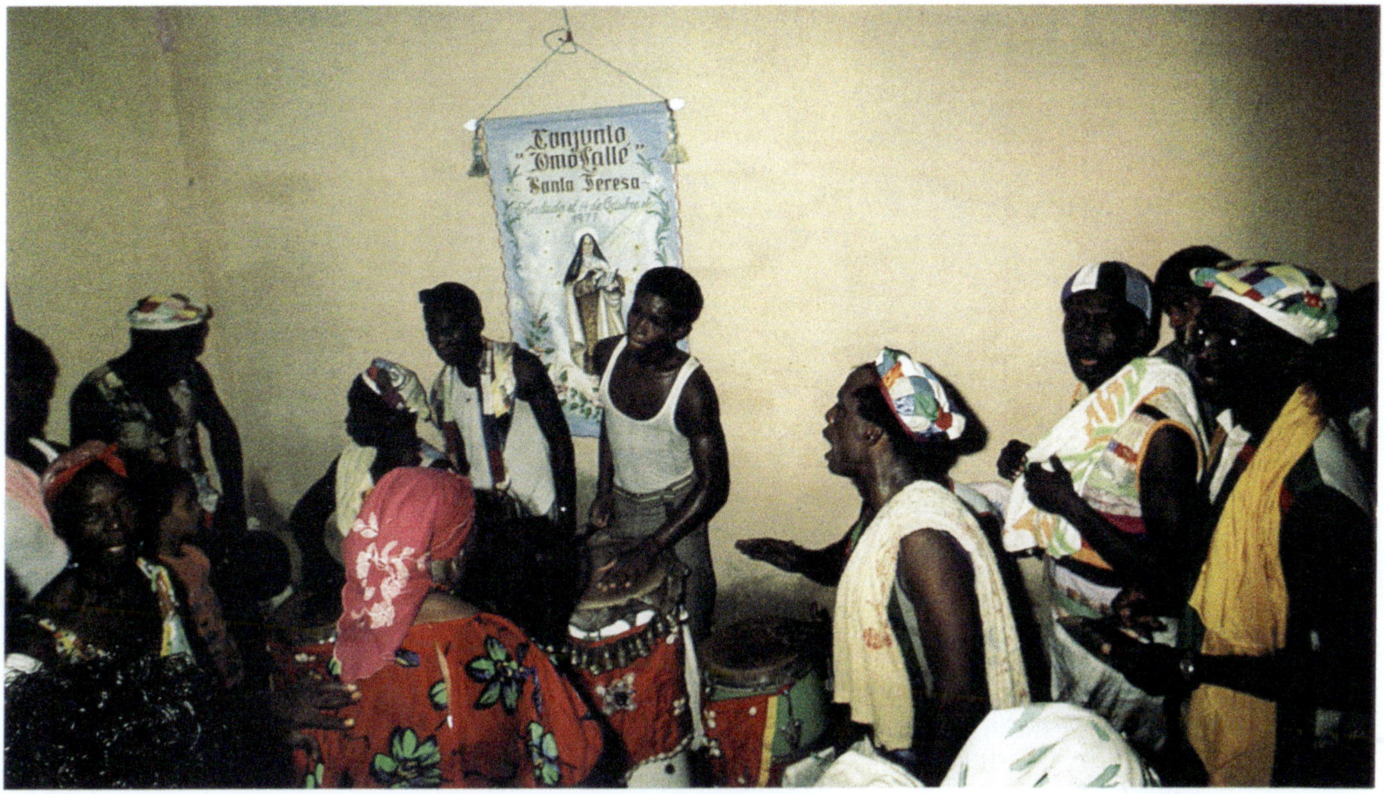

Plate 4.—*Bembé* given to the Oyá of Tomassa Villamil by Conjunto Omó Lallé at the Cabildo de Santa Teresa, Matanzas, August 1989. The *cabildo*'s matriarch, the late Tomasa, in her mideighties, "mounted" by Oyá, dances in the center, in the red flower-print dress and headtie; the *cabildo*'s director, Osvaldo Cárdenas Villamil, is at right center, with a cloth over his shoulder. (Photograph by David H. Brown, 1989.)

Plate 5.—*Trono del asiento* (initiation throne) for Obatalá, designed by Antonio Queiro for the exhibition *Orisa/Orixá/Orisha: Africa/Brazil/New York*, spring 1984. (Courtesy Caribbean Cultural Center. Photograph by David H. Brown.)

Plate 6.—Throne for Ochún and Obba styled as a satin- and lace-canopied bed with prominent representation of the Holy Sacrament, by the late Juan Boza, 1986. (Courtesy Caribbean Cultural Center. Photograph by David H. Brown.)

Plate 7.—Drumming throne for the Changó of the late Adolfo Fernández (Obbadelé), with red and gold *paño* shaped as thunderax, designed by the late Ramón Esquivel. The sacred *batá* drums, constructed by the temple's *babalawos*, rest before the throne during the intermission between the drumming's first and second segments. Templo Bonifacio Valdez, New Jersey, 3 April 1983. (Photograph by David H. Brown.)

Plate 8.—Throne for Yemayá (with Ochún and Obatalá), framed by a dossal painting of the Virgin of Regla, a fringed shawl, and *pañuelos*, in the house of Enrique Hernández, Armenteros, Guanabacoa, 1989. The gown of the doll representing Yemayá and the Virgin of Regla acts as a *paño* to cover the *oricha's sopera*. (Photograph by David H. Brown.)

Plate 9.—"Birthday" throne for the Changó of Adolfo Fernández (Obbadelé) with beaded attributes for Changó (bat and thunderax) and beaded and cowrie-encrusted crown for Dadá. The throne was designed by Ramón Esquivel, 16 August 1985. White *paños* for Obatalá and Ochanlá form the "Hill of Oke" (*rear*), beneath the spoked, monstrance-like lamp. The "Warriors" (Ochosi, Ogún, and Eleguá) sit in the foreground. (Photograph by David H. Brown.)

Plate 10.—Isabel Castellín Domínguez, "Chola" (Ocha Ilé), priestess of Obatalá, with her "birthday throne," also mounted for a drumming for Ochún and Babalú Ayé, Barrio Obrero, Havana, January 1994. Obatalá is highest and is represented by a *paño* hand painted with the Holy Sacrament. The backdrop curtain and a hand-painted icon of La Caridad del Cobre (out of view) represent Ochún. The burlap curtain on the right represents Babalú Ayé (also known as Asojuano and San Lázaro). Babalú Ayé's clay vessel is covered in a mass of the plant Cundiamor. (Photograph by David H. Brown.)

Plate 11.—Eleguá throne for drumming, made of pine boughs, adorned with little bottles of liquor, toys, and cigars, designed by Ramón Esquivel, New Jersey, 1984. (Photograph by David H. Brown.)

Plate 12.—*Ropa de santo* of Eleguá, by Lourdes López, 1984. (Courtesy Caribbean Cultural Center and Lourdes López. Photograph by David H. Brown.)

Plate 13.—*Ropa de santo* of Ogún, by Lourdes López, 1987. (Courtesy Caribbean Cultural Center and Lourdes López. Photograph by David H. Brown.)

Plate 14.—*Ropa de santo* of Ochosi, by Lourdes López, 1987. (Courtesy Caribbean Cultural Center and Lourdes López. Photograph by David H. Brown.)

Plate 15.—*Ropa de santo* of Yemayá, by Lourdes López, 1984. (Courtesy Caribbean Cultural Center and Lourdes López. Photograph by David H. Brown.)

Plate 16.—*Ropa de santo* of Ochún, with *paño* (*background*), by Lourdes López, 1984.
(Courtesy Caribbean Cultural Center and Lourdes López.
Photograph by David H. Brown.)

Plate 17.—Shrine vessel, pedestal, cut-out wood thunderax, shakers, *mazos,* and figure for Changó. Rigoberto Rodríquez Duque collection, Madruga, Havana. (Photograph by David H. Brown, 1986.)

Plate 18.—Eleguá *de cabecera* (of the head) in beaded calabash atop a stone initiation seat, with *mazos, garabato* staff, and a painted and dressed store mannequin representing Eleguá, designed by the late Ramón Esquivel, New York, 1987. (Photograph by David H. Brown.)

Plate 19.—Lucumí mortar (*odó,* or *pilón*) for Changó, with polychromed relief carving and nailed wood thundercelt, nineteenth century. 15 inches high x 11 inches in diameter. Fernando Ortiz Collection, Casa de Africa, Havana. (Photograph by David H. Brown.)

Plate 20.—Plaster saints (La Caridad del Cobre, San Lázaro, La Virgen de Regla, and Santa Bárbara) over *soperas* of Yemayá, Obatalá, and Ochún, with plastic ducks, La Correa, Guanabacoa, Havana, 1986. (Photograph by David H. Brown.)

Plate 21.—Participant in 7 September 1999 procession of the Virgin of Regla. She wears Yemayá's colors and carries a doll, also in those colors, representing Yemayá or a spirit that followed Yemayá/the Virgin of Regla "in life." During the colonial era, such dolls were known as *anaquillé*. (Photograph by David H. Brown.)

Plate 22.—Hybrid Palo Monte throne for the 4 October 1987 celebration of Francisco Siete Rayos, designed by Ramón Esquivel, Union City, New Jersey. This spirit's plaster and painted representations rise above a Spiritist *bóveda* table set with water goblets for the dead beneath a Cuban Lucumí-style throne canopy. (Photograph by David H. Brown.)

Plate 23.—Porcelain tureen (*sopera*) with coat of arms of Los Marqueses de la Real Proclamación, owned by descendants of Gonzalo Recio y Oquendo, Regla, produced by the Limoges factory, France, late nineteenth century. Porcelain, 6½ inches high x 14½ inches long. The blue and white color pattern reproduces the colors of the Virgin of Regla, for whom the town was named. Museum of Regla. (Photograph by David H. Brown.)

Plate 24.—*Top*, lidded Santería tureen (*sopera*) containing Ochún's *fundamento*, produced in the factory of Alfred Meakin of Staffordshire, England, c. 1890–1930. High-fired earthenware ("Creamware"). The tureen was owned by the priestess Tomasa de la Caridad Córdoba Medina of Regla (d. 1988), salvaged from her house after she died in isolation, and accessioned into the collection of the Museum of Regla. *Bottom*, underside of the same Alfred Meakin tureen, showing pottery mark. (Photographs by David H. Brown.)

Plate 25.—María Sirgelina Martínez before what Cubans call a *canastillero* (*armario vitrina*), displaying china *soperas* and creamers, a covered bowl made of *losa* (*third shelf from top, far right*), and china plates. The vessels contain *orichas*. Regla, 1992. (Photograph by David H. Brown.)

Plate 26.—Gilt porcelain *sopera* for Ochún with jewel-encrusted triple-arch gold crown, brass fans, oars, bells, mortars and pestles, mirrors, bracelets, china plates, beaded *mazos,* and porcelain chinoiserie. The objects belonged to the late Rigoberto Rodríguez Duque. Private collection, Madruga, Havana. (Photograph by David H. Brown.)

Plate 27.—*Canastillero,* Marianao, Havana, 1989. The cabinet contains, from top to bottom, Orula and Ibeyi (*top of cabinet*), Obatalá (*top shelf*), Yemayá, Ochún, and *kofá* de Orula. The *tinajas* on the floor, are, from left to right, three Olokuns, two Oyás (spray-painted with her "nine colors"), a large, shell-encrusted pot (the *babalawo's* Olokun), and a classic *batea* (stave and metal band, painted red) on a pedestal, for Changó. The *canastillero* embodies the hierarchy, or chain of being, of the *oricha* pantheon, as it organizes the *orichas* along the vertical axis of heaven and earth. A painting of Saint Lazarus hangs above the cabinet. (Photograph by David H. Brown.)

Cloth serves other important purposes, which are performative, artistic, and epistemological. The throne installation organizes a complex visual drama of secrecy and knowledge. Throne cloth visually radiates the *orichas' aché* but physically conceals its source. In a visual paradox, *oricha* thrones are simultaneously compelling invitations to knowledge, spiritual communion, and aesthetic experience—especially given the theatrical device of parted curtains, which promotes the sense of revelation—*and* a strategic concealment of the *oricha's fundamentos,* which are enclosed beneath cloth in lidded *soperas* (plates 7, 8, 9). This effect recalls the use of cloth in Yoruba *egúngún* masquerades, as poetically described by Judith Gleason: using layers of dazzling, expensive cloth, these masquerades "dramatiz[e] . . . the surfaces in order to stress the depth of what is thereby concealed. The delighted eye teases the mind to contemplation of the unseen force behind the apparition" (Gleason 1987, 102). Gleason's cloth example functions as a device of ritual exclusion, also serving to veil the secret from the eyes of the uninitiated.

Part of these performative and aesthetic roles played by throne cloth include the aesthetic evaluation of the maker's or makers' artistic virtuosity by the audience (see Bauman 1975; Thompson 1973; Chernoff 1979; Hardin 1993; Brown 1996), who discuss and debate the qualities and details of the installation: for example, its place on a scale of "beauty" or "tackiness,"[45] its effectiveness in "communicating" *patakís* about the *orichas,* and its success in creating an ineffable spiritual sense or tone, a "harmonious environment . . . associated with a specific *oricha*" (see Flores-Peña and Evanchuck 1994, 15). Equally important, the act of throne building is a performance in itself, the primary audience of which comprises the *orichas as subjects,* who must be aesthetically content with their presentation, physically comfortable in the space, satisfied with the appropriateness of the iconography selected to represent them, and fully respected by a worthy amount of work and elaboration. Though the audience of "the people" evaluates these features to an extent, they are reflected upon mostly within the private relationship between the *orichas* and their priests—not to mention that perhaps the most crucial meanings of the throne installation have to do with the event's private objectives, which may be to solve a delicate problem, such as vanquishing enemies or healing a grave illness (see Friedman 1982, 96, 217; Brown 1996).

The first phase of throne building entails mounting the backdrop, the canopy, and, finally, the parted curtains to finish and "close" (*cerrar*) the space.[46] Within this protective enclosure, the next phase entails figuring out how best to organize the *orichas* hierarchically, according to their relative importance to the priest's spiritual profile: for example, though Obatalá normally is placed "highest," followed by the owner of the head, a third *oricha,* which serves as the priest's secret source of protection and defense (the *onilé*), is given a prominent position (see Brown 1996, 110–15).[47] Still, the problem of "teasing the mind" with "dazzling" surfaces is not resolved simply by attractive bolts of cloth. It is also a problem of effective and affective sculptural form, which has important phenomenological implications. The draping of the *orichas* entails solving the artistic problem of how best to cover the *soperas* so that the rising, mound-like cloth form adequately hides the *sopera* but also *comes alive* as a three-dimensional, quasi-anthropomorphic figure (see Brown 1993b).

If one function of draped African cloth was and is to enhance, if not also constitute, the "secret" (Barber 1981), in the African Diaspora, the cloth *paño* took on an additional "secrecy function": like other adornments borrowed from the church and popular Catholic practice, cloth covered the deities with the veil of "licitness" (*licitud*) in a colonial society in which discretion was the better part of valor (see Ortiz 1952–55, 4:79). Though the worst police persecutions and desecrations ended in the mid-1920s, practitioners could not really cease to "hide the *santos*" until the height of the "Special Period" (1993–94), when the government sought to let off steam by lifting restrictions on religious practice.[48] Clearly, throughout Cuban history, the *mantos* and dresses of the Catholic saints, the *paños* and skirts (*sayas*) of the *orichas*, and the decorative *frontal* of elevated altar tables have, in fact, physically hidden the *soperas* of the *orichas* from view, as Bascom noted in his summer 1948 research in Matanzas (Bascom 1950, 65). In sum, the "hiding" of the *orichas* is morphologically and semantically complex: thrones constitute and hide secrets within fraught social contexts, functions realized in and through artistic and performative devices. It is thus difficult to tease apart unequivocal motives for particular altar components. Analytically distinct forms such as Catholic *mantos* and *oricha paños* tend to blur together as unified "traditional" (i.e., traditionalized) presentational strategies.

A spectacular Yemayá throne, erected for a 1989 drumming celebration in the Guanabacoa house of Enrique Hernández Armenteros (plate 8),[49] nicely demonstrates hybrid presentation, particularly in the morphological and semantic "fit" of the saint's and *orichas'* cloth (*manto*, gown, *paño*, and *ropa de santo*); it also exemplifies the complexities of the drama of the secret. A blue satin dossal, which frames a large hand-painted icon of the Virgin of Regla, provides the framed background for the central, elevated *sopera* of Yemayá. A decorative fringed blue Spanish shawl with a colorful floral print forms the throne's prominent valance, and two floral silk *pañuelos* add the decorative flourish of swags on either side of this dramatic proscenium arch. Yemayá's *sopera*, raised on a covered pedestal, is enclosed and hidden by the light blue lamé gown of a black plastic doll. This *muñeca*, with its sparkling silver tiara, crucifix in hand, and tiny figure of the Christ child, directly echoes the dossal's hand-painted icon—itself copied from popular chromolithographs—as well as stands as an attribute of Yemayá herself. The fecund, protective, secret enclosure of the doll's skirts (*saya*) blends the *manto*, gown, *paño*, and *ropa de santo* forms.

A similar array of morphological and semantic associations was reiterated in the striking style in which female *iyawós* were "presented to the *batá* drums" during a 1989 *tambor* in Union City, New Jersey. Many houses might have chosen to cover the *iyawós'* heads with a white cotton headwrap (*pañuelo*) to hide recently shaved scalps. Others might have chosen to leave the heads uncovered, but for the open circular crown. However, in this case, their godparent chose to hide and adorn the *iyawós'* heads with *oricha paños*, over which the circular crowns were then placed. Elegant domes of luminous brocade (i.e., over the head's calvarium) filled the apertures of the open, bejeweled crowns. Dressed in their luxurious *ropa de santo* gowns, the *iyawós* looked as if they had stepped right out of a chromolithograph, or an *oricha* throne for that matter. If these decorative head cloths recall the initiation throne's *paños* (plates 5, 7, 8, 9, 10), they also echo the *mantos* and *mantillas* that cover the heads of Virgin and saints, upon which are placed the crown and halo (cf. fig. 5.30, *B*, *C*). Of course, the effect also reiterated the typical manner of dressing the *orichas' soperas*. The *paños* of Ochún and Oyá, for example, are gently coaxed up through their miniature metal crowns to form a "bun" (see Brown 1993b, 51; fig. 5.30, *A*). Despite differences of detail, it remains difficult to discern where the Catholic "robes of the saints" begin and the Lucumí *ropas de santo* end.

In his seminal study of Cuban Santería's Yoruba content, in which he assessed the role of Catholic additions, William Bascom concluded that the "chromolithographs and plaster images of the Catholic saints . . . prominently displayed in the shrines and houses of the santeros . . . are regarded as empty ornaments or decorations, which may be dispensed with. The real power of the santos resides in the stones, hidden behind a curtain in the lower part of the altar, without which no santeria shrine could exist" (Bascom 1950, 65). Bascom was clearly correct that the stones (*otán*) were the defining feature, the sin qua non, of Lucumí *oricha* shrines. Grounded by their *fundamentos*, which were consecrated with fresh plants and sacrificial blood, Lucumí shrines stand as distinct from domestic altars for the Catholic *santitos*—who preferred incense, oil, candles, and chromolithographs. For Bascom, "stones, herbs, and blood" constituted the essential and historically enduring Yoruba "focus of Cuban Santería," which embodied these shrines' "real power." The Catholic overlay was simply nominal.

Still, insofar as the Yemayá throne demonstrates cloth's potential to "hide," it also demonstrates that several important social and cultural functions (protection against stigma or persecution, veiling the "secret" in order to enhance its power [see Barber 1981], and protection against the eyes of the uninitiated) cannot easily be teased apart. Indeed, the motives behind particular altar components overlap and are overdetermined. Moreover, in historical perspective, as the documentation of Bremer (1853), Roche y Monteagudo (1908), and Wright (1910) suggests, the adorning of the *orichas' fundamentos* with cloth types that apparently have their origin in "European" and Catholic practice (the *manto*, the *saya*, and the "curtain in the lower part of the altar") had, by the time of Bascom's fieldwork (summer 1948), served as a cherished aesthetic mode of presentation for perhaps a century or more, and it continues fifty-five years later in the twenty-first century. In sum, the cloth of Mary and the cloth of the *orichas* became presentational features of a popular religious "faith," with its own range of diversity, which could regard Catholic saints and *orichas* as parallel "roads," as distinct registers on the matter-spirit continuum, or as an identity (see Murphy 1988, chap. 11; Wafer 1991, 14–15). As Bascom astutely observed, the saints' statues or chromolithographs and the *orichas'* stones resided in a hierarchical, up-down configuration (saints up–*orichas* down; fig. 5.9, plates 8, 10, 20), in which the latter could be hidden beneath cloth. The Guanabacoa Yemayá throne exemplifies this pattern (see also Cabrera [1954] 1983, plates). Yet such a presentation was, perhaps, more unified and irreducible than Bascom realized.

In distinguishing "real power" from mere "ornament" in his ostensibly informant-based account, Bascom deprived throne arts of multiple "power effects." Bascom's quite brief Cuban fieldwork did not permit him to illuminate Lucumí altar cloth as integral to efficacious sacrificial practice, that is, to powerful *ebó* directed at cleansing and protecting (see Brown 1996). He did not consider the very "hiding" function of cloth as a "power" in and of itself. Indeed, insofar as the "curtain in the lower part of the altar" prevented "anything" of the "real power of the santos" from being "shown" (e.g., to noninitiates, nosy neighbors, the local priest, the police), it clearly harbored a socioritual power that could not be "dispensed with" so easily. Second, he did not consider the throne's cultural and affective "power" to iconographically delineate the rich Lucumí cosmos and its dramatis personae. Finally, he did not consider the capacity, in Robert Plant Armstrong's sense, that diverse and distinct aesthetic means can constitute "powers of presence" in particular objects and assemblages (1981).[50]

It is true that many contemporary houses in Cuba and the United States dispense with chromolithographs and statues of the saints. However, cloth "ornament," particularly for the *asiento*, does remain that "without which no santeria shrine could exist." Thrones that do dispense with Catholic statues and chromolithographs still depend upon the baroque dramatic devices of the canopy, valance, parted curtains, draped *paños*, and, often, a cloth-covered altar table and its *frontal* to elevate, focus, reveal, and conceal the *aché* of the *orichas* (plates 7, 9, 22). For the late Ramón Esquivel, it was not whim that determined the inclusion or exclusion of Catholic statues. For him performance context—appropriateness in relation to the occasion at hand—determined the presence or absence of explicit saint representations. He typically used statues, chromolithographs, covered altar tables, candelabras, monstrances, and crucifixes for thrones honoring the *orichas* on the double feast days of the Catholic calendar, for example, 1 January for San Manuel (Odudúwa Obatalá Yekú-Yekú) and 17 December for Babalú Ayé and San Lázaro (plate 3; see also plate 10 and app. 5). He also used altar tables in combination with canopies on Palo Monte spirit feast days, as these spirits are typically called within the modified Spiritist mass called the *misa palera* (plate 22). In contrast, his thrones for *oricha* drummings and birthdays dispensed with those forms and emphasized artistically draped and gathered cloth (plates 7, 9). As a result, these latter thrones stood as more abstract tableaux.

Esquivel's thrones, through shape and color (though not exclusively), effectively delineated the rich Lucumí cosmos and its powerful dramatis personae. A kind of transitory sacred architecture, like soaring gothic churches, albeit in entirely different media and scale, his thrones limned the spirit-matter hierarchy in a way that elegantly remodeled African and Catholic cosmologies. Like Catholic altar baldachins, the upper reaches of his canopies of transluscent or reflective cloth (chiffon or lamé) evoked the firmament, sometimes with abstract, cloudlike formations (plate 7). In one birthday throne, a high, central pedestal elevating the *soperas* of two Obatalás, which he covered with white and silver *paños*, evoked for him the "hill of Oké"—Obatalá's mythical companion, firm "support" (*bastón*), and transcendent dwelling place (plate 9). Oké's white hill (Lucumí *oké;* Yoruba *òkè*) serves as the classic *axis mundi* of Obatalá, the old arch-*oricha* who mediates between God and the world (see epigraphs to chap. 3). As the origin place of Obatalá, the hill is an important figure in Yoruba and Lucumí oral literature, wherein Obatalá is the "King of the White Mountain," as well as "King of the White Cloth" (Mason 1992, 219–21, 246, 251, 255; 1985a, 34; Angarica [1955?] n.d, 20–21, 34; Ojo 1966, 159–62; Abraham 1946, 464; Cabrera [1957] 1986, 249). In turn, in direct vertical opposition to God's firmament and Obatalá's rising white mountain, this thronescape's "foreground," as it were, contains a *plaza* of fruits and prepared foods, a dense and colorful thicket of the earth's products spread over a straw mat (*estera*). Within this earthly thicket, the attributes of Eleguá and the Warriors, as well as other-*orichas* connected to the earth (Oricha Oko, Babalú Ayé), are ensconced. Taken in two dimensions, this stunning tableau could claim as its virtual blueprint Guzmán's 1955 cosmological representation of Obatalá and Echú, set within an idealized hierarchical landscape of sky, clouds, mountains, forest, earth, and stone (fig. 3.2).

Esquivel regularly played with the dynamics of these hierarchical representations through further embellishment, using cloth and other furnishings. Depending upon the elements he selected, the "syncretic" dimension of his relatively abstract thrones was more or less explicit. For example, he often mounted on the wall, between the spiritual registers of Oké's "hill" and the "sky," a golden-spoked metal lamp fitted with light bulbs in the four cardinal Lucumí ritual colors: white, yellow, blue, and red (plate 9, see also plate 6). For him, the lamp represented the Holy Sacrament (*Santísimo Sacramento*). That is, it approximated the monstrance form—the Roman Catholic altar attribute developed in the fourteenth century to display the consecrated Host for adoration and meditation (Apostolos-Cappadona 1994, 244). Cast metal and carved wood versions are ubiquitous on the domestic altars of *santeros, paleros*, and *abakuás* and have been carved and cast by Lucumí priests for perhaps two centuries or more (fig. 4.9, see also plate 10). A representation of the Eucharist, the *Santísimo Sacramento* also can serve as one attribute of the head of the pantheon, Obatalá (plate 10). As indicated in chapter 3, Obatalá and Christ each play the role of the "son" of the Supreme Being (Dios Todopoderoso or Olodumare/Olorun/Olofin). Employing simile, Agayú priest Idalberto Cárdenas elaborated upon the significance of such adornments in his explication to me of a throne Esquivél made for him—a drumming throne Cárdenas had to present to Obatalá (fig. 5.31). The throne's central, upwardly aspiring draped *paño* of silver *lamé* represented a "bird" or "airplane going to heaven . . . you know, *height*! Like something that looks toward the sky. Because Obatalá, is, you know, God's son. Like Jesus; Obatalá is like Jesus. It's like something [going] to his father, very symbolic . . . to open the ways to heaven from earth."[51]

Of course, this "heaven" is not at all a remote one, and

Figure 5.31.—Drumming throne for the Obatalá-Ayáguna of Idalberto Cárdenas with representations of Ochún, Yemayá, and Changó, New Jersey, 1984. Note the ascending bird- or airplane-shaped silver *paño* in the center over Obatalá's covered vessel. (Photograph by David H. Brown.)

not in any way dichotomously distinguished from an impure world of temptation. "The sky [is] really close to the earth," a source told Lydia Cabrera ([1954] 1994, 365). As a reconstituted Yoruba altar form, the throne situates and presents the *orichas'* spiritual "power" (*aché*), *right here.* It is embodied precisely in elements of nature—the stones, which are washed with herbs and fed with sacrificial blood—enclosed in ceramic vessels. Not least, the throne locates, makes present, and makes legible the *orichas' aché* precisely through the voluptuous and immediate means of a resplendent baroque aesthetic of "ornament": dense layers and folds of prestige cloth and brilliant metallic trimmings. Parted curtains create intimate, charged relations of spectatorship and interactive performance. Along with rich, saturated color and dramatic texture, these throne features promote the immediate, sensuous, revelatory experience of divinity. Satin, metallic brocade, sequins, and lamé reflect light, an effect that seems to transcend the earthly materials themselves, transmitting from within the *aché* or *gracia* that charges the *santo*'s presence. Chiffon miraculously plays with the limits of its own materiality, given its diaphanous and transluscent quality. As Erwin Panofsky lyrically observes, a fundamental and paradoxical effect of the baroque aesthetic is that "the unutterable bliss of a heavenly apparition—now within reach of a mortal being—becomes so strong that it begins to hurt, which makes the pleasure all the more intense" (Panofsky [1934] 1995, 51).

The very materiality of displays of rich, bejeweled cloth embodies the *orichas'* status, their wealth, and the virtually unlimited devotion of their priests to them (see Brown 1996). The luminosity or translucency of cloth brings heaven down to earth, while the material richness and density of layered cloth figures heaven in terms of legible signs of high earthly status, wherein the *orichas* occupy the apex of a sumptuary hierarchy (see Freudenberger 1963).[52] Yet ornament does more; it accomplishes the bridging of domains, as well as the constituting of difference. As Georg Simmel wrote on the effect of jewelry and adornment, "the *material* means of its social purpose is its *brilliance*. By virtue of this brilliance, its wearer appears as the center of a circle of radiation in which every close-by person, every seeing eye, is caught. . . . [It is a] flash . . . which returns to the subject as the enlargement of his own sphere of significance. The radii of this sphere mark the distance which jewelry creates between men—'I have something which you do not have.' But, on the other hand, these radii not only let the other participate: they shine in his direction; in fact, they exist only for his sake. By virtue of their material, jewels signify, in one and the same act, and increase in distance and a favor" (Simmel 1950, 342).

The paradoxical effects suggested by Panofsky and Simmel apply to the pan-Caribbean creole aesthetic effect Robert Farris Thompson poetically describes as "heaven's glamor" (Thompson 1993, 164). In Haiti, for example, Vodou's "physical tangibility of belief" is realized in the voluptuous baroque figures and bursting foliage, the resplendent martial uniforms and gowns of the *lwa* seen in the paintings of Hector Hyppolite (1940s) and Andres Pierre (1960s), as well as the ornate temple wall murals of crowned, haloed, and cloth-draped *lwa*. These paintings and murals, Donald Cosentino observes, "achieve the . . . spiritual realness . . . the hard heaven Catholics only imagine" (Cosentino 1995a, 52).[53] As limned by the priest-artists in the Cuban Lucumí tradition, the "glamor" of this "heaven" claims a particular cultural history. In the Cuban Lucumí "theater of God" (Thompson 1984), a liturgical cast of *orichas* is accustomed to appearing realistically as kings, queens, and warriors sitting in state.

CULTURAL BORROWING, TRANSATLANTIC DECORATIVE ARTS, AND *ADORNOS A GUSTO CRIOLLO*: THE *SOPERA* AND THE EUROPEAN CHINA EXPORT TRADE

El Museo Polivalente de Regla, an ethnographic, decorative arts, and local history museum on the busy Calle Martí, just up the hill from the church of the town's black Virgin, houses a collection of former possessions of the town's colonial aristocracy and middle class. It also owns objects salvaged from local houses of Ocha, their elderly owners having died without the support of ritual families to properly bequeath or dispatch their *oricha* attributes. Prominently exhibited in the foyer of the Museum, in a display of Regla's early history, sits a nineteenth-century blue and white gilt porcelain *sopera,* a harmonious modified oval form with chamfered corners and prominent upturned gilt handles (plate 23). The tureen embodies Cuba's colonial ties to the European continent and the Spanish crown as well as the fortunes and deeds of Cuba's urban creole elite. The tureen bears the coat of arms of the Marqueses de la Real Proclamación. The Marqués de la Real Proclamación was one of seventy-eight nobility titles granted by the Spanish king to European-born or creole men and women in Cuba between 1708 and 1866 (Marrero 1986, 13:35–49). This porcelain tureen belonged to the descendants of Gonzalo Recio de Oquendo, a creole born in Havana, who served as lieutenant governor during the English occupation of Havana (1762). Granted the title of Marqués de la Real Proclamación in 1764, Gonzalo Recio was the inheritor of the *mayorazgo* (estate) of Antón Recio (d. c.1570; Marrero 1986, 13:39), who, according to the museum's director, was the original owner of the lands on which the town of Regla was founded in 1687.[54] Commissioned in the late nineteenth century as part of a grand table setting (*vajilla*) by one branch of the Recio family to mark their status as noble title holders, the tureen was produced by a famous porcelain factory in Limoges, France. The tureen's color scheme of blue and white follows directly from the pattern of the Virgin of Regla, the town's patron saint and the town's coat of arms.[55] Across the lobby from the Recio tureen are exhibited weapons and other revolutionary mementos from Reglanos who fought in the Cuban wars of independence and the 1959 Revolution. Next to these are stunning artifacts and documents of Regla's African heritage, including slave manacles, ritual objects, and an elegant photograph of another kind of Regla nobility: the famous Ño Remigio Herrera (Adechina), the Yoruba *babalawo* who founded Regla's Cabildo de Yemayá and was greatly responsible for the establishment of Cuba's Ifá tradition (figs. 2.1, 5.8). In the succeding salons, displays of bourgeois decorative arts, furniture, and paintings find their counterparts in rich examples of Lucumí altar objects: the *soperas, collares de mazo, herramientas,* and *ropas de santo* belonging to the *orichas* of deceased Regla Ocha priests.

In the Museum's cramped storage room sits a cream white *sopera,* a simple oval tureen with plain flat handles. It is decorated with gilt trim and a printed pink and green floral motif. Made by the English firm of Alfred Meakin, this inexpensive, mass-produced soup tureen belonged to Tomasa de la Caridad Córdoba Medina, a Regla *iyalocha,* who was probably initiated in the 1920s and died in 1988 (plate 24). The tureen contains the stones, cowrie shells, and *herramientas* of the *oricha* Ochún. The Recio and Meakin tureens confront one another as varieties of prestige forms that marked, and circulated between, social classes and cultural domains. The first is an expensive porcelain object produced by a famous French factory to mark and enhance the titled nobility and colonial class position of a Cuban creole family; still, this tureen remains an imitation of an imitation of an imitation, which was chosen from a catalog and produced by a large, though selective, international china export industry.[56] The second tureen is a cheaper, nonporcelain, mass-produced object that was marketed for middle-class secular domestic use but was rerouted for sacred purposes within Regla's working-class Lucumí houses. The Meakin tureen, in its sacred context, continued to be informed by certain "original" messages of material well-being and class prestige, but these were redirected to mark the wealth and splendor of the *orichas.* Presently, both tureens, housed within a museum building that used to be the sprawling mansion of a wealthy white family, refer not only to Regla's social and cultural history, but also to the Triumph of the Revolution. The objects of Cuba's elite, left behind or expropriated by the Revolution, remain as museum relics, reminders of a colonial past. The objects of Regla's old

Lucumí houses, consistent with the tradition of Fernando Ortiz, revolutionary folklore programs and the 1970s politics of "Afrocastroism" (see Moore 1988), have been elevated in stature. The museum's Afro-Cuban director, Pedro Cosme Baños, has sought to recover and recognize the contribution of Regla's previously marginalized, multiracial, working-class priestly population. Antón Recio may have owned the *tierra* on which Regla was founded, but Adechina Ño Remigio Herrera and his colleagues founded Regla's Lucumí *tierra* (i.e., nation, new homeland), which was not officially valued until well after 1959.

Soup tureens were integral to the prestigious porcelain dinner services that became popular in Europe in the second half of the eighteenth century (Howard and Ayers 1978, 181). Whereas earlier porcelains on the European continent were tokens of prestige in the households of kings, in the second half of the eighteenth century, "a wider public began to interest itself in [c]hina and to have an influence on its decoration. In imitation of the king, the nobility began to have their table services made of faience [fine painted ceramics], especially in the second half of the century, when the demand for table services and other utilitarian objects became widespread. For a vast public, objects in porcelain, which had formerly been unknown, except in the upper ranks of society, began to become almost essential luxuries. . . . A large number of factories came into existence" to satisfy this upper class demand (Faniel 1957, 63). *Faïence fine* was a fine French earthenware. Not of porcelain (made of kaolin), it was a "cream-colored ware . . . made with calcinated flint to whiten, harden, and stabilize the clay body and then covered with a lead-oxide based glaze." This earthenware product was, in fact, developed by Josiah Wedgwood in England about 1760 to compete with porcelain, and it achieved great commercial success througout Europe (Harris Cohen and Hess 1993, 29–31). The fabulous glazed earthenware product, called *terraglia* in Italy, *Steingut* in Germany, *faïence fine* in France, and *Queen's ware* in England, was known generically as "creamware" (Harris Cohen and Hess 1993, 29).

At the level of surface decoration, the characteristically Chinese blue and white wares dominated in Europe until the eighteenth century. These gave way, with the expansion in eighteenth-century manufacture and trade, to "motifs of oriental style derived from novels," nature, and other arts (Palmer 1976, 19). Over time, however, decorative surface designs came to reflect more strictly European, particularly French tastes. Such "[d]ecoration in the naturalistic style included the use of flowers, birds, and landscapes, as well as 'trompe-l'oeil.' . . . Flowers, in particular, became a favorite form of decoration" (Faniel 1957, 66).

The most popular soup tureen shapes in the European-centered mass-manufacture and export trade of the second half of the eighteenth and the nineteenth centuries were oblong, oval, and, to a lesser degree, octagonal forms. These mass-produced objects were made in new, sprawling factories in Strasbourg (Alsace), Lille, Chantilly, Vicennes, and Sèvres (France), and Staffordshire (England) and in older, revived factories in Rouen, Marseilles, and Limoges (France). They were shipped throughout the world, increasingly in the first half of the nineteenth century (Fay-Halle and Mundt 1983, 11–12; Palmer 1976; Godden 1979). While the "round pottery tureen for soup was used in Europe long before 1700," by the "beginning of the eighteenth century, it formed an important part of European upper class dinner services" (Lunsingh [1966] 1974, 120). The oblong shape was established as a conventional and much-desired model by about 1765. The "shape that occurs over a long period is the oblong tureen with chamfered corners and handles in the form of boars' heads" (Lunsingh [1966] 1974, 114). The oblong style was apparently modeled after early silver sets (Howard and Ayers 1978, 181). In the history of the ceramic export trade to the New World, the Spanish were involved early on, long before the advent of European mass manufacture. "The first Chinese porcelains to reach the American continent came to the West Coast [i.e., Mexico] in the sixteenth century on Spanish ships from the Philippines," notes Arlene Palmer (1976, 25). Still, the majority of decorative domestic ceramics that entered the Spanish possessions in the nineteenth century were from England and France. British export records show a large, healthy export trade in ceramics to Cuba by the beginning of the nineteenth century, and Britain was probably the leading exporter of fine earthenware to the New World through the first half of the twentieth century.[57]

White Cubans remember the *sopera* as a cherished object of Cuban middle- and upper-class domestic life.[58] The *sopera,* and the *vajilla* of which it was a part, were saturated with the meanings of domestic well-being and social class status. Since the eighteenth century, porcelain objects, status tokens of European aristocracy, were profuse in the Cuba's Palace of the Captain General and the homes of Cuba's aristocracy during and after the colonial period (see figs. 5.19, 5.20). Members of the Spanish and creole nobility and the upper classes in Cuba, such as the count of the Revilla de Camargo and the family of José Martí, continued to acquire eighteenth- and nineteenth-century European-made porcelain objects, as well as earlier Chinese dynasty porcelains, for their lavish Havana residences. This custom continued, in some cases, as late as 1961.[59] With the increasing diversity and reach of transatlantic commercial nineteenth-century trade, imitations, often of less elaborate materials and design, were disseminated widely across class lines.

In nineteenth- and early-twentieth-century Cuban homes of means, "china" (porcelain and its competitors, "creamware" and "ironstone") plates, sugar bowls, creamers, and tureens that made up the *vajilla* were meticulously arranged in *armarios vitrinas,* multishelved armoires with glass doors, for prominent display in formal dining rooms. Cuban decorative arts curator Carmen Trujillo Pardo, describing a particularly beautiful example from the colonial period that is displayed in Havana's Museum of Decorative Arts (fig. 5.32) writes: "[this *armario vitrina*] utilized in the dining rooms of Cuban homes, [is] constructed of cedar and inlaid with rosewood, with the interior of maple. It displays figured forms on the upper section, and below [inside] can be observed the various porcelain objects that [typically] belonged to Cuban families" (Trujillo Pardo, Méndez-Plasencia, and Suárez García n.d., 82–83).

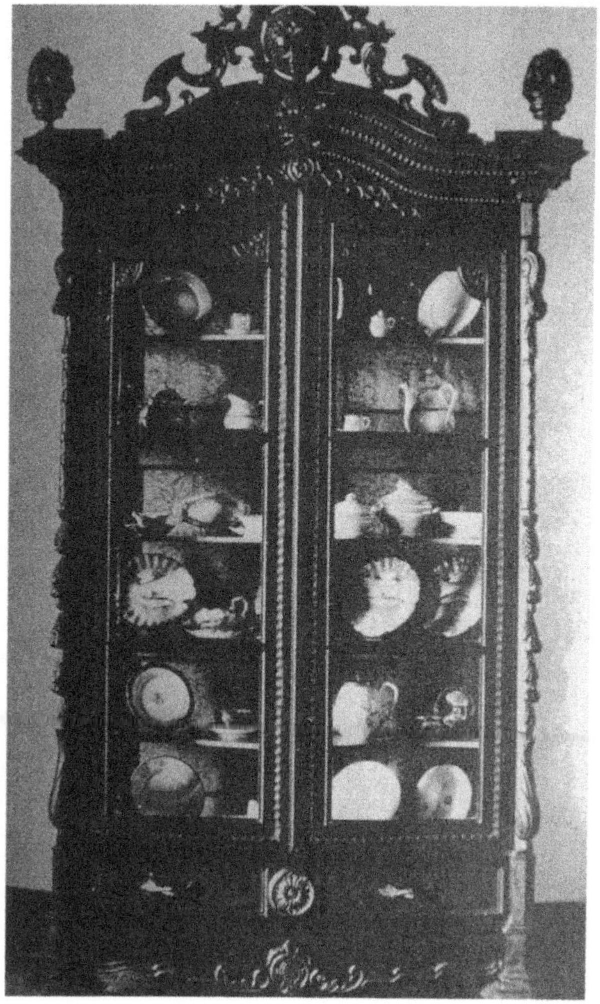

Figure 5.32.—*Armario vitrina* (glassed-in china cabinet) containing porcelain dinner service and table settings (*la vajilla*) of colonial Cuban bourgeoisie. Cabinet made of cedar, rosewood, and maple. (From Trujillo-Parte n.d. [*sic;* her actual name is Trujillo Pardo]. Courtesy Museo de Arte Colonial, Havana.)

At least by the time of Roche y Monteagudo's and Irene Wright's accounts of Papá Silvestre Erice's "African *cabildo*" in El Cerro, the "soup tureen . . . that held a holy secret" was also an established central feature of the Cuban Lucumí altar (figs. 5.10, 5.11). The white *soperas* reposing beneath lace-trimmed satin curtains and Yoruba gourd shakers in Roche's 1908 photographic documentation (Roche y Monteagudo 1908, 79), are simple, white, oval tureens with flat, modular handles at each extreme, and plain round knobs on their lids. Changó's favorite foods, plantains and okra, hang from the knob of one *sopera*, and metal *oricha* bracelets encircle the knob of the other. Elevated upon their altars, these are the centerpieces of a very different kind of table setting.

As Cuba's Lucumí practitioners utilized the *sopera* form to contain the *orichas'* stones, shells, and *herramientas*, so they also utilized the genre of decorative furniture in which china was customarily displayed by the middle and upper classes. Since the nineteenth century, Lucumí priests have typically arranged their *orichas' soperas* in multishelved closets or in *canastilleros*, the common term for the preferred form of permanent Lucumí domestic altar: a standing cabinet with hinged doors—which may be glass, revealing lace valances and curtains on the inside (i.e., the *armario vitrina;* see González Huguet 1968, 34, 35, 43, 48, 49, 50–51). Lydia Cabrera observed that the *soperas* "are disguised [*se disimulan*] in an armoire that is called '*canastillero*'" (Cabrera [1974] 1980, 131). In the most humble of Cuban homes, where priests themselves may suffer materially, the *orichas* can repose resplendently, as in the Ocha house of María Sirgelina Martínez on the impoverished Loma Adriano, one of the *favela*-like hills above the town of Regla's busy port (plate 25).

The simple, cream white oval *sopera* for Ochún in the Regla museum collection was produced by the firm of Alfred Meakin of Tunstall, Staffordshire, England, the northernmost production center of the many pottery producers in Staffordshire—a great source of fine clays. Alfred Meakin, somewhat late in coming, began producing in 1875 and concentrated his production not around porcelain, but around *faïence fine*, or creamware (Cushion 1987, 548), the very composition of this *sopera* for Ochún. Marked under its base with the label "Alfred Meakin, England" (plate 24, *bottom*), this tureen was likely produced after the early 1890s, possibly as late as 1930, and may have passed through the United States before arriving in Cuba.[60]

The story of Alfred Meakin and the Regla tureen forms part of a larger success story, that of the famous Meakin pottery dynasty of north Staffordshire, which rapidly became an international business boasting of huge sales by numerous agents throughout the world. James and George Meakin ("J. and G.") opened their sprawling Eagle Factory in the north Staffordshire town of Hanley in 1859. These ambitious and upright sons of James the Elder Meakin (1807–52), the great patriarch of "yeoman farming stock" who had begun producing pottery as early as 1846 in Staffordshire, made their fortune on their special "White Granite China," also known as "Ironstone China," a fine earthenware competitor to porcelain, which "won a wide popularity throughout North America and subsequently in South America" (Hollowood 1951, 5–15; see also Weatherbee 1985, 129–30). Hard, brilliant, and white ironstone was a cut above, and more expensive than, creamware. By 1951, J. and G. Meakin had been exporting to Latin America for at least seventy years, since about 1880—five years after Alfred Meakin began producing at his own factory. Under the Spanish motto "J. and G. Meakin Cumplen" (deliver), the brothers proudly claimed agents in Havana, Montevideo, Caracas, Bogotá, Medellín, and Port of Spain. One Señor Vincente M. Gómez represented Meakin at 201 Calle Amargura (Hollowood 1951, 55) in the bustling business district of Old Havana, a street directly parallel to, and two blocks south of, the main commercial throroughfares of Obrapía and Obispo. In 1951, the several large J. and G. Meakin potteries were producing more than one million pieces a week. Alfred Meakin, probably one of the many sons of James Meakin, Jr.,[61] undoubtedly rode the same business curve as the factories of his family members. J. and G. Meakin soup tureens and other mass-produced

Figure 5.33.—*Vajilla* (dinner service) with soup tureen by J. and G. Meakin, Staffordshire, England, the pottery family dynasty to which Alfred Meakin belonged. The pattern is the "Century" model of "ironstone China" for export and middle-class consumption marketed in the Caribbean and South America as of 1870. (From Hollowood 1951.)

creamware objects were aggressively and creatively marketed to the middle class as part of elegant dinner and serving sets, such as the "Duchess" and the "Century." These charming sets were photographed for advertising purposes along with flatware, wine glasses, vases of flowers, bowls of fruit, lace doilies, and linen table napkins. "The great majority of Meakin's white ironstone tureens had plain round or oval bodies" (Wetherbee 1985, 129–30). The Alfred Meakin Regla *sopera* utilized for Ochún mirrors the oval form, flat handles, and floral print of the popular J. and G. Meakin "Century" tureen (fig. 5.33).

In Havana, the porcelains of the Spanish and creole nobility and upper classes were undoubtedly seen and handled by domestic slaves and later by domestic wageworkers but were undoubtedly beyond the reach of their ownership. Nevertheless, as the foregoing discussion suggests, a chain of imitations, graded in quality and cost, were undoubtedly marketed to the different rungs of Cuba's colonial and postcolonial socioeconomic ladder. For example, *soperas*, pitchers, plates, bowls, and cups of creamware or less expensive forms of glazed ceramics, such as the utilitarian cafeteria stonewares Cubans know as *loza*, were evidently widely available to humble Havana consumers at least by the time the meticulous realist Víctor Patricio de Landaluze published his *Tipos y Costumbres de la Isla de Cuba* in 1881. A white oval *sopera* with simple handles and a knobbed lid, among other pieces of utilitarian table service, prominently occupies the background of his realist lithograph of a typi-

Figure 5.34.—Víctor Patricio de Landaluze, *El Mascavidrio* [The fool; or "Glass chomper"], 1881, approximately 11 x 9 inches. The lithograph depicts two drunken fellows in a colonial Cuban *bodega* with its various household wares, including white plates and a white oval *sopera* (see the shelves in background, *top center*). (From Landaluze 1881.)

cal Cuban *bodega,* a kind of neighborhood general store that sold dry goods, food, and household supplies and in which patrons could also gather socially and drink (Landaluze 1881, 69–76; fig. 5.34). Before the background of well-stocked shelves, two grizzled, drunken fellows stand and lounge. Empty and broken bottles litter the tile floor. These white working-class "types"[62] and the *bodega*'s utilitarian household goods occupy a social space that is decidedly not upper or, even, middle class. Though the type and source of the *bodega*'s *sopera* cannot be ascertained, the context for its display and consumption represented, one speculates, a significant contrast to the middle-class china market of Sr. Vicente Gómez's Old Havana outlet, not to mention the more specialized import market for elite porcelains such as the late-nineteenth-century Recio tureen. In short, the social and cultural distance from this 1881 *bodega*'s common houseware shelves to relatively humble practitioners' homes and their altars was not at all insuperable. Though it is not possible to determine the precise type and source of the Sociedad Santa Rita y San Lázaro *soperas* (figs. 5.10, 5.11), it may be observed that these simple oval tureens, as well as the Landaluze *bodega* tureen, were typical of the most common forms of the creamware and ironstone mass-export trade and closely match the form of the Regla museum's Ochún *sopera* (Wetherbee 1985, 129–30).

Many questions remain unanswered. What kinds of import goods could the poorest and darkest Cubans afford, and what goods and market domains were accessible to them, particularly from the end of the Spanish-American War (1898) through the first several decades the Republic, when Afro-Cubans suffered serious disenfranchisement and social marginalization (Helg 1995)? Where did the Lucumí Papá Silvestre Erice and his congregation—the *mulato* bandleader-priest who escorted Irene Wright to his *cabildo,* or the young Yemayá priestess "who might have 'passed for white'"—purchase their altar objects and *soperas?* Clearly, well-to-do, white, early-twentieth-century practitioners, such as the late Rigoberto Rodríguez Duque of the Havana provincial town of Madruga, acquired authentic porcelain tureens (plate 26); at the same time, some of the poorest houses in the most impoverished Afro-Cuban *barrios* of Guanabacoa acquired admirable tureens earlier in the twentieth century (plate 20).[63] It is not inconceivable that wealthier or socially mobile white godchildren acted as patrons for their more impoverished black initiators, providing, in the form of gifts to the house, luxuries for the *orichas.* Lydia Cabrera's old Afro-Cuban informants in the 1940s, for example, remembered that the most lavish religious adornments during the late colonial period were encountered in Ocha houses whose initiations were sponsored by well-to-do Spanish patrons. "'The [*oricha*] thrones in the period of Spain (of the Colony) in the houses of the famous Santeros were very beautiful,' an old woman tells us, 'as when one of those *mulatas* was initiated, the kind that takes your breath away and that were kept by Spanish gentlemen like Don X . . . who spared no expense on his lovers, who were always women of color'" (Cabrera [1974] 1980, 176). The same informants noted that the *oricha* adornments in impoverished houses were usually "nothing of luxury! [*¡nada de lujo!*]." Such *oricha* thrones were "no more than a white sheet . . . hung from the wall and nothing more."

Fernando Ortiz's observations on the history of Afro-Cuban Abakuá objects may help explain the rise of increasingly more lavish and expensive adornments within Afro-Cuban practices as a whole. Ortiz noted that the addition of expensive and ostentatious *adornos a gusto criollo* ("adornments in the creole taste") within the Abakuá society corresponded historically to the growing initiation not only of working-class whites, but also many "boys of the 'Acera del Louvre' [an upper-class café hangout on Old Havana's Prado], that is, the dissipated young men of Havana's 'best familes'" (see Ortiz 1952–55, 4:55, 69; Robreño 1925). Beginning in the last third of the nineteenth century, with the founding of the first "white" lodge, called Akanarán Efó Ocobio Mukarará, Abakuá altars hungrily adopted Cuban secular and sacred forms and exploded in their ostentation. The lodge's name means the "Efó Mother of the White Brethren," and they were seen to put on an air of superiority.[64] Given their unique and protected access to burgeoning Havana sea commerce, these "white brethren" presumably were able to enhance their well-being.

Havana's Akanarán Efó and its "white" offspring, particularly in Regla, mounted cloth-covered altar tables that featured painted crucifixes and large gilt monstrances with Jesuit insignia—all forms inspired by the furnishings of the church. Their tubular staffs of office (*itones*) boasted finials of silver and gold, religious medals, and military-style decorative cords and tassels. Similar to the *oricha sopera* styles and their adornments, the urnlike symbolic drum (*sese de copón*) of these new white Abakuá lodges of the Efó branch was fitted with silver jewel-encrusted crowns inspired by those of the Bourbon kings and local Virgins and saints (Ortiz 1952–55, 4:55, 58, 59, 69). And, as in the emerging creole Lucumí aesthetic, lavish prestige cloth was added: thick red velvet adorned the staffs; great bolts of satin were used as altar dossals and curtains across the threshold of the *fambá*, the Abakuá temple space. Through conspicuous displays of lavish adornment, these "white" lodges aggressively competed with one another, as well as with the older black lodges (Cabrera [1958] 1970, 54–55), which, according to Ortiz, eventually adopted many of the *adornos a gusto criollo* (1952–55, 4:49–84). As Cabrera's Abakuá informants noted, "[t]he whites adorned [their altars] with [finials] of gold and silver on their ends. If Abakuá Efó had them with [finials] of silver and of gold, those of Nyegueyé made all of them of gold" ([1958]1970, 54). Such lavish altar displays were apparently made possible by increasing workers' well-being and the patronage of Akanarán Efó (founded in 1863), the members of which included sons of the wealthy, and a general and noble or two. The top officer of the white Regla lodge Nyegueyé, Manuel de Jesús "Chuchú" Capáz (b. 1881; d. c. 1961), originally a stevedore and member of Akanarán Efó, accumulated considerable resources and patronage power in his later years as a wharf boss, labor leader, and politician (López Valdés 1985b, 170–71). Not least, Chuchú, some Abakuá of his lineage believe, was paid twenty thousand dollars as one of Lydia Cabrera's principal informants.[65] In effect, as internationally known figures, such as Jorge Amado and David Byrne, have been patrons of the Bahian Candomblés, so was Lydia Cabrera a patron, as well as ethnographer, of Cuba's Abakuá.

It is worth hypothesizing that Abakuá lodges began to compete in symbolic ways that reflected and expressed

Figure 5.35.—Living room shelves with two white china *soperas* (*left and center*), two bisque-fired and spray-painted clay *soperas* adorned with relief floral designs touched up with gold paint (*center left and center right*), and a *sopera* of *loza* (cafeteria stoneware, *right*), in the house of an *oriaté* of El Cerro, Havana, 1994. (Photograph by David H. Brown.)

material competition within expanding mid- to late-nineteenth-century urban job markets in western Cuba. The latter competition could include street violence (see Roche y Monteagudo [1908] 1925b, 68–69, 77). The white Spanish immigrant working class—mostly male workers—increased 86% with the government's efforts to offset the island's feared black majority by importing whites in the middle decades of the century (1846–61). "White workers were extending their control over urban jobs at the expense of free people of color," especially in Havana. Related to these crucial demographic changes, labor activism boomed (Pérez 1988, 117–21). Abakuá lodges began to control labor in numerous industries—for example, in the cigar-making, shipping, warehousing, meatpacking, and outdoor agricultural market sectors—helped organize strikes, and fought to take wharf and other jobs away from the members of black lodges. Still, given the strong articulation of lodge membership with specific *barrio* loyalties (see López Valdés 1985b; Palmié 1994), competition apparently also ensued between the white lodges themselves for material success and reputation. Symbolic competition for resources and reputation, which could parallel, or substitute for, actual street battles between neighborhood-based male institutions, is a pan-Latin American and Caribbean historical phenomenon originating in the slavery era; it has been documented for Trinidadian stick fighting and Pierrot Grenade bands, Haitian Rara secret societies, New Orleans's Black Mardi Gras Indian Tribes, and coastal Brazil's Capoeira subculture (see Pearse [1956] 1988, 38–39; Carr [1956] 1988, 200; McAlister 2002, 135–57; Smith 1994, 65, 111–12; 1984, 95–97; Lewis 1992, 42–50; Capoeira 1995, 6–12).

The religious brotherhoods and clubs of the colonial period in Cuba (*cabildos*) and Brazil (*irmandades*), competed aesthetically with one another for power, recognition, and earnings, especially on the occasion of public festivities—often with the added component of violence (see Bastide [1960] 1978, 114; Ortiz [1920] 1960, 10–17; Deschamps Chapeaux 1968, 50).[66] Similarly, Lucumí *casa-templos*, like their cousins of the Bahian Candomblés, continue to influence, and compete with, one another in their aesthetic elaboration of the gods (see Brown 1996, 119–21). In some cases, as in the Candomblés, Lucumí houses have cultivated patrons for such purposes, including ethnographers. If this agonistic pattern at all derived from a West African ethos (Omari 1984, 27–28), it also had precedents in the competition between local religious brotherhoods (*cofradías*) of the Iberian Peninsula (see Christian 1981, chap. 3, and 117–19). In Lucumí religious practice, aesthetic elaboration, such as beautiful *soperas* displayed in an elegant *canastillero*, or lavish thrones, *paños*, and *ropa de santo*, express not only the house owner's devotion to the *orichas*, but also the grace and fortune the *orichas* have bestowed, in turn, upon the house (see Brown 1996).

Clearly, many Ocha houses in Cuba, perhaps even a majority, have never possessed the means for the most prestigious and expensive objects. However, through a variety of connections and opportunities—for example, through business and political relationships, including initiating rich and powerful godchildren—a number of houses have acquired significant resources. The early- to mid-twentieth-century Ifá houses of Bernardo Rojas, Tata Gaitán, and Quintín Lecón Lombillo are cases in point (see chap. 2). Prior to the 1959 Revolution, famous, well-to-do Ocha houses, such as the that of Guanabacoa's Arcadio Calvo and Madruga's Rigoberto Rodríguez Duque (plate 26) acquired valuable *soperas*, expensive cloth, gold and brass attributes, and the like. Under the post-1959 government, patronage became a state affair under the Cultural Ministry, and a number of Afro-Cuban institutions, such as those of Guanabacoa's Enrique Hernández Armenteros ("The Sons of Saint Lazarus") and Madruga's late Rigoberto Rodríguez, now under the direction of Fredesvinda Rosell, Antonio Castañeda's state sponsored Yoruba Cultural Association of Old Havana, and several other houses co-opted for "religious tourism," have done very well (plates 8, 26).[67] The well-attended massive feasts of Arcadio Calvo, for example, like Papá Silvestre Erice's, were showcases that may have constituted new desires and significances with respect to *oricha* adornment; they may also have set stylistic trends that were, in turn, copied in budget media by the less fortunate. Cheaper *oricha* objects could still send messages of heightened, albeit relative, value, in contrast to what priests materially permit for themselves. Marked aesthetic and material investment in the *orichas'* possessions has included intensive decorative handiwork in bright paint and embroidery (fig. 5.7). A priestess in one of Guanabacoa's most impoverished *barrios*, La Correa, brightened her altar of saints and *oricha soperas* with colorful plastic ducks (for Yemayá) and a smattering of blue paint (plate 20, see also fig. 5.35).[68] María Andó de Cárdenas, whose humble house was photographed by Cabrera's assistant at midcentury, surrounded her corner *canastillero* with a canopy and dossal improvised from a semicircle of bright cloth flags and appliqué cutouts of stars along with colorful chromolithographs of the Catholic saints on the back wall (fig. 5.9). The "folkloric" programs of dance companies and the exhibition salons of "ethnographic" museums continue to place before the Cuban, as well as international, public the most elaborate *oricha* objects and assemblages. Indeed, the Ethnographic Museum of Guanabacoa houses many of the fine altar objects of the late Arcadio Calvo (fig. 5.36), and other fine objects were specifically commissioned for the museum's opening in

Figure 5.36.—Tourist postcard of a tableau mounted in the Ethnographic Museum of Guanabacoa, with *oricha* objects including a fine *armario vitrina* with porcelain *soperas* and small side thrones for Yemayá and Ochún (to the right and left of the *armario*) showing a traditional arrangement of plates around a vessel set into a bowl atop a mortar.

1964. As amplified below, museum displays have formed one source for numerous imitations, albeit produced with budget means.

Substitutions, Compromises, and Inventions: The Universe of Cuban "Vessels of Domestic Use"

Soperas have, ultimately, replaced the lidded calabashes (*igbá*) and figured wood and clay pots (*ìkòkò*) in which the Yoruba historically contained the secrets of their *òrìṣà*, and which formed the core of their shrines (see Pemberton 1975, 20–22; Thompson 1993, 146–280; Drewal, Pemberton, and Abiodun 1989, 153–56; Matory 1994, 155–63; figs. 5.37, 5.38, 5.39). Clearly, by the 1940s and 1950s, when Cabrera's photographer, Josefina Tarafa, documented a priest's *orichas* reposing upon a straw mat, the *soperas* had been standard, or at least desired, equipment for Cubans of even limited means for fifty to seventy years if not more (Cabrera [1954] 1983, plates; see also Dornbach 1977; fig. 5.40). *Soperas* had been commercially available since the early nineteenth century, and their ap-

Figure 5.37.—The Agbeni Ṣàngó shrine in Ìbàdàn, Nigeria, 1910. (Photograph by Leo Frobenius. Courtesy the Frobenius Institute, Frankfurt, Germany.)

Figure 5.38.—Yoruba ceramic or wood *ìkòkò* (wide-mouthed pot). This pot bears a surface relief of Ṣàngó's iconography and is probably used as a pedestal to support a bowl or calabash of thunderstones (see, e.g., fig. 5.37). (From Abraham 1946, 774.)

parently wide religious use, as indicated, had been documented as early as the first decade of the twentieth century (Landaluze 1881; Hollowood 1951; Roche y Monteagudo 1908; Wright 1910).

Still, the transatlantic leap from African pots to porcelain *soperas* belies the great historical diversity of Cuban Lucumí *oricha* vessels. It also belies the historical and regional variations in ritual pot types throughout Yorubaland. For example, Ọ̀yọ́ North practice tends to favor calabashes, whereas southwestern groups favor earthenware (see Matory 1986, 101).[69] At the same time, many of the Cuban *orichas* never accepted the china *sopera* at all, re-

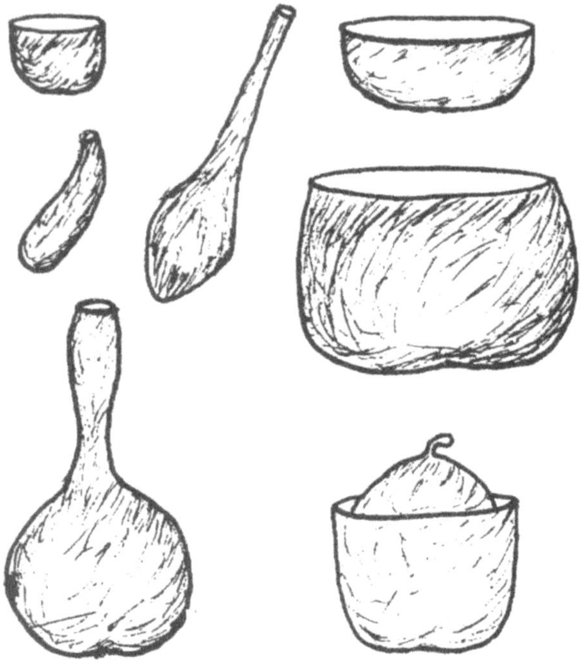

Figure 5.39.—Various types of Yoruba *ìgbá* (calabash). *Left, top to bottom: ahá*, a small calabash for giving medicine or for drinking palm wine; *atọ́*, a long, thin calabash used as a receptacle for medicine; *agbè*, a calabash that can be used to make shakers; *center: ṣẹ́rẹ́*, a calabash with a long, thin neck that, when cut in half, can be used as a ladle and, uncut, can be used as a rattle announcing Ṣàngó (*ṣẹ́rẹ́ẹ̀*); *right, top to bottom: pọ̀kọ́*, either the upper half or the lower half of a small, ovoid type of calabash; *koto*, a very broad and basket-shaped calabash; *igbá kòtò*, a deep calabash used for hot *ẹ̀kọ*, with a lid. (From Abraham 1946, 282.)

Figure 5.40.—*Soperas* and *palanganas* containing *orichas*. *Clockwise from front left:* Agayú, Oyá, Ochún, Oricha Oké, Yemayá, and Changó, with Obatalá in the center (covered in cotton). The small, white plate might contain an Eleguá or a prepared *ñame* (white African yam, for Obatalá). (From Cabrera [1954] 1983, plates. Courtesy the Estate of Lydia Cabrera.)

quiring, instead, other vessel forms and materials. In general, the female *orichas* and/or those of the domains of sky and water, such as Yemayá, Ochún, Oyá, Obá, Inle, and Obatalá, have taken the *soperas*, as is apparent in the documents of Roche y Monteagudo, Wright, and Tarafa (figs. 5.10, 5.11, 5.40).[70] The *sopera*'s reflective surface and materials—fine clays produced from waterborne sedimentation and glacial movement—were consistent with these *orichas*' qualities. Still other *orichas* required different vessels appropriate to their particular characters and domains. The squat oval soup tureen form was never appropriate to the mysterious *oricha* of the ocean's bottom, Olokun, who required a vessel of significant depth. Olokun uses a deep earthenware storage jar (*tinaja*), which is glazed on the inside so it holds water.[71] Olokuns are normally painted blue, though the Olokuns of *babalawos* are encrusted with cowries, seashells, and cemented *carga* upon their surface (fig. 5.41). Babalú Ayé/Asojuano/San Lázaro, patron of the poor, owner of illnesses (internal organs and the skin), and specialist in the domain of the *egun*—the dead—resides in a bisque-fired, terra-cotta pot, which may or may not be painted. The pots of the Asojuanos are perforated with holes, which are likened to the sores that pock this *oricha*'s skin (fig 5.42). Asojuanos of the Arará Sabalú of Matanzas and Havana are sealed with cement, while those of other Arará groups in rural Matanzas towns (e.g., Perico) and their descendants in the United States remain unsealed.

Figure 5.41.—Three *tinajas* for Olokun, painted blue. The rear two have decorative surface designs; the *tinaja* in front is an Olokun *de babalawo*, because it is encrusted with seashells and, on the lid, with cowries. The cowries are embedded in cement, and the pot's surface is covered with a ring of cement—the medium of *masa*, an *osain*-based mixture that carries a *carga* (ritual "load"). Fernando Ortiz Collection, La Casa de Africa, Havana. (Photograph by David H. Brown.)

Oricha Oko, Owner of the Land and its products, takes a classic Spanish terra-cotta roof tile and lives in a basin (*palangana*) or platter (*fuente*) filled with earth. The terracotta tile (*teja*) not only embodies the earth, but also carries associations of rainfall and the effective channeling of water, including in early agricultural irrigation systems—in other words, the critical procreative relationship of sky and earth. Osain, the forest-dwelling master of leaves and medicines, uses a lidded calabash gourd, which may be covered with multicolored bead strands (fig. 5.43). Osain's forest comrades, the fierce male Warriors Eleguá, Ogún, and Ochosi, have never used the dainty, lidded *sopera* form of the other *orichas,* who live in the "house" beneath a roof; instead, they are outdoorsmen, who take rustic terra-cotta or iron pots that remain open to the sky (fig. 4.22), or, like Osain, large beaded gourds (plate 18).[72] The fiery hot Changó, and, nowadays, Agayú, utilize not ceramic or metal vessels, but lathe-turned lidded containers of cedar or mohogany, called *bateas.* Early Changó vessels were constructed, barrel-like, of staves and rings, with a flat wood lid, after the classic pan-Caribbean *batea* form, which served as a washbasin and feed trough for animals (plates 17, 27, *far right*).[73] Cedar and mohogany (*cedro* and *caoba*) are considered to be "male" woods;[74] they come from tall, hard, thick trees bearing a reddish color (Cabrera [1954] 1983, 221–30, 368, 372). Odudúwa (Odúa), the Creator of the Earth, the origin of all births and deaths, and a pivotal mediator between the material and the celestial, life and death, requires a *cofre*—a silver or polished stainless steel box that resembles a reliquary chest. And, finally, Olofin requires a metal "can" (see chap. 2).

Figure 5.42.—Asojuano terra-cotta pot (two bowls, one inverted as a lid), painted dark red and encrusted with cowries. The top is perforated, which is appropriate to Asojuano's iconography of sores or breaks in the skin. The perforations also permit this deity to be "fed" when the pot is sealed shut, a practice found among Arará, Sabalú houses. Fernando Ortiz Collection, La Casa de Africa, Havana. (Photograph by David H. Brown.)

Figure 5.43.—Lidded calabash of Osain wrapped in multicolored beads, Miami, 1984. It is meant to be hung. (Courtesy Dr. Charles Wetli.)

Figure 5.44.—Seashell-encrusted *tinaja* for Ochún with bird-topped double-arched and pointed brass crown, *collares de mazo* (probably Ochún Ibú Acuaró), five chased fine brass *manillas,* and brass *campanilla* (bell). From a special exhibition at the Museo Nacional de Bellas Artes, Havana, 1986. (Photograph by David H. Brown.)

Fernando Ortiz's observations help locate the *soperas* documented by Landaluze (1881), Roche y Monteagudo (1908), Wright (1910), and the Meakin example in the Regla collection within a universe of domestic vessel forms. In place of "the earthenware vessels of the rustic African potter's workshop," Ortiz wrote in 1906, the Afro-Cuban religious practitioners "substituted pots [*cazuelas*], cups [*tazas*], tureens [*soperas*], basins [*palanganas*], goblets [*copas*], plates [*platos*], and other vessels of domestic use" ([1906] 1973, 79). *Soperas* have, therefore, competed with many other domestic vessel types that could serve the same functions, if not always send the same messages of prestige. "Other vessels of domestic use" have also included iron cooking cauldrons (Ogún), *bateas* (stave-and-band wood basins for Changó), and earthenware water storage jars (*tinajas*). Beyond their faithful service to the *orichas* Nanú, Olokun, and Naná Burukú, *tinajas* could substitute for *soperas* when painted or glazed with an *oricha's* signature colors, or when encrusted with lustrous seashells for Yemayá and Ochún (plate 27, figs. 5.35, 5.44). A small, lidded *tinaja* continues to be used to carry water back to the house following the *iyawó's* ceremony of the river.

The time-honored *chumba,* of which Ortiz provided an

Figure 5.45.—*Chumba* dedicated to an *orisha*. The *chumba* is a lidded vessel improvised from two china bowls, a form that reproduces the Yoruba *igbá* (covered calabash). (From Ortiz [1906] 1973, 79. Courtesy María Fernanda Ortiz Herrera, Representante Sucesores de Fernando Ortiz.)

illustration in 1906, consists of two simple bowls, one inverted as a lid (fig. 5.45). The apparently impoverished house of María Andó de Cárdenas used white bowls covered with plates (fig. 5.9). In truth, most houses from the second half of the nineteenth century down through the present have experimented and improvised with different vessel types, adding the highly prized *soperas* when possible. Of all of these vessels, the *chumba* and the *tinaja* have remained very common solutions during Cuba's current "Special Period" of economic austerity.

Among the diverse vessel alternatives, though the humble *chumba* might appear to be an economic and aesthetic compromise, in fact, it most closely reproduces the morphology and meaning of the classic Yoruba *òrìṣà* container of two opposed gourd halves or stacked and covered wood bowls (see Drewal, Pemberton, and Abiodun 1989, plates 3, 167, 172; Pemberton 1975, 20–22; fig. 5.37). It is possible that some Cuban houses have preferred the *chumba* to the *sopera* for precisely that reason: two rounded bowls, one inverted as a lid, closely reproduce an important Yoruba cosmological model of *orun* and *ayé* (the other world and this world), which are envisioned as opposed calabashes, a concept that also permeates Lucumí cosmological thinking. In his own practice *oriaté* Ernesto Pichardo of Miami explicitly interprets the use of the lidded vessel in the Lucumí religion in this way. Instead of keeping his Changó inside a contemporary lathe-turned *batea*, he acquired two widely flaring wood bowls, painted them in Changó's colors, and created the kind of *orún*- and *ayé*-patterned container seen in the early-twentieth-century photographs taken by Leo Frobenius in Ọ̀yọ́ (fig. 5.37; see Drewal, Pemberton, and Abiodun 1989, 14–15; Brandon 1983, 112–14).[75]

Indeed, beyond the issue of affordability, some houses have consciously chosen not to use *soperas* at all. As late as 1968 in Cuba, "houses where the old African traditions survive[d] most purely" resisted not only the luxury of decorative *soperas*, but also the *soperas'* great domestic companion, the *armario vitrina* or *canastillero*, preferring to keep their *orichas* in calabashes (*jícaras*) arranged over a small straw mat on the floor (González Huguet 1968, 34). Older practitioners and traditionalists argue that, in the beginning, the *ochas nacieron en güira* (were born in gourds), not in pots or *soperas*. Some Cuban and Cuban-American houses acquire for their *iyawós* a set of large half calabashes, ten or more inches wide, for the *asiento*.[76]

Hence, "vessels of [interior and exterior] domestic use," along with natural alternatives, such as gourds, have formed a continuum of types, which may correspond to specific motives. Still, ingenious blends of forms within this continuum abound. One midpoint solution between calabashes on the mat and *soperas* in the *canastillero* was employed in the house of Havana Lucumí founder Ña Margarita Armenteros (Ainá). She is remembered by her descendants for her "humble" approach to sacred vessels and altar arrangements. When Ña Margarita's "great-grandson" in the religion, "Papo" Reinaldo Remberto Chaguayceda, visited her house as a boy in 1926, the year of the last initiation she conducted before her death, he found "nothing of luxury." Ña Margarita's typical *oricha* vessel, "the most primitive form of that epoch," Papo related, was the *taza bola*, or *tazón chino:* an eating bowl of half spher-

Figure 5.46.—Alberto Druyat, painted hybrid *soperas* with gourd bodies, wood lids, and wood and metal bases, Matanzas, 2000. The vessels use a time-honored African-Cuban medium, the gourd (*güira*), to contain the *orichas* but render it in the style of a *sopera*, with a knobbed lid and shiny floral surface design. *Left to right:* Eleguá, Changó, Yemayá, and Eleguá (vessels for Eleguá are to contain the Eleguá to which one has been initiated, not the Eleguá of the warriors). Collection of the author. (Photograph by David H. Brown.)

ical form, typical of Chinese table services. Made of *loza*, they were covered with china plates. Ña Margarita arranged her set of *tazas bolas* atop a "rustic wood table," which served as an altar—just the kind of rustic table documented by Fernando Ortiz in 1906 (fig. 5.13, *bottom*). On the floor before the table, she would present the *orichas* with their *plaza* of fruit, cakes, and sweets, along with candles.[77] In contrast, Papo himself, a medical doctor who was initiated in the 1940s, is a descendant of the well-to-do Regla family that owned the Museum of Regla mansion before the Revolution moved them to a smaller house around the corner. Papo has always kept his *orichas* in authentic porcelain *soperas*, within a fine *armario vitrina* in his lavish *cuarto de santo*.

An ingeniously blended vessel style is seen in the religious artwork of septuagenarian Alberto Druyat of Matanzas. His "*soperas*" consist of open, elliptical gourds set upon little metal and wood cruciform bases. Their lids are smoothly carved wood covers. Thick coats of glossy enamel paint with decorative surface designs blend and unify the diverse materials—gourd, wood, metal—so they appear to be *soperas*, albeit of a curious shape (fig. 5.46).

"The Family of Soperas" and the "Porcelain House": Symbolic Interpretations of a Vessel Type

All of the mass-produced china and other domestic earthenwares used as *oricha* vessels could become appropriate "substitutes" for several apparent reasons, which I offer as hypotheses. First, they were morphologically similar and functionally identical to vessel types that had long served in West Africa. That twentieth-century Yoruba, as Andrew Apter discovered in Ayédé, Èkìtì, have turned to mass-produced domestic ceramics for their shrine pottery, replacing the work of traditional artisans with lidded casserole dishes and enameled decorative metal bowls, suggests how appropriate the Cuban substitutes were (see Apter 1992, plates 5, 9; Brown 1989, 579, fig. 5.40).

Second, in urban Cuban settings, where most of the *orichas* have shared living spaces with their priests, such domestic wares must have offered practical convenience and social discretion. High-fired stoneware or glazed earthenware ceramics, because of their impermeable surfaces, were sanitary and easily cleanable. Following blood sacrifices that had to be conducted in small homes, they could be effortlessly restored to their luster and returned to their *canastilleros;* this may have been important for reasons of discretion, for as late as the middle of this century, practitioners still worried about having "their *ochas* . . . thrown . . . into the street" (Angarica [1955?] n.d., 81), or worse, being attacked, lynched, or jailed (see Chávez Álvarez 1991; Helg 1995, 107–16; Palmié 2002, 210–43). After 1959, any open religious practitioners (Jehovah's Witnesses received the worst treatment) were denied jobs and rights; those found out could be humiliated, beaten, and denied jobs, ration rights, and services.[78]

Third, in their ritual context, vessels of the kitchen and the table setting drew upon their secular domestic associations as vehicles of family nurture and alimentation, themes associated with women. In Yoruba sacred arts, women were often idealized as generous, hardworking, and dedicated to giving birth and nurturing; they were often represented as kneeling figures that offered bowls or as caryatid figures supporting vessels of foodstuffs and *òrìṣà* secrets on their heads. In the religious arena, women and calabashes or bowls were, and continue to be, symbols of spiritual renewal. Thus, in the arts for the thunder god in Ọ̀yọ́, for example, the vessels women carry are "metaphor[s] for the devotee's womb" and, thus, "contain evidence of Sango's [procreative] power" (Drewal, Pemberton, and Abiodun 1989, 162–63). The Olóòkun priestesses of Ayédé, Èkìtì, process from the sacred bush grove and spring, where spiritual power is "raised," to the town, where it is transmitted within the king's throne room. As they carry on their heads calabashes of sacred water and the deity's secrets, prayers uttered wish for the "safe delivery" of these vessels, which renew the king's power, and embody the "future" of the king's rule and patrilineage in the form of male children (Apter 1992, 103–5). In the southwest, among the Ẹ̀gbádò Yoruba, as Thompson has shown, the ceramic lidded vessels for the deity called Eyinle, which are filled with cool river water and smooth river stones, incorporate the iconography of a female figure holding a bowl in a gesture of service and generosity (1993, 157). "Within these visibly hollow icons of community," James Lorand Matory lyrically writes, "priestesses nourish images of *motherhood* in the service of healing and the [strategic] projection of female priestly lineages across the landscape of the new patriliny.[79] . . . [T]he Yemoja shrine in Onigboho palace houses the two most important Yemoja calabashes (*igbá*) in the town. . . . They are full of river stones, cowries, and larger *cypraeidae* shells, and they sit atop large, whitened clay pots. . . . The entire contents are covered with windings of white cloth (*àlà*)" (Matory 1994, 155; Apter 1992, 101–6, 109–10).

More research, theorizing, and exposition than are permitted here would be required to launch and substantiate a transatlantic argument about the critical relation of iconography, gender, and spiritual power, a project that J. Lorand Matory has, in fact, already begun (1988, 1994, 225–30; forthcoming; see also Gleason 1987; Wafer 1991; Apter 1992, 111–14). However, it is worth noting that the Cuban counterparts of Yoruba pots and calabashes are also socially and ritually invested emblems of intergenerational sacred reproduction: of *orichas,* "heads," the *rama,* and the Lucumí tradition as a whole. Nicolás Angarica astutely employed the phrase "family of *soperas*" to refer to the ritual kinship network of an Ocha house. In his exposition, the sacred connections of house members (*familia de santo*), as well as the ties of blood family (*familia de sangre*), are subsumed and explained by the guiding proverb of the divination sign, Oché. Oché, five cowries, is dominated by the passionate, feminine "Owner the River," Ochún. Oché has to do with the family home, its kinship, codes of respect, and vicissitudes. Its guiding proverb, "Sangre que corre por sus venas" (Blood that runs in the veins; Angarica [1955?] n.d., 61), poetically traces the continuous current of life force that connects family members and their ancestors, *orichas* and humans, and links all the generations of *santo*, past and present. In the consecration and "birth" rituals of the *asiento*—most dramatically, in the "feeding" of *aché*-imbued blood and food offerings to the *orichas* in their fecund vessels—sacrifices help create the ritual kinship lines of "heads" and *oricha fundamentos* through "blood metaphors" (Matory 1994, 191; Mason and Edwards 1981, 26–31 and passim; Mason [1985] 1993, 61–75; Cabrera [1974] 1980, 165–73; Brandon 1990). In its largest semantic reach the proverb marks a continuum of domains, from blood coursing through human veins to rivers coursing through the land, and from the life-carrying blood and reproductive capacity of the human body to the sentiments and fellow feeling between individuals and groups. Historically, the river was the cradle and connector of civilizations (see M. Mason 1993).

Though the *orichas* utilize particular vessel types appropriate to them,[80] the *sopera*—the lidded soup tureen form—became so widespread that the term is often applied generically to all *oricha* vessels. All *oricha* vessels clearly share common functions and meanings: regardless of type, all participate in the "containment," "storing," "regulation," and "circulation" of *aché* (Apter 1987, 246–47; Matory 1986, 15, 138). All function as "containers" (Matory 1986, 84–91): of *fundamentos*, and as receptacles in which the *orichas* and, by extension, their priests, are nourished. As such, Matory astutely notes, all bear direct analogy to other kinds of "containers" or "vessels" that store, generate, and transmit energy, knowledge, genetic material, semantic codes, and/or vital liquids: the head, the breasts, the womb, round fecund stones, the *odu* of the divination systems, as well as the family, the compound, the kinship group, the town, and the kingdom (in Yorubaland; see Matory 1986, 77–94). Within the Lucumí idiom, all of the vessels play a central role in giving "birth" to new *orichas*, all participate in the consecration of new priests when presented to the head or body of the initiate, and all bear relation to another set of social and genealogical "containers"—the *casa* and the *rama* or *fundamento*. For these reasons, Angarica's turn of phrase, "family of *soperas*," is exquisitely apt, and Ogún's cauldron and Olokun's *tinaja* belong to this category as much as the "soup tureens" of Obatalá, Ochún, and Yemayá (see also Ecún 1985, passim).

Just as the mortar (*pilón*) came to be "shared" by all the *orichas*, so did the "*sopera*" form. In the modern Lucumí *regla*, the West African mortar and the English and French soup tureen converged on the same hybridized stage, yet coming to it from different legs of the transatlantic triangle (Africa, Europe, and the Americas). Both function within a meticulously organized scheme of attributes that classify and and embody each *oricha*'s particular *aché*. This scheme includes iconographically appropriate vessels; a determinate set of color- and number-coded "stones" (*otán*), standard sets ("hands") of cowrie shells (*dilogún*), and symbolic metal or wood "tools" (*herramientas*). In the modern initiatory scheme, all of the *orichas*' "*soperas*" are lined up within a determinate sequence on the floor, presented to the head, "fed" sacrifices, and interrogated through divination in much the same way (see chaps. 3 and 4). At the same time, within this unity, groups of the *orichas* would distinguish themselves with vessels and seats that differered in significant detail in order to mark their special domains, for example, in the case of the Warriors.

Internationally, and in Cuba, in the nineteenth through the twentieth centuries, the porcelain *sopera* has represented prestige. As an invested and valorized social and cultural currency, its acquisition could lend the *orichas* of the "house" a sense of distinction. Hence, soup tureens in porcelain, ironstone, creamware, and stoneware have been highly sought after. At one level, "porcelain is just white clay,"[81] and, therefore, no different from Yoruba pots of natural materials. Since it is made of kaolin, it just happens to be a very fine clay. It is simply more decorative. Like stoneware and earthenware clays, it is a by-product of glacial movement and water borne sedimentation and belongs to the same grand cycle of geologic transformation.[82] As the earth and waters, with their flora and fauna, the sun, and the wind are constitutents of *la naturaleza,* which embodies *poderes astrológicos* (astrological powers, as my *madrina* likes to say), so is clay, and so are the smooth, rounded stones contained within ceramic and wood vessels. Still, it is not unimaginable that the Cuban priests and priestesses who were attracted to porcelain and its imitations were as sensitive to its exceptional aesthetic qualities as those who originally discovered the medium and those who imported porcelain products from China into Europe. Porcelain, in its whiteness, purity, luster, and translucency, was seen to embody prestige and heavenly grace (see Palmer 1976, 13; *Compact OED,* s.v. "porcelain").[83] According to received accounts, undoubtedly apochryphal, the Italian Marco Polo was so impressed by porcelain's surface qualities and hardness during his trek through China that he named this rare and prestigious material after the cowrie shell (*porca, porcella, porcellana;* see Palmer 1976, 13; *Compact OED,* s.v. "porcelain"). In a bit of historical poetry, the oval Lucumí *sopera* would contain objects bearing the very qualities and ingredients for which porcelain became known: the lustrous cowrie shell, which was used as currency and as oracular equipment in Africa, as well as ancient, hard stones, worn smooth by water: the river and the sea. If there is something of heavenly grace in porcelain, so are there messages from heaven in the cowrie shells and immortality in the spirit-embodying stones.[84]

The special regard for "porcelain" (actual porcelain and its "china" facsimiles) within Havana Lucumí communities is evidenced, albeit anecdotally, in the name given to a well-known Ocha house on Calle Estrella. It is called La Porcelana, and the name became synonymous with its late owner, an Afro-Cuban *madrina.* When I visited the house in 1994, La Porcelana, a tiny, stooped octogenarian, had meticulously arranged on her living room walls, all the way up to the fifteen-foot ceiling, her prodigious collection of decorative porcelain plates gained over her more than fifty years in the religion. The plates, along with other decorative porcelain objects, including *soperas* and decorative animals, were gifts from the numerous priests she had initiated, as well as from the houses she visited during her *yaworage.* The plates given as gifts to La Porcelana embody in lustrous decorative porcelain the bonds of ritual family kinship, the status of this famous priestess, and the gratitude of her *ahijados* and admirers. The china plate, given as a gift to *iyawós* who enter a house of Ocha for the first time, also represents a concrete wish or prayer that the new priest always find nourishment and nurture. Later, the plates may be displayed along with the *soperas* in the *canastillero,* making this cabinet look even more like the Cuban bourgeois *armario vitrina* (cf. fig. 5.32 and plate 25).[85] La Porcelana is a priestess of Ochún, the *oricha* of ideal feminine beauty, for whom lustrous decorative domestic objects in porcelain (especially chinoiserie), as well as expensive cloth, gold, and brass, are particularly appropriate (see plate 26, fig. 5.44).

The special regard for the porcelain *sopera* form is also revealed by the treatment of *oricha* vessels that are neither *soperas* nor porcelain, but that aspire to reproduce in a variety of ways the *sopera*'s form and/or aesthetic qualities. It is a case of the exception that proves the rule. Where *soperas* may not be available or affordable, approximations of their form, luster, and decorativeness are sought through the hand painting of bisque-fired earthenware pots (*tinajas*) with the *orichas'* colors and with the surface application of floral designs typically found on *soperas.* Apparently, the surface luster and repertoire of organic decorative motifs from the nineteenth century export trade are so highly prized that they have also been applied to the wood vessels and pedestals (*batea* and *pilón*) of Changó (plate 17) and the painted gourd *"soperas"* of Alberto Druyat. With Cuba's material privations, spray paint provides a glossy, if not fine, finish. Gold paint is often added in order to gild molded floral reliefs or stamps applied to the surface of bisque-fired *tinajas* before firing (fig. 5.35). As indicated, in what became an elegant tradition for adorning the vessels of Yemayá and Ochún, makers encrust the surface of earthenware *tinajas* with seashells. In examples exhibited in Havana museums, while the shells appropriately refer through metonymy to the sea floor or the shoreline, their opalescent surfaces invoke the luster of porcelain, and their decorative patterns reproduce the floral motifs characteristic of export *soperas* (fig. 5.44).

In sum, the *sopera* and the *canastillero* became signs of prestige for the Lucumí *orichas* meriting the royal, luxury aesthetic of the "palace" as early, perhaps, as the last third of the nineteenth century, if not before. The porcelain, creamware, ironstone, stoneware, glazed earthenware *sopera*, and even cheaper approximations, such as the painted terra-cotta pot, were consistent morphologically, aesthetically, and semantically with the emerging system of *adornos a gusto criollo*, which included other colonial-era signs of prestige and authority: the satin *ropa de santo*, the jewelry-encrusted pasteboard crown, the canopied throne, *oricha* pedestals shaped like classical columns or amphoras, and even gilt candelabra. Aesthetically, the quality of surface richness, luminosity, and density of decoration, particularly romantic organic motifs, is common to the principal royal *oricha* attributes (crowns, garments, thrones, *soperas*, and *paños*) and is shared, as well, by the principal attributes of the saints. In contrast, itinerant *orichas* of the "outside," who are also unequivocally male deities, such as the Warriors and Osain, and *orichas* of the poor and the land (San Lázaro and Oricha Oko), typically utilize unrefined vessels of unpainted clay, metal, or gourd.[86] Correspondingly, they live, unlike the *orichas* who reside in *soperas* and the *canastillero*, on the floor year-round. The Warriors live on the floor behind the front door to the house (see González Huguet 1968; Brown 1999).

For the throne displays of the Middle Day, drummings, and birthdays, such "borrowed," modified, and reinvented object types, dedicated to the public presentation of *orichas*, were integrated with four principal Yoruba-derived ritual art forms that completed the hybridized ensemble of Lucumí initiatory kingship: the *iyawó*'s painted head (the *osu* and *peinado*), the *collares de mazo*, the beaded or painted dance wands, and the royal mortar (*odó*, or *pilón*). Still, many of these putatively Yoruba-derived forms were remodeled according to the creole aesthetic of Cuba's palace of the Obá Lucumí. As indicated, the painted representations that complement the *osu* on the Middle Day—pendant earrings, handlebar mustaches and goatees, and crisscross boot lacings on the legs—theatrically conjure into this palace the fancy nobility of ladies and gentlemen who might have inhabited a royal "court." Changó, the archetypal "king" of this court and its palace, would enforce a special sumptuary clause to highlight his own exceptionalism: rather than directly mingling with the *orichas* of the *canastillero* or the Warriors behind the door, he would reign throughout the year on the palace's most essential throne, the *pilón*.

The mortar, a quintessential attribute of the Ọ̀yọ́ imperial cults, was first reproduced in Cuba with the same squat, tapered cilindrical form, low-relief carved surface, and polychrome adornment of documented West African prototypes (plate 19, fig. 4.21). Yet it, too, was eventually captured and transformed by the *gusto criollo*. Late-nineteenth- and early-twentieth-century mortar examples in Havana's Fernando Ortiz collection resemble urns and garden pedestals. Their profiles vary from the whimsical curve-reverse-curve rococo to the sober, contained neoclassical style (see, e.g., plate 17). Unsurprisingly, the mortars most commonly sold in *botánicas* in the United States and Cuba, like some examples in the Cuban museum collections, gild the pedestal form with the decorative impulse of the *sopera*, adding organic motifs of flowers, leaves, and sometimes fish, and a high-gloss, transluscent finish. Furthermore, many mortars overdetermine their messages of royalty and prestige by adding the crenelated brickwork tower motif of Santa Bárbara's chromolithographs and statues—a motif that doubles as the royal "castle" of Changó. Others have recast the mortar altogether as the goblet form from Santa Bárbara's chromolithograph (fig. 5.47).

Figure 5.47.—Cosme Guio, pedestal (*odó*, or *pilón*) and vessel (*batea*) for Changó, which takes the form of the goblet and host of Santa Bárbara, Havana, 1998. Lathe-turned cedar, varnish, and gold paint. Hand-carved roosters, male sheep, and Changó's six "tools" (thunderaxes) are represented. The six standing "tools" of Changó take the form of the radiating grace lines of the Eucharist. Collection of the author. (Photograph by David H. Brown.)

The mortar and *batea* of Rigoberto Rodríguez Duque's Changó exemplify the riotous extreme of the decorative continuum. The compound object integrates an urnlike mortar shape with a *batea* that features five rising crenelated towers (plate 17). The mortar and *batea* surface appears to be seamlessly painted with bold, highly contrasting red and white floral designs. Still, these designs are polyvocal: they read as floral abstractions and as thunderaxes and rams' horns (fig. 4.21). Moreover, while the Changó figure atop the *batea* styles himself as the *negrito guarachero* of the vernacular theater and cabaret rumba genres, he carries on his head, in Yoruba fashion, the upright thunderax (*oché*). Consistent with the hybrid persona of *rumbero* and thunder god, his two handheld instruments read, from afar, as the maracas of an Afro-Cuban bandleader. However, upon close inspection, they are two of Changó's principal attributes, the thunderax and the thunder rattle (*acheré*), which are held parallel and upright in a classic transatlantic pattern that mirrors the symmetry of the double thunderbolts upon his head (cf. plates 17, 19). If the figure's clothes update, albeit in a stereotyped manner, more soberly dressed Yoruba-styled nineteenth-century Changó shrine figures, they not only maintain Changó's signature colors. They also project a popular Afro-Cuban conception of Changó as the master of percussion-driven ritual music, the "king of dance," a lover of life, and a flashy, irrepressible macho performer.

INNOVATION AND RE-AFRICANIZATION: THE *ORICHAS* AND THE TRANSATLANTIC MARKETPLACE

Lydia Cabrera's elderly mid-twentieth-century sources told her that the *orichas'* most lavish altars and consecration garments in the nineteenth century were embellished not only with imported European luxuries, but also with trade goods of another kind. An extraordinary array of African adornments and ritual materials were imported "in the limited but lucrative business waged by the Canary

Islanders, who supplied themselves with merchandise on the West Coast of Africa in order to sell it to the priests of the Lucumí and other African cults in Cuba. . . . 'Many adornments of the Santo came from Guinea, [such as] skins, teeth, animal horns, necklaces, cloth, rugs, caps that were called "fila," and everything else that was missing [cowries, animal claws, *obí* (kola nut), *loros* (African gray parrot), calabash gourds, monkeys]. In their houses, the Padres [*padrinos*] and the Babalá [*babalawos*] dressed in African style'" (Cabrera [1974] 1980, 176).[87]

The existence of the shipbound transfer of West African goods directly to Cuba gains some support in the growing literature on the extensive nineteenth-century maritime interaction between major Atlantic port cities, including Havana (Salvucci 1991, 46; Price 1991). The importation from Lagos of similar West African goods into Brazil during the nineteenth century, particularly black soap, red parrot feathers (*ìkóòdẹ*), four-lobed *kọ̀lá* nuts (*obì àbàtà*), palm oil nuts (called *dendê* in Brazil), and African Malagueta pepper (*ataare*), is more strongly documented (Omari 1984, 40; Voeks 1997, 45). According to Hugh Thomas, by the middle of the nineteenth century, the illegal slave trade "went direct Havana-Africa-Havana or Brazil-Africa-Brazil" (1971, 137), and it is possible that trade goods accompanied slaves on the same ships; indeed, it is also possible that black sailors, and religious agents, such as Salvador Montalvo, utilized this transatlantic route to recover the secrets of Olofin for Cuba's Yoruba *babalawos* (see chap. 2; see also Linebaugh and Rediker 2000, 152–67).

While Lucumí altars and garments must have undergone innovations by the late nineteenth century with prestige objects borrowed from secular and sacred Spanish-Cuban material culture, they were also, apparently, "reafricanized" (Bastide [1960] 1978, 66) by the West African trade goods, as Cabrera's sources suggested. Yet, just as innovation did not mean the dilution of diasporic cultural forms on a mechanical continuum from "more African" to "more European" "traits" (Herskovits [1945] 1966), "re-Africanization" did not necessarily mean an essential return to Yoruba origins. Even for Herskovits, the "reabsor[ption of] Africanisms" occurred in critical relation to changing social relationships and processes (1941, 133). In the Bahian case, for example, the nineteenth-century importation of West African religious goods, knowledge, and institutions by free people of color who traveled back and forth across the Atlantic occurred in the context of reform-like movements, the purist agendas of which were permeated by their leaders' strategies of institutional invention and self-promotion (Bastide [1960] 1978, 165; see also Wafer 1991, 56–58; Matory 1999).[88]

In Cuba, just as the "reforms" of Efuche and Obadimelli were strategic innovations of Lucumí practices based on highly selective utilizations of West African resources, so the imported religious goods must also have been used selectively. For example, though the African trade goods that arrived in Cuba evidently included *kọ̀lá* nuts (*obì-àbàtà*), which were embraced, and endure, in Bahia as a fundamental Yoruba-derived divination instrument, the Lucumí substituted the coconut (*obi-agbón* [from the Yoruba *àgbọn*]) to serve the same purpose (see Mason [1985] 1993, 76–92). It is worth asking what status imported West African goods would have had in nineteenth-century urban, coastal Cuba, and what criteria of selection were operative when they were encountered by Lucumí priests in the sacks and baskets of Canary Island and other traders. Were they essential "historical sources" to be reclaimed, or did they take their places among other "forms current in the [heterogeneous commercial] environment" (Reisman 1970), which were subject to selective utilization? By the turn of the twentieth century, some *cabildos* with African leaders, as Irene Wright and Roche y Monteagudo documented, had felicitously embraced and "traditionalized" imported soup tureens and decorative European-made cloth, but not necesarily the "calabashes" and *fila* caps that appeared on Cabrera's import lists. In contrast, some purist houses apparently continued to contain their *orichas* in calabashes up through the 1960s research of Lydia González Huguet (1968).

Notwithstanding these sharp contrasts between certain of the foregoing media, one issue remains clear: a reestablished continuity with the West Coast of Africa enabled Cuban Lucumí religious practice in very essential ways. Though the Ochún of the El Cerro Sociedad Santa Rita y San Lázaro could live in a china *sopera* surrounded by a Canary Island shawl, or repose before a yellow satin bed-throne, Ochún's priests could not have been initiated at all without the essential "African seeds" of Cabrera's West African trade list. These ingredients constituted the *aché del santo* ("African seeds"), which is no less indispensable for the *asiento* within Ocha than the secret of Olofin for the initiation of *babalawos* within Ifá. Moreover, no initiation, no sacrifice, no festival could take place without the transmission of ritual knowledge and bodily practice (oracular narratives, liturgical music, dance movement language, and drum fabrication) of West African origin, which has been documented by researchers who emphasize the continuity and conservation of Yoruba practices in Cuba (see, e.g., Thompson 1983; Mason 1992, 1996).

Still, the possibility that priests could "choose," through purchase, the way their Ocha houses and ceremonies looked by selecting from an array of African and European trade goods, as well as from the mundane houseware shelves at the corner *bodega*, renders quite uninteresting any essentialist argument for African origin as a determinant of any given diasporic cultural arrangement. In late-nineteenth- and early-twentieth-century Cuba, which priests "dressed in African style" and which dressed in "the robes of the saints"? The African leader of the El Cerro Santa Rita *cabildo*, Papá Silvestre Erice, the "last Lucumí pontiff," who died in about 1915, remained in the memory of his flock wearing not a Yoruba *agbada* gown, but a royal "mantle of precious stones and fringes of all colors" (Castellanos 1916, 57). Roche y Monteagudo's 1908 photographs of this *cabildo* only begin to suggest the kinds of radically bricolaged assemblages of saints, satins, china, candelabra, and Canary Island shawls, animal skins, horns, necklaces, calabashes, cowries, specialized sacrificial offerings, and Lucumí musical instruments that could be constituted (figs. 5.10, 5.11).

In short, the place of "origin" of Cuban Lucumí iconography belongs to the specific historical conjunctures, spaces, and cultural and countercultural imaginations of the "modern" Atlantic world (see Gilroy 1993; Linebaugh and Rediker 2000; Palmié 1994). Within, and as a result of, the brutal capitalist Atlantic triangle, hybrid societies and cultures among continentals, colonists, and subject peoples were produced. The peculiarly Cuban *adornos al gusto criollo* of the palace of the Obá Lucumí emerged out of the fertile meeting of transatlantic movement, exchange, conservation, resistance, and innovation; its strategies combined the bricoleur's "consuming symbolic ambition," which both perpetuates and revises dominant discourses and, as Zora Neale Hurston aptly put it, the "will to adorn."[89] Yet these strategic "cultural" innovations cannot, and should not, be disengaged from their local and global contexts of struggle within specific colonial and neocolonial arenas (see Smith 1957; Comaroff 1985; Comaroff and Comaroff 1992, 1994; Palmié 1993). Thus is encountered, for example, the "origin" of Changó's crenelated neoclassical urn with its polyvocal surface design; Changó's satin thrones and garments, which are adorned with leopard skin, raffia fiber, and cowrie shells; the *orichas'* pasteboard crowns, which proudly sprout the red tail feathers of the African gray parrot sewn into theatricalized regalia of royal display (fig. 4.12); Ogún and Eleguá's Cuban farmer's *sombrero* adorned with cowrie shells (plate 13); the altars of Oricha Oko, which embed brightly painted Spanish terracotta roof tiles, coconuts, and a miniature ox-drawn plow or sugar-plantation cart in plastic basins of consecrated earth; and china soup tureens filled with cowries and stones that descend from those putatively swallowed by the slaves and carried on ships in the Middle Passage to the New World.

When Oddedeí located the origin of Ocha initiation in the palace of the Obá Lucumí, she was right, but the palace had been remodeled. The prestige adornments of the *obá's* palace—the pasteboard crown, satin throne and *ropa de santo*, brocaded *paño, soperas, collares de mazo*, beaded staff, and Changó's royal mortar—along with the essential "focus" of stones, herbs, blood, shells, and *herramientas*—had become standardized as the modern iconographic and ritual repertoire of Lucumí initiatory kingship. The Lucumí palace occupied an imperial landscape differentiated according to the dramatis personae of a condensed and reworked Lucumí *oricha* pantheon, which was grouped into the kings and queens of the "house" and *canastillero*, on the one hand, and the itinerant Warriors of the "street" and the "bush" on the other hand. The remodeled individual characteristics of the Lucumí *orichas* could "resemble" both their putative West African "sources" and the particular "forms current in the environment" of Cuban cultural history. For example, Changó is a Cuban macho, the loyal but volatile guy who is always in your face. Ochún is the flirtatious, vain, cinnamon-skinned *mulata* who flutters her eyelashes behind her fan and reposes on gold satin beds, or else the "witch" who makes fearsome potions. Agayú, the powerful volcano, has so seamlessly blended with aspects of Saint Christopher that even the most purist accounts of this *oricha*'s character delineate him as the "ferryman . . . who carries people across great obstacles," distances, and bodies of water (Mason 1985a, 38; Kelly and Rogers 1993, 60–62). Oricha Okó, the Owner of the Earth, condenses the iconography of Saint Isidor and Cuba's colonial sugar industry: two miniature oxen pulling a plough or a miniature sugar cane plantation cart, as well as the instantly recognizable architectural detail of the Spanish-style roofing tile, the concave terra-cotta (*teja*). Yemayá's nautical iconography is of a piece with the popular adornments of the Virgin of Regla's chapels: boats, ships' wheels and anchors, skeleton keys, oars, and mermaids. If the Lucumí Warriors, Eleguá, Ogún, and Ochosi, owe their forest occupations and iconography to the itinerant Yoruba hunter-herbalist prototype, they were remodeled in the historical experiences of conquest, slavery, revolution, and urbanization as fierce, path-clearing paramilitary *cimarrones* and combatants who wear *sombreros* and wield hooked branches, machetes, and bows and arrows. This differentiated dramatic landscape, on which such royalty and warriors engage in warfare, resistance, sacrifice, human sustenance, healing, and social transformation, built its scenery over a Cuban cultural geography and environment that was itself historically emergent: the opposed categories of *occidental* and *oriental, la ciudad* and *el campo, la casa* and *la calle, lo africano* and *lo criollo, la esclavitud* and *la libertad, lo masculino* and *lo feminino*. The culturally and politically invested landscape of "town" and "bush," and its corresponding attributes, were manifested not only in the historical imagination and mythologies of the wars of independence and the revolution (loyalist west vs. revolutionary east, the "ditch" across the island, etc.), but also in nineteenth-century African carnival's orderly, decorous royal processions and athletic "African" *diablitos:* African street performance both revised and perpetuated the codes of colonial social and cultural space. The iconography of the "royal" *orichas* and the warriors follows a similar typology: thrones of satin versus "leaves," elegant mortars versus jagged stones and raw trunks, crowns versus straw hats, royal hand regalia versus weapons and work tools. Obatalá's house of order and hierarchy can be subverted by the ethos of the forest and the street.

The emergence and establishment of the resilient modern Lucumí initiatory system and its multivocal iconography coincided with the period of emancipation, but also with the greatest repression, marginalization, and disenfranchisement of Afro-Cubans (1880s–1920s), which was substantiated and rationalized through witchcraft accusation, show trials, and blackface comic theater, with its parodies of Afro-Cuban music, religion, and carnival processions (see Helg 1995; Moore 1997; Chávez Álvarez 1991; Ortiz [1906] 1973). Further historical research might illuminate specific links between emergent Afro-Cuban labor and political organization on the one hand, and religious institutionalization on the other hand (see Scott 1985). It remains clear, for example, that most of the "transitional" Afro-Cuban *sociedades* or *cabildos* were founded or reorganized during the first twelve years of the twentieth century, coterminous with two violent political bookends—the first American occupation (1899–1902) and the "race war" of 1912. On the cultural front, further study of the feedback loop of reciprocal appropriations between racist commercial theatricalizations and the Afro-Cuban music of the *barrios* documented by Robin Moore from the 1880s through the 1930s might illuminate processes in iconographic innovations within the Lucumí religion. In any event, it is obvious that changes in the Lucumí religion during this same period did not occur in a social, political, and cultural vacuum. If Lucumí ritual and iconography owe their foundations to Yoruba precedents, they are also heavily indebted to the vision and strategies of Cuban Lucumí founders and followers within religious communities that struggled within the "conditions" they encountered in their houses, *ramas, barrios,* towns, and the country as a whole. It is clear, for example, that influential practitioners have engaged in dialogue with ethnographers, and have read, revised, and applied elements of ethnological discourse since the first decade of the twentieth century, that is, since the moment at which Fernando Ortiz penned the first Afro-Cuban ethnography ([1906] 1973; Palmié 2002, 248–59). And, since the early 1960s, state-sponsored displays of Cuban "national folk culture"—ethnographic museums and cultural performances, particularly of music and dance—have fed back in varying degrees into Lucumí practice (Hagedorn 2001; Velez 1998). Ritual artists regularly use ethnographic museum exhibits and catalogs, and photographs in cultural magazines as models to refashion new altar objects. Similarly, Odeddei's laconic statement of the origins and ethos of Ocha initiation, "To make a Santo is to make a king, and *kariocha* is a ceremony of kings, like those of the palace of the *Obá Lucumí,*" finds meaning not merely within a narrowly conceived Yoruba tradition, but within a context of Cuban historical nomenclatures.

It would, perhaps, be willful and simplistic, at this point, to assert that innovations in Lucumí institutions, ritual, and iconography were motivated entirely by "resistance" to dominant institutions and narratives. Many practitioners have not been politically self-conscious in any explicit way or politically active within explicitly oppositional institutions. At the same time, within the *habitus* of Afro-Cuban religious practice, for example, the strategies of the secret—the dynamic of "hiding" and revealing—have generated multivocal fruit in complicated, "syncretic" *oricha* displays, not to mention esoteric and coded ways of speaking about the religion and an ethic of "discretion" in relation to multiple audiences (the uninitiated, ritual juniors, nosy neighbors, and government authorities). Practitioners who have taken on the added role of public performer, no less in 1937, when Ortiz first presented Lucumí *batá* drumming, than within the National Folklore Group of Cuba, have had to negotiate ritual and "folkloric" modes of "working *santo*" and doing their "job," respectively. Before any given heterogeneous audience, the *orichas* that appear during stage and carnival performance are apprehended in multiple ways (Hagedorn 2001, 85, 98). While skeptical practitioners regard state-sponsored performance as "mere folklore," others accept it as a public affirmation of their private practices. It is indisputable that *oricha* references and rhythms within Cuban popular music (in such groups as N.G. La Banda, Los Van Van, and Orishas) have permitted young practitioners to bridge their old family traditions with vital participation in "new" national and international cultural currents, while also introducing nonpractitioners to themes of real importance.[90] As observers condescended to the splendidly dressed *cabildo* royalty of the nineteenth century, some mainstream contemporary observers might also misunderstand the aesthetic and meaning of *oricha* kings, queens, and deified warriors of the Día del Medio as nothing more than amusing Halloween-like costumes or the Three Musketeers. Enthroned *orichas,* like the old *cabildo* kings and queens, are neither "kings for a day" nor objects of amusement. The royalty and warriors of this semiunderground religion, La Regla de Ocha, formed the beloved and heroic dramatis personae of an epic alternative narrative or "counter-narrative" (see Lipsitz 1990), built upon themes of ancestral continuity and connection to nature's forces, spiritual empowerment, agency, personal transformation through initiation and priesthood, respect and mutual aid through membership in a "house," healing and self-defense through ritual work, and, in Maxine Kamari Clarke's eloquent phrase, "reclaimed nobility" (Clarke 1997). However, as the Lucumí religion was adopted and developed among the Black American Yoruba Movement studied by Clarke, its context became more explicitly political and its enabling narrative more explicitly about resistance. Consonant with the themes of this chapter, the closing section explores another case of innovations within the Lucumí religion and suggests just how swiftly and comprehensively such innovations can occur (see also Mintz and Price [1976] 1992, 48–49). The aesthetic of the Cuban *gusto criollo,* which developed in the late nineteenth and early twentieth centuries by people who are venerated today in ancestral *moyuba* prayers, has been subject to successive revisions by new generations of creative agents, whose experience is both similar to and different from that of Cuban practitioners.

CODA: REVISING *SANTERÍA* AND THE *ADORNOS A GUSTO CRIOLLO:* "REVERSIONISM" AND THE BLACK AMERICAN YORUBA MOVEMENT

> Possibilities of "traditional" life and magic are realized on a ten-acre plot hidden in the "bush" of Beaufort Count, South Carolina
> —Maxine Kamari Clarke, 1997

The first African American initiated into the Afro-Cuban Lucumí system went on to inaugurate in Harlem a movement of Black American Yoruba, whose nationalist agenda included establishing an "African state" on American soil (Hunt 1979, 28). In the 1950s, the nascent group's ambitious and creative leader, Walter Serge King, who had immersed himself in studies of Haitian Vodou and ancient Egyptian religion, was inspired by Ghanaian independence (1957) to advocate the wearing of West African clothing, and later participated in the movement to learn the Swahili language, which is spoken throughout eastern and southeastern Africa. Yet, after his exposure to the "Santo" in Harlem by his Afro-Cuban-American friend and colleague, Christopher Oliana (Hunt 1979, 26), and the eventual initiation of the two men into the *rama* of Fermina Gómez in Matanzas, Cuba, in August 1959, the Yoruba of southwestern Nigeria became their specific reclaimed connection to African heritage and served as the social, cultural, and religious model for the elaboration of the cultural nationalist movement.

In 1960 King, Oliana, and others opened the Shango Temple on 125th Street in Harlem. Among their many cultural objectives was to purge what they saw as the religion's colonialist legacy, particularly its European and Catholic elements. The community of New York Cuban Santería priests, who were, technically, their religious elders, "objected to the fact that [King] began wearing Yoruba clothes and refused to use Catholic saints and statues in the worship ceremonies" (Hunt 1979, 27). King explains that "numerous other Afro-Americans were entering the traditional Cuban Santo system and only timidly and surreptitiously substituting Yoruba images in place of Christian images. These for the most part avoided Yoruba attire which was angrily prohibited by their Afro-Cuban God-parents. Indeed, there was some resentment among certain white Cubans when informed that the Religion was of African origin" (quoted in Gregory 1986, 63). Given the spirit of militancy among many young activists of the time, nonblack Cuban priests themselves became antithetical to the emerging Yoruba movement, just as whites were deemed antithethical to the Black Power Movement, which grew out of Malcolm X's early 1960s self-reliance and anticolonialist vision and the Student Non-Violent Coordinating Committee's (SNCC) Black Power platform under Stokely Carmichael as of 1966 (Van Deburg 1992, 134). According to Walter Serge King, "we had introduced a racism into the religion that didn't exist among the Cubans . . . and . . . they couldn't understand my extremely severe racial attitudes at that time. So that naturally alienated a lot of them" (quoted in Palmié 1995, 79). It was not long before King and his group split entirely with the Cubans (Hunt 1979, 28). After founding the Yoruba Oyotunji community in 1971, which they eventually established permanently in Shelton, South Carolina, in 1974, King traveled to Nigeria, where he was initiated as a *babalawo* in 1972 (Hunt 1979, 63; Clarke 1997, 221). The Ọ́ọ̀ni of Ifẹ̀ ordered the Ifẹ̀ chiefs to perform initiation rites upon him in order that he become Oba Oseijeman Adefunmi I, "the first of a line of New World Yoruba kings consecrated" by the Ọ́ọ̀ni. In August 1972 he was proclaimed the Alaṣe Ọba and made the King of Oyotunji in October (Clarke 1997, 221). Ultimately, he became known as His Royal Highness Oba Ofuntola Oseigeman Adelabu Adefunmi I (Ofuntola or Adefunmi, for short). He is addressed respectfully as *Ká biyè sí* ("Your Royal Highness"), the formal greeting addressed to Yoruba kings and chiefs (see Adefunmi 1982; Abraham 1946, 357).[91]

Within its utopian cultural nationalist agenda, and its narrative reconfiguration of a direct West African–African-American "genealogy of reclaimed nobility" (see Clarke 1997), the Black American Yoruba Movement sought to uncover and embrace an ancient African origin in order to remake black American identity on American soil. With its emphasis on reconstructing a culture, as well as a "village" society and an "African state," the revision of iconography was central to the project of reforming hitherto colonialized social space, mind, and body—particularly through the living environment, rituals, and everyday dress (see Comaroff 1985). Appropriate iconography was central to black American cultural and religious identity, and, therefore, the modern Lucumí system's *adornos a gusto criollo*, as well as its initiatory system, would have to be thoroughly revised.

Oyotunji Village foregrounded the same chronotope that animated Oddedeí's folk history, the "king's palace," but it was not the creolized Cuban palace of the Obá Lucumí; it was an applied ethnographic recreation of "traditional" Yoruba imperial institutions and material culture. The recreation of the "traditional" depended, in part, upon a picture of the Yoruba sketched over and over again in the "ethnographic present" by any number of texts to come out of West African fieldwork (see below). The model of "Yoruba tradition," in short, relied upon historically specific modes of knowledge production that had developed within the field of anthropology since the late nineteenth century (see, e.g., Fabian 1983; Asad 1973). Traditional Yoruba culture should appear as it did on the eve of colonialism, that is, as it had from time immemorial: the *orichas* of Cuba would become the *orishas* or *òrìṣà* of New York and North Carolina.

This is an intriguing case in which the agenda to reclaim an essential African identity was also a creative and conscious self-refashioning on a newly plotted African Diaspora "map-history" (see Gilroy 1993, 1–40; Clifford 1994, 315–19; see also Scott 1991). In its attempt to reconnect directly with Africa by leapfrogging one proximate diasporic location—Cuba—the movement chose another location of proximate origins—South Carolina, near Beaufort, in which to settle. As Paule Marshall's New York protagonist, Avey Johnson, in *Praisesong for the Widow*, looks to the proximate, African-derived "big drum dance" on the Caribbean island of Carriacou as a "step closer" to Africa in negotiating her complex identity (Kendrix 1998, 12, Marshall 1983, 74–83, 149–256; Washington 1981, 322–23), the movement selected an already-familiar "southern home"[92] directly associated with black American "roots" and "routes" (see Gilroy 1993, 133; Clifford 1994, 1997). South Carolina represented a "ritual ground" for an identity-transforming *communitas* (Stepto 1979, 68, 73) and, like Carriacou, was a "step closer" to Africa on the American north-south axis. Going south meant "going home," a figure deployed in a variety of African Diaspora secular and sacred performance contexts (see Marks 1974, 109)[93] Indeed, this "return" to the South, traced over a real and imagined diasporic "map-history" or "symbolic topography," reproduces the literal and figurative journeys of "descent" or "immersion," in Robert Stepto's seminal formulation, that black writers and artists have pursued since W. E. B. Du Bois's 1903 *Souls of Black Folk* (see Stepto 1979, 67, 78, 80, and 52–91). "Descent" is also the diametrical opposite of stealing away to freedom, following the North Star, the underground railroad, and the great migration northward (1877–1920s). Still, though Paule Marshall's protagonists do not usually get to Africa itself (Kendrix 1998), the Black American Yoruba made formative pilgrimages back and forth across the Atlantic, seeking "authentic" origins in their ultimate, newly reclaimed homeland in Yoruba country, particularly in the kingdom of Ọ̀yọ́ (Hunt 1979, 63; Clarke 1997, chap. 2, 95). Apropos of this Yoruba diasporic extension, the name given to the African village, Oyotunji, means "Oyo rises again" (Curry 1997, 6). In contrast, in the Cuban setting seventy years earlier, though the African Adechina had clearly directed the creole Bernardo Rojas to plumb the deep knowledge of Yoruba culture within his religious practice, on the social axis, he directed Bernardo Rojas and other creoles to "go west," rather than go "home," in the capitalist sense of building fortunes in business.

Iconographic and Bodily Reform

Oyotunji Village became the principal site for the elaboration of a particular version of the Yoruba religion in the United States, in its social, ritual, environmental, architectural, linguistic, and aesthetic dimensions. Within the movement's identity politics, many aspects of the creole Cuban version of the Lucumí religion were irrelevant, if not antagonistic, to the African-American historical experience and to the village's agenda of self-determination: "the Cubans had decided for themselves how they wanted to reorganize the religion and culture and so, too, had the Brazilians. Therefore, it was time for Black Americans to decide what the religion and culture meant to them and how they were going to preserve it" (Hunt 1979, 39).

The wearing of "African attire at all times" became village law. Village life was based upon a reading of Yoruba social structure, entailing the organization of the stratified institutions of Yoruba kingship and chieftaincy, such juridical and ancestral societies as Ogboni (Hunt 1979, 58, 70, 72; see also Bascom 1969b; Clarke 1997, 100), and traditional gender hierarchies. The religious system was reorganized around the principle that each deity should have its own temple and priesthood (Hunt 1979, 75; Clarke 1997, 58),[94] a notion that had currency in the ethnographic literature prior to revisionist scholarship in the 1980s and 1990s (see chap. 3).

The village's *orisha* iconography in carved and painted shrine images was reformulated upon an interpretation of African models. *Babalorisha* John Mason, one of the movement's luminaries of the second generation, and following the direction of Robert Farris Thompson, recently interpreted the aesthetic agenda of the movement, dubbing its aesthetic production "Yoruba-American art." "Oyotunji served as the focal point in the United States for the renaissance of traditional Yoruba art from earlier times. There was a conscious, all-out effort to remove Catholic/slave vestiges from Yoruba worship and to reclaim the best parts of an ancient and valued past in order to build a free and enlightened future" (J. Mason 1994, 244). The bold idea of reclaiming the "best parts of an ancient and valued past" as a blueprint for the nation of the future remains as indebted to Herder's Romantic Nationalism and Matthew Arnold's seminal, but conservative, concept of culture ("the best that has been thought and said") as it is to American pan-Africanist philosophy (see Wilson 1973; Arnold 1966; Williams [1976] 1983, 89–91; Locke [1925] 1992; Schomburg [1925] 1992). The idea of a *renaissance* of Yoruba-American art, which follows the Dark Ages of slavery, colonialism, and racial oppression, has key precedents in the writings of twentieth-century African-American pan-Africanists and Romantic Nationalists, such as W. E. B. DuBois and Alain Locke. Having studied in Berlin, they were conversant with nationalist historiography and theory, including nineteenth-century Zionism, and acted as principal "midwives" of the Harlem Renaissance (see Fredrickson 1987; Rampersad 1992, xi–xii, xvi; Locke [1925] 1992, xxv–xxvii, 14). In addition, the Yoruba movement's intellectual precedents, as well as those of the Harlem Renaissance, are encountered in the centuries-old tradition of Ethiopianism, which revolved around the promise and ultimate redemption of the "African race" ("Ethiopia"), its prophesied restoration to the level of world esteem (formerly possessed by such great classical black civilizations as ancient Egypt), and its political, cultural, and psychological liberation from the shackles of colonialism (see Appiah 1992; Raboteau 1983; Locke [1925] 1992, 14).[95] Ironically, the notion of "a renaissance" depends upon conventional Western definitions of the Renaissance, as encountered in any art history textbook: a "*rediscovery*," following the Middle Ages, "of the principles already known to the ancient Greeks and Romans" (Tansey and Kleiner 1996, 686; emphasis in original), not least among which were humanism, subject matter, aesthetics, and scientific canons of proportion from the Greek classical period (fifth century B.C.E.). Finally, the culturological idea that pure and authentic "African" elements could, analytically, not to mention practically, be disengaged from "European" ones—that is, that the "Yoruba" could be cleanly extracted from the Cuban Lucumí—was squarely in the intellectual tradition of Melville J. Herskovits and the trait diffusion theory of modern cultural anthropology (Herskovits 1938, 1941, 1964, [1945] 1966). The question remains whether the genuine essences of traditions and cultures can be uncovered, reclaimed, and preserved or must, of necessity, be reimagined and re-invented (see Handler and Linnekin 1984).[96]

The movement's intention to purify the religion of "Catholic/slave vestiges" was central to the project that became known as "Yoruba reversionism." Gary Edwards, penning a manifesto-like statement of the Black American Yoruba Movement, writes that the Catholic saint images and terms were "modifications" that "did not change the character of the religion itself, but did contribute to some misunderstanding, and served to hide the idea that there was a direct link to Africa." Efforts by Black American Yoruba "fostered a philosophical approach to the study of Yoruba culture which is based on the idea that the religion should return to its origins. By this I mean that the language which is used in ceremony should be Yoruba in toto, and the Orìṣa concepts, where possible, should be returned to their pre-slavery state minus the influence of the Catholic saints. . . . This approach we will call, for lack of a better term, 'Yoruba Reversionism'" (Mason 1985a, iv–v).

In order to uncover and revive "traditional Yoruba art from earlier times" and "return . . . the religion . . . to its origins," reversionist aesthetics sought to disengage the Lucumí pantheon's Yoruba-based iconography from the styles and adornments of the *gusto criollo cubano*. The canons of this Yoruba-American art were drawn, in part, through intensive research into the abundant ethnographic and art historical literature on Yoruba art and culture and, later, through travels by black Americans to West Africa. "Adefunmi's imagination was restless," art historican Robert Farris Thompson writes, "and he ceaselessly studied the Yoruba language, handbooks with illustrations of the *classical* art of the Yoruba, lectures by New York–area Africanists, and many other sources. In the process, the art of New York Yoruba became a willed phenomenon, a self conscious *renaissance* that was distinguishable from modern Afro-Cuban work" (1983, 90; emphasis added). Black American Yoruba artists' renderings of Ṣàngó at Oyotunji, for example, preserved the thunder god's signature colors and thunderax form, jettisoned the crenelated tower and brickwork motifs the Cuban Changó had borrowed from Santa Bárbara, and dressed representations of the deity's possessed priests in Yoruba clothes. Thus, the Cuban Changó became the Yoruba-American Shango, after the Yoruba Ṣàngó (see Thompson 1983, 90–91; Omari 1991; Matory 1994, 172, 174; cf. fig. 5.48). Some of the quite impressive and meticulously worked Oyotunji iconography appears to be modeled directly on the ethnographic photographs of transatlantic researchers such as Pierre Verger

Figure 5.48.—Interior of the town shrine to the deity Ṣango, Oyotunji Village, Shelton, South Carolina, 1989. (Photograph copyright © Mikelle Smith Omari-Tunkara. All Rights Reserved. Courtesy Mikelle Smith Omari-Tunkara.)

(e.g., compare Adefunmi 1982, 2; and J. Mason 1994, 244; with Verger 1954, plates 134 and 118).

Still, Black American Yoruba altar assemblages themselves changed over time. For example, the permanent altar installation for Oyá in the "Hall of Man in Africa" in New York's American Museum of Natural History, which was donated by Chris Oliana in 1969, is replete with Cuban Santería-style objects (e.g., soup tureens and metal, pointed crowns), while objects produced in the 1970s through the 1990s rely heavily on Yoruba models (see, e.g., Drewal and Mason 1998, 129, 116, 103; and fig. 5.48). With the multicultural 1990s and renewed interest by Black American Yoruba in Cuba itself, recent examples, produced by Cuban and Latino artists who work in New York with multiple communities (Manuel Vega, José Rodríguez, Felipe García Villamil), or through collaborations between Latino and African-American practitioners, have combined Cuban-based, black American, and Yoruba forms—for example, Yoruba and Cuban Lucumí iconography and beadwork, and satin cloth (see Drewal and Mason 1998, 129–67).

Though not necessarily typical, perhaps the most radical contrast between the Yoruba reversionist sensibility and the *gusto criollo* of Cuban, Cuban-American, and other Latino *santeros* is dramatically captured in Stephan Palmié's lively interview with Chief Ajamu, head of the Yoruba temple of Miami. "[W]hen a person is . . . as they say, 'saint'—and that's right, it's saint, it's not orisha—when the saint descends upon him, on his horse, and they rush 'em off to dress them, they come back with these little early English outfits on them, they look like the Three Musketeers with the little knickers, knickerbockers coming up to here [pointing to his knee] and the little . . . almost like a beret to one side with a feather in it . . . ah, it's disgusting!" (Palmié 1995, 80). Not only are the modern Lucumí ritual garments anathema here, but also the Cuban *oricha* (*santo*) that is dressed in such fashion is not granted the status of a genuine Yoruba deity. For this Black American Yoruba descendant of Oyotunji, the Lucumí *santo* is a white mask over black skin—the colonized shell of its former self—bereft of the genuine presence of African spirituality. The Cuban *ropa de santo* emerges as nothing more than the "robes of the saints"—or, more precisely, the robes of seventeenth-century swashbuckling musketeers imagined by Alexandre Dumas *père* (1802–70; *Les Trois Mousquetaires*, 1844), a writer now claimed within the African Diaspora literary canon.[97] For an American audience raised on predominantly Protestant cultural ideas and uninformed of Afro-Cuban cultural history, including the festive Caribbean "fancy" carnival aesthetic sensibility, with its "Spanish flavor" (see Nunley and Bettelheim 1988; Bettelheim 1991), the plumed headgear and *pantalones de bombachas* of the Warriors (Eleguá, Ogún, and Ochosi) survive only as the kitsch outcropping of the white Western, Roman Catholic baroque imagination, rather than as the ingenious local fashionings of the Cuban Lucumí imagination. In contrast, when Miami *iyalocha* Nydia Pichardo visited Spain on vacation, she effortlessly assimilated the iconography of Spanish palace royal symbols to Cuban Lucumí aesthetic and religious categories: "We went to Spain to a palace and saw a throne that was red. And I said, 'Look!, you could have an *iyawó* of Changó here.' If you look at [our Santo through the eyes of] someone who is not a *santero*, you see a European king of the seventeenth or eighteenth century, starting with the crown and [jacket] that is used in European royalty."[98] Pichardo, a Puerto Rican–American *santera* initiated into the Cuban house of Rudiberto Domínguez, a descendant of the seminal Lucumí *rama* of Efuche, Andrea Trujillo, and Susana Cantero, was raised to expect the Warrior *orichas* to come down in plumed hats, satin jackets, and *pantalones de bombachas.* Palmié's interlocutor, a black American, received his deities from a lineage rooted in the Lucumí of Matanzas, but he did not identify himself as a *santero* in the Cuban sense; rather, he saw himself as a "chief" in the sense of Yoruba lineage or town-quarter leaders.

Yoruba reversionism's return of the religion to a "preslavery state" in Oyotunji and its offshoots around the country meant not only iconographic revision, but also institutional innovation—the deconstruction of the modern Lucumí initiatory system, which had been established by the African and creole founders of the Regla de Ocha around the turn of the twentieth century. The pantheonized initiatory architecture of the Four Pillars of Ocha, in which the *iyawó* came to receive a core group of four or five *orichas* along with the "head" and the Warriors, was revised. "Ofuntola and his growing African American following advocat[ed] a return to 'African style' initiations," Palmié notes (1995, 79, 96 n. 24), which means the head-and-foot initiatory model wherein the initiate receives only the deity of the head and Elegba along with the Warriors.[99] The village reconfigured its initiatory practice around a reading of transatlantic Yoruba religion that preserved the condensed, hierarchical New World pantheon of major deities but revised the particular solution of "the first slaves of Cuba and Brazil [who] decided that in order for the tradition to survive there, it was necessary to have initiates receive more than one Orisa [*orisha*] or two, as they had in Africa" (Marta Moreno quoted in Caribbean Cultural Center 1984).

The head-and-foot system, according to one Cuban priest who directed some ceremonies in Oyotunji in the 1980s, meant significant changes in the initiation's protocols and aesthetic presentation. For example, the painted signature (*firma*) on the modern Lucumí initiate's shaved head, which invokes multiple *orichas* that work with the *cabecera*, was reduced to a single set of colors representing the principal owner of the head, as in Yoruba initiation (see Drewal, Pemberton, and Abiodun 1989, 33; Matory 1994, 184). By the same logic, the extended sequences of Lucumí initiatory chants (*oro*) to multiple *orichas*, as well as the *itá* divination reading, were revised, in some contexts, to focus upon the principal deity of the head.[100] An Oyotunji initiate would become the priest of a particular deity's shrine on the village's grounds. Priests could, however, still receive the other *orichas* as later additions.

The modern Lucumí religion was a negotiated distillation of remembered and encountered sociocultural principles wrought on the island of Cuba by Africans and their varied ethnic and racial descendants. As such, the religion had left behind the "wealth of institutional detail" of Yoruba social structure (Bascom 1944, 1950) and took on a new wealth of insititutional detail when it was reformulated in the "niches" provided by the stratified colonial society and early Republic, particularly the networks of *cabildos* and houses of Ocha (Bastide 1972, [1960] 1978). The modern houses of Ocha, in turn, left behind the mortal kings and queens who had ruled the colonial-era *cabildos*, yet continued to be "ruled," symbolically, by *orichas* whose iconography expressed their royal status and grandeur in the terms of colonial-era sumptuary codes. In contrast, Oyotunji Village and its reversionist ideology revived a versioin of "the palace of the Oba Lucumí," not as a chronotope informed by Cuban cultural history, but as a chronotope figured as a literal, ethnographically researched neo-Yoruba kingdom.[101] His Royal Highness Oba Ofuntola Oseigeman Adelabu Adefunmi I was dubbed by Yoruba authorities in Nigeria "King of the New World Yorubas" during one of his trips to Africa. He practices polygyny, lives in a royal compound, and rules from his throne like an African monarch.[102] He wears elegant Yoruba cloth and carries a royal fly whisk. Enthroned and surrounded by his "royal family," he observes the proceedings of annual and periodic festivals (see Hunt 1979, 69, 92; and Omari 1991). Still, he wears multiple hats, which rarely characterizes Yoruba kings. He not only functions as royal ruler, but also performs the role of *babalawo* and *oriaté*, as he apparently divines with the Ifá oracle, supervises the initiation of Yoruba priests, and conducts sacrifices.[103] Therefore, if Oyotunji represents the successful and thoroughgoing re-Africanization of black American religion and the personal identities of the movement's members, it is also an extraordinary and bold gesture of collective self-fashioning in the heart of the Old South, Shelton, South Carolina, a short distance from the Old Slave Mart in Charleston. This "reinvention" and "naturali[zing]" of "Yoruba 'traditions,'" was part of a strategy of "reclaiming nobility" through the narrative manipulation of "genealogy" (Clarke 1997, chap. 1).

The refashioning of the Lucumí religion and African-American identity in terms of Yoruba categories and cultural nationalist ideology required a particular reading of, and argument about, the processes of the African Diaspora. The field of Afro-American anthropology was based on the idea that not only African peoples, but also their cultures were dispersed in the slave trade. In the tradition of Boas, culture was understood as a learned phenomenon, although essentialized, blood-based metaphors clearly seeped into Herskovits's reckoning of the culture process (see Apter 1991). African culture was seen to have been transmitted to other peoples, including dominant groups, in the "two-way flow of cultural materials" in multiethnic New World settings (see Herskovits 1941; Ellison [1964] 1972;

Mintz 1974a; Mintz and Price [1976] 1992). In the Yoruba-American and Black Nationalist conception, the idea of a Yoruba diaspora was revised along more literal blood-based lines; modern liberal concepts of culture that were based on shared and learned "traits," "rules," and meanings were supplanted by pan-Africanist racial theory, which was, significantly, derived from nineteenth-century Euro-American racialist thought (see Appiah 1992). One result of the application of such theories to the "creole question" already implicit in the earliest statements of Adefunmi I was that Lucumí founders and their Afro-Cuban descendants who were phenotypically identifiable as African descended should be embraced and inscribed as the authentic religious forebears (e.g., Mason 1996),[104] particularly Fermina Gómez (Ocha Bí). Meanwhile, one Miami white, Puerto Rican–American *oriaté* relates that he was told by Black American Yoruba practitioners that the "white priests . . . were seen as merely the caretakers of the religion, to which the black Americans are the legitimate heirs."[105]

The movement's self-fashioning in Africanist and exclusivist terms, as Maxine Kamari Clarke brilliantly demonstrates, was accomplished not only through ambitious pilgrimages to Africa and artistic modifications in South Carolina, but also narratively through the strategic and selective revision of chanted ancestral genealogies. References to West African "high ancestors" were added to the beginnings of the religion's *moyuba* chants, followed by selected Cuban ancestors in the Matanzas line of Adefunmi I (in particular, "Osha Bi," Fermina Gómez) and the "exclusion of other related priests from the Cuban/Santería line." As Clarke notes, "since Africa was seen as originary, anyone perceived to be 'black' could be located within a homogeneous African line of descent" (1997, 167). Whites represented passing blips on ethnic radar screens. Such narrative practices within the movement's rituals are "indicative of the politics of determining which Yorùbá practices and Yorùbá priests are 'authentic' and 'traditional' and which are not" (Clarke 1997, 132–34).

Nevertheless, these principles seem to vary by individual, region, and historical period. If more extreme voices dominated in the 1960s, 1970s, and 1980s, the Black American Yoruba base, at least in New York, has become diverse in viewpoint and practice; some individuals who helped found the movement are now connected, or reconnected, to Cuban houses, and, in some cases, have been initiated by white Cuban godparents.[106] A recent Cuban- and Puerto Rican–sponsored initiation in New York brought together, for example, Cuban godparents, a Latina *iyawó*, and her African-American husband, also a priest. The Middle Day celebration gathered a greater blend of backgrounds: a Black American Yoruba drumming group, Puerto Rican and white American musicians, a noted Yoruba reversionist writer, a famous Bahian Candomblé Mae de Santo, and a throne containing nine *iyawós*, among whom were Puerto Ricans, Cubans, Mexicans, Jews, and African-Americans. Still, any glib conclusion drawn from such apparently harmonious public behavior among the religion's faithful might not hold up in relation to the private beliefs and practices within individual houses. Anyone who has spent time within these religious circles has heard white priests in Havana and New York voice racist views about black practitioners and has heard just as extreme nationalist statements with respect to white practitioners.

The racial continuity of Diaspora blacks with the continent of Africa is an idea with a long history in the United States (Woodson [1936] 1968; Du Bois [1903] 1969; Appiah 1992). Yet the movement's identification with the Ọ̀yọ́ Yoruba cemented a specific ethnic and cultural link that was selected out of any number of imaginable alternatives. Would Oyotunji be a "Kongo" village named after Mbanza, the ancient Kongo capital, had King and Oliana been initiated into the Afro-Cuban Palo Monte/Regla de Congo? As it happened, they were drawn into the Cuban Lucumí tradition because of the dominant religious strain that post–World War II Cuban migration had brought to New York and, perhaps, because the Yoruba had already been inscribed as a representative, stately

West African civilization in the academic literature (see Adefunmi 1962).[107]

The Yoruba identity of many movement members was naturalized through permanent bodily reform, which was manifested not just in the wearing of clothes. La Regla de Ocha was a *regla* or "religion," albeit a suppressed one, within the larger Cuban society; Oyotunji sought to build a "neo-Yoruba" society and an African state of Yoruba men, women, children, and ancestors on bounded and resacralized soil within the American nation. Where the Cuban Lucumí tradition has used tempera paints to mark the cheeks of initiates, symbolizing their spiritual embodiment of particular regional *orichas' aché*, many Oyotunji followers had their faces permanently etched with cicatrizations to reinscribe their bodies with marks of a specific Yoruba ethnic identity. They had discovered through divination, Hunt reports, "that each person who lived in Oyotunji should receive tribal [scarification] marks so that the ancestral spirits would know that they were a different people. The villagers themselves also preferred the marks so that they could be distinguished from the other Afro-Americans as worshippers and preservers of the culture of their ancestors. The villagers chose one of the three marks of the Oyo, which are three parallel lines on each cheek" (Hunt 1979, 58; see also Clarke 1997, 91). Moreover, the freedom, pan-Africanist, and self-determination movements had empowered the descendants of Africans in the United States to forge a series of "changes of name"—from "colored" to "Negro" to "black," to "African-American"—in order to mark newly claimed identities and rights (see Gates 1990, xxxiii). The founders and members of Oyotunji rejected these effectively "creole" or New World "ethnic" denominations—for example, "black" (see Hoetink 1979, 26–27; Powell 1997, 8–16). They renamed themselves "Yoruba"—in particular, Oyo-Yoruba. Within the United States, the Oyotunji Villagers would represent a "naturalized" (Clarke 1997) African vanguard or chosen people, not only in relation to the population as a whole, but also in relation to other black Americans. Indeed, initiated villagers received not only distinguishing ethnic facial marks, but also Yoruba names. As one delighted new initiate exclaimed, "'[the diviner] helped me explain my true African identity.' She added, 'No more slave master's name and no more shame. That's all I wanted and that's what I got'" (Clarke 1997, 173).

Though the original charge to aspring Black American Yoruba was to "go south," as well as back to Africa, in the historical terms of Ethiopianism and Garveyism, Oyotunji also found itself having to "go west." In order to survive economically within the American economy, the African village and state had to rely on a time-honored American commercial enterprise—the theme park. The village hosts a schedule of public festivals that can be attended by tourists (see Omari 1991; J. Mason 1994; Clarke 1997). A recent brochure encourages travelers to "Come to South Carolina and visit North America's first and only authentic African Village!" Like Stepto's notions of ritual "immersion" and "descent" in African-American literature, such visits, in the words of Oyotunji's brochures, represent "A Pilgrimage to Africa in America" (Oyotunji brochure, n.d.; Stepto 1979, 66–82).[108] Still, any such pilgrimage would be mediated by cash transactions, not to mention plane tickets and automobile association maps.

The iconography, rituals, and institutions of the modern Lucumí religion were not the natural, passive results of Cuban cultural history, but were the products of self-conscious agents of innovation and audiences of reception. As the tenor of Nicolás Angarica's 1955 manual suggests, such innovations reflected a certain progressive reform agenda, not least, perhaps, because the organization of the turn-of-the-twentieth-century *cabildos* and houses emerged in the context of the independence movement from Spain and the organizing of Afro-Cuban political parties and institutions to combat political disenfranchisement and social marginalization. These innovations were subject to various revisions over time within the Cuban setting, producing a continuum of divergent ritual practices that were imported to the United States with post–World War II Cuban migration. King, Oliana, and others transformed their Lucumí priesthood from the proportions of leaders of a "temple" into leaders of an antisyncretic nationalist movement that stressed Yoruba identity (see Palmié 1995). After 1959, Black American Yoruba innovations swiftly followed upon practices leaders perhaps imagined to have been long held in the Cuban system, but which were also recent and had been swiftly instituted. The modern initiatory system according to which King and Oliana were initiated in 1959 in Matanzas, as discussions with Osvaldo Cárdenas Villamil suggest, had only been "modernized" from the "head-and-foot" system to the pantheonized system in the preceding decade.

The antisyncretic movement to "purify" the religion of its supposed European and Catholic elements has not been confined to black American practitioners; it has been taken up by Spanish-speaking practitioners as well, such as the leader of Miami's Church of the Lukumí, Babalú Ayé, Ernesto Pichardo, who published an incisive critique of syncretism in his own practitioners' manual (see Palmié 1995; Pichardo and Nieto 1984, 20–28). Pichardo and many others reject the terms *santería* and *santero* and prefer to call their religion Yoba, Ayoba, or Yoruba. The late Yrmino Valdés Garriz ("Chiqui"), who practiced in Puerto Rico, following his research trip to Yorubaland in the 1980s, proposed a campaign of "rectification" (*rectificación*) in the newsletter of his *oricha* temple. In rhetoric reminiscent of that used by Oyotunji and the re-Africanized Cuban descendants of Ọ̀ṣogbo's Ifá Yemí (chap. 2), Valdés wrote:

> Within our Western, syncretized, and incorrect practices of the ceremony of *Ka Ori Cha* [*kariocha*], *Greco-Roman* elements have been added in the making of thrones and in imitations of the European hierarchies in the form of the crown used, the Middle Day, and various other syncretic elements from the Roman Catholic religion in the colors of the garments of the Middle Day.
>
> Those interested in rectifying their understanding should study the true practice of the religion, and one of the best ways is returning to the root. Through research trips to the country of origin, Nigeria, we will make anew all the priests, priestesses, and members of our *Culto de Estudios y Culto Religioso Yoruba.* (Valdés Garriz 1988)

These antisyncretic interventions grew not entirely out of Black American Nationalist sentiments but, it seems, out of newly fashioned agendas to claim greater authenticity within an increasingly diverse, competetive, politicized, commercializing, and transnational religious marketplace (see Palmié 1995). For example, Pichardo's long-held intellectual interest in the Yoruba basis of the Lucumí religion has taken on a particular stridency in the context of exile politics, namely, his efforts to enlarge his Church of the Lukumí's visibility, legitimacy, and constituency since its rousing victory in the Supreme Court over Hialeah animal sacrifice ordinances in 1993 (*Church of the Lukumi Babalu Aye, Inc. and Ernesto Pichardo, Petitioners, v. City of Hialeah*, 508 U.S. 520; 113 Sup. Ct. 2217). Thus, in the late 1990s, he was seeking ways to represent Cuba's Ocha-practicing population, defend it from the recently renewed strength of the Catholic Church on the island, and question the assumed monopoly the pope would have over Cuba's religious population. By emphasizing the Yoruba basis of the religion and rejecting "syncretism" with Catholic practices, Pichardo rhetorically located Africa as Cuba's religious mother and the Roman Catholic Church as Cuba's "other."

Emphasizing similar intellectual reasons, but using the rhetoric of 1980s and 1990s multiculturalist identity politics, Ysamur Flores-Peña, a "Puerto Rican with African ancestry," rejected the conventional Cuban *ropa de santo* for his own initiation and those of his Southern California godchildren. "'Don't you dare dress me like that!'" he told his godmother. Flores, the spiritual consultant to a heterogeneous constitutency that includes stars in the Hollywood movie industry, has dressed many of his ethnically diverse *iyawós* in neo-Yoruba outfits. For the recent Middle Day of a white American *iyawó*, Flores skirted what he defined as the "'minstrel dilemma' . . . a white man wearing the clothing of a black man imitating the clothing of a white man!" by developing a kind of postmodern sartorial solution, a self-conscious syncretism. In other words, the work of disenchantment always begets new enchantments. Thus, "Ysamur modified the eighteenth-century style by blending it with African and [W]estern fashion, an acknowledgement of the derivations of the religion as well as the background of the initiate" (Flores-Peña and Evanchuck 1994, 35). It is not likely that the major labels of Western fashion will begin to produce *ropas de santo*, and we do not know how far *oricha* iconography is capable of being pushed before it tilts into something unrecognizable as an African-derived pattern (see Barnes 1989b, 13). Still, the diversity of the contemporary Ocha community may produce as many sartorial solutions as there are new emergent urban identities. As Nydia Pichardo's godfather, Rudiberto Domínguez, reported, the Los Angeles initiation of a Chicano man to the Changó priesthood produced an "*iyawó* [who] looked like a Mexican mariachi."

CONCLUSION

The figure of divine royalty, most specifically as delineated by the palace of the Obá Lucumí, served as a connecting thread in my exploration of three areas of innovation in the history of the Lucumí religion: institutional organization, ritual practice, and iconographic elaboration. The palace of the Obá Lucumí, as a capacious and versatile chronotope, could refer to the ethos and authority of the nineteenth-century *cabildos* and the initiatory protocols of the twentieth-century *casa-templos* and serve as the connective tissue in diasporic historical narratives. Crowned and enthroned kings and queens ruled the old *cabildos*, the miniature "kingdoms" of Cuba's African "nations" prior to emancipation from slavery. Kings, queens, and warriors also have ruled over the societies and houses of the Lucumí religion since at least the 1820s.

The old-style *cabildos*, formidable institutions under the Spanish crown and church, revived, transformed, and replaced aspects of West African social, political, and cultural life in the Cuban context. As colonial institutional templates were both accommodated to and manipulated by the "nations," *cabildos* were formative in creating shared ways of surviving, organizing, ritualizing, and sometimes rebelling, among Cuba's African populations. The *cabildos* and less formal organizations, as well as other institutional arrangements in the *barrios extramuros*, provided channels for becoming Afro-Cuban and "niches" or "hiding places" (Bastide [1960] 1978, 160) for the elaboration of distinctive diasporic subcultures. If the "nation" structure and the *cabildos* followed a "creolizing" trajectory, they also served, along with independent nineteenth-century "houses" (aka *cabildos*), as "incubating cells" and training grounds for the distinct, neo-African religious orders (*reglas*) and societies of the twentieth century: Lucumí, Congo, Arará, and Abakuá (Palmié 1993). The early-twentieth-century "transitional" Lucumí *cabildos* and *sociedades*, which were founded and led by freedmen and women and their "Lucumí" *ritual*, as well as blood family, descendants, maintained selected patterns of the old-style *cabildos* of the previous century, including official inscription, Catholic saint patronage, the "double" festival cycle, the *bandera*, and a formalized administrative hierarchy, yet they were reorganized within the new form of legalized voluntary associations during the American occupation and the early years of the Republic.

Undergirding their public hierarchy of patron saints, presidents, treasurers, and committee members, these transitional *sociedades* and *cabildos* were, in fact, collectives of *casa-templos* ("house-temples"), which were ruled by specific Yoruba-Lucumí deities and governed by recognized elders according to their ritual seniority. Their ceremonies, and those of the many houses they sponsored, were directed by ritual specialists called *obás* ("kings"). To extend the "palace" metaphor, the priests and priestesses "formed a court"—an earthly one—in the understanding of Lydia Cabrera's mid-twentieth-century sources, while the *orichas* of the Lucumí "pantheon" formed a "celestial court" (*corte celestial*).

In the ritual domain, as the personnel of the court were

"just like" the ones in the palace of the Obá Lucumí, so were the "coronation" ceremonies of new priests imagined to be like the coronation of the West African king himself. The verb *coronar* (to crown) became interchangeable with "making the god" (*hacerle ocha*) to the initiate—the momentous *kariocha* ceremony in which an *oricha* is mounted on the head. The *babalawos, babalochas, iyalochas,* and *obá-oriatés* of the *casa-templos* were, in effect, New World versions of the ritual "kingmakers" of Yoruba quarter and lineage cults (see Apter 1992, 83–84). They were the ritual authorities and midwives of innumerable kings, queens, and warriors, and filled their houses with the "godchildren" they had "crowned."

Though not all *òrìṣà* of Yorubaland were "royal" deities, the *orichas* created in the Lucumí coronation ceremonies were considered kings, queens, and warriors, who would rule over houses, the "heads" of priests, and the "year"—following their selection in annual divination ceremonies that echoed the annual election of old-style *cabildo* kings and queens. In the *kariocha* initiation ritual of "mounting the saint," the *oricha* "arrives" in an enthroned, sitting position upon Changó's royal mortar or its facsimile in alternate media and then is installed beneath a lavish canopied "throne" (*trono*). Thus crowned and outfitted with royal regalia, the *orichas* would receive salutations and gifts from "the people" in an aesthetically marked public performance of affirmation and legitimation.

The sumptuary codes of *oricha* royalty and warriorhood called for expensive fabrics, elaborate beadwork regalia, and prestige accessories, such as fine china—which they and only they could utilize. Thrones, crowns, satin garments, handheld regalia, and china soup tureens became the distinctive aesthetic markers of altar display and public celebration. While the Regla Lucumí or Regla de Ocha reworked the basic iconography of the Yoruba deities—for example, thunderaxes, fans, fly whisks, and cutlasses, prodigious color-coded beadwork—the *orichas'* crowns, garments, and decorative sensibility found their proximate sources in the finery of the old *cabildo* monarchs, the pomp of colonial black and mulatto military battalions, and the Catholic saints. Other accessories, in contrast, such as the soup tureens and domestic altar forms, were adapted from the prestige forms of the *vajilla* and *armario vitrina* of the Cuban bourgeoisie. As a whole, this aesthetic was nicely summed up by Fernando Ortiz as the *adornos al gusto criollo,* and it became the preferred aesthetic marker of what Oddedeí called the palace of the Obá Lucumí.

The *orichas'* thrones and garments became marvelous hybrids. Stylized, highly legible figures of monarchs, gentlemen, ladies, and soldiers of the court and army were presented in the theatricalized performance setting of the throne's proscenium arch and curtains; they would wear pasteboard crowns or floppy musketeers' hats, satin jackets, riding knickers, flowing gowns, painted-on mustaches, beards, riding boots, and earrings; at the same time, they would also wear Yoruba-derived beadwork—the *collares de mazo*—painted facial markings that recalled the cicatrizations of West African ethnic groups, and coiffure-like painted head designs that recalled the meticulous head adornments of Yoruba shrine sculpture and possession priests. In effective, often aesthetically jarring ways, imported fine satins and china combined with animal skins, horns, cowrie shells, beadwork, palm fronds, and African gray parrot's red tail feathers (*ikodidé*), as well as fabrics from agricultural shipping bags of jute taken directly from the wharves of Havana and Matanzas.

Some observers have regarded such innovations, including, at times, Catholic chromolithographs, as a merely decorative, "dispensable" colonial window dressing over the gods' "real power," as superfluous to the *Yoruba* "focus of Cuban *santería*" (stones, herbs, and blood; Bascom 1950). Yet these multimedia adaptations clearly represented traditionalized and cherished expressive means to celebrate the greater glory of the *orichas.* Moreover, these means have never remained without their own power. As constituents of "thrones," they have shaped the experiential dynamic of secrecy and revelation, "syndetically" adding aesthetic force to the *orichas' fundamentos* during public performances. They have served as important "gift" media within ongoing human-divine exchanges and, not least, acted as, or formed part of, efficacious ritual *ebós* (sacrifices; see Brown 1996). In short, historically specific aesthetic adornment is crucial to the development of a religious practice. The real power of the *santos* resides not only in objects technically identifiable as "ritual" but also in "innovations" that might otherwise be dismissed as merely decorative and "foreign."

It remains somewhat easier to describe the surfaces and structure of such hybrid end products than to thickly detail the historical contexts and "processes" of their making (Palmié 1993). For example, how, and under what sets of opportunities and constraints, did Africans and creoles acquire and utilize prestige cloth, china, and an array of ritual ingredients for their emergent practice? What were the criteria of selection among variant groups of practitioners? What kinds of struggles took place among them? And how should such acquisitions of prestige objects be considered in relation to the rungs of class, race, and gender in colonial and postcolonial society which crosscut the practitioner population? A study of imports from the triangular Atlantic trade in relation to the internal market systems and class-color hierarchy of western Cuba would make it possible to contextualize more precisely the novel use and the local meanings of satins and ceramics—for example, the white oval *sopera* in the 1881 Landaluze lithograph (fig. 5.34) and items of the West African trade. When exactly did these objects become accessible? On what bases were they selected? How did such objects circulate within urban communities? To whom, and how, were they affordable? What implications did patronage have, particularly as far as Ocha personnel formed cross-class and race linkages, as in the case of Adechina's relations to Regla's bourgeoisie and the rich white sponsorship of a branch of the Abakuá society? And what did the possession of particular objects along a large spectrum from lavish to humble, from "European" to "African," signify?

Moreover, it remains difficult, if not futile, to pinpoint and tease out the precise "sources" of the *orichas'* royal iconography. Of course, the notion of "sources" may itself obscure the question of how complex cultural processes are. In cases of multivocal forms that embody highly mediated "sources," the search for origins cannot represent the best approach. For heuristic purposes, and in order to give art historical iconographic methodology its chance to provide useful data, I have sought to suggest multiple proximate formal and textual sources based upon formal comparisons—"visual similarities." These include such sources as the finery of *cabildo* kings and queens, the Virgins and royal saints, and bourgeois material culture. However, I cannot but agree with the conclusions of my colleagues in the field that the sources and inspirations of ongoing artistic production within *la melange* are highly overdetermined (see, e.g., Cosentino 1995a, 1995b).

In any event, I have sought to evoke a sense of historical process and change through an approach to innovation along an epochal time line that is pegged to changing Cuban historical formations. La Regla de Ocha's *adornos al gusto criollo*, for example, were well established in the major *sociedades*, it seems, by the time Ortiz (1906), Roche y Monteagudo (1908), Wright (1910), and Castellanos (1916) visited these Lucumí institutions during the first decade of the twentieth century. Such adornments may have entered Lucumí practice at a moment paralleling the emergence of the "white" Akanarán Efó branch of the Abakuá, as of 1863, if not before. For the Abakuá, such material innovations were linked to patronage arrangements, shifts in the class and color of personnel given demographic changes in western Cuban labor markets, competition between lodges for scarce resources, and the need to present "licit" voluntary associations to the larger society. Just around 1863, Adechina Ño Remigio Herrera established himself in Regla, acquired property, began to elaborate the *cabildo* he had founded, and gained a stunning reputation. These advances were made possible, in part, thorough his relationships with, and patronage by, members of Regla's white establishment. As a result,

Adechina could support his freed colleagues; in turn, their ritual offspring supported their elders as well as their juniors. Such networks of mutual aid and collective action developed in greater force from the era of emanciption (1880–86) through the founding of the Republic (1902), when African and creole ex-slaves arrived in the cities with new knowledge and experience, but with pressing needs for resources and ethnic and religious belonging.

Though self-conscious political action by religious Afro-Cubans has yet to be documented in depth—other than, for example, the direct engagement of the Abakuá in labor advancement between the 1880s and 1940—it is clear that intensive organizing within Lucumí circles to form official "societies" paralleled unprecedented organizing among Cuban people of color for political, social, and economic rights between the Second War of Independence and 1912. If religion was the inspiration for the 1891 and 1900 reorganizations of Havana's Cabildo of Saint Barbara and the 1902–12 reorganizations of other Havana and Palmira "societies," the religious motive cannot easily be separated from the organizations' important collectivizing, mutual aid functions and programs of cultural self-identification and self-assertion. In the context of widespread public claims for visibility and recognition among Cuban people of color, Saint Barbara's banner proclaiming the presence of "the Lucumí nation and its children and descendants" could not have been insignificant to an Afro-Cuban collective consciousness, if not also the society at large. It is also not insignificant that, though the political movement of people of color was effectively crushed by the state in 1912, the Afro-Cuban *reglas* persisted—despite police persecutions in order to destroy them. Though further research might establish a causal relationship between state repression and strategic responses in the form of organizing or reorganizing, the *reglas* clearly persisted through, it might be hypothesized, further shape-shifting. The religions went further underground, and "houses" became far more privatized than they had been during the reign of the old and transitional *cabildos*—which were visible umbrella organizations of multiple houses. At the same time, leaders of many houses, for protection, if not also personal enrichment, went on to form significant relationships of exchange and patronage with local and national politicians and with businessmen; many, particularly *babalawos*, were or became recognized artisans and businessmen themselves; their religious and professional careers were mutually reinforcing and provided channels of mobility and resources for the advancement of their houses. The issue of color and class cannot be discounted in this series of changes. Many of the emergent Ifá leaders were *mulatos* (*pardos* in colonial parlance) and *blancos* of Spanish descent; they descended from creole families with significant mobility, and many were more ambitious *hombres de movimiento*. Their resources and education permitted them to compile (*recopilar*) and transmit religious knowledge in textualized form and establish spaces for highly organized religious practice, such as Bernardo Rojas's "Vatican" in Marianao. It is, perhaps, not coincidental, that such Ifá houses began to expand significantly with the prosperity of the World War I period and its immediate aftermath (the "Dance of the Millions"). Moreover, the formidable social, political, and intellectual connections secured by religious leaders seem to have expanded with the cultural openings of the Afrocubanismo period (1923–1930s), including a degree of public legitimization of certain Afro-Cuban practices through the works and organizations of Cuban intellectuals and statesmen, and reached their apogee during the putatively more politically open, albeit grossly corrupt, Constitutional Period (1940–53), when Quintín Lecón Lombillo acquired funds from his godchild in Ifá, President Carlos Prío Socarrás (1948–52), to found and build his socioreligious institution in Regla. At the same time, larger political divides created divisions within the religion itself. Some *babalawos*, including Miguel Febles, distanced themselves from Tata Gaitán, because they believed he had initiated Cuba's brutal dictator, Gerardo Machado, into Ifá.

Undoubtedly, some leaders of Cuba's predominantly female-directed Ocha houses, such as Aurora Lamar, benefited directly from the mobility and prosperity of the foregoing *babalawo* social types—in her case, her husband, the *mulato blanconazo* José Ramón Gutierrez (one of Bernardo Rojas's protégés). Lamar's huge Ocha practice functioned within Gutierrez's large house and, early on, also her brothel. Many of the most important *madrinas* of the twentieth century were married to *babalawos.*[1] After 1936, Gutierrez's house also functioned as the base of Bernardo Rojas's Luz de San Francisco association of *babalawos.* Gutierrez, and other prosperous *babalawos* such as Tata Gaitán and Ramón Febles, had the resources to support large constituencies and to travel regularly. Thus, for example, Gutierrez and Lamar were able to launch La Regla de Ocha in Santiago de Cuba at the other end of the island.

At the same time, further research might bear out that the kinds of hitherto-undervalued or unrecognized cooperative work characterizing African Diaspora women's networks (see e.g., Landes 1947; Stack 1974; Bush 1990; White 1999) pertained as well within houses of Ocha. Though its social and religious effect remains to be documented, Aurora Lamar, for example, devised an "easy payment plan" by which candidates—a majority of whom were probably women—could pay off their initiations over time. Other examples of women's networks would include the powerful and prolific houses of 80 San José (directed by Ña Margarita Armenteros, Efuche, and others) and that of Apoto Belén González. Early on (1900), these houses were institutionally linked to the women's division of the Society of Saint Barbara, the male leadership of which consisted of powerful *babalawos.*

By numbers and influence, women have dominated the leadership positions of Ocha houses and their ranks since the nineteenth century. The principal *ramas* and sub-*ramas* in Havana and Matanzas were led by women: Ma Monserrate González, Fermina Gómez, Ña Caridad Argudín, Ña Margarita Armenteros, Efuche Ña Rosalía, Belén González, Tiburcia Sotolongo, Aurora Lamar, Pilar Fresneda (fig. 3.5), and others. Women founded and led two of the three Lucumí societies in Palmira (Sociedad San Francisco's Ma Lugarda and Ma Fea; Sociedad San Roque's Francisca Entensa) and three *cabildos* of Yemayá in Regla (Josefa Herrera; Susana Cantero; and Panchita and Marcelina Cárdenas). Women, such as "the Bishop," Felipa Calderón, as well as Ma Monserrate González and Fermina Gómez, have also dominated positions of ritual authority in Matanzas and Havana since the nineteenth century. Through the mid-1930s, it seems women, such as La Tuán Timotea Albear and Guillermina Castel, dominated the *oriaté* profession. The same pattern has been noted throughout the African-derived religions of the Caribbean and Brazil (see e.g., Landes 1947; Brown 1991). It would be well worth a study to determine how women's leadership roles and rank-and-file predominance within La Regla de Ocha articulated with Cuban society and its demographics, and even challanged it's entrenched patriarchies, as has been addressed, at times, in the literature on women in the African Diaspora (e.g., Belasco 1980; Lloyd 1963, 1974; Hafkin and Bay 1976; Sudarkasa 1973; Derby 1980; Baer 1984, 164–65; Amadiume 1987; Awẹ 1972; Bush 1990; Matory 1994, 91–125; Daniels 1997)

During the socialist revolutionary period, from 1959 to the present, though all religious practice was repressed in the 1960s, and heavily regulated, at least, through 1993, the co-optative strategies of the state's cultural apparatus to wipe out "negative folklore" had the effect of inscribing the Afro-Cuban religions into the public transcript and some Afro-Cuban values into the national culture. In contemporary Cuba, the *orichas* are everywhere, including high-profile performances, tourist magazines, popular music, and the agendas of the Central Committee in their funding of "Yoruba" organizations (e.g., the Yoruba Cultural Association of Old Havana), as well as in the tourist-stop houses of certain practitioners. During the Special Period, the increased public presence of the *orichas* was not merely owed to the state's loosening of the steam valve and foreign patronage (the initiation of foreigners with dollars). It is also worth hypothesizing that the collectivizing, mutual aid, and resource-circulating functions of the *casas de santo* were crucial to the survival of significant urban constituencies.

Beyond innovations in *oricha* iconography and institutional organization, profound and thoroughgoing structural innovations in ritual characterized the emergence of a "modern" Regla Lucumí. Examples of such far-reaching innovations are seen in at least three thoroughgoing revisions of initiatory practice from perhaps the middle of the nineteenth century to 1945 in Matanzas, and, in Havana, in numerous cases from the second half of the nineteenth century through the 1950s. The broadest structural innovations may be seen in the reorganization of multifarious Yoruba deities into a hierarchical "pantheon" under the roof of Obatalá's "house" (and, as often, Orunmila's house), which produced significant local and regional variation in the pantheon. By the middle of the twentieth century, variant forms of initiation—such as the early head-and-foot model—had been relatively standardized according to the pantheonized Havana model developed around the turn of the twentieth century. Each initiate, following the Warriors ceremony, would "make" a single *oricha* "owner of the head," "receive," at minimum, the Four Pillars of Ocha (Obatalá, Ochún, Yemayá, and Changó), and, in all but two cases, receive Oyá. However, the rules, attitudes, and shifting alliances of priests and priestly groups, as well as historical additions, losses, and modifications of *orichas*, created variant cosmological hierarchies and pantheons.

Important organizing principles of this new initiatory template and related ceremonies owe much to the protocols and iconography of the cult of Changó, suggesting that leaders selected from myriad resources specific patterns considered efficacious and meaningful and sought to standardize them. Though apparently exclusive to the Ọ̀yọ́ Ṣàngó cults in West Africa, the mortar, the *batá* drums, and the crown of the Dadá, as well as new ideas of royalty titling, came to be shared by the other principal *orichas* in Cuba. The notion of the *asiento* as a coronation, and the Middle Day's luxurious throne and garment displays, were elaborated on the basis of the idea that the *orichas* were kings and queens, as well as deified warriors.

Consistent with such standardizing tendencies, the *orichas'* iconographic attributes, mythology, prayers, and ceremonies were highly codified and were comprehensively organized and implemented in relation to the enhanced Lucumí cowrie divination system of *odu.* The oracular corpus of Ifá and the *dilogún* were increasingly textualized, recompiled, and, ultimately, published, over the course of the twentieth century. The secrets of all Yoruba deities were contained in a regional variety of pot types, and their contents also appear to have varied regionally. In Cuba, variant domestic pot types distinguished groups of *orichas,* such as those of the *canastillero* (associated, e.g., with soup tureens), those of the earth and the Warriors behind the door (terra-cotta and iron pots), and Changó, the archetypal king (pots of carved cedar). The oval china *sopera* became the preferred, if not always the most affordable, form of container for the first group. Each *oricha* would possess a determinate number of color-coded stones (seven black for Yemayá, five yellowish for Ochún, four or eight white for Obatalá, etc.) and divination shells (twenty-one for Eleguá, eighteen for most of the others), as well as a kit of highly legible miniature iconographic wood or metal "tools" to distinguish them and to perform their "work."

The standardization and dissemination of these fundamental institutions and practices were facilitated by emergence of the "professionalized" master of Ocha ceremonies, the *obá-oriaté,* and the textualization of religious knowledge during the first half of the twentieth century. These innovated ritual, mythological, and oracular systems, which clearly owed much to religious resources brought to Cuban shores from Yorubaland, were also elaborated, rationalized, and crystallized in narrative form with reference to other ancient and world religions (Egyptian, Greek, Roman Catholic, etc.) by erudite practitioners who drew on oral teaching and ethnographic and popular published sources.

The predominance of oral data and the dearth of hard historical documentation kept by practitioners themselves (e.g., diaries, chronicles) or by scholars and journalists make it difficult to date religious innovations with any precision or to make fully fleshed out identifications of specific actors. The most highly recognized Cuban ethnographers, Fernando Ortiz and Lydia Cabrera, were far more interested in their "informants" as transparent folkloric repositories than as agents whose biographies and social conditions were significant and would compel attention. Nevertheless, stories that circulate among contemporary Havana and Matanzas practitioners fuel my hypotheses that religious innovations resulted from deliberations made by historically self-conscious individuals and "commissions" or "councils." In the processes of resource selection that contributed to innovations and systemic changes, resources were chosen and put to work based upon emergent criteria of ritual efficacy, correctness, and authenticity, if not also personal prestige, with an eye to the long-term resilience of the religious system. Religious credentials, claims to authority, and priestly capacity were subject to "witnessing" and validation within local and regional networks of legitimation. Priests presenting themselves in any given locale often had to submit to confirmatory rituals, a principle embodied in the name of one of the religion's most famous figures, Obadimelli, the "king who was made twice."

In the same spirit of agency, this study has argued that the successful "cultural transfer" of institutions, ritual practices, and arts from West Africa to Cuba occurred not merely as the passive result of the arrival of massive numbers of slaves. Though perhaps one-third of Africans taken to Cuba in the nineteenth century embarked from the Bight of Benín (about one hundred thousand, comprising Yoruba, Nupe, Fon, Mahi, Adja, Evhe, Popo, etc.), clearly not all were initiates and religious leaders. Although contemporary priests may cite studies they have read about the great numbers of Yoruba slaves who arrived in the "last wave" (in the middle third of the nineteenth century), their orally transmitted stories emphasize the particular and the local. The advent of enduring institutions, such as the pantheonized initiation, the *Pinaldo,* the office of the *oriaté,* and the enhancement of the *dilogún* divination system, are traced to the intervention of particular specialists and their winning of authority and respect, as well as their creation of controversy, among particular local groups. The most important innovations were apparently conceived through council-based deliberation and were implemented bit by bit, through individual initiations over time. Atandá (Ño Filomeno García) and Añabí were responsible for launching the sacred *batá* drum tradition in Regla; Adechina and two or three colleagues were responsible for the Olofin tradition. The Olokun masquerade traditions were reinstituted around Fermina Gómez's *cabildo* in Matanzas and the *cabildo* in Regla of Adechina and his immediate collaborators, Atandá (the masks' carver), Tata Gaitán, and Matilde Zayas, an intimate of the García and Herrera families. The three families lived within a two- or three-block radius in Regla's Third Barrio—ground zero, as it were, of fundamental bases of Havana's Ifá and Ocha origins and development.[2] Efuche Ña Rosalía of El Cerro and Obadimelli, originally of Matanzas, were responsible for major structural innovations in Ocha initiation. Guanabacoa's Pilar Fresneda was responsible for extending the Cabildo Arará Sabalú into Havana, with the help of her goddaughter Taurina Montalvo (Enujere).

In short, numbers do not necessarily reflect cultural influence or persistence. Perhaps the most poignant argument in favor of this point in all of the literature is Calazán Herrera's savvy statement to Lydia Cabrera in the middle of the twentieth century: "the mandingas, so many of whom came to Cuba, were so proud of their straight hair and small lips[;] with their God Allah, who had a miraculous book, they taught the creoles; when they disappeared they left neither a *cabildo* nor even a trace of music . . . — Who still speaks mandinga? No one" (Cabrera [1954] 1994, 380).

Of course, the narrower consideration of origins and official agendas to codify and disseminate standardized practices take one only so far. Reform and innovation were not necessarily acquiesced to. They were launched in the face of apparently divergent, eclectic, and "incorrect" local practices; they generated heated contest; if they produced consensus in some quarters, they produced further contest and variation in others. Orthodoxies or traditional and traditionalized strongholds that resulted from the assuming of authority by particular leaders and their credentialing of newcomers through confirmatory ceremonies produced reactions: either the hardening of previously entrenched practices or breakaway heterodoxies. For example, though Havana *babalawos* sought to supervise and control Ocha practice, and in many cases succeeded, the Lucumí religion came to form a continuum of variations, the extremes of which may be designated "Ifá-centric" and "Ocha-centric" ritual fields. Following many decades of variation in the ritual roles and authority assignments around initiatory practice in Ocha, the *obá-oriaté* emerged in the first decades of the twentieth century as a powerful, professionalized ritual leader ("king") who would not only assume an overarching role in relation to the houses of Ocha in which he worked. Given innovations in sacrificial protocol and divination—for example, the *Pinaldo* "Knife" ceremony and the enhanced *dilogún* system—the *oriaté* might complement, compete with, or substitute for the *babalawo*. To this day, while so many revere the name of Obadimelli Octavio Samar Rodríguez, the "first" great professional *oriaté*, not a few Havana *babalawos* believe that Obadimelli was also the first great "deceiver" and charlatan for initiating the "fraud" that is Ocha-centric practice, not least through his use of the *Pinaldo* to confer sacrificial authority in the killing of four-legged animals.

To the extent that the presence and status Orunmila and his *babalawos* vary across the continuum of ritual fields, "the Religion" is, in fact, crosscut by divergent cosmological schemes and systems of authority, which are relatively more centralized or decentralized. The value and status of particular practices and the authority of the groups behind them are the focus of constant rhetorical struggle, in which truth claims and arguments about ritual correctness are cast in terms of primacy of origins. It is often difficult to distinguish original products from innovations; yet what is an efficacious or necessary innovation in one camp is mere invention in another. For example, a Lucumí *oricha* called Asojuano (Babalú Ayé San Lázaro) has circulated with great force among Matanzas and Havana *ramas* for more than a century. However, the Arará Sabalú of Matanzas and Havana recognize neither the initiated priests of Asojuano made "indirectly" or the Asojuano auxiliar *orichas* "received" within the Lucumí system. "Asojuano Lucumí" simply does not exist for the Arará Sabalú; they vociferously claim that their Oluwó Popó and Awó Bokonó priests retain the exclusive right to "make" and "give" Asojuano, and thus the Arará Sabalú Asojuano does not circulate like that of Lucumí, which can be given by anyone who has already received it. Evidently, this more strident Arará theory and practice were begun via Pilar Fresneda and Taurina in Havana, as they are credited with "giving Asojuano Arará to all of Havana's *babalawos*."[3] Yet Havana's dean of Arará Sabalú practice, Pedro Abreu, concedes that he personally reformed Asojuano practice according to his own research into and interpretation of the Asojuano cult and the *odu* of Ifá. Still, the Arará Sabalú protocol undoubtedly resulted in something of a scarcity of Asojuano priests and recipients, because Asojuano's cult among the Arará Sabalú cannot, in theory and practice, grow exponentially as it has among the Lucumí.[4] It may be that Armando Zulueta of the famous Zulueta Arará *cabildo* of Perico, Matanzas, whom the Sabalú credit with inventing "Asojuano Lucumí," acted out of necessity, if not also, as some suggest, "commercial motivation." The liberal making and giving of Asojuano has meant that more people in need could be served if this *oricha* could circulate more freely through a wider cadre of authorized sources. Though Arará Sabalú criticize Armando Zulueta for "inventing" Asojuano Lucumí, in fact, the origins of his ostensibly new Asojuano date well back to the last third of the nineteenth century, to an Arará ex-slave, Octavia Zulueta (Jundesi), according to Michael Mason's research. Efuche Ña Rosalía accomplished an effect similar to the triumph of Zulueta's "Asojuano Lucumí" when she "gave the shells to the Arará" of Havana. This meant that the priests of the Arará gods would not have to rely on *babalawos* or the small and hermetic order of the Oluwó Popó Awó Bokonó (male priests of Asojuano who have undergone Ifá ceremonies) to read their *foduces* with Ifá's divining chain (*opele*); instead, Arará priests of all the *fodú* pantheon could, like their counterparts within the Lucumí *regla*, read their deities with the shells. Nowadays, particularly in the United States, even "Asojuano Arará" is liberally given out by *babalawos*, not Oluwó Popó, who claim this highly specialized authority.

The case of the Black American Yoruba Movement suggests how swiftly self-conscious agents can "reform" a religious system and its iconography, extending even further the range of variant practices and kinds of ideological argumentation used to rationalize them. It also introduces the question of race into the mix more explicitly, a question that has not been satisfactorily addressed in the Cuban historiography in general and in the study of the Afro-Cuban religions in particular.[5] The case also raises questions about the nature of "diaspora" and the terms of the "cultural transfer" of Yoruba religion to the Americas. It appears that the "Lucumí" identification was quite elastic during Cuba's slavery period, and increasingly so afterward, including non-Yoruba-speaking people, blood descendants, and ethnically and racially diverse ritual descendants under its umbrella—though a more widespread *Afro*-Cuban consciousness among the historical and contemporary practitioner community may yet be revealed by further research. In any case, the first Black American Yoruba, who were initiated in Matanzas, strictly construed Lucumí (Yoruba) genealogy in terms of North American categories of racial phenotype. In New York, nonblack practitioners went the way of the Catholic statues, the *gusto criollo*, and "Three Musketeers" costumes in the staking out of black nationalist boundaries linked to a Yoruba identity. Still, the Oyotunji African state, an earnest political and cultural corrective to past violent deracination, which sought to reveal and cultivate original connections to the continent, was also a brilliant invention in the heart of the American South. At the same time, the idea of original, purified connections to Yorubaland has, since the 1970s, been increasingly used by nonblack Cuban practitioners, some of whom advocate strictly antisyncretic agendas, to increase their religious authority and lend their practices greater authenticity.

This study has focused on innovations of institutional, ritual, and iconographic practice in the Afro-Cuban Regla de Ocha and Regla de Ifá. The study builds on the insights of previous studies that emphasize historical process and creative change by active agents. Though I fall toward the "creolist" end of the historiographical and theoretical continuum, focusing upon innovations among emergent social groups and religious lifeways in Cuba, I also rely, for appropriate balance, upon relatively more "Africanist" considerations of the two *reglas* as clear descendants of the religion of the Yoruba-speaking peoples of southwestern Nigeria. Though I trace a history of selected innovations from the middle of the nineteenth century down through the present, this history is more narrowly cast as a one of changing institutional, ritual, and iconographic forms over a series of epochs, as it were. I gesture toward process—one that locates reflective agents and their "choices" at the center. I also gesture towards context, to the extent that I link cultural changes to their immediate socioinstitutional bases as well as refer to changes in Cuban social and political history. Thus, I intend to provide some sense of the sets of opportunities and constraints within which agents have found themselves. I skirt the thicker explanatory approaches of social historians, who would wish to see those agents and their choices and constraints, and the Afro-Cuban culture in question, fully contextualized in relation to race, class, and gender, more rigorously periodized, and more clearly linked to changing local and global histories.

As indicated, my interest in form as an art historian and visual anthropologist, with an abiding passion for the Afro-Cuban religions, has led me to de-emphasize thicker historical explanation in favor of the opportunity to closely focus upon the details of internal changes on an epochal "time line."

Clearly, the study of the Afro-Cuban religions deserves greater dialogue with the full range of Black Atlantic historiography, including studies that contextualize black cultures in relation to national and Atlantic histories (e.g., Butler 1998; Matory forthcoming; Palmié 2002; Bennett 2003). At the same time, I would not wish to see detailed local ethnographic, closely focused art historical and ethnohistorical inquiry fall by the wayside in such historical investigations. As scholars, we continue to labor under an extremely undeveloped ethnographic and chronological picture of the Afro-Cuban religious systems and their local variations. We have few biographies or close historical studies of Black Atlantic or African Diaspora religious or artistic practitioners (Smith 1963; Rosengarten [1974] 2000; Price 1983; MacGaffey 1983; Brown 1989; Abreu Alonso 1992; Flores-Peña and Evanchuck 1994; Hagedorn 2001; Brown 1996; Wexler 1997; Vélez 1998). No intensive ethnohistorical studies exist on the differences in practice among religious houses in Havana and Matanzas, within and among northeastern Brazilian cities in the Candomblé, or between Haitian regions in Vodou, let alone between practices in New York, Miami, and California. A growing number of self-reflexive ethnographic studies of Santería, Vodou, and Candomblé, which revolve around their authors' experiences in relation to these religions, are welcome but do not always paint the kind of detailed historical picture most needed (Wafer 1991; Hagedorn 2001; Mason 1997). In this sense, there is much to be said for straightforward antiquarian studies of local religious history, as well as social histories and postmodern anthropological interventions.

Among the special causes of the dearth of basic studies of the Afro-Cuban religions have been the isolation of Cuba, the lack of resources and training for Cuban scholars, the lack of basic resources in general—for example, computers, paper, and ink for publishing—the difficulties of travel for foreign researchers, and the disorganization, poor condition, and, in some cases, destruction of Cuban archives and libraries. Of course, an outstanding problem that characterizes all study of "folk" practices is the dearth of detailed historical documentation, though parish and local archives hold extraordinary potential for research, if only they were more accessible. As indicated, the greatest Cuban ethnographers of this century did not focus on agents' lives and practices, because they were enchanted and limited by the discourses of nation and culture. However, a number of recent works are based on practitioner documents or attend to locale and show sensitivity to particular agents (e.g., Menéndez 1998; Vinueza 1986; Abreu Alonso 1992; Brice Sogbossi 1998).

An achievement of this study is to bridge questions of ritual arts, religious institutions, and ethnohistory, which continue to be explored within the distinct disciplines of art history, religious studies, and history and historical anthropology.[6] This study combines the methods of ethnographic fieldwork, oral history, visual documentation, and archival inquiry with art historical and ethnohistorical approaches, in order to illuminate institutional, ritual, and iconographic innovation in one African Diaspora religion. We can hope that historically contextualized studies emerge that combine a close focus upon reflective agents of change and attention to linked local and global systems, questions of modernity, and knowledge production within the fields that foment African Diaspora or Black Atlantic studies (see, e.g., Palmié 2002; Matory forthcoming; Bennett 2003). Still, the greatest and possibly most interesting challenge to scholars will be to respond to studies by practitioners themselves. Practitioners are starting to produce self-conscious works that continue to "blur the genres" further, forcing university scholars to question their methods, positionality, and authority.

APPENDIX 1

FREDRIKA BREMER'S DESCRIPTION OF A SUNDAY AFTERNOON DRUMMING IN A HAVANA LUCUMÍ *CABILDO*, 1853

I. [On her arrival in the *extramuros* to visit an event in "the Luccomées *cabildo*"]

As these clubs generally meet in the afternoons and evenings of the Sunday, we set off in the afternoon to the street in which the *cabildos* are situated, for they occupy a whole street near one of the toll-gates of the city. The whole street swarmed with negroes, some decked out with ribbons and bells, some dancing, others standing in groups here and there. There prevailed a wild but not rude sort of lawlessness, and on all hands, near and afar off, was heard the gay, measured beat of the African drum. Round the gates of the different halls were collected groups of white people, most of them evidently sailors, who were endeavoring to get sight of what was passing inside; but a couple of negroes, stationed at each with sticks in their hands, kept the entrance closed with good-tempered determination, and did not allow the doors to open beyond half way (Bremer 1853, 2:379).

II. [Inside the *cabildo*]

Chairs were offered to us not far from the door; we were presented to the queen and the king of the assembly who made demonstrations of good-will, and we were then left to look about us in quiet. The room was tolerably large, and might contain about one hundred persons. On the wall just opposite to us was painted a crown, and a throne with a canopy over it. There stood the seats of the king and queen. The customary dancing was going forward in front of the seat. One woman danced alone, under a canopy supported by four people. Her dancing must have given great delight—though it was not very different from that of the negro ladies which I have already described—for all kinds of handkerchiefs were hanging about her, and a hat, even, had been placed upon her head. The women danced on this occasion with each other, and the men with the men; some struck the doors and benches with sticks, others rattled gourds filled with stones, and the drums thundered with deafening power. They were apparently endeavoring to make as much noise as possible. While this was going on, a figure was seen advancing with a scarlet hat upon his head, and with a great number of glittering strings of beads round his neck, arms, and body, which was naked to the waist, from which hung scarlet skirts. This figure, before which the people parted to each side, approached me, bowing all the time, and as he did so the whole upper portion of his body seemed to move in snake-like folds. Still making these serpentine movements, he stood before me with extended hands, I being not at all certain whether he was inviting me to dance, or what was the meaning of his apparently friendly grimaces, and his great, black, outstretched hands. At length he uttered, with other words, "per la bonita!" and I comprehended that all his bowings and bedizenment were intended as a compliment to me, and I made my reply by shaking one of the black hands, and placing within it a silver coin, after which we exchanged friendly gestures, and my friend made a serpentine retreat, and began to dance on his own account, receiving great applause from the by-standers.

The nation is regarded as rich, in consequence of the

great prizes which it has won in the lottery, and this wealth it is said to apply to a good use—the purchasing the freedom of slaves of this tribe.

These cabildoes are governed, as I have already said, by queens, one or two, who decide upon the amusements, give tone to the society, and determine its extension. They possess the right of electing a king, who manages the pecuniary affairs of the society, and who has under him a secretary and master of the ceremonies. The latter presented me with a small printed card, which gave admission to the "Cabildo de Señora Santa Barbara de la nacion Lucumi Alagua."

After this, and when we had made a little offering to the treasury of the society, we took our departure, in order to visit other cabildoes (Bremer 1853, 2:380–81).

APPENDIX 2

IRENE WRIGHT'S DESCRIPTION OF HER VISIT TO AN "AFRICAN CABILDO" IN EL CERRO, 1910

I. [On the "colony of the African-born negroes" (in Cuba, 7,948 in 1910), the El Cerro *cabildo*, and the sociolegal status of Afro-Cuban religion]

These [of the "colony"] are almost all surviving slaves, for the Census shows only 10 immigrants from Africa in 1902–1907. My acquaintance with these is limited to seeing one, an old man, who seemed to be a leader in charge of an African *cabildo*, which used to hold forth on Sunday afternoons from one to four o'clock in a house on the outskirts of the suburb of Cerro. It was a social-religious organization licensed by the municipality under a name in which figured that of a Catholic saint. When we attended its dance, we were accompanied by a member, a mulatto, the leader of an orchestra well known in Havana. Before we reached the house we heard the nervous beat of the drum which takes the place of the tomtom, forbidden by law, and the accompanying rattle of gourds shaken up and down inside a beaded net. Three young negroes standing on a bench manipulated the gourds; another, seated below them, pounded the drum in maddening rhythm. The music was unquestionably African. In the open space, on the stone floor, before the players, members of the organization danced, not together, but singly, jerking and gesticulating in a circle, round and round. They sang in an African dialect. We were told that one song, movements to which simulated a snatching from above, was a prayer to Saint Barbara for blessings. In an adjoining room we were shown altars. One was to Our Lady of Mercy,[1] one to Saint Joseph,[2] and one to Saint Barbara, at the base of whose shrine was an iron image of a black jockey such as used to stand, before good taste made them scarce, on sidewalks before houses in the North as hitching posts. These altars were decorated with cheap hangings and tawdry trinkets, which had, probably, their secret meanings. In another room, in which also was a bed elaborately trimmed with yellow satin and ribbon, was an altar to the Virgin of Cobre. There were dishes of food before it, in the process of being blessed, I gathered, and there was a covered soup tureen we were given to understand held a holy secret. We returned to the dancing in time to see one apt performer throw a fit. "The saint" had entered into her. Immediately other women unbound her hair and removed her shoes. They hustled her into the other room and returned her clad in a garment which seemed to imitate the robes altar images of the Virgin and saints wear. She wore gold and brass bracelets which jingled as she danced forth. She proceeded to salute all present by throwing her arms about the shoulders of men and women alike, one after the other, kissing them on the cheek, if they were women, and rubbing each of her shoulders to each of theirs, in turn, if they were men. As she went she collected offerings of pennies and dimes. She approached us, and with more or less good grace we, too, submitted to these caressings. It seemed to me the frenzied creature took a particular delight in seizing hold of one of our number, a very precise and very religious young woman from Kentucky, whose face fairly froze with horror as she was smacked soundly on both cheeks. We were told that sometimes in this condition of hysteria those who had "the saint" prophesied and prescribed remedies for the sick. Later, I asked police headquarters to tell me exactly what this *cabildo* was, and learned that it, and organizations like it, are all the law allowed, at that time, of the old ñanigo clans. It was, as it were, the threshold beyond which lie their nefarious mysteries and the trickery of witchcraft.

The ñanigo clans were, I understand, a revival in Cuba of tribes that existed in Africa. I am not sufficiently informed, nor is there space here, to tell of their objects, their rites, and known and suspected ramifications. There was a time when on the "Day of Kings" their leaders were actually received in the palace of the governor-general; on that date their bands paraded the street and whites kept within closed doors. They had their jealousies, and members of rival clans killed and were killed in the public streets. One Spanish governor collected all their paraphernalia and boasted that he had persuaded them to disband. The police force of the American Government of Occupation declared that it had suppressed them. The spontaneity with which, during one carnival season not so long ago, certain groups of maskers appeared upon the streets, leads an observer to suspect that neither was successful. Later still, after two white children had been killed and cut up by "witch doctors" in the country, and the perpetrators of the crimes caught and convicted, the Provisional Administration grew critical of even such societies that we visited. I venture to say, however, that openly or secretly, they still exist, and if ever there is a negro uprising in Cuba they will play their prominent part (Wright 1910, 149).

Yet not all their members are negroes. Our guide was, as I have said, a mulatto. He was an officer in the organization, and as such those entering after he had arrived saluted him. One pretty young girl, who might have "passed for white" in her clean lawn dress with blue sash and neck ribbons he compelled by a glance to do as the rest,—to throw herself prone on the floor before him, and turn from hip to hip. We had no manner of knowing what immoralities lay behind many of the suggestive details we noticed. Taken [at] its surface value, the performance we saw that afternoon was a demonstration of fanaticism and ignorance it would be hard to equal anywhere. It was the most astounding confusion of heathenish and Catholic worship one could imagine: they sang in barbarous tongue to Christian saints, and to them they sacrifice white cocks occasionally; in the dances, which must have originated about African campfires, they flaunt yellow as the color of Our Lady of Cobre, white for Mary of Mercies, purple and green for Saint Joseph, and red for their favorite saint, protecting Barbara, each of whom has an African name. In honor of these respective patrons they wear copper, silver, bead, and coral trinkets. The local Catholic church recognizes this same symbolism in color and ornament (Wright 1910, 150).

APPENDIX 3

THE "REGULAR" IFÁ-CENTRIC INITIATION VERSUS THE OCHA-CENTRIC INITIATION

The "Regular Santo"

The Ocha house "uses" the *babalawo*, through Orula, to "take out the guardian angel" of the individual's head.[1] The *babalawo* also prepares and delivers the *guerreros* and the *mano de orula* (*awofaka* or *ikofá*). Two or three days before the *asiento*, the *babalawo* conducts the *vista*—an Ifá reading with the *opele* divining chain, in order to "mark" a protective *ebó* that must be performed on the eve of the initiation: the *ebó de entrada* (sacrifice and cleansing of entering) prior to the river ceremony (see also Cabrera [1974] 1980, 137–38).[2] For initiations of the *orichas* Eleguá, Ogún, and Ochosi, three *babalawos* "take the initiate to the *monte*" for a series of special sacrifices, followed by the ceremony of the river (Cabrera 1980, 183–84). The supervising *babalawo* and the *oriaté* contracted to work the initiation as "master of ceremonies" communicate about the results of the *vista* and the *ebó de entrada*, which deal with potential problems to be avoided.[3] The *oriaté* officiates during the principal phases of the *asiento*—shearing, shaving, painting the head, and "mounting" it with the *oricha*—except the *matanza*. Though Cabrera's informants insisted that the *babalawo* delivers the fresh plants and the *aché de santo* (the four African seeds), blesses the initiation's herbal cleansing liquids (*osains*), and "presents the razor to the *iyawó*'s head," other priests often conduct these tasks and some are often omitted, such as the razor ceremony.[4]

In the third day's *itá* reading, in which the *orichas* "speak for the first time" through their cowrie shells, the *oriaté* gives a comprehensive reading of each *oricha* in the line of *soperas* on the floor in order to map out the *iyawó*'s "past, present, and future" through a series of *consejos* (advice), which reveal applicable taboos (*egües* or *ewaws*) and sacrifices (*ebó*). The *oriaté* should explain how the sign of each *oricha* brings its particular blessings, if it is in *iré* ("positive" valence), or explain why an *osobo* ("negative" valence) came out, what its role will be in the initiate's life, and how its consequences should be managed. The *oriaté* determines the particular "roads" of the *orichas* Obatalá, Yemayá, and Ochún, and of Eleguá or Ogún, if one of these is the guardian angel. The *nombre de santo*—the initiate's sacred name in Lucumí—is determined,[5] and the identity of a second *oricha* "parent," which accompanies the guardian angel, is determined. The *oriaté* also determines what auxillary *oricha* protectors or powers the initiate must receive in the course of her life, such as the Twins, Oricha Oko, San Lázaro, and *Pinaldo*. Those prioritized, given the signs that have emerged, can be received as early as three months later, in the important *Ebó de los Tres Meses* (Sacrifice of the Three Months), a major blood offering of two- or four-legged animals, depending upon the house, in which the original initiation gains confirmation and firmness (see Cabrera [1974] 1980, 230–32).

The Ocha-Centric Santo

The *padrino* or *madrina* of the house or an *oriaté* takes out the guardian angel with the *dilogún*. The *guerreros* are received from an *oriaté* or the Ocha godparent (male godparents often make *guerreros* themselves). Few, if any, members of these Ocha-centric houses receive the *mano de orula*. The *oriaté* performs the *vista* and the *ebó de entrada*, and the *oriaté* or *oyubona* takes initiates of Eleguá, Ogún, and Ochosi to the *monte*. The *oriaté* officiates throughout the *asiento* and performs the major sacrifices, the *matanza*. The *oriaté* conducts the *itá* in the same way as in the "regular *santo*" model. Houses in which *padrinos* or *madrinas* arrogate to themselves tasks now considered central to the *oriaté*'s professional role open up additional variations within the Ocha-centric ritual field (see Ecún 1985, 25 and passim).

APPENDIX 4

THE *ORIATÉ*'S COUNTERNARRATIVE TO IFÁ-CENTRIC OCHA PRACTICE

Point by point, Ernesto Pichardo challenges every exclusive claim *babalawos* have put forward with respect to the four *guerreros* (Eleguá, Ogún, Ochosi, and Ósun), the herbalist Osain, the Creator Odúa, the mysterious master of the deep, Olokun, and the dead (the *egun*). In a form of argumentation perfected also by the Black American Yoruba Movement in the 1970s and 1980s (see Hunt 1979; Adefunmi I 1982; Mason 1985a), Pichardo appeals to the authority of African origins as the anchor of a counternarrative to the vociferous authority claims of Cuban creole *babalawos*. This mode of argumentation also recalls the Yoruba rhetorical strategy of "critical revision," in which protagonists on contested ritual and political terrains mobilize "deep knowledge" to subvert established hegemonic structures of authority (Apter 1992, 210–11; 222–24; see also Lipsitz 1990). Yet Pichardo's counternarrative proposes not only his possession of ritual deep knowledge. The currency of Pichardo's rhetorical strategy, his symbolic capital, also contains historical knowledge gleaned from scholarly research. He and other learned priests have upped the ante of ritual debate within the religion by adopting forms of knowledge, argumentation, and presentation based in the apparatuses and resources of the academy. Their self-conscious scholarly works act not merely as neutral sources of information, but as material demonstrations of their social and intellectual competence—in the Lucumí idiom, their *aché*—which have the potential to dislodge other entrenched ideological narratives (see, e.g., Pichardo and Nieto 1984; Pichardo 1989a, 1989b; J. Mason 1992, 1994, 1996; Flores-Peña and Evanchuck 1994; Epega and Neimark 1995; and see Bell 1992, 82).

Thus, on the ritual and rhetorical battleground that Pichardo paints as the history of Lucumí religion, Cuban *babalawos* "took the initiative early on to document and compile written works, but they did so in order to acquire knowledge and power." The turn-of-the-twentieth-century literate creole *babalawos*, who conducted a kind of ethnographic fieldwork among surviving Africans, appropriated and mobilized the resulting information as their own symbolic capital, according to Pichardo. However, "In Cuba, in fact, the most renowned contributor of knowledge to the *babalawos* was not even a priest, but an *aleyo* [noninitiate], an African whose name was Ayayí. The African master of Olokun was an *aleyo*. The *babalawos* came to possess [Olokun] and they said, 'Screw you!' They came to possess it and wouldn't talk to you."[1] In the same way, he argues, Cuban *babalawos* attempted to extend their monopoly to the *guerreros* Eleguá, Ogún, Ochosi, and Ósun. Utilizing scholarly research and ethnohistorical argumentation, Pichardo revises the Cuban *babalawo*'s exclusive claim over the *guerreros* by citing the structure and logic of Yoruba cult organization. "*Babalawos* insist that they have exclusive right to and control over Eleguá and the Warriors—Ogún, Ochosi, and Ósun. But if we go to Nigeria, is it the *babalawo* who is giving out Ogún, or is it the Ogún priest? The same goes for Eleguá, Ochosi, and Ósun. The Ósun is the status symbol, the staff, for the priest in general. The *babalawos*' idea that in the New World only they can give the Ósun is nonsense because in Africa Ósun was generalized. [The] Ifá [corpus] even says this. Ósun begins [in Africa] as an extension of the [cult of] Odudúwa. In the New World the *babalawos* say only they can give Odudúwa. This is nonsense again."[2] The logic of West African ritual arrangements grants Cuban Ocha priests, Pichardo argues, an original claim of authority and competence with respect to Eleguá, Ogún, Ochosi, Ósun, and Odúa (Odudúwa). Thus, for example, like their original counterparts in Africa, *oriatés* and *santeros* confect, with perfect competence and authority, the *fundamentos de cabecera* that are seated on the heads of initiates who become priests of Eleguá, Ogún, and Ochosi. Therefore, nothing but an arbitary and politicized New World proscription, a function of La Regla de Ifá's agenda to establish its authority and power to extract tribute (*derechos*), prevents *oriatés* and *santeros* from preparing these *orichas* as they appear in the *guerreros*.

Indeed, for Pichardo, the *guerreros*, particularly Ogún and Ochosi, stand as a test of the *babalawo*'s limitations. The original authority and deep knowlege *oriatés* and *santeros* possess with respect to these two *orichas* reduce the *babalawo*'s version of Ogún and Ochosi to less profound "representations" in the form of iron tools: the seven implements of Ogún and the bow and arrow of Ochosi—precisely the same representations the *oriaté* and *santero* give within their *guerreros*. "The *babalawo* cannot process Eleguá, Ogún, Ochosi, and Ósun as we do. What *babalawos* give is a representation of Ogún, and a representation of Ochosi. They do truly give Echú. However, when a person goes into the initiation, we now have to redo this Eleguá [Echú] and we have to make and finish off Ogún [and Ochosi] so that it is no longer a representation of Ogún but an Ogún [*de cabecera*]."[3] By extension, the *babalawo*'s special claim over the ceremony of the *monte* for initiates of Eleguá, Ogún, and Ochosi evaporates. "Their role is not significant. You can do Eleguá [Ogún, and Ochosi] any day of the week and not bring the *babalawo* in the door."[4]

In sum, Pichardo's counternarrative radically relativizes the *babalawo*'s historical and ritual claims to all of interconnected points of defense of the Ifá-centric Maginot Line: Olofin, Odúa, Eleguá, Ogún, Ochosi, Ósun, Osain, Olokun, and the dead. For Pichardo, the *babalawo* is left with his tutelary *oricha*, Orula (Orunmila), and his special road of Echú. "If you leave them with Echú and Orunmila, but you take Ogún and Ochosi away from them, what do they have left? The rhetoric is that they're the only ones that are supposed to have Osain; they're the only ones that are supposed to have Olokun. . . . In the early days, it was [also] said: 'the *babalawo* is the only one who can feed *egún* [the dead].' But when we started talking to Yoruba people it blew up in the *babalawos*' faces. . . . 'We are the *babalawos*,' they say. They try to create this distinction. . . . It's become a tradition for other motives."[5]

APPENDIX 5

CALENDAR OF *ORICHA* AND SAINT FEAST DAYS

ORICHA	ROMAN CATHOLIC SAINT	FEAST DAY
Oyá	Candelaria/Santa Teresa	2 February
Ochagriñán	San José	19 March
Aguema	La Purísma Concepción	5 May
Orichaokó	San Isidro	15 May
Ochosi	San Norberto	16 June
Eleguá	San Antonio/El Niño de Atocha	13 June
Naná Burukú	Nuestra Señora del Carmen	16 June
Ogún	San Pedro	29 June
Yewá	Santa Clara/Nuestra Señora de los Desamparados	11 August
Yemayá	La Virgen de Regla	7 September
Ochún	La Caridad del Cobre	8–12 September
Obatalá	La Virgen de las Mercedes	24 September
Los Ibeyi	Santos Cosme y Damián	26 September
Inle	San Rafael	29 September
Orula	San Francisco de Asís	4 October
Dadá	Nuestra Señora del Rosario	7 October
Agayú	San Cristóbal	16 November
Changó	Santa Bárbara	4 December
Babalú Ayé/Asojuano	San Lázaro	17 December
Osain	San Silvestre/San Ambrosio	31 December

APPENDIX 6

ORAL DATA FROM FIELDWORK: INTERVIEWS, PERSONAL COMMUNICATIONS, AND CORRESPONDENCE

Formal interviews are extended discussion and question-and-answer sessions, on tape and/or with extensive note taking. *Personal communications* are informal, relatively brief discussions, with some note taking. *Personal correspondence* is more or less formal correspondence by E-mail, with questions and answers.

Formal Interviews

Oluwó Popó Awó Bokonó Arará Pedro Abreu, 21, 24, 29 July, 1 August 2000, El Cerro and Matanzas

María Eugenia Álvarez Pérez (with her grandson Jorge Díaz, a *babalawo*), 31 August 1999, 1, 2 September 1999

Babalawo Mario Angarica ("Papo"), 10 July 1992, central Havana

Babalawo Juanito Angulo, 16 June 1993, Mantilla, Havana

Olorisha Gisela Arandia, 25 June 1992, central Havana

Babalawo Francisco Aristola ("Pancho"), 3, 7 July 1992, 27 June 1998, 14, 18 August 1999, Pogolotti, Havana

Babalawo Reinaldo Blayó, 17 June 1993, El Vedado, Havana

Babalawo Fran Cabrera Suárez, 4 January 1994, 4, 12 July 1994, 1 June 1998, 11 August 1999, Párraga, Havana

Iyaloricha Olga Calvo Püig and *babalawo* Radamés Corona, 21 August 1999, central Havana

Babalawo Elpidio Cárdenas, 15, 18, 23 June 1998, central Havana

Oloricha Idalberto Cárdenas, 29 November 1986, Brooklyn, N.Y.

Osvaldo Cárdenas Villamil, 20, 25 July 1997, Matanzas

Iyaloricha Melba Carillo, 7 August 1987, New Jersey; 6 May 1990, New York; 1 September 1987, New York; 20 March 1987, New York; 4 April 1995, telephone

Teruel Rolando Cartaya, 29 August 1999, Matanzas

Babalawo Luis Castillo, 25 May 1986, Elizabeth, N.J.

Babalawo Radamés Corona, Havana, 21 August 1999, 2, 5 September 1999, Havana

Lic. Pedro Cosme Baños, 15, 21 June 1993, 5, 13 January 1994, 20 December 1995, 12, 18, 30 June 1998, 15 December 1998, Regla

Babaloricha Reinaldo Raimundo Chaguayceda ("Papo"), 6 January 1996, Regla; 17 July 1997, Regla; 7 April 2000, telephone

Iyaloricha Candelaria Cruz, 6 July 1994, 24 June 1998, Guanabacoa, Havana

Babalawo Lázaro CuestaValdés, 3, 4 January 1996, 26 June 1998, 5, 15 September 1999, Mantilla, Havana

Babalawo Antonio de Armas, 16 June 1998, El Vedado, Havana; 7 March 2002, Cayotlueso, Havana

Iyaloricha Ángela Rosa Delgado Entensa, 9 July 1994, Palmira, Cienfuegos

Eusebia Febles, 14 July 1994, Buena Vista, Havana

Musician Juanito Febles, 17, 22 June 1998, Havana

Iyaloricha Josefina García, 21 May 1988, Bronx, N.Y.

Iyaloricha Gloria Gónzalez, August 30, 1987, Elizabeth, N.J.

Babalawo Cosme Guio, 29 July 1997, 14 June 1998, Central Havana

Oriaté Agustín Hernández, 9 July 1994, Palmira, Cienfuegos

Tata Nkisi Rolando Rodríguez Hernández, president of La Sociedad de San Antonio, 9 July 1994, Palmira, Cienfuegos

Babalawos Andrés Kolá and Hermes Valera Ramírez, 16, 19 July 1992, 26 June 1993, 2 July 1993, Lawton, Havana

Iyaloricha Lourdes López 27 February 1987, West New York, N.J.

Mae de santo, 28 February 1988, Cabula, Salvador, Bahia

Iyaloricha Mercedes Melo González ("La China"), 24, 30, 31 August 1999, El Cerro, Havana

Inocencia Mola, 25 August 1999, Havana

Babalawo Fernando Zacaria Molina Puente, 11, 23 June 1998, Lawton, Havana

Julia and Juan Montalvo, 25 June 1998, Cárdenas, Matanzas Province

Babalawo Feliberto O'Farril, 30 December 1993, 4 January 1994, 28 December 1994, 1, 5 July 1993, Reparto Poey, Havana

Babalawo Ángel Padrón ("Bebo Mokongo"), 20, 27 August, 7, 9 September 1999, San Miguel del Padrón, Havana

Obá Ernesto Pichardo, 14 January 1988, 12 September 1989, 12 October 1989, 24 December 1994, 12 March 1995, 24 May 1995, 11 July 1995, 26 July 1996, 21 January 1997, 21 January 1998, telephone and in person

Iyaloricha Nydia Pichardo, 26 March 1995, telephone

Olorichas Gualberta Püig and Ricardo Navarro, 4, 7, 14 July 1994, 17, 18 June 1998, Guanabacoa, Havana

Babalawo José Manuel Pulido, 14, 16, 18, 20 August 1999, San Miguel del Padrón, Havana

Oriaté Miguel "Willie" Ramos, 9 March 1995, telephone; 6 April 1995, telephone; 7 November 1996, telephone

Babalawo Evelio Real Orduña, 19 June 1998, Guanabacoa, Havana

Babalawo Gilberto H. Rojas, 2 January 1993, 29 December 1993, 1 January 1994, 26 June 1998, 15 December 1998, Marianao, Havana

Cabelo Rolim, 15 April 1998, telephone

Arará Sabalú priestess Mitagros Sequiera Palma, 26 March 2002, Matanzas

Babalawo Antonio Sevilla, 10 July 1994, Palmira, Cienfuegos

Babalawo Pablo Sevilla, 5 July 1994, Havana; 9 July 1994, Palmira, Cienfuegos

Babalawo Orlando Sierra Justiz ("Pipo"), 24 July 1997, Old Havana

Sociedad San Roque members, 9 July 1994, Palmira, Cienfuegos

Babalawo Ignacio Tartabull, 23 June 1993; 16 August 1999, Lawton, Havana

Lic. Carmen Trujillo Pardo, curator, Museum of Colonial Art, Havana, 16, 24, 27 June 1998

Babalawo José Valdés ("Joseito"), Guanabacoa, 1 January 1994

Babalawo Hermes Valera, 20, 23, 24, 25, 29, 30 June 1992, 8, 9, 15, 17 July 1992, 23, 25 June 1993, 31 December 1993, 27 June 1986, 21 July 1997, 23 July 1997, 6, 11 June 1998, 24, 25, 27 August 1999

Babalawo Jesús Varona Puente, 1 July 1994, 23 July 1997, 22 June 1998, 25 June 1998, 5 January 1996, Havana

Babalawo Pancho Veitia, 7 July 1994, 16 June 1994, 7 July 1994, 17 June 1998, Guanabacoa, Havana

Villalonga family, 7 July 1996, 7 September 1999, Luyanó, Havana

Babalawo Roberto Villanueva, 17 June 1993, 24 June 1994, 29 July 1997, 15 June 1998, Central Havana

Personal Communications

Dr. Isabel Castellanos, 2 July 1997, telephone

Dr. David Dorris, 3 November 2002, telephone

Babaloricha Adolfo Fernández, 1 May 1988, Union City, N.J.

Dr. Franklin W. Knight, fall 1994

Dr. John Howett, 10 October 1995, Atlanta

Dr. Jean Howson, 22 April 1998, New Brunswick, N.J.

Dr. Alice Jarrard, 20 September 1993, Atlanta

Elliot Klein, 12 April 1997, telephone

Kunle, 12 August 1992, Ibeji Temple, Atlanta

Babaloricha John Mason, 20 October 1993

Dr. Michael Mason, 30 May 1995, 20 August 1997, 10 October 1996, 7 November 1996, 20 August 1997, 10 January 1999, 1 November 2000, 3 December 2000, all telephone

Dr. J. Lorand Matory, 7 September 1996, telephone

Babalawo and Alañá Salvador Ortiz, Jr., 30 September 2000, Bronx, N.Y.

Lic. Luis Alberto Pedroso, 12 June 1998, 18 August 1999, El Vedado, Havana

Obá Ernesto Pichardo, 24 May 1995, 21 January 1997, 30 January 1998, all telephone

Oriaté Miguel Ramos, 9 March 1995, April 9 1995, all telephone

Babalawo Pedro Rodríguez, 30 August 1987, Elizabeth, N.J.

Dr. Rafael L. López Valdés, 10 June 1993, El Vedado, Havana

Babaloricha Dagoberto Ventura Herrera, 2 January 2000, central Havana

Babaloricha Francisco Zamora Chirino ("Minini"), 3 August 1989, Matanzas

Personal Correspondence

Babalawo Ronald Harris, 22 April 2001

Dr. Michael Mason, September 2000 (marginal comments made upon his reading of drafts of chapters in this book)

Oloricha William Muldro (Sim-El Fatunmishe), E-mail correspondence during September 2000

Obá Ernesto Pichardo, 6 December 1999, E-mail

Oriaté Miguel Ramos, 29 March 1995, 26 March 1995, 6 April 1995, 11 April 1995, 19 July 1995, 19 July 1995, 28 July 1995, all E-mail

Cuban researcher Jorge Rodríguez, 6 December 1999, E-mail

NOTES

PREFACE

1. See Richard Drinnon's harsher perspective, which the title to his book reveals up front (Drinnon 1980).

2. I include cultural descent in the sense that culture is learned and borrowed—Americans who are not "black" have been influence and changed in a variety of ways by African-derived cultures (see Mintz 1974a, 5–6; Mintz and Price [1976] 1992, chap. 2).

3. Some important scholars, direct students of Herskovits, had never stopped working (e.g., Simpson 1978). Other scholars such as Sidney Mintz had, of course, been working tirelessly all along in Afro-America, since the early 1950s (see bibliography in Mintz 1974a). John Szwed traces a general hiatus after Herskovits's *Myth of the Negro Past* (1941) until the 1970s, due to the direction of integrationist and "melting pot" politics, in which Herskovits's argument about the exceptionalism of black culture was conveniently ignored—because it was taken to suggest that blacks could not be assimilated into the mainstream of American life (Szwed 1969). In the 1970s, a huge number of writings by anthropologists, folklorists, historians, and art historians that stressed black *culture* were produced, such as Thompson 1969; Vlach [1978] 1990; Szwed and Whitten 1970; Szwed and Abrahams 1978; Abrahams 1983; Reisman 1970; Marks 1974; Blassingame 1979; Genovese 1976; Raboteau 1978; Levine 1977; and Brown 1976).

INTRODUCTION

1. *Rompe zaragüéy* is used for "breaking" particular problems; *siempre viva* means "always alive"; *ètìpọn' ọlá* is the common name of *Boerhavia diffusa* [Nyctaginaceae]. "The whole plant in an infusion . . . is a mild laxative and febrifuge for children: it is given for convulsions in children . . . and for producing regular menstruation in women" (Abraham 1946, 168). *Atipolá* in Cuba (*atikuanlá* in Lucumí) is good for the urinary tract and to "refresh the head" (Cabrera [1954] 1983, 332).

2. This "scale" is a chart of trait diffusion of cultural elements ranging from "very African" to "a little African" and then to "absent"—read European.

3. Hagedorn writes that Martínez Furé "promoted the transformation and development of folklore, essentially by cleaning up the folk" in an attempt to fashion an appropriate revolutionary national culture (Hagedorn 2001, 173–74; Martínez Furé 1979, 267).

4. See also Robinson, Foster, and Ogilvie 1969; John Szwed's important essay (1969) addresses the politics of black culture study from the moment of Herskovits's *Myth of the Negro Past* (1941) until the eve of the 1970s.

5. See Lippard 1990 for a panorama of 1980s multicultural art and identity expressions.

6. The vocalists of Grupo Orishas, particularly Roldán, utilize rap modes as well as the richly voiced, polyphonous, and exclamatory *timba* styles of N. G. La Banda and David Calzado. Their percussionist on recordings is the famous Miguel Angá Díaz. Their current DJ is an Algerian living in Paris who does not speak Spanish. Singer "Ruzzo" and singer Yotuel "Guerrero" are priests of Eleguá and *Changó*, respectively. They introduce *oricha* themes, chants, and dance movements into their song performances.

7. More generally, Herskovits's work's falling out of favor is attributable to the fact that evidence of the potential to integrate blacks within the American mainstream was preferred by the sociologists of the "Negro problem" to evidence of cultural "difference" (see Szwed 1969 and Jackson 1986).

8. The works of Richard Price (1983), as well as Herskovits (1941), are subjected to a brilliant critique by David Scott (1991). Herskovits and Price, though apparently different in their approaches to history (Price treats process, whereas Herskovits's "ethnohistory" is static), are nevertheless seen to be bound up in the enterprise of verifying and documenting a "Negro past," which is built upon the received American anthropological construction of "the New World Negro," and makes them feel compelled to speak to the racist discourse of "pastlessness" while ignoring alternate, local, imaginary constructions of "African Diasporas."

9. For example, a recent Rutgers Center for Historical Analysis "Black Atlantic Project" seminar, in which Michael Gómez (1998, 1999) presented his work, the historians of Africa and the Diaspora present concluded that the 1970s and 1980s works in the tradition of Herskovits were "useless" as far as respectable historical investigation was concerned (i.e., for data), not least because the writers had no training in African history (see Gómez 1999). At the same time, it is clear, Gómez (1998) and others regard Stuckey (see 1987) as a key model for future historical studies, though clearly, Stuckey's work relies for some of its core ideas upon the 1970s and 1980s historiography in the Herskovits school.

10. I say "ironic," because Stuckey utilizes the figure of the "circle" or "ring," which Thompson traced through the aforementioned formalist and iconological methods, to Kongo-Angola cultures (see Thompson 1983, chap. 2), yet the new positivists (Gómez 1998) reject what appears to them as overly generalized, static treatments of African-based cultures in the Americas, believing that specific evidence of, for example, "Iboisms," can and should be documented in transatlantic histories of cultures (e.g., Chambers 1997; Gómez 1998, 1999). Herskovits is most roundly criticized on all sides for his ahistorical reliance on the idea of "Africanisms."

11. Palmié and I had met in December 1986 in Miami, and I had the early benefit of reading his work—particularly his paper for a 1989 conference, a later version of which he published in 1993—and discussing our common interests. Mintz and Price refer to "new social ties" as the institutional basis of their creolization model ([1976] 1992, 44).

12. "Improperly contextualized," they insist, "the stories of ordinary people past [and present, presumably] stand in danger of remaining that: stories. To become something more, these partial, 'hidden histories' have to be situated in the wider worlds of power and meaning that gave them life." For them "ethnography . . . calls upon us to ground subjective, culturally configured action in society and history—and vice versa" (Comaroff and Comaroff 1992, 11). Thus their main questions: "*How* . . . do we connect parts to 'totalities'? How do we redeem the fragments? How do we make intelligible the idiosyncratic acts, lives and representations of others? How do we locate them within 'a historically determinate environment'?" (17).

13. From talks by, and personal communications with, Michael Fried, Marc Gottleib, and James Meyer, 1992–97, as well as readings of the works of Fried (1990) and T. J. Clark (1973, 1984).

14. For example, "kinship" is an analytical model; however, as a set of generative principles, it is embodied in dance performance. An elder or big man must dance in a satisfying way with particular female authorities in order to maintain, or change, kinship relations and alliances.

15. A future book about Cuba's *babalawos* will deal with these "edges" in a more self-reflexive account.

16. David Scott (1991) has critiqued the use of "Africa" and "slavery" as conventional beginnings of narratives of the African Diaspora, along with its enabling anthropological object (the "New World Negro") constructed by Boas, DuBois, and Herskovits between the 1890s and 1941. These narrative beginnings sought to counteract the "myth of the Negro past" (i.e., the absence of a history) but had the effect of reducing and obscuring many possible constructions of diaspora by contemporary African-descended peoples, Scott argues.

17. Iconological analysis consists of three analytical and interpretive phases: formal description, a first-level interpretation of motifs or types, and then a second-level interpretation to illuminate a greater horizon of cultural (in Panofsky's time, read "national") meanings (see Panofsky 1955; Brown 1996, 81–85).

18. Since the early 1970s, the king has initiated three hundred priests. He established temples in New York, Chicago, Los Angeles, Philadelphia, Milwaukee, Indiana, Georgia, and North and South Carolina (Clarke 1997, 221). There are also related groups in Miami and Gary, Indiana.

CHAPTER ONE

1. Siliman's Proclamation reports on the heavy losses the French suffered on 4 June 1808 in Barcelona and on 14 June in Cádiz, where the French naval squadron was forced to surrender. Yet, on 15 June, confronted by an armed populace, the French killed half the population of Zaragossa. Siliman's anti-French proclamation and a series of anti-French demonstrations in Havana around that time followed upon similar anti-French demonstrations in Spain in May of 1808. By 2 May, a great anti-French insurrection had begun in Madrid, the scene of the bloody repression of the Spanish crowds by French troops depicted by Goya in his famous painting *El Dos de Mayo.* Napoleon proclaimed the ceding to him of the crown on 11 May, and on 7 June, Joseph Bonaparte, Napoleon's older brother, arrived in Spain, having been proclaimed king (see Bergamini 1974, 129–63).

2. King Ferdinand VII (1784–1833), son of Charles IV (1748–1819) and María Luisa of Parma, was King of Spain in 1808 and then again from 1814 to 1833. He was followed by Isabella II (1830–1904), queen of Spain from 1833 to 1868).

3. For the best discussion of the features of *bozal,* see Castellanos 1990 and 1977. Siliman's speech is characterized by a reduced grammatical structure (e.g., a single conjugation of the infinitive is used for all tenses and subjects, *veni* [to come] and *sabi* [to know] for *venir* and *saber:* yo veni/sabi, tu veni/sabi) and

phonologically shaped features characteristic of Cuban creole pronunciation. However, its lexicon derives predominantly from Spanish, and it lacks many of the African terms and aspect markers that characterize historically earlier or "deeper" versions of the *bozal* (see Castellanos 1990; Todd 1974).

4. These nations had their putative origins in the western Sudan region of present-day Mali, Senegal, and Sierra Leone (Mandinga), the Gulf of Guinea region of present-day Togo, Ghana, the Republic of Benín, and southwestern Nigeria (Arará, Fanti, Mina, Lucumí), the "semi-Bantú" regions spanning the Niger River and Cross River deltas (Carabaly, Brichi), the Bantu Kongo-Angola regions (Congo, Luango, Mondongo, Intuanza), and the eastern Bantu region of Mozambique (Macuá). See Ortiz [1916] 1987, 40–59, for the ethnonyms applied to Africans during the slave trade.

5. *Palente, mingo, y crabela* are approximations of the *bozal* morphology through the reporter's transcription of the speaker's phonology. The terms are characterized by typical creole elisions and "liquids" (exchanges of 'r' and 'l'). The Spanish lexical equivalents of *palente* and *mingo* are *pariente* (relative) and *amigo* (friend), while *crabela* is the elided form of *carabela*, a *bozal* word meaning African "countryman" (*paisano*) or "shipmate" (*combarcano*). The last has apparent roots in both Congo and European continental languages, such as an old term for a particular seagoing vessel (*caravelle*). See Ortiz 1924, 103–4. Mintz and Price show that the "shipmate" relationship (*carabela*), was understood both literally and figuratively to cover various surrogate kinship relationships created throughout the Americas. *Carabela* emblematizes the "new social ties" and incipient institutions at the heart of diasporic experience and "culture building" (Mintz and Price [1976] 1992, 42–44).

6. "Yó má negro que tó unté": though it literally means "I'm more African (or "black") than all of you," it seems to connote his claim of seniority, authority, and reputation through his African origin.

7. "Ordinary experiences" are day-to-day experiences, which may be more or less marked; "extraordinary experiences" are highly marked or framed performance events, such as speech making and carnival displays (see Abrahams 1986).

8. Here I use the term "creole"—a term borrowed from historical linguistics—in its simplest sense, as "island born" as opposed to Old World born, and in its "social-relational" rather than "cultural" sense. "Social-relational" has to do with the ways and contexts in which new social groups are formed from hitherto disparate elements (in sociolinguistics, a new "speech community" is formed), whereas the "cultural" dimension refers to the "expressive" (e.g., morphological, phonological, semantic, and performative) aspects of language use (see Mintz and Price [1976] 1992, 21).

9. Appearing on maps dated 1798, to the southwest of the *intramuros* (the walled "Old City of Havana") are found the *barrios* of Jesús María, El Horcón, and Guadalupe; these were contiguous with the swampy edge of the Bay of Havana. By 1842, *barrio* San Lázaro appears on maps directly to the west and northwest of the *intramuros*, along the Atlantic seawall (now the Malecón); by 1853 San Lázaro had been been subdivided to produce Barrio Colón. Jesús María by 1853 had been subdivided to include *barrio* Chávez (from 1798, 1842, and 1853 Havana maps in the Smithsonian Institution's map collection, National Museum of American History).

10. Kiple 1976, 47 ff., suggests that the 1841 census overstated some figures. Kiple estimates about 324,000 slaves for all of Cuba in 1841 (1976, 55).

11. I do not wish to reify Ortiz's five "types" in the present work. However, Ortiz's typology reflects Cuban historiography and scholarly and popular thinking in the nineteenth and early twentieth centuries.

12. For example, Pérez, citing an 1862 Cuban statistical study, shows 355,849 total slaves distributed in the following manner: 172,671 on sugar plantations (48%), which were predominantly in the western section of the island; 75,977 in urban centers (21%); and 107,201 on coffee estates, tobacco plantations, and miscellaneous agricultural establishments (30%), predominantly in the central and eastern parts of the island. In other words, as Knight suggests, at the height of the sugar boom, around 80% (78% in Pérez' numbers) were in the rural agricultural domain in 1862, with the largest percentage in sugar (48%), while 21%, very significant in a diaspora-wide perspective, found themselves in urban centers (Pérez 1988, 98).

13. By the middle of the nineteenth century, conditions of slave life worsened: plantation family relationships became more tenuous, small independent plots for subsistence (*conucos*) gave way to sugar, and the possibilities for *coartación* vastly diminished with the great demand for labor (see Knight 1970, 68).

14. Knowledge of such an "internal market" system and material culture among slaves and free creoles in Cuba in the rural and urban settings—and the relation of those systems to larger Cuban and global networks—remains undeveloped. It is richer in the research of other areas of the Caribbean and North America (see, e.g., Mintz 1974b; Higman 1991; McDonald 1993; and the fine edited collection by Berlin and Morgan [1991]). Undoubtedly, however, African and Afro-Cuban internal markets were linked to transatlantic trade circuits in which Havana was integral in the eighteenth century and nineteenth century (see Kuethe 1991). In the early nineteenth century, for example, a huge trade, carrying a great variety of goods, circulated between Havana and Philadelphia (see Salvucci 1991), and Havana was the destination

for imports of English cloth of all kinds and ceramics (personal communication with Jean Howson, who researched British exports to the Caribbean, including Cuba, during the nineteenth century).

15. See n. 13. After the Moret Law of 1870, the offspring of enslaved persons were legally free (see Pérez 1988, 127).

16. See also Klein's discussion of urban slaves and free blacks in the artisanal trades (1967, 160–62, 194–227). In 1832, José Antonio Saco lamented that "the arts [including artisanal trades] are in the hands of the people of color. . . . Among the greatest ills that this race has brought to our soil, is the retreating of the arts from our white population" ([1832] 1946, 93).

17. Aponte's insurrection, the "Aponte Conspiracy" of 1812 for which he and others were jailed and executed, included members of the various African nations, as well as free creoles. Plans were apparently hatched and carried out through the social networks of the multifarious Afro-Cuban *cabildos* (Franco 1963, 8–13, 18–19, 26; 1977, 23).

18. José Luciano Franco reports that Aponte led the famous Lucumí *cabildo* called Changó-Tedúm, was a member of the "Ogboni society," and was a priest of Changó. It remains unclear how Franco arrived at such conclusions. Changó is the Yoruba-Lucumí thunder god; Ogboni is a Yoruba society of elders that has judicial, ancestral, and kingmaking functions. The contents of Aponte's home, as searched by the authorities, are silent on the question of the *cabildo*'s name and Aponte's African religious identity. However, the homes of his colleagues contained some African religious attributes; for example, a "red box with religious attributes of African origin" is reported to have been found in the house of one coconspirator, Clemente Chacón, and "African religious objects that the colonial authorities evaluated as witchcraft" were found in the house of another, Salvador Ternero (Franco 1977, 23–24). The "red box" may have suggested to Franco the presence of the Yoruba thunder god.

19. This flag was probably the tricolor *bandera nacional* of the earlier "separatist conspiracy" of 1809–10, in which Aponte participated. Seeking to liberate Cuba from Spanish control, and directed by Román de la Luz, Luis F. Basabe (Bassave), Manuel Ramírez, and Joaquín Infante, it raised the horizontal tricolor of green, purple, and white (see Roig de Leuchsenring 1950, 71–72; Franco 1977, 9–11). Bassave was a white creole captain of the Calvary Militias and a member of the wealthy classes of Havana. Aponte, first corporal of the Black and Mulatto Battalion, according to Franco, was "recruited by Bassave for the work of the conspiracy" (1977, 10).

20. Aponte's books included *Historia Natural, Arte de Nebrija, Guía de Forasteros de la Isla de Cuba, Maravillas de la Ciudad de Roma, Estado Militar de España, Sucesos Memorables del Mundo, Historia del Conde Saxe, Formulario de escribir cartas, Catecismo* [sic] *de la Doctrina Cristiana,* and *Vida del Sabio Hicosopo tomo tercero de D. Quijote* (Franco 1977, 132). For a discussion of the historical significance of *Arte de Nebrija,* see Illich 1980.

21. I tend to favor Homi Bhabha's definition of "hybridity" as an "interstitial passage between fixed identifications"; in other words, hybrids resist identification with binaries and constitute a kind of "third space." Hybrids are constituted through "cultural engagement," "enunciation," or "performance." They mark "difference" that "must not be hastily read as the reflection of *pre-given* ethnic or cultural traits set in the fixed tablet of tradition. The social articulation of difference, from the minority perspective, is a complex, on-going negotiation that seeks to authorize cultural hybridities that emerge in moments of historical transformation" (Bhabha 1994, 4–5). This notion resonates with some creolist formulations in which creole morphology is overdetermined and resists singular etymologies (see Reisman 1970). Such forms do not mediate between two reified "sides" but are emergent through performance. In the case of Aponte's collage-like "book of pictures," though it would be tempting to tease out the iconographic sources of this text, the ultimate sources and their particular contexts would not determine the meanings of their enunciation in Aponte's book. The work could be called a *bricolage* (an improvised assemblage or structure from an available storehouse of potentially polyvocal elements). Bricolages can be ambiguous and ambivalent through the compounding of their semantic load; most important, within hegemony, they both resist and perpetuate received traditions (see Comaroff 1985, 197–98; see also Hebdige 1979).

22. According to Ortiz, "The *negros curros* are distinguished from other mortals by a multitude of details. Their figure, their hairstyle, their walk, their shirts, their trousers, their footwear, their hat, their handkerchief, their teeth, etc., everything that denotes the *curro*. . . . In him no mimetic adaptation of the social environment could be observed, rather he seemed set upon struggling to separate himself and distinguish himself from all other individuals, in order that they recognize, admire, or fear him" (Ortiz 1927, 285; see also 323). Ortiz, elaborating on their linguistic "exhibition[ism]" (285), notes that they adopted an old, "disused" Spanish creole more characteristic of Andalusian and Sevillan working class and minority populations brought to Cuba. Even if they had been able to speak the standard Spanish of white Havana, insists Ortiz, they would have done so only as a kind of stylized performance to amplify their difference 1928, 161–62. "No mimetic adaptation of the social environment" seems to mean that the *curro* does not conform to any social category.

23. Ortiz insists that "the African *cabildos* of Cuba have a wise Spanish origin: they are an overseas survival of a medieval Sevillan institution (1921, 14).

24. In Brazil, the "divide and rule" policy was similar (see Bastide [1960] 1978, 55).

25. See Ortiz (1921) and Deschamps Chapeaux (1968, 50–51) for a description of *cabildo* offices, powers, and funding. Similar structures were found in the United States in both northern and southern cities (see Ortiz 1921, 31–32; Aimes 1905, 15–32; and Piersen 1988).

26. In the case of West African regions colonized by the British, systems of indirect rule made for levels of "collaboration" between the colonial authority and various local "chiefs, headmen, and elders," a collaboration that was "a very practical affair of exchanged benefits" (Ranger 1983, 229). It is not clear in the Cuban case how much *cabildo* kings were collaborators in this sense, if at all, and whether their "subjects" ever resisted them. Clearly, the government identified the *cabildos* as sites of organization for rebellion (see Aponte case above). As the *cabildos* were intended as institutions in a "divide-and-rule" strategy, and as mechanisms of enculturation and Hispanicization, they can be likened to aspects of Louis Althusser's "ideological state apparatuses" (ISAs)—sites of negotiation and struggle within hegemony (1971, 143–51).

27. For the richest description, with contemporaneous engravings, of Afro-Cuban street processions, see Ortiz [1920] 1960.

28. In the City of Havana, the *cabildo* establishments housing the African nations had, until 1792, occupied many streets *within* the walled *intramuros* of Old Havana. However, in 1792, they were "banished" by law to the *extramuros*, ostensibly because of the "raucous and disagreeable sound of the[ir musical] instruments" during their regular cycle of weekend and annual festivals (Ortiz 1921, 17). As likely, they were driven out for fear of subversion following the onset of the 1791 black revolution on the island of Hispaniola.

29. It is a commonplace by now that carnival practice and ethos contain the potential for status inversion and transformation. The literature is characterized by debates over, and revisions of, the thinking of Van Gennep (1960), Max Gluckman (1954), and Victor Turner (1969). See T. Turner (1977) and Alonso (1990) for the most useful summaries and critiques.

30. The militias of color had their advent in the defense of Havana against the British in 1762 and were established more officially with a *reglamento* in 1769. During the Aponte (1812) and Escalera (1844) conspiracies, however, they became greatly open to suspicion as sites of resources, organization, and personnel for the purposes of revolt (see Marrero 1986, 140–43).

31. The Fernando Ortiz Collection has been housed in Old Havana's Casa de Africa, which was inaugurated in 1986.

32. Deschamps Chapeaux writes that the Arará nation in Cuba preferred the Espíritu Santo (Holy Spirit) as its patron; the Congos preferred King Melchior—the black member of the Three Kings who visited the baby Jesus on Epiphany; the Carabalís preferred Saint Christopher and the Holy Trinity; the Lucumís preferred Santa Bárbara; and the Mandingas preferred the Virgin of Regla and the Virgin of the Immaculate Conception (Deschamps Chapeaux 1968, 50).

33. The ruling classes believed that "All the horrors of San Domingo's [Saint Domingue] massacres were to have been repeated. Many of the whites were to have been flayed and broiled while alive, and with the exception of the young women, reserved for a worse fate, all, without discrimination of age or sex, were to have been massacred" (Wurdemann 1844, quoted in Pérez 1988, 103).

34. This is the "colored captain" of a *cabildo* in Regla. See Ortiz [1920] 1960, 19, fig. 3; and Bettelheim 1993, fig. 3.

35. I retranslated and revised this account from Ortiz's Spanish quotation in order to present a more generous version for the purposes of the chapter epigraph (see above). However, I reproduce here the version in the Aimes account in order to suggest earlier translations' condescending tone and racist stereotyping.

36. Fernando Ortiz dates Landaluze's Day of Kings depiction to 1870 (see Ortiz 1952–55, 4:187, fig. 327). The Royal Museum of Fine Arts catalog (1992, fig. 280) dates the work as 1878 and incorrectly credits one "M. Puente" as the painter and "Nañigo feast" as the title.

37. Charles DeForest Fredricks first visited Havana in 1853, but it was in 1857 that he opened his studio on Calle de la Habana, in which the carnival group *carte de visite* may have been photographed, if not in a makeshift studio on the street (see Levine 1990, 28–32).

38. In descending order of size, the drums were and are called *caja*, *mula*, and *cachimbo* and played by straddling the instrument. Ortiz uses Landaluze's Day of Kings painting (plate 1) to illustrate how they were played (only two are depicted; see Ortiz 1952–55, 4:187, fig. 327). Of western Central African derivation, the drums were also called *fumabata ngoma* by the Congos in Cuba. In Matanzas, they were specifically called *engóma* (Ortiz 1952–55, 4:181). Using Bentley's *Dictionary and Grammar of the Kongo Language* (1887), Ortiz found these terms' origins in the listing for *ngoma* (see Ortiz 1952–55, 4:193–94).

39. The Kongo-Angola rattles, called *ensansi*, were worn on the drummer's wrists; because of that, they reiterated and accentuated the drum rhythms—played with the hands—and could be heard above the welter of percussion, given their higher sound frequency (see Ortiz 1952–55, 2:87–89).

40. The arched crown, according to Goodall, "was the pattern for later imperial crowns in Austria and Russia. . . . The arched crown was . . . adopted by France [in] the sixteenth century and became general thereafter. Many Continental crowns have four arches; two arches were [mostly] the standard for England" (Goodall 1995, 79–80).

41. The use of of royal and courtly garments and other accessories of prestige also appeared in eighteenth-century New England among elected and hereditary black kings (Aimes 1905; Piersen 1988), and throughout the Caribbean, as the signs of authority of community and carnival group leaders. Since the middle of the nineteenth century, the elected carnival kings and queens of Port of Spain, Trinidad, for example, have worn crowns and prestige cloth, have been elevated upon thrones, and have led street processions and participated in costume competitions (see Hill 1972).

42. For example, pre-1898 headgear associated with five Yoruba kings between 1854 and 1892 reproduced the arched crown, though topped with a royal bird rather than a crucifix, the cleric's hat, and the ecclesiastical miter (Drewal and Mason 1998, 70, figs. 76, 93, and 95, fig. 77, and fig. 80, respectively).

43. Precedents for the dichotomous idea of a "separate" or "autonomous" slave sphere (separate from the master's sphere), whether it be phrased in spatial, temporal, psychological, or cultural terms, comes from the 1970s American historiography, for example, the "sundown to sunup" and "slave community" theses of a distinct "culture" that developed in the slave quarters, maroon communities, and so on (see Blassingame 1979; Rawick 1972; Genovese 1976; Joyner 1984).

44. Servile and buffoon-like characteristics and physiognomic distortions in representations of blacks entered American high and popular arts after the War of 1812 (e.g., the "Jim Crow" figure of 1820s–1830s engravings). Such representations were increasingly influenced by minstrel performances, which emerged as early as the 1820s in American cities such as Philadelphia (see McElroy 1990, xvi, 28–29). Given intensive commercial exchanges between Philadelphia and Havana in the early nineteenth century (Salvucci 1991), it would not be surprising if reports of such performances by travelers, traders, and sailors—the transmitters par excellence of the era (see Linebaugh and Rediker 2000; Scott 1986)—if not also mimickings of them, appeared in Havana and contributed to popular culture and representations on the island.

45. Of course, African borrowings of prestige materials from European monarchial, military, and ecclesiastical formal display, such as flags, umbrellas, fancy cloth, crucifixes, sculptures, uniforms, gowns, thrones, and podiums, were documented in Western and western Central Africa from at least the sixteenth century forward (see Balandier 1968; Blier 1995a; Cosentino 1995a, 1995b; Polk 1995).

46. Indeed, as Ortiz himself noted, "the attributes of European origin" worn by Congo *cabildo* kings—mantles, scepters, peaked hats, long coats and pants, and so on—had been used by kings in central West Africa for hundreds of years (1921, 7). Such borrowings, and more, were documented in western and central West Africa from at least the sixteenth century (see Balandier 1968; Blier 1995; Cosentino 1995a, 1995b; Polk 1995).

47. See Pérez 1988, 91–95, for a breakdown of Cuban elite social structure and the rivalry between the Creole planter and landowner elite and the Spanish *Peninsulares*, who were the merchants and administrators of the colony.

48. See Thomas 1971 on the buying of nobility titles (142), on the building of palaces (146), on their interior appointments (148), and on the costumed balls, theatrical performances, and decked-out footmen and guards (147).

49. See Argeliers León's insightful discussion on French and other European cultural influences in Cuba during the early nineteenth century (1984, 16–23).

50. Of course, as Victor Turner noted many years ago, the everyday "social interactions of a conflictive, competitive, or agonistic type" (i.e., the "social drama") from which performative material is stylized are already "processually 'structured' before any story about [them has] been told" (Turner 1986, 33–34). In a slightly different vein, James Wafer begins his work on ritually performative spirit possession in Salvador, Bahia, noting that Bahians are culturally attuned to the notion of *estrelismo*, literally "the desire to be a star." They are determined to "distinguish [themselves] from the crowd"—and, thus, always on stage, or within the performance frame (Wafer 1991, 8).

51. Intriguingly, in postemancipation Trinidad, participants in many carnival masquerades commemorated and commented upon their prior condition of enslavement in a sugarcane economy with molasses-smeared bodies, for example, the *negue-jadin* and *jab-molassi* masquerades (see Pearse 1956; Crowley 1956; Hill 1972).

52. This interpretation is indebted to Richard Schechner's notion of "restored behavior"; social material subject to the framing and stylization of theater permits and encourages critical reflection and the experience of epiphany (1985, 35 ff.).

53. Such stops and dance circles (*corros*), which potentially earn money for the performers, are pan-Caribbean; they are called "breakouts" in the Anglophone Caribbean (see Bettelheim 1988; 1985). Stops are also integral to the New Orleans procession style of the "second line" parades of the "social and pleasure clubs" and the "Mardi Gras Indian tribes" (see Smith 1984, 95–97). For example, I followed and photographed second-line parades and

Mardi Gras Indian tribes on several occasions. The Sudan Social and Pleasure Club's fancily dressed members processed through black neighborhoods to the music of a brass band; it made stops at various locations along the route, forming a dance circle, and displaying its individual and collective moves. The stops were marked on a handbill distributed weeks before the event.

54. The central-standing *diablito* in Landaluze's 1878 depiction of the Day of Kings (plate 1) was identified as La Kulona. Ortiz attributed it to the Gangá nation (Ortiz 1952–55, 2:3), though Thompson has, more recently, attributed the skirt style to Cross River peoples (Carabalí in Cuba; see Thompson 1983, 265–67).

55. In Samuel Kinser's pan-Caribbean interpretation of carnival performance, important meanings generate from this contrast of the aesthetic of "royalty" and the aesthetic of "wildness" (Kinser 1990; see also Bettelheim 1988; Crowley 1956).

56. These individual Corpus Christi grotesques were variously called *mojigangas, mamarrachos,* and *moharraches* (Ortiz [1920] 1960, 28; Brown 1993a, 79, 80; León 1984, 19).

57. Ortiz (1953) makes a persuasive claim for the verisimilitude of Landaluze's depictions. And C. D. Fredricks's mid-nineteenth-century *carte de visite* corroborates many of Landaluze's details. However, Miahle and Landaluze clearly drew upon art historical conventions of representation, such as the compressed and composite groupings of figures found in European late-eighteenth-century realistic history painting, with doses of baroque drama thrown in (see Miahle 1838). Landaluze emphasized more plausible groupings and gestures within his compositions, so that, for example, individuals logically figure within a *cabildo* procession's organization. Miahle, in his own Day of Kings, packs diverse figures together in a kind of promiscuous carnival abandon, framed by numerous visual sidebars of interracial dancing, balcony observers, and so on. Landaluze seems to have combined actors from different carnival groups, in a composite, in order to represent the diversity of colorful types, as well as a single *cabildo*'s dance circle. For example, his Day of Kings representation features a *culona* masquerade (the central horned figure with a hoopskirt of raffia, which Ortiz etymologically traces to Malinke or Mand[e] languages, but which Thompson's work places in the Carabalí tradition (Ortiz [1920] 1960, 33; Thompson 1983, 265–67). The *íreme,* which also generated from the Carabalí *cabildos,* is depicted as an individual performer; it is not clear whether he belongs to this group. At the same time, the drummers, who play nailed-headed *ngomo* drums and wear *ensansí* wrist rattles, as well as the feather-crowned dancer, were more likely to be associated with Congo *cabildos.* And, as Ortiz himself carefully documents, the "ferocious" Carabalí or *ñáñigo cabildos,* with their inimitable *íreme diablitos,* typically processed in more marginal sections of the city (Ortiz [1920] 1960, 12).

58. Ortiz, through nineteenth-century accounts, documents groups of *mulatas* who wore expensive and opulent layered skirts, stockings, shoes, head adornments, and jewelry and were protected from above by umbrellas ([1920] 1960, 13). These were undoubtedly carnival queens.

59. See Wafer's use (1991, 55–56, 59–60) of M. M. Bakhtin's terms, "grotesque body" and the "carnivalesque," in discussions Afro-Brazilian performance. Bakhtin's carnivalesque regards carnival as the "temporary liberation from the prevailing truth and the established order . . . [through] the suspension of all hierarchical rank, privileges, norms, and prohibitions" (Bakhtin 1984, 10).

60. See useful discussions by Reisman (1970) and Morton Marks (1974) on the dynamic opposition of "noise" and "order" in Caribbean expressive performances. Reisman and others (e.g., Abrahams 1983; Marks 1974) have shown how actors "code-switch" between varieties of speech and performance. In the Caribbean, this often manifests itself in switching between "lower" or "deeper" versions of Afro-Caribbean creole varieties and performance rules and "higher" ones on a continuum, depending upon context. From the point of view of the "higher" varieties, such as the theoretical "standard language," the "lower" varieties may be perceived as "noise."

61. The documents of Landaluze, Miahle, and Ortiz show, for example, that white observers and government authorities "participated" in carnival by watching from balconies and exchanging *aguinaldo* for amusing, if also frightening, performances. Some non-African men ventured out into the streets to witness at close range the processions and dance circles, while women and children stayed inside. Carnival apparently provided public opportunities for nonblack men and *negras* or *mulatas* to engage socially, as in mixed-race dancing (see Miahle's Day of Kings document [fig. 1.3], *far left*). It is likely that, notwithstanding the relative physical distances that observers put between themselves and the performances, many experienced vicarious pleasure.

62. Ortiz documents that the police, often around 2:00 P.M. on carnival day, already had to move out of the *intramuros* great swelling crowds indulging in dancing, drinking, and, sometimes fighting ([1920] 1960, 12).

63. In Taussig's work, for example, Amerindian peoples were subject to gross labor exploitation, horror, torture, and killing (in a word, "terror") by the Peruvian Amazon Rubber Company near the Putumayo River in Colombia in the early twentieth century. In turn, the Amerindian came to figure as a magical being and shaman in the popular culture; he was called to "cure" the ills of the peasant colonizing class—wherein sickness and misfortune are interpreted by Taussig as the fetishized embodiments of class struggle, social contradiction, and the fallout of the history of ter-

ror. Somewhat similarly, Renato Ortiz shows how "scientific" Umbandista practitioners in Brazil, who reject what they see as primitive African *macumba* practice, nevertheless require a mediator, the fierce Yoruba god of iron, Ogum, in order to do their bidding in the darker and more dangerous spheres of the spirit world (Ortiz 1989).

In Trinidad carnival, observers participated in stylized street exchanges for amusement as well as to be rid of "bad" or "evil" presences, such as the "Midnight Robber" or various dragons and "devils." The Robber, fashioned as a "bad man" and murderer, carrying guns, knives, coffins, etc, threatened his "victims" with stylized speeches of his exploits. Certain death could be exchanged for a payment (Crowley 1956).

64. Aimes dates Bremer's visit to Cuba as 1851 (Aimes 1905, 21).

65. The "Luccomees *cabildo*" was probably on Calle Monserrate, where numerous historic *cabildos* were established. Monserrate (now the Avenida de Bélgica, which runs into the main Egido artery), ran roughly north-south, bordering and facing the western wall of Old Havana.

66. The new restrictive slave law of 1842 reflected the demands of the booming sugar economy (1820–60) and the presence of huge numbers of slaves on the island; it restricted the movements and activities of the slaves and provided more detailed regulations for work, and "the stronger emphasis upon the obedience of slaves to white persons and the constituted authorities revealed a severe hardening of attitudes of the master group toward their slaves" (Knight 1970, 131).

67. It remains unclear exactly who the "Alagua" were as a subgroup of the larger Lucumí nation. "Lucumí" was the metaethnonym for Yoruba-speaking and related Bight of Benín peoples and those of the several northern hinterland peoples (i.e., to the north of old Ọ̀yọ́, such as the Tapa, Nupe, and Bariba. The most recognizable Yoruba-speaking subgroups were defined by hyphenated second elements such as Eyó (Ọ̀yọ́), Egua (Ẹ̀gbá), Agguado (Ẹ̀gbádò), Iyecha (Ìjẹ̀ṣà), and many groups were not Yoruba-speaking, such as "Lucumí Achanti," "Lucumí Fanti," "Lucumís Popos," "Lucumís Ararás," who belonged, more strictly speaking, to areas to the west of the Yoruba in present-day Benín, Togo, and Ghana (see Ortiz [1916] 1987, 50–51; López Valdés 1986). Rafael L. López Valdés uncovered fifteen Havana Lucumí *cabildos* listed between 1728 and 1868 in Cuban archives. The five listed as having existed before 1792 would probably have been encountered in the *intramuros*, in the Fourth Distict of the capital, but after that date probably would have been moved to the *extramuros*. Of the fifteen, only two list Santa Bárbara as their patron—although the others' patrons simply may not have appeared in the lists he encountered. The two with Santa Bárbara as their patron, Lucumi Bragurá (1843, at 49 Monserrate in Havana) and Lucumi Ayones (1868), do not seem to be identifiable from the name printed on the business card given to Bremer (Lucumí Alagua) (López Valdés 1994), though "Alaguá" could have been a contemporaneous variation of "Bragurá." It might also have meant Nación Lucumí "The Elder," (Alaguá). It is also possible that such names changed over time.

68. "[O]thers rattled gourds filled with stones" could refer to *maracas*, but might also be an imprecise description of the common Yoruba-derived seed- and bead-covered gourds called *chekeré* (*ṣẹ̀kẹ̀rẹ̀* in Yoruba; see Abraham 1946, 614).

69. In Cuban Regla de Ocha, the elevating of a sheet or canopy over the head of individuals or groups of individuals marks the activation of a cleansing (*ebó*) or prophylactic precautions.

70. Fernando Ortiz explained the contrast of fancily dressed kings and fearsome *diablito* masquerades on the Day of Kings as the difference between African secular political rulers and religious priests. The raffia and horns of the masquerades preserved the "savage taste" of the African "fetish" priests, who controlled the *cabildos'* primitive, subterranean religious domain. The *diablitos*, Ortiz thought, like the "fetish" staffs (*anaquillé*) carried by female Day of Kings participants (plate 1), were the most visible public "survivals" of the "partially religious character of the *cabildos*" ([1920] 1960, 31, 32; see also 1921, 18).

71. Of course, in Yorubaland itself, given British colonization in the second half of the nineteenth century, local kings and chiefs themselves were incorporated into the system of "indirect rule" (see above) where the new "top" would have included the queen of England, the local colonial administration, and emerging British-trained and educated elite Yoruba classes (e.g., missionaries and the civil service, see epigraph of this chapter from Ranger 1983). The British presence actually increased the number of local kings—including numerous new leaders of "crowned towns." Thus, the kinds of dual structures and institutional checks and balances that Apter describes seem to have been created, or were intensified, during this period (see Pemberton and Afolayan 1996, 2). Ortiz's readings of late-nineteenth-century West African arrangements probably reflected this fact; thus, I do not want to suggest the *cabildos'* dual structure as the simple linear descendant of the former arrangements, for similar kinds of leadership patterns may have developed on both sides of the Atlantic in relation to colonial hierarchies.

72. *Ñañiguismo* was the historical (now pejorative) term for the Abakuá society, the putative origins of which lie in the men's gerontocratic trading, judicial, recreation, and slaving "leopard societies" of Old Calabar and the hinterlands of the Cross River Delta at the border of Nigeria and Cameroon (see Thompson 1983; Sosa Rodríguez 1982). Roche y Monteagudo believed that

the revelation of their practices, shrouded in mystery, would help realize the extinction of *ñañiguismo*, that is, ridding the nation of what he considered a " grave offense to our culture" (1925a).

73. Textually, Ortiz's *Los Negros Brujos* (1906) manifests the interrelation of scholarly enterprise and police work in its content and form—for much of Ortiz's data was gleaned from police reports detailing aggressive raids on cult houses. Fifty-five criminal cases are listed in appendixes and referred to in the text against "*brujos*" (sorcerers, witches) between September 1902 and September 1905; eleven were in the city of Havana (Ortiz [1906] 1973, 181–220). In such raids, houses were desecrated by the police and sacred objects were confiscated (see Ortiz [1906] 1973; Roche y Monteagudo [1908] 1925b, 50–73).

74. Ortiz studied neocorrectionalist penal theory in Barcelona between 1900 and 1901, and anthropometry and anthropology after that; his thesis was inspired by the positivist theories of Enrico Ferri and Garófalo; he published articles on criminology in Havana in 1903, and audited courses in sociology and criminal anthropology with Cesare Lombroso in Turin while chief secretary of the Cuban consulates (he resided in Genoa, Italy); the same year he collaborated with Lombroso on the latter's criminology journal, and from 1904 though 1916 contributed articles on the spread of criminology in Cuban journals (see InterAmericas Society 1988, 35–26). Lombroso wrote the *carta-prólogo* to Ortiz's 1906 work, *Los Negros Brujos* (see Ortiz [1906] 1973, xx–1).

75. The gathering of personnel for the first "white" lodge of Abakuá (it was sponsored by, and probably included, *mulatos*), Akanarán Efó Okobio Mukarará, dates to 1857; but it was officially inaugurated in 1863 (Roche y Monteagudo [1908] 1925b, 4). Akanarán Efó then initiated a series of "white" lodges between 1874 and 1882 in Havana, El Cerro, Regla, and Guanabacoa, which, in turn, initiated others (see Sosa Rodríguez 1982, 143; and Roche y Monteagudo [1908] 1925b, 24). My fieldwork among Abakuá in Havana (1991–present) corroborates these dates.

76. "The white male population more than doubled (230,986 to 468,107), while the number of white males of economically productive ages (16 to 60) increased even more dramatically, from 132,738 to 300,926). Of these 300,926 males, almost 86 percent were located in the west" (Pérez 1988, 116).

CHAPTER TWO

1. For example, Curtin shows that Yoruba-speaking peoples made up 53% of all recaptives (from interdicted slaveships off West Africa's Atlantic coast—indicating the demographics of the trade) in 1848 (Curtin 1969, 244). Directly neighboring peoples—for example, Nupe, Tapa, Fon, Mahi, Adja, Evhe, Gun, Popo, and Benín (Edo)—made up 10% that year, making Bight of Benín imports into Cuba 63% of that year's total. Earlier, between 1817 and 1843, the years of the greatest slave imports into Cuba, 31.1% were taken from the Bight of Benín. Perhaps 26% (more than one quarter) of the total of 280,000 imported into Cuba from 1817 to 1843 (Curtin 1969, 40) were Yoruba-speaking (1969, 244, 247). In the longer run, the total number of Africans imported into to Cuba between 1808 and 1865 was 570,200 (Curtin 1969, 40). Prior to that, 1774–1807 imports were 119,000 as a whole (Curtin 1969, 31, 35). It is possible to estimate that a quarter to a third of Cuban slave imports from the last decades of the eighteenth century all the way to 1865 were Yoruba-speaking peoples—conservatively considered, perhaps, amounting to just under 150,000, but possibly over 170,000. See Smith (1969) for extended discussions of Yoruba imperial warfare and its relationship with the Atlantic slave trade in the late eighteenth and the nineteenth centuries.

2. One "Remigio Lucumí" was baptized in 1833 by the parochial church of Nueva Paz, according to his certificate of baptism. According to historian Franklin Knight, newly arrived Africans were often subjected to three years of "seasoning," including learning enough Spanish to fulfill the catechistic requirements of the baptism (personal communications with Franklin Knight, 1994). This suggests that this individual, bearing the African name Adechina (in Spanish, "Remigio Herrera," taking the surname of his master), arrived in Cuba about 1830. In Regla's 1881 census, Ño Remigio Herrera is listed as seventy years old, which puts his birth at 1811; his 1891 marriage certificate lists his age as seventy-five years, which puts his birth at 1816. By these numbers, he would have been twenty-two (by the 1881 document) or seventeen (by the 1891 document) in 1833, the year of his baptism (baptism, marriage, and census documents were kindly shared with me by Pedro Cosme Baños, director of the Regla Museum, 1992–94).

It is not clear that Atandá Ño Filomeno García was an "old slave" in the 1830s, in terms of numerical age. For documents of *defunción* in the Regla Parish archives show that he died at age seventy-seven in 1876 (*Iglesia Parroquial de Regla, Libro de Defunciones de Pardos y Morenos, 1866–1886*, no. 5, folio 115, partido 833). Therefore, he would have been forty-one years old in 1835; still, perhaps twenty years of plantation labor would have rendered him prematurely "old." I am grateful to Licenciado Luis Alberto Pedroso for sharing this document with me.

3. Various interviews and personal communications with *babalawos* Hermes Valera Ramírez, Andrés Kolá, Gilberto Herrera Rojas, and Pedro Cosme Baños, in the summers of 1992, 1993, and 1994.

4. The discovery of a document of Remigio's manumission or

coartación could reveal that someone had purchased his freedom or that he bought his own freedom. However, the oral history relates that his mentor, Ño Carlos Adé Bí, another Reglano, bought his freedom (see epigraph to chap. 2).

That he was a property owner, stonemason, and person of connections and influence is suggested in the 1881 census and later property documents: in 1881, he appears, along with a listing of immediate and extended family members, as living in his own house at 31 Calle San Ciprián (later renamed Calle Fresneda). A 1900 set of documents shows the significant value of his house and another piece of land: the former was valued at fifteen hundred *pesos* in *oro español*), and he also took rental income there from others (six *pesos* of silver per month); he also owned an empty lot on Calle Morales (later renamed Perdomo), valued at three hundred pesos gold. That he was economically independent is also suggested by the fact that no *hipotecario* (financial sponsor or cosigner) was necessary to secure these properties (*Provincia de la Habana, fincas urbanas, Ayuntamiento de Regla,* folio 492, no. 32, 12 November 1900 [for the house]; *Provincia de La Habana, fincas urbanas, Ayuntamiento de Regla,* folio 1665 [for the lot]).

That Adechina had significant social connections among Regla's elite is suggested by the witnesses and godparents to his 1891 marriage: a white businessman, a magistrate, a pharmacist, and a housewife (from documents shared with me by Pedro Cosme Baños).

Though the Cabildo de Yemayá may been conceived earlier along with Atandá and Añabí, it is likely that it was not inaugurated in an establishment until later. That is, the partnership of Remigio and his future wife Francisca Burlet, and the births of Josefa and Teodoro in the mid-1860s, flags the beginning Adechina's life as a free person *of means,* that is, able to house and support the *cabildo.* That Adechina was in Regla by 1864 is indicated by the births there of his daughter, Josefa Herrera, in 1864 and her brother Teodoro in 1866 (from baptism documents shared with my by Pedro Cosme Baños, July 1992). Prior to that, according to oral sources, Adechina lived in Matanzas, where he met his future wife, a Lucumí named Francisca Burlet (interviews with Teruel Rolando Cartaya, Adechina's grandson, Matanzas, 29 August 1999).

Probably, the *cabildo* was first established in the family home, and later on the Morales lot (later 63 Perdomo), following Adechina's death, his daughter's maturity and inheritance, and the lot's development. This probably did not occur until after 1921, when Josefa returned from Havana, where she had taken refuge during antiblack violence in Regla in 1912 (see n. 32).

5. I am grateful to Stephan Palmié for drawing my attention to Castellanos's 1916 documentation of Papá Silvestre Erice.

6. The El Cristo compound was built around 120–30 years ago (ca. 1870–80) by Nicolás Sevilla (who changed his name from Iznaga upon his freedom, according to an interview with the current director, Pablo Sevilla, 9 July 1994, Palmira). The Sociedad de Santa Bárbara, founded by the African ex-slave Ma Lugarda Fernández, was legalized in 1904 and probably not founded much earlier (interview with the organization's current director, *oriaté* Agustín Hernández, 9 July 1994, Palmira). And the Sociedad San Roque was founded by the African ex-slave Francisca Entensa Pino, who died in 1959 at eighty-two years of age. Perhaps founded around the turn of the twentieth century or afterward, it was reorganized and rebuilt in 1930 (interviews with San Roque members, 9 July 1994, Palmira). Palmira's Congo society, the Sociedad San Antonio, was legalized in 1904, although its current "king" said it was founded originally in 1700 (interview with Rolando Rodríguez Hernández, 9 July 1994, Palmira). The progeny of and succeeding generations to Nicolás Iznaga/Sevilla (he had twenty-seven children) included people with the surnames Iznaga, Sevilla, Reyes, and Estables, as the earliest children were Iznagas, the next group were Sevillas, and the rest took their mothers' surnames (interview with Nicolás's grandson Antonio Sevilla, 10 July 1994, Palmira).

7. Besides documenting the Sociedad Lucumí Santa Rita de Casia y San Lázaro in El Cerro, in 1904 Rafael Roche y Monteagudo also visited La Sociedad Religiosa Lucumí de Nación Llová, under the patronage of Nuestra Señora de la Caridad del Cobre (Our Lady of Charity/Ochún) in El Cerro's Barrio Pilar, as well as the Sociedad de Socorros Mútuos Lucumí, under the patronage of Santa Bárbara (Changó) in the La Ceiba section of Marianao (Roche y Monteagudo [1908] 1925a, 209–13). The last may have been one of the several Societies of Santa Bárbara referred to by Lydia Cabrera ([1954] 1983, 24 n. 1), which, she reports, existed in the *barrio* of Pogolotti, also in Marianao. Pogolotti is very close to La Ceiba. "Llová," probably pronounced "Yobá," may have been a contraction of "Yorubá" but more likely reflected a specific Lucumí ethnonym of the slave trade: "Lucumí-Yobá" appears on a list of 137 ethnonyms used in Cuba to refer to various Lucumí groups (López Valdés 1986, 73).

8. See n. 3. That it was not built upon until the 1920s is calculated from estimations based upon research kindly shared with me by Luís Alberto Pedroso, summer 1999.

9. According to the 1899 census, of the 12,898 African-born inhabitants of the island, 1,784 lived in Havana Province, 4,390 in Matanzas Province, and 4,159 in Santa Clara, while 836 lived in the City of Havana, 144 in the City of Cienfuegos, and 244 in the City of Matanzas (Thomas 1971, 429).

10. I am indebted to Stephan Palmié for sharing this important document with me, from the War Department's archives of

the American Occupation of Cuba in the National Archives in Washington, D.C.

11. The seven men I can positively identify as leading *babalawos* were Ño Remigio Herrera/Adechina (African, Lucumí, eighty-three to eighty-nine years old), Eulogio Rodríguez (Gaitán, creole, thirty-nine years old), Pedro P. Pérez, Bernabé Menocal, Bonifacio Valdés, Luis Pacheco, and Esteban F. Quiñones. José Cornelio Delgado, Francisco Roche, Ricardo Domeneche, Isidoro Somodevilla, Isidoro Sandrino, and Hermenegildo Albear were also very likely *babalawos* (from personal communications with Jesús Varona Puente, summers of 1998 and 1999 [Varona, a *babalawo*, is a recognized specialist in reciting the names of deceased *babalawos* in ancestral rites]). The first roster is composed primarily of men and the second primarily of women. The only name appearing on both is the sole female "founder" (*fundadora*) of the first, Caridad Argudín, who also appears as the *presidenta* of the second. Beneath the second list's male *director*, Isidoro Somodevilla, and *colector*, Leopoldo Aragón, all of the officers are women. The relationship of the two hierarchies is not entirely clear, though the second appears to have been the women's division of the same society, a quite common organizing principal in institutions of this kind. There appear surnames that ring out as the key family names in the history of the religion in Havana: Somodevilla, Argudín, Sotolongo, Albear, Corrales, Arriera (probably Arrieta). Belén González ("Apoto"), and Margarita Armenteros were founders of Lucumí lineages (see below).

12. Death date from the Regla cemetery register.

13. The African *babalawo* godparents of Eulogio Rodríguez, Bernabé Menocal, and Esteban F. Quiñones were, respectively, Oluguеré Kó Kó (Oyekún Melli), Ifá Omí (Ogunda Teturá), and Ño Carlos Ade Bi (Ojuani Boká). Luis Pacheco was a godchild of Pedro P. Pérez, who was initiated by Quiñones.

14. The oral research on Lucumí Ocha ramas by Natalia Bolívar Aróstegui, which she shared with William Muldro (Sim-El Fatunmishe), seems to be corroborated by Valdés Garriz's list of notable founders and *oriatés* (Valdés Garriz 1997, 135), though Valdés may have served as an informant for Bolívar, diminishing the possiblity of independent verification. Still, I am grateful to William Muldro for sharing his sources with me.

15. See Cabrera's suggested chronology of this *cabildo* (Cabrera [1954] 1983, 25 n. 1) and Fernando Ortiz's important references to it (1952–55, 4:217), particularly its widely respected *batá* drums.

16. Bernabé Menocal and Tata Gaitán worked closely with the godchildren of Adechina, and all of their *ramas* were related by interlocking ritual kinship.

17. Though Ortiz does not make the explicit connection between Cabildo Africano Lucumí and Erice's *cabildo*, he does make the connection between Erice and Fernando Guerra and Changó Tedúm. Given that Erice was on Cabildo Africano Lucumí's board, it is quite possible that we are talking about the same *cabildo*, Changó Tedún.

18. I am grateful to Stephan Palmié for pointing out the historical significance, agenda, and connections of Fernando Guerra, particularly as he was connected to Papá Silvestre Erice and Fernando Ortiz,(personal communications, spring 1995).

19. The 137 hyphenated Lucumí ethnonyms López Valdés discovered were quite heterogeneous, at least according to how ethnologists have reckoned differences among African ethnic subgroups. More than forty of the ethnic suffixes in the Lucumí hyphenated compounds are shown by López Valdés to belong to regional, but non-Yoruba-speaking peoples, such as "Lucumí-Baribá," "Lucumí-Benín" (i.e., Edo), "Lucumí-Magí" (Mahi of Dahomey), "Lucumí-Mina" (of Ghana), "Lucumí-Popo" (of Togo), "Lucumí-Jausa (Hausa of Islamicized northern Nigeria), "Lucumí-Ibo" (of eastern and southeastern Nigeria), and "Lucumí-Takua" (i.e., Tapa, of northern Nigeria).

20. Gaitán's *tabaquero* profession is known from his last will and testament, kindly shared with me by his inheritors in Guanabacoa, Gualberta Püig and Ricardo Navarro, in the summers of 1994 and 1998. I learned that he worked in Tampa from Tata's grandchild in Ifá, *babalawo* Pablo Sevilla, 5 July 1994, in Havana.

21. Gaitán is believed to have been formally "consecrated as *obá*" by Asunción Villalonga and others, probably in the first decade or so of the twentieth century (interviews with Andrés Kolá, Fran Cabrera, Francisco Aristola, Ángel Padrón [Bebo el Mokongo], Hermes Valera, Juanito Angulo, Pablo Sevilla, Radamés Corona, and others, 1991–2000).

22. Quotation from Hermes Valera, summer 1991. This point was reiterated in repeated interviews with *babalawos* Hermes Valera, Andrés Kolá, Jesús Varona, Antonio Martín de Armas Arredondo, Joseíto Valdés, and others, 1991–98.

23. Tata Gaitán was a member (*obonekue*) either of Havana's Usagaré Kamawá or Mutanga lodge (interviews with Joseíto Valdés [1992] and Jesús Varona [1998], both of whom are *babalawos* and Abakuá members). According to interviews with a number of Havana *babalawos* (1991–99), Tata's elder and colleague, Adechina, was the Mokongo of Efí Abarokó Taibá; Tata's godson, Quintín García, was the Mokongo of Regla's Abarakó Chiquito; Bonifacio Valdés was the Mokongo of Efí Embemoró of Cayo Hueso; Pedro P. Pérez was the Mokongo of Aroko Kujuáo; and Guillermo Castro was an *obonekue* of Orú Papá. Mokongo, the "supreme chief," is the second highest grade of the Abakuá society.

24. Interviews with the inheritors of Gaitán's estate, Gual-

berta Püig and Ricardo Navarro, in the summers of 1994 and 1998.

25. I am grateful to Stephan Palmié for pointing out the significance of this detail.

26. Cádiz was the homeport of major slavers who illegally traded in Africans after the 1820 formal ban (Thomas 1971, 137).

27. Interviews with *babalawos* Hermes Valera, Andrés Kolá, Fran Cabrera, Feliberto O'Farril, Havana, summers of 1992 and 1993. Kolá added that he was told the story of Joaquín Cádiz by Cádiz's grandchild in Ifá, Joaquín Salazar (Osalofobello); Salazar had related that the Odí Melli sign and its interpretation were produced by Ifá Bí Francisco Villalonga (interview, 26 June 1993, Havana).

28. This was reported to Licenciado Pedro Cosme Baños in the early 1980s by an elderly Reglano who said that when he was a child he witnessed such demonstrations of respect toward Adechina (personal communication with Cosme, Summer 1993).

29. Quotation from the Sociedad Santa Rita's 1915 "manifesto" (see Castellanos 1916, 57).

30. See n. 21.

31. For example, Joaquín Salazar (Osalofobello) occupied the office of *obá* within the "Vaticano" of Bernardo Rojas for many decades until his death in 1978. Menocal's other famous godchildren, Eustaquio Delgado ("Caretica" Obara Rete), Cornelio Vidal (Obeché), Aurelio Estrada ("Babel" Elliogbe), and Miguel Febles y Padrón (Odí Ká), were some of the most important *obás* of the twentieth century. Other premier Ifá *obás* of this century were Guillermo Castro (Obeché) and José Antonio Tamayo (Obewole) of the Ifá Bí lineage, and Miguel Febles's brother, Francisco Febles del Pino (Otura Nico).

32. Susana Cantero (Omí Toké), known as the owner of one of two early *cabildos* of Yemayá/the Virgin of Regla was the granddaughter in Ocha of the Yoruba priestess Efuche (see below). According to Licenciado Luis Alberto Pedroso, Cantero had no family or formal affiliation with a *cabildo de nación;* a native of, and migrant from, Cienfuegos, she arrived in Havana Province in 1914, having merely "attended" Lucumí festivals in Cienfuegos and Palmira. Her Cabildo de Yemayá was probably not established until the second half of the 1910s, as she apparently remained uninitiated until that point, and the *cabildo* did not "come out" on the 7 September holy day until 1921, when documents show she petitioned the municipal government to conduct the festivities. Indeed, very little open Afro-Cuban religious activity took place between the end of the War of Independence (1898) and 1913, given island-wide discrimination, which led to brutal antiblack violence against the Independent Party of Color in 1912 (see Helg 1995, 116–248). Antiblack violence infected Regla—indeed, prominent Regla practitioners took refuge in Havana during these years, including Josefa Herrera Echubí Pepa (Adechina's daughter), who did not return to Regla until 1921 or 1922. It is possible that Cantero was initiated by Efuche's goddaughter Andrea Trujillo after 1914, possibly in Havana, at the very end of Efuche's life, probably in the teens (data on Cantero and Herrera in relation to Regla's social history are from personal communications with Luis Alberto Pedroso and notes he kindly shared with me from a paper in progress ["La salida de los cabildos: Una fiesta pública de Yemayá-Virgen de Regla en el Puerto de La Habana"], 18 August 1999).

33. El Palenque, according to Cabrera's sources, was a *finca* (farm) in Marianao that was converted into a *barrio* of Africans and creoles, all of whom were godchildren of the famous Lucumí twins and priests Perfecto and Gumersindo, called *los Papás Jimaguas* ("The Daddy Twins"). They were wealthy and had multiple houses, in each of which lived a different wife, as in an African-style compound. El Pocito ("The Little Spring") was another Lucumí compound nearby in Pogolotti (see Cabrera [1954] 1983, 25 n. 1).

34. See John Mason's outline of the founders and the relationships between families and rituals of the Regla and Matanzas *cabildos* (Mason 1996, 18–19, 26–28).

35. Esteban Baró (Achó, 1866–1956) founded the Sociedad Arará San Manuel y sus descendientes of the town of Jovellanos in 1921, which was inherited by his children, the late Maximilliano Baró Céspedes (Gbövi) and Miguelina Baró Céspedes (Sogbosí, the current director); Esteban was the son of the Dahomean-Cubans Patricio Baró (Tösu, 1810?–1900) and Carlota Baró (Asönsie Se, 1820?–1918; see Brice Sogbossi 1998, 82). Ta Facundo Zulueta, an African who died at 105 years of age in 1933, and Ma Florentina founded the Cabildo of Perico—later the Sociedad Africana Santa Bárbara; the Sociedad Africana de San Lázaro of Agramonte was founded by the Dahomean Manuela Fernández (Ma Gosé), Andrés Fernández (Coso-Coso), Sisto Fernández, and Pilar Fernández (Caletú) and others in 1912. Ma Gosé was an ex-slave from the large sugar *central* "La Unión" of Agramonte (see Vinueza 1986, 22–27, 37–50; Brice Sogbossi 1998, 41–48, 82–83). A descendant of the Zuluetas, Armando Zulueta of Perico, is believed to be the root—some say "inventor"—of the cult of Babalú Ayé (San Lázaro) Lucumí of Perico, Matanzas, and the United States, as opposed to San Lázaro Arará (from my interviews with Ernesto Pichardo, Michael Mason, and Oscar Rodríguez, the director of the Cabildo Arará Sabalú of Matanzas City).

36. See Vinueza 1986, 43, for the connection of Flora Heredia to the Arará Sabalú/Espíritu Santo *cabildo*. Oluwó Popó Awó Bokonó Arará Pedro Abreu of Havana, an apparent ritual grandchild of Pilar Fresneda, states that Fresneda, the founder and dis-

emminator of Arará in Havana, descended from Flora of the Arará Sabalú *cabildo* (personal communciations, August 2000).

37. Such terms are also found in patronage relations in the society at large. Cubans speak of their patrons in the workplace—business, government, and the Communist party—as *padrinos*, "godfathers."

38. In one sense, *fundamento* can refer to the extended sacred kinship relations, past and present, of Lucumí sacred genealogy. In a narrower genealogical sense, it refers to the consecrated stones that are "born" to each new generation of priests (see Brandon 1983, 492–93). In a more philosophical sense, *fundamento* can refer to a corpus of highly restricted traditional secrets (see Mason [1985] 1993, 3–4).

39. *Babalawos* refer to the "system" (*sistema*) of practice of different *ramas*, for example, the widely generalized "system of Bernardo Rojas" and the more restricted "system of Asunción Villalonga."

40. "Adechina" was rendered back into the Yoruba and translated for me as "crown makes fire" (*Adé ṣe iná*) by Dr. David Dorris and as "crown opens the road" (*Adé ṣí ọ̀na*) by my former Emory master's student Babatunde Naṣiru in spring 1993.

41. Ortiz does not report Atandá Ño Filomeno García to have been a *babalawo*, but rather a master of drums (*olúbatá*) and drum or image sculptor (*agbégui*; Ortiz 1952–55, 4:315–16). However, Havana *babalawos* state unequivocally that Atandá was a *babalawo*. No one can say who Atandá's initiated Ifá descendants are, if any—indeed, it is said that he "left no [Ifá] family." The other putative Africans were Ño Blas Cárdenas, Ño José Akon Kon, Achadé, Luzaracó, Año Bí, Oro Bí, Adé Olokun, Awé Ití, Awé Iwí, Ño Hermenegildo, and Obá Yenú Ifá. They were great teachers of Ifá (Ño Blas Cárdenas and Ño José Akon Kon), notable founders or officials of Lucumí societies in Palmira, Matanzas, and Havana (Año Bí, Oro Bí, Ño Hermenegildo, Ño Blas Cárdenas), and masters of confecting Ifá powers, such as Olofin (Achadé). The *babalawo* Kaindé (or Caindé), said to have been an African, was, in fact, a creole lawyer of great means, born in Havana, named Jacinto Fernández Bramoso. An early famous figure, called Adofó, is recognized as a great herbalist (*osainista*) and participant in the *batá* tradition, but *babalawos* are divided as to whether he was a *babalawo*. Ño Hermengildo was, possibly, Hermenegildo Albear, the third vice president of Cabildo Africano Lucumí (Cabildo Africano Lucumí 1900).

42. Interviews with Matanceros Osvaldo Cárdenas Villamil, Francisco Zamora Chirino ("Minini"), Pedro Abreu, Oscar Rodríguez, and Habaneros Hermes Valera, Antonio de Armas, and Jesús Varona, 1992–2000.

43. Vicente Goytizolo was described as "'The Congo King' and noted fetishist of Santiago de Cuba. . . . Goytizolo was a prince of one of the royal families of an African tribe, and like many of them, figured into the individuals captured" and brought to Cuba (Castellanos 1916, 76).

44. The story about Ño Blas as "brother" of Olugueré and teacher of Tata Gaitán comes from interviews with Hermes Valera Ramírez and Andrés Kolá, 16 July 1992, Havana. Additional historical information about Ño Blas comes from Cuban researcher Jorge Rodríguez, based upon his collaborative work with Matanzas's Israel Moliner Castañeda (from the Afro-Cuba Web Discussion Group page and correspondence with Ernesto Pichardo and Jorge Rodríguez, 6 December 1999 [http://www.afrocubaweb.com/ceilidh/cdbcc32900A-3601-144-90.htm]).

45. For example, Olugueré is remembered as the master of ceremonies for Adechina and others and the confector of Olofin. Achadé, an *osainista* (herbalist), ran the "laboratory" of this group. Adofó, who some believe to have been a *babalawo*, confected the *batá* drums, which were normally consecrated under Ifá supervision. However, Ortiz locates Adofó, who died in 1946, as a master *batá* builder of the Republican era—he built drums for Cabildo Changó Tedún; still, his midcentury date of death suggests him as a creole, not an African (though possibly of African parents (Ortiz 1952–55, 4:38). As I detail below, Ño Carlos Adé Bí, possibly Cuba's premier Ifá founder, and the most elder among the *babalawos* in the nineteenth century, is believed to have "reconsecrated" the Ifá of Adechina, effectively becoming his Cuban godfather, regardless of Adechina's prior training in Africa.

46. These forebears, along with the long lists of founders and members of Cabildo Africano Lucumí (Cabildo Africano Lucumí 1900), would have lived and worked during the period of the worst religious persecution of *brujería*, from the end of the nineteenth century until the mid-1920s.

47. The Arará have been known to say, "Arará no cruce agua" (Arará does not cross water), which means that their traditions should not leave their immediate territory or home (i.e., *tierra*). In other words, they do not travel. Pedro Abreu, the dean of the Arará Sabalú in Havana, who is of Matanzas roots, and Francisco Zamora Chirino, a Lucumí, Palo, Abakuá, Mason, and professional performer, both lamented that the Arará have mostly "taken their knowledge to the grave" because of their hermeticism and reluctance to teach anything to the young (personal communications, August 2000 and July 1989, respectively).

48. "Big man" is a term more indigenous to Africa than to Cuba. Such a man in Cuba's political sphere would be called a *caudillo*. In the social and religious sphere, as much in the workplace as in the temple, such a man would be called a *padrino* ("godfather"). A "godfather" in the workplace helps one get a job, advance, secure perks, and so on.

49. The Yoruba *ọ̀pẹ̀lẹ̀* is made of eight halves of the seed shells or pods of the oil palm, which are joined together by short sections of chain or beading (Bascom 1969a, 29, and plate 2; see also Bascom 1952, 170).

50. From interviews with Hermes Valera Ramírez and Andrés Kolá, summers of 1992 and 1993, Havana.

51. Practitioners speak of a "representative" godparent as one who assumes one's religious sponsorship after one's separation from an original godparent of initiation.

52. According to one story, "Adechina, when he was captured, swallowed his Ifá; in the ship, he defecated it and guarded it." According to another, "After [the Middle Passage], in order to continue [as a *babalawo*], Adechina washed his Ifá in the back of a *bodega* of *españoles*, together with Adé Bí, who bought [Adechina] his liberty." The stories come from taped conversations between Valera and Kolá, 16 July 1992 and 26 June 1993, in Havana. In the first interview, Kolá characterized Adé Bí as un "hombre duro, que era mayordomo y hombre de confianza de un español." Valera and Kolá are five generations in Ifá from Adechina and Adé Bí, respectively.

53. These deductions are from an interview of 29 August 1999 with the late Teruel Rolando Cartaya (1905–99), the last blood descendant of Adechina in Cuba, through Adechina's Matanzas relationship with Manuela Cartaya. Teruel was the grandson of Adechina and called himself a *bastardo*, as both his grandmother and mother had out-of-wedlock children. Teruel, researcher Luis Alberto Pedroso, and I pursued a genealogical discussion, from which I constructed a genealogy of Adechina's blood family. During the Matanzas period, Adechina also became involved with the Lucumí Francisca Burlet, with whom he produced Josefa Herrera Echubí Pepa (1864–1947), Teodoro (b. 1866), Faustino Herrera, and Marcelino Herrera. All were born in Regla, which is why it can be hypothesized that he moved there in the early 1860s, leaving behind at least one other family in Matanzas (see n. 4 above). That these children were born in Regla—a major clue to Adechina's residence there as of the early 1860s, came out of extended discussions between Pedro Cosme Baños and myself, 1992–96; following my interview with Teruel Rolando Cartaya and discussions with Luis Alberto Pedroso in 1999, the chronology could then be amplified in time to include the Matanzas period prior to the 1860s.

54. See n. 4 for documentation. The Morales (Perdomo) vacant lot was a sizable property, measuring more than twelve yards across the front and three hundred from the street to the back of the yard.

55. C. D. Fredricks's 1860 photograph of a *cabildo* group represents an important exception (figure 1.7).

56. During the nineteenth century, photographic portraits in Latin America and Cuba were largely for the affluent and white (Levine 1990, 26). Among Ño Remigio Herrera's Lucumí contemporaries who were photographed were "Papá" Silvestre Erice and Domingo Boucourt. A photograph of the former in his coffin and a police mug shot of the latter appeared in racist criminological treatises on the themes of evolutionary atavism and social delinquency among Africans, which supposedly manifested themselves in the form of "witches" *(brujos)*, who were hunted tried, and executed, if not summarily, by the police (e.g., Castellanos 1916, 78–79 [Erice], 88–89 [Boucourt]; see Roche y Monteagudo [1908] 1925a, 230); see mug shots in Trujillo y Monagas 1882, passim; Castellanos 1916, figs. 16–20, between pp. 80 and 85; and Ortiz [1906] 1973, 136, and contrast them with the fine formal portraits of government, military, and police heroes in Roche y Monteagudo [1908] 1925a, 282–85, 386–97). Boucourt was accused, convicted, and garroted to death in 1906 for the supposed ritual murder of a white child, La Niña Zoila, in 1904. Photographs of Africans as anthropological specimens of atavism and pathology, including one striking formal portrait, appear in Henri Dumont's works published in Cuba in the 1910s (see Scott 1985, plates; and Dumont 1915–16; see also Castellanos 1916, passim; and Dumont 1915–16). The late-nineteenth-century studio portrait of Adechina, in contrast, is a large, oval enlargement in three-quarter pose, with a slightly elevated head and illuminated forehead, conventions to signify intelligence and civilization. In tone, it is similar to the formal portraits of officials in Roche y Monteagudo ([1908] 1925a). A survey of published Cuban photography, 1860–1920 (Museum of Arts and Sciences 1988) shows landscapes and some group portraits but no studio portraits of Africans.

57. For Díaz Fabelo (1960, 28), Olofin signifies "law," "mandate," and "the beginning of the beginning." Pichardo and Nieto (1984, 35) say that Olofin, "in his basic form, represents the beginning, the end, and the evolution of existence." Díaz Fabelo associates Olofin with "the Eternal Father" (28). For him, *Olórun* is the sun, the sky, the firmament, the (macro)cosmos, the total Creation—"the creator and owner of the light, of all fire, colors, the air, the wind, of the breath of life." Olórun "is the manifestation of [the mandate of] Olofin . . . Olofin in another form" (Díaz Fabelo 1960, 32–33). Scholars and practitioners have regarded Olodumare as the All-Powerful (e.g., Angarica [1955?] n.d., 12). With respect to the concrete powers the *babalawo* receives, Díaz Fabelo says both that Ordun (Odun) is a "power of Olofin that the *babalawo* receives from his *padrino*" and then makes the two synonymous: "Ordun is The Most Holy, it is Olofin" (1960, 35).

58. Interviews with Hermes Valera, June 1983, Havana; Ernesto Pichardo, summer 1994.

59. The sources of Adechina's and Oluguere Kó Kó's Olofins

and/or the means to fabricate them remain mysterious. One *babalawo* I interviewed identified one "Salvador Montalvo" as a godchild of Adechina (interview with Francisco Aristola, summer 1992); another insisted that "Salvador Montalvo" was both a real person—Adechina's alter ego—and an alias Adechina used to mask himself when sought or addressed by unknown inquisitors. Andrés Kolá told me the story of Odun-Montalvo's returns to Africa and the use by Adechina of the alias (interview of 19 July 1992). Kolá says these stories were told to him by Miguel Febles.

60. Ortiz identifies Ño Ernesto Noriega as an African ("The local tradition of the *santeros* notes that a famous *babalawo negro,* Ernesto Noriega . . . brought [the ancestor staff's] use from Africa when he returned from a trip that he made to his homeland" (1952–55, 2:299). The late Feliberto O'Farril (July 1991) and Orlando Justiz Sierra (24 July 1997) also identified him as an African, and Andrés Kolá (16 July 1992) and Lázaro Marqueti (11 June 1998) identified Noriega as an Arará diviner (Bokonó). The photograph I have of Ernesto Noriega depicts him as a phenotypically Spanish creole, perhaps a *mulato.* However, formal portraits of putatively African figures were commonly modified to give them non-African features (for example, this one, and the photograph and painting of Ta Vicente Goytisolo, supposedly a Congo *cabildo* king of Santiago de Cuba [see n. 43]).

61. Like the Ortiz account, a story related by Natalia Bolívar Aróstegüi resonates with those I collected about Lucumí *babalawos* returning to Africa and bringing back ritual secrets. In her story, she identifies one "Eulogio Gutiérrez" as a *babalawo* who returned to Africa where he "received Olofi on two occasions"—which would explain how the Adechina group got the basis for its Olofins. However, because many key details in her account of Ifá's beginnings are highly inaccurate—starting with this figure's name, which she confuses with that of Tata Gaitán (Eulogio Rodríguez)—it is unreliable evidence. Bolívar is also incorrect in asserting that this "Eulogio Gutiérrez" initiated Bernabé Menocál, Bernardo Rojas, and Tata Gaitán (Bolívar Aróstegüi 1990, 25–26).

62. Interview with *babalawo* Feliberto O'Farril, 4 January 1994.

63. The rough estimate of perhaps two score *babalawos* working in Havana between the 1880s and 1910 is based on a count of all the names of men I encountered who were initiated during that period on top of the ten or more noted Africans. These include Ño Carlos Adé Bí, Adechina, Ifá Bí, Ifá Omí, Ño José Akón Kón, Olugueré, Isidoro Somodevilla, Isidoro Sandrino, José Cornelio Delgado, Ricardo Domeneche, Francisco Roche, Achadé, Ño Ernesto Noriega, Adé Olokun, Awé Ití, Awé Iwí, Ño Hermenegildo, Obá Yenú Ifá, Kaindé Jacinto Fernández Bramoso, Bernabé Menocal, Félix Mulita, Asunción Villalonga, Miguel Castellón, Tata Gaitán, Ramón Febles, Secundino Crucet Landa, Valentín Cruz, Esteban Quiñones, Marcós García, Quintín García, José Antonio Ariosa, Bonifacio Valdés, Pedro Pablo Pérez, Federico Acosta, Luís Pacheco, José Carmen Batista, Lino Espejo, Bernardo Rojas (thirty-seven *babalawos;* Atandá had died in 1876; Año Bí and Oro Bí worked in Palmira, not Havana, as did most of the early godchildren of Tata Gaitán). This small number of male *babalawos*—perhaps two of them were white—belonged to a Havana male population of color of 50,990 in 1899, out of a total Havana population of color of 112,214, and a total white and colored population of 424,804 (see Kiple 1976, appendixes).

64. Bernardo Rojas would live in an upscale section of Marianao, while most of his godchildren and colleagues lived in its poorer *barrios* (e.g., Juan "Chiquito" Aristola and Joseíto Herrera [Pogolotti], and Guillermo Castro [La Ceiba]).

65. El Cerro *babalawos* from the first decades of the twentieth century through the 1970s have included Ramón Febles, Panchito Febles, Bernardo Rojas, Gerardo de las Mercedes Valdés Montalvo, Hilario Barbón, José Ramón Gutiérrez, Joaquín Salazar, Enrique Santa Cruz, and many others.

66. For example, Asunción Villalonga, the son of the Yoruba Francisco Villalonga Ifá Bí, was born about 1858 and was initiated into Ifá about 1878. Ramón Febles Molina, a second-generation creole *babalawo,* was born in the mid-1840s and was initiated about 1887; Bernabé Menocal was probably initiated before Villalonga, in the 1870s; Tata Gaitán was probably initiated just after Villalonga, in the early 1880s. Bernardo Rojas was initiated in 1902 (from my oral history research among a score or more of *babalawos* between 1986 and 2000).

67. Cuba's economy soared during and after World War I, just as it did during and after World War II. See Pérez 1988, 222–25.

68. Ifá Bí's Francisco Villalonga's son was Asunción Villalonga (Ogunda Masá), and his grandson was Angelito Villalonga (Ogunda Leni). In the 1960s, Ángel Padrón ("Bebo Mokongo"), initiated by Párraga's Juan Angulo of the Adé Bí lineage, developed close working relations with the Villalonga line and its two great *obás,* Guillermo Castro and José Antonio Tamayo. Padrón would inherit mantle of the Villalonga line after the death of Angelito Villalonga in the 1970s.

69. One of my Havana sources says that Marcos García died in 1903, that is, while Adechina was still alive (interview with Andrés Kolá, 19 July 1992). John Mason reports, from an interview with Marcos's nephew Quintín Lecón Lombillo (Jr., aka Tín), that Marcos died in 1909 (Mason 1992, 48 n. 19).

70. These include Bernabé Menocal, about 1927; Bonifacio Valdés, about 1938; Ramón Febles and Secundino Crucet, about 1939; Tata Gaitán, 1944; Asunción Villalonga, 1953; Bernardito Rojas, 1955; and Bernardo Rojas, 1959.

71. The "Knife" (*Wanaldo,* or *Guanaldo*) gives a *babalawo*

the power (*poder*) to initiate his own godchildren, but he cannot do so without the authority of Olofin, which belongs to the *rama* and which he inherits or otherwise acquires or which he borrows for the purpose of initiation.

72. Chronologies that I have assembled from oral and archival data suggest that a great many initiations occurred during and just after the First World War (1916–early 1930s, particularly in the houses of Bernabé Menocal, Ramón Febles, Bernardo Rojas, Pedro P. Pérez and his son Pedro Pérez Sánchez, and Pedro Ruiz Armenteros). Though a number of significant initiations and events did occur during the Great Depression (e.g., the inscribing of Bernardo Rojas's Luz de San Francisco organization), some of the greatest organizing triumphs came after the depression and the new constitution (1940), continuing through the economic prosperity from World War II through the 1950s, such as the building of the twentieth century's two principal Ifá instititutions (Bernardo Rojas and Quintín Lecón Lombillo; see below). With respect to the World War II period and afterward, Pérez writes: "Good times arrived in spectacular form. Sugar exports accounted for nearly a 40% increase in national income between 1939 and 1947 . . . [although] not all enjoyed the new prosperity" given an increase in food prices and cost of living (Pérez 1988, 282–85).

73. Data on Tata Gaitán's parents come from his will. Property documents show that the house and land, purchased in 1916 were worth fifteen hundred pesos, the equivalent of approximately thirty thousand now. The tomb, purchased in the Colón Cemetery in 1924, cost five hundred pesos (according to documents held by the descendants of the estate's inheritor, Ramón Hugues, kindly shared with me by Gualberta Püig and Ricardo Navarro, Guanabacoa, 17 June 1998).

74. Interviews with Fran Cabrera, 12 July 1994 (who said that "Bernabé Menocal worked for politicians and the rich"), and the descendants of Ramón Hugues on the subject of Tata Gaitán's relationships, 7 July 1994 and 17 June 1998.

75. Interview with Gisela Arándia, 25 June 1992.

76. Febles was born in Matanzas about 1849 to the son of white wealthy family and a *negra de nación* (African). Febles's son Juanito says the father was "white," though his grandson, Pancho Veitia, says that one side of Febles family was of Spanish–Canary Island stock. Disinherited and cast out, his father took Febles and his mother to Güines, where he apparently had some family. The father soon abandoned the family, returning to Matanzas. In Güines, the young Febles learned carpentry and cabinetmaking from an uncle. Probably there, or in Havana, he encountered Rojas. Later, Febles owned multiple houses and shops and built some of Havana's most luxurious horse-drawn funeral coaches (from interviews with Ramón Febles's son, Juanito Febles, 17 June 1998, Havana). Pancho Veitia, Febles's grandson, believes that Ramón was of Canary Island descent (interviews, 7 July 1994, Havana).

77. Interviews with Andrés Kolá (of this lineage), Pancho Veitia and Eusebia Febles, grandson and daughter, respectively, of Ramón Febles, and Gilberto Rojas, grandson of Bernardo Rojas, during the summers of 1992, 1993, and 1994. The date of Adechina's death comes from the register of the cemetery of Regla. The conditions of Rojas's birth come from his baptismal and death documents, kindly shared with me by his grandson, Gilberto Rojas Herrera (3 January 1994). Dagoberto Ventura Herrera, an elder *santero* of Central Havana, tells the same story about Bernardo's "moving" to Regla to study with Adechina (personal communication, 2 January 2000).

78. "This sign signifies Two Kings, the birth of wealth, and the wealth of children" (*Tratado de Oddun de Ifa* 1992, 128; see also *Tratado de Odduns de Ifá* n.d.b). One of its proverbs is, "When gold speaks, man listens." One important theme in the sign is "commerce" (other themes include the problem of "the tongue" and its potential to betray as well as save). These proverbs and themes were discussed in my hearing and written up by *babalawos* who interpreted the sign of 2000, Obara Meyi, after it emerged on 1 January: Lázaro Cuesta, Víctor Betancourt, Guillermo Diago, Hermes Valera, Roberto Villanueva, Antonio de Armas, and Radamés Corona.

79. Story told by *babalawo* Hermes Valera Ramírez, 2 January 2000.

80. During the first decades of the twentieth century, Ramón Febles had moved from a house in the City of Havana's Jesús María *barrio*, where Tata Gaitán was born, through three different houses in Barrio Pilar in El Cerro, where he maintained his coach shop, called El Lorigado (interviews with Juanito Febles, 22 June 1998).

81. One story tells that the cantankerous Ño José Akón Kón was a willing teacher but would not allow his words to be transcribed. According to several stories, Rojas, Pedro Pablo Pérez Rodríguez, and Ramón Febles (who housed, clothed, and fed Ño José) would visit the old man's home; two would engage him in conversation while a third crouched outside the louvered window and transcribed the information.

82. Kolá, Valera, and others use the phrase "the system of Bernardo Rojas" (interviews with Andrés Kolá and Hermes Valera Ramírez, 19 July 1992 and 26 June 1993). All of the following, and many of their godchildren, worked together from the first decades of the twentieth century through the 1970s, particularly in the house of Rojas in Marianao: Bernardo Rojas and all his godchildren (Adechina line); Tata Gaitán, Ramón Hugues, José Antonio Erize, Felix el Negro (Olugueré line); Bernabé Menocal—Rojas's second godfather (*oyubona*)—and his godchil-

dren, Joaquín Salazar, Cornelio Vidal, "Babel" Aurelio Estrada, and Miguel Febles (Ifá Omí line); Ramón Febles, Panchito Febles, Pedro Pablo Pérez, Pedro Pérez Sánchez, and Juan Angulo (Adé Bí line), and Guillermo Castro and José Antonio Tamayo (Ifá Bí line). Rojas's and Menocal's ritual families were interlocking, as many of Rojas's godchildren had Menocal as their *oyubona* and vice versa. Salazar was the *obá* of Rojas's house for perhaps thirty years. Following the death of Bernardo Rojas in 1959, Salazar, in his role as *obá*, and Joseíto Herrera (Ogbe Dí), Rojas's Ifá godchild, confidant, protégé, and Olofin heir, maintained the organization until their deaths in the mid 1970s.

83. From a private collection of documents on Rojas's organization, kindly shared with me by Rojas's Ifá grandson, Francisco Aristola, 15 June 1998, Havana.

84. Data and photographs from the private collection of the late *babalawo* Fernando Molina "El Marinero," Roja's grandson in Ifá, 15 June 1998, Havana.

85. Tín gave Prío the "Hand of Orula," signifying the protection of Ifá and making the president Tín's ritual godchild, and Prío Tín's economic patron. This is widely known among Havana *babalawos*, including the *babalawo* son of Tín's confidant and first godchild, Felix Pulido (interview with José Manuel Pulido, 16 August 1999).

86. Photographs of Quintín Lecón Lombillo (Tín) receiving the check from Prío and the laying of the first stone were kindly shared with me by *babalawo* José Manuel Pulido, 8 July 1999. Previously, the late Reinaldo Blayó had shared an alternate photograph of the laying of the first stone with me (1991–92).

87. Dates and facts from documents shared with me by *babalawo* Andrés Kolá, 19 July 1992 and 26 June 1993, and Francisco "Pancho" Aristola, Havana, 15 June 1998, as well as from research in Regla civil archives (see *Provincia de la Habana, fincas urbanas* in my works cited). I was shown the structural hulk of the building in 1994 by the director of Regla's museum, Pedro Cosme. Various unflattering stories circulate about the causes of the failure of the project.

88. Tín, initiated in about 1939, became Cuba's senior *babalawo* following the deaths of Bernabé Menocal's godchildren Miguel Febles (1986) and Eustaquio Delgado ("Tatica") in the mid- to late 1980s. If the *itutu* rites (the ritual dispatching and bequeathing of the priest's *orishas*, followed by a ceremony called the *honras*, do not take place, one may not be chanted to as an *egun* (ancestor), as one has not been ritually transferred to the *ará orún* ("other world").

89. The term, appears, likewise, in lower case in modern Yoruba dictionaries as "legislator" (*olóòfin;* Abraham 1946, 452).

90. There is an *Ọlọ́fin-ọ̀run*, "which signifies the high office of Olódùmarè as the Supreme Sovereign Ruler Who is in heaven. Sometimes, it is used in contrast to *Ọlọ́fin-Aiyé*—'The supreme ruler on earth'—which, according to Yoruba belief, was the title of the first priest-king from whom the title has passed on to the successive Ọni of Ile-Ifẹ̀" (Idowu [1962] 1963, 36).

91. While Ortiz [1906] 1973, 28–29, surveying the Cuban Lucumí religious cosmology against the background of extant Yoruba ethnography, does not mention Olofin among the High Gods he cites (Olodumare and Olorun), Olofin turns up much more frequently in the statements of Cabrera's informants than either Olodumare or Olorun (see the *O* section of Cabrera's index [1954] 1983 and pp. 77–81). In 1955 Angarica identified Olofi as "the primary one in charge, after Oloddumare [the Almighty], of all the heads and things that exist in this world," whose "image or consecrated secrets" are possessed by the high authorities of Ifá (Angarica [1955?] n.d., 14). In a way that has become common and persuasive among practitioners, though not literally correct as a translation, "Olofin" breaks down as Olo ("extension," "expansion") and Fi (*pintica* or *manchita*), that is, a materialized trace or instantiantion "within the great extension or space of this world." In this view, in other words, Olofin is a primordial materialization in "the World" of Olodumare, the All-Powerful (Angarica [1955?] n.d., 14). Of course, Olofin still translates more precisely as "Owner of the Law"—a version of Abraham's (1946) "legislator" more apt to the cosmological role of the being bearing this proper name *(Olóòfin)*.

92. According to the first Cuban-born *babalawo* to have made Ifá in the United States, José Miguel Gómez Barberas, the Lucumís "created the first sixteen Olofins and then stopped. As of that moment, Olofin could only be inherited" (interview of Gómez Barberas by Ernesto Pichardo, 28 July 1990, in Miami, kindly shared with me).

93. A small number of Olofins were fabricated "in the past century" (nineteenth century) by a collective of Lucumí founders, said to include Adechina and Oluguеré, while Ifá Bí Francisco Villalonga, as indicated, is said to have brought his Olofin from Africa (interviews with Hermes Valera Ramírez and Andrés Kolá, together and separately, 19 July 1992 and 26 June 1993; and Fran Cabrera, 12 July 1994). For example, accounts diverge: Tata is said to have inherited his Olofin from Oluguеré; alternately, Adechina is said to have fabricated one for him. Some *babalawos* say all these men had Olofins and others say many did not and had to borrow them.

94. The "Knife" (*Wanaldo*) is normally given when a *babalawo* godchild has achieved a requisite body of Ifá knowledge, a level of maturity, and secure trust of his godfather; the "Knife" is sometimes denied in order to hold back and control, and perhaps even frustrate, *babalawos* who raise ire or jealously among their colleagues or fall out with their *ramas* for one reason or another.

Still, a *babalawo* with the "Knife" must get permission to use his *rama*'s Olofin to initiate others.

95. Occasionally, the most senior godchild would be found lacking in moral character (*la moral*) if he was a drinker, for example, or if he was involved in crimes or personal indiscretions. In a famous case, the rightful inheritor of the Olofin of Gerardo de las Mercedes Valdés Montalvo (Cheché) was denied it because he was seen to lack *la moral.* The Olofin was kidnapped at gunpoint from an initiation for which it was being used by an indignant faction of the *rama;* never delivered to the designated inheritor, it remains "hidden somewhere in Pogolotti."

96. Data on Rojas's restriction of Olofin come from interviews of Berta Prajedes on 24 July 1990 and 1 August 1990 by Ernesto Pichardo in Miami, which he kindly shared with me. Several Havana *babalawos* told me that Rojas would not fabricate Olofins, or the other special Ifá *orichas,* such as Odúa, for anyone; and his contemporaries, Asunción Villalonga and Pedro Pablo Pérez, refused to give Olofin to anyone (interviews with Hermes Valera and Gilberto H. Rojas, 1 January 1994). The members of his "*rama* Marianao" remained dependent upon Rojas's Olofin, which was inherited in 1959 by Rojas's preferred heir, José (Joseíto) Herrera y Herrera (Obe Dí), over the head of Rojas's rightful senior godchild, Enrique Santa Cruz (my interviews with Hermes Valera and Andrés Kolá, 2 July 1992; Hermes Valera, 3 July 1993, and Reinaldo Blayó, 17 June 1993).

97. Interview with José Miguel Gómez Barberas by Ernesto Pichardo 28 July 1990, kindly shared with me.

98. Interviews by Ernesto Pichardo of Berta Prajedes (the partner of Miguel Febles), who owned the house in Mantilla where Febles had his Olofin "laboratory," 24 July and 1 August 1990, kindly shared with me.

99. Francisco Febles del Pino was initiated by his own father in 1923, and Miguel Febles Padrón by Bernabé Menocal in 1924.

100. Francisco was his father's eldest son and senior godchild in Ifá; whereas the younger Miguel, who was not the most senior of Bernabé Menocal's eminent godchildren, had no immediate inheritable Olofin.

101. Interview with Hermes Valera Ramírez, 25 June 1993, Havana.

102. Divination with the Ifá system and the execution of healing *ebós* are a central, but not the sole, task of the *babalawo. Babalawos* are often called upon to "go to war" on behalf of clients, or themselves against the agents of witchcraft (*brujería*). With their intimate knowledge of Osain, *babalawos* prepare *inche-osains,* fierce Echús, and defensive and offensive *trabajos* ("works") against perceived malign forces. Although many *oricha* priests are specialists in Osain, *babalawos* see themselves as the most effective defenders within the Lucumí religion against the *brujería* (witchcraft) of the Kongo-Cuban Palo Monte priests (*Tata-Nganga*), who work with "charged" cauldrons called *prendas, ngangas,* and *nkisis* (see Cabrera [1954] 1983, 118–46; Cabrera [1979] 1986). Indeed, many *babalawos* refer to their Osain pots as *la prenda del babalawo.* These metal or ceramic vessels, "charged" (*cargado*) with earths, plants, animal parts, and, sometimes, human skulls, bear a striking resemblance to the *prendas,* or *ngangas,* of Palo Monte (see Cabrera [1954] 1983, 102–4). In concert with their *prendas de babalawo,* they "work both sides" of Orula's divination equipment. When they perform their regular Ifá divining and healing work, they utilize the "top" face of their circular divination boards (*tablero de Ifá*). When they engage in offensive *brujería,* like "breaking marriages" or "getting back at your employer who is giving you trouble," some invert their *tablero* and work with its bottom face, which may be painted black (data from interviews with *babalawo* Antonio Sevilla of Palmira, Cienfuegos, 10 July 1994). Others work with a special rectangluar tray for Osain. Tata Gaitán initiated all of his godchildren into Palo before Ifá, such as Walfredo Rivera Ules, and many *babalawos* conducted protracted "wars" against each other with their *prendas,* such as Hilario Barbón and Pedro Pérez Sánchez during the first half of the twentieth century (interviews with Hermes Valera Ramírez, 29 June 1992, 17 July 1992, 11 June 1998).

103. This characterization of Miguelito's ability to select and "block" Olofin recipients comes from Ernesto Pichardo's interviews with José Miguel Gómez Barberas in 1991 and 1992 in Miami, kindly shared with me.

104. From interviews with three Havana *babalawos,* who shall remain anonymous, summers of 1994 and 1995.

105. Pedro Pablo Pérez (d. c. 1936), Bonifacio Valdés (c. 1938), Miguel Febles's father, Ramón Febles (c. 1939), Secundino Crucet (c. 1939), Miguel Febles's *oyubona,* Tata Gaitán (1944), Asunción Villalonga (1953), Bernardo Rojas's son Bernardito Rojas (1957), and, last, Bernardo Rojas (1959).

106. Interviews with Andrés Kolá, 19 July 1992 and 26 June 1993.

107. Miguel Febles's contemporaries who received Olofins were Facundo Sevilla (Obé Dí) and Mario Fernández (Ojuani Bofún) of Palmira, Aurelio Estrada ("Babel" Baba Elliogbe) of Regla, and Walfredo Rivera (Oturukpon Benon Wa) of Guanabacoa; among his mentorees in Ifá and contemporaries in age was Juan Angulo (Obetuará Morá) of Parraga. Febles godchildren who received Olofin from him included José Ramón Ávila, Papito Adakoy, and Panchintín Francisco Álvarez Pérez (from interviews by Ernesto Pichardo with Berta Prajedes, 8 January 1990, 24 July 1990, kindly shared with me; my interviews with Fran Cabrera, 12 July 1994; Andrés Kolá, 19 July 1992 and 26 June 1993; and Hermes Valera and Gilberto H. Rojas, 1 January 1994).

108. From interviews with *babalawos* Hermes Valera Ramírez, Andrés Kola, and Fran Cabrera, summers of 1992, 1993, and 1994.

109. This is the opinion of Havana *babalawos* interviewed during 1991–99, including Hermes Valera, Andrés Kolá, Gilberto H. Rojas, Fran Cabrera, Francisco Aristola, Francisco Pancho Veitia, Fernando Molina, and Ignacio Tartabull, as well as Miami's José Miguel Gómez Barberas and *santera* Berta Prajedes (the last two by Ernesto Pichardo).

110. At the top of the list of these prolific *babalawo* houses are those of Elpidio Cárdenas (Otura Sá), the late Agapito Piloto (Otura Irá), and the late Luciano Canto (Iwori Bobe) of Central Havana, Fran Cabrera (Obeché) of Parraga, Norberto Díaz (Baba Elliogbe) of Regla, Ángel Padrón of San Miguel del Padrón, and Lázaro Cuesta of Buena Vista and Mantilla. All of them have initiated scores of *babalawos*. The beneficiaries also included Carlos Ojeda and Diego Fontela of Miami and Roberto Bolufer of Puerto Rico (list compiled from numerous interviews, 1992–2000 in Havana and Miami). To date, Elpidio Cárdenas is the most prolific of all, having initiated over 115 *babalawos* since the early 1960s (interviews with Orlando Sierra Justíz, 24 July 1997; Elpidio Cárdenas, 15 June 1998; also from research I commissioned from Ernesto Valdés Janet and Orlando Sierra Justiz, 1997–98).

111. A popular Cuban expression for one who "fucks with you" and "fucks you over" all the time.

112. Interviews with Fran Cabrera (Obeché), one of Miguel's last, closest protégés, 12 July 1994.

113. Angarica believed that only *babalawos* of the highest rank (*omocolabbá*), could rightfully possess Olofin, but doubted that any *omocolabbá* had ever existed in Cuba, because no one thus far had had the oracular "sign" authorizing the occupation of this rank ([1955?] n.d., 14).

114. Murphy (1988, 50) reports the year of Francisco "Pancho" Mora's arrival in the United States as 1946; Marta Moreno's interview of Pancho Mora reports his arrival date as 1950 (Caribbean Cultural Center 1984).

115. Tín had descended from the sub-*rama* of his adoptive father, Secundino Crucet Landa (Osalofobelló) of Reparto Juanelo (San Miguel del Padrón), the ultimate roots of which lay in Tata Gaitán and Oluguere Kó Kó.

116. The first of three major post-Revolution "waves" of Cubans was predominantly white, the second was mostly white. Miami became the mecca for white Cubans and the Northeast (New Jersey and New York) for Afro-Cubans (see Dixon 1982, 1983).

117. The following account is owed to my interviews with Ernesto Pichardo and Pichardo's interviews with a number of Miami *babalawos* and others during 1990, which he kindly shared with me.

118. Ojeda and Campos were initiated by José Ramón Gutiérrez (Ogundá Bedé) of El Cerro's Barrio Ataré in the early 1950s, and their *oyubona* was Bernardo Rojas, Gutiérrez's godfather.

119. The first five *babalawos* made in the U.S. were (1) Bobby Bolufer (Ogunda Leni) and (2) Orestes Menezes (Elliobe), made the same day in 1970 by Diego Fontela (Obe Yono) and Rogelio Facenda, respectively; (3) Aurelio Arango (Odifún) and (4) José Miguel Gómez Barberas (Otura Adakoy), made together some months later by Fontela and Silvio Rodríguez (Ofún Sá), respectively; and (5) José Ojeda (probably Diego Fontela). (Data on the first Ifá initiations are from Pichardo and Nieto 1984, 7–8, and Cintrón 1979, 7). In the cases of several participants, I have completed the names, signs, and godfathers with information from Cintrón, gathered in an interview in 1979 with "Babi" Bolufer in Puerto Rico, and from my own fieldwork in New Jersey and Havana, 1986–2000.

120. Interviews with Ernesto Pichardo, a Miami godchild of Ojeda's, and Fernando Pichardo, 1992–95, who has seen the "contract"; interviews with Lázaro Cuesta, 15 September 1999; correspondence between José Miguel Gómez Barberas and Radamés Corona, 1989, and between Miguel Febles and Miami *babalawos*, 1979–80 (from the collection of Radamés Corona).

121. From a collection of correspondence kept by Radamés Corona and generously shared with me.

122. Ernesto Pichardo related to me that Orestes Menezes, the second of the first two Ifá initiates in the United States (the first was Boluffer), had been brainstorming the return to Africa for years, which was picked up and realized by José Miguel Gómez Barberas (interview with Ernesto Pichardo, 12 March 1995). As the works of Hunt (1979), Pichardo and Nieto (1984), Clarke (1997), and Curry (1997) reveal, Walter King and Chris Oliana traveled from New York to Matanzas in 1959 to be initiated into the rama of Fermina Gómez, and King returned to Africa in the early 1970's to be initiated as a *babalawo* (see Hunt 1979, 63). African-American artists and intellectuals had "returned" to Africa to connect with roots as had exponents of the various late-nineteenth-century "colonization" movements and twentieth-century pan-Africanist movements. African-American artists also traveled to Africa intensively in the period of African independence (late 1950s; see, e.g., Wardlaw 1995; and Dallas Museum of Arts 1989).

123. In Ọ̀ṣogbo, using his own Olofin, Gómez initiated three Cuban-born men into Ifá. Each ceremony cost eight hundred dollars. Priests who worked in these ceremonies included a Puerto Rican *babalawo* living in Miami, Anajaku Fagbemi (the *obá* of Lagos), Kajote Atanda (a *babalawo* from Ifẹ̀), and Mmonka Laide Amensu—a *babalawo* from Ọ̀ṣogbo. The ceremonies were conducted in a bush grove and were well documented with photo-

graphs and official-looking typed documents. These data are from documents in the collection of the late Reinaldo Blayó of Havana (summer 1992) and the collection of Radamés Corona, kindly shared with me (21 August 1999).

124. The documents I have seen indicate that Ifá Yemí first gave Olofin to Gómez in Òṣogbo, along with Odudúwa, Broncia and Bromú (4 September 1975); He next consecrated four *babalawos* to Olofin in Òṣogbo in October and November 1978; then, Ifa Yemí went to Miami and gave three more Olofins—eight altogether. These last three *babalawos*, with the addition of himself, Gómez saw as "emulat[ing]" the arrival of the first four Yoruba *babalawos* in Cuba. Data from letter by Gómez to Radamés Corona, 21 October 1989, from the collection of Radamés Corona). This data is reinforced by an interview Ernesto Pichardo conducted with Gómez (28 July 1990).

125. From the private collection of Radamés Corona.

126. These names refer or appear to refer to Atandá (Ño Filomeno García) and his colleague Añabí (Ana[b]í, Ño Juan el Cojo), [A]caidé (Kaindé)—who was, in fact, a creole *babalawo* of El Cerro—and a fourth, whose identity is uncertain.

127. From a 21 October 1989 letter from Gómez in Radamés Corona's collection.

128. See how Maxine Kamari Clarke (1997, 131–44) demonstrates that the Black American Yoruba reconfigured their spiritual genealogies by inserting African ancestors uncovered in trips to Africa into their Cuban-derived *moyuba* prayers. African names learned on trips and in research appear, in a hierarchical ranking, above the name of Osha Bí (Fermina Gómez, the putative Afro-Cuban root of the Matanzas lineage from which the Black American Yoruba Movement descended, given the 1959 initiations of the Movement's founders Walter King and Chris Oliana in Matanzas; see my chap. 5). Obá Teró, Fermina's senior and godmother, mentioned universally in the *moyubas* of priests descending from this *rama*, does not appear, however.

129. The verso of another photograph, taken in Miami, reveals that the Cuban *babalawos* also brought back a set of Yoruba *bàtá* drums from Nigeria. It depicts Ifá Yemí with a Cuban *babalawo* holding the hourglass-shaped drums. The verso says: "Miami, Fl, Dic. 2, 1978; Dagoberto Calzado 'Iwori Bobe', godchild of Miguel Febles together with Yemi Elebuibon, with the legitimate batá drums, brought from Africa, in the house of Omo Ordun Ifa Adakoy, with the Oba of Ifa of Osogbo, Nigeria, West Africa, the *sole place where the root, tradition, and pratice of Ocha and Ifá are to be found*" (emphasis added). "Omo Ordun" refers to the fact that Gómez (Ifa Adakoy) had received Olofi (alternatively Odun or Ordun)—he was a "child of Ordun."

130. Some *babalawos* and *santeros* in Miami like to believe that Ojeda's Olofin was never really brought out of Cuba, and that those Olofins actually brought are not legitimate because they were never formally conferred through ceremonies of *adjudicación* (inheritance) or *entrada* (installation in the house). Many *babalawos* in Cuba deny that Olofin was taken out of Cuba, except in the cases of the well-known José Ramón Avila, José Miguel Campos, Agapito Piloto, and Panchito Erize—and that Reinaldo "Pipo" Peña, the grandson of Arturo Peña, received a legitimate Olofin from Piloto.

131. The other *babalawos* were Reinaldo Peña and Agapito Piloto.

132. Excerpted from an undated document (probably 1979–80) penned by Miguel Febles, from the the collection of Radamés Corona; emphasis added.

133. Excerpts from a series of letters and documents penned by Miguel Febles, undated (probably 1979–80), in the collection of Radamés Corona.

134. These are my calculations from data in a letter from Gómez in the collection of Radamés Corona, wherein Gómez reports that Ifá Yemí was thirty-seven years old in 1978 and had twelve years in Ifá. Data on Febles come from a variety of interviews with his surviving colleagues and family in Havana, including Andrés Kolá, Lázaro Cuesta, Fran Cabrera, Pancho Veitia, Candelaria Cruz, Eusebia Febles, and Juanito Febles, 1996–99.

135. From undated letter from Gómez to Radamés Corona (probably 1979–80), in Corona's collection.

136. Ernesto Pichardo of Miami recited to me Efuche, Apoto, Monserrate, Aratakuá, Trapito, and Obadimelli. Miguel Ramos of Miami mentioned to me Efuche, Apoto, Monserrate, Ferminita, Palmira, Culo Verde, Trapito, and Obadimelli. Michael Mason informed me of San José Ochenta as the name of his *rama* and identified, through his field research, the connection of Efuche, Ña Margarita Armenteros, Tiburcia Sotolongo, Atí Keké, and Adewa(ro) to San José Ochenta. My godparents Hermes Valera Ramírez and Zenaida Justiz have discussed with me the *rama* of our house, which includes José Pata de Palo and Aurora Lamar. Valera and Jesús Varona Puente of Havana have mentioned Los Jimaguas to me on a number of occasions; see also Cabrera [1954] 1983, 25 n. 1. Yrmino Valdés Garriz (1997, 135), Sim-El Fatunmishe William Muldro (personal correspondence October 2000), Natalia Bolivar (personal correspondence shared with William Muldro), and the researchers for an important summative article on Cuban religion (Latin American News Agency (Prensa Latina) 1996) note Igoro (aka Aigoro, Aiworo).

Other names cited in the very good Prensa Latina piece include Aldewaró, Aramitó, Ashakún, Atún, Awapiticó, Oddun Tawadé, Tillakó, Ochailú, Obbilumí, Imalé, Oyatagún, Abbita, Efuche Atiquequé, Maleque la grande, and Maleque la chica. All of these are the sacred Lucumí names of priests, and at least two,

Aldewaró and Efuche Atiqueque (Efuche's two daughters), are included within the San José Group. Awapiticó was undoubtedly Changó priestess Ramona Collazo (Valdés Garriz 1997, 135).

Mercedes Melo González, an Ochún priestess of El Cerro, cites her *rama* as that of the "La Gumisa." The root of this *rama* was Juana Talabí, who Melo says was an "africana." The *rama* was called "Gumisa" because Juana's goddaughter, Siliaca López, was an Ochún priestess named Ochún Gumí (interview with Mercedes Melo González, 31 August 1999).

See next footnote for sources on Asiñabí, Abonse, and San Lorenzo de Samá.

137. Among others, Monserrate Asiñabí, a Yemayá priestess, was cited by Hiali-Ricardo Quiñonez (personal correspondence of 19 April 2001) and Afolabi, in his website (http://www.yemoja.com/teaching.htm). Afolabi claims that she was "brought from Africa during the slave trade," and is the root of his lineage. These two sources believe Monserrate Asiñabí to be the root of the line that runs from Arabia Oviedo Shangó Funke, through Adela Alonso Oduanla, through Rigoberto Rodríguez Duque of Madruga Oshún Yemí. Tía Julia Samá Abonse was cited to me by Eguin Lety of Miami (personal correspondence, 15 January 2001). This *rama,* also called "San Lorenzo de Samá," is said to include members of the famous Samá (aka Samar) family, including Obadimelli. It is likely that José Pata de Palo and quite possible that Obadimelli were *criollos.*

138. John Mason believes that Ma Monserrate González was of Yoruba Ẹ̀gbàdó descent and a priestess of Ṣàngó (Mason 1996, 26), though his sources remain uncited. Reinaldo Raimundo Chaguayceda ("Papo") of Regla says he believes Monserrate was a priestess of Yewá, an *oricha* associated with an important Virgin enshrined in Matanzas, Our Lady of Monserrate.

139. Cabrera reports that "The liturgical masks of Olokun, which at one time were kept in a *casa-templo* in the village of Regla, were found many years ago in the city of Matanzas, in the *ilé* ['house'] of the deceased *iyalocha* Fermina Gómez. I saw the seven goblet-shaped drums that were played in God's honor, painted blue and white, but they didn't show me the masks, which were considered ancient relics. . . . It was known that the custodian of these masks didn't know the liturgy and the handling of these masks, and that no *babalawo,* after the famous, and now dead, Adechina (initiated in Nigeria) had the boldness to dance them" (Cabrera [1974] 1980, 27).

140. Some say that Ma Monserrate and Ferminita Gómez were related by initiation and by blood: Miguel Ramos was told by elder priests that Ma Monserrate Obá Teró, an African ex-slave, was the mother *and* godmother of Ferminita (interview of 9 March 1995). John Mason reports, but without revealing his sources, that Ferminita's first initiator was the Lucumí Ochún priestess Adèlé (Omodelé), but that later Ferminita came under Ma Monserrate's "guidance" (Mason 1996, 26).

Osvaldo Cárdenas Villamil relates that Ferminita's original *padrino* was a Cuban-born child of an African slave; he was was Ño Cordá-isí, a one-legged priest who may or may not have been José Pata de Palo Urquiola, a famed Matancero ("José Wooden Leg"). After Cárdenas's story about the wooden-legged Eleguá priest named Ño Córda-Isí, whose Spanish name he could not remember, I asked him if this might have been José Pata de Palo, and he wholeheartedly agreed and then went on to repeat and clarify his story. This identification deserves to be verified.

According to John Mason's anonymous sources, Ma Monserrate was originally Ferminita's *oyubona,* who, because of complications with Ferminita's initiation, had to become her principal godparent (*madrina*). Mason identifies Ferminita's first initiator as Kúdáasí—who prepared to initiate Ferminita to Ochún, but it was Yemayá that possessed her during the rites. Kúdáasí, because of some ritual taboo, was banned from dealing with Yemayá, and, hence, Ma Monserrate stepped in and became the de facto godmother of Ferminita (Mason 1996, 26). Michael Atwood Mason's interviews with Matanzas-Havana *oriaté* Saúl Fernández, who descends from the Fermina Gómez line, mostly confirms Mason's data on the shifting of Fermina's godparents (personal communication with Michael Mason, 1 November 2000).

141. Discussions with Hermes Valera Ramírez and Zenaida Justiz, Havana, summer 1999. Cabrera lists one "Ña Pilar" as one of the wives of Gumersindo; she might be the Pilar Valdés of Cabildo Africano Lucumí (Cabildo Africano Lucumí 1900). Valera believes that Belén González (Apoto; see below) may have descended from El Palenque.

142. Miguel Ramos (personal communication, 9 March 1995) believes that "the rama of Palmira" had as its founder Guadalupe Estables. Ernesto Pichardo locates his own line in Palmira, the founder of which he says was "Francisca Estencel."

My field research in Palmira (8–10 July 1994) suggests that Guadalupe Estables descended from Palmira's Sevilla family (the owners of Sociedad El Cristo), as Estables was and remains one of five surnames among the twenty-seven children of Nicolás Sevilla, this society's founder (those surnames being Sevilla, Iznaga, Estables, Solano, and Reyes). "Estencel" is an alternate pronunciation and spelling of Entensa, the surname of the founders and owners of Palmira's Sociedad San Roque. Francisca Entensa was called Shangó Gumí (interview with Ángela Rosa Delgado Entensa, a great-grandchild of Franscisca, Palmira, 9 July 1994).

143. Interview with the current director of Palmira's Society San Roque, Angela Rosa Delgado Entensa, a great-grandchild of Franscisca, 9 July 1994.

144. Ernesto Pichardo believes that Efuche was a priest of Ochosi and that she arrived in the 1880s (personal communications with Ernesto Pichardo, fall 1994 and spring 1995). An elder *santera* and granddaughter in Ocha of Efuche, María Eugenia Álvarez Pérez of El Cerro, insists that Efuche arrived in Cuba enslaved (interview of 31 August 1999). Miguel Ramos seconds the Ochosi identification, but believes she was a twentieth-century free arrival (personal communications of fall 1994 and spring 1995); others say she was a priest of Obatalá or Yewá (e.g., Valdés Garriz 1997, 35). According to Irene Wright, the Cuban census for early Republican period showed that ten immigrants had arrived from Africa during the 1902–07 period (1910, 149).

145. John Mason identifies Efuche as Doña Victoriana Rosalia-Ẹ́fúnṣẹ̀ Wáríkọndó but believes she lived in Regla (see Mason 1996, 18). His source is not revealed. Elder Reglanos, Michael Mason, and other priests I queried in Havana never heard of Efuche, Efushe, or Fushe; however, Havanans of the San José Ochenta *rama* (see below) root their lineage in one Ña Rosalía, among others; moreover, María Eugenia Álvarez Pérez insists Efuche lived in El Cerro (see below).

146. María Eugenia Álvarez Pérez, one of Cuba's oldest living *santeras* (seventy-six years in Ocha as of 2000), a "granddaughter" of Efuche, told me that Efuche lived on Fifth Avenue (Calle Quinta), between Fernandina and Castillo in El Cerro, near María's own house in Barrio Ataré, El Cerro. As oral history contains divergent viewpoints, some insist that Efuche's name was not "Ña Rosalía" but María Trujillo, that she was the elder sister of Andrea Trujillo, and that the figure of Arabia Oviedo represents an intermediate generation between the two (personal correspondence with Robin Filson Villanueva, 22 November 2001, who received this information from her grandfather in Ocha, Orlando Martín Baba Funke, in a recent visit to Cuba).

147. Margot Fundora Sotolongo was Tiburcia's daughter and goddaughter (personal communication with Michael Atwood Mason,3 December 2000, based upon interviews with various descendants of the San José rama, 1996–2000).

148. Data from personal communications with Michael Mason, 1995–2000—based on his Havana and Matanzas interviews, particularly with *oriaté* Saúl Fernández, and from a conference call interview between Michael Mason, myself, and "Papo" Reinaldo Raimundo Chaguayceda of Regla, Ña Margarita's "grandson" in Ocha, 7 April 2000.

149. An ancestral *moyuba* shared with me by Ernesto Pichardo, spring 1995. In addition, Miguel Ramos identifies Apoto as a priestess of Yemayá who originally was from Matanzas (interview of 9 March 1995). Both Valdés Garriz (1997, 135) and Natalia Bolívar (from personal correspondence between her and William Muldro, 10 April 1999, kindly shared with me by the latter) identify Apoto as an Ochún priestess with the Lucumí name Ochún Alaibó. Bolívar locates González as the penultimate root of the line that includes José Pata de Palo and Aurora Lamar (see below).

150. Interview with Osvaldo Cárdenas Villamil, 25 July 1997. Ño Córda-isí is undoubtedly the figure that John Mason identifies as the Matanzas initiator of Ferminita Gómez. Mason apparently renders back into Yoruba (Kúdáasí) Cárdenas's Lucumí pronunciation of the name (1996, 26). The parenthetical *r* in a typical rendering of Cuba Lucumí phonology (*Có(r)da-isi*) seeks to mark the *o* sound as in the English *bought;* in Cuban Spanish, the *or* is gruffly stopped and swallowed at the back of the throat. Abraham's dictionary transcribes the Yoruba equivalent of *Có(r)da-isi* as *Kú-dáày'ií-sí* ("Death spared this one") which is rooted in the term *ikú* (death) (see Abraham 1946, 395, 298).

151. Interview with Mercedes Melo González, 30 and 31 August 1999, El Cerro, Havana. Melo is the goddaughter of Lamar's *babalawo* husband, José Ramón Gutiérrez, and inherited the Gutiérrez-Lamar house.

152. Data around the names and genealogical relationships of Apoto, José Pata de Palo Echú Bí, Aurora Lamar, Culo Verde, and Trapito are from an interview with Miguel Ramos, 9 March 1995. These names, though not always with knowledge of their relationships, were also mentioned to me on a number of occasions between 1996 and 2000 by Hermes Valera and Zenaida Justiz of Central Havana (who described José Pata de Palo as the initiator of Aurora Lamar), Mercedes Melo González of El Cerro (who described the relation of José Pata de Palo, Aurora Lamar, and Pimienta), and William Muldro of New York (who provided the meaning of "Culo Verde" and various important relationships of Lamar, including her family and ritual intimacy with the Samar family [Obadimelli and his son Lamberto Samár]).

153. Personal correspondence with William Muldro (Sim-El Fatunmishe), who conducted interviews with a descendant of José Pata de Palo who claims that a ritual grandson of José, Apolinar González, was also called "Green Ass" when he arrived from the countryside (correspondence of 20 September and 13 October 2000).

154. The identities and relationship of Culo Verde (as José Pata de Palo's *rama*) and Trapito (as Lamar's *rama*), the "easy payment plan," and Lamar's imagined one thousand Ochas or seven hundred priestesses of Yemayá come from an interview with Miguel Ramos, 9 March 1995. The nickname of Lamar, "La China de Maximiliano" (including that Maximiliano was a prior partner, whose name was tatooed on her leg), comes from Mercedes Melo González (interview, 30 and 31 August 1999, El Cerro). The suggestion that Lamar made six hundred Ochas, confirmation of the nickname "La China de Maximiliano" and the

tatoo text, as well as the epithet "La China of the Ten Cent [Plan]," come from Natalia Bolívar via William Muldro (correspondence, 20 Sept 2000). In Cuba, the nicknames "China" or "Chino" are typically given to non-Asian Cubans with light skin, a round face, and *ojos achinados*, almond-shaped eyes. And all Asians, regardless of nationality, are called *chinos*.

155. Interviews with Mercedes Melo González and Hermes Valera Ramírez, El Cerro, 30 and 31 August 1999.

156. Interview with Mercedes Melo González, 30 and 31 August 1999, El Cerro. For the Yoruba term for alligator (malagueta) pepper, see Abraham 1946, 74; see also Cabrera [1970] 1983. This *barrio* thus historically connects, within social proximity, and family and ritual relationships, Aurora Lamar, Efuche, the Samar family (Obadimelli and Lamberto), and *babalawos* Ramón Febles and José Ramón Gutiérrez, who lived in El Cerro (in 1913 Febles became the godfather of María Eugenia, Efuche's granddaughter in Ocha, and in the late 1910s or early 1920s María Eugenia became the godmother in Ocha of Gutiérrez). Given Efuche's close relationships with Ña Margarita Armenteros and Tibúrcia Sotolongo, it would be surprising if they did not know and work with Lamar also. It is also quite likely that Ayayi La Tuán Timotea Albear worked as *oriaté* for these groups, followed by Obadimelli and Lamberto (see below).

157. The two Yoruba epithets mean, roughly, "yokel," "rustic," or "boor"; see Abraham 1946, 61). *Ará óké* literally means dweller (*ará*) of the "hill" and *ará oko* means dweller of the bush, that is, "hillbilly."

158. I thank William Muldro for sharing with me the story of "Havana-centric" practice, José's "conversion," and the contextual translation of "Culo Verde" as "Green Ass" (correspondence of 20 September 2000).

159. Personal communication with Michael Atwood Mason, who heard the story in Cuba, March 1995. It remains unclear which *oricha*'s tureen broke and in whose initiation the event happened. William Muldro reports the same story from his oral history research (correspondence of 20 September 2000).

160. When I first asked my *madrina*, Zenaida Justiz, about our *rama*, she identified it as "Aurora Lamar"; on another occasion she said it was "José Pata de Palo" and recited the genealogy down to the present, locating Aurora Lamar as José's goddaughter. The identifiers "*rama* of Aurora Lamar" or "*rama* Pimienta" would seem to distinguish the descendants of this prolific house from their ritual "cousins," who were descendants of another, perhaps less prolific, godchild of José Pata de Palo (that is, one of Aurora's "sisters" or "brothers"), whose agency in genealogical memory remains subsumed by the great figure of José Pata de Palo. It may also be that primary citation of Lamar marks the beginning of a distinctively Havana *rama*, as opposed to a Matanzas one. *Babalawos* typically refer, for example, to proximate rather than ultimate *rama* names in identifying their descent, because their *moyubas* do not always conserve the chronological order or all of the names of the *rama*. For example, *babalawos* distinguish between the members of the very prolific "*rama* of Cheché" and those of the "*rama* of Pedro El Policía," even though both of these *ramas* have their ultimate roots, two and three generations back, respectively, in the African Ño Carlos Adé Bí. *Babalawos* typically refer to the "*rama* of Secundino Crucet," because most, including Crucet's descendants, are unsure of his initiator (I've been told, over fifteen years, that it was, variously, Adechina, Marcos García, Quintín García, and Tata Gaitán).

161. The connection of La Pimienta and El Trapito is complicated by the account of *iyaloricha* Hilda Herrera, a descendant of La Pimienta who lives in the Bronx. She was told that the name "Pimienta" marks a *rama* that relied and relies on *babalawos*, while "Trapito" did not and does not (personal communication with priestesses Lourdes López and her daughter Ana Vidal, of West New York, N.J., 17 October 2000).

Robin Filson Villanueva was convinced by her grandfather in Ocha in Cuba that the two *ramas* are distinct (personal correspondence of 27 November 2001). *Babalawo* Ron Harris ("Facundo") of Philadelphia was told this revised "Culo Verde" story by his godfather in Ocha, Apolinar González himself (personal correspondence of 23 April 2001).

162. From personal correspondence with William Muldro, September 2000, based partly on his correspondence with Natalia Bolívar in Cuba, 10 April 1999.

163. I speculatively put two and two together to identify "Ña Caridad" and the founder of Cabildo Africano Lucumí, Caridad Argudín: the Cabildo's *reglamento* document (Cabildo Africano Lucumí 1900) and Valdés Garriz's identification of Ña Caridad as Igoró and founder of a Sociedad of Santa Bárbara/Changó. He writes that Ña Caridad was a priestess of Ochosi, named "Igoró," and was head of the "Head of the [Cabildo] Changó Tedún" (1997, 135). As indicated, Changó Tedún and Cabildo Africano Lucumí were probably the same organization, or the latter was a descendant of the former.

164. For example, Regla's "Papo" Reinaldo Raimundo Chaguayceda regards Ña Margarita as his *rama* root; he never heard of Efuche or San José Ochenta and did not learn about her relationship with Ña Margarita or Tiburcia Sotolongo or about the the relationship of the three to the San José *rama* until Michael Mason revealed his research to him. Similarly, the blood and ritual descendants of Tiburcia Sotolongo in Barrio Príncipe in Havana (Olga Calvo Püig and Radamés Corona) never heard of Efuche or San José Ochenta (interview of 21 August 1999).

165. At least, the closeness of the Samar family and Aurora

Lamar's house is hinted by the fact that Obadimelli's son, Lamberto Samar, married Chela, Lamar's daughter.

166. See my chap. 3. John Mason believes that Obadimelli was born in Africa and arrived in Cuba about 1850 (see Mason 1992, 169). I have not independently verified his African birth. I learned that his career and ascent overlapped that of La Tuán, whose contemporary was Guillermina Castel, from personal communications with Michael Mason, 1998–2000. Mason learned in various interviews with Saúl Fernández, "Papo" Reinaldo Raimundo Chaguayceda, and others that Obadimelli was active by 1926 in Havana and that he dominated the practice after the death of La Tuán in 1935.

167. According to Miguel Ramos and Ernesto Pichardo, Obadimelli is the root of one of New York's most venerated *santeros* and *obás*, Eduardo Rodríguez (Changó Dina).

168. From interviews with Ernesto Pichardo and Miguel Ramos, fall 1994 and spring 1999.

169. The other source of identification and genealogy on Obadimelli is the Matancero *oriaté* Saúl Fernández (data from Michael Mason, kindly shared with me, 5 November 2000).

From the point of view of simple, flattened retrospect, "two initiations" seems transparent: he had one, then another. From a historically specific point of view, each initiation had its own historicity. His "second initiation," or "reinitiation," was *not foreseen* from the experiential and historical perspective of the first. As Catherine Bell notes, citing Louis Althusser, practices, considered in diachronic perspective, will give an answer to a question that was never posed (Bell 1992, 87). Hence, his "second initiation" gave an answer to a question that was never posed in relation to the first.

170. From an interview Michael Mason conducted with two independent sources, including Matancero Saúl Fernández of the Fermina Gómez line (personal communication, 1 November 2000).

171. From a telephone interview with Ernesto Pichardo, 26 July 1996.

172. Aratakuá means "people [*ará*] of Takuá" (Tápà becomes "Takuá" in Lucumí and Spanish orthography). The Aratakuá (Tápà-Nupe) were, and are, not among the groups ethnographically classified in the twentieth century as Yoruba-speaking peoples from southwestern Nigeria. They did, however, historically share many cultural features with the Yoruba, such as glass bead making, brass casting, and ancestral masquerade types, and were specifically influenced by the Old Ọ̀yọ́ kingdom to their south (see Matory 1994, 292, 127). Still, by the time the Yoruba-speaking peoples began to be shipped in great numbers to Cuba (1820s–1840s), the Nupe had been Islamicized (this happened by the early nineteenth century, as they had been conquered by the Fulani; see Bascom 1973, 84–85). In any event, the Tápà-Nupe were classified under the "Lucumí" metaethnonym during the slave trade, probably because they were a hinterland people to the north, who were sold and marched to the coast, embarking from Bight of Benín slave ports. Ernesto Pichardo is aware of their ethnographic identification as the people Tápà-Nupe people to the north of Old Ọ̀yọ́, a fact that López Valdés also notes (1986, 72). The influence of the Aratakuá in Western Cuba's Lucumí religion is suggested, moreover, by the fact that it was felt neccesary to publish a glossary of its idiom (see Angarica [1955?] n.d. [*The Yoruba-Arataco Dialect; Arataco* is his spelling of *Aratacuá*]).

173. From an interview with Osvaldo Cárdenas Villamil, 25 July 1997, Matanzas.

174. Virtually all of Palmira's *babalawos* descend from Tata Gaitán: Miguel Iznaga, Ta Genaro Benítez, Ta Vicente Goytizolo, Facundo Sevilla, and Mario Fernández are outstanding among them. Many Palmira *babalawos* owe their Osains to Havana's Miguel Febles. Tata's godchildren and their colleagues, such as Walfredo Rivera Ules and Félix "El Negro" Quesada, and Miguel Febles's godchild Carlos Martínez, regularly traveled back and forth on this route. The director of Palmira's Sociedad El Cristo, Pablo Sevilla, Tata's Ifá grandchild travels back and forth between his Havana apartment and Palmira every weekend, and his son, Antonio, was initiated in Havana.

175. The Fernández family history derives from my Palmira fieldwork of July 1994 and dicussions with Havana *babalawos* Hermes Valera, Fran Cabrera, and Pablo Sevilla during that period. According to John Mason's reseach, Ma Fea "was the first person to be initiated by Josefa Herrera-*Ẹ̀ṣù Bí*, from Regla and Felipa Calderón of Matanzas" (Mason 1996, 27).

176. Michael Mason uses the term "opportunistic" in several cases in which contemporary practitioners marshal alternate genealogies in order to legitimate the particular ceremonies they are undertaking. For example, a priest who has initiated gochildren in the Babalú Ayé "direct" method (see chap. 3), emphasizes his Matanzas ancestors in his background, as Matanzas is where the direct ceremonies began and continue. In other cases, where he conducts a ceremony the "Havana way," he might emphasize his Havana ancestors (from personal communication with Michael Mason, 1 November 2000). Mason's "performance" theory of communication, which revolves around the notions of "genre" (a set of codes shared by performer and audience), "competence" (the appropriateness and quality of the performance vis-à-vis its "style"), and "context," is influenced by his mentor Richard Bauman (see Bauman 1975, 1986, 1992), as well as Bauman and Briggs's important collaboration (1990; see also Fowler 1989). These have been very helpful to my thinking.

177. Personal communication with John Mason, October 1993.

178. Telephone interview with Ernesto Pichardo, 14 January 1988.

179. Efuche is credited with introducing the *Pinaldo,* with restructuring the Ocha initiation, and with modifying Arará practice by introducing the oracle of the Lucumí cowrie divination shells into the cults of the Arará *fodduces,* wherein, since the middle of the eighteenth century in Dahomey, these deities had supposedly "spoken" through the "Fá" (Dahomean Ifá system) of the *bokono* diviner. In Havana, they eventually spoke through the divining chain of the Oluwó Popó Awó Bokonó, a priest of Asojuano (Babalú Ayé) who received credentials from the Lucumí *babalawos* (from various discussions with Oluwó Popó Awó Bokonó Pedro Abreu and *babalawo* Oscar Rodríguez, summer 2000).

180. Miguel Ramos relates that Obadimelli "was initiated in the campo but there was no trust of initiations done in the *campo,* so when he came to city he had to be initiated all over again" (interview with Miguel Ramos, 9 March 1995). Mason (1992, 169), without citing sources, writes that Obadimelli (Mason uses the Yoruba spelling Ọbadaiméjì) was a "Lùkùmí priest of Aganjú [who] arrived [from Africa] with his parents, as slaves, about the year 1850. . . . Nothing is known of the father but the mother was said to have been an íyálòrìṣà in Africa and was responsible for educating Ọbadiméjì, who had also been initiated in Africa."

181. Interview with Osvaldo Cárdenas Villamil, 25 July 1997, Matanzas.

182. Personal communications with the late *babalawo* Cosme Guío and *babalawo* Antonio de Armas, August 1998. See Brown 1989, 219–21, and the following chapter in this book for discussions of the *oriaté-babalawo* debate over "rights" and their "usurpation" (see Cabrera 1980, 183–84). *Babalawos* undergo the Knife ceremony within the Regla de Ifá, in which it is called *Wanaldo. Pinaldo* developed within the Regla de Ocha, it is believed, through the efforts of Efuche and Obadimelli (see the following section).

183. The authorization, and immunity from culpability, for "taking a life" derives from the sanction of Obatalá, Olofin, and Olodumare, although Ogún performs the actual killing with his swift, forceful, and unhesitating iron blade (see Angarica [1955?] n.d., 79; see also Mason [1985] 1993, 62). "Ifá-centric *ramas*" assert that the *Pinaldo* of *santeros* does not grant the right to sacrifice four-legged animals. Only the *babalawo*'s *Wanaldo* (the Knife as received in Ifá), confers such a right (see my chap. 3).

184. In today's *Pinaldo* model, a senior priest confers the knife upon an initiate when both coparticipate in the feeding of four-legged animals to all the *orichas* received in the initiate's original initiation. Following the same pattern of the original initiation, including its ritual period of seven days, the *orichas* are interrogated on the third day through divination (*itá*). That *Pinaldo* "confirms" one's original initiation was first explained to be by Josefina García, 16 May 1986. Josié García explains: "the *cuchillo* is just like making Santo all over again. It confirms what came out in your *Itá* from the Santo, but the person that gives you that *cuchillo* [knife] becomes your real godfather or godmother. The one that gave you the basic [Santo], [whom] you did Ocha with, is like an outsider." In another case, a woman broke from her *padrino de santo* in the mid-1970s. Later, in 1981, she took on a "representative" *padrino* who gave her *Pinaldo.* He "became" her "real godfather" when she received the *cuchillo* from him: "He's my godfather; he gave me the knife and that topped it" (interviews with Gloria González, August 30, 1987; Josi García, May 21, 1988; and Melba Carillo, August 7, 1987.

185. Conversations with Melba Carillo, 1997; and see Brown 1989, 207–11, 219–23; Brandon 1983, 485–500).

186. Pichardo believes that *Pinaldo* today "say[s] the same thing that Efuche said: it validates and establishes a sense of completion" (interview with Ernesto Pichardo, 11 July 1995)

187. Personal communication with Michael Mason, 20 August 1997. Saúl Fernández descends from the Matanzas house of Ferminita Gómez but lives in Havana.

188. Interview with Osvaldo Cárdenas Villamil, 25 July 1997, Matanzas.

189. As indicated, Mason reports that Obadimelli arrived from Africa in the 1850s with his mother, as an already initiated young boy. Havana priests relate that Obadimelli was not established in Havana until at least 1926 and did not begin his reign as top *oriaté* until at least 1935 with the death of Ayayi La Tuán. Given Mason's dating, this would mean that Obadimelli did not reach his apogee until he was perhaps eighty-five years old. Others assert that Obadimelli was a creole, not African born.

190. Matory proffers this same narrative around the Yoruba-Atlantic shrine vessel form (1994, 223–224), rehearsing the earlier argument of Bascom (1950, 68).

191. This is very much the sense of Palmié's important revisionist work (1993).

192. See J. Mason 1994, 173 n. 5 for a description of the ritual issues associated with Agayú initiation and the fears of death or insanity. Michael Mason reports that in his Havana house they fear doing Agayú directly because he is so hot that the initiate could "die" (personal communications, April 1995).

CHAPTER THREE

1. Cabrera writes, "Olofi and his family, like Zeus and his—this Lucumí polytheism curiously recalls the Greek—who are

omnipotent and immortal, are not much different from Calazán, Calixta, Catalino, Baró or any other of these good friends [her Afro-Cuban informants] who narrate their stories to me" ([1954] 1983, 77–78).

2. Palmié (1993, 346) suggests that the institutionally "cross-cutting" nature of Yoruba *òrìṣà* cults—based in initiation as much as familial descent—was crucial in their role in the reconstitution of neo-African populations in the New World; that is, they could serve in the reaggregation or resocietalization of heterogeneous populations. As a heuristic exercise for the purposes of this chapter, it might be useful to identify some principal gods belonging to major Yoruba regions. Clearly, most are now found throughout Yorubaland given migration and the spread of Ọ̀yọ́ influence long after its collapse in 1835. Still, heartland Ọ̀yọ́ gods were or are Ṣàngó, Ọya, Aganjú, Òrìṣà Oko, and Erinlẹ̀. Yẹmọja, goddess of the Ògún River, who is most prominent in the city of Abẹ́òkùta among the Ẹ̀gbá Yoruba, has also been prominent historically in Ọ̀yọ́ (see Apter 1992; Matory 1994), for the Ògún River flows from Ọ̀yọ́ to the Ẹ̀gbá (personal communication with J. Lorand Matory, 7 September, 1996). Ọ̀ṣun is the goddess of the river by the same name, which rises in Ekiti in the northeast and flows past the city of Òṣogbo, the site of her principal shrine (Bascom 1969b, 90). Heartland Ifẹ̀ gods include Odùduwà, Ọbàtálá, Ọrúnmìlà (or Ifá), Ọranyàn, Àràmfẹ̀, Òrìṣà-oko, and Èṣù (Abraham 1946, 483–84). Àràmfẹ̀, a god of lightning, was distinct from the Ṣàngó of Ọ̀yọ́. Èṣù, according to Matory, is found almost universally where Ọrúnmìlà is found (Ifá has spread far and wide), including the Yoruba-Fon borderlands where his counterpart Legba is prominent. Ọ̀ṣọ́ọ̀sì is strong in Kétu, the westernmost Yoruba city (Ẹ̀gbádò Yoruba), in the Republic of Benín. Nana Burúkú and the "smallpox complex," which includes Omolu and Ṣakpata, are found far and wide but are very prominent in the Republic of Benín (formerly Dahomey) and the western borderlands of Yorubaland, alongside Dahomey. See Dennet's regional and town lists of deities ([1910] 1968, 104, 183–88), showing both a certain exclusivity and sharedness between locales. Contemporary shrines in Ọ̀yọ́ include deities who might claim "origins" in other kingdoms, such as Òsóòsì, Ọ̀ṣun, and Ifá (Ọrúnmìlà; see Matory 1994, 160).

3. See Pierre Verger's mentions of deities that were or are shared among the Fon and Yoruba, such as Ṣakpata/Ṣọ̀npọ̀nnọ́n and Nana Buku/Nana Burúkú (1957, 239–304). In the eighteenth century and before, the imperial penetrations of Ọ̀yọ́ into the "Benín gap," now known as the People's Republic of Benín, all the way to the coast, resulted in the sending of religious and secular "delegates" (*ìlàrí*) to rule. They carried and installed many Yoruba cults into this area (personal communication with J. Lorand Matory, 7 February 1999). However, by the 1820s, according to the report of John M'Leod, imperial Dahomey's northeastern border had extended to the "Eeyo" (Ọ̀yọ́-Yoruba; M'Leod cited in Herskovits 1938b, 1:9). See Herskovits 1938b, vol. 1, for a discussion of the reach of the Dahomey kingdom (pp. 3–25). See Verger 1957, passim, for an exhaustive accounting of the Yoruba and Fon pantheons, institutions, rituals, and praise poem repertoires.

4. "Fá is a *vodu* who, originating with the Nago [Yoruba], came to Dahomey in the time of Agadja," Herskovits quotes a source as saying (1938b, 2:209). Another source explains the eventual dominance of Fá over the widespread *gbo* oracular possession cults: "In the early days, those who divined Fá were called *babalawo*, the Nigerian name for the diviners of the Afa [Ifá] cult. When Fá came to Dahomey, it encountered the *gbo* as a rival. However, when people saw that Fá told the truth better than *gbo*, they said, '*Gbo-kwe-no*,' meaning '*gbo*-money-remains'—that is, 'money for *gbo* is not spent.' Therefore, when people went to Fá the name of those who divined for them was changed to *bokono*." (Herskovits 1938b, 1:208). A particular *gbo*, the first source says, was "hated" by the King, "because it permitted too many alliances against him," which led to (I)Fá's importation from the Nago Yoruba (1938b, 1:209, see pp. 209–22 for an explanation of the Fá system, which follows the Yoruba model).

5. Personal communications with Stephan Palmié, spring 1997.

6. Particularly influential in Cuba were the gods from the Fon, Mahi, Adja, and Evhe and the interstitial Fon-Yoruba borderlands, such as Ṣakpata and Nana Buruku—in Cuba they are called Asojuano and Naná Burukú. In the Regla Arará, concentrated in Matanzas but with an important presence also in Havana, are found the Ewe-Fon deities, called *fodduces* (from *voduns*); though they bear variant names among the different Arará "nations," the *fodduces* in the pantheon of the Baró Society of San Manuel in Jovellanos include Jurajó (Eleguá), Ajuangún (Ogún), Aggé (Ochosi), Ebioso (Changó), Fereketé (Yemayá), Addañó (Oyá), Foddú Masén (Ochún), Dalúaa (Babalú Ayé), Ajosi (Obatalá); as indicated, each *foddú* is correlated with a Lucumí deity (Galzagorry Madán 1983, 4; see also Vinueza 1986, 95; Brice Sogbossi 1998, 44–53).

7. Verger documented praise songs for Aira in Kétu in the Yoruba-Dahomean borderlands; this deity is is also known there as Agbonan or Aira Igbonan, and he is known as a great friend of Ṣàngó in the town of Sabẹ (Verger 1957, 397, 315; see also Bascom 1969b, 87). Jàkúta, an earlier, nonhuman incarnation of a Ṣàngó type (lightning and retribution), is also the name of the fifth day of the week, when this deity is worshiped (Mason 1992, 170; Abraham 1946, 339). A Jakuta or Djakuta is also documented as a *vodun* in Abomey by Verger (Verger 1957, 528). "Airá" and

"Yakuta" are encountered as praise names for Changó in Cuba (Cabrera [1970] 1983, 40, 319). Obá Ecún defines Yakuta as the "name of Changó when he hurls the thunderbolt" (Cabrera [1979] 1986, 182). "Airá" appears as the "god of fire" in some of the Bahian Candomblés (Carybé 1980, 146). See Mason 1992, passim, for very rich and concise discussions of the deities in their Yoruba and Cuban contexts.

8. See Balandier 1968; MacGaffey 1986; and Thompson and Cornet 1981 for discussions of Kongo history, society, religion, and art. See Thompson 1983, 101–60 for a discussion of Kongo-Angola transatlantic visual traditions. See Ortiz [1916] 1987, 37–78; and Lachatañeré 1961a and 1961b for the ethnic identifications of Kongo-Angola peoples within the Cuban colonial and slavery period. See Cabrera [1979] 1986 for an in-depth discussion of the religions of Kongo-Angola derivation in Cuba. See Castellanos and Castellanos 1992, 3: 138 for a cross-indexed chart of Lucumí and Kongo pantheons.

9. However, James Wafer reports that in Bahia, "[i]n smaller [poorer] *terreiros* all the *orixás* may be seated together in a single house, or in a room, called the 'room of the saints'" (Wafer 1991, 16).

10. Interview with a *mae de santo* at Ilê Axé Apô Afonjá, 28 February 1988.

11. One Lucumí *oro* sequence, as Angarica provides it ([1955?] n.d., 65) is Eleguá, Ogún, Ochosi, Oricha Oko, Inle, Osain, Babalú Ayé, Oke, Dadá, Agayú, Ibeyi, Changó, Obatalá, Yeguá, Obba, Oyá, Yemayá, Ochún, and Orunmila (nineteen altogether). A slightly varied *oro* provided by Obá Ecún (1985, passim) goes Eleguá, Ogún, Ochosi, Inle, Osoguano (Babalú Ayé) Oricha Oko, Dadá, Oggué, Oke, Ibeyi, Agayú, Changó, Obatalá, Yewá, Obba, Oyá, Yemayá, Ochún, and Orula (nineteen altogether). These *oros* would be used in the singing to the deities during initiations. Pichardo and Nieto list twenty-six (1984, 36).

John Mason (1992, 20–22) provides the *oro* (he spells it *oru*) of an alternate ritual context, a sacred *batá* drumming. The "*oro* of the *igbodú*," the drum rhythm sequence played directly to the deities, without singing (Cubans call it *oro seco* ['dry']), he presents as the following, wherein some of the deities receive two rhythms: (1) Elegba, (2) Elegba, (3) Ogun, (4) Osoosi, (5) Osoosi (but he says it is called Obaloke, "king of the mountain"), (6) Erinle, (7) Babaluaiye, (8) Babaluaiye, (9) Osanyin, (10) Osun (the staff, not the deity Oshun), (11) Obatala, (12) Dada, (13) Oge (companion of Shango), (14) Aganju, (15) Orunmila, (16) Ibeji, (17) Orisa Oko, (18) Sango, (19) Yewa, (20) Oya, (21) Ọṣun [Oshun], (22) Yemoja, (23) Oba, (24) Oduduwa—there are twenty-two deities if one counts Osun, the staff. Several other deities discussed in the work, that do not appear in this *oro*, are Oke, Korikoto, Nanú, Naná Burukú, Olokun, and Iroko.

12. "Traditional" is a relative term. Candomblés that present themselves as "traditional," and which root themselves in specific founders in the nineteenth and early twentieth centuries, have self-consciously purified any "whitening" influences (*blanqueamento*). They exclude the diety Exú from all but symbolic participation in ceremonies as a mark of their protocols (see Omari 1984, 16; Wafer 1991, 9, 56–57).

13. The recordings of Brazilian *xirés* I have purchased commercially are from Rio de Janeiro Candomblés associated with Bahian ones. For example, Toninho de Oxossi's Kêtu *terriero* invokes ten *orixás*, while Carlinhos de Oxum's invokes fourteen (see *Candomblé* n.d.; and Oxum 1997). The former calls Exu, Ogum, Oxossi, Obaluaiê, Ossanhê, Oxumarê, Nanã, Obá, Ewa, Oxum, Iansã, Iemanjá, Xangô, and Oxalá. The *xirê* taught to Cabelo Rolim of New York by Jorge Alabê of Bahia's Casa Branca is Exu, Ogum, Oxossi, Obaluaiê, Ossanyin, Oxumarê, Xangô, Oxum, Logunédé, Yemanjá, Iansã, Obba, Ewa, Nanã, and Oxala. These sequences vary from, but clearly share certain grouping principles (e.g., the warriors Exu, Ogum, and Oxossi, followed by Obaluaiê and Ossanyin, and the cluster of females) with, Lucumí versions (personal communication of 15 April 1998). Whereas in Cuba, different *oros* and drum ensembles are employed for the rhythms of different "nations" or *reglas* (e.g., Lucumí, Iyesá, Arará), in Brazil, a single *xirê* often makes reference to a series of nations. For example, according to the Toninho de Oxossi recording's notes (p. 12), a Kêtu rhythm called *avaninha* opens and closes the sequence; the *ijexá* rhythm is played for Oxalá, Logunédé, Oxum, or Ogun; in Cuba, the Iyesá *oro* to all the *orichas* is played primarily in ceremonies to Ochún.

14. As summarized by Loreto Todd, Suzanne Sylvain, for example, proposed an "African syntax" as the basis of Haitian Creole (Sylvain 1936, 178; quoted in Todd 1974, 38–39); similarly, Robert A. Hall, Jr., though a supporter of a polygenesis theory of the world's creoles (i.e., they derive not from one source), nevertheless believed that "with regard to the Atlantic varieties, the majority of the speakers shared 'a common West African substratum'" (Hall 1966, 77; quoted in Todd 1974, 31). In 1960, DeCamp and Le Page questioned the "African substratum" model, arguing that "[n]o one African language can account for all or even a majority of the 'African' elements in Caribbean creole, nor is any significant 'African feature' in creole shared by all or even a majority of the native languages of all the slaves" (see DeCamp 1971, 20). As early as 1957, "as Le Page pointed out in an attack on the African substratum theories of Herskovits (Le Page 1957–58, 374–75), many of the common features of Caribbean and African creoles are also shared by other creoles such as Pitcairneses, where there have been no African influences, only English and Polynesian. . . . (This is not to deny significant, particu-

lar African influences on particular languages)" (DeCamp 1971, 20).

15. I am grateful to my colleague at the Black Atlantic Project of Rutgers Center for Historical Analysis, Herman Bennet, for suggesting the use of these terms ("narrative production" and [narrative] "recrystallization," which Carlos Ginzburg has deployed incisively (e.g., Ginzburg 1980).

16. Herskovits, an early proponent of the idea of an African substratum, argued that syncretic outcomes were mostly "congruent" with older culture patterns (1958). The culture "pattern followed by survivals of African custom in New World Negro life" were "set" by the cultures of the "focal area of slaving" (i.e., the Guinea coast; Herskovits 1941, 77). Thus the identities and relationships of the African gods in the New World would remain essentially constant; "syncretism" in this case would amount to little more than "parallels" with the Catholic saints; Herskovits did observe, however, that Haitians "identified" saints and gods in a more thoroughgoing way than Cubans and Brazilians (1966, 322). Thus, Verger, agreeing with and quoting the straighforward observation of Nina Rodrigues, writes that the correspondence between the Cuban Lucumí deities and the Catholic saints "seems to be based on the similarity of colors used by the religious confraternities and those which are symbolic of the African deities" (Verger 1993, 35 n. 36). These are conclusions that Ortiz ([1906] 1973, 63–66) and Irene Wright (1910, 150) early made in Cuba. As Thompson would later concisely summarize much of the historiography, "New World Yoruba were introduced to the cult of the Roman Catholic saints, learned their attributes, and worked out a series of *parallelisms* linking Christian figures and powers to the forces of their ancient deities" (Thompson 1983, 17; emphasis added). Moreover, most prominent observers throughout the twentieth century, such as Nina Rodrigues (1945), Herskovits (1941, 224; 1966, 322), Bascom (1950), Michel Leiris (1953) Verger (1993, 25–28), Métraux ([1959] 1972), and Bastide ([1960] 1978), have defined the saints as fulfilling a camouflaging function (e.g., as a *mask* or *guise*). For example, Bastide writes that "the whites believed [the Africans] to be dancing to the glory of the Blessed Virgin or the saints, but the Virgin or the saints were no more than *masks*" ([1960] 1978, 49, 162; emphasis added; see also Lawal 1996a, 28). And the historiography has mostly rejected any question of the internalization of belief in favor of nominal or outward Catholic practice only. Thompson writes, for example, "Yoruba-Americans, outwardly abiding by the religious properties of the Catholics who surrounded them, covertly practiced a system of thought that was a creative reorganization of their traditional religion" (1983, 18). Bastide did, however, develop the more interactive notion of "symbiosis" between saints and gods, which was taken up by Murphy (1988) and Desmangles (1992). For general historical and theoretical overviews and specific cases of syncretism, see Colpe (1987) and Stewart and Shaw (1994). For fine revisionist treatments of African and African Diaspora syncretism, see Comaroff 1985; Apter 1991; and Palmié 1995.

17. Bastide's "structural parallels" were accompanied by two equally important parallels: the "cultural parallel between the functional conception of the saints, each of whom presides over a certain human activity or is responsible for healing a certain disease, and the equally functional conception of the *voduns* and *orixás*, each of whom is in charge of a certain sector of nature and who, like the saints, are the patrons of trades and occupations, protecting the hunter, the smith, the healer, etc." There was also the "sociological parallel between the Brazilian 'nations' or the Cuban *cabildos* and the Catholic fratenities." Moreover, "these parallels, which facilitated the approximate equation of saints and gods, were complemented by more specific parallels between individual saints and gods" (i.e., their visual attributes and legends; see Bastide [1960] 1978, 262).

18. Structuralism, to the extent that it emphasizes, if not reifies, the *langue*, is a formalism (see Eagleton 1983, 91–113; see also Bennet 1979, 65–75).

19. As Apter emphasizes, in *practice*, it is the ambiguity and "slippage" between the gods and saints, rather than a static correspondence, that defines their relationship and enables syncretism (1991).

20. Leroy Jones (Imamu Amiri Baraka) writes: "The Negro's music changed as he changed, reflecting shifting attitudes or (and this is equally important) *consistent attitudes within changed contexts*" (1963, 153). James Clifford, in his seminal 1994 piece, "Diasporas," writes that, even in the "current theoretical climate of anti-essentialism, diaspora discourses such as Gilroy's refuse to let go of a 'changing same,' something endlessly hybridized and in process but persistently there—memories and practices of collective identity maintained over long stretches of time" (Clifford 1994, 320; see also Handler and Linnekin 1984).

21. Though they present a hierarchical model of the Yoruba cosmos for heuristic purposes, Drewal, Pemberton, and Abiodun rightly insist that "the gods are not ranked in any hierarchy. Their relative importance in any given part of the Yoruba world reflects their relative local popularity, reputation, and influence, and the order in which they are invoked in ceremonies has to do with their roles in the ritual and their relationships to each other" (1989, 14–15).

22. I am grateful to Herman Bennet for his insights into this subject, expressed and developed during the ongoing Rutgers Center for Historical Analysis "Black Atlantic Project" (1997–2000), which have I attended as a senior fellow and participant (see Bennett 2003).

23. On the subject of "monotheism," Idowu writes: "I do not know of any place in Africa where the ultimacy is not accorded to God. That is why, because this is very true of the Yoruba, I conclude that the religion can only be adequately described as monotheistic. I modify this 'monotheism' by the adjective 'diffused,' because *here we have a monotheism in which there exist other powers which derived from Deity [with] such being and authority that they can be treated, for practical purposes, almost as ends in themselves.* The descriptive phrase 'implicit monotheism' will serve as well as '*diffused monotheism*'" (1973, 135–36; emphasis added).

24. Ellis (1894, 34), Frobenius (1913, 1:198), and Parrinder (1949, 26) characterized the Yoruba Supreme being as otiose—for example, "idle," "asleep," and "reposed" (Ellis); of an "entirely Platonic and mythological existence" (Frobenius); and as "a supreme but unworshipped God" (Parrinder). Idowu cites these views ([1962] 1963, 140) in order to revise them—they are mistaken for various reasons, including "incomplete" reasearch. In another work, Idowu critiques the Roman Catholic missionary Père Noel Baudin's idea of a *deus otiosus* as a "definite reading in of the Western deistic idea into African belief" (1973, 140, 144) yet Idowu does not seem to reflect upon his own "reading in" of Western categories in his accounts of Yoruba religion.

25. For example, see Crowther 1848 and Bowen 1858. According to Verger (1993, 35 n. 12), of the eighteen principal authors who approached the issue of the Yoruba High God between 1845 and 1962, thirteen were Catholic or Protestant missionaries and two were anthropologists. They were M. d'Avezac, Bishop Samuel Crowther, T. J. Bowen, Richard Burton, R. P. Noel Baudin, Abbé Pierre Bouche, Rev. James Johnson, A. B. Ellis, R. E. Dennett, Leo Frobenius, Rev. Samuel Johnson, R. P. Thomas Mulero, P. Amaury Talbot, Stephen S. Farrow, Rev. D. O. Epega, Rev. J. Olumide Lucas, Geoffrey Parrinder, and E. Bolaji Idowu. Nothwithstanding their career differences, they were all influenced by the notion of overarching cosmological models.

26. Pichardo and Nieto 1984, for example, cite Bowen, Burton, Dennett, Ellis, Frobenius, Bishop Samuel Johnson, and Rev. James Johnson in their bibliography, as well as Bascom and Herskovits.

27. From *Tratado de Odduns de Ifá* n.d.b: 419–22. Wallis Budge's [Egyptian] *Book of the Dead* ("El Libro de los Muertos") is cited throughout the final seventy-seven-page section of this widely circulated Ifá manual. Cuban *babalawo* Hermes Valera Ramírez wrote out an explication of the diety Olokun for me, which proceeds as follows: "In accordance with the Egyptian mythology, Tum/Atomu (Adumú), was the god of the ocean, the soul of the abyss, the deepest seas. In Egyptian cosmology, he was identified with Pa and was known as Atm-Ra or Ra-Tum; that which has survived as Ra in the Yoruba Territory suggests also the vigilance of Tum. So close is the resemblance between Tum and Olokun that it is difficult to consider one without the other. It should be remembered that Tum is the Egyptian god of the Ocean, which is well described in the Egyptian books, 'The Soul [Khu] of Ra.' Now, the significance of Olokun (*o-lo-ku-n*) is 'the owner of "ku" or "khus"': this is: the one who possesses the soul or souls" (transcribed personal lecture, Havana, 23 July 1997).

28. Deren lists in her bibliography Campbell's influential 1949 work, *A Hero with a Thousand Faces* (Campbell [1949] 1973).

29. Campbell assumed that universals connected the religious cosmologies of the world. The 1948 preface to his 1949 *Hero with a Thousand Faces* (written during the period of Maya Deren's fieldwork trips to Haiti between 1947 and 1951) lays out the second of two paths of Campbell's research plan: "The second step will be then to bring together a host of myths and folk tales from every corner of the world, and to let the symbols speak for themselves. The parallels will be immediately apparent; and these will develop a vast and amazingly constant statement of the basic truths by which man has lived throughout the milenniums of his residence on the planet" ([1949] 1973, vii).

30. African-American Ethiopianism and Protestant prophetic religion commonly have employed the ancient Israelites and the Exodus and Promised Land figures as sacred typologies for the destiny of the scattered African peoples (see Raboteau 1983; and Smith 1989). See also my chap. 5.

31. For example, Olofin was documented in Yorubaland as early as 1848 as a lowercase noun, meaning "lawgiver" (Crowther 1848, 172). Indeed, "Ọlọ̀ọ̀run" (Owner of the Sky), Verger notes, was used by "Christians and Muslims in their work with the infidels." He also notes that Idowu ([1962] 1963) gives Olódùmarè as the name of the Yoruba Supreme God (Verger 1993, 22).

32. Ernesto Pichardo graphically represents the *panteón Lukumí* and the vertical spiritual hierarchy in this way: (1) Olodumare, (2) Olofin—Olorun, (3) Oduduwa—Obatalá, (4) *Orichas*, (5) Araonu, (6) Egun, (7) Tierra (Earth).

33. For example, the late *babaloricha* Ramón Esquivel of Union City, New Jersey, emphasized the imagery of Christ, the Eucharist, and the Immaculate Conception on the Catholic calendrical feast day of Saint Manuel (1 January), which he associated with his "path" of Obatalá, Yecú-Yecú (as well as Odudúa), but did not do so on other Obatalá celebration days, such as his "birthday" in Ocha and drummings to Obatalá.

34. These conceptions of Changó are widely held among Cuban practitioners and are typically expressed in answer to questions about Changó's identity; however, many—erro-

neously, in Angarica's opinion—do not hesitate to add the aforementioned references to Santa Bárbara.

35. Olofi ("in charge of everything after Olodumare"), Odúa ("time," "longevity"), Olokun ("the sea," "all that is good and bad that covers the world"), Oricha Oko ("represents the earth"), Oke ("represents the hills in this world"), Obatalá ("he is the head of all people and things in this world"), Nana Burukú ("the spirit that represents the sweet waters"), and so on (see Angarica [1955?] n.d., 5, 37).

36. Echú ("penetrates the house and destroys and ruins everything"), Eleguá (Echú as "neutralized" by Obatalá, opens and closes people's roads), Ogún ("war, blood spread over the world as in Dante's Inferno"), Ochosi ("hunter and warrior-sorcerer"), Agayú ("hot volcano capable of great destruction"), Changó ("fire," "problems"), Ibeyi (represents "infancy"), Obba, Oyá ("hurricane"), Yemayá ("seas," "mother of the world"), Ochún ("river," "the vibration of life") (see Angarica [1955?] n.d., 38–61).

37. Little is known about the popular religious painter Guzmán other than that he was a close relative of Nicolás Angarica, according to his son, Mario "Papo" Angarica, a *babalawo* and renowned *olubatá* of Havana (interview with Mario Angarica, 10 July 1992). Angarica's apartment is full of baroque-like oil paintings of religious subjects by Guzmán.

38. Ernesto Pichardo defines the roles of the "three important *orichas*, Eshu, Obatalá, and Changó" in this way: "Eshu represents the Guide of Destiny [*Orí*], Obatalá—the Creator [and Owner of Human Heads, *orí*], and Changó—the Problems of Life" (interview with Ernesto Pichardo, 14 January 1988). See also Angarica [1955?] n.d., 34–36, 38–42, 52–54). Karin Barber nicely explains how the individual must must "pick . . . his way (aided by his Orí or Destiny, chosen by himself before coming to earth) between a variety of forces, some benign, some hostile, many ambivalent, seeking to placate them and ally himself with them in an attempt to thwart his rivals and enemies in human society" (1981, 729).

39. The *Dictionary of the Yoruba Language* ([1913] 1979), recently republished by Oxford, was first published by the Church Missionary Society Bookshop of Lagos in 1913, and it is heavily indebted to Crowther (1848). Verger writes that Olódùmarè resides in the other world or *ọ̀run*, which is generally translated by the word "heaven"—given the "misunderstanding" on the part of investigators who were Christian, or Christianized (Verger 1993, 21). The Yoruba *ọ̀run* appears in Angarica's text (as is typical of Cuban Lucumí usage) in creolized form as *onú*, where the *r* is elided and the *u* and *n* are reversed (Angarica [1955?] n.d., 5), as in the term for "ancestors in the other world" (*ará-onú*). This concept of *ará-onú* is present in the *moyuba* invocation of *orichas* and ancestors, who occupy the *ará onú* at the "foot of Olodumare," which is commonly understood as "Heaven" among Cubans. Moreover, Angarica clearly states, for example, that the spiritual energy of blood sacrifice, a kind of "spiritual fluid," "arrives in the *ará-onú*" so that "our elders of the other world" can authorize the ceremonies of divination (*itá*) that follow the sacrifice (65). Still, *ará onú*, understood as *el mas allá* (other world), is not at all remote. It is a spiritual dimension just the other side of "this world" (*aye, la tierra*).

40. Similarly, in Ernesto Pichardo's graphic representation of the Lucumí cosmos, the trinity (Olodumare, Olorun, Olofi) are at the top of the hierarchy, Obatalá follows, the *orichas* are in the middle, and closest of all to the human lifeworld, are the spirits of the deceased (see Pichardo and Nieto 1984, 36–37) and my nn. 32, 35, and 36 above.

41. Angarica notes that he was born on the Perico, Matanzas, sugar mill estate called "Central España." He belonged to the Partido Popular Cubano, the Partido Acción Republicana, and the Partido Realista and was an executive member of the last (Angarica [1955?] n.d., 8)

42. Though my Cayo Hueso (a *barrio* of Havana) house pays homage to the *egun* of Nicolás Angarica, who lived in the same neighborhood, other Havana and U.S. houses and *oriatés* do not necessarily recognize him as having achieved the same level of renown as other *oriatés*, such as, La Tuán, José Roche, Tomás Romero, Maximilano Ordaz, Liberato Valdés, Lamberto Samá (from personal communications with Michael Mason, who researched this topic in Havana among members of the Efuche and Ña Margarita Armenteros *ramas*, 1999–2000).

43. Angarica notes three other books he wrote, *El Lucumí al Alcance de Todos* (*Lucumí* [language] *within Reach of All*), *Obras Mágicas (Magical Works)*, *El Dialecto Yoruba-Arataco (The Yoruba-Aratac[ua] dialect)*; Angarica [1955?] n.d., 8.

44. The title of Lachatañeré's 1942 religious "manual" is *Manual de Santería*.

45. These sentiments, as penned in 1955, recall Joseph Campbell's universalist formulations about religious "truths" (see Campbell [1949] 1973, vii; see nn. 28 and 29 above).

46. I use the term "modern," primarily in the sense that Osvaldo Cárdenas Villamil used it in our interview (see discussion below and nn. 99, 101), essentially to distinguish a series of "earlier" (*primitivo* in Cárdenas's terms) and heterogeneous practices carried by Africans to Cuba, which were subject to piecemeal modifications, from new and comprehensive, systemic changes instituted in Matanzas during the middle of the twentieth century, the results of which were profound and lasting. My use of "modern" also refers to self-conscious reform at the turn of the twentieth century, which included systematization and codifica-

tion of institutions and practices, textualization of oral tradition, the professionalization of certain ritual roles, such as the *oriaté*, and a progressive, ideological program to rectify the dominant society's view of African practices by re-presenting them as consistent with universal religious truths.

47. The prologue to Angarica's work, by Dr. José Roque de la Nuez, is dated 3 August 1955.

48. Interview with Miguel Ramos, 9 March 1995.

49. Further research could more precisely and profoundly connect changes in Lucumí institutions with particular sociopolitical conditions, such as the Cuban economy and the demographics and migration of African and creole populations within Cuba during the emancipation period, increasing urbanization and proletarianization in western Cuba during the second half of the nineteenth century, the destruction of the countryside in the Second War of Independence, the waning of the African-born generations, racial discrimination and disenfranchisement and political organizing among people of color after abolition, and religious persecution from the 1880s to the 1920s (see, e.g., Helg 1995 and López Valdés 1985b for views on these historical contexts).

50. Interview with Miguel Ramos, 9 March 1995.

51. From recent conversations with *babalawos* Hermes Valera Ramírez and others, summer 1998.

52. Ifá's 256 compound *odu* signs are permutations of a set of sixteen ranked principal or parent signs, called *melli* (Yoruba *méjì*, i.e., 16 x 16 = 256; see Bascom 1952, 1969b). The elaborate and complex Ifá corpus, as it was recompiled and textualized in Cuba, consists of sets of invocational prayers in the Lucumí ritual language (*rezos*), cogent proverbs that encapsulate the meaning of the *odu* signs (*refranes*), a narration of "taboos" and "advice" (*egües* or *consejos*), typological narrative legends (*historias*), the sign's particular "secret" (*secreto*), "works" that may include the execution of *ebós* on the Ifá tray, recipes for making Echús corresponding to the sign in question, and *inche osains* (see Castillo 1976; *Tratado de Odduns de Ifá* n.d.a.). See Abimbola 1971, 1975, 1976, 1977; Bascom 1952, 1969a; and Dennett [1910] 1968; as well as the exhaustively cited sources in Bascom 1969a, for Ifá divination in Yorubaland and neighboring parts of West Africa. See Bascom 1952, Castillo 1976, and *Tratado de Odduns de Ifá* n.d.a. for examples of the Cuban Ifá system. Cuban *babalawos* believe that while at one time the *dilogún* was a somewhat simpler system with less oracular reach, today, "the *dilogún* are divining Ifá." Some *oriatés*, somewhat more boldly, insist that they have always "divined Ifá." The *babalawo* perspective comes from personal communications with Roberto Villanueva (Osa Kana), Antonio de Armas (Irosun Sá), Hermes Valera Ramírez (Otura Sá), and others, Havana, 1993–2000.

Babalawos explain that the Ifá system works on the basis of *permutations*, that is, Obara-Oche is unique, and different from its converse Oche-[O]Bara. In contrast, they explain, the *dilogún* work on the basis of *combinations* only, that is, that Obara-Oche is, for all intents and purposes, is really the same as Oché-[O]bara. The diviner simply relates the gist of one, and then the other, though he might seek some kind of dominant emphasis. For this reason (i.e., combinations only), *babalawos* like to explain that the *dilogún* "really" have only twelve signs, while Ifá has 256 (16x16); for though sixteen shells are cast, the *oriaté* cannot "read" the last four (13–16) and must pass the interpretation on to a *babalawo*. However, *oriatés* vary in their practice. Many do read the shells' signs as if they were Ifá signs, that is, as permutations, having studied Ifá intensively. Some say that they are fully capable of interpreting 13–16; others say that they only pass to a *babalawo* signs that have 13, 14, 15, 16 as the first "throw" in the compound sign (e.g., 13-4, but not 4-13). In this latter practice, along with the permutation method, the *dilogún* can produce 192 compound signs (12 x 12 + 12 x 4; see, e.g., Elizondo [1934?] n.d., 59–61). Many *babalawos* today will concede that *oriatés* "really are now reading Ifá" and that, whereas before, shell readings were based more on the signs' proverbs than complex *historias* (legends), now they are much more comprehensive. In the foregoing, the *oriaté* perspective derives from Miguel Ramos, Ernesto Pichardo, Michael Mason, and Mason's interviews and study with Havana *oriaté* Saúl Fernández. The *babalawo* perspective derives from my interviews with Havana *babalawos* Hermes Valera, Roberto Villanueva, and Antonio de Armas and observations of Ifá practice from 1986–2000. That the *dilogún* "borrowed" from Ifá is a term used by Miguel Ramos. See Fatunmbi (1992, 75) for a comparison of Ifá and cowrie signs, and where the latter black out on 13–16 (i.e., call for interpretation by a *babalawo*).

53. Personal communications with Stefanía Capone, who worked in Brazil for ten years, September 2000 (see also Capone 1999).

54. The single figure that results from the casting of the shells in the *lavatorio* is written down, but, depending upon the house, it is given more or less significance. One Cuban *oriaté* explains that the number or its interpretation is less significant than the fact that in the washing (*lavatorio*), the shells (standing in for the embryonic *orisha*) are "saluting the earth" (*moforibale*) as the *oricha* is "coming" (being born); in the *itutu* funerary ceremony, in contrast the shells are saluting the earth as the *oricha* is "leaving" (going to the other world; personal communications with Ernesto Pichardo and Michael Mason, September 2000).

55. From interviews with Ernesto Pichardo and Miguel Willie Ramos in Miami, 1994–98, and interviews in Cuba with *babala-*

wos Hermes Valera Ramírez, Roberto Villanueva, Antonio de Armas, Jesús Varona Puente, and Radamés Corona and *santeros* Osvaldo Cárdenas Villamil, María Eugenia Álvarez Pérez, and Michael Mason, 1992–99.

56. Many of the priests I have talked to in the United States use the term *adimú-oricha* to describe any auxiliary deity received before or after the initiation (e.g., Ibeyi, Olokun, Babalú Ayé, Dadá, Odúa, and even the Knife). A Cuban *babalawo*, Antonio de Armas, recently made the argument to me that *adimú-oricha* cannot be a blanket designation; it depends entirely upon the identity of the *oricha* in question, what status it has, what kind of sacrifice contributed to its "birth," and what rank, if any, it confers. For example, *orichas* received with four-legged sacrifices, which thus "talk" with their shells, have the status of independent *orichas* in themselves and cannot be qualified by *adimú*, which has the sense of merely adding to something else. *Orichas* that are washed and fed two-legged animals and, therefore, do not "talk" through shells, may be more appropriately called *adimú;* they are not "independent" and must speak through Eleguá's shells. The *orichas* received by *babalawos* on the "road of Ifá" are called *ori-ochas* by some.

57. Discussions with James Wafer (1992), Katya Wilson (1994), and Stefanía Capone (2000), all of whom are initiated, at some level, in the Candomblé. Still, unambiguous data on how many *orixás* and in what configurations they are received are hard to come by, because, it seems, there is so much variation among Candomblé practices, and there are more differentiated levels of initiation than in the Lucumí religion. See also Wafer's description of Candomblé initiation (1991, 17).

58. "The Four Pillars" and "the Four Cardinal Points" are terms used by Miguel Ramos (personal correspondence with Miguel Ramos, 19 July 1995). Obatalá priestess Marta Moreno uses a similar idiom in her text for Caribbean Cultural Center 1984, but does not use these terms explicitly.

59. The Four Pillars are important referents of the four principal "colors" of *ocha* yet do not exhaust these colors' symbolic reach. A number of other *orichas*, cosmological principles, and philosophical concepts, and material objects fall under these color categories. For example, as sketched by Angarica, white "symbolizes peace, tranquility, and the material [world]" and takes in those *orichas* connected to the sky and the head (e.g., Obatalá, Odudúwa, and Orí); red "symbolizes our Ochas of action, struggle, war"—e.g., Changó, Oyá, Agayú, Eleguá, and Ogún—and "symbolizes life, because it is the color of blood and this is concentrated in our life"; blue takes in *orichas* related to the sea (e.g., Yemayá and Olokun) and "symbolizes . . . the oscillating action of everything that moves in this world . . . [and is the color of] the Sky and the Sea . . ."; yellow is color of Ochún, and it "represents all the vicissitudes of life" (Angarica [1955?] n.d., 72–73). Beyond these *oricha* references, for example, are a series of more practical, sometimes ineffable associations: white is associated with *efun*, chalk, which connects to a whole range of meanings and practices having to do with the head, purity, the *egún*, etc..

60. This does not mean that the "child" of every *oricha* can or should have that *oricha* "seated" on the head. Some cases require "indirect" arrangements (see below) or that the person simply receive a "washed" *oricha* to aid him or her, and which is "delivered" without a complex ceremony.

61. In Ernesto Pichardo's view, the proximity of Changó's "fire" on the head with the fierce and stormy Oyá represents too dangerous a combination (personal communication of 21 January 1997). Moreover, the strained relationship of Oyá and Yemayá—Changó's protective mother—is considered irreconcilable by some.

62. Ernesto Pichardo uses the term "protocol" to elaborate the term *oro* (interview with Ernesto Pichardo, 21 January 1997).

63. The *oro* sequence of sung invocation occurs several times during the *asiento*. Similar, in some respects, to the order of chanted and drummed *oro* versions, the basic order of *orichas* on the floor diverges significantly from these other much longer *oro* sequences. Nineteen or more *orichas* are called in sung chants multiple times during the initiation, including the culmination of the *asiento*, when, theoretically, one of perhaps fourteen of those *orichas* called could possess the initiate in order to stake a final claim to the head or interrupt the initiation to reveal a problem (at least five of the nineteen—Orunmila, Oricha Oko, Ogué, Oké, and Ibeyi—do not possess people for various ritual, mythological, and historical reasons). What the order of the *orichas* in line on the floor shares most basically with other *oros* is that Eleguá and the warriors stand at the beginning, and guardian angel stands at the end. One of the most important principles behind the order of *soperas* on the floor, according to Ernesto Pichardo, revolves around the symbolic and practical requirements of the *matanza*, the sequence of sacrifices in which the *orichas* "eat." Groups of the *orichas* in the line "eat together" (*comen juntos*)—they consume the same class of principal sacrificial animals in the *matanza*, conducted just after the mounting of the guardian angel on the head. The male fraternity of Warriors, Eleguá, Ogún, Ochosi, and Ósun, eats rooster and male goat (and Ogún, Ochosi, and Ósun eat doves together). Then comes a series of male and female *oricha* couples who can eat together ("together" means the same kind of animals, although in the *matanza* each *oricha* must get its own set of animals, particularly its four-legged animal, so that it can later "talk"): e.g., Obatalá and Oyá eat female goat, hen, dove, and guinea fowl; Ochún and Agayú (when he is included) eat male goat, though Ochún's own goat should be cas-

trated (*chivo capón*); and, finally, Yemayá and Changó eat male sheep (*carnero*), along with roosters and guinea hens.

64. Interview with Ernesto Pichardo, 21 January 1997.

65. As I explain below, depending upon the house, the Eleguá (made by a *santero*) or the Echú (made by a *babalawo*) may or may not be "put to the head." In general, Eleguás made long before the full initiation may have embedded within them ingredients that are unknown, or turn out to be "taboo" to the initiate's head. Many initiators, whether they be *oriatés* or *babalawos* supervising the ceremonies, often put Eleguá's cowrie shells to the head instead, or choose some other alternative, such as having another Eleguá or Echú fabricated for the initiate.

66. Personal communication with Michael Atwood Mason, 10 January 1999.

67. When Oyá is the guardian angel, Yemayá is not excluded because she is one of the crucial Four Pillars; however, special measures are taken to rigorously segregate these two antagonists, especially at the moment of the *matanza* when Oyá eats *chivo* (goat) and Yemayá and Changó eat *carnero* (ram) (see Ecún 1986, 104).

68. When Agayú is initiated "indirectly," that is, when Changó is "made" and Agayú is put to the shoulder (Agayú *con oro para* Changó or Changó *con oro para* Agayú), Oyá is also not received, as Changó goes to the head (see below for this concept of *con oro para . . .*).

69. From my oral history research in Havana, 1986–present, based on interviews with numerous *babalawos*.

70. Nicolás Angarica proudly relates that early in the century, his great master, Obadimelli, initiated María Antonia Alfonso (Angarica's sister in Ocha) as a priestess of Dadá in the "direct" form ([1955?] n.d., 49).

71. Babalú Ayé/San Lázaro (aka Asojuano) is made "directly" only in Matanzas in the Regla Arará and among the Havana Arará, who claim Matanzas descent. Certain Lucumí houses in Matanzas and Havana also make Asojuano "directly," but this practice is not accepted by the the Matanzas Arará Sabalú Cabildo or its extension in Havana under Pedro Abreu; neither do they accept that the "indirect" Matanzas and Havana method of initiating San Lázaro through the mediation of (*con oro para*) Obatalá, Yemayá, or Ochún. Indeed, for the Arará, the terms "direct" and "indirect" have no meaning, as they make Asojuano only one way.

Agayú is made "directly" only in those *ramas* that adopted the controversial method established in Matanzas and Havana by Obadimelli, who claimed that it was *the* authentic form of Agayú initiation (Mason 1992, 169; Angarica [1955?] n.d., 51). Obadimelli was one such priest of Agayú "direct." Otherwise, Agayú is made *con oro para* Changó (or Changó *con oro para* Agayú).

72. In some cases, such as initiations of Inle, additional *orichas* that accompany him are included. An *oricha* called Abata, Inle's wife, accompanies him in the penultimate position (see Angarica [1955?] n.d., 34; Ecún 1985, 101 and passim). Inle also accompanied by his guardian or "staff" (*bastón*), called Ibú Joto or Ibú Yoto (from marginal comments on this draft by Michael Mason, September 2000).

73. Obá Ecún says, for example, "Inlé is not made directly, but *con oro para* Yemayá. This is to say, when Inlé is going to be initiated, Yemayá is [in fact], made *con oro para* Inlé" (Ecún 1985, 101). Technically, the latter is correct, because, in the *asiento* ceremony, Yemayá is *made* and presented to the head, and Inle is received and presented to the body.

74. Likewise, the target-like painted "signature" (*firma*) of the mediating *oricha* is painted on the head, while the *firma* of the indirect *oricha* is painted on the floor beneath the *iyawó*'s feet, that is, under the mortar and mat (see chap. 4). This practice may vary by the house.

75. For example, the famous *babalawo* Ramón Febles Molina is reported to have been a child of Odúa who made Obatalá (from interviews with Havana *babalawo* Andrés Kolá, summers of 1992, 1993, and 1994). Melba Carillo initiated a child of Ósun *con oro para* Obatalá on 4 February 1989. According to her, Ósun's initiation proceeds under the supervision of sixteen *babalawos* and sixteen priests of Obatalá. The *asiento* is performed outside so that the sun, the principal manifestation of God, shines directly upon the *iyawó*'s head during the ceremony (interview with Melba Carillo, 6 May 1990).

76. For example, *babalawo* Quintín García (Otura Nico) was a child of Dadá who made Changó (from interviews with Havana *babalawo* Andrés Kolá, summers of 1992, 1993, and 1994).

77. For example, this is evident in an explanation by Obá Ecún of the strong relationship of Oricha Oko to the *odu* called Odí (seven cowries), which is dominated by Yemayá and Olokun—the progenitor of all the Yemayás. "Together with Olokun, [Oricha Oko] is the most powerful *oricha* in the world. . . . Oricha Oko is the land, all of the land, which is one part of this planet—since the other part is water. . . . From the marriage of the land and the sea all the *orichas* of our religion are born; [here] the love of Oricha Oko and Yemayá originates. . . . Oricha Oko speaks only through the mouth of Yemayá, and when he is going to be made, Yemayá is made *con oro para* Oricha Oko, because he speaks through her mouth. . . . Oricha Oko and Yemayá are *ocaninis* (one heart); one doesn't exist without the other; their sign is 7, and that means sky, water, sea, and land" (Ecún 1985, 115). Angarica seconds this explanation: "Oricha Oko speaks through the mouth of Yemayá, because Oricha Oko is the husband of Olokun, the mother of all the Yemayás." A principal re-

lationship that evolves in the Creation is the "marriage" of Olokun and Oricha Oko, that is, the relation of sea and land, along with the great cycle of natural processes that create and sustain life as well as lead to death (Angarica [1955?] n.d., 19).

78. From interview conducted in El Cerro with ninety-six-year-old María Eugenia Álvarez Pérez (2 September 1999). Her memory is like a tack. Born 29 January 1904, María Eugenia received her Kofá de Orula in 1913 from Ramón Febles, with the help of Bernabé Menocal, and made Ocha at twenty years of age in 1924. In 1999, she turned ninety-six years old and had seventy-five years in Ocha. Initiated by Luisa Arango (Changó l'adé), a goddaughter of Efuche, with Bernarda Padrón (Ochún Migüá) as *oybona*, María Eugenia was made, she told me, in the head-and-foot tradition. *Babalawo* Ramón Febles presided over the initiation. Ayayi La Tuán Timotea Albear conducted the initiation as its *oriaté*.

79. Phone interview between "Papo," Michael Mason, and the author, 7 April 2000.

80. Phone interview between "Papo," Michael Mason, and the author, 7 April 2000.

81. Phone interview between "Papo," Michael Mason, and the author, 7 April 2000.

82. "Ña La Tuá[n] . . . lived at Vapor 36" [next door to José Miguel Barberas, Vapor 34—the Solar de la Santa Malteza—in Barrio Príncipe]. Ña Tiburcia Sotolongo lived just across the street from Gómez" (Gómez letter to Radamés Corona, 21 October 1989, kindly shared with me by the latter, summer 1998).

83. From my fieldwork among *babalawos* Pablo Sevilla and Pablo's sons Chiqui Sevilla and Antonio Sevilla and *santeros* Agustín Hernández and Ángela Rosa Delgado Entensa in Palmira, 9–11 July 1994.

84. The kinship relations of the "family of *soperas*" are regulated by proscriptions, some of which are, in effect, incest prohibitions. Priests recognize rules that limit relations between certain *orichas* and between priests themselves, though these rules vary quite a bit. There exists a consensus that priests of Yemayá cannot make priests of Oyá and vice versa, as the two *orichas* are "enemies" (my godmother says that the combination of the wind and the sea is catastrophic). Though some disagree, most priests will tell you that Changó may not initiate the children of the female *orichas* that were, in mythology, his wives: the problematic and stormy Oyá; the tricked, spurned, and world weary Obba; and the inaccessible "virgin" Yewá. The combination of Changó and Oyá is too dangerous and volatile, as they produce "storms" together (from an interview with Ernesto Pichardo, 24 May 1995). Changó's marriage to Obba turned sour when the naive Obba was tricked by her sister and rival Oyá, who wanted Changó back. Oyá convinced Obba to cut off her ear and put it in Changó's favorite dish in order to bind him to her side. Changó "recoiled in disgust" from this meal and banished Obba forever from his palace (see Mason 1992, 263; Ecún 1986, 109–14). The macho, procreative Changó cannot touch Yewá because she is the archetypal virgin (*doncella;* see Ecún 1986, 119–22). It is not coincidental that the three women whom Changó (the embodiment of vital, procreative life) cannot "touch" live around, or go into, the cemetery (Oyá is on the cemetery border, Obba is on the cemetery grounds, and Yewá is at the *fosa* or open grave). A number of *babalawos* and *santeros* I have talked to find no justification or logic in the prohibition of Changó's making Ochún and vice versa. Several *babalawos* point to the example of María Eugenia Álvarez Pérez, an Ochún priestess made by Changó priestess Luisa Arango. They believe this initiation was correct, and, for erroneous reasons, the prohibition arose later.

85. Data on exogamous relationships come from an interview with Ernesto Pichardo, 24 May 1995.

86. Discussions with *babalawos* Antonio de Armas, Jorge Díaz, and others, August 1999.

87. Interview with María Eugenia Álvarez Pérez (Ochún Niké) and her grandson Jorge Díaz, 2 September 1999.

88. Babalú Ayé/St. Lazarus/Asojuano, who embodies the sufferings of the world and whose afflictions include irruptions of fluid through painful perforations of the skin, failures of the immune system, severe blood disorders, and the puncturing of internal organs, can be made indirectly, according to some Lucumí lines, through Obatalá, Yemayá, or Ochún (see Ecún 1985, 131–34). Angarica says that Babalú Ayé can be made through all of those three ([1955?] n.d, 113). Ernesto Pichardo insists that Babalú Ayé should be made indirectly through Obatalá and disputes that he can be made through Ochún and Yemayá (interview, 21 January 1998). As indicated, the Arará Sabalú reject these initiations entirely as "inventions"—you make Asojuano either directly in the Arará fashion, or not at all.

89. Interviews with *babalawo* Oscar Rodríguez, director of the Cabildo Arará Sabalú Nonjó of Matanzas, and Pedro Abreu, a leader of the Arará Sabalú of Havana, July 2000.

90. The largest, most recognized group that performs the reading of the year is the Comisión Organizada para la Letra del Año, which has proceeded under the direction of Lázaro Cuesta, Hermes Valera, Víctor Betancourt, Guillermo Diago, Andrés Kolá, and others.

91. Taurina Montalvo Enujere married Nino "El Cojo" (Otura Ogbe), a godchild of Bernardo Rojas. Taurina, an Oluwó Popó (priestess) of Asojuano and goddaughter of Pilar Fresneda, was the Ifá godchild in *kofá* of Pilar Fresneda's son, *babalawo* Bartolo Rodríguez Fresneda (from interviews with Lázaro Cuesta [4 Jan-

uary 1996] and *babalawo* Evelio Real Orduña [member of the surviving Rodríguez Fresneda family, 19 June 1998]).

92. Palmira's Facundo Sevilla (Obe Dí) made Ifá with Guanabacoa's Tata Gaitán. Later, Facundo's nephew, Antonio Sevilla, claims, Facundo Sevilla "traded powers" (*intercambio de poderes*) with Havana's Miguel Febles—Facundo Sevilla received Olofin from Febles, and Febles received an Osain from Sevilla (interview with Antonio Sevilla, 10 July 1994).

93. Rafael L. López Valdés reports that La Regla de Ocha was brought eastward to Santiago de Cuba in the 1940s (personal communication, Summer 1993, Havana). Judith Bettelheim's sources in Santiago claimed that one or two priests arrived in Santiago in 1912 (personal commumication, August 1996). In any case, it is clearer from my interviews with Mercedes Melo González (31 August 1999) that José Ramón Gutiérrez and Aurora Lamar carried Ocha initiation to Santiago de Cuba; this may have been in the 1920s, 1930s, or 1940s.

94. Interview with Julia and the late Juan Montalvo, 25 June 1998, Cárdenas. Though "most people don't know her any longer," the elderly couple explained to me, Naná Burukú was a major highlight of Lucumí ceremonies in the city of Cárdenas early in the twentieth century, where she "danced in possession wearing an apron of hennequen decorated around the waist with *tocoloro* (parrot) feathers. Naná carried an oxtail fly whisk, wore a sombrero, smoked *tabaco* (cigars), and received blood sacrifices conducted with a knife made of *caña brava* (cane) or glass, rather than steel."

95. Interview with Hermes Valera Ramírez and Andrés Kolá, 19 July 1992, Havana. There were a number of famous figures with versions of this name (Bamboché, Bangoché). Calazán Herrera, one of Lydia Cabrera's principal informants, was named "Bangoché" (Cabrera [1947] 1994, 353). Obadimelli was also known as Banboshé (Valdés Garriz 1997, 135).

96. Interviews with Pedro Abreu, 21, 24, 29 July and 1 August 2000.

97. Miguel Ramos, an *oriaté* of Miami, traveled to Brazil.

98. This is a case of a Cuban-born priestess in New York "receiving" a Lucumí Asojuano and an "Arará road" of Asojuano. In her house, the latter is given by *babalawos* who claim the authority to fabricate Asojuano Arará. They presumably ignore or disagree with the Arará principal that this is the exclusive right of the Oluwó Popó.

99. The meaning of these terms is not clear, although the *obé weo* and *aberikiti* may refer, in part, to protocols of the *Pinaldo* (Knife; *obé* or *abé* in Lucumí) within initiation practice. The introduction of certain knife rituals, among other things, according to Cárdenas, radically changed Matanzas practice.

100. Tomasa Villamil died during the summer of 1998 at age ninety-seven.

101. Interview with Osvaldo Cárdenas Villamil, 25 July 1997. Additional details in this paragraph come from a followup phone interview with Cárdenas by Elliot Klein, 3 June 1998, which he kindly shared with me. Though Cárdenas apparently received the full complement of Lucumí *orichas* in his initiation in the "modern" form, that he "has San Lázaro and Ogún" probably refers to special relationships one forms with particular *oricha* protectors, as well as with those *orichas* that are accustomed to possessing a person. It is common to hear that one may be possessed by one's own "head *oricha*," but also by Obatalá, "the Owner of All Heads," as well as San Lázaro, who is considered as much of an *egun* (dead spirit) as *oricha*.

102. Bascom states, more generally, for example, that "Ọramfé has not been reported outside of Ifẹ̀, Ileṣa, and Ọ̀yọ́, nor Agbona and Oriṣa Madoga outside of Mẹkọ (Ọ̀yọ́ region). Oṣumare, Iroko, and Nana Buruku are important in Mẹkọ and in Dahomey, but not among the eastern Yoruba" (1969b, 43).

103. This is suggested by the differentiated title rankings of Ifá diviners in Yorubaland (Dennett [1910] 1968, 152): in ascending order, Babalawo, Olowo, Odofin, Asawo; beneath the Babalawo, in descending order, are Ajigbona, Awaro, Aro, Asareparo, Apetehí or Ayaro (each of whom has an assistant). Some contemporary Havana *babalawos* who, as of the mid-1990s, came under the influence of 'Wande Abimbola's son, Taiwo Abimbola, who was living in Havana, adopted what they were taught were the royal and Ifá title rankings from Ifẹ̀: in descending order, "Oní of Ifé, Araba, Agbonbon, Aseda, Amosun, Awise, Agestinyowa, Afedigba, Jolofinpe, Adifolu, Babalawo, Awo" (from Ile Tum Tum 1997). Castellanos and Castellanos provide a list of Cuban *babalawo* rankings: in ascending order, Omofá (Hand of Orula), Awó (a *babalawo* initiated in Ocha first), Oluo (a *babalawo* of rank), Adofín—next after Oluo, Aró—third in rank at this high level (1992, 3:84–86).

104. For example, the recent recompilations by Ofún Oyekún Yemiló's group, based mostly on mid-twentieth-century manuals by Pedro Arango, as well as the more private notebooks and the memorized knowledge of contemporary *babalawos*, though corrected in some ways, mostly repeat what is found in any given "Tratado" or "Dice Ifá." Compare for example, *Tratado de Oddun de Ifá* 1992, ed. Ofún Oyekún Yemiló, and *Tratato de Odduns de Ifá* n.d.a and n.d.b. The latter, older texts are based also on versions of the Arango texts. I tested this hypothesis by opening at random several different texts and asking a couple of *babalawos* to give a summary of the major points of a sign. Not only the general content, but also the order and distinct word usage were similar if not the same.

105. Cuban *babalawos* who have interacted with Nigerian Yoruba *babalawos* remark on the latter's level of specialization in

contrast to what they take to be their own more encompassing and diverse generalist practice. Cuban *babalawos,* depending upon the *rama,* for example, engaged in ancestral masquerades for the *egun* not only through ancestral prayer, but also, historically—and down through 1963—through the Olokun masquerades conducted in Regla. Olokun's masks belonged to Adechina, then Tata Gaitán, then Quintín García, and finally, the late Quintín Lecón Lombillo (Tín). *Babalawos* in the *rama* of Ño Carlos Adé Bí who were students of Miguel Febles possess powers that they call Ogboni. The *babalawos* receive an Osain that they claim is distinct from the lesser version received by *santeros* (*inche osain*), unless the *santero* undergoes a special initiation to receive the *fundamento* of Osain.

Babalawos and *oriatés* contest authority over Eleguá, Ogún, Ochosi, Ósun, Olokun, Odúa, *egun,* and many other deities (see below).

106. That Orunmila is considered *eleri küín* in Cuba comes from an interview with Hermes Valera Ramírez, 27 June 1986, Havana.

107. Interview with Hermes Valera Ramirez, 27 June 1986, Havana.

108. In an important myth, Olofin contrives a "difficult test to see if Orula is capable of handling such an important responsibility"—Ifá divination. It is only through the intervention of Eleguá, "who is everywhere and sees everything," that Orula is able to pass the test, for Eleguá leads Orula to the right answers (Cabrera [1954] 1983, 88).

109. These discussions are reported by Hermes Valera Ramírez, who attended Ifá readings of the opening of the year from the late 1950s through the 1970s in the house of the late Bernardo Rojas (when it was run by José Herrera and Joaquín Salazar) (personal communication, Havana, 23 June 1993).

110. As a function of an emerging colonialized order, entailing accommodation to and negotiation with British indirect rule as of 1860, Yoruba kings, considered members of a "traditional" elite, sought to define and strengthen their authority and legitimacy over the local or regional constituencies they sought to represent before the British (Pemberton and Afolayan 1996, 2).

111. In other words, in the Ọ̀yọ́-centric myths, "[t]he idiom of migration, as opposed to cosmological descent, underplays the political and ritual authority accorded to Ife by the creation myth, for Ife figures as a place of arrival and temporary kingship and not the locus of origin. In fact, the attribution of Oduduwa's paternity to a Meccan king places the founder of the Yorubas outside the Ife cosmological scheme altogether" (Apter 1991, 16).

112. "One of the obvious results of African acculturation in the New World," Bascom wrote in 1952, "is the transition from a non-literate to a literate tradition. As a result of this change the teachings of the santeros, which were once handed down solely by word of mouth, have been copied in notebooks by those learning the names and the verses of the divination figures, the sacrifices and salutations of the African deities, the uses of the herbs, Lucumi phrases and vocabulary . . . etc." (1952, 169–70).

113. Regla's Ilé Adé Yerí, directed by Ofún Oyekún Yemiló, has produced a seventeen-volume "encyclopedia" of Ifá (Ofun Yemiló 1997). On a per-order basis, the group of researchers also works up a personalized, custom manual of the Ifá signs of an individual *babalawo,* a compilation that might otherwise take years to research. Another Havana compiler, named "Luisito," competes with Adé Yerí with his own seventeen-volume "encyclopedia." Both series can be found in the bookstalls of Old Havana's Plaza de Armas, and Adé Yerí's works are sold in Librería Cervantes in Havana, as well as internationally on the Web, e.g., at Folkcuba.com.

114. Four hundred pages in photocopied manuscript form.

115. Dennett's chart draws on A. B. Ellis (1894), Bishop James Johnson (1899), R. Dennett ([1910] 1968), and S. Farrow [1924] 1926), among others. I am indebted to Obá Ernesto Pichardo for bringing this crucial point to my attention, for outlining to me the differences between the various manuals, and for detailing which ethnographies and kinds of information the *libretas* draw upon. I have examined selected pages in the manuals referred to and compared them to examples in Dennett ([1910] 1968, 149–50).

116. Mintz and Price, as have others, astutely note the transatlantic Ifá tradition as a dynamic of continuity and change ([1976] 1992, 59). New Jersey *babalawo* Luis Castillo does not regard Bascom 1969 as a "bible."

117. Texts that present Ifá's oracular wisdom in the form of *historias* (legends) are often called *dice Ifás,* and the exposition of each *odu*'s information begins with the framing phrase, *dice Ifá,* "Ifá says." Ifá knowledge is inherently distributed and shared.

118. Though I am foregrounding here the interpretations of Ernesto Pichardo (interviews from June 1994), I have attended several *bajones de Orula* in Cuba and witnessed the proceedings. I have attended two Readings of the Opening of the Year in Cuba (1994, 2000); though non-*babalawos* may not enter the room, I have heard the interpretations from outside, and *babalawos* have explained the protocol and interpretations to me as they proceeded. The reciprocal effect of the *babalawos'* interpretations is clear to anyone who has attended a *bajón*—particularly since *babalawos* explicitly refer to, cite, revise, and summarize the previous statements of their colleagues. Still, that older *babalawos* always have greater synthetic and analytical capacity is not clear. Indeed, many "younger," highly "prepared" *babalawos,* may surpass their elders in knowledge but do not publicly boast about

it. Many *babalawos* will tell you that *capacidad,* as much as "years," is important.

119. The "hierarchy of power and prestige" is as follows (top to bottom): (1) persons who have received Olofin; (2) persons who have received *Wanaldo* (the Knife); (3) Oluos (*babalawos* who made Ocha before making Ifá); (4) *babalawos* (those who did not make Ocha before); (5) *santeros* with *Pinaldo;* (6) *santeros;* (7) persons who have received the hand of Orula; (8) persons who have received the Warriors; (9) persons who have received the necklaces; (10) persons who have received a protective charm or *inche osain,* (11) nonbelievers (Sánchez 1978, 33; Brandon's ranking is, in descending order, "Omocolabbá, Wanaldo, Oluo, Babalawo, Obá Oriaté, Pinaldo, Italero, Babalocha/Iyalocha, Olorisha, Aleyo, Abirinkulu" [Brandon 1983, 512]).

120. For example, Ifá-centric *babalawos* vociferously reject the authority of *oricha* priests to prepare the Warriors (Eleguá, Ogún, Ochosi, and Ósun). Their perspective on a range of ritual practices decisively shapes Cabrera's late summative descriptions of the religion ([1974] 1980, 1980), while in her *El Monte,* where she wrote down and re-presented basically whatever her range of informants told her, she reports that *babalawos* and *oricha* priests, both men and women, prepare the Warriors ([1954] 1983, 88).

121. These other tasks, according to Cabrera's sources, have included three *babalawos'* leading the inaugurating forest (*monte*) ceremonies for initiates of Eleguá, Ogún, and Ochosi (see chap. 4); delivering the plants and the *asiento*'s sacred ingredients (four African "seeds" called the *aché del santo*), and consecrating the fresh plants and the herbal baths and infusions (*osains* and *omiero*) with his *aché de Orula* and other media. However, in my observations, having provided transportation for priests and *babalawos* on their rounds to contract herbalists *oriatés,* and providers of animals, and in witnessing the events I was allowed to see in my own initiation, as well as working an initiation in the summer of 2003, I have not seen the *babalawo* deliver the plants—they are delivered by *osainistas.* Michael Mason, who has worked at a number of initiations involving *babalawos* in various houses, reports that he has never heard of, or seen, the *babalawo* adding this *aché* or blessing the herbal liquids. However, the *aché de Orula* from the Ebó de Entrada conducted by a *babalawo* is often added to the *osains* in Ifá-centric ritual (from marginal notes by Michael Mason from his reading of this draft, September 2000).

122. In this view, the *babalawo,* through Orula, is on the most intimate terms with Eleguá, Ogún, Ochosi, and Ósun. Ifá divination is best qualified to make the determination of the guardian angel and perform the *vista,* the opening Ifá reading that takes out a sign that guides the coming initiation and sets out the *ebó de entrada* to be performed on the evening of the *asiento.* This *ebó,* some believe, makes Olofin aware of the proceedings. Only the "knife" (*wanaldo*) of the *babalawo* is authorized to kill four-legged animals in the *matanzas* (*babalawos* believe that the "knife" of *santeros,* called the *pinaldo,* is a "fraud" (a summary from discussions with numerous *babalawos* in Cuba and the United States, 1985–2000).

123. After the passing of Havana's two chief female masters of ceremony, Guillermina Castel and La Tuán (c. 1935), Havana *oriatés* would all be males, with the exception of Adelfa Teheran Ambiro, who would continue to practice in New York in the 1970s, though she was not widely accepted (personal communication with Miguel Ramos, 9 March 1995).

124. *Obá* means "king," *orí* means "head," and *até* refers to the divination tray or mat. This sense of *até* refers not only to the divination and *ebó* that the *oriaté* conducts on the "mat" (*estera*) on the third day of the initiation, but also to all of the other activities conducted over the "mat," including the "shaving" and "mounting" of the *oricha* on the head.

125. See my discussion above of premodern initiation formats and John Mason's brief discussion of the initiation of Ferminita Gómez in Matanzas (Mason 1996, 26).

126. For example, Cabrera lists the ingredients for fabricating an Eleguá, reporting neutrally that "the babalawo, the babalocha, and the iyalocha prepare him" ([1954] 1983, 88). The last suggests that women may have fabricated Eleguás as late as the 1950s, although this is inconceivable to most practitioners today. Still, debates did rage as to what kind of Eleguás women could prepare, some conceding that women could certainly give Eleguás consisting of a "stone" to initiates, while the Eleguá of cement (*masa*) was the bailiwick of the *babalawo* only (1980, 187). At least one female *oriaté* was married to a conservative *babalawo* (La Tuán to Bernabé Menocal). One can only wonder what regulations were in force at that time. A set of traditions was apparently established in the central Cuban town of Placetas in the last third of the nineteenth century by a line of women, some of whom were not fully initiated in the modern sense and who may have conducted sacrifices of four-legged animals themselves, a task now reserved to *oriatés* and *babalawos,* male offices reserved for men (Gómez Abreu 1982).

127. *Babalawos* are mentioned in Angarica's discussion of Olofin, though not in the most favorable light ([1955?] n.d., 14).

128. Obá Ecún (1985), each of whose chapters outlines the initiation ceremonies for a different *oricha,* mentions that, just prior to the mounting of the *oricha* on the head, a *babalawo* may "present the razor" to the head if the initiate has a *babalawo* for a godfather (see below).

129. I am grateful to Andrew Apter for articulating the point in this way to me.

130. The Hand of Orula for men is called *awofacá*, and for women, *(i)kofá* or *ikofafún* (however, for some reason, some priests call the man's version "Hand of Orula" while they call the woman's version *kofá de orula*). Heterosexual men who received the *mano de orula* may "pass to Ifá," that is, become initiated as *babalawos*. Women who receive the *mano de orula* (*kofá*) are authorized to act as *apetebí*, the female assistants of Orula and the drum spirit, Añá. This often means cooking and serving food during Ifá initiations and drummings. Women and men commonly receive the Hand of Orula long prior to their intiations as *santeros*. Among these, the men, historically, could pass to Ifá without making Ocha first, leaving them as *babalawos* who might not be admitted into the room of Ocha in some houses because they did not have Ocha made first.

131. Interview with Ernesto Pichardo, 12 September 1989. Pichardo and others insist that the *babalawo*'s Eleguá is, strictly speaking, an "Echú," which is different in its value and valence from the Eleguá given by the *oriaté* and *santero*. The latter is "restrained," controlled, and transformed into a useful presence by Obatalá, whereas the former is controlled by Orunmila, and remains, from the standpoint of Ocha, a "negative" presence. See also González Wippler 1989, 31, 168.

132. In many houses in Cuba and the United States, the *collares* of the *orichas* may be received first if a person's first formative contacts are with an *oricha* priest (*santero*). But if a person's first formative contacts are with a *babalawo*, as in my case, the *guerreros* may be received from him before anything else. For a description of the *imposición de collares* ceremony, see Murphy 1988, 77–83; Brandon 1983, 355–61; Cabrera [1974] 1980, 120–27; Ecún 1988, 11–20; Sánchez 1978, 70–71).

133. Interview with *babalawo* Antonio de Armas, 16 June 1998, Havana.

134. One gets a primary *padrino* and secondary *padrino* (called the *oyubona*) in Ifá through the *mano de orula* ceremony. One gets a primary *padrino* or *madrina* and a secondary one (*oyubona*) in Ocha through the receiving of the *collares* of *santo* (though this *oyubona* may remain nominal, and another may be selected before the full initiation). The primary *padrino* or *madrina* of Ocha initiates the person into the priesthood of an *oricha*, and the *oyubona* of this initiation becomes very important as a nursemaid, teacher, and guardian during the initiation week, the year of white apprenticeship, and in the course of the priest's life.

135. From conversations with *iyaloricha* Gloria González and her *babalawo* son, Freddie González, members of Templo Bonifacio Valdez, Elizabeth, New Jersey, 30 August 1987.

136. The *babalawo*'s exclusive right to prepare the *guerreros* prevails in the accounts of Teodoro Díaz Fabelo (1960, 66–71), Julio Sánchez (1978, 72), and Lydia Cabrera ([1974] 1980, 1980). For example, *babalawos* consider the *pinaldo* of *santeros* as nothing more than the protection of Ogún and reject its authority to perform animal sacrifices (see, e.g., Sánchez 1978, 97–99). They also believe *santeros* have no authority to prepare and give Odúa (alternatively Odudúwa), and that the Olokun of *santeros* is really just a "road of Yemayá," called Mayeleo, whereas Ifá has the "true" Olokun (it is true that the contents and appearance of the *Olokun de Babalawo* and the *Olokun de Santero* are quite different. The *santero*'s contains shells, coral, and metal "tools," while the *babalawo*'s contains "charged" wood tools, and its outside is layered with charged loads of cement and shells. Contemporary *babalawos* in Havana describe the *santero*'s Warriors and *pinaldo* as "plagiarisms" and "frauds."

137. From interviews with Ernesto Pichardo, 12 September 1989. According to an early explanation to me by my Ifá *padrino*, during the *asiento*, the Echú he originallyprepared for me as part of the Warriors would be incorporated within the domain of La Regla de Ocha by receiving its cowrie shells. So transformed, this modified Eleguá would then take up the first position and opening role in the line of *orichas* made and received—for example, when the *orichas* are "put to the head" in the *asiento* and when they "speak" during the *itá* divination reading on the third day of initiation. I was also told by Ifá-centric *santeras* and *babalawos* in New Jersey in the 1980s that their initiates received only the Echú of the Babalawo, augmented with shells. Still, this way of regarding Echú through the initiatory ladder that bridges the two *reglas* is one of a number of contested models. In Ocha-centric houses, *oriatés* who encounter initiates that have an Echú of the Babalawo—an unknown quantity that is often regarded as "negative" and "dangerous"—fabricate a new one that they feel can be safely put to the head. And, despite my *padrino*'s early explanation to me, I received a new Eleguá, consecrated by the *oriaté*, though my Echú of the Babalawo remained present throughout the ceremonies.

138. This was my experience in receiving an auxiliary *oricha* in a Miami house. I had had my Echú of the Babalawo for nine years, and my Eleguá of Ocha for three months. I was told to "put away" the Echú, as he would not participate at all. The "context" of the ceremony had nothing to do with him (i.e., it was an "Ocha" context), and this Echú would "understand" this. In contrast, solidly Ifá-centric houses, such as those connected to New Jersey's Templo Bonifacio Valdez, always have their *babalawos'* Echus "eat" with every Ocha ceremony conducted in the house, and they may, or may not, depending upon the event, exclude the Eleguás owned by participants, Eleguás they received in former relationships with *santeros*.

139. From an interview with Hermes Valera Ramírez, 27 June 1986, Havana.

140. This myth cycle is primarily from Oche Melli. For example, "All the *orichas* were always bothering Orula for things. 'Divine this, divine that for me,' they said. He was tired of it. When Ochún came to him to divine for her, instead he gave her five cowrie shells to divine with. Then Yemayá came and he gave her seven shells to divine with; twelve altogether. But he kept the *ikín* to himself. Only Orula divines with the *ikín*" (story told to me in an interview with Luis Castillo, 25 May 1986). A story collected by Lydia Cabrera at midcentury identifies Yemayá as the most unabashed thief of Orula's secrets. Warned by Eleguá that Yemayá was trying to divine with the *ikín* and *tablero de Ifá*, Orula "gave her seven cowrie shells and complained to Olofin that his woman wanted to know as much as he" (Cabrera [1954] 1983, 84).

141. As Ifá-centric *babalawos* and *santeros* have expressed to me, the "loss" of secrets from Ifá is the greatest practical threat to the survivability of the religion; such views are often expressed as a problem of "women's" essential characteristics. For example, Melba Carillo explains that "many of secrets of the religion have been lost . . . because there is *always*, you know, a *woman talking*" (emphasis added). While the secrets of La Regla de Ocha have been revealed in numerous published accounts and films, she notes, the secrets of Ifá have been "preserved" (interview with Melba Carillo, 1 September 1987).

Any linking of Afro-Cuban constructions of secrecy along gender lines to the interpretive findings of recent Yoruba scholars should be highly qualified, though the idea remains suggestive. Recent studies of Yoruba religion, for example, identify, by analogy, the preservation of secret knowledge and the integrity of "vessels": literally, the covered pots of shrines and, figuratively, the human body and the corporate body of cult-organizations. The sexual "penetration" of women's and gay men's bodies and the "leakage" or "spillage" of menstrual blood from the former are theorized as analogous to the undue revelation or "loss" of the cult-group's secret knowledge, in a word, its *àṣẹ* (Matory 1986, 57–99, esp. 84, 91–92; 1994, 17, 18, 84, and his chap. 5 generally). The relation of the female body to the symbolic issue of "containment" is nicely encapsulated in Gleason 1987, 69–76, 83–86. While no comparable literature exists with respect to Afro-Cuban religions, the African literature's insights might be (carefully) extended to the New World case, as Matory has extended his gender theorizing to observations of the Afro-Brazilian Candomblé (Matory 1988). One might interpret a famous Lucumí *patakí* with the foregoing Yoruba principles in mind. For example, a hunter's wife endeavors to discover what happened to "the blood" of his hunt—as the animals always return home already drained. She introduces ashes into the bottom of her husband's game bag, punctures three holes in the bag, and then follows the trail of ashes back to a tree—a sacred grove, where the hunter always secretly left the animals' blood for Olofin. For "wanting to see blood," Olofin punished woman eternally with the curse of menstruation. In other words, if she wanted to "see blood," she would see it every month (Elizondo [1934?] n.d., 17–18). One might interpret the narrative's leaking bag as the leakage or "spillage" of a cult secret; moreover, the ashes—dead matter—and the resulting menstrual blood (a sign that pregnancy has not occurred) could be taken, in the Yoruba sense, to figure the antithesis of procreative, life-giving blood. Menstrual blood is linked in Yoruba religion to the dessicating power of the witch—a postmenopausal woman who "hordes blood," and whose bird avatars peck holes in wombs in order to destroy the wealth and "future" of the King's patrilineage (see Thompson 1983, 7, 47; Apter 1992, 111–14; Elizondo [1934?] n.d., 47).

142. As indicated above, some heads are proscribed from making other heads; for example, a Yemayá priest cannot make Oyá and vice versa. Many people believe that unscrupulous priests proceed against such prohibitions in order to make money (e.g., an Oyá priest will proceed with making Changó anyway rather than saying he or she cannot do it, thereby losing a client).

143. Contestation over oracular practice has a long history, involving the politics of the religious authority behind imperial rule. For example, in mid-eighteenth-century Dahomey, the Fon king imported the Yoruba Ifá system to reign in and delegitimize the "centrifugal" and subersive tendencies of the country's numerous *gbo* possession oracles. What became "Fá" divination in Dahomey was intended to strengthen and revitalize the authority of the royal center—the king. Zuesse writes: "the oracular cults were part of a socially and cosmologically centrifugal diversity, one family over against another, and even one individual against others (in witchcraft accusations). The logic of passionate desire even led to alliances against central authority. The Fá system, on the other hand, is an entirely conscious, rational attempt to order the whole reality into one vast classification system" (1979, 208).

144. In response to my verbal account of Hermes Valera's identification of Orula as "witness at Creation," Ernesto Pichardo shrewdly revised Orula's status by rhetorical inversion and substitution. The full quotation from Pichardo is, "*Babalawos* take Orunmila and glorify him to the status of Ifá, which is Total Knowledge. Orunmila is nothing but the interpreter. Orunmila is a force or energy, just as Eshu or Changó are. The *babalawo* has to obtain the blessing of three important *orichas*, Eshu, Obatalá, and Changó. Eshu represents the Guide of Destiny [*Orí*], Obatalá—the creator [and owner of human heads, *orí*], and Changó—the Problems of Life. Orunmila is said to be a 'witness,' but before the witness, Destiny [and its guide], Echú, had to exist

already. Ifá means 'proper exploration of the problems of life.' Who comes first, the 'witness' or the 'problems of life'? First we have to go through Changó [the source of 'problems']." According to Pichardo, the creator of heads (Obatalá), the guide of heads on the road of life (Echú-Eleguá), and the problems of life (Changó), are three forces with which the Ocha priest and *oriaté* have intimacy and competence. They were seminal in the birth of each of these domains, and the *dilogún* system, used by these *orichas* and their human representatives, is optimal for divining and resolving *any* issue (from a telephone interview with Ernesto Pichardo, 14 January 1988).

145. Some contemporary *babalawos* agree with this assessment, though they insist that the oracular sophistication of the *dilogún* is not an original or essential feature, but resulted precisely from its relatively recent appropriation of the Ifá corpus and its divination methods These opinions were voiced in discussions with Havana *babalawos* Hermes Valera Ramírez, Roberto Villanueva, and Antonio de Armas, in the summer of 1998. Villanueva says that *dilogún* "is Ifá now" but used to be much simpler; it was based more in the verbal interpretation of the basic proverbs assigned to the cowrie *odu* (*dicharachos*), considered as combinations. "Now," the *dilogún* diviners interpret the *historias* (legends) they took from the corresponding Ifá *odús*, and many diviners consider the *dilogún odu* as permutations, not just simple combinations. The three *babalawos* believe that such changes are less than forty years old, though they probably date to Obadimelli's Havana period (early twentieth century through the 1930s).

146. Interviews with Ernesto Pichardo, 12 October 1989 and 24 May 1995.

147. A restless young lawyer from Washington, D.C., dissatisfied with a shell reading indicating his head was Ogún, appealed to three *babalawos*, it seems, shopping around for a satisfactory answer. A Washington, D.C., *bajón de Orula* determined his head *oricha* was Yewá; a Miami *bajón* said Eleguá. He, nevetheless, remained convinced that his head *oricha* was Ochún. One of the *babalawos* who had read him found out about his "shopping around" and was furious (from discussions with Michael Mason, 1997).

148. Eleguá's cowrie shells are used for day-to-day readings—for Eleguá is the universal messenger, mediator, and speaker of all languages. When readings are conducted with the cowrie shells of most of the other *orichas* (some have no cowries, some do not speak, and some must speak through other *orichas*), the deity's *sopera* is "brought to the floor" in a divination ceremony called the *bajón de santo*. In some ways, this pattern is analogous to the difference between the *babalawo*'s divining chain (*opele*), a kind of messenger, which is used in day-to-day divinations, and divination with Orula's circular wood tablet (*tablero*) and *ikín* (palm nuts). Orula's *sopera* and this equipment are also brought to the floor (*bajón de orula*), and the session must be conducted and interpreted by at least three *babalawos*. As indicated, *babalawos* do not accept the finality of the two classes of *oricha* readings and regard the *tablero* as surer than the chain.

149. Interview with Ernesto Pichardo, 12 September 189.

150. The seeds of La Regla de Ocha and La Regla de Ifá were planted outside of Cuba with the emigration of practitioners from the island in the decade or so before the Revolution (1959), though the practice of Ocha and Ifá grew rapidly and spread widely from the mid 1960s through 1980. Today, Cuban *olorichas* and *babalawos* reside in numerous cities in the United States, as well as in Puerto Rico, Panama, Venezuela, and Mexico City. Cubans arrived in the United States in three post-Revolutionary "waves," although an earlier "wave" had already begun in the early to mid-1940s. In 1980 the total number of Cubans living in the United States was close to 1,000,000. In that year, approximately 469,000 lived in greater Miami, 84,000 lived in New Jersey, and 79,000 lived in New York City (Dixon 1983; see also Clarke 1981). Significant Cuban populations are found in Chicago, Los Angeles, Oakland, and New Orleans, among other cities. Over the years, the religion's membership has come to include large numbers of other North American groups, including other Latinos, African-Americans, and Americans of European descent.

Luis Castillo, a Cuban-born and Cuban-made *babalawo*, founded Templo Bonifacio Valdez in 1972, naming it after his great-great "grandfather" in La Regla de Ifá, Bonifacio Valdés (Obe Weñe). The temple was incorporated legally under the laws of the State of New Jersey in 1975 as a non-profit, tax-exempt corporation. In 1980, thanks to collectively saved monies, the members purchased a pre-war house in a town in Union County, New Jersey. The interrelated houses of the Temple became a demographic microcosm of the entire Cuban migration as it encountered the already multi-ethnic context of the New York Metropolitan area (see Brown 1989, chap. 2).

151. See Díaz-Fabelo 1960, 42; Sánchez 1978, 81–90; Cabrera 1980, 102, 182–84; [1974] 1980, 128–202; Murphy 1981, 285–95; 1988, 84–91; Gleason 1992; Murphy 1994; Brandon 1983, 388–423; Ecún 1985; and González Wippler 1989, 164–89. Díaz-Fabelo, Sánchez, Cabrera ([1974] 1980, 1980), and Murphy (1981, 1988) tend to represent, and endorse, the Ifá-centric model. Gleason's film (1992) and Ecún (1985) repesent Ocha-centric models. Brandon (1983) presents a variety of positions without judging them. None document such an extreme Ifá-centric model as the temple's.

152. See Lydia Cabrera ([1974] 1980, 128–203) for her discus-

sion of the *kariocha*. See also Cabrera's Lucumí glossary ([1957] 1986, 185) for her definition and breakdown of the word as *Ka-Orí-Ocha:* "putting (*ka*), on the head (*orí*), the *Orichas* (*ocha*)." Murphy (1981, 293; 1994, 94) follows Cabrera's breakdown and reports a set of standard initiatory ceremonies. Brandon (1983, 399) quotes Murphy's use of Cabrera and provides a description of the ceremonies similar to Murphy's.

153. Interview with a temple priestess, 26 September 1987.

154. For example, Ernesto Pichardo and other *oriatés*, when fabricating an Eleguá for a client, may determine its road identity through divination in advance, build it according to the appropriate ingredients marked in the divination reading, and then wash and feed it. The *oriaté* can also make a "generic" Eleguá as a stone or head. It is washed and fed, its identity is divined through the shells of the *oriaté*'s own Eleguá, and then the *oriaté* "calls" the particular "road" of this Eleguá (road) to the figure. As is common in the full initiation setting, particularly where the initiate already has an *Echú de babalawo*, the *oriaté*, in most cases, makes a new Eleguá, which may be nothing more than a simple stone. This Eleguá is washed, put to the initiate's head, and fed sacrifices. Then its "road" is determined in the *itá* session on the third day. As of information gleaned in the Ifá, the stone may have to be modified accordingly, for example, embedded in cement and/or a large seashell, with the addition of other ingredients (phone interview with Ernesto Pichardo, 12 September 1989, and various other personal communications with him, as well as Michael Mason, 1991–98). Still, as Michael Mason adds, in ceremonies to consecrate Babalú Ayé in order to be received, the road must be marked in advance of the ceremony (from marginal comments made upon his reading of this draft, September 2000).

155. Personal communication with the late *babalawo* Pedro Rodríguez, Elizabeth, New Jersey, 30 August 1987.

156. In the case of a conventional *itutu* (funerary ceremony) for a deceased priest, some of the *orichas* are dispatched to the other world and the *soperas* are broken; other *orichas* may be inherited in their *soperas* by living priests (see Cabrera [1974] 1980, 342–59; Valdés Garriz 1991).

157. Interviews with Hermes Valera Ramírez, June 1991 and June 1993.

158. Interview with Ernesto Pichardo, 24 December 1994.

159. Gómez writes, "The *babalawo* shaved my head, performed on me the Fifi Okán [painting of the head], the *babalawo* sacrificed for me the animals." Gómez's godfather was Miguel Menocal and his Oyubona was Mercedes del Monte ("Mercedes Chiquita") of Cabildo Africano Lucumí fame. Gómez was first a godchild of La Tuán, the famous female *oriaté*, who was probably present at the initiation, as well as Tiburcia Sotolongo, both Gómez's neighbors. Tata Gaitán's godchild, Secundino Crucet Landa, was Gómez's Ifá godfather of the Hand of Orya(from a letter from Gómez to Radamés Corona, 21 October 1989, kindly shared with me by the latter). It remains unclear how widespread this early Ifá- and *babalawo*-centric practice was, or whether it was a kind of ceremony that was demanded in particular cases. In any case, very well known and accredited *santeros* and *babalawos* whose lives bridged the nineteenth and twentieth centuries are placed at the scene of such a practice: Mercedes del Monte, Tiburcia Sotolongo, La Tuán and Miguel Menocal (the second to last wife, and the last, probably a relation, of Bernabé Menocal), Secundino Crucet, and others.

Cabrera's "old" mid-twentieth-century sources told her that in Africa, *babalawos* had extraordinary input into Ocha initiation, including the shaving of the initiate's head, a practice retained in some Cuban Lucumí (as indicated), and in Havana Arará houses long after the shearing, shaving, and painting of the head became central to the *oriaté*'s task (Cabrera 1980, 184).

160. Luis Castillo told me, in conversations in 1985–86, that his late colleague Miguel Ángel Castillo (Oyekún Biroso) sent from Cuba, and brought out of Cuba in the Mariel exodus, information on many secret ceremonies.

Miguel Ramos says he gained awareness of ceremonies similar to the temple's distinctive *kariocha* model in the late 1970s. He heard rumors that a Miami *babalawo* purchased for twenty thousand dollars a set of "secret papers" from Havana's Miguel Febles when exiles were permitted to return to the island in 1978 and disseminated them to a very few *babalawo* groups in the United States upon his return—at a high price. According to Ramos, these papers distinguish between two Ocha initiatory models, the modern model, which either does or does not use the *babalawo*, called *sodoricha* (alternatively *sode-oricha*), and the *kariocha*, which grants extraordinary oracular authority and capacity to Orulą and the *babalawo* (phone interview with Miguel Ramos, 9 March 1995, and personal correspondence of 6 April 1995).

161. Ilé Tun Tun conducts its Ifá Reading of the opening of the Year in June, which the members believe coincides with the Yoruba Yam Festival in Ifẹ̀, Nigeria. Information on Ilé Tun Tun (also called Ilé Titún and Ilé Tum Tum) comes from an interview with its director, *babalawo* Fran Cabrera, 11 August 1999, Havana; and from *Ilé Tum Tum* 1997 (a newsletter; "Ilé Titún" is defined as "The New Sacred Homeland" after Ilé Ifẹ̀ in Nigeria); see also the organization's webpage: http://members.aol.com/iletuntun/index.html.

Víctor Betancourt's reversionist and traditionalizing practices are widely known among Havana *babalawos*.

162. A house in Vedado had not used *babalawos* in a generation or more, but, recently, when one of its Ocha godchildren was initiated in Ifá, the house began to use *babalawos* again, and house members began to receive the *mano de orula*.

CHAPTER FOUR

1. The proverb comes from the divination *odu* or *letra* called *Eyionle* (Elizondo [1934?] n.d., 9, 39). George Brandon first sought to explain the *asiento* via the throne metaphor, drawing on that same divination proverb: "As the king sits on a throne so does the newborn santero(a); as the head rules the body so is the orisha seated there in the head as the throne from which it rules the priestess" (Brandon 1983, 388).

2. In the temple's initiatory system, the particular "road" of the guardian angel is known, via Ifá divination, prior to the initiation. In most houses, this information is not known until the third day of the initiation period (see below).

3. All initiates except those of Yemayá and Changó also receive Oyá, along with the main group. Oyá is "hot" like Changó, and red can stand for all such "hot" or warrior types, *orichas* of "action," such as Eleguá and Ogún.

4. Obatalá's white cloth and birdlike forms are often combined with embroidered and painted representations of the *Santísimo Sacramento:* the Holy Sacrament, represented by the goblet and Host, the baroque forms of which radiate light.

5. *Iyawós* who make a number of other *orichas*—Agayú, Inle, Obba, Yewá—also wear royal iconography.

6. Interview with Nydia Pichardo, 26 March 1995.

7. "Closeness" invokes the discourse of Spiritism (*Espiritismo*, based on the teachings of Allen Kardec (see Kardec n.d.; and also Wafer 1991, 62, 85, 105, 106).

8. The Warriors' thrones of *yerba,* ideally made of specific fresh leaves associated with these *orichas,* are often made of pine, because it "lasts longer" (it does not turn brown during the seven-day initiation period). Obá Ecún (1985) instructs the use of *laurel, muralla,* or both leaves for Eleguá and Ogún's thrones (pp. 25, 54) and *almendra/o* for Ochosi (p. 78).

9. Clearly, other *orichas,* such as Changó, Oyá, and Agayú, and certain "roads" (*caminos*) of Obatalá and Yemayá have "hot," warlike qualities. Yet, as Miami *italero* Ernesto Pichardo argues, "warrior" in these cases (m. *guerreros* or f. *guerreras*) is adjectival not archetypal (warrior with a capital *W*): "The Warriors are *Warriors.* They don't belong to the royal extension. Changó possessed these qualities as a strategist in guiding war, but he's really seen as the Alafin ['king'], not the Warrior" (interview with Ernesto Pichardo, 24 May 1995).

10. The richest literary evocation of nineteenth-century themes of slavery and revolution, city and countryside, plantation, forest, and marronage (running away), and the Afro-Cuban religions is found in Miguel Barnet's "biography" of Esteban Montejo (Barnet [1966] 1980).

11. *El patio* can refer to the courtyard of a Spanish style dwelling or backyard space.

12. See J. Mason (1985a, 6–27).

13. Sacrifices are made to the Warrior in question in the *monte* (forest). The hot-blooded *jutía* (a large bush rodent with sharp teeth) is fed there to Echú and Ogún, followed by rum, toasted corn, smoked fish, smoked bushrat, cigar smoke, and candy, which are utilized to further appease the *oricha* in question and to cleanse the participants, who must leave any unwanted spiritual influences behind before they move on to the river. Prior to the river, however, Ogún, the strong *oricha* of iron, requires an additional ceremony: special sacrifices must be made to him at a "live" railway line (see Ecún 1985, 55; see also Brown 1999, 166–70). See Ecún (1985, 23–100) for variations between the initiations of Eleguá, Ogún, and Ochosi. Saint Lazarus's initiation appears to be the only other that has a major *monte* ceremony. Obá Ecún writes that this *oricha* cannot be "touched" with water. The initiate is brought to the river so Ochún can be "informed" of the proceedings, and offerings are made there, following a ceremony in the *monte.* The initiate is "taken out of the *monte*" covered in *cundiamor,* a plant sacred to Saint Lazarus (see Ecún 1985, 134–35).

14. "The honey neutralizes Elegba and Ogún so the better side of them comes out through the presence of Ochún," Ernesto Pichardo explains (interview with Ernesto Pichardo, 24 May 1995). This practice finds mythical justification in a well-known Lucumí *patakí* (legend). Ochún was the only one who could coax Ogún back out of the forest following Obatalá's curse upon him for the rape of Ogún's mother, Yemayá. Ochún seduced Ogún by smearing honey over his lips (see Rolando 1992).

15. The gourds contain the very foodstuffs and condiments that served to appease the Warriors in their *monte* ceremonies (African pepper [*pimienta guinea*], smoked fish and bushrat [*pescado ahumado* and *jutía ahumada*], toasted corn [*maíz tostado*], etc.). Eleguá's gourds are additionally filled with sweets [*caramelos*], of which this child-trickster is particularly fond (Ecún 1985, 25, 54; see also Mason and Edwards 1981, 34–35). Eleguá has three or seven gourds painted red and black, and Ogún has seven, painted green and black.

16. See Brown 1996 for a discussion of creativity and variation within these iconographic requirements.

17. Lourdes López's designs for Ogún, Ochosi, Obatalá, and Changó employ the same basic jacket style, but in green, mauve, white, and red satin respectively. Each is trimmed with broad metallic braid and, in cases, sequins, for brilliance and color contrast. Changó's tunic features sparkling rosettes of red and white rhinestones (*piedrecitas de boreales*) on the chest, each of which bears a cowrie in the center.

18. Each of the *orichas* claims a signature number, which, in some cases, corresponds to the oracular sign (*odu*) in *dilogún* div-

ination that the *oricha* dominates (e.g., for Ochún, five cowries; Changó, six cowries; Yemayá, seven cowries; Obatalá, eight cowries; Oyá and Agayú, nine cowries).

19. "I tried to make it look like the bottom of the sea, like buried treasure," she explained (interview with Lourdes López and her daughter Ana Vidal, 27 February 1987, West New York, N.J.).

20. Many houses omit the *pluma de loro* for the Warriors; they may substitute red and black rooster feathers for Eleguá and various others plumes for Ogún and Ochosi. Ernesto Pichardo, for example, uses three feathers for Eleguá: rooster, vulture, and African gray parrot; for him, only the first and last are appropriate to Ogún (interview with Ernesto Pichardo, 24 May 1995). Lourdes López gives Ogún a vulture feather and Ochosi a fuzzy pink ostrich plume.

21. "Hey hah, we are alive (because) Ṣàngó turns aside habitually to save the red parrot feather" (J. Mason 1994, 195). "When all else fails," John Mason glosses the song text, "invoke Ṣàngó; he is the savior of the babalórìṣà and ìyálóríṣà" (J. Mason 1994, 214 n. 15).

22. Interviews with Ernesto Pichardo, 24 May 1995, and with Nydia Pichardo, 26 March 1995, Miami, and from personal communication with *babaloricha* Adolfo Fernández, 1 May 1988, Union City, N.J.

23. For some, the feather is contrary to ritual logic. "You cannot do something that has already been done" (i.e., a king can only be crowned once; interview with Ernesto Pichardo, 24 May 1995). Accordingly, just before a 1988 Día del Medio presentation in New Jersey, the *oriaté*, Adolfo Fernández, removed the six *plumas de loro* that the seamstress had mistakenly sewn to this *oricha*'s pasteboard crown.

24. The story comes from the divination sign *ogbe oché* (*obeché;* interview with Miguel Ramos, 6 April 1995). At the same time, Changó receives, for example, special protection by virtue of the presence of his elder brother, Agayú—the embodiment of some of nature's hottest formations, the sun and the volcano. Nine wicks of palm-oil-soaked cotton are burned in a terracotta dish, on the floor, over a painted concentric *firma* of Agayú (see Ecún 1985, 195–96; Gleason 1992). One Havana priest explained the ceremony to Michael Mason in this way: "you need something as strong as Agayú to protect Changó from the jealousy that surrounds him because he is so special" (personal communication with Michael Atwood Mason, 30 May 1995).

25. *Yarey*, an Amerindian word, refers to the straw from an Antillean palm tree, which is abundant and much used in the Cuban countryside. Lourdes López referred to this *sombrero* as made of *yarey*, but it looks to be a commercially produced straw hat. The red parrot feathers are stuck into the bands of the Warriors' *sombreros.*

26. The cape undoubtedly protects this wily but "mild" outdoorsman from the elements; in contrast, the more physically powerful and brutish Ogún goes bare chested. The hunter's apron, as a recent exhibition of Yoruba beadwork and ritual accessories suggests, falls over the hunter's genitalia, acting as a charm to protect him from being cuckolded while away from home (Drewal and Mason 1998 [object exhibited at exhibition venue at the Museum for African Art, New York, but not included in their book]). It is not at all clear that the Lucumí apron follows directly from its Yoruba counterpart. Ecún insists that the apron should have two pockets. Depending upon the house, the apron is magically "loaded" with a "powder" (*afoché*) (Ofún Yemiló 1994, 4). The pockets undoubtedly permit the hunter quick access to the powder in order to capture and subdue his ususpecting prey.

27. Interview with Ernesto Pichardo, 24 May 1995. See, for example, the legend of the hunter called Oddé, from the *odu* Ellioco (two cowries; Elizondo [1934?] n.d., 17–18).

28. The Yoruba word *òde* literally means "outside" (Abraham 1946, 449).

29. From personal correspondence with Miguel Ramos, 6 April 1995. In Cuba, the bags are also called *apó* (see Cabrera [1970] 1983, 55). Yoruba *àpò*-Ifá, often of leather or cloth, may be adorned with cowries and representational beaded panels and are used by *babalawos* to transport divining equipment and as a surface for divination when they travel away from home to conduct consultations (see Bascom 1969a, 32 and plates 3, 4, 16).

30. See Ortiz [1951] 1985, 296–350, for an in-depth discussion of the "pantomime" of each *oricha*'s dance repertoire and how the *herramientas* are incorporated into each (see also M. Drewal 1989 for African and Brazilian examples).

31. As Thompson's account suggests, the air activated by the fans of Yemayá and Ochún is as easily a refreshing breeze as a carrier of disease, blight, and witchcraft (Thompson 1983, 73–74, 80). Yemayá can be a Warrior, and both Ochún and Yemayá, witches.

32. The late Obatalá priest Ramiro Hernández Almirall, master drummer, singer, dancer, and costume maker for the National Folklore Group of Cuba, referred to his ax-surmounted crenelated crown as "the Alafin de Oyó" (interview of 3 August 2000, Vedado, Havana).

33. I witnessed this efficient machete-and-*garabato* action while traveling through the Cuban countryside in June 1989.

34. One for the guardian angel; one for each of the four standard *orichas* acquired in the modern initiation (Obatalá, Yemayá, Changó, and Ochún); one for Oyá (except for initiates of Changó, Agayú, and Yemayá); and one for Eleguá, whose *mazo* represents the Warrior group. If Changó is made, Agayú is given also; when

Ochún is made, Agayú is often given. If the guardian angel is Ogún or Ochosi, an additional *mazo* is worn. The foregoing protocol is used by the houses of New Jersey's Templo Bonifacio Valdez. Houses vary in their use of *mazos*. The *collares de mazo* are worn by *iyawós*, in concert with the *ropa de santo*, on two occasions only: the afternoon of the Día del Medio and the "presentation to the drums" (*presentación al tambor*). On the latter occasion, at Templo Bonifacio Valdez, only two *collares de mazo* are worn (those of the guardian angel and the second *oricha* parent), as the full set of five to seven would greatly limit the *iyawó*'s ability to dance before the *batá* drums.

35. The order of placing the *mazos* in Melba Carillo's house is a variation on the fundamental sequence in which all ritual work is done: Eleguá, Obatalá, Oyá, Ochún, Yemayá, and Changó, with the sequence adjusted to culminate in the guardian angel in question. For example, the guardian angel Obatalá is taken out of the sequence and located at the end, in order that the protocol's trajectory culminate in him.

36. Correspondence and discussions with bead makers Terri-Dawn Trosclair of Los Angeles and Gloria of Botánica El Tumí in the Bronx, April to November 2000, and "Papo" Reinaldo Raimundo Chaguayceda, Regla, Havana, August 2000.

37. The terms *moña* and *moña principal* were taught to me by bead worker and Obatalá priestess Melba Carillo of New York. Others might pronounce it *moño*.

38. Ayáguna, a "warrior" road of the pure white Obatalá archetype, takes the red beads of Changó to indicate his connection to the hotter domain of youth, action, struggle, and war. He rides a white horse and carries a sword. Yekú-Yekú is a very old, gentle road of Obatalá, whose beads are dominated by white. In contrast, a *mazo* for another road of Obatalá, Obámoro, would use purple in place of red, an motif arguably borrowed from Jesus of Nazareth, with whom he is associated. In contrast, a *mazo* for Yemayá would employ strands, bunches, and *moñas* patterns of seven and its multiples, counterpointing opaque or transluscent blue beads (e.g., Prussian blue or aquamarine) with beads that are opaque white, a soapy white (*jabón*), or clear/colorless (*agua*). Depending upon the road, these may be punctuated by red or coral; Changó's *mazo* employs six and its multiples in red and white beads; Oyá's employs nine and its multiples in brown or more caramel beads (*matipó*), along with a *matipó* bead with black and white stripes; Eleguá's red and black bead pattern uses multiples of three; Ogún uses alternating green and black (1x1 or 3x3), though he can take seven *moñas;* Ochosi uses seven and its multiples, alternating, for example, amber and prussian blue, punctuated by red and black; though Cubans tend to alternate orange and a royal blue.

39. Three pounds is an approximated sum from my picking up of several examples and comparing them with the weight of my three-pound camera. The number twelve-thousand comes from a study of one example in which I counted its constitutent beads. It actually had 12,615 beads. *Mazos* are lighter if fewer strands are used and if plastic *gloria* beads dominate; they are heavier if crystal and metal *glorias,* not to mention more strands, are used. *Mazos* sold in *botánicas* are usually of cheaper quality, since fine materials are expensive and would price the work out of the market. Nevertheless, people are apparently willing to pay around $175 for plastic-dominated, unprepossessing or tacky *mazos*.

40. From my experience as a bead maker at four bead shops in New York's Garment District (Thirty-seventh Street, between Fifth and Sixth Avenues), as well as Soho's Leekan Designs, on Mercer Street near the corner of Spring.

41. Personal correspondence with Miguel Ramos, 11 April 1995. Cowries historically served as money in West Africa, were integral to ritual payments included in sacrificial exchanges with the deities among the Yoruba, and served as divination instruments (Bascom 1980, passim).

42. A priest takes a *mazo* from the altar or throne and, using the element of surprise, drops it over the body of the prospective initiate. Upon receiving divination results that decisively identify the *oricha* "owner" of the head (*dueño de la cabeza*) and the necessity of "making *santo*," the person being read in the divination might find himself or herself suddenly snared with a *mazo* by his or her *padrino* or *madrina*, who is acting on the *santo*'s behalf.

43. Telephone interview with Miguel Ramos, 6 April 1995. Chango's influence and protection is reiterated in the bunch of large *plátanos verdes* that may hang over the threshold of the initiation room (as an *ebó*) if need be.

44. Mortars are between nineteen and twenty inches tall—the height of the seat of a standard straight-backed chair, and are ten or so inches in diameter. In other words, the mortars used for initiation purposes are ergonomically geared to support the body in a sitting position with the feet flat on the floor.

45. That Ochosi sits on "stone" is contradicted by Obá Ecún (1985, 78) and by most other accounts (see n. 47). The use of initiatory chairs (*sillas*) for the female *orichas* and Obatalá represents an intriguing alternative tradition to the *pilón* (mortar) and the *piedra* (stone). According to Miguel Ramos, "some houses use the *pilón* for the masculine Orishas, and a chair for the females. The chair [like the *pilón*] is consecrated. It can be extended to Obatalá because of his/her [gender] duality" (Obatalá has eight male and eight female roads; personal correspondence with Miguel Ramos, 29 March 1995). In another variation, according to Ernesto Pichardo, female *orichas* may be initiated in the *asiento* upon Changó's *pilón* but are formally presented on chairs on the Día del Medio (interview of 24 May 1995). The female

oricha called Obba, as it is done in one New York house, is initiated upon a bamboo stool.

46. Interview with Ernesto Pichardo, 24 May 1995.

47. Cabrera represents an informant as telling her that Ochosi takes a stone (Cabrera [1974] 1980, 162), though no sources I have polled agree with her. Ochosi's stool "must be a trunk" of the almond tree (interview with Nydia Pichardo, 27 March 1995). Miguel Ramos also specifies that the trunk of an almond tree is used (personal correspondence, 26 March 1995). Cabrera does report, in another work (1980, 184), that Ochosi takes the trunk of an almond tree (*almendro*).

48. Miguel Ramos reports that the trunk of the *guayaba* (Guava) tree can be used for Eleguá (telephone interview of 6 March 1995).

49. Personal correspondence with Miguel Ramos, 29 March 1995.

50. Telephone interview with Ernesto Pichardo, 24 May 1995. In order to be consecrated (not at every initiation, but when it is used in a Changó initiation) "The *pilón* gets washed like an *oricha*, then later it is painted. . . . It's fed turtle, quail, rooster." Cabrera's informants gave a similar explanation (Cabrera [1974] 1980, 162) and they insisted that the consecration of Changó's mortar be performed by a priest of Changó (*omó-Changó*, 163).

51. That the *pilón* is considered a "throne" was indicated to me by Miguel Ramos in personal correspondence, 29 March 1995.

52. I am grateful to J. Lorand Matory's notion of "iconopraxis," which he coins to refer to structuring principles that constitute the expressive "template" of ritual and the experience of the initiate and provide an enduring model for structuring social relations over time (see Matory 1994, 4, 220). In the terms of Pierre Bourdieu (1977), the *pilón* is integral to the initiatory *habitus*.

53. Personal correspondence with Miguel Ramos, 29 March 1995.

54. The presentation of *iyawós* to the drums can, and, in Cuba used to, occur often after the Itá is completed on the third day. My presentation took place after the visit to the Plaza on the seventh day, though many *iyawós* must wait longer. The ceremony authorizes—via Añá, the *oricha* of the sacred drums—full participation in the religious community (some insist that one must be presented to the same drum *fundamento* that was used for the house's elders). *Iyawós* emerge solemnly in a formal procession headed by a praise singer (*akpwón*), ritually prostrate themselves before the *iyá*, the "mother" of the three *batá*, and then touch their heads to each of the drums, depositing a tribute of money to Añá. Dressed in *ropa de santo* or white, depending upon the house, the *iyawó* must salute the initiating godparent and then dances in the center of a circle of priests, wherein he or she might be possessed, and finally is whisked out of the room.

55. The Yoruba Dàda is seen to be male (Abraham 1946, 121) or female (Gleason 1987, 88–95), whereas the Cuban Lucumí Dadá (spelled differently) is female (see Angarica [1955?] n.d., 46–49). The crown of Dadá owned by Adolfo Fernández (see plate 9) of Union City, New Jersey, was constructed and displayed in the following manner. The crown itself is composed of alternated concentric rings of cowries and beads encrusting a half gourd the size of Fernández's head. Its surface design features four bands of cowries that alternate with four bands composed of bead strands. From the widest band at the edge to the center, the pattern is: (1) cowries, (2) four rows of red and white bead strands in the pattern two white–four red–two white–four red, (3) five rows of red and white bead strands in the pattern two white–two red–two white–two red, (4) cowries, (5) four rows of red and white bead strands in the pattern two white–four red–two white–four red, (6) cowries, (7) four rows of red and white bead strands in the pattern two white–four red–two white–four red, and, finally, (8) a single cowrie at its zenith. Each of twelve fringes (*ese*, "legs") descending from the rim of the gourd is composed of bead strands consists of twelve cowries separated by units of red and white beads in the pattern two red–two white–two red–two white–two red–two white–two red–two white—twelve units in all. When displayed, the crown descends from the ceiling on a double strand of red and white beads in the pattern red red–white white–red red–white white, and so on. Near the crown itself, each strand has two cowries separated by a strand of sixteen beads: that is, one strand of sixteen beads—cowrie—two red–two white–two red–two white–two red–two white—cowrie—two red–two white–two red–two white–two red–two white—crown.

56. In Lucumí, *igüoro* is spelled, alternately, *iworo*, which is close to the Yoruba generic term for priest (*àwòrò*; Abraham 1946, 80). I was told by priests in New Jersey and New York that Dadá is received after a priest has received all the other Lucumí *orichas*.

57. Taking a cue from my reading of Cabrera (Brown 1989, 387; Cabrera [1974] 1980, 162), Matory cites the Cuban Lucumí contrast of Changó's mortar and Ogún's stone to demonstrate the continuity of a fundamentally Yoruba binary Ṣàngó/Ògún model in the New World (Matory 1994, 228). The basis of Matory's Ṣàngó/Ògún distinction in the Ọ̀yọ́ region depends on the critical relation of gendered iconography and possession practice. For Matory, Ògún's anvils and iron and his all-male hunter cult resist the metaphors of "penetration" and "mounting" (*gùn*), which are, by contrast, characteristic of the female priesthoods of Ṣàngó worship, whose shrines are filled with "hollow" vessels and mortars. In Ọ̀yọ́, Ògún does not possess—mount, penetrate,

and "feminize" his all-male worshippers. However, in Cuba, Ogún is seen as one of the "greatest *montadores*"; he regularly and very powerfully possesses some of his priests. In this sense, Lucumí possession practice, like other ritual practices, does not necessarily reflect Yoruba distinctions, but operates on the basis of Cuban developments.

58. These differences and similarities were discussed in my telephone interview with Miguel Ramos, 6 April 1995.

59. Telephone interview with Nydia Pichardo, 26 March 1995. Miguel Ramos reports that "some houses employ *saco* for initiation [of the Warriors]. . . . Others initiate in white" (personal correspondence with Miguel Ramos, 29 March 1995). At the double Middle Day I attended in Guanabacoa in August 2000, the *iyawós* of Ogún and Eleguá had worn *saco* during the previous day's *asiento.*

The initiates of the Warriors, regardless of gender, wear shirt-and-pants outfits. Presumably, these unequivocally male *orichas,* whose *iyawós* wear the animal skin side bags and carry *garabatos* or machetes as they sit upon the rough stone under the *trono del patio,* prefer not to "arrive" in dresses. The Museum of Regla collection contains a charming early-twentieth-century child's *initiation* outfit made entirely of *saco de yute* (see fig. 4.26).

60. Beyond the color white's reference to Obatalá, the *orí,* and spiritual associations with "purity," it is possible that the white clothes of the *iyawó*'s first year have picked up associations with the sanitary customs of medical practice—particularly in the context of childbirth—and with white's association with the purity of a woman's bridal status. However, this may be a relatively recent practice. Priests in Havana (Jesús Varona) and Matanzas (Osvaldo Cárdenas Villamil) relate that decades ago, *iyawós* in many houses wore their *oricha*'s gingham outfits for the year when they went out on the street, not white (personal communication with Osvaldo Cárdenas Villamil and Jesús Varona, summer 1998).

61. In Melba Carillo's house, as the normal (not the ritual) breakfast and lunch are taken in this outfit, she sometimes refers to it as the *traje del desayuno* (breakfast outfit).

Nydia Pichardo of Miami relates that, in her house, *iyawós* take breakfast in their white pajamas, bathe, and then are dressed in the *traje de almuerzo* by 9:30 A.M. They take lunch in the late morning. Before their light breakfast, all *iyawós* are given their "African breakfast" (a square of coconut and other ingredients, along with a drink of the *omiero,* a composite of the *osains,* the sacred herbal liquids of the *asiento;* telephone interview with Nydia Pichardo, 26 March 1995; see also Cabrera [1974] 1980, 156–58, 175).

62. Gingham (*guinga*), an industrially made, yarn-dyed cotton in a plain weave, was imported into Cuba along with many other types of cloth from England during the nineteenth century. Checks and prints first made in India and other British colonies were, by the nineteenth century, beginning to be mass-produced in England and shipped increasingly throughout the world: first to Africa and then the countries of the Caribbean and Latin America. Nineteenth-century British commercial export shipping lists do not list "gingham" specifically but refer to various "checked" fabrics (personal communications in spring 1998 with anthropologist and archaeologist Jean Howson, who researched exports of cloth and ceramics to the Caribbean in the nineteenth-century British parliamentary records).

63. Those *orichas* whose colors include white, such as Changó and Yemayá, have their alternating bead pattern represented in this mass-produced cloth medium. Ochún takes yellow and white gingham; Ogún may take green and white gingham; and Eleguá, whose bead colors are black and red, may take black and white gingham (presumably so as not to confuse him with Changó; Obá Ecún 1985, 44). However, New Jersey designer Lourdes López was lucky enough to find a green and black checked gingham for a *traje de almuerzo* she made for Ogún. The *traje de almuerzo* for Obatalá is, of course, all white (a white blouse and skirt for women, a slightly elaborated shirt or blouse and dress pants for men.

64. The Warriors' lunch outfits are distinguished along gender lines. In most houses, it seems, for every *oricha* but the Warriors, the *traje de almuerzo* is worn according to the gender of the initiate, not the *oricha.* Male initiates wear shirt-and-pants outfits and female initiates wear a gingham dress. Thus, while female initiates of Changó wear red and white dresses of gingham, female initiates of the Warriors dress like their male counterparts: a shirt of gingham and pants of *saco de yute.*

65. Miguel Ramos suggested to me that slaves may have constructed their daily attire of agricultural shipping bags and sacks (telephone interview with Miguel Ramos, 6 April 1995). *Saco* also became the typical clothing in religious representations of spirits of the old, strong Africans, sometimes called *carabelas* or *africanos/africanas,* who were brought across the sea in the Middle Passage to work the plantations (see Ortiz 1924, 103–4; [1923] 1983, 124–25; Brown 1993a, 64–65). Yet not only plantation workers, but also urban dockworkers had, and still have, daily contact with agricultural shipping bags of *yute. Saco de yute* was and continues to be used for the conical hoods of the *íreme* masquerade costumes of the men's Abakuá Society, which dominated wharf labor from the second half of the nineteenth century through 1942 in the port cities of Havana, Matanzas, and Cárdenas (see Castellanos 1928, 30–32; López Valdés 1985b). The masquerade costumes themselves are called *sacos.* Finally, the *traje de almuerzo* of Babalú Ayé/Saint Lazarus's is made entirely of *saco de yute.*

66. In Yorubaland, it is the *òṣù*, "ball of medicine" (Matory 1994, 178, and see Drewal 1992, 182). In Brazil, it is a "cone" borne on the head (Omari 1984, 18)

67. The head *orichas* of the *oriaté*, each of the *levantados*, the *oyubona*, and the *padrino* or *madrina* have been paid a ritual tribute (*derecho* or *acheddín*) to authorize their human representatives' participation in the ceremonies of Ocha (see Cabrera [1970] 1983, 26; Brown 1989, 193–94, 271; González Huguet 1968, 57).

68. "Putting forth their *aché*" refers to the fact that they are working on behalf of their "heads"—their respective *orichas*—whose *aché* is seated in the bodies of their priests.

69. *Fín* in Yoruba can mean "to inscribe" or "to carve patterns on a calabash" (Abraham 1946, 214). The phrase *ó fín wìn:nin'-wìn:nin'* and *ó fín kàlá-kìní* both mean "it is variegated: it is multicolored." Much of this phrasing is found, in modified form, in the Lucumí chant (which does vary from house to house—see Brandon's version below) that accompanies the painting of the head: "Fin fín Okán kini kini dekún. . . . Fin fín Okán wi ni ki Eleguá" (transcribed in Cabrera [1974] 1980, 161).

70. The photographs and drawings of Yoruba and Brazilian practices cited here, along with Cabrera's photograph of an *iyawó* (see fig. 4.29), show Brazil and Cuba to emphasize spots, and the Yoruba to emphasize allover linear marks, forming geometric shapes within which spots are placed—all of which is applied over a base of white.

71. Brandon speculates that the act of painting, *fin fin okán osú*, "empowers the yawo with the attributes of the leopard [*ẹkùn* in Yoruba, *ekún* in Lucumí] and brings about an identification of the [i]yawo with the leopard, a traditional representative of kingship (Lucas 1948, 156–57). The Fin Fin Okan makes the yawo, his godparents, and Eleggua all kings."

Fin Fin Okan kini kini dekun.
Iya dekun.
Ba[ba?] *dekun loni o.*
Fin Fin Okan winikin dekun.
Bara dekun loni o.

The engraving of one changes one to a leopard.
Mother changes to a leopard.
Father changes to a leopard today.
The many lines of the leopard are engraved one by one.
Eleggua becomes a leopard today
(Brandon 1983, 398–99)

72. Telephone interview with Miguel Ramos, 6 April 1995.

73. Telephone interview with Miguel Ramos, 6 April 1995.

74. Telephone interview with Ernesto Pichardo, 24 May 1995. In this interpretation, the scalloped or diamond designs are painted versions of a beaded African fringe. In Cuba, as is evident, they descend from westernized pasteboard crowns rather than from conical Yoruba beaded crowns. In the Brazilian Candomblé, the westernized metal crowns of many of the *orixás* in fact feature a curtain of bead strands over the forehead (see Verger 1957, fig. 117; Carybé 1980, 161, 163, 173, 174, 175, 178, 181, 187, 188). They also appear in scalloped form (Galembo 1993, 127, 155).

75. Children of Inle are initiated via the mediation of Yemayá, and children of Obba are initiated via the mediation of Ochún (see chap. 3 and below).

76. I have seen such marks painted on the legs of initiates of Eleguá, Changó, and Agayú. Brandon notes "hashmarks" but does not explain their significance (Brandon 1983, 405–6).

77. The Warriors, as well as Agayú and Changó are unequivocally male, though some say that female representations of Changó, beyond Santa Bárbara, exist. Obatalá has eight male roads and eight female roads.

78. Telephone interview with Nydia Pichardo, 26 March 1995.

79. In Bahia, it seems to vary by the house and priest. Sometimes the deity's gender is emphasized, and sometimes the gender of the priest is emphasized. In my visits to the Bahian *terriero* of Lidio on the Bahian island of Itaparica in 1988, I observed male priests of the female deities, such as Yansam (Oya) and Oxum, in dresses. Phyllis Galembo (1993) documents a priestess of the male Xangô in jacket and pants (terriero Sao Joao Batista in Recife, p.130); meanwhile, Naomi Katz documented male priests for Xangô both in pants and in dresses among *terrieros* in Cachoeira in the interior of Bahia (field photographs shared with me, 1991). Carybé depicts priestesses of Xangô in dresses and priests of Xangô in pants (1980, 131, 133), while he depicts male priests of the male Oxossi in dresses (p. 65), as did Galembo (1993, 141). Galembo documents a female priestess of the male Ogum in a dress (144); one male priest of Oxum is seen in a dress (157), and another male priest of Oxum is seen in pants (159).

80. Interview with Melba Carillo, 6 May 1990.

81. At this point, Obá Ecún writes, the *iyawó* "can now receive visits" (1985, 45). However, Miguel Ramos disagrees with this practice, though he seems to be in the minority. In Miguel Ramos's view, the hiding of the repainted *osu* with cloth during the morning is symptomatic of the larger aura of guardedness that has descended upon the Día del Medio in the United States. He insists that in Cuba the heterogeneous public is permitted into the room as soon as the *iyawó* is dressed in the *traje de almuerzo*. This day is the "only day that people are permitted to see *orí*. . . . People are allowed into *igbodú* before twelve noon, although there are a lot of taboos being born every day. People could view the *iyawó* with the *traje de almuerzo* in Cuba and the head would be bare" (interview with Miguel Ramos, 6 April 1995). However, priests in Miami and Havana reported to me that they follow the

tradition that the *iyawó*'s head should always be covered and no one is allowed into the room until twelve o'clock noon. In my initiation, my head remained uncovered until about 1:00 P.M., yet only priests could enter the room. An uninitiated friend of mine who entered before the curtain was raised was asked to leave.

82. Interview with Melba Carillo, 4 April 1995.

83. Interviews with Miguel Ramos, 6 April 1995.

84. At "high noon. . . . Olorún [God; Owner of the Sky] is at full manifestation: he's the principal witness to the initiation" (telephone interview with Miguel Ramos, 6 April 1995). In contrast, Ernesto Pichardo points out that the standard moment for God (i.e., the Sky, Olorún) to "witness" the *orí* of the *iyawó* is the sixth day: "The only point in which you uncover and present the head to Olorún is on the sixth day. Just before the Day of the Plaza, you take the *iyawó* out at noon and present him to Olorun for the first time" (telephone interview with Ernesto Pichardo, 21 January 1997).

85. These tributes (*derechos*) come in the form of marked sums of money, figured according to the *orichas'* signature numbers. Obatalá get sums in multiples of $8.00, Yemayá in multiples of $7.00, Changó in multiples of $6.00, Ochún in multiples of $5.00, and so on.

86. The *moforibale* gesture invokes the two overlapping dimensions of the *orí: orí* as the locus of a "seated" *oricha* and *orí* as the maturing head of spiritual eldership. In the first movement of reciprocated salutations, visiting initiated priests put their *orí* to the ground to salute the *oricha* crowned on the head of the *iyawó*. In the second movement, the newly born *iyawó* not only salutes the *oricha* crowned on the head of the visiting elder priest, but also recognizes the seniority of the elder's *orí* (see M. Mason 1994).

87. This ancient Yoruba gesture is known in Spanish as *tirarse al suelo al pie del santo* (throwing oneself to the floor at the feet of the *santo* or *oricha*). Burgess-Polcyn (1986) writes: "The raising is a blessing which elevates, strengthens, and honors the junior . . . a sign of ritual recognition: symbolically conveying, affirming and supporting membership in a relationship." Priests of male *orichas* make their *moforibale* as a prone submission to the floor, forehead to the mat, hands at their sides, palms up. Priests of female *orichas* go to the floor in a gesture that has two phases: first, they lie on the left side, knees slightly flexed, left hand supporting the head, right hand upon the hip with elbow pointing to the ceiling; then, they turn over to the right side and mirror the first set of movements. While on the floor, priests deposit their *derechos* in the *jícara*, sometimes combined with the Christian gesture of crossing themselves and kissing their flexed hand, which holds the *derecho*. The eldest visitors "pick themselves up" and receive the *iyawó*'s salutation, and then, in "picking up" the *iyawó*, the elder bends, touches the *iyawó*'s back with extended fingers several times—first with the arms extended straight, then with arms crossed over one another, and then with arms extended straight again. The elder then grasps the prostrated *iyawó* at the collarbones and lifts the *iyawó* to resume the standing position. Once again the two come into contact with arms across their respective torsos. The blessing and support received by the junior in this cycle of reciprocal salutation is initiated by the intoned words of the elder, who says, in a version recorded by Lydia Cabrera: *awá wantó* [name of the *oricha*, e.g., Obatalá] *bé odidé* (Cabrera [1974] 1980, 177). "By paying homage," Ramos explains, "the junior receives the blessings of the [elder] priest, who asks the tutelary Orishas of both [persons] to bless the [junior]" (personal correspondence with Miguel Ramos, 19 July 1995). Michael Mason learned the blessing as *awá wadó* [e.g., *Changó*] *sodidé* (*odidé* means "stand") (personal communication, 7 November 1996).

88. The reciprocated salutations across the throne's threshold—between visiting priests and *iyawós*—represent one of several appropriate occasions for the *moforibale* gesture. The relative emphasis on *oricha*, eldership, and mutual support (picking up) in these several *moforibale* contexts varies. Priests *moforibale* before several kinds of consecrated sites: (1) *orichas* enshrined in their private domestic altars or formally presented on drumming and birthday thrones, (2) the bodies of priests possessed by *orichas* during drumming events, (3) the set of three sacred *batá* drums (*batá de fundamento*), and (4) elder heads encountered in any given ritual context.

89. Such deceptions have, in fact, occurred, and they are regarded as extreme profanations. The New York Cuban priestess of Oyá, Margot Torres, was "deceived"—through a terribly shoddy initiation by impostors in order to take her money, she claims (personal communication with Michael Mason, 10 October 1996).

CHAPTER FIVE

1. Lydia Cabrera was born in Havana on 20 May 1900; she studied, worked, and wrote there until 1927, when she traveled to Paris to paint. She was photographed with Oddedeí in Pogolotti, Marianao, Havana, in 1930, upon her brief return to Cuba from Europe that year, although her first research encounters with practioners had actually been in 1928 while on an earlier brief vacation in Havana. In 1938 she returned permanently from Paris and moved into the Quinta San José, an abandoned eighteenth-century colonial mansion, which she and her companion restored—the project apparently lasted through 1941. The Marianao mansion was relatively close to the poor *barrio* of Pogolotti, where Oddedeí lived. According to a recent chronol-

ogy, in 1942 Cabrera recommenced her research into Afro-Cuban religions, working intensively through the 1950s; in 1954 she published *El Monte* (see Cabrera [1954] 1983), significant parts of which had appeared in earlier pieces (e.g., Cabrera [1947] 1994). In short, despite two earlier, brief fieldwork experiences, the intensive Havana fieldwork that lead to her major ethnographies lasted from 1942 to 1958, when she published on the Abakuá society (for the source of the above chronology, see Intar Gallery 1984, 14–15; Cabrera [1958] 1970). She left Cuba in 1960 for Miami, where she began to publish works based on prior fieldwork (e.g., Cabrera [1974] 1980, 1980).

2. I hypothesize that Oddedeí's explanation came in the context of a Día del Medio because the footnote in which these quotes are found elaborates upon the passage in which she discusses the women taking her to such a ceremony (Cabrera [1954] 1983, 26–27). Still, Cabrera more concretely ties this ritual occasion to her first meeting of Oddedeí in an article she wrote later (see [1947] 1994, 278–79), suggesting that this occasion took place around 1930, the year she is supposed to have met Oddedeí (see previous note).

3. For perhaps the most influential contemporary use of "chronotope," see Bakhtin (1981, 84–85). Though I had not read Maxine Kamari Clarke's dissertation at the time of my use of this term, I was grateful to see her similar use of it in the case of the Black American Yoruba Movement's Oyotunji Village. Drawing on literary theory and recent cultural studies (e.g., Bakhtin 1981; and Gilroy 1993), Clarke shows how Oyotunji Villagers used particular chronotopic (spatiotemporal) narratives to reconstruct their collective history, most notably their genealogies of "belonging" and "nobility," through which Oyotunji Village is imagined as the rebirth of the Ọ̀yọ́ kingdom (Clarke 1997, 4–5 and chap. 1).

4. The "Angola" chronotope derives from my years of experience with Mestre João Grande in his Capoeira academy in New York. The Mestre traveled throughout Africa in the 1960s to perform, and he sings about these experiences, though songs referring to "passing through Congo and arriving in Angola" also conjoin verses referring to the *roda* itself, for example, chorus: "Vou-m'mbora, vou-m'mbora, vou-m'mbora pra Angola" / solo: "Berimbau 'ta me chamando / vamos logo e vadiar" [I'm leaving for Angola. . . . The *berimbau* is calling me, lets play [Capoeira] now].

5. The long, tapered, modular cap looks like the French/Belgian military *bonnet de police*, which is as old as the Napoleonic wars (see Arnoldi and Kreamer 1995, 17). *Fìlà* means "cap of any kind" (Abraham 1946, 213). Given the configuration of six cowries in the form of an abstract double axe (for Changó), I take the outfit to be red satin and the *mazos* to be red and white.

6. Presentations to the drums may occur closer in time to or long after the *asiento*. There is a strong tradition of presenting *iyawós* on the third day, the Day of the Itá, when the throne is still mounted. When presentations occur on the occasion of a drumming to an *oricha*, the *iyawós* waiting to be presented congregate, are changed into their *ropa de santo* outfits, and rest in the throne room. Some *iyawós* are presented in white to the drums, rather than in the *ropa de santo*.

7. José Miguel Gómez Barberas reports that he introduced *babalawos* Eulogio Rodríguez Gaitán ("Tata Gaitán," Ogunda Fún) and Guillermo Castro (Obeché) to Fernando Ortiz (probably in the late 1930s or early 1940s), and that they used information he made accessible to them (see chap. 3).

8. *Omocolabá*, according to some, is the highest title *babalawos* receive (Angarica [1955?] n.d., 14; Brandon 1983, 512), though others use the term *obacolabá* (from my fieldwork with Cuban *babalawos*, summer 2000). The *obacolabá* also refers to a power (*poder*) that *babalawos* who are priests of Changó receive. The title, if translated via the Yoruba, means, roughly, "king of the beaded epaulettes" (*ọba-ìkọ̀làbà;* Abraham 1946, 298, 498; Abiodun 1975)—which suggests the kinds of honorific beaded regalia worn by Yoruba kings (see Drewal and Mason 1998). Women who receive the *mano de orula* (*kofá* or *ikofafún*) are authorized to act as *apetebí*, the revered female assistants of Orula and the drum spirit, Añá.

9. A *tambor* is a "drumming." At New Jersey's Templo Bonifacio Valdez, the temple's *bandera* bearing the colors of this institution's patron, Orula, as well as images of the three *batá* drums owned by the temple, flies over all drum celebrations. In Cuba, for example, the town of Regla's Conjunto de San Francisco and Conjunto San Cristóbal fly fringed *banderas* bearing the images of their patrons; the banner of the Cabildo of Santa Teresa flies over drummings given there in Matanzas (see plate 4; from my fieldwork there in August 1989).

10. For discussions of "traditionalization," see Kirshenblatt-Gimblett 1983, 208–22; and Schoemaker 1994.

11. My first introduction to the relation of crowns to the "royal" lineage of saints derives from discussions with my former Emory colleague, Rennaisance specialist John Howett, in April 1995; this idea is confirmed in Apostolos-Cappadona 1994, 90–91).

12. Obatalá (the Virgin of Mercy), Yemayá (the Virgin of Regla), Changó (Santa Bárbara), and Ochún (the Virgin of Charity of Cobre). Oyá is associated with Our Lady of Candlemas, although she is also associated with Santa Teresa, who does not wear a crown; Naná Burukú is associated with Our Lady of Carmen, and Dadá with Our Lady of the Rosary.

13. Errol Hill, describing early-twentieth-century Trinidad

Calypso competition during carnival, writes that the Calypsonian would "sometimes . . . be a king of the band and would lead his subjects, like a medieval prince of war, to engage rival bands." They would often be attired in courtier-style garments; the status of competitors and the nicknames or titles given them has continued through the present (Hill 1972, 64).

14. In the United States, we have the Duke (Duke Ellington), the Count (Count Basie); the Empress (Bessie Smith); the King (King Oliver, and the King of Jazz [Benny Goodman]), the Pres[ident] (Lester Young), the Judge (Milt Hinton), and so on.

15. The set of *herramientas* for Yemayá that I purchased in a *botánica* in Carrol City in North Miami, consists of stereotyped nautical and cosmological icons in cast lead: a set of two oars (*remos*) and seven smaller low-relief forms: the sun, a half moon, a ship's wheel, an anchor, a life preserver, a skeleton key, and a mermaid (see also J. Mason 1996, plates 80 and 81, for an identical set, though belonging to Olokun). For Obá Ecún, who likes to assign specific, pithy significations to symbols (though others do not), the ship's wheel (*timón de barco*) signifies Yemayá's quality as the "good mother . . . who seeks to carry human beings over the right road"; the pair of oars "signifies the balance of good and bad that we make in this life"; the mermaid (*sirena*) "represents [Yemayá's] mysterious beauty . . . because she is . . . the Absolute Queen"; the full moon signifies the fertility of Yemayá (he does not include a half-moon in his set; Ecún 1985, 298). The two little brass oars, which go inside the *sopera* of Ochún, are also central to the iconography of her counterpart, the La Virgin de la Caridad del Cobre: three sailors, called the "Three Johns" (*Los Tres Juanes*) navigate a rowboat in the stormy Bay of Nipe in eastern Cuba, where this saint's church is located (Cabrera [1974] 1980, chaps. 1, 3).

16. For example, using the Gramscian hegemony model, Eugene Genovese argues that "acceptance," as well as forms of resistance, characterized Afro-American life under slavery (Genovese 1976, 4–7, 25–49). Though Genovese was heavily criticized unfairly in the politically charged 1970s for his "accommodation" model, its Gramscian basis makes it consistent with Jean Comaroff's notion that signifying practices perpetuate as much as resist.

17. Personal communication with Luis Alberto Pedroso, 12 June 1998; Pedroso participated in the accession of of the objects to the museum and mounted them in a permanent exhibition in the museum's salon within the Regla church compound.

18. One of Cabrera's sources told her that "'all the children of [Ochún] like the men of other women.' She is the quintessence of coquetry, of grace, of fawning, cajoling, insinuating, and captivating . . . the true reflection of the uniquely Cuban *mulata de rumbo*, the inspiring . . . *mulata* of colonial times . . . the *mulata fina* . . . Oshún Yeyé Carí, idealization of the beatiful mixed-race person, of a certain lower class (*baja*) generally, happy and charming, but with the arrogance . . . of a proud sovereign." Another source described her as *la santa puta* (the whorish saint; Cabrera [1954] 1983, 37, 86).

19. The archetypal Cuban *mulata* entered the literature as early as the first versions of Cirilio Villaverde's *Cecilia Valdés* in 1839 but was most fully developed in the first complete printing of Villaverde's novel in 1882, a year after Landaluze's depiction of the *mulata de rumbo* in his famous *Tipos y costumbres de la isla de Cuba* (1881). *Mulatas* also appeared with frequency in the commercial *marquillas cigarreras* of the nineteenth century (see Kutzinski 1993, chaps. 1, 3). *De rumbo* (literally "of the route" or "the way") characterizes this *mulata* as a fixture of "the street"—an interzone of social intercourse, including interracial meeting, petty trade, and what Fernando Ortiz would later term delinquency (see chap. 1). As noted, Cabrera's informants in the 1950s referred to Ochún as *la dueña del oro* ("the owner of gold") and *la santa puta* (Cabrera [1954] 1983, 85–86), "the whorish saint." The latter term, is, of course, an oxymoron in Christian terms, but remains appropriate to the complex Cuban, Afro-Cuban ethos (which might be seen as a Diaspora-wide phenomenon) in which seduction can be a strategy for negotiation and survival. For example, Karen Brown explicates Vodoun priestess Mama Lola's prostitution ("selling her land") as a survival tool, which Brown locates in the symbolic domain of the beautiful, vain, light-skinned Ezili Freda, Ochún's Haitian equivalent (K. Brown 1991). John Mason refers to this transatlantic and diasporic goddess in one facet as "a prostitute in the sense that she does and gives favors for sex" (Mason 1985a, 76). The *mulata* in Cuban cultural conception, and arts and letters, mediated the experience of culture and race mixing (*mestizaje*) and became an icon for the creolized and indigenous core of the modern nation born of colonialism and the slave trade but that intended to distinguish itself from Europe and, officially, would be a harmonious racial democracy.

20. Roche y Monteagudo's descriptions of the Santa Bárbara altar, identical in the 1908 and 1925 editions, apply precisely to the photograph he published in the 1925 edition, which carries the same text (p. 182). His photograph of the "witchcraft tabernacle" in the 1908 edition (p. 79) is identical in formal structure to the 1925 edition but is placed differently, near a window, and employs different cloth. I deduce that both photographs are from the same early period. A single "black jockey"–like figure is present in the 1908 photograph. The same kind of figure, along with another of similar size, is present in the 1925 photograph. That Wright and Roche visited the same El Cerro house is suggested by the fact that they both describe an altar for Santa Bárbara, as

well as altars to Our Lady of Mercy and Our Lady of Charity—in addition to Wright's observation of the "jockey" figure. Roche y Monteagudo correctly identifies the three altars as dedicated to Changó, Obatalá, and Ochún, respectively (Roche y Monteagudo [1908] 1925a, 186). Roche and Israel Castellanos (Castellanos 1916, 38, 54, 56, 78) identify the *cabildo* by name, and the latter gives biographical details of its African founder, Papá Silvestre Erice.

21. Figure 5.13, *bottom*, may very well be an altar to deceased spirits (*bóveda*), since it features glasses and cups, probably filled with water.

22. *Baldachino* comes from the Italian term for Baghdad. The canopy was "identified with Baghdad, the source of the finest silk brocades." The *baldachino* (or baldachin in English) was "placed above the altar and [its meaning] derived from the Old Testament symbolism of the Temple of Solomon" (Apostolos-Cappadona 1994, 48–49).

23. Personal communication with Renaissance specialist John Howett, fall 1995, Emory University.

24. Personal communications with baroque scholar Alice Jarrard, Emory University, fall 1993.

25. Eighteenth-century monarchs conducted their state business from their beds, as the kingdom and subjects were an extension of their household. See Elias 1983.

26. The child may have been Philippe, duc d'Anjou, who became king of Spain as Philip V; more likely, however, it was the child Don Carlos, enthroned in 1759; see *Encyclopaedia Britannica*, 15th ed., s.v. "Bourbon, house of").

27. The presence of gold and brass bracelets identifies the agent of this possession as Ochún. In her memory or notes, Wright apparently confounds the initial onset of possession with the subsequent reentrance of the dressed *oricha:* metal jewelry is normally removed from the body of the person mounted at the onset, and the *orichas* do not return to dance with such jewelry.

28. The English *robe* and the Spanish *ropa*, as well as the Portuguese *roupa* and the Italian *roba*, have the same root (*Compact OED*, s.v. "robe"). See Cabrera [1979] 1986, 27–28 for the Lucumí term *achó* (*-oricha*); and Abraham 1946, 72, for the Yoruba *aṣọ* (*òrìṣà*). *Robe* and *ropa* can refer to clothing and general, but retain particular historical connotations of an ankle-length garment of prestige material marking special status (*Compact OED*, s.v. "robe"). *Santo*, in popular Cuban discourse, can refer, of course, interchangeably to saints and *orichas*—though this popular use of *santo*, a noun, derives important meanings from its adjectival form: something *santo* is something holy, sacred, or consecrated, particularly a *fundamento*, for example, stones and drums. "The *Santo*" refers, most broadly, to the religion, or the collective spiritual force of its metaphysical agents. *Santero* refers to the priests of the Lucumí religion, though during the period of the Inquisition it referred to ostensibly Christian believers who were in error, though they worshiped "good celestial entities" (Brown 1993a, 59–60; Ortiz 1939; (Rodríguez Herrera 1958–59, 2:498–99). In Spain, *santero* referred to the caretakers of the reigious brotherhoods (*cofradías*) associated with local churches, a submayordomo- or mayordomo-like role (see Christian 1981, 107).

29. In Christian belief, the "robe" is a "symbol of the Passion of Christ and of unity, and thereby the wholeness of the Tradition," its white color embodying "light, joy, purity, virginity, faith, glory, holiness of life, and the soul." The belt is "a sign of virginity and chastity when worn by a woman. . . . On a male figure, the belt signified preparation for service, as this was the last item one put on when dressing" (Apostolos-Cappadona 1994, 303, 342, 57; see, e.g., my figs. 5.5, 5.6, 5.15, 5.21, 5.22).

30. The halo, from the Latin for "cloud," represents a "circle of light surround[ing] the head of a divine or sacred person. . . . [C]ircular halos were reserved for Mary, saints, and angels" (Apostolos-Cappadona 1994, 154). A triangular halo was reserved for God the Father, a cruciform halo for the Resurrected Christ, a square halo for persons who were alive when a work of art was made, and a hexagonal halo for an allegorical or legendary person (Apostolos-Cappadona 1994, 154).

31. It is not clear whether this Virgin of Regla statue belongs to the church or to one of Regla's *cabildos*, though the mantle's visual presentation and effect remain the same.

32. Displayed in its glassed-in cabinet (*armario vitrina*), the *manto* resembles the *paño* of an *oricha* throne. It is not clear whether this is an original form of Roman Catholic display that influenced the *oricha* throne or whether the church appropriated this manner of display as a strategy of cooptation to draw *santeros* into the church, stressing the primacy of the Virgin over Yemayá.

33. For example, Ogún raped his mother, Yemayá; a female manifestation of Obatalá was coerced into sex by the ferryman Agayú; Changó engages in trysts with his various conquests; and so on.

34. From a research document by Museum of Regla museologist Concepción Morales, commissioned by David Brown, dated 20 June 1996 (she interviewed old *santeras* in Regla for me).

35. The Church of Saint Lazarus Obispo is located in the village of El Rincón, just beyond the town of Santiago de Las Vegas, about fifteen miles from the City of Havana.

36. In colonial times, these were called *anaquillé* (Ortiz [1920] 1960, 40, and his fig. 9). The doll in plate 21 may represent Yemayá, but more likely, a deceased spirit who, in life, was a follower of Yemayá and/or the Virgin.

37. *Orichas* possessing their mounts often use the *paños* to

rub down the body of participants in order to take away ills. In a drumming for Changó in 1987 in New Jersey, I witnessed Changó remove his belt of lappets—hanging cloth strips adorned with thunderaxes—and wrap the torso of a *babalawo* whom Changó was in the process of "cleaning."

38. Telephone interview with Nydia Pichardo, 26 March 1995.

39. Further research could be done, for example, in Cuban magazine archives in Havana's Biblioteca Nacional and the University of Miami.

40. Robin Moore's recent work on Cuban music (1997), which treats vernacular theater (*teatro vernáculo*, or *teatro bufo*) in the late nineteenth and early twentieth centuries, suggests an entire field of popular imagery that remains to be explored. Marylyn and Richard Wilmeth (1977) suggest that the costumes and dramatic patterns of Haitian Vodou possession performance were decisively influenced by the Parisian version of the Italian *commedia dell'arte*, which swept St. Domingue in the eighteenth century, a hypothesis that Donald Cosentino uses to great advantage in his interpretation of Vodou costumes, characters, and drama (Cosentino 1995a, 39–42).

41. I have passed significant time in twenty or more houses in the New York area, two in Los Angeles, one in Atlanta, two in Washington, D.C., one in Miami, and a score or more in Havana and Matanzas, 1983–2003.

42. The *orichas* received in the original initiation, Obatalá, Oyá, Ochún, Yemayá, and Changó, for example, are elevated. The Warriors are placed on the floor. And certain auxiliary *orichas* connected to the earth, such as Babalú Ayé and Oricha Oko, are also placed on the floor.

43. At any time, an unpacified *egun* could "jump in" and take advantage of the *iyawó*'s delicate spiritual condition as a "newborn baby." At least one initiated person, usually the *oyubona*, suspends a white sheet or towel over the *iyawó*'s head.

"When we hold the cloth over his head, we say that "he's out of his house," so he must be covered, and a *santero* must always be there and stands right by the door to the bathroom. The *santero* doesn't go in there, but the *iyawó* can't lock the door. It's to protect the person. That's his protection, no *eguns*, nothing comes near. Anything floating in the air the *santero* receives rather than the *iyawó*" (Interview with Melba Carillo, 20 March 1987, New York).

44. The "protective custody" metaphor comes from personal communication with Salvador Ortiz, Jr., September 2000, New York.

45. Personal communications with Melba Carillo, 1997, New York.

46. My *madrina* in Havana uses the verb *cerrar*, as does New York throne maker Salvador Ortiz, Jr.

47. Obatalá always goes highest, in most houses, and the *oricha* of honor is located in the center; other *orichas* are arranged according to their relationships with the guardian angel; for example, Yemayá is normally separated from Oyá. Ochún may be placed next to Yemayá or Oyá, and Agayú next to Changó (see Brown 1993b, 1996).

48. Though some authors date the loosening of religious restrictions to earlier "conciliatory" measures by the state in the mid-1970s (see Velez 1998, 92–93), many Cuban practitioners I have talked to point to the worst of the "Special Period" of austerity (1991–94) as the moment when, in practice, they could openly wear their necklaces and show themselves publicly as *religiosos*. A song by N.G. La Banda, recorded in 1992 (N.G. La Banda 1992), captivated the country through the summer of 1994. Called "Santa Palabra" (Holy Words), it warned listeners not to "hide the santos."

> A saying told me sacred words,
> Don't hide the *santos* or they'll condemn you,
> There are many people that hide their *santos*,
> By day they laugh and by night they cry.
> In order to open the road (*Echú beleké*) look for an Elegguá,
> Because, without this *santo*, everything is blocked. . . .

Within the group's innovative *timba* beat, developed around 1990, N.G. La Banda incorporated *oricha* rhythms, praise names, and chants. In clubs, the youth danced to this song, incorporating the *orichas*' characteristic steps and gestures. When the Conjunto Folklórico Nacional de Cuba toured the United States shortly after this, they used "Santa Palabra" as their principal example of contemporary Cuban popular music, presenting this very dance style.

49. Enrique Hernández Armenteros is a *palero*, *babalawo*, and *abakuá*. His house in the La Hata section of Guanabacoa was one of the first (mid- to late 1980s) to be converted into a folkloric showplace for tourists, who are brought by bus to participate in *palo* drummings.

50. Armstrong argues that through the "syndetic" accumulation of ritual media (e.g., the stones, herbs, and blood of Santería), an "affecting presence" (i.e., the *presence* of an object, which is aesthetically marked and emotionally powerful, is created; in effect, the object has become a subject or agent in its own right). The aesthetic of "syndesis" entails a process of "invocation" through addition or accumulation, which can include prayer, music, sacrifices, festival gathering, and dance. Still, the "powers of presence" are realized, and, indeed, depend upon, another presence-building aesthetic, an aesthetic of "virtuosity" or "excellence." For Armstrong,"ornament" stands "in attendance," rather than "in invocation." For example, if the Yoruba king's

power and authority are produced by the medicines and relics embedded in his sacred crown and incorporated by his body (i.e., syndetically; see Apter 1992, 125–26, 82–83; Pemberton and Afolayan 1996, 169, 196–99), the finely carved house posts of the king's palace, not to mention his resplendent beaded cloth regalia, amplify the king's power, through an increase in his visual presence, which makes for reputation (see Drewal and Mason 1998, 58 and passim; Brown 1996). In sum, the "aesthetics of invocation" and "virtuosity" exist in complementary relationship: the former is enriched syndetically with the addition of the latter (Armstrong 1981, 71–86).

51. Interview with Idalberto Cárdenas, 29 November 1986, New York.

52. Sumptuary laws enforced social distinctions within the feudal system in Europe. Later, traditional elites restricted the "use of fine cloth and other luxuries . . . to retain a visible position of eminence," particularly to prevent rising monied classes from imitating them. Moreover, civic or religious authorities, on moral grounds, have controlled avarice or idolatry by restricting the use of rich fabrics and gold and silver threads (see Freudenberger 1963, 37). Analogously, satins, brocades, silver and gold trimmings, and bejeweled adornments are owned exclusively by the *orichas* and are to be used only for thrones and *ropa de santo*. The use of these fabrics and trimmings in secular fashion and domestic furnishing would be highly inappropriate. The *orichas' ropa de santo* is taken out only when the *orichas* come down during *tambores*, when *iyawós* are formally presented on the Día del Medio and the Presentation to the Drums, and when a priest is buried.

53. Los Angeles Ochún priest and throne maker Ysamur Flores-Peña explains his own Día del Medio designs in the same manner: "I always like the [consecration] garments to reflect heaven. The person who becomes the Orisha's mirror must look like an apparition from the spirit world" (Flores-Peña and Evanchuck 1994, 17). See also Thompson's earlier treatment of Caribbean carnival aesthetic, "Recapturing Heaven's Glamour" (1988, 17–30).

54. Levi Marrero notes, it appears, that A. Recio died in 1570. The Regla museum director's accession files for the Recio tureen say that he died in 1575. The latter date was kindly shared with me by director Pedro Cosme Baños, summer 1997.

55. According to decorative arts historian Carmen Trujillo Pardo, curator of Old Havana's Museum of Colonial Art, following a dispute between two Recio family factions, this *vajilla* was commissioned from a Limoges factory in the late nineteenth century by one faction to imitate an earlier *vajilla* produced by the Calle de París factories and presumably kept by the other faction (interviews with Trujillo Pardo, 16, 24, 27 June 1998, Havana). Historian Isabel Castellanos suggests that such a tureen, along with other prestige objects, would have been commissioned as a "vanity exercise" to mark the commissioners' status as noblity titleholders (personal communication, 2 July 1997). Castellanos pointed out that in the coat of arms on the object, Marqueses, is to the plural, referring to the Marqués and the Marquesa, the title holder and his wife.

56. Thus, this is an imitation of an earlier family *vajilla* (see n. 55), which may itself have imitated the eighteenth-century *vajillas* of the family's previous generations. Regressing further in time, the latter objects were, of course, imitations of the repertoire of prestige objects that the contintental bourgeoisie had copied from kings and nobles in the second half of the eighteenth century. (Personal communication with Carmen Trujillo Pardo, 2 July 1997.)

57. Personal communications with Jean Howson, an archaeologist and Caribbeanist historian specializing in transatlantic export from Europe to the Caribbean, spring 1998.

58. Natalia Revuelta Fernández, a member of Havana's social elite prior to the Revolution, and José Piedra, who was born into an upper-middle-class home in Matanzas in the early 1950s, fondly remember the *sopera* as an integral part of the family table setting, signifying prestige and domestic well-being. The tureens were used to serve hot and cold soups and *frijoles dormidos* (black bean soup).

59. In the late 1920s, the Spanish count of the Revilla de Camargo built a mansion in Havana's El Vedado neighborhood (1924–27), which he filled with eighteenth- and nineteenth-century French porcelain (e.g., Sévres, Meissen, Chantilly), eighteenth-century woodwork (Baudin, Chevalier, Simoneau, Chippendale), Chinese dynasty porcelains, French bronzes, and so on. The vast dining room is now devoted to a display of porcelain *vajilla* belonging to the daughter of José Martí (María Teresa Martí Zayas Bazon); the *vajilla*, including a number of *soperas*, was made between 1856 and 1864 in a Sévres factory. The house was taken over by the Cuban government in 1961 ("when its owners abandoned it") and was made into the Museum of Decorative Arts. The count's decorator in the 1920s was the House of Jansen of Paris (*Museum of Decorative Arts*, n.d.).

60. From 1875 to 1897, "Alfred Meakin" appears as the pottery mark. "Alfred Meakin, Ltd." appears from 1897 to about 1913. "Alfred Meakin (Tunstall) Ltd." appears from about 1913 to about 1930. After 1930, "Ltd." ceases to be included in the stamp (Cushion 1987, 548). As of 1891, all exports in this trade had to be marked with the country of origin (Wetherbee 1985, 129–30). Godden's (1964) encyclopedia of pottery marks suggests that a piece with "Alfred Meaken, England" would probably have been produced after 1930. I am grateful to Jane Rehl for her research assistance on the Meakin family dynasty.

61. Alfred is not mentioned in the Meakin's vanity press history by Hollowood but was probably one of the sons of James Meakin, Jr. (see Hollowood 1951, 14).

62. Landaluze's title for this lithograph is *El Mascavidrio*, which means, in this case, the drunken "fool," or "halfwit."

63. All of these questions form part of another, new, research project; I will seek to contextualize objects in historical collections by asking questions about their sources, the demographics of their owners, and circulation, including an internal market system.

A *sopera* I photographed in the poor Afro-Cuban *barrio* of La Correa, Guanabacoa, was owned by a priestess of very humble means, Francisca Morales Cruz (Ochún Falá), who was initiated in Guanabacoa more than 110 years ago(ca. 1890). The tureen was inherited by a ritual family godchild (see plate 20, *far right*).

64. From my readings of Ortiz 1952–55, 4:1–85; Sosa Rodríguez 1982; Trujillo y Monagas 1882; Rodríguez 1881; and interviews with Jesús Varona Puente, the Nasakó officer of Regla's Eforitongó lodge.

65. Personal communication with a ritual descendant of the late Chuchú Capáz, Jesús Varona Puente, the Nasakó of Regla's Eforitongó lodge, which is the "nephew" of Chuchú's Nyegueyé in the Akanarán Efó #1 genealogical line (August 2000).

66. Displays of flamboyant, expensive costuming, loud drumming, and vigorous, athletically danced performances during carnival were observed by spectators on balconies who could, if moved to do so, deliver *aguinaldo* (tips). The intensive work put into the costume, particularly that of the kings and queens, undoubtedly was intended to impress not only the elevated spectators, but also other carnival groups.

67. From the mid-1980s to the early 1990s, according to a number of *babalawos, santeros,* and Cuban scholars I spoke to, select Havana priests had been approached to function within a program of state-sponsored religious tourism, wherein they would receive spacious houses by the beach and complete access to resources (religious goods, sacrificial animals) in order to initiate foreign tourists at elevated prices. The state would receive hard currency from tourists, and the priests would be paid in Cuban pesos. Rafael L. López Valdés coined the term "Ochatur" to name this project (discussion with López, Havana, June 1993).

68. Most of the *oricha* garments and *paños* in the Museum of Regla collection, which are from humble Ocha houses, are adorned with hand-embroidered or hand-painted floral designs.

69. Moreover, as Apter documented in Yorubaland's northeast (Ayédé, Èkìtì), priests have, for some time, substituted commercial casseroles and serving tureens for calabash and earthenware forms.

70. In Josefina Tarafa's photograph (fig. 5.40), from right to left, rear, Yemayá and Ochún own plain oval *soperas;* Oyá owns a circular *sopera* with zigzag trim. The *sopera* in the center is probably the road of Obatalá called Ochanlá, who is swathed in cotton. The stones of Changó and Agayú are in enameled metal bowls (*palanganas*), which is highly uncommon, as they prefer wood *bateas*.

71. John Mason notes that Olokun's vessel is made of a "hard-fired terracotta (coral colored) . . . glazed on the inside to make it watertight" (Mason 1996, 48). However, Cuban priests have also used tall Chinese porcelain vases, which are impermeable to water; Yemayá and Ochún also take water; therefore, if they are not kept in receptacles impervious to water, the vessels must be sealed or painted inside.

72. Ogún takes a three-legged iron cooking pot; the Ochosi of the Warriors lives inside Ogún's iron pot; when received as an independent *oricha*, Ochosi lives in a large, flat terra-cotta dish (*cazuela*); Eleguá lives in a small *cazuela*. All are open to the sky; however, when Eleguá is "made" as the guardian angel, he lives inside a covered gourd, often beaded (plate 18).

73. The Yoruba Ṣàngó's pots in West Africa were mostly of calabash or wood, although Thompson documents a ceramic pot with this deity's iconography (1983, 7), though it probably is used to elevate a bowl holding his stones. Ernesto Pichardo reports that Agayú used to be contained in ceramic vessels (personal communication, 30 January 1998), examples of which are exhibited in the Fernando Ortiz collection of Havana's Casa de Africa. These deep ceramic vessels are called *lebrillos* in Cuba. *Batea* refers to an old Caribbean work vessel noted early on by Bartolomé de las Casas (in his *Historia de las Indias*. It was a circular or square wood bucket or trough, often constructed of staves and rings, which Cubans used to wash clothes and, a long time ago, used to wash minerals (see Rodríguez Herrera 1958–59, 1:171).

74. Conversations with *babalawo* Antonio de Armas, who was initiated as a *palero*, and Jesús Varona Puente, who is a *palero*, Abakuá, and *babalawo*, summer 1999, Havana. Many of the Afro-Cuban drums—sacred drums are played exclusively by men—are made of cedar, and Varona explains that the male Abakuá secret society uses cedar for all of their drums because it is a "male wood."

75. Personal communication with Ernesto Pichardo, 27 December 2000, Miami.

76. My own *padrinos* in central Havana wanted my *ochas* to be "born in *güira*," but we could not find ones large enough. My *orichas* were, however, "fed" in the Sacrifice of the Three Months in gourds, and the Ochosi I received was born in *güira*, though later transferred to a *cazuela*.

77. When the *orichas* were fed sacrifices, Ña Margarita Ar-

menteros would put each *taza bola* in a *palangana* (basin) on the floor (interview with Papo Raimundo Reinaldo Chaguayceda, Regla, 17 July 1997). "Great-grandson" in the religion refers to his ritual descent—two generations removed from Ña Margarita, through his ritual "grandmother," Tiburcia Sotolongo, and his godmother, Margot Fundora Sotolongo.

78. Cubans tell many shocking stories about such incidents, especially during the 1960s and early 1970s. For example, a party militant who was the chief of nurses in a Havana hospital was ambushed during a surprise "assembly" organized for her benefit when it was discovered she was a *santera;* she was verbally insulted and beaten so badly by her co-workers that she required hospital treatment, and lost her job. Spies regularly photographed Cubans entering churches and used the evidence to deny them privileges in the workplace (personal communication with an eyewitness who was the chief's close friend, August 2000).

79. Power and authority are gendered and contested in Yoruba kingdoms. The "calabash" and the woman's body itself are symbolic sites of ideological struggle. Female priestesses marshal special forms of "deep knowledge" in order to "revise" the king's patrilineally based motivations to claim and use power (Apter 1991, 97–116; see also Matory 1986, 1994, 130–69).

80. The range of vessel types extends to *tinajas* of terra-cotta (Olokun, Nanú, Naná Burukú), *bateas* of wood (Changó, and now Agayú), *palanganas* of metal, plastic, or terra-cotta and *tejas* of terra-cotta (Oricha Oko), terra-cotta *cazuelas* (Eleguá, Ochosi), *calderos* of iron (Ogún), *cofres* of chromed metal or stainless steel (Odúa), large lidded *güiras* (Osain and Eleguá *de cabecera*), and metal *latas* (Olofin). *Güiras, chumbas,* and Chinese-style *tazones chinos* or *tazas bolas* of *losa* stoneware may also be used for some *orichas,* in place of *soperas.*

81. So argues Miguel Ramos, who is more interested in the morphological relation of Lucumí to natural, earthenware African pots (personal correspondence with Miguel Ramos, 28 July 1995).

82. See several very good discussions of the history of pottery, the classes of clay as related to geology, region, and technology, and their economic and cultural values, particularly during the slavery period in the American South in Horne 1990.

83. "The Chinese made porcelain from two kinds of earth: a very pure white clay known as *kaolin,* and a feldspathic stone called *petuntse.* Plastic and infusible, kaolin was considered the 'flesh' of porcelain, while petuntse—the 'bones'—provided translucence and resonance" (Palmer 1976, 13). The *Compact OED* defines porcelain as "a fine kind of earthenware, having a translucent body and a transparent glaze. . . . The name properly belongs to the hard paste or *natural* procelain, composed of kaolin combined in China with Petuntse, elsewhere with some siliceous material; but [the term] is also applied to soft paste or artificial porcelain, which is essentially a substance, intermediate between glass and earthenware, and a *hybrid* or *mixed* porcelain, which contain a certain amount of kaolin." These last products could be, for example, Wedgwood, creamware, and ironstone.

84. The erosion-smoothed stone is the product and index of transhuman geologic time and phenomena. The stones are immortal because they come from and return to *la naturaleza* and, therefore, always remain as potential earthly supports or "foundations" for the *orichas' aché*—living spiritual force. When a priest dies, some or all of the *orichas* are dispatched—pots, stones, shells—yet the stones return.

85. In general, china plates are used to organize and present sacred objects during Ocha initiations, such as the ritual scissors, razor, and comb set, the four paint colors and brushes, the *aché del santo* and other ingredients, the necklaces and bracelets, and the foodstuffs used in the cleansings involved in the receiving of Babalú Ayé and Olokun (see Brandon 1983, 370–84). It is also proper "form" to feed participants and guests during Ocha events with food on on china plates. Moreover, when *iyawós* visit the houses of other priests for the first time, cool water is sprinkled across the door threshold and a *moyuba* and blessing are intoned by the house-owner; then *iyawós* customarily receive at least a china plate, often decorative. Some never learned this tradition; others argue that, in addition to the plate, the *iyawó* should receive two coconuts, two candles, and a small sum of money. This compound gift is, in fact, a blessing: "The plate is so the *iyawó* should always have food; the coconuts are so the *iyawó* will always be able to talk to the *orichas;* the candles are so the *iyawó* will always have light; and the money is so that the *iyawó* will always have it" (from my first visit, following initiation, to Melba Carillo's New York house, February 2000).

86. However, when Eleguá is "made" as the *oricha* of the head, he lives inside a lidded gourd that is often painted or beaded in red and black (plate 18).

87. I have condensed two of Cabrera's paragraphs into one, using an ellipsis. In the bracketed passage above, I listed some of the goods she named, which also included things called *Akán, Apá,* and *bikoko,* which she could not identify (Cabrera [1974] 1980, 177). *Fila* is from the Yoruba *filà,* "cap of any kind" (Abraham 1946, 213). *Obí* is the kọ̀lá nut that was and is used in West Africa and Brazil as a divination instrument, and it is also used to prepare the *aché de santo* in Ocha. *Apá* could be the mahogany bean (*Afzelia africana caesalpinaceae;* see Abraham 1946, 57). *Bikoko* could be what Cubans came to call *obicoco,* the coconut used for divination, but more likely, since coconuts were plentiful on the island, it could be ìkòkò, pots. The nineteenth-century trade in

African goods, as well as European luxury items, awaits further research, and, thus, this section is essentially conjectural, based on the suggestions of Cabrera's sources.

88. Roger Bastide provides an interesting example of the dynamic of recovery and invention, self-promotion and authority building: "Martiniano de Bomfim went [from Brazil] to Lagos to learn the art of divination and later became the most prestigious *babalaô* in Bahia. He used his considerable authority to prevent the degeneration of the African cults and to reform the Opô Afonja *candomblé* by introducing certain institutions that did not exist in Brazil but that he had seen, or thought he had seen, in Africa" (Bastide [1960] 1978, 165). Bastide's footnote is interesting and alludes to the practices of innovation and reform: "I am alluding to the introduction of the twelve ministers [*mogba* or *Oba*] of Shangô. And I say 'thought he had seen' rather than 'had seen' because, although some writers do state that there were twelve *Obas*, the names of these ministers include extremely heterogeneous titles" (441 n. 23).

89. In contemporary historical writing, the notion of an emerging modern Atlantic space or "unit" within which African diasporic cultures emerged is expounded most powerfully by Linebaugh and Rediker (2000), as well as in the more culturally based work of Gilroy (1993; see also Palmié 1994). From Levi-Strauss's theorizing about bricolage comes "consuming symbolic ambition" (1966, 220). The way that bricolages perpetuate and resist dominant discouses is inspired by Comaroff (1985, 198) and Apter (1991, 245, 253–54, 1992, 113–14); the "will to adorn" comes from Hurston's writing on black American cultural aesthetics (1983, 50–51).

90. Producer Lisa María Salb reports that during the recording sessions of Cuba's premier ritual drummer from Matanzas, Esteban Vega ("Chachá"), the young female singers in the group jammed to the CD of new young group, *A lo cubano* by Orishas, at every free moment. *A lo cubano* begins with a Lukumí *moyuba* prayer and follows with "Represent," a savvy blend of Cuban popular music and rap to a heavy dance beat.

91. A handbill I was given in New York in the 1980s announced the visit to New York of H.R.H. Obá Ofuntola Oseigeman Adelabu Adefunmi I. I heard him addressed and addressed him as *Ká biyè sí* at a conference at the Art Institute of Chicago in 1989.

92. I borrow the phrase "southern home" from the title of William Wells Brown's famous ex-slave narrative (1880).

93. Morton Marks brilliantly demonstrates the figurative journey of "going home" as a central feature of African-American and Caribbean sacred and secular music, such as gospel and Puerto Rican *salsa*. "The theme of 'going home' is widely distributed throughout New World Negro contexts, and in general is derived from the eariest slaves' consciousness of exile, and of their desire to return to Africa." For example, in the context of the black church and gospel music, the "ritual transition" into the state of receiving the Holy Spirit through "shouting" is a symbolic movement of "going home"; and in *salsa*, going *pa'l monte* ("back to the woods") or entering *monte adentro* (inside the sacred forest) can mean "going home," spiritually, to "the island" (Puerto Rico or Cuba) and the *tierra* of one's ancestors (see Marks 1974, 98–109).

94. According to Clarke (1997, 58), Oyotunji Village has ten separate shrines arranged around the grounds.

95. These themes are encapsulated in a key biblical prophecy (Psalms 68:32): "Princes shall come out of Egypt and Ethiopia shall soon stretch forth her hands unto God" (see Raboteau 1983).

96. See Handler and Linnekin 1984; Hobsbawm and Ranger 1983; Anderson 1983.

97. Alexandre Dumas *père*, born near Paris in 1802, was one eighth of African descent—his grandfather, Marquis Antoine-Alexandre Davy de la Pailleterie, had married Marie-Céssette Dumas, a black slave on St. Domingue (see www.africana.com; search on "Dumas").

98. Telephone interview with Nydia Pichardo, 26 March 1995.

99. Ernesto Pichardo and Miguel Ramos also report the revival of the head-and-foot initiatory system in some houses. Kunle, the head priest of the Black American Yoruba Ibeji Temple in Atlanta, who was initiated at Oyotunji, reported the same. However, Kunle says that he will perform the initiation either according to the head-and-foot system or the Cuban model, depending upon the wishes of the initiate (personal communication, August 1992, Atlanta).

100. Personal communication with Ernesto Pichardo (24 May 1995), who participated in Oyotunji rituals and delivered Babalú Ayé to the village. The deity of the head and Elegba would be the primary foci of the *itá* reading, according to Pichardo.

101. According to Clarke (1997, 63 n. 8; see also 117), Oyotunji residents were particularly fond of the works of Rev. Samuel Johnson (1921), N. A. Fadipe (1970), and J. F. A. Ajayi and Robert S. Smith (1969).

102. According to Hunt (1979, 69), "The government of Oyutunji . . . according to Kabiyesi, is one of 'monarchial socialism.' Under this system all of the main resources such as water, minerals and land belong to the [African] state. The state is represented by a King who must be the Chief Priest of the Village and the Ogboni Society. The Ogboni Society at Oyotunji is comprised of all the Chiefs with the king at its head. As the Council of State, it administers the religious, health, legislative, judicial, administrative, executive and police functions. The King has the final word on all decisions, and his word is law."

103. Personal communication with Ernesto Pichardo 24 May 1995 (see also Pichardo and Nieto 1984, 8–9).

104. For example, John Mason's research on the founders of the Lucumí religion in Cuba focuses exclusively on Africans and their immediate blood and ritual descendants.

105. Personal communication with Miguel Ramos, April 1995.

106. I know of several cases, including a woman who participated in the first groups of Black American Yoruba in the late 1960s but now belongs to a New York Cuban house headed by a white *madrina*.

107. I am grateful to Stephan Palmié for his suggestion that, had it been otherwise, Oyotunji might have been a Kongo village. Herskovits's deemphasis of the influence of Kongo-Angola culture in the Americas (Herskovits 1941) was not revised until Robert Farris Thompson's important work of the late 1960s and particularly the late 1970s (Thompson 1969, 1978; Thompson and Cornet 1981; see also Thompson 1983). The tradition of African ethnography has, perhaps invidiously, distinguished between the ostensibly more complex societies of West Africa, which featured kingship, stratified societies, and elaborated theologies, and the "lower-level," "less advanced" civilizations of western Central Africa, which lacked political sophistication and mythologies (see, for example, how this historiographical distinction affects an important New World ethnology: Bastide distinguishes between the firmly organized collective memory and mythological basis of the Yoruba and Dahomean Candomblés and the ostensible disorganization and individualism of the Bantu practices [Bastide [1960] 1978, 285–303, esp. 293]). Cuban practitioners of Palo Monte did not arrive in the United States in very great numbers until 1980.

108. Under the brochure's banner heading, the cover features a photograph of a billboard designed like an African thatched house, with "Oyotunji African Village" and an arrow pointing to the left. Underneath, the address is provided: Highway 17, Post Office Box 51, Shelton, South Carolina 29941. The brochure provides the history of the village and its events—for example, "monthly annual festivals, opened to the public and filled with entertainment and information on the lives of African Americans. . . . Weekly religious services of worship for residents and for the general public who may attend regularly. . . . The Yoruba Temple Dancers, Drummers and Singers featuring costumed presentations, including the Rites of Passage program" (Oyotunji brochure, n.d.).

CONCLUSION

1. Many famous, prolific *santeras* were married to *babalawos*. Ayayi La Tuán Timotea Albear was apparently married to Bernabé Menocal; Carmen Peñalver Teherán (Ochún Dína) was married to Guillermo Castro; Matilde Sotomayor of the Arara Sabalú was married to Víctor Rodríguez Fresneda ("Victor Abuela"); Taurina Montalvo Enujere of the Arará married Bernardo Rojas's godchild Nino el Cojo; Amelia Silva ("Mellí") married Bernardo Rojas; América Padrón was married to Ramón Febles; Caridad Rosado (Omí Toké) had a common-law relationship with Aurelio Estrada (Babel). There are many other examples.

2. Matilde Zayas was the godmother in the church of Atandá Ño Filomeno García's son Marcos (1862; *Libro de Bautismos de Pardos y Morenos, 1860–1874*, vol. 6, folio 54, no. 228, Parroquia de Regla); Atandá and Adechina were collaborators, and the latter initiated the former's son, Marcos, into Ifá. Fernando Ortiz documents that Olokun masquerades were early held in the house of Matilde Zayas in Regla. Ortiz credits Atandá as the Olokun carver (Ortiz [1951] 1985, 452–53). Zayas (Laguení) lived on Morales Street (now Perdomo); the García home by 1868 was located at the corner of Morales and Santa Rita (now Millar; *Actas Capitulares del Ayuntamiento de Regla*, vol. 1, act 19, 6 June 1868); and Adechina's house was just around the corner at 31 San Cipriani (now Fresneda; *Provincia de la Habana, fincas urbanas, Ayuntamiento de Regla*, folio 492, no. 32, November 1900). The secret Olokun masks and authority over them were passed from Adechina to Tata Gaitán to Quintín García, and finally to the latter's son, Tín Lecón Lombillo, who died in August 1999. Their destiny is unclear.

Just as Cuba's Abakuá tradition, unique in the African Diaspora, claims the small Havana seaport town of Regla as the birthplace of its root, Efik Buton (1836), so must Ifá. Three of the five major Ifá *ramas* began there: Adechina was first reconsecrated and mentored there by Ño Carlos Adé Bí of Regla. Ño Francisco Villalonga Ifá Bí lived, worked, and gave birth to Asunción Villalonga in Regla. Regla was also home to the two major *cabildos* of Yemayá, and, as indicated to the first consecrated *batá* drums, which were produced by Atandá and Añabí.

3. Interview with Lázaro Cuesta, summer 1998.

4. In other words, if, as in the Lucumí version, one can give Asojuano as soon as one receives him, then the tree, so to speak, branches quickly, exponentially: for example, 1 gives 5; 5 give 5; 25 give 5; 125 give 5. If a slowly expanding cadre of Asojuano priests gives him exclusively, there is no exponential effect, because the recipients are priests of many other *orichas*, and they must send their godchildren back to the same cadre of Oluwó Popó.

5. Three recent works on Afro-Cuban history, society, and culture look at the issue of race in quite black-and-white terms (Moore 1988; Helg 1995; Moore 1997).

6. I am thinking, for example, of the work of Robert Farris Thompson, Joseph Murphy, and Stephan Palmié, respectively.

APPENDIX 2

1. The Virgin de las Mercedes, Obatalá.

2. Saint Joseph (San José) is associated with Ochagriñá or Ochaquiriñán, the road of Obatalá that also takes red and whose day is March 19 (I consulted the annual dual calendar in the *Cultural* Santería magazine). See also app. 5

APPENDIX 3

1. Orula's oracular equipment includes the divining chain (*ekuelé, okuelé,* or *opelé*), used by one *babalawo* in day-to-day sessions, and the circular wood tray (*tablero* de *Ifá*), along with the sixteen sacred palm nuts (*ikín*), used in high-level sessions in which Orula's secrets are "brought to the floor" (*bajón de orula*), and which require at least four *babalawos* total as witnesses and speakers. Depending on the practice of the particular *rama* of Ifá, in order to determine the guardian angel, some *babalawos* begin with the lower-level *opelé* (divining chain), moving to the higher-level *bajón de Orula* if more certainty is required. Many houses use only the *bajón* to take out the guardian angel (see, e.g., Díaz Fabelo 1960, 42).

2. The *ebó de entrada* is basically the same format, whether performed by a *babalawo* or an *oriaté*, although *babalawos* say that only their *ebó* actually makes Olofi aware of the initiation and gets his blessing. Ecún (1985, 25) outlines the Ocha-centric version, performed by the *oriaté:* the initiate sits before the mat and the diviner "invokes the blessing of Olodumare and Olofi and all the principal dead [*mayores*] of the *rama* of *santo* of the *Oriaté* . . . [and performs] the same operation [the *moyuba*] for [the *mayores*] of the *Padrinos* . . . and also those of the [initiate]. The *ebó* of this reading is then taken out of the house and dispatched [*dar camino*] in an appropriate site."

3. Pichardo reports that communication around the results of the *ebó de entrada,* should take place between the *babalawo* who performs it and the *oriaté,* who needs the information to effectively carry out the *santo* (interview with Ernesto Pichardo, 27 December 1993).

4. Cabrera's quoted informants insisted that the *babalawo* "delivers to the Madrina or Padrino [of the *iyawó*] the *Aché* of Orula for the consecration of the plants in the ceremony of the *Osain* and [also delivers] the 'secrets of the Santo' [*aché de santo/ocha*], the African seeds that will be put in [the *iyawó*'s] head" (Cabrera 1980, 183). These four seeds, Obí, Orun, Osun, and Kolá, are the "essence of the Oricha" and are "indispensable" for the consecration of Ocha (Cabrera [1974] 1980, 158). Cabrera's sources told her that the *babalawo* consecrates the bunches of fresh plants on the mat with a special spray of water and coconut; in other words, "the *babalawo* endows the fresh plants with the blessing (*aché*) of God, Olodumare and Olofin" (Cabera [1974] 1980, 149). Next, they added, the *babalawo* also brings his blessing to the "seasoning" of the initiation's consecrating herbal liquid, the *omiero,* by adding his prayer and his divining powder, the *aché de orula,* or *yefá* (Cabrera [1974] 1980, 158).

5. These are names such as Obanyoko for priests of Changó, Ogún Bí for Ogún, Igbin Letí for Obatalá, Oyadina for Oyá, and so on.

APPENDIX 4

1. Telephone interview with Ernesto Pichardo, 12 September 1989. It is clear, for example, that the *babalawos* of Havana, particularly Regla (Adechina, Quintín García) and Guanabacoa (Tata Gaitán), were masters of the Lucumí rites of dancing Olokun complete with carved wood masquerades, ceremonies now extinct (see Cabrera [1974] 1980, 27; and Mason 1996).

2. Telephone interview with Ernesto Pichardo, 12 September 1989. John Mason reports that a Lucumí priestess—that is, not a *babalawo*—"Eña Rafaela Odun . . . is the person credited with bringing Odùa to Habana at the turn of the century" (Mason 1992, 223). In fact, the staff of the Yoruba *babaláwo* is an iron bird-topped staff called *òsùngàgà* (two birds atop a flat disk, in turn, atop four inverted bells, resembling the Afro-Cuban Ósun and Ósun *de tamaño* of Odúa), strengthening the counterargument that the latter two do derive from the former. The iron staff of the Yoruba Ọsanyín (*ọpá ọsanyín*) features a circle of birds surrounding a larger bird; the personal staff of particular *òrìṣà* priests, such as those of Ọbàtálá, is not a bird-surmounted staff but an iron "staff rattle" (*ọ̀pá ọ̀ṣọ̀orò;* see Lawal 1996a, 14–15,18–18; Thompson 1975; 1983, 48–51).

3. Telephone interview with Ernesto Pichardo, 12 September 1989.

4. Interview with Ernesto Pichardo 24 May 1995. However, the *babalawos*' counterargument is that they fabricate Eleguá, Ogún, and Ochosi in their own special ways as elaborated *fundamentos* apart from the iron representations given in the Warriors' group. And it is clearly the case that in many houses the *babalawo* prepares the *fundamentos* of Eleguá, Ogún, and Ochosi for the *iyawó.*

5. Telephone interview with Ernesto Pichardo, 12 September 1989.

GLOSSARY

aché Spiritually transformative power or "life force" distributed by God throughout the natural world, to be channeled, contained, and used by consecrated priests for the benefit of human beings.

adimú (*oricha de adimú*) Auxiliary *orichas* that may be "received" before or after one's full initiation in order to resolve specific problems of health or increase a priest's versatility, for example, when one needs to own a given *oricha* in order to "give" it to another person. *Adimú* (apart from *oricha de adimú*) refers to putting fruit before an *oricha.*

ahijado, ahijada A ritual godchild (see *casa de santo*).

apetebí A priestess who has received the "Hand of Orula" for women (*ikofá de Orula*). She cares for Orunmila and is authorized to assist *babalawos* in their work.

asiento The weeklong full initiation in *ocha* or the initial intensive first day in which the guardian angel *oricha* is "seated" (*asentado*) on the head (see *kariocha*).

babalawo "Father of the secret": an initiated member of the all-male order of the diviners of the Ifá system, whose tutelary head is Orunmila (Orula). *Babalawos* divine with the *tablero de Ifá* and the *ikin* palm nuts or the *opelé* divining chain.

bajón de orula, bajón de santo A high-level Ifá divination session in which Orula is "brought to the floor." The sixteen palm nuts are used to extract the Ifá *odu,* which are marked upon Orula's *opon-ifá* or *tablero,* which has been dusted with Orula's divining powder, *iyefá.* At least three *babalawos* must be present to interpret the results. In the *bajón de santo* or *ocha,* an *oricha* is "brought to the floor" and is divined directly through its own cowrie shells, rather than through those of Eleguá. In order for an *oricha* to "talk" in this fashion, it must be given a sacrifice, and the *itá* divination session is normally performed three days later, though some houses conduct the *itá* the same day if the sacrifices do not involve four-legged animals.

bandera The official flag or banner of *cabildos* and Afro-Cuban drum ensembles. Figuratively, *bandera* refers to the "colors," in cloth or beads, that identify particular *orichas,* as well as to the *orichas* themselves. For example, "Changó is my *bandera*" means that he "rules my head."

batá Three hourglass-shaped, double-headed drums, which can be consecrated (*fundamento*) or profane (*aberikula*). The heads of *iyawós* are "presented to the drums" in a special ceremony to complete their initiations. The drums "talk" to each other in a "conversation." The drum spirit, Añá, animates consecrated drums.

batea The cedar, lathe-turned vessel that contains Changó's consecrated thunderstones (*eduará*). The *batea* was an ancient Caribbean work vessel, a circular or squarish wood trough, often constructed of staves and rings, that Cubans used to wash clothes and, a long time ago, to wash minerals (see Rodríguez Herrera 1958–59, 1:171).

botánica Urban commercial outlet for essential sacred flora, images, beadwork, and so on, of the Lucumí, Palo Monte, and Spiritist religions.

cabildo A colonial-era club, mutual-aid association, or religious fraternity of Africans, creoles, and other groups. *Cabildos* were, strictly speaking, *cofradías,* if they were official religious associations with saintly devotions under the auspices of the church. The *cabildos de nación* had African-born slave membership (*negros de nación*) and worked to buy their nation members out of slavery. The "houses" (*casas*) of the Afro-Cuban religions were, and still are, in some cases, called *cabildos.*

camino The particular "road" or "path" that *aché* takes in the world. *Camino* can refer to a specific manifestation of an *oricha,* for example, Ochún has "five" different paths with distinct names; Obatalá has sixteen. It can also refer to a person's "road" in the world, in the sense of "destiny."

canastillero A common cabinet with shelves and doors, within which the *orichas' soperas* and attributes are kept. More elaborate cabinets with glass doors are technically called *armarios vitrinas.*

casa de santo, casa de ocha (Lucumí *ilé-ocha*) The "house" or basic social unit of Lucumí religion, referring to the kinship group of godchildren (*ahijados*) initiated by a single priest—their "godparent" (*padrino/madrina*). The term *casa-templo* may be synonymous with "house" but also may refer to a house used solely for *oricha* practice and shared by a number of groups.

cocos (Lucumí *obi*) A form of divination used by all levels of Lucumí priesthood, beginning with those who have received the Warriors. It is performed by casting four coconut shards on the mat following a *moyuba* prayer. The *Obì àgbọn* (coconut) replaced the West African *obì àbàtà* (kọ̀lá nut) in Cuba.

collares The *orichas'* beaded necklaces (see *ilekes*).

collares de mazo Literally "bunches of necklaces": thick, clusters of bead strands worn diagonally across the body by *iyawós* on the Día del Medio and the Presentation to the Drums, or arranged about the *sopera* of an *oricha* on an altar or throne.

coronación espiritual A spiritual "mass" held one or two nights prior to the initiate's entry into the house of *ocha*. It delineates a set (*cuadro espiritual*) of spirits of the dead (*muertos*) that the initiate must pay attention to and informs them that the *asiento* of *ocha* is going to take place.

criollo An island-born—"creole"—individual, as opposed to African-born or Spanish-born (*peninsular*). *Criollo* has historically been applied to island-born social and cultural practices, most simply referring to mixtures of, for example, European and African elements, making for something uniquely "Cuban."

dilogún The cowrie shell oracle, from the Yoruba term for "sixteen." Each *oricha* owns a "hand" (*mano*) of eighteen shells that are kept in the *sopera* or in another guarded place, sixteen of which are cast to the mat (Eleguá owns twenty-one shells, and five remain as *testigos* [witnesses]).

ebó Protective, defensive, cleansing offerings, sacrifices, or "works," which are advised by oracles and prepared by specialists, in order to transform situations. *Ebó* may involve the simple offering of fruit, a blood sacrifice, and/or a drumming.

ebó de entrada The offering conducted just prior to an initiate's trip to the "river." It is based upon a prior reading, sometimes called the *vista*, which provides information about the spiritual state of the initiate and all of the participants on the eve of the initiation—particularly things that must be done, avoided, and watched out for through this delicate process.

egun Generally, spirits of the dead (*muertos*). Strictly speaking, the *egun* category refers to the deceased members of one's priestly "line" (*rama*) and the deceased members of one's natural family.

ekuelé/okuelé/opelé The divining chain of Orula, used by *babalawos*. It consists of eight concave disks of coconut shell, brass, ivory, or sometimes halved shells of Orula's palm nuts. The chain forms two "legs" of four disks and is cast so that it produces two columns, with the disks "up" or "down," forming an *odu*. It is cast twice to produce Ifá's compound *odu*, such as Ogbe Bara or Iroso Oché.

eledá That spark of the Creator (*edá*) embodied in the "head" (*orí*) of each person.

fundamento As a noun, the *orichas'* material "supports" or "foundation," in particular, the consecrated stones (*otán*, or *piedras*) that embody the *orichas' aché*, which are kept in the *soperas*. *Fundamento* is also synonymous with the genealogical line of initiatory descent (*rama*) and its spiritual kinship relationships. As an adjective, it refers to objects that have been formally consecrated, such as *batá* drums.

guardian angel/angél de guardia A person's tutelary *oricha* as determined by divination, also called the "owner of the head" (*dueño de cabeza* or *oricha de cabecera*).

guerrero "Warrior": a "strong" or hot *oricha* whose qualities and history find it engaged in battle, such as Changó, Oyá, Eleguá, Ogún, or Ochosi, or the strong "road" of another *oricha*, such as Ayáguna (of Obatalá) or Achabá and Okute (of Yemayá). "The Warriors" refers to a set of protective powers—Eleguá, Ogún, Ochosi, and Ósun—received from a *babalawo* or *santero* as an important early initiatory passage. They "open the road" and fight for the person's head (*orí*). Warriors from the *babalawo* are called *guerreros de babalawo* and those from a *santero* or *oriaté* are called *guerreros de santero* or *de oriaté*. To some, strictly speaking, the *babalawo*'s Eleguá is called Echú and the *santero*'s, Eleguá.

herramienta "Tool": any of the iconographic metal, and sometimes wood, tools and symbols that go inside or atop the *orichas' soperas*.

historia A precedent-like story within the corpus of divination *odu*, which details the exploits, failures, and successes of particular personages, usually involving problems that are resolved through sacrifice. These stories are interpreted by diviners to draw wisdom from a particular *odu*.

Ifá The system of divination with the *tablero* or *opon* (tray) or *opelé* (chain). The term may also be applied to La Regla de Ifá, the fraternity of male diviners, and, philosophically, to "Total Knowledge," which is contained and distributed in the *odu*, the categories of the oracular systems (*Ifá* and *dilogún*).

Igbodú(n) Literally "sacred festival grove": the "sacred room" (*cuarto sagrado, cuarto de ocha*) in which initiatory rituals are performed and where the *orichas* are kept in their *soperas*.

ilekes See *collares*.

itá A high-level divination session with the cowries of a particular *oricha* or Ifá's *tablero,* which often follows two days after sacrifices of four-legged animals. An *itá* is integral to the *asiento* and to "receiving" auxiliary *orichas* that are fed "four-legs" (four-legged animals) so that the *orichas* may "talk." *Orichas* "received" having been fed "two-legs" do not "talk" in an *itá* session. *Itá* can also refer to Ifá's divination sessions that occur on the third day after sacrifices.

iyawó The novice initiated in the "coronation" or *asiento* ritual. It literally means the "junior wife," but refers, in practice, to a spiritual "newborn" who must observe strict taboos for one year—the "Year of White"—following initiation. From the moment that the initiate leaves the "river" ceremony for the house of *ocha,* he or she is known as *abokú* until the mounting of the *oricha* upon the head, after which the term *iyawó* is used.

kariocha Lucumí term for the full initiation ritual ("put the *oricha* on the head"; alternately, in Spanish, *asiento*).

madrina (*padrino*) "Godmother" ("godfather"): a priestess or priest who initiates others and heads a house. People take on a *madrina* or *padrino* when they receive the *collares* from an *oricha* priest, or the *guerreros* from a *babalawo* or from an *oriaté.*

moyuba Lucumí for "I pay homage": a chanted prayer that praises God, the ancestors, living elders, and *orichas.* The *moyuba* prayer precedes all ritual activity. *Moyubas* contain praise name recitations for the *orichas* and the deceased *rama eguns.*

obá The master of ceremonies of the Ocha initiation or the ceremonies of Ifá.

odu The knowledge-organizing categories or "containers" of the Lucumí oracular systems, each of which has specific prayers, advice, narrative legends, and sacrifices associated with it.

oloricha Literally "owner of the *oricha*": a priest who has gone through the *asiento.* A priest who has initiated others is an *iyaloricha* (female, "mother of *oricha*") or *babaloricha* (male, "father of the *oricha*").

orí "Head": the physical head, the inner spiritual head, or one's "destiny."

oriaté Master of ceremonies of Ocha ritual. The word is derived from *orí* (head) and *até* (divination tray or mat). Also called *obá* (king) or *obá-oriaté.*

oricha A deity of the Lucumí pantheon, each of whom controls a particular kind or range of *aché* and a domain within the cosmos, nature, society, and human experience. John Mason nicely translates it as "selected head" (see Mason 1992).

oyubona (*oyugbona,* pronounced "ojubona") The "second" godparent to whom the *iyawó* becomes linked in ritual kinship and who tends to the *iyawó* most intimately during the initiation.

padrino See *madrina*

paños Color-coded lavish squares of expensive cloth that cover the *soperas,* adorn the throne, and are worn and used by the *orichas* in possession ceremonies.

patakí Lucumí term for myth, legend, or story (alternately, *historia*).

pilón (Lucumí *odó*) The mortar of Changó that is used as a ritual stool in initiations of virtually all the *orichas* except the Warriors, who use large stones or tree trunks.

pinaldo The strong, protective "knife" (Spanish *cuchillo;* Lucumí *obé*) of Ogún received during the ritual career. It serves to confirm one's initiation in Ocha. It may have begun as a reinitiation or confirmatory ritual to legitimize the credentials of priests who arrived in a new place, for example, in Havana from Matanzas.

plaza The marketplace, or, in a different context, the mat under a throne upon which fruit and sweets are offered to the *orichas.*

rama The genealogical branch or line of descent to which a particular house of *ocha* is attached.

ropa de santo (*traje del medio*) The sumptuous consecration garments often of satin worn by *iyawós* and by *orichas* when they come down in possession during drummings. They include a gown or combination of jacket and pants and a pasteboard crown (Spanish *corona;* Lucumá *adé*).

santero The priest or devotee of the *oricha* (*santo*). The term is used specifically to distinguish the *oricha* priests of La Regla de Ocha from the *babalawos* of La Regla de Ifá. Some consider it pejorative, although it was a welcome replacement in the 1930s for *brujo* (sorcerer; see Ortiz 1937b; and Lachantañeré 1961c).

sopera Color-coded porcelain or other glazed ceramic lidded vessel used to contain the *orichas'* stones, shells, and metal iconographic attributes (*herramientas*). The term has become generic and also can refer to all *oricha* pots.

tambor Literally "drum," but more loosely "drumming": an *oricha* festival event of drumming, dancing, and spirit possession.

tinaja A relatively deep, bisque-fired lidded earthenware vessel in which some *orichas* reside (Olokun, Nanú, Naná Burukú). The basic *tinaja,* which has a vertical contour and is unglazed, was historically used in the house for water storage (it breathed and kept the water cool). However, the term is applied to a vessel glazed on the inside for Olokun (master of the deep). The *iyawó* also carries a small *tinaja* filled with river water back to the house after the opening river ceremony.

trono The "throne": a temporary canopy-like installation of lavish cloth, coded to the *orichas'* colors, or leaves, under which initiates are presented to the community and protected from undue influences following their *asientos.* Thrones also present the *orichas* themselves, as enclosed in their various vessels.

Orichas

Eleguá: Messenger, crossroads, and trickster. With qualification (see below) Eleguá takes the form of a small cement head with cowrie shell eyes and mouth, which may be embedded in a conch shell, or else may be a simple stone. Eleguá carries the *garabato*—a hooked staff (in Cuba). His colors are black and red, and he is associated with the Catholic Child of Antioch and Child of Prague in the syncretic conception. His vessel is a terra-cotta dish (*cazuela*), or a large painted or beaded lidded gourd if Eleguá is "made."

Echú generally refers to the unrestrained—some say "negative"—side of a complex figure called Echú-Eleguá, which lives "outside" in the street or the bush. *Eleguá* refers to the side of this figure that has been "calmed" by the presence of Obatalá, for example, when this figure is brought into the house in a "transformed" state, via ritual. *Echú* is also used, in another sense, to refer to the particular *oricha* that is fabricated by the *babalawo,* while *Eleguá* refers to the figure made by the *oricha* priest. At the same time, every Echú and Eleguá carries a special compound name, of which there are 21 or 101 (depending upon who makes it), which begins with *Echú,* such as Echú Alaguana, Echú Bekeké, and Echú Laroye.

Ogún: Iron, violence, brute strength, sacrifice, eternal work, struggle, war, technology, and defense. His principal tool is the machete. His colors are green and black, and he is associated with the Catholic Saint Peter and Saint Anthony. His vessel is an iron cooking pot with three legs, containing seven iron tools, an anvil, and a stone.

Ochosi: Hunting, the law, and sustenance. His attributes are the *arco y flecha*—an iron bow and arrow. His colors are combinations of royal or Prussian blue, amber, red or coral, black, and gold, and he is associated with Saint Michael the Archangel. He is a shrewd, brainy, solitary hunter, the younger brother of Ogún. He lives inside Ogún in the form of an iron bow and arrow. When "made" or "received," his vessel is a large terra-cotta dish containing a large stone and metal tools, such as bows and arrows, shields, machetes, a trident, and deer horns, which may be magically charged.

Odúa: (Odudúwa) Creator of the world and the origin of all births and deaths. A primary material extension of the High God complex, Odúa is a principal mediator between the celestial and the material, life and death. He is represented by the "Ósun of Height" and other secrets prepared by the *babalawo.* He is associated with San Manuel. He lives inside a polished white metal *cofre* (box) and is accompanied by his helpers, Bromú and Bronciá.

Olokun: The great mystery of the bottom of the sea. A great constituent of the Creation—the sea—Olokun is associated, like Odúa, with great transitions of life and death. The Olokun of the *santero* lives inside a tall porcelain or terra-cotta lidded pot. The Olokun received by *babalawos* is encrusted with seashells and magical substances on the outside.

Oricha Oko: The earth (*tierra*) and all of its products. Oricha Oko is a great constituent of the Creation. He is represented by a miniature lead plowman and two oxen, and sometimes by a sugarcane cart pulled by oxen. A Spanish terra-cotta roof tile stands upright in the basin of earth that contains his secrets, along with two coconuts, a stone, and the plowman.

Babalú Ayé: (also called Asojuano) Archetypal deity of skin diseases such as leprosy, of all the world's suffering, and of decomposition. In Cuba he is the poor beggar with sores on crutches (associated with the Catholic parable of Saint Lazarus) and is the patron of the poor and the sick. He carries a broomlike dance wand made of the newest shoots of the royal palm, burlap, cowries, and beads (*ajá* or *chachará*). Burlap is one of his main symbols, since it is the cloth of penitence and poverty and has a texture like rough, diseased skin. His beads may be brown (*matipó*), white with blue or red stripes, along with Jet, depending upon the road. The Asojuano of the Arará Sabalú of Matanzas and Havana lives inside a sealed terra-cotta lidded pot perforated with holes; the Asojuano of the Arará Dajomé of Perico lives in an unsealed terra-cotta pot.

Ósun (not to be confused with Oshún or Ochún): The essence of a person's being and stability. Ósun is, in effect, a shrine to a person's sacred inner head (*orí*). His attribute is a metal staff (*òsun* means "staff" in Yoruba). In Cuba the Ósun staff consists of a cup on a stem, topped by a little rooster, hung with four little bells, on a heavy lead base. The rooster is ever vigilant, and the bells "scare away" malevolent influences from the head. Recipients of Odúa receive an "Ósun of height" (a tall Ósun the height of the recipient surmounted by a silver winged bird, not a rooster).

Osain: The owner of the *monte,* specificially, all sacred plants and medicines. Osain in Cuba lives in a lidded gourd and may be represented by a magically charged doll or a carved figure with one eye, one arm, and one leg. His colors are the colors of all the *orichas.*

Obatalá: The father of the *oricha* pantheon: whiteness, purity, and tranquility. Despite these characteristics, he can be a "young" brash warrior (Ayáguna), who is close to Changó. His principal attribute is a white horsetail fly whisk (*rabo de caballo* or *irúke*). He is associated with the Virgin Mercedes and the Immaculate Conception. Known as the "Owner of All Heads," he creates heads like a potter, and controls and "restrains" all the other *orichas.* Obatalá lives inside a white vessel, which may be a porcelain *sopera* or an earthenware pot painted white.

Oyá: Wind, lightning, and the "winds of change" and transition—especially death. Her attribute is a black oxtail fly whisk (*rabo de buey* or *irúke*). She has nine colors and is associated with the Catholic Saint Teresa and Candlemas. She is alternately dispassionate (still, watchful, and vigilant) and furious (like a whirlwind). She controls the perimeter and threshold of the cemetery. She is one of the wives of Changó, though not the ideal wife, as they make storms together—he is lightning and thunder, and she is the wind. They form a fearsome, unstable couple. Oyá lives inside a brownish *sopera,* though it sometimes is pink, or painted with "nine colors."

Ochún: River, "sweet" fresh water, sensuality, love, and also a witch (*bruja*) in some incarnations. Most important, as expressed by the proverb, "blood that runs in the veins," she is the mediator of connections on many levels, such as reproduction, family, and kinship, and between Olofin and the world. Her attribute is a yellow or gold fan (*abebé*). Her colors are yellows, honey, amber, coral, red, and green, depending upon her road, and she is associated with Our Lady of Charity of Cobre. Ochún lives in a yellow *sopera.*

Yemayá: The sea, the archetypal mother of the world, the source of all life, a great enveloping mother and nurturer, and also a warrior (as the sea is rough) and strong "witch." Her attribute is a blue fan (*abebé*). Her colors are blues, crystal, and coral, and she is associated with the Virgin of Regla. She is the mother of Changó. Yemayá lives inside a blue or blue and white *sopera.*

Changó: The Fourth Alafin of Oyó, a thunderbolt, "fire," "problems" on the head, a procreator, and the loyal "defender of all of Obatalá's children." His attribute is the thunderax, called *oché.* His colors are red and white, and he is associated with Saint Bárbara. Changó lives inside a *batea,* which may be a lathe-turned cedar vessel or a wood, barrel-like stave-and-band pot with a flat cover.

Orunmila (also Orula): Diviner-*oricha* of the Ifá oracle, and tutelary head of *babalawos.* His implements are *opón, opelé, irofá* (tapper), and *iruke* (fly whisk). His colors are yellow and green. Orunmila may live inside a wood, lathe-turned vessel, which is divided into quadrants, or a *sopera.*

WORKS CITED

Abimbola, 'Wande. 1971. Ifa as a body of knowledge and as an academic discipline. *Lagos Notes and Records* 3, no. 1:30–40.

———. 1975. *Sixteen great poems of Ifa*. N.p.: Unesco.

———. 1976. *Ifa: An exposition of Ifa literary corpus*. Ibadan: Oxford University Press.

———. 1977. *Ifa divination poetry*. New York: Nok Publishers.

Abiọdun, Rowland. 1975. *Ifa art objects: An interpretation based on oral traditions*. In *Yoruba oral tradition*, ed. 'Wande Abimbola, 421–68. Ile-Ife: University of Ife.

Abraham, R. C. 1946. *Dictionary of modern Yoruba*. London: Hodder and Stoughton.

Abrahams, Roger D. 1968. "Pull out your purse and pay": A St. George mumming from the British West Indies. *Folklore* 79:176–201.

Abrahams, Roger, (with John Szwed). 1983. After the myth: Studying Afro-American cultural patterns in the plantation literature. In *The man-of-words in the West Indies: Performance and the emergence of creole culture*, 40–54. Baltimore: Johns Hopkins University Press.

———. 1986. Ordinary and extraordinary experience. In *The anthropology of experience*, ed. V. Turner and E. Bruner, 45–72. Chicago: University of Chicago Press.

———. 1992. *Singing the master: The emergence of African American culture in the plantation South*. New York: Pantheon Books.

Abrahams, Roger, and John Szwed, eds. 1983. *After Africa*. New Haven, Conn.: Yale University Press.

Abramson, Charles, and Jorge Rodríguez. 1985. *Orisha/santos: An artistic interpretation of the Seven African Powers*. Exhibition. New York: Museum of Contemporary Hispanic Art (MOCHA).

Abreu Alonso, Guillermo. 1992. *Los Ararás en Cuba: Florentina, la princesa dahomeyana*. Havana: Editorial de Ciéncias Sociales.

Actas capitulares del Ayuntamiento de Regla. Vol. 1, act. 19, 6 June 1868. Archives of the Museum of Regla.

Adefunmi, Oba Oseijeman. 1962. *The African state: An outline of the ancient Yoruba kingdom of West Africa (pre-European period)*. Shelton, S.C.:Yoruba Academy Research Division, Oyotunji African Village.

Adefunmi I, Oba Ofuntola Oseigeman Adelabu. 1982. *Olorisha: A guidebook into Yoruba religion*. Shelton, S.C.: Igbimilosha Priests Council and the Orisha Academy of the Yoruba Village of Oyotunji.

African Arts. 1978. Special issue on Egungun masquerade. Vol. 11, no. 3 (April).

Aimes, Hubert, H. S. 1905. African institutions in America. *Journal of American Folklore* 8:15–32.

Ajayi, J. F. Ade, and Robert Smith. 1964. *Yoruba warfare in the nineteenth century*. Cambridge: Cambridge University Press.

Akinjogbin, J. A. 1972. The expansion of Oyo and the rise of Dahomey, 1600–1800. In *The history of West Africa*, ed. J. F. A. Ajayi and Michael Crowder, 305–43. New York: Columbia University Press.

Akoni (El). 1975. *La voz de Orunla: El cordón del orilé*. New York: n.p.

Alén Rodríguez, Olavo. 1992. *De lo afrocubano a la salsa*. San Juan, Puerto Rico: Editorial Cubanacán.

Alleyne, Mervyn C. 1971. Acculturation and the cultural matrix of creolization. In *Conference on pidginization and creolization*, ed. Dell Hymes. Cambridge: Cambridge University Press.

Alonso, Ana María. 1990. Men in "rags" and the devil on the throne: A study of protest and inversion in the carnival of post-emancipation Trinidad. *Plantation Society in the Americas* 3, no. 1: 73–120.

Althusser, Louis. 1971. *"Lenin and philosophy" and other essays*. Translated by Ben Brewster. New York: Monthly Review Press.

Althusser, Louis, and Etienne Balibar. 1979. *Reading capital*. Translated by Ben Brewster. London: Verso.

Amadiume, Ifi. 1987. *Male daughters, female husbands: Gender and sex in an African society*. London: Zed Books.

Anderson, Benedict. 1983. *Imagined communities: Reflections on the origin and spread of nationalism.* London: Verso.

Angarica, Nicolás Valentín. [1955?] n.d. *Manual de Orihaté: Religión Lucumí.* Havana: n.p.

Apostolos-Cappadona, Diane. 1994. *Dictionary of Christian art.* New York: Continuum.

Appiah, Kwame Anthony. 1992. *In my father's house: Africa in the philosophy of culture.* New York: Oxford University Press.

Apter, Andrew. 1987. Rituals of power: The politics of orisha worship in Yoruba society. Ph.D. diss., Yale University.

———. 1991. Herskovits' heritage: Rethinking syncretism in the African diaspora. *Diaspora: A Journal of Transnational Studies* 1 (winter): 235–60.

———. 1992. *Black critics and kings: The hermeneutics of power in Yoruba society.* Chicago: University of Chicago Press.

———. 1995. Notes on Orisha cults in the Ekiti Yoruba highlands: A tribute to Pierre Verger. *Cahiers d'Etudes Africaines* 35, nos. 2, 3.

Ardener, Edwin. 1987. "Remote Areas": Some theoretical considerations. In *Anthropology at home,* ed. Anthony Jackson, 38–54. London: Tavistock.

Armstrong, Robert Plant. 1989. The etymology of the word "Ogún." In *Africa's Ogun: Old World and New,* ed. Sandra Barnes, pp. 30–38. Bloomington: Indiana University Press.

———. 1981. *The powers of presence: Consciousness, myth, and affecting presence.* Philadelphia: University of Pennsylvania Press.

Arnold, Matthew. 1966. *Culture and anarchy.* Edited by J. Dover Wilcon. Cambridge: Cambridge University Press.

Arnoldi, Mary Jo, and Christine Mullen Kreamer. 1995. *Crowning achievements: African arts of dressing the head.* Los Angeles: Fowler Museum of Cultural History.

Arozarena, Marcelino. 1961. Los cabildos de nación ante el registro de la propiedad. *Actas del Folklore* 1, no. 3:13–22.

Asad, Talal, ed. 1973. *Anthropology and the colonial encounter.* New York: Humanities Press.

Asante, Molefi Kete. 1988. *Afrocentricity.* Trenton, N.J.: Africa World Press.

———. 1990. African elements in African-American English. In *Africanisms in American culture,* ed. Joseph E. Holloway, 19–33. Blacks in the Diaspora series. Bloomington: Indiana University Press.

Atkins, Robert. 1990. *Art speak: A guide to contemporary ideas, movements, and buzzwords.* New York: Abbeville Press.

Awolalu, J. Omosade. 1979. *Yoruba beliefs and sacrificial rites.* London: Longman.

Baer, Hans A. 1984. *The black spiritual movement: a religious response to racism.* Knoxville: University of Tennessee Press.

Bakhtin, M. M. 1981. *The dialogic imagination: Four essays.* Edited by Michael Holquist. Translated by Michael Holquist and Caryl Emerson. Austin: University of Texas Press.

———. 1984. *Rabelais and his world.* Translated by H. Iswolsky. Bloomington: Indiana University Press.

Balandier, Georges. 1968. *Daily life in the kingdom of the Kongo, from the sixteenth to the eighteenth century.* London: George Allen and Unwin.

Balea, Mirta. 1984. Guanabacoa museum, black roots: African slaves had a powerful influence on Cuban culture. *Prisma* 2 (July): 24–26.

Barber, Karin. 1981. How man makes god in West Africa. *Africa* 5, no 3: 724–44.

———. 1990. Oriki, women and the proliferation and merging of orisa. *Africa* 60, no. 3: 313–37.

Barnes, Sandra, ed. 1989a. *Africa's Ogun: Old World and New.* Bloomington: Indiana University Press.

———, ed. 1989b. The many faces of Ogun. In *Africa's Ogun: Old World and New,* ed. Sandra Barnes, 1–28. African Systems of Thought series. Bloomington: Indiana University Press.

Barnet, Miguel. 1961. La religión de los Yoruba y sus dioses. *Actas del Folklore* 1, no. 1: 9–16.

———. [1966] 1980. *Biografía de un cimarrón.* Havana: Editorial Letras Cubanas.

———. 1983. *La fuente viva.* Havana: Editorial Letras Cubanas.

———. 1997. La Regla de Ocha: The religious system of Santería. In *Sacred possessions: Vodou, Santería, Obeah, and the Caribbean,* ed. Margarite Fernández Olmos and Lizabeth Paravisini-Gebert, 79–100. New Brunswick, N.J.: Rutgers University Press.

Baron Robert. 1994. Africa in the Americas: Melville J. Herskovits' folkloristic and anthropological scholarship, 1923–1941. 2 vols. Ph.D. diss., University of Pennsylvania.

Barth, Fredrik, ed. 1969. *Ethnic groups and boundaries: The social organization of culture difference.* Bergen: Universitets Forlaget and George Allen.

Barthes, Roland. [1957] 1972. *Mythologies.* Translated by Jonathan Cape. New York: Hill and Wang.

Bascom, William. 1944. *The sociological role of the Yoruba cult group.* Titles in the Memoir Series of the American Anthropological Association, no. 63. Menasha, Wis.: American Anthropological Association.

———. 1950. The focus of Cuban Santeria. *Southwestern Journal of Anthropology* 6, no. 1:64–68.

———. 1951. The Yoruba in Cuba. *Nigeria Magazine* 37:14–20.

———. 1952. Two forms of Afro-Cuban divination. In *Acculturation in the Americas.* Vol. 2 of *Proceedings and selected pa-*

pers of the Twenty-ninth International Congress of Americanists, 3 vols., ed. Sol Tax, 169–79. Chicago: University of Chicago Press.

———. 1969a. *Ifa divination: Communication between gods and men in West Africa.* Bloomington: Indiana University Press.

———. 1969b. *The Yoruba of southwestern Nigeria.* New York: Holt, Rinehart and Winston.

———. 1972. *Shango in the New World.* Austin, Tex.: African and Afro-American Research Institute.

———. 1973. *African art in cultural perspective: An introduction.* New York: W. W. Norton.

———. 1980. *Sixteen cowries: Yoruba divination from Africa to the New World.* Bloomington: Indiana University Press.

Bascom, William Russell, and Melville J. Herskovits, eds. 1959. *Continuity and change in African cultures.* Chicago: University of Chicago Press.

Bastide, Roger. [1960] 1978. *The African religions of Brazil: Toward a sociology of the interpenetration of civilizations.* Translated by Helen Sebba. Baltimore: Johns Hopkins University Press.

———. 1972. *African civilizations in the New World.* Translated by Peter Green. New York: Harper and Row, Harper Torchbooks.

Bauman, Richard. 1975. Verbal art as performance. *American Anthropologist* 77 (June):290–311.

———. 1986. *Story, performance, and event: Contextual studies of oral narrative.* Cambridge: Cambridge University Press.

———. 1992. *Contextualization, tradition, and the dialogue of genres: Icelandic legends of the Kraftskáld.* Cambridge: Cambridge University Press.

Bauman, Richard, and Charles L. Briggs. 1990. Poetics and performance as critical perspectives on language and social life. *Annual Review of Anthropology* 19:59–88.

Bearak, Barry, and Brian Jones. 1978. Neighbors living in fear of cultists. *Miami Herald,* 9 April.

Beauvallet, Leon. 1856. *Rachel and the New World: A trip to the United States and Cuba.* New York: Dix, Edwards. Microfiche, Louisville, Ky.: Lost Cause Press, 1970.

Beier, Ulli, comp. 1980. *Yoruba myths.* Cambridge: Cambridge University Press.

Belasco, Bernardo I. 1980. *The entrepreneur as culture-hero: Preadaptations in Nigerian economic development.* New York: Praeger Special Studies.

Bell, Catherine. 1992. *Ritual practice, ritual theory.* New York: Oxford University Press.

Benjamin, Walter. 1969. The work of art in the age of mechanical reproduction. In *Illuminations,* ed. Hannah Arendt, trans. Harry Zohn, 217–54. New York: Schocken.

Bennet, Tony. 1979. *Formalism and Marxism.* London: Methuen.

Bennett, Herman. 2003. *Africans in colonial México: Absolutism, Christianity, and Afro-Creole consciousness, 1570–1640.* Bloomington: Indiana University Press.

Bentley, W. Holman. 1887. *Dictionary and grammar of the Kongo language.* London.

Bergamini, John D. 1974. *The Spanish Bourbons: The history of a tenacious dynasty.* New York: G. P. Putnam's Sons.

Berlin, Ira, and Philip D. Morgan, eds. 1991. *The slave's economy: Independent production by slaves in the Americas.* London: Frank Cass.

Bettelheim, Judith. 1985. The Jonkonnu festival. *Journal of Ethnic Studies* 13 (fall): 85–105.

———. 1988. Jonkonnu and other Christmas masquerades, chap. 2. In *Caribbean festival arts: Each and every bit of difference,* ed. John Nunley and Judith Bettelheim, 39–83. Exhibition catalog. St. Louis: St. Louis Art Museum; Seattle: University of Washington Press.

———. 1991. Negotiations of power in carnaval culture in Santiago de Cuba. *African Arts* 24 (April): 66–75, 91.

———, ed. 1993. *Cuban festivals with annotated glossary. The Afro-Cuban festival: "Day of Kings."* New York: Garland.

Bhabha, Homi. 1994. *The location of culture.* London: Routledge.

Binger, Louis Gustave. 1892. *Du Niger au Golfe de Guinée para le pays de Kong et le Mossi, par le capitaine Binger.* Paris: Hachette et cie.

Blanc, Giulio V., Julia P. Herzberg, and Lowery S. Sims. 1992. *Wifredo Lam and his contemporaries.* Exhibition catalog. New York: Studio Museum in Harlem.

Blassingame, John. 1979. *The slave community: Plantation life in the antebellum South.* New York: Oxford University Press.

Blier, Suzanne Preston. 1995a. *African Vodun: Art, psychology, and power.* Chicago: University of Chicago Press.

———. 1995b. Vodun: West African roots of Vodou. In *Sacred arts of Vodou,* ed. Donald Cosentino, 61–87. Los Angeles: Fowler Museum of Cultural History.

BMI. 1976. *Salsa: The Latin dimension in popular music.* The Many Worlds of Music, no. 3.

Bois, Yves-Alain. 1990. *Painting as model.* Cambridge, Mass.: MIT Press.

Bolívar Aróstegui, Natalia. 1990. *Los orichas en Cuba.* Havana: Ediciones Unión, Unión de Escritores y Artistas de Cuba.

Bourdieu, Pierre. 1977. *Outline of a theory of practice.* Translated by Richard Nice. Cambridge Studies in Social Anthropology, vol. 16. Cambridge: Cambridge University Press.

Bowen, T. J. 1858. *Grammar and dictionary of the Yoruba language.* Washington, D.C.: Smithsonian Institution.

Boza, Juan. 1986. *Afro-Cuban altars by Juan Boza.* Exhibition, October. New York: Caribbean Cultural Center.

Bradford, Sarah. 2000. *America's queen: The life of Jacqueline Kennedy Onassis.* New York: Penguin-Putnam, Viking.

Brandon, George E. 1983. "The dead sell memories": An anthropological study of Santería in New York City. Ph.D. diss., Rutgers University.

———. 1990. Sacrificial practices in Santeria, an Afro-Cuban religion in the United States. In *Africanisms in American culture,* ed. Joseph E. Holloway, 119–47. Blacks in the Diaspora series. Bloomington: Indiana University Press.

———. 1993. *Santeria from Africa to the New World: The dead sell memories.* Blacks in the Diaspora series. Bloomington: Indiana University Press.

Bremer, Fredrika. 1853. *The homes of the New World: Impressions of America.* 2 vols. Translated by Mary Howitt. New York: Harper Brothers.

Brice Sogbossi, Hippolyte. 1998. *La tradición ewé-fon en Cuba: Contribución al estudio de la tradición* ewé-fon (arará) *en los pueblos de Jovellanos, Perico y Agramonte, Cuba.* Havana: Fundación Fernando Ortiz.

Briggs, Charles L. 1988. *Competence in performance: The creativity of tradition in Mexicano verbal art.* Philadelphia: University of Pennsylvania Press.

Brown, David. 1989. Garden in the machine: Afro-Cuban sacred art and performance in urban New Jersey and New York. Ph.D. diss., Yale University.

———. 1993a. Annotated glossary for Fernando Ortiz's *The Afro-Cuban festival "Day of the Kings."* In *Cuban festivals: An illustrated anthology,* ed. Judith Bettelheim, 49–98. Studies in Ethnic Art, vol. 3. New York: Garland.

———. 1993b. Thrones of the orichas: Afro-Cuban altars in New Jersey, New York, and Havana. *African Arts* 26, no. 4 (October): 44–59, 85–87.

———. 1996. Toward an ethnoaesthetics of Santería ritual arts: The practice of altar-making and gift-exchange. In *Santería aesthetics in contemporary Latin American art,* ed. Arturo Lindsay, 77–148. Washington, D.C.: Smithsonian Institution Press.

———. 1998. Thrones of the orichas/Tronos de los orichas. *Church of the Lukumí-Babalú Ayé Journal,* 22 January. Available on line at http://church of the lukumi.org/thrones.htm.

———. 1999. Altared spaces: Afro-Cuban religions and the urban landscape. In *The gods of the city: Religion and the contemporary American urban landscape,* ed. Robert A. Orsi, 155–230. Bloomington: Indiana University Press.

Brown, Karen McCarthy. 1976. The "vèvè" of Haitian Vodou: A structural analysis of visual imagery. Ph.D. diss., Temple University.

———. 1991. *Mama Lola: A Vodou priestess in Brooklyn.* Berkeley: University of California Press.

———. 1995. *Tracing the spirit: Ethnographic essays on Haitian art.* Davenport, Iowa: Davenport Museum of Art; Seattle: University of Washington Press.

Brown, William Wells. 1880. *My Southern Home.* N.p.

Budge, Sir Ernest Alfred Wallis. 1894. *Book of the dead: Facsimile of the papyrus of Ani in the British Museum.* N.p. [British Museum?].

———. 1923. *Book of the dead: An English translation of the chapters, hymns, etc. of the Theban recension.* New York: E. P. Dutton.

Burgess-Polcyn, Yvette. 1986. Dobale: Respect gesture as greeting ritual. Paper presented at the Third International Conference on Orisha Tradition, New York.

Bush, Bárbara. 1990. *Slave women in Caribbean society: 1650–1838.* Kingston, Jamaica: James Currey; Bloomington, Ind.: Heinemann Publishers.

Butler, Kim D. 1998. *Freedoms given, freedoms won: Afro-Brazilians in post-abolition São Paulo and Salvador.* New Brunswick, N.J.: Rutgers University Press.

Cabildo Africano Lucumí. 1900. *Cabildo africano Lucumí, Sociedad de socorros mutuos bajo la advocación de Santa Bárbara: Reglamento con permiso de la superior autoridad de esta isla.* Habana: Impresa "La Biblioteca."

Cabrera, Lydia. [1940] 1972. *Cuentos negros de Cuba.* Madrid: Imprime Ramos (Ediciones C.R.).

———. [1947] 1994. Eggüe o Vichichi Nfinda. In *Páginas sueltas,* ed. Isabel Castellanos, 273–357. Miami: Ediciones Universal. Originally published in *Revista Bimestre Cubana* 60:47–120.

———. [1954] 1983. *El monte: Igbo-finda, ewe orisha-vititi nfinda: Notas sobre las religiones, la mágia, las supersticiones, y el folklore de los negros criollos y el pueblo de Cuba.* Miami: Colección del Chicherekú en el Exilo.

———. [1954] 1994. El sincretismo religioso de Cuba. In *Páginas sueltas,* ed. Isabel Castellanos, 363–82. Miami: Ediciones Universal. Originally published in *Orígenes* 11, no. 26:8–20.

———. [1957] 1986. *Anagó: Vocabulario Lucumí (el Yoruba que se habla en Cuba).* Miami: Ediciones Universal.

———. [1958] 1970. *La sociedad secreta Abakuá: Narrada por viejos adeptos.* Miami: Ediciones C.R.

———. [1974] 1980. *Yemayá y Ochún.* New York: C. R. Publishers.

———. [1979] 1986. *Reglas de Congo, Palo Monte, Mayombe.* Miami: Colección del Chicherikú.

———. 1980. *Koeko iyawó: Aprende novicia; pequeño tratado de regla lucumí.* Miami: Ediciones C.R.

Campbell, Joseph. [1949] 1973. *The hero with a thousand faces.* Princeton, N.J., Princeton University Press. Original publication, New York: Pantheon.

Candomblé: Brésil: Les eaux d'Oxalá. n.d. Compact disk. Paris: Buda Records.

Canet, Carlos. 1973. Lucumí: Religión de los Yorubas en Cuba. N.p.

Canizares, Raúl. 1993. *Walking with the night: The Afro-Cuban world of Santeria.* Rochester, Vt.: Destiny Books.

Cantero, Justo G., and Eduardo Laplante. [1857] 1984. *Los ingenios: Colección de vistas de los principales ingenios de azúcar.* Barcelona: Gráficas M. Pareja; distributed by La Moderna Poesía, Coral Gables, Fla.

Capoeira, Nestor. 1995. *The little Capoeira book.* Berkeley: North Atlantic Books.

Capone, Stefanía. 1999. *La quête de l'Afrique dans le candomblé: Pouvoir et tradition au Brésil.* Paris: Karthala.

Caribbean Cultural Center. 1984. *Orisa/orixá/orisha//Africa/ Brazil/New York: An exhibition on the survival of African belief systems among Yoruba descendants in the Americas.* Exhibition. Curator/complilor, Marta Moreno Vega. New York: Caribbean Cultural Center.

Carpentier, Alejo. [1933] 1979. *Ecue-yamba-o.* Barcelona: Bruguera.

———. [1946] 1984. *La música en Cuba.* Mexico City: Fondo de Cultura Económica.

Carr, Andrew. [1956] 1988. Pierrot Grenade. In *Trinidad carnival: A republication of the Caribbean Quarterly Trinidad carnival issue, vol. 4, numbers 3 and 4 of 1956,* 197–207. Port of Spain: Paria Publishing Company.

Carybé. 1980. *Iconografía dos deuses africanos no Candomblé da Bahia.* Salvador, Brazil: Fundação Cultural Do E. Da Bahia, Instituto Nacional Do Livro Universidade Federal Da Bahia.

Castellanos, Isabel Mercedes. 1977. The use of language in Afro-Cuban religion. Ph.D. diss., Georgetown University.

———. 1983. *Elegua quiere tambó: Cosmovisión religiosa afrocubana en las canciones populares.* Cali, Columbia: Universidad del Valle.

———. 1990. Grammatical structure, historical development, and religious usage of Afro-Cuban Bozal speech. *Folklore Forum* 23, nos. 1, 2:57–84.

Castellanos, Israel. 1916. *La brujería y el ñañiguismo en Cuba desde el punto de vista médico-legal.* Habana: Lloredo y Compania.

———. 1928. El "diablito" Ñáñigo. *Archivos del Folklore Cubano* 3 (October–December): 27–37.

Castellanos, Jorge, and Isabel Castellanos. 1990. *Cultura afrocubana.* Vol. 2, *El negro en Cuba, 1845–1959.* Miami: Ediciones Universal.

———. 1992. *Cultura afrocubana.* Vol. 3, *Las religiones y las lenguas.* Miami: Ediciones Universal.

Castillo, José M. 1976. *Ifá en la tierra de Ifá.* Newark, N.J.: Castillo House.

Chambers, Douglas B. 1997. "My own nation": Igbo exiles in the Diaspora. In *Routes to slavery: Direction, ethnicity and mortality in the Atlantic slave trade,* ed. D. Eltis and D. Richardson, 72–98. London: Frank Cass.

Chávez Álvarez, Ernesto. 1991. *El crimen de la niña cecilia: La brujería en Cuba como fenómeno social (1902–1925).* Havana: Editorial de Ciencias Sociales.

Chernoff, John Miller. 1979. *African rhythm and African sensibility.* Chicago: University of Chicago Press.

Christian, William A. 1981. *Local religion in sixteenth-century Spain.* Princeton, N.J.: Princeton University Press.

Christian Dior advertisement. 2001. *New York Times,* 23 January, Fashion section.

Cicero, Linda. 1980. In our rich ethnic culture, Voodoo (Santeria) is a "matter of faith." *Miami Herald,* 6 March.

Cintròn, Isabel. 1979. "Babalawos" cubanos in Puerto Rico: Babi Bolufer explica la Santería. *El Miami Herald,* 1 December, *Galería* section.

Clark, Timothy J. 1973. *Image of the people: Gustave Courbet and the 1848 revolution.* London: Thames and Hudson.

———. 1984. *The painting of modern life: Paris in the art of Manet and his followers.* Princeton, N.J.: Princeton University Press.

Clarke, Juan M. 1981. *The 1980 Mariel exodus: An assessment and prospect: A special report.* Washington, D.C.: Council for Interamerican Security.

Clarke, Maxine Kamari. 1997. Genealogies of reclaimed nobility: The geotemporality of Yoruba belonging. Ph.D. diss., University of California, Santa Cruz.

Clifford, James. 1988. *The predicament of culture: Twentieth century ethnography, literature and art.* Cambridge, Mass.: Harvard University Press.

———. 1994. Diasporas. *Cultural Anthropology* 9, no. 3:302–38.

———. 1997. *Routes: Travel and translation in the late twentieth-century.* Cambridge, Mass.: Harvard University Press.

Cohen, David William. 1994. *The combing of history.* Chicago: University of Chicago Press.

Colpe, Carsten. 1987. Syncretism. In *The encyclopedia of religion,* ed. Mircea Eliade, 218–27. New York: MacMillan Publishing.

Comaroff, Jean. 1985. *Body of power, spirit of resistance: The cul-*

ture and history of a South African people. Chicago: University of Chicago Press.

Comaroff, John, and Jean Comaroff. 1992. *Ethnography and the historical imagination.* Boulder, Colo.: Westview Press.

———, eds. 1994. *Modernity and its malcontents: Ritual and power in post-colonial Africa.* Chicago: University of Chicago Press.

Cornelius, Steven Harry. 1989. The convergence of power: An investigation into the music and liturgy of Santería in New York City. Ph.D. diss., University of California, Los Angeles.

Corporación Nacional del Turismo. 1950. *La pintura colonial en Cuba: Exposititón en el Capitolio Nacional.* Exhibition catalog. Havana.

Cortéz, Rev. Enrique. 1980. *Secretos del oriaté de la religión Yoruba.* New York: n.p.

Cosentino, Donald J. 1995a. Introduction: Imagine heaven. In *Sacred arts of Haitian Vodou,* ed. Donald J. Cosentino, 25–55. Los Angeles: Fowler Museum of Cultural History.

———. 1995b. It's all for you, Sen Jak! In *Sacred arts of Haitian Vodou,* ed. Donald J. Cosentino, 243–63. Los Angeles: Fowler Museum of Cultural History.

Coulson, John, ed. 1958. *The saints: A concise biographical dictionary.* New York: Hawthorn Books.

Courlander, Harold. 1944. Abakua meeting in Guanabacoa. *Journal of Negro History* 29 (October): 461–70.

Cros Sandoval, Mercedes. 1975. *La religión Afrocubana.* Madrid: Colección Plaza Mayor Libre.

———. 1979. Santería as a mental health care system: An historical overview. *Social Science and Medicine* 13B:137–51.

Crowley, Daniel J. 1956. The traditional masques of carnival. *Caribbean Quarterly* 4 (March–June): 194–223.

Crowther, Bishop Samuel. 1848. *Vocabulary of the Yoruba language. London.*

Curry, Mary Cuthrell. 1997. *Making the gods in New York: The Yoruba religion in the African American community.* New York: Garland Publishing.

Curtin, Philip D. 1969. *The Atlantic slave trade: A census.* Madison: University of Wisconsin Press.

Cushion, John P. 1987. *Manuel de la céramique européene: Faïence, faïence fines, grès, terre cuites.* Fribourg, Switzerland: Office Du Livre.

Dallas Museum of Arts. 1989. *Black art/ancestral legacy: The African impulse in African American art.* Dallas: Dallas Museum of Art.

Damian, Carol. 1995: *The Virgin of the Andes: Art and ritual in colonial Cuzco.* Miami Beach: Grassfield Press.

da Motta Lody, Raul Giovanni. n.d. *Símbolos mágicos na arte do metal: Magic symbols in metal and art.* Trans. Nilda dos Santos. N.p.

Daniels, Donna D. 1997. When the living is the prayer: African-based religious reverence in everyday life among women of color devotees in the San Francisco Bay Area. Ph.D. diss., Stanford University.

Debret, Jean Baptiste. [1834–39] 1940. *Viagem pitoresca e historica ao Brasil.* 2 vols. Sao Paulo: Livraria Martins. Original publication, Paris: Didot Freres.

DeCamp, David. 1971. Introduction: The study of pidgin and creole languages. In *Conference on pidginization and creolization,* ed. Dell Hymes, 13–39. Cambridge: Cambridge University Press.

de Certeau, Michel. 1984. *The practice of everyday life.* Translated by Steven Rendall. Berkeley: University of California Press.

Dennett, R. [1910] 1968. *Nigerian studies.* London: Macmillan.

Derby, Doris Adelaide. 1980. Black women basket makers: A study of domestic economy in Charleston County, South Carolina. Ph.D. diss., University of Illinois, Urbana-Champaign.

Derby, Lauren. 1995. Research report on Afro-Cuban cultures and criminological discourse. Unpublished paper.

Deren, Maya. [1951] 1970. *Divine horsemen: The Voodoo gods of Haiti.* New York: Delta.

Deschamps Chapeaux, Pedro. 1964. Margarito Blanco: Ocongo de Ultán. *Boletín del Instituto de Historia del Archivo Nacional* 65 (July–December): 97.

———. 1968. Cabildos: Solo para esclavos. *Cuba: Revista Mensual,* January, 50–51.

———. 1969. Marcas tribales de los esclavos en Cuba. *Etnología y Folklore* 8 (July–December): 65–78.

Desmangles, Leslie G. 1992. *The faces of the gods: Vodou and Roman Catholicism in Haiti.* Chapel Hill: University of North Carolina Press.

Díaz Fabelo, Teodoro. 1960. *Olórun.* Havana: Ediciones del Departamento de Folklore del Teatro Nacional de Cuba.

Dictionary of the Yoruba language. [1913] 1979. Lagos: Church Missionary Society Bookshop; Oxford: Oxford University Press.

Dixon, Heriberto. 1982. Who ever heard of a black Cuban? *Afro-Hispanic Review* 1 (September): 10–12.

———. 1983. *An overview of the black Cubans among the Mariel entrants.* ERIC Documents (ED 233104).

Dornbach, María. 1977. Gods in earthenware vessels. *Acta Ethnografica Scientiarum Hungaricae* 26, nos. 3, 4:285–308.

Douglas, Mary. [1966] 1985. *Purity and danger: An analysis of concepts of pollution and taboo.* London: ARK Paperbacks.

Drewal, Henry John. 1989. Art or accident: Yorùbá body artists and their deity Ògún. In *Africa's Ogun: Old World and New*, ed. Sandra Barnes, 235–60. African Systems of Thought series. Bloomington: Indiana University Press.

Drewal, Henry John, and John Mason. 1998. *Beads body and soul: Art and light in the Yorùbá universe.* Exhibition catalog. Los Angeles: UCLA Fowler Museum of Cultural History.

Drewal, Henry John, John Pemberton III, and Rowland Abiodun. 1989. *Yoruba: Nine centuries of African art and thought*, ed. Allen Wardwell. Exhibition catalog. New York: Center for African Art and Harry N. Abrams Publishers.

Drewal, Margaret Thompson. 1986. Art and trance among Yoruba Shango devotees. *African Arts* 20 (November).

———. 1989. Dancing for Ogun in Yorubaland and Brazil. In *Africa's Ogun: Old World and New*, ed. Sandra Barnes, 199–234. African Systems of Thought series. Bloomington: Indiana University Press.

———. 1992. *Yoruba ritual: Performers, play, agency*. Bloomington: Indiana University Press.

Drinnon, Richard. 1980. *Facing west: The metaphysics of Indian hating and empire building*. Minneapolis: University of Minnesota Press.

Duarte, Patricia. 1987. Primera iglesia santera en Hialeah. *El Miami Herald, 15 May.*

Du Bois, W. E. B. [1903] 1969. *The souls of black folk*. New York: Signet.

Dumont, Henri. 1915–16. Antropología y patología comparada de los negros esclavos. *Revista Bimestre Cubana* 10, no. 3 (May–June 1915); and 11, no. 2 (March-April, 1916).

Duque de Estrada, Nicolás. 1989. *Doctrina para negros (Explicación de la doctrina cristiana acomodada a la capacidad de los negros bozales.* Transcribed and introduced by Javier Laviña. Barcelona: Ediciones Sendai.

Eagleton, Terry. 1983. *Literary theory: An introduction.* Minneapolis: University of Minnesota Press.

Ecún, Obá (Cecilio Pérez). 1985. *Oricha: Metodología de la religión Yoruba.* Miami: Editorial Sibi.

———. 1986. *Itá: Mitología de la religión "Yoruba."* Gráficas Maravillas.

———. 1988. *Addimú: Ofrenda a los orichas.* Miami: Editorial Sibi.

———. 1989. *Ita: mythology of the Yoruba religion.* Miami, Fla.: Obaecun Books.

Edmonson, Munro S. [1956] 1988. Carnival in New Orleans. In *Trinidad carnival: A republication of the Caribbean Quarterly Trinidad carnival sssue, vol. 4, numbers 3 and 4 of 1956*, 108–32. Port of Spain: Paria Publishing Company.

Edwards, Brent Hayes. 2003. *The practice of diaspora: Literature, translation, and the rise of black internationalism.* Cambridge, Mass.: Harvard University Press.

Eliade, Mircea. [1957] 1959. *The sacred and the profane: The nature of religion.* Trans. Willard R. Trask. New York: Harcourt Brace.

Elias, Norbert. 1983. *The court society*. Translated by Edmund Jephcott. New York: Pantheon.

Elizondo, Carlos. [1934?] n.d.. *Manual de la religión Lucumí.* Union City, N.J: n.p.

Elkins, Stanley. [1959] 1963. *Slavery: A problem in American institutional and intellectual life.* New York: Universal Library Edition.

Ellenberg, Todd. 1987. Santeria showdown: Authentic religion or satanic cult? *Wave: Miami's Alternative Newspaper* II (October 8–21):7–9, 17.

Ellis, A. B. 1883. *The land of fetish.* London.

———. 1894. *The Yoruba-speaking peoples of the Slave Coast of West Africa.* London: Chapman and Hall.

Ellison, Ralph. [1964] 1972. Blues people. In *Shadow and act*, 247–60. New York: Random House, Vintage Books.

Epega, Afolabi A., and Philip John Neimark, trans. 1995. *The sacred Ifa oracle: The first English translation of the complete sacred texts of Ifa—the ancient African religion underlying Santeria, Candomblé, and Voduu.* San Francisco: Harper San Francisco.

Evans-Pritchard, Edward Evan. 1956. *Nuer Religion.* Oxford.

Fabian, Johannes. 1983. *Time and the other: How anthropology makes its object.* New York: Columbia University Press.

Fadipe, N. A. 1970. *The sociology of the Yoruba.* Ibadan: Ibadan University Press.

Fane, Diana, ed. 1996. *Converging cultures: Art and identity in Spanish America.* New York: Brooklyn Museum and Harry N. Abrams Publishers.

Faniel, Stephane. 1957. *French art of the eighteenth century.* New York: Simon and Schuster.

Farmer, David Hugh. 1978. *The Oxford dictionary of saints.* Oxford: Clarendon Press.

Farrow, Stephen S. [1924] 1926. *Faith, fancies, and fetich, or Yoruba paganism.* New York: Macmillan.

Fatunmbi, Fá'Lokun. 1992. *Awo: Ifá and the theology of orisha divination.* Bronx: Original Publications.

Fay-Halle, Antoinette, and Barbara Mundt. 1983. *Porcelain of the nineteenth century.* New York: Rizzoli.

Feduchi, Luis. [1965.] *Colecciones reales de España: El mueble.* Madrid: Editorial Patrimonio Nacional.

———. 1969. *Estilos del mueble español.* Barcelona: Rieusset.

Fermoselle, Rafael. 1974. *Política y color en Cuba: La guerrita racial de 1912.* Montevideo: n.p.

Fernández, James W. [1974] 1986. The mission of metaphor in expressive culture. In *Persuasions and performances: The play of tropes in culture.* Bloomington: Indiana University Press.

Fernández Carillo, Enrique. 1881. El Ñáñigo: Carta cerrada y abierta. In *Tipos y costumbres de la isla de Cuba,* by Víctor Patricio de Landaluze. Havana: Miguel de Villa.

Fernández Robaina, Tomás. 1994. *El Negro en Cuba, 1902–1958: Apuntes para la historia de la lucha contra la discriminación racial.* Havana: Editorial de Ciencias Sociales.

Flores-Peña, Ysamur, and Roberta J. Evanchuck. 1994. *Speaking without a voice: Santería garments and altars.* Folk Art and Artists series. Jackson: University of Mississippi Press.

Fowler, Alastair. 1989. Genre. In *The international encyclopedia of communication,* ed. Erik Barnouw, 2:215–17. New York: Oxford University Press.

Franco, José Luciano. 1963. *La conspiración de Aponte.* Havana: n.p.

———. 1977. *Las conspiraciones de 1810 y 1812.* Havana: Editorial de Ciencias Sociales.

Frazier, E. Franklin. 1934. Traditions and patterns of Negro family life in the United States. In *Race and culture contacts,* ed. E. B. Reuter, 191–207, New York: McGraw Hill.

———. 1939. *The Negro family in the United States.* Chicago: University of Chicago Press.

Fredrickson, George M. 1987. *The black image in the white mind: The debate on Afro-American character and destiny, 1817–1914.* Middletown, Conn.: Wesleyan University Press.

Freudenberger, Herman. 1963. Fashion, sumptuary laws, and business. *Business History Review* 37:37–48.

Fried, Michael. 1990. *Courbet's realism.* Chicago: University of Chicago Press.

Friedman, Robert Alan. 1982. Making an abstract world concrete: Knowledge, competence, and structural dimensions of performance among bata drummers in Santería. Ph.D. diss., Indiana University.

Frigerio, Alejandro. 1983. The search for Africa: Proustian nostalgia in Afro-Brazilian studies. M.A. thesis, Dept. of Anthropology, University of California, Los Angeles.

Frobenius, Leo. 1913. *The voice of Africa.* Vol. 1. London: Hutchinson.

Galembo, Phyllis. 1993. *Divine inspiration: From Benín to Bahia.* Albuquerque: University of New Mexico Press.

Galzagorry Madán, Juventino. 1983. Desarollo del rito Arará en Jovellanos. Unpublished Paper. Primer simposio de la cultura Matancera.

García Cortéz, Julio. 1971. *El Santo (La Ocha): Secretos de la religión Lucumí.* Miami: Ediciones Universal.

———. 1980. *Pataki: Leyendas y misterios de los orishas africanos.* Miami: Ediciones Universal.

García-Pelayo y Gross, Ramón. 1983. *Gran diccionario moderno: Español/Inglés—English/Spanish.* México, D.F.: Ediciones Larousse.

———. 1984. *Pequeño Larousse ilustrado.* México, D.F.: Ediciones Larousse.

Gates, Henry Louis, Jr. 1988. *The signifying monkey: A theory of African American literary criticism.* New York: Oxford University Press.

———. 1990. The face and the voice of blackness. In *Facing history: The black image in American art, 1710–1940,* ed. Guy C. McElroy, xxix-xlv. Washington, D.C.: Bedford Arts Publishers and Corcoran Gallery of Art.

Geertz, Clifford. 1983. "From the native's point of view": On the nature of anthropological understanding. In *Local knowledge: Further essays in interpretive anthropology,* 55–70. New York: Basic Books.

Genovese, Eugene. 1976. *Roll Jordan roll: The world the slaves made.* New York: Vintage Books.

Giddens, Anthony. 1979. *Central problems in social theory.* Berkeley: University of California Press.

Gilroy, Paul. 1993. *The black Atlantic: Modernity and double consciousness.* Cambridge, Mass.: Harvard University Press.

Ginzburg, Carlo. 1980. *The cheese and the worms: The cosmos of a sixteenth-century miller.* Baltimore: Johns Hopkins University Press.

Glassie, Henry. 1995. Tradition. *Journal of American Folklore* 108, no. 430 (fall): 395–410.

Gleason, Judith. 1975. *Santería Bronx.* New York: Atheneum.

———. 1987. *Oya: In praise of the goddess.* Boston, Mass.: Shambhala.

———. 1992. *The king does not lie: Initiation of a Shango priest.* Film. Distributed by Filmakers Library, New York.

Gluckman, Max. 1954. *Rituals of rebellion in south-east Africa.* Manchester: Manchester University Press.

Godden, Geoffrey A. 1964. *Encyclopedia of British pottery and porcelain marks.* New York: Crown Publishers.

———. 1979. *Oriental export market porcelain and its influence on European wares.* London: Granada.

Goffman, Erving. 1959. *The presentation of self in everyday life.* Garden City, N.Y.: Doubleday.

Gómez, Michael. 1998. *Exchanging our country marks: The transformation of African identities in the colonial and antebellum South.* Chapel Hill: University of North Carolina Press.

———. 1999. African identity and slavery in the Americas. *Radical History Review* 75:111–20.

Gómez Abreu, Nerys. 1982. Estudio de una casa-templo de culto Yorubá: El Ilé-Ocha Tula. *Islas* 71:113–38.

González Huguet, Lydia. 1968. La casa-templo en la Regla de Ocha. *Etnología y Folklore* 5 (January–June): 33–57.

González Wippler, Migene. 1982. *The Santería experience.* New York: Original Publications.

———. 1989. *Santería: The religion: A legacy of faith, rites and magic.* New York: Harmony Books.

Goodall, J. A. 1995. Regalia. In *The dictionary of art,* 26:77–83. New York: Grove Press.

Gregory, Stephen. 1986. Santería in New York City: A study in cultural resistance. Ph.D. diss., New School for Social Research.

Gutman, Herbert George. 1976. *The black family in slavery and freedom, 1750–1925.* New York: Pantheon.

———. 1977. *Work, culture, and society in industrial America: Essays in American working class and social history.* New York: Vintage.

Hafkin, Nancy J., and Edna G. Bay, eds. 1976. *Women in Africa.* Stanford, Calif.: Stanford University Press.

Hagedorn, Katherine J. 1992. The negotiation of aesthetic boundaries in the transformation of Afro-Cuban religious ritual into folkloric theater in Cuba. Paper presented at the Society for Ethnomusicology annual national meeting, Seattle, 23 October.

———. 2001. *Divine utterances: The performance of Afro-Cuban Santería.* Washington, D.C.: Smithsonian Institution Press.

Halifax, Joan, and Hazel Weidman. 1973. Religion as a mediating institution in acculturation: The case of Santeria in greater Miami. In *Religious systems and psychotherapy,* ed. R. H. Cox, 319–31. Springfield, Ill.: Charles C. Thomas.

Hall, Robert. 1966. *Pidgin and creole languages.* Ithaca, N.Y.: Cornell University Press.

Handler, Richard, and Jocelyn Linnekin. 1984. Tradition, genuine or spurious. *Journal of American Folklore* 97, no. 385: 273–90.

Hardin, Kris L. 1993. *The aesthetics of action: Continuity and change in a West African town.* Washington, D.C.: Smithsonian Institution Press.

Harris Cohen, David, and Catherine Hess. 1993. *Looking at European ceramics: A guide to technical terms.* Los Angeles: J. Paul Getty Museum; London: British Museum Press.

Hartigan, Lynda Roscoe. 1991. *Made with passion.* Washington, D.C.: Smithsonian Institution Press.

Harwood, Alan. 1977. *RX: Spiritist as needed: A study of a Puerto Rican community mental health resource.* New York: John Wiley.

Hebdige, Dick. 1979. *Subculture: The meaning of style.* London: Methuen.

Helg, Aline. 1995. *Our rightful share: The Afro-Cuban struggle for equality, 1886–1912.* Chapel Hill: University of North Carolina Press.

Herskovits, Francis S., ed. 1966. *The New World Negro: Selected papers in Afroamerican studies.* Bloomington: Indiana University Press.

Herskovits, Melville J. [1925] 1992. The Negro's Americanism. In *The new Negro: Voices of the Harlem Renaissance,* ed. Alain Locke, 353–60. New York: Atheneum.

———. 1930 The Negro in the New World: The statement of a problem. In *The New World Negro: Selected papers in Afroamerican studies,* ed. Francis Herskovits, 1–12. Bloomington, Ind.: Minerva Press.

———. [1937] 1975. *Life in a Haitian valley.* New York: Octagon.

———. 1938a. *Acculturation: The study of culture contact.* New York: J. J. Augustin.

———. 1938b. *Dahomey: An ancient West African kingdom.* 2 vols. New York: J. J. Augustin.

———. 1941. *The myth of the Negro past.* New York: Harper and Brothers Publishers.

———. [1945] 1966. Problem, method, and theory in Afroamerican studies. In *The New World Negro: Selected papers in Afroamerican studies,* ed. Francis S. Herskovits, 43–61. Bloomington: Indiana University Press.

———. 1958. Preface to the Beacon Press edition. In *The myth of the Negro past.* Boston: Beacon Press.

———. 1964. *Cultural dynamics.* New York: Alfred A. Knopf.

———. 1966. African gods and Catholic saints in New World Negro belief. In *The New World Negro: Selected papers in Afroamerican studies,* ed. Francis S. Herskovits, 321–29. Bloomington: Indiana University Press.

Herskovits, Melville J., and Francis S. Herskovits. 1934. *Rebel destiny: Among the Bush Negroes of Dutch Guiana.* New York: McGraw-Hill.

Higman, Barry. 1991. Jamaican port towns in the early nineteenth century. In *Atlantic port cities: Economy, culture, and society in the Atlantic world, 1650–1850,* ed. Franklin W. Knight and Peggy K. Liss, 117–48. Knoxville: University of Tennessee Press.

Hill, Errol. 1972. *Trinidad carnival: Mandate for a national theater.* Austin: University of Texas Press.

Hobsbawm, Eric, and Terence Ranger, eds. 1983. *The invention of tradition.* Cambridge: Cambridge University Press.

Hoetink, Harry. 1979. The cultural links. In *Africa and the Caribbean: The legacies of a link*, ed. Franklin W. Knight and Margaret E. Crahan, 20–40. Baltimore: Johns Hopkins University Press.

Hollowood, Bernard. 1951. *The story of J. and G. Meakin*. Derby: Bemrose Publicity.

Horne, Catherine Wilson, ed. 1990. *Crossroads of clay: The southern alkaline glazed stoneware tradition*. Columbia, S.C.: McKissick Museum, University of South Carolina.

Houlberg, Marylin Hammersley. 1979. Social hair: Tradition and change in Yoruba hairstyles in southwestern Nigeria. In *The fabrics of culture: The anthropology of clothing and adornment*, ed. Justine M. Cordwell and Ronald A Schwarz, 349–97. The Hague: Mouton Publishers.

Howard, David, and John Ayers. 1978. *China for the West: Chinese porcelain and other decorative arts for export*. Vol. 1. London: Sotheby.

Hunt, Carl. 1979. *Oyotunji Village: The Yoruba movement in America*. Washington, D.C.: University Press of America.

Hurston, Zora Neale. 1983. Characteristics of Negro expression. In *The sanctified church*, 49–68. Berkeley: Turtle Island.

Hymes, Dell, ed. 1969. *Reinventing anthropology*. New York: Pantheon Books.

———, ed. 1971. *Conference on pidginization and creolization*. Cambridge: Cambridge University Press.

Idowu, E. Bolaji. [1962] 1963. *Olodumare: God in Yoruba belief*. New York: Frederick A. Praeger. Original publication, London: Longmans, Green.

———. 1973. *African traditional religion*. London: SCM Press.

Ile Tum Tum. 1997. *Los orichas: División informativa de la religión Yoruba Afro-Latina en Latino America*. Newsletter, Caracas, Venezuela.

Illich, Ivan. 1980. Vernacular values. *CoEvolution Quarterly*, no. 26 (summer): 22–50.

Intar Gallery. 1984. *Lydia Cabrera: An intimate portrait*. Exhibition catalog. New York: Intar Latin American Gallery.

InterAmericas Society. 1998. *Miscelanea II of studies dedicated to Fernando Ortiz (1881–1969)*. New York: InterAmericas Society of Arts and Letters of the Americas.

Jackson, Michael. 1989. *Paths toward a clearing: Radical empiricism and ethnographic inquiry*. Bloomington: Indiana University Press.

Jackson, Walter. 1986. Herskovits and the search for Afro-American culture. In *Malinowski, Rivers, Benedict and others: Essays on culture and personality*, ed. George W. Stocking, Jr., 95–126. Madison: University of Wisconsin Press.

James, Henry. 1907. *The American scene*. London: Chapman and Hall.

Jarrard, Alice. 1993. Theaters of power: Francesco I D'Este and the spectacle of court life in Modena, Italy. Ph.D. diss., Columbia University.

Johnson, Bishop James. 1899. *Yoruba heathenism*. Lagos.

Johnson, Samuel. 1921. *The history of the Yorubas*. Lagos: C.M.S. Bookshops.

Jones, Leroi. 1963. *Blues people: Negro music in white America*. New York: Morrow Quill Paperbacks.

Joyner, Charles. 1984. *Down by the riverside: A South Carolina slave community*. Urbana, University of Illinois Press.

Karasch, Mary. 1979. Commentary one. In *Roots and branches: Current directions in slave studies*, ed. Michael Craton, 137–41. Toronto: Pergamon Press.

Kardec, Allan. n.d. *Nuevo devocionario espiritista: Colección de oraciones escogidas*. N.p.

Karp, Ivan. 1986. Agency and social theory: A review of Anthony Giddens. *American Ethnologist* 13, no. 1 (February): 131–37.

Karp, Ivan, and Mary Jo Arnoldi. 1986. Review of *The flash of the spirit: African and Afro-American art and philosophy*, by Robert Farris Thompson. *Art in America*, November.

Kelly, John D, and Martha Kaplan. 1990. History, structure, and ritual. *Annual Review of Anthropology* 19:119–49.

Kelly, Sean, and Rosemary Rogers. 1993. *Saints preserve us! Everything you need to know about every saint you'll ever need*. New York: Random House.

Kendrix, Piper. 1998. Mapping the African Diaspora: Materialism and cultural (re)connection in Paule Marshall's *Praisesong for the Widow*. Paper presented at seminar series, The Black Atlantic Project, Rutgers Center for Historical Analysis, 10 March.

Kinser, Samuel. 1990. *Carnival American style: Mardi Gras at New Orleans and Mobile*. Chicago: University of Chicago Press, 1990.

Kiple, Kenneth. 1976. *Blacks in colonial Cuba, 1774–1899*. Gainesville: University of Florida Press.

Kirshenblatt-Gimblett, Barbara. 1983. The future of folklore studies in America: The urban frontier. *Folklore Forum* 16 (winter): 185–234.

Klein, Herbert. 1967. *Slavery in the Americas: A comparative study of Virginia and Cuba*. London: Oxford University Press.

Knight, Franklin W. 1970. *Slave society in Cuba during the nineteenth century*. Madison: University of Wisconsin Press.

Kopytoff, Igor. 1986. The cultural biography of things: Commoditization as process. In *The social life of things: Commodities in cultural perspective*, ed. Arjun Appadurai, 64–94. Cambridge: Cambridge University Press.

———. 1987. The internal African frontier: The making of an

African political culture. In *The African frontier*, ed. Igor Kopytoff, 3–84. Bloomington: Indiana University Press.

Koster, Henry. 1817. *Travels in Brazil*. Vol. 2. London: Longman, Hurst, Reese, Orme and Brown.

Kubler, George. 1962. *The shape of time: Remarks on the history of things*. New Haven, Conn.: Yale University Press.

Kuethe, Allan J. 1991. Havana in the eighteenth century. In *Atlantic port cities: Economy, culture, and society in the Atlantic world, 1650–1850*, ed. Franklin W. Knight and Peggy K. Liss, 13–39. Knoxville: University of Tennessee Press.

Kutzinski, Vera M. 1993. *Sugar's secrets: Race and the erotics of Cuban nationalism*. Charlottesville: University Press of Virginia.

Lacan, Jaques. [1973] 1981. *The four fundamental concepts of psycho-analysis*. Edited by Jacques-Alain Miller. Translated by Alan Sheridan. New York: W. W. Norton.

Lachatañeré, Romulo. 1938. *¡Oh, mío Yemayá!* Havana: n.p.

———. 1942. *Manual de Santería (el sistema de cultos Lucumís)*. Havana: Editorial Caribe.

———. 1961a. Notas sobre la formación de la población afrocubana. *Actas del Folklore* 1, no. 4.

———. 1961b. Tipos étnicos africanos que concurrieron en la amalgama Cubana. *Actas del Folklore* 1, no. 3:3–12.

———. 1961c. Las creencias religiosas de los afrocubanos y la falsa aplicación del término brujería. *Actas del Folklore* 1, no. 5:11–15.

Landaluze, Víctor Patricio de. 1881. *Tipos y costumbres de la isla de Cuba*. Havana: Miguel de Villa.

Landes, Ruth. 1947. *City of women*. New York: Macmillan.

Latin American News Agency (Prensa Latina). 1996. Prensa Latina especial: Religión en Cuba, 1996 (http://www.jewishcuba.org/curelig.html).

Lawal, Babatunde. 1996a. From Africa to the Americas: Art in Yoruba religion. In *Santería aesthetics in contemporary Latin American art*, ed. Arturo Lindsay, 3–38. Washington, D.C.: Smithsonian Institution Press.

———. 1996b. *The Gelede spectacle: Art, gender, and social harmony in an African culture*. Seattle: University of Washington Press.

Leib, Elliot, and Renee Romano. 1984. Reign of the leopard: Ngbe ritual. *African Arts* 18, no. 1:48–56, 95, 96.

Leiris, Michel. 1953. Note sur l'usage de chromolithographies catholiques par les vaudouisants. *Memoires do l'Institut Français d'Afrique noire* 27:201–7.

León, Argeliers. 1964. *Concierto de música Abakuá*. Concert playbill. Havana: Consejo de la Cultura.

———. 1984. *Del canto y el tiempo*. Havana: Editorial Letras Cubanas.

León, René, and Emilio J. León. 1986. *Fernando Ortiz: Bibliografía sobre el tema negro*. N.p.

Le Page, Robert B. 1957–58. General outlines of creole English dialects in the British Caribbean. *Orbis* 6:373–91; 7:54–64.

Le Page, Robert B., and David DeCamp. 1960. *Jamaican creole*. Creole Language Studies, no. 1. London: Macmillan.

Levine, Lawrence. 1977. *Black culture and black consciousness: Afro-American folk thought from slavery to freedom*. Oxford: Oxford University Press.

Levine, Robert M. 1990. *Cuba in the 1850s: Through the lens of Charles DeForest Fredricks*. Tampa: University of South Florida Press.

Lévi-Strauss, Claude. 1966. *The savage mind*. Chicago: University of Chicago Press.

Lewis, John Lowell. 1992. *Ring of liberation: Deceptive discourse in Brazilian Capoeira*. Chicago: University of Chicago Press.

Lewis, R. W. B. 1955. *The American Adam: Innocence, tragedy, and tradition in the nineteenth century*. Chicago: University of Chicago Press.

Libro de bautismos de pardos y morenos. 1860–74, vol. 6, fol. 54, no. 228. Havana: Parroquia de Regla.

Lindsay, Arturo. 1992. *New work by Arturo Lindsay: Las siete potencias: Mestizaje and the aesthetics of Santería*. Exhibition, July–September. Atlanta, Georgia: Chastain Gallery.

Linebaugh, Peter, and Marcus Rediker. 2000. *The many-headed hydra: Sailors, slaves, commoners, and the hidden history of the revolutionary Atlantic*. Boston: Beacon Press.

Lippard, Lucy. 1990. *Mixed blessings: New art in a multicultural America*. New York: Pantheon Books.

Lipsitz, George. 1990. Mardi Gras Indians: Carnival and counter-narrative in black New Orleans. In *Time passages: Collective memory and American popular culture*. Minneapolis: University of Minnesota Press.

Lloyd, P. C. 1963. The status of the Yoruba wife. *Sudan Society* 2:35–42.

———. 1968. Conflict theory and Yoruba Kingdoms. In *History and social anthropology*, ed. I. M. Lewis. London: Tavistock.

———. 1974. *Power and independence*. London: Routledge and Kegan Paul.

Locke, Alain. [1925] 1992. *The new Negro: Voices of the Harlem Renaissance*. New York: Atheneum.

López, Lourdes, and Antonio Keiro. 1987. *Ritual dress of initiation designed and constructed by Lourdes López and Antonio Keiro*. Exhibition, May 8–June 13. New York: Caribbean Cultural Center.

López Valdés, Rafael L. 1985a. *Componentes africanos en el etnos cubano*. Havana: Editorial de Ciencias Sociales.

———. 1985b. La sociedad secreta Abakuá en un grupo de trabajadores portuarios. In *Componentes africanos en el etnos cubano*, 151–85. Havana: Editorial de Ciencias Sociales.

———. 1986. Notas para el estudio etnohistórico de los esclavos Lucumí de Cuba. *Anales del Caribe* 6:55–74.

———. 1987. Las religiones de origen africano en Cuba: Tiempos y conjugaciones. Unpublished paper.

———. 1994. Cabildos de Africanos y religiones afro-cubanas: Un nuevo enfoque. Unpublished paper.

Lucas, J. Olumide. 1948. *The religion of the Yorubas, being an account of the religious beliefs and practices of the Yoruba peoples of southern Nigeria, especially in relation to the religions of ancient Egypt*. Lagos: CMS Bookshops.

Lumsden, Ian. 1996. *Machos, maricones, and gays: Cuba and homosexuality*. Philadelphia: Temple University Press.

Lunsingh, Scheurleer, D. F. [1966] 1974. *Chinese export porcelain*. London: Faber and Faber.

MacGaffey, Wyatt. 1983. *Modern Kongo prophets: Religion in a plural society*. Bloomington: Indiana University Press.

———. 1986. *Religion and society in Central Africa: The religion of the Bakongo of Lower Zaire*. Chicago: University of Chicago Press.

Marks, Morton. 1974. Uncovering ritual structures in Afro-American music. In *Religious movements in contemporary America*, ed. Irving I. Zaretsky and Mark P. Leone, 60–134. Princeton, N.J.: Princeton University Press.

———. 1982. You can't sing unless you're saved: Reliving the call in gospel music. In *African religious groups and beliefs: Papers in honor of William Bascom*, ed. Simon Ottenberg, 305–31. Delhi: Folklore Institute.

———. 1987. Exploring El Monte: Ethnobotany and the Afro-Cuban science of the concrete. In *En torno a Lydia Cabrera (cincuentenario de "cuentos negros de cuba," 1936–1986)*, ed. Isabel Castellanos and Josefina Inclán, 227–44. Miami: Ediciones Universal.

Marrero, Levi. 1986. *Cuba, economía y sociedad*. Vol. 13. Río Piedras, Puerto Rico: Editorial San Juan.

———. 1988. *Cuba, economía y sociedad: Azúcar, ilustración y conciencia (1763–1868)*. Vol. 14. Madrid: Editorial Playor.

Marshall, Paule. 1983. *Praisesong for the widow*. New York: G. P. Putnam's Sons.

Martínez-Alier, Verena. [1974] 1989. *Marriage, class, and colour in nineteenth century Cuba: A study of racial attitudes and sexual values in a slave society*. Ann Arbor: University of Michigan Press.

Martínez Furé, Rogelio. 1979. *Diálogos imaginarios*. Havana: Editorial Arte y Literatura.

Marx, Karl. 1976. *Capital: A critique of political economy*. Vol. 1. Translated by Ben Fowkes. New York: Vintage Books.

Mason, John. 1985a. *Black gods: Orișa studies in the New World*. Brooklyn, N.Y.: Yoruba Theological Archministry.

———. 1985b. *Four New World Yoruba rituals*. Brooklyn, N.Y.: Yoruba Theological Archministry.

———. [1985] 1993. *Four New World Yoruba rituals*. 3d ed. Brooklyn, N.Y.: Yoruba Theological Archministry.

———. 1992. *Orin òrìsà: Songs for selected heads*. Brooklyn, N.Y.: Yoruba Theological Archministry.

———. 1994. Yoruba-American art: New rivers to explore. In *The Yoruba artist: New theoretical perspectives on African arts*, ed. Rowland Abiodun, Henry J. Drewal, and John Pemberton III, 241–50. Washington, D.C.: Smithsonian Institution Press.

———. 1996. *Olóòkun: Owner of rivers and seas*. Brooklyn, N.Y.: Yoruba Theological Archministry.

Mason, John, and Gary Edwards. 1981. *Onje fun orisa (Food for the gods)*. New York: Yoruba Theological Archministry.

Mason, Michael Atwood. 1993. The blood that runs in the veins: The creation of identity and a client's experience of Cuban-American dilogún divination. *Drama Review* 37 (summer): 119–30.

———. 1994. "I bow my head to the ground": The creation of bodily experience in a Cuban-American Santería initiation. *Journal of American Folklore* 106 (423–24): 1–17.

———. 1997. Practicing Santería, performing the self: The social construction of subjectivity in humans and gods in an Afro-Cuban religion. Ph.D. diss., Indiana University.

———. 2002. *Living Santeria: Rituals and Experiences in an Afro-Cuban Religion*. Washington, D.C.: Smithsonian Institution Press.

Matory, James Lorand. 1986. Vessels of power: The dialectical symbolism of power in Yoruba religion and polity. M.A. thesis, University of Chicago, Department of Anthropology.

———. 1988. Homems montados: Homossexualidade e simbolismo da possão nas religiões afro-brasileiras. In *Escravidão e invençāo da liberdade: Estudos sobre o negro no Brasil*, ed. João José Reis, 215–31. Sao Paulo: Editora Brasiliense.

———. 1991a. Futures in "blood" and money: The initiation of the Santo possession priest in a post-modern era. Unpublished paper, 15 September.

———. 1991b. Sex and the empire that is no more: A ritual history of women's power among the Oyo-Yoruba. 2 vols. Ph.D. diss., University of Chicago, Department of Anthropology.

———. 1994. *Sex and the empire that is no more: Gender and the politics of metaphor in Oyo Yoruba religion*. Minneapolis: University of Minnesota Press.

———. 1998. Yoruba imperialism and the Americanization of Africa: On the rhizomatic roots of the contemporary "Yoruba revival" in the United States. Paper presented to colloquium, Religion outside the Institutions, Center for the Study of Religion, Princeton University, 5–7 June.

———. 1999. The English professors of Brazil: On the diasporic roots of the Yoruba nation. *Comparative Studies in Society and History* 41, no. 1:72–103.

———. Forthcoming. *The transatlantic nation: Tradition, transnationalism, and matriarchy in Afro-Brazilian Candomblé.* Princeton, N.J.: Princeton University Press.

McAlister, Elizabeth. 1995. "Men Moun Yo," "Here are the people": Rara festivals and transnational popular culture in Haiti and New York City. Ph.D. diss., Yale University.

———. 2002. *Rara! Vodou, power, and performance in Haiti and its diaspora.* Berkeley: University of California Press.

McDonald, Roderick A. 1993. *The economy and material culture of the slaves: Goods and chattels on the sugar plantations of Jamaica and Louisiana.* Baton Rouge: Louisiana State University Press.

McElroy, Guy C. 1990. *Facing history: The black image in American art, 1710–1940.* Washington, D.C.: Bedford Arts and Corcoran Gallery of Art.

Melion, Walter. 1992. Piety and pictorial manner in Hendrick Goltzius's early life of the Virgin. In *Hendrick Goltzius and the classical tradition,* exhibition catalog, ed. G. Harcourt, 44–51. Los Angeles: Fisher Gallery and University of Southern California Press.

Menéndez, Lázara. 1998. Libreta de Santería de María Antoñica Fines, Libreta de Santería de Jesús Torregrosa. In *Estudios afrocubanos: Selección de lecturas,* ed. Lázara Menéndez, 3:17–268. Havana: Facultad de Arte y Letras, Universidad de la Habana.

Métraux, Alfred. [1959] 1972. *Voodoo in Haiti.* Translated by Hugo Charteris. New York: Schocken Books.

Miahle, Pierre Toussaint Frédéric. 1838. *Album pintoresco de la isla de Cuba.* Berlin: Storch and Kramer.

Mintz, Sidney W. 1974a. Afro-Caribbeana: An introduction. In *Caribbean transformations,* 1–42. Baltimore: Johns Hopkins University Press.

———. 1974b. The origins of the Jamaican market system. In *Caribbean transformations,* 180–214. Baltimore: Johns Hopkins University Press.

Mintz, Sidney W., and Richard Price. 1976. *An anthropological approach to the Afro-American past: A Caribbean perspective.* Occasional Papers in Social Change, no. 2. Philadelphia: Institute for the Study of Human Issues.

———. [1976] 1992. *The birth of African-American culture: An anthropological perspective.* Boston: Beacon Press.

Miralda, Antonio, and John Mason. 1985. *Santa comida/holy food.* Exhibition catalog. New York: El Museo del Barrio.

Moore, Carlos. 1986. "Congo or Carabalí": Race relations in socialist Cuba. *Caribbean Review* 15, no. 2 (spring): 12–15, 43.

———. 1988. *Castro, the blacks, and Africa.* Los Angeles: Center for Afro-American Studies.

Moore, Robin. 1994. Representations of Afrocuban expressive culture in the writings of Fernando Ortiz. *Latin American Music Review* 15 (spring–summer): 32–54.

———. 1997. *Nationalizing blackness:* Afrocubanismo *and artistic revolution in Havana, 1920–1940.* Pittsburgh: University of Pittsburgh Press.

Moore, Sally F., and Barbara G. Myerhoff. 1977. Introduction: Secular ritual: Forms and meanings. In *Secular ritual,* ed. Sally F. Moore and Barbara G. Myerhoff, 3–24. Amsterdam: Van Gorcum.

Morales, Beatriz. 1990. Afro-Cuban religious transformation: A comparative study of Lucumi religion and the tradition of spirit belief. Ph.D. diss., City University of New York.

Moreno Vega, Marta. 2000. *The altar of my soul: The living traditions of Santería.* New York: Ballantine, One World.

Morton-Williams, Peter. 1964. An outline of the cosmology and cult organization of the Oyo Yoruba. *Africa* 34, no. 3:243–61.

Mosquera, Gerardo. 1996. Elegguá at the (post?)modern crossroads: The presence of Africa in the visual arts of Cuba. In *Santería aesthetics in contemporary Latin American art,* ed. A. Lindsay, 225–58. Washington, D.C.: Smithsonian Institution Press.

Mullen, Edward J. 1987. Los negros brujos: A reexamination of the text. *Cuban Studies* 17:111–32.

Murphy, Joseph. 1981. Ritual systems in Cuban Santería. Ph.D. diss., Temple University.

———. 1988. *Santería: An African religion in America.* Boston: Beacon Press.

———. 1994. *Working the spirit: Ceremonies of the African Diaspora.* Boston: Beacon Press.

Museum of Arts and Sciences. 1988. *Salon and picturesque photography in Cuba 1860–1920: The Ramiro Fernández collection.* Daytona Beach, Fla.

Museum of Decorative Arts. n.d. Exhibition brochure. Havana.

Nelson, Robert S. 1996. Appropriation. In *Critical terms for art history,* ed. Robert S. Nelson and Richard Shiff, 116–28. Chicago: University of Chicago Press.

New York: Fifty-two "sacrifice animals" are siezed by police. 1983. *Miami Herald,* 18 September.

N. G. La Banda. 1992. *Échale Limón.* Compact disk. Havana: Artex.

Nina Rodrigues, Raimundo. 1945. *Os Africanos no Brasil.* 3d ed. Sao Paulo: Companhia Editôra Nacional.

Núñez, Luis Manuel. 1992. *Santería: A practical guide to Afro-Caribbean magic.* Dallas: Spring Publications.

Nunley, John, and Judith Bettelheim, eds. 1988. *Caribbean festival arts: Each and every bit of difference.* Exhibition catalog. St. Louis: St. Louis Art Museum; Seattle: University of Washington Press.

Oduyoye. Modupe. 1971. *The vocabulary of Yoruba religious discourse.* Ibadan: Daystar Press.

Offner, Richard. 1950. Guido da Siena and A.D. 1221. *Gazette des Beaux Arts,* 6th ser., 37:51–90.

Ofún Yemiló. 1994. *Tratado de Ochosi.* Regla, Havana: Ilé Adé Yerí.

———. 1997. *Tratados Enciclopédicos de Caminos de Ifá.* 17 vols. Regla, Havana: Ilé Adé Yerí.

Ojo, G. J. Afolabi. 1966. *Yoruba culture: A geographical analysis.* London: University of Ife and University of London Press.

Omari, Mikelle Smith. 1984. *From the inside to the outside: The art and ritual of the Bahian Candomblé.* Monograph Series of the Museum of Cultural History, no. 24. Los Angeles: Museum of Cultural History, UCLA.

———. 1991. Completing the circle: Notes on African art, society, and religion in Oyotunji, South Carolina. *African Arts* 24 (July): 66–75, 96.

Orishas. 1999. *A lo cubano.* EMI compact disk CD7243 522052 2 6.

Orsi, Robert. 1985. *The madonna of 115th street: Faith and community in Italian Harlem, 1880–1950.* New Haven, Conn.: Yale University Press.

Ortiz, Fernando. [1906] 1973. *Los negros brujos: Apuntes para un estudio de etnología criminal.* Miami: Ediciones Universal.

———. [1916] 1987. *Los negros esclavos.* Havana: Editorial de Ciencias Sociales.

———. [1920] 1960. *La antigua fiesta afrocubana del "día de reyes."* Havana: Ministerio de Relaciones Exteriores, Departamento de Asuntos Culturales, División de Publicaciones. Originally published in *Revista Bimestre Cubana* 15, no. 1:5–26.

———. 1921. Los cabildos Afrocubanos. *Revista Bimestre Cubana* 16 (January–February): 5–39.

———. [1923] 1983. *Nuevo catauro de cubanismos.* Havana: Editorial de Ciencias Sociales.

———. 1924. *Glosario de afronegrismos.* Havana: Imprenta "El Siglo XX."

———. [1926–28] 1986. *Los negros curros.* Havana: Editorial de Ciéncias Sociales.

———. 1927. Los negros curros. *Archivos del Folklore Cubano* 2, no.4 (June): 285–325.

———. 1928. Los negros curros. *Archivos del Folklore Cubano* 3, no.2 (April–June): 160–75.

———. 1937a. La música sagrada de los negros yorubas en Cuba. *Ultra* 3, no. 13:77–86.

———. 1937b. Brujos o santeros. *Estudios Afrocubanos* 3, no 3:85–90.

———. 1950. *La africanía de la música folklórica de Cuba.* Havana: Ministerio de Educación, Dirección de Cultura.

———. [1951] 1985. *Los bailes y el teatro de los negros en el folklore de Cuba.* Habana: Editorial Letras Cubanas. Original publication, Havana: Ediciones Cárdenas.

———. 1952–55. *Los instrumentos de la música afrocubana.* 5 vols. Havana: Publicaciones de la Dirección de la Cultura del Ministerio de Educación.

———. 1953. Dos "diablitos" de Landaluze. *Bohemia* 45, no. 44:36–38, 99–101.

Ortiz, Renato. 1989. Ogun and the Umbandista tradition. In *Africa's Ogun: Old World and New,* ed. Sandra Barnes, 90–102. African Systems of Thought series. Bloomington: University of Indiana Press.

Oxum, Carlinhos d'. 1997. *Cânticos aos* orixás *de Candomblé.* Rio de Janeiro: Natasha Records.

Oyotunji brochure. n.d., n.p..

Palmer, Arlene. 1976. *A Winterthur guide to Chinese export porcelain.* New York: Winterthur and Routledge.

Palmié, Stephan. [1988]. Santería and the contest of cultures in South Florida. Unpublished paper.

———. 1989. Ethnogenetic processes and cultural transfer in Afro-American slave populations. Unpublished conference paper.

———. [1990]. "Kulturkamf" in South Florida: The case of the Church of the Lukumi Babalu Ayé. Paper presented at the meeting of the Gesellschaft für Karibikforschung, Vienna, 20–23 June.

———. 1991. *Das Exil der Götter: Geschichte un Vorstellunswelt einer afrokubanischen Religion.* Frankfurt: Peter Lang.

———. 1993. Ethnogenetic processes and cultural transfer in Afro-American slave populations. In *Slavery in the Americas,* ed. Wolfgang Binder, 337–63. Würtzburg: Königshausen Un Neumann.

———. 1994. Some notes on space, time, and units of analysis in the historiography of Ekpe/Abakuá. Paper presented at the Centre for African Studies and Latin American Studies Centre, University of London, October 7.

———. 1995. Against syncretism: "Africanizing" and "Cubanizing" discourses in North American *òrìsà* worship. In *Counterworks: Managing the diversity of knowledge,* ed. Richard Fardon, 73–104. London: Routledge.

———. 1996. Which center, whose margin? Notes toward an archeology of US Supreme Court case 91-948, 1993. In *Inside and outside the law: Anthropological studies of authority and ambiguity,* ed. Olivia Harris, 184–209. London: Routledge.

———. 2000. Una salación científica: The work of witchcraft and science in Cuban modernity. Paper presented to the Black Atlantic Seminar of the Rutgers Center for Historical Analysis, 14 October.

———. 2002. *Wizards and scientists: Explorations in Afro-Cuban modernity and tradition.* Chapel Hill, N.C.: Duke University Press.

Panofsky, Erwin. [1934] 1995. What is Baroque? In *Three essays on style,* ed. Irving Lavin. Cambridge, Mass.: MIT Press.

———. 1955. Iconography and iconology: An introduction to the study of Renaissance art. In *Meaning in the visual arts,* 26–54. Garden City, N.Y.: Doubleday, Anchor.

Parrinder, Geoffrey. 1949. *West African Religion.* London: Epworth.

Peacock, John. 1991. *The chronicle of Western fashion: From ancient times to the present day.* New York: Harry N. Abrams Publishers.

Pearse, Andrew. [1956] 1988. Carnival in nineteenth-century Trinidad. In *Trinidad carnival: A republication of the Caribbean Quarterly Trinidad carnival issue, vol. 4, numbers 3 and 4 of 1956,* 4–41. Port of Spain: Paria Publishing Company.

Pemberton, John, III. 1975. Eshu-Elegba: The Yoruba trickster god. *African Arts* 9 (October): 20–27, 66–70, 90 92.

———. 1989. The dreadful god and the divine king. In *Africa's Ogun: Old World and New,* ed. Sandra Barnes, 105–46. African Systems of Thought series. Bloomington: Indiana University Press.

Pemberton, John, III, and Funso S. Afolayan. 1996. *Yoruba sacred kingship: "A power like that of the gods."* Washington, D.C.: Smithsonian Institution Press.

Pérez, Louis A. 1988. *Cuba: Between reform and revolution.* New York: Oxford University Press.

Pichardo, Ernesto. 1989a. *Lukumí dialect and herbs.* Miami: Church of the Lukumí, Babalú Ayé.

———. 1989b. *Lukumí Ebó and prayers/oraciones y ebó Lukumí.* Public Education in the Yoruba Religion series, no. 2, booklet 2. Miami: Church of the Lukumí, Babalú Ayé.

Pichardo, Ernesto, and Lourdes Nieto. 1984. *Odudúwa/Obatalá.* Miami: St. Babalú Ayé, Church of the Lukumí.

Piersen, William D. 1988. *Black Yankees: The development of an Afro-American subculture in eighteenth-century New England.* Amherst: University of Massachusetts Press.

Pietz, William. 1996. Fetish. In *Critical terms for art history,* ed. Robert S. Nelson and Richard Shiff, 197–207. Chicago: University of Chicago Press.

Podro, Michael. 1982. *The critical historians of art.* New Haven, Conn.: Yale University Press.

Polk, Patrick. 1995. *Sacred banners and the divine cavalry charge.* In *Sacred arts of Vodou,* ed. Donald Cosentino, 325–47. Los Angeles: Fowler Museum of Cultural History.

Powell, Richard J. 1997. *Black art and culture in the twentieth century.* London: Thames and Hudson.

———. 2000. Sartor africanus. Paper presented at the Black Atlantic/African Diaspora Seminars, Rutgers Center for Historical Analysis, 20 April.

Price, Jacob M. 1991. Summation: The American panorama of Atlantic port cities. In *Atlantic port cities: Economy, culture, and society in the Atlantic world, 1650–1850,* ed. Franklin W. Knight and Peggy K. Liss, 262–76. Knoxville: University of Tennessee Press.

Price, Richard. 1972. Saramaka onomastics: An Afro-American naming system. *Ethnology* 11:241–67.

———. 1983. *First time: The historical vision of an Afro-American people.* Baltimore: Johns Hopkins University Press.

———. 1990. *Alabi's world.* Baltimore: Johns Hopkins University Press.

Price, Sally, and Richard Price. 1980. *Afro-American arts of the Suriname rain forest.* Los Angeles: Museum of Cultural History and University of California Press.

Provincia de la Habana, fincas urbanas, Ayuntamiento de Regla. Fol. 492, no. 32, November 1900. Archives of the Museum of Regla.

Quintana, Steve. 1986. Calendario 1986. *Cultural Magazine,* no. 1 (May–June).

Rabinow, Paul. 1977. *Reflections on fieldwork in Morocco.* Berkeley: University of California Press.

———. 1986. Representations are social facts: Modernity and post-modernity in anthropology. In *Writing culture: The poetics and politcs of ethnography,* ed. James Clifford and George E. Marcus, 234–61. Berkeley: University of California Press.

Raboteau, Albert J. 1978. *Slave religion: The invisible institution in the ante-bellum South.* Oxford: Oxford University Press.

———. 1983. "Ethiopia shall soon stretch forth her hands": Black destiny in nineteenth-century America. University Lecture in Religion at Arizona State University, Tempe, Ariz., 27 January, 1983.

Ramos, Miguel "Willie." 1982a. *Ase omo Osayin, ewe aye.* Carolina, Puerto Rico: n.p.

———. 1982b. *Ceremonias de Obaluaye.* Carolina, Puerto Rico: n.p.

———. 1982c. *Dida obi: Adivinación a través del coco.* Carolina, Puerto Rico: n.p.

———. 1982d. *Oro egungun: Honras de egungun.* Carolina, Puerto Rico: n.p.

———. 1996. Afro-Cuban orisha worship. In *Santería aesthetics in contemporary Latin American art*, ed. Arturo Lindsay, 51–76. Washington, D.C.: Smithsonian Institution Press.

Rampersad, Arnold. 1992. Introduction. In *The new Negro: Voices of the Harlem Renaissance*, ix–xxiii. New York: Atheneum.

Ranger, Terrence. 1983. The invention of tradition in colonial Africa. In *The invention of tradition*, ed. Eric Hobsbawm and Terrence Ranger. Cambridge: Cambridge University Press.

Rawick, George. 1972. *The American slave: A composite autobiography*. Vol. 1, *From sundown to sun up: The making of the black community*. Westport, Conn.: Greenwood.

Reisman, Karl. 1970. Cultural and linguistic ambiguity in a West Indian village. In *Afro-American anthropology: Contemporary perspectives*, ed. John F. Szwed and Norman Whitten, 129–42. New York: Free Press.

Riis, Jacob. [1890] 1971. *How the other half lives*. New York: Dover.

Roberts, John Storm. [1979] 1985. *The Latin tinge: The impact of Latin American music on the United States*. Tivoli, N.Y.: Original Music.

Robinson, Armstead L., Craig C. Foster, and Donald H. Ogilvie, eds. 1969. *Black studies in the University: A symposium*. New Haven, Conn.: Yale University Press.

Robreño, Gustavo. 1925. *La Acera de la Louvre: novela histórica*. Havana: Imprenta y Papelería de Rambla, Bauza y Ca.

Roche y Monteagudo, Rafael. 1908. *La policía y sus misterios*. Havana: Imprenta "La Prueba."

———. [1908] 1925a. *La policía y sus mist e rios*. Havana: n.p.

———. [1908] 1925b. Los Ñañigos: Su origen y progresos. In *La policía y sus mistérios*, 1–154. Havana: n.p.

Rodríguez, Alejandro. 1881. Reseña histórica de los ñáñigos de Cuba desde su creación hasta la fecha. Handwritten ledger manuscript.

Rodríguez Herrera, Esteban. 1958–59. *Léxico mayor de Cuba*. 2 vols. Havana: Editorial Lex.

Rogers, Andrés R. 1973. *Los caracoles: Historia de sus letras*. Washington, D.C.: Rico Publishing.

Rogg, Eleanor, and Rosemary Cooney. 1980. *Adaptation and adjustment of Cubans: West New York, New Jersey*. New York: Hispanic Research Center.

Rohlehr, Gordon. 1990. *Calypso and society in pre-independence Trinidad*. Port of Spain: Gordon Rohlehr.

Roig de Leuchsenring, Emilio. 1950. *Banderas oficiales y revolucionarias de Cuba*. Havana: Oficina del Historiador de la Ciudad de La Habana.

Rolando, Gloria. 1992. *Un eterno presente: Oggún*. Video. Havana: ICAIC. For distribution, see www.afrocubaweb.com/gloriarolando/html.

Rosaldo, Renato. 1980. *Ilonglot headhunting, 1883–1974: A study in society and history*. Stanford. Calif.: Stanford University Press.

Rosengarten, Theodore, comp. [1974] 2000. *All God's dangers: The life of Nate Shaw*. Chicago: University of Chicago Press.

Royal Museum of Fine Arts. 1992. *America, bride of the sun: Five hundred years, Latin America and the Low Countries*. Exhibition catalog. Antwerp: Imschoot Books and Royal Museum of Fine Arts.

Saco, José Antonio. [1832] 1946. *La vagancia en Cuba*. Havana: Publicaciones del Ministerio de Educación.

Said, Edward W. 1983. *The world, the text, and the critic*. Cambridge, Mass.: Harvard University Press.

Salvucci, Linda K. 1991. Supply, demand, and the making of a market: Philadelphia and Havana at the beginning of the nineteenth century. In *Atlantic port cities: Economy, culture, and society in the Atlantic world, 1650–1850*, ed. Franklin W. Knight and Peggy K. Liss, 40–57. Knoxville: University of Tennessee Press.

Sánchez, Julio. 1978. *La religión de las orichas: Creencias y ceremonias de un culto afro-caribeño*. Hato Rey, Puerto Rico: n.p.

Sarno, Gerardo. 1978. *Iawo*. Film. Distributed by the Cinema Guild, New York (www.cinemaguild.com).

Sarracino, Rodolfo. 1988. *Los que volvieron a Africa*. Havana: Editorial de Ciencias Sociales.

Schechner, Richard. 1985. *Between theater and anthropology*. Philadelphia: University of Pennsylvania Press.

Schoemaker, George H. 1994. Mai '68 and the traditionalization of French shadow theatre. *Journal of American Folklore (JAF)* 197, no. 425: 364–77.

Schomburg, Arthur. [1925] 1992. The Negro digs up his past. In *The new Negro: Voices of the Harlem Renaissance*, ed. Alain Locke, 231–37. New York: Atheneum.

Scott, David. 1991. That event, this memory: Notes on the anthropology of African diasporas in the New World. *Diaspora* 1 (winter): 261–84.

Scott, Julius Sherrard, III. 1986. The common wind: Currents of Afro-American communication in the era of the Haitian Revolution. Ph.D. diss., Duke University.

Scott, Rebecca Jarvis. 1985. *Slave emancipation in Cuba: The transition to free labor, 1860–1899*. Princeton, N.J.: Princeton University Press.

Shryock, Andrew. 1997. *Nationalism and the genealogical imagination: Oral history and textual authority in tribal Jordan*. Berkeley: University of California Press.

Siliman, Monfundi. n.d. *Proclama: Que en un Cabildo de negros congos de la ciudad de la Havana, pronunció su Presidente Rey Monfundi Siliman, un domingo por la tarde con motivo de la llegada de Cádiz del navío San Justo.* Manuscript group no. 1350, ser. III, fiche no. 89 (ID 801 2735). Latin American Pamphlet Collection, Yale University Library, New Haven, Conn.

Simmel, Georg. 1950. *The sociology of Georg Simmel.* Edited by Kurt Wolff. New York: Free Press.

Simpson, George Eaton. 1978. *Black religions in the New World.* New York: Columbia University Press.

Slotkin, Richard. 1985. Myth and ideology. In *The fatal environment: The myth of the frontier in the age of industrialization, 1800–1890,* 21–32. New York: Atheneum.

Smith, Henry Nash. 1950. *Virgin land: The American West as symbol.* New York: Vintage Books.

Smith, M. G. 1957. The African heritage in the Caribbean. In *Caribbean studies: A symposium,* ed. Vera Rubin, 34–122. Jamaica: Institute of Social and Economic Research, University College of the West Indies.

———. 1963. *Dark Puritan.* Kingston: University of the West Indies.

Smith, Michael P. 1984. *Spirit world: Pattern in the expressive folk culture of Afro-American New Orleans.* Baton Rouge: Louisiana State Museum.

———. 1994. *Mardi Gras Indians.* Gretna, La.: Pelican Publishing.

Smith, Robert S. 1969. *Kingdoms of the Yoruba.* London: Methuen.

Smith, Theophus H. 1989. The spirituality of African-American traditions. In *Christian spirituality: Post-Reformation and modern,* ed. Louis Dupré and Don E. Saliers. World Spirituality: An Encyclopedic History of the Religious Quest, no. 18. New York: Crossroad.

Sosa Rodríguez, Enrique. 1982. *Los Ñáñigos.* Havana: Ediciones Casa de Las Américas.

Southern, Eileen. 1971. *The music of black Americans: A history.* New York: W. W. Norton.

Spitzer, Nicolas R. 1986. Zydeco and Mardi Gras: Creole identity and performance genres in rural French Louisiana. Ph.D. diss., University of Texas at Austin.

Stack, Carol. 1974. *All our kin: Strategies for survival in a black community.* New York: Harper and Row.

Stepto, Robert. 1979. *From behind the veil: A study of Afro-American narrative.* Urbana: University of Illinois Press.

Stewart, Charles, and Rosalind Shaw. 1994. *Syncretism/anti-syncretism: The politics of religious synthesis.* London: Routledge.

Stuckey, Sterling. 1987. *Slave culture: Nationalist theory and the foundations of black America.* New York: Oxford University Press.

Suchlicki, Jaime. 2001. *Historical dictionary of Cuba.* Latin American Historical Dictionaries, no. 27. 2d ed. Lanham, Md.: Scarecrow Press.

Sudarkasa, N. 1973. *Where women work: A study of Yoruba women in the marketplace and in the home.* Anthropology Papers, Museum of Anthropology, no. 53. Ann Arbor: University of Michigan.

Sylvain, Suzanne. 1936. *Le créole haitien: Morphologie et syntaxe.* Port-au-Prince: Wetteren.

Szwed, John F. 1969. An American anthropological dilemma: The politics of Afro-American culture. In *Reinventing anthropology,* ed. Dell Hymes, 153–81. New York: Pantheon.

Szwed, John F., and Roger D. Abrahams, eds. 1978. *Afro-American folk culture: An annotated bibliography of materials from North, Central, and South America and the West Indies.* 2 vols. Philadelphia: Institute for the Study of Human Issues.

Szwed, John F., and Norman Whitten, eds. 1970. *Afro-American anthropology: Contemporary perspectives.* New York: Free Press.

Taussig, Michael. 1980. *The devil and commodity fetishism in South America.* Chapel Hill: University of North Carolina Press.

———. 1987. *Shamanism, colonialism, and the wild man: A study in terror and healing.* Chicago: University of Chicago Press.

Tansey, Richard G., and Fred S. Kleiner. 1996. *Gardner's art through the ages.* Vol. 2, *Renaissance and modern art.* 10th ed. Fort Worth: Harcourt Brace College Publishers.

Thomas, Hugh. 1971. *Cuba: The pursuit of freedom.* New York: Harper and Row.

Thompson, Edward Palmer. 1964. *The making of the English working class.* New York: Pantheon Books.

Thompson, Robert Farris. 1969. African influence on the art of the United States. In *Black studies in the university: A symposium,* ed. Armstead L. Robinson, Craig C. Foster, and Donald H. Ogilvie, 122–70. New Haven, Conn.: Yale University Press.

———. [1969] 1983. African influence on the art of the United States. In *Afro-American folk art and crafts,* ed. William Ferris, 27–66. Jackson: University of Mississippi Press.

———. 1970. The sign of the divine king: An essay on Yoruba bead-embroidered crowns with veil and bird decorations. *African Arts* 3, no. 3:8–17, 74–80.

———. [1971] 1976. *Black gods and kings: Yoruba art at UCLA.* Bloomington: Indiana University Press.

———. 1973. Yoruba artistic criticism. In *The traditional artist in African societies,* ed. Warren L. d'Azevedo, 19–61. Bloomington: Indiana University Press.

———. 1974. *African art in motion: Icon and act.* Exhibition catalog. Washington, D.C.: National Gallery of Art; Los Angeles: University of California Press.

———. 1975. Icons of the mind: Yoruba herbalism arts in Atlantic perspective. *African Arts* 8, no. 3:52–59, 89–90.

———. 1983. *Flash of the spirit: African and Afro-American art and philosophy.* New York: Random House.

———. 1984. Ten Haitian paintings: Stage notations for the theatre of God. In *Master painters of Haiti in the collection of Siri von Reis,* 35–49. Exhibition catalog. Rochester, Minn.: Meadow Brook Art Gallery, Oakland University.

———. 1988. Recapturing heaven's glamor. In *Caribbean festival arts: Each and every bit of difference,* ed. John W. Nunley and Judith Bettelheim. Exhibition catalog. St. Louis: St. Louis Art Museum; Seattle: University of Washington Press.

———. 1993. *Face of the gods: Art and altars of Africa and the African-Americas.* Exhibition catalog. New York: Museum of African Art.

———. 1994. The three warriors: Atlantic altars of Esu, Ogun, and Osoosi. In *The Yoruba artist: New theoretical perspectives on African arts,* ed. Rowland Abiodun, Henry Drewal, and John Pemberton III, 225–40. Washington, D.C.: Smithsonian Institution Press.

Thompson, Robert Farris, and Joseph Cornet. 1981. *The four moments of the sun: Kongo art in two worlds.* Exhibition catalog. Washington, D.C.: National Gallery of Art.

Todd, Loreto. 1974. *Pidgins and creoles.* London: Routledge and Kegan Paul.

Tratado de Oddun de Ifá. 1992. Edited by Ofún Oyekún Yemiló. Regla, Havana: Proyecto Orunmila.

Tratado de Odduns de Ifá. n.d.a., n.p. [Havana?].

Tratado de Odduns de Ifá. n.d.b., n.p. [Havana?].

Trescott, Jacqueline. 1992. Haley, the master storyteller whose "Roots" ran very deep. *Washington Post,* 11 February.

Troulliot, Michel-Rolph. 1991. Anthropology and the savage slot: The poetics and politics of otherness. In *Recapturing anthropology: Working in the present,* ed. Richard Fox, 17–44. Santa Fe, N.M.: School of American Research Press.

Trujillo Pardo, Carmen, Miriam Méndez-Plasencia, and Margarita Suárez García [the book mistakenly gives the first author's name as Trujillo-Parte]. n.d. *El museo de arte colonial.* Havana: Editorial Letras Cubanas.

Trujillo y Monagas, D. José. 1882. *Los criminales en Cuba y el inspector Trujillo: Narración de los servicios, prestados en el cuerpo de policía de La Habana.* Barcelona: F. Giró.

Turner, Terence S. 1977. Transformation, hierarchy and transcendance: A reformulation of Van Gennep's model of the structure of rites de passage. In *Secular ritual,* ed. Sally F. Moore and Barbara G. Myerhoff, 53–72. Amsterdam: Van Gorcum.

Turner, Victor W. 1969. *The ritual process: Structure and anti-structure.* Symbol, Myth, and Ritual series. Ithaca, N.Y.: Cornell University Press.

———. 1977. Variations on a theme of liminality. In *Secular ritual,* ed. Sally F. Moore and Barbara G. Myerhoff, 36–52. Amsterdam: Van Gorcum.

———. 1982. *From ritual to theater: The human seriousness of play.* New York: Performing Arts Journal Press.

———. 1983. Carnaval in Rio: Dionysian drama in an industrializing society. In *The celebration of society: Perspectives on contemporary cultural performance,* ed. Frank E. Manning, 103–24. Bowling Green, Ohio: Bowling Green University Popular Press.

———. 1986. *The anthropology of performance.* New York: PAJ Publications.

United States District Court, Southern Division, Miami Division. 1989. *Federal Supplement.* Vol. 723. *Church of the Lukumi Babalu Aye v. City of Hialeah,* 1467–88.

Valdés Garriz, Yrmino. 1988. Es de sabios el rectificar. *Bulletin of CECRY* [Centro de Estudios y Culto Religioso Yoruba] 1 (January–March).

———. 1991. *Ceremonias fúnebres de la Santería afrocubana: Ituto y honras de egun.* San Juan, Puerto Rico: Sociedad de Autores Libres.

———. [1995] 1997. *Dilogún.* Havana: Ediciones Unión.

Van Deburg, William L. 1992. *New day in Babylon: The Black Power movement and American culture, 1965–1975.* Chicago: University of Chicago Press.

van Gennep, Arnold. 1960. *The rites of passage.* Translated by Solon T. Kimball. Chicago: University of Chicago Press.

Vansina, Jan. 1985. *Oral tradition as history.* Madison: University of Wisconsin Press.

Vélez, María Teresa. 1998. *Drumming for the gods: The life and times of Felipe García Villamil, Santero, Palero, and Abakuá.* Philadelphia: Temple University Press.

Verger, Pierre. 1954. *Dieux d'Afrique: Culte des orishas et vodouns à l'ancienne Côte des esclaves en Afrique et a Bahia, la baie de Tous les saints au Bresil.* Paris: P. Hartmann.

———. 1957. *Notes sur le culte des orisa et vodun à Bahia, la baie de Tous les saints, au Brésil et à l'ancienne Côte des esclaves en Afrique.* Memoires de l'Institut français d'Afrique noire, no. 51. Dakar: Ifan Dakar.

———. 1993. *Orixás: Deuses iorubás na Africa e no novo mundo.* Sao Paulo: Corrupio Ediçoes Ltda.

Villaverde, Cirilo. 1996. *Cecilia Valdés.* Havana. Editorial Letras Cubanas. Original manuscript, 1839; original publication, 1879.

Vinueza, María Elena. 1986. *Presencia Arará en la música folclórica de Matanzas.* Havana: Casa de las Américas.

Vlach, John M. [1978] 1990. *The Afro-American tradition in decorative arts.* Cleveland: Cleveland Museum of Art.

Voeks, Robert A. 1997. *Sacred leaves of Candomblé: African magic, medicine, and religion in Brazil.* Austin: University of Texas Press.

Wafer, Jim. 1991. *The taste of blood: Spirit possession in the Brazilian Candomblé.* Philadelphia: University of Pennsylvania Press.

Wafer, Jim, and Hédimo Rodrigues Santana. 1990. Africa in Brazil: Cultural politics and the Candomblé religion. *Folklore Forum* 23, no. 1/2:98–114.

Wardlaw, Alivia J. 1995. *The art of John Biggers: View from the upper room.* New York: Harry N. Abrams; Houston: Museum of Fine Arts.

Washington, Mary Helen. 1981. Afterword. In *Brown girl, brownstones,* by Paule Marshall, 311–25. Old Westbury, N.Y.: Feminist Press.

Waterman, Richard Alan. [1952] 1971. African influence on the music of the Americas. In *Anthropology and art: Readings in cross-cultural aesthetics,* ed. Charlotte Ottenberg, 227–44. Garden City, N.Y.: Natural History Press.

Wetherbee, Jean. 1985. *A second look at white ironstone.* Lombard, Ill.: Wallace Homestead Book Company.

Wexler, Anna. 1997. "I am going to see where my Oungan is": The artistry of a Haitian Vodou flag maker. In *Sacred possessions: Vodou, Santería, Obeah, and the Caribbean,* ed. Margarite Fernandez Olmos and Lizabeth Paravisini-Gebert, 59–78. New Brunswick, N.J.: Rutgers University Press.

White, Deborah Gray. 1999. *Ar'n't I a woman? Female slaves in the plantation South.* New York: W. W. Norton.

White, Hayden. 1973. *Metahistory: The historical imagination in nineteenth-century Europe.* Baltimore: Johns Hopkins University Press.

Williams, Raymond. 1973. *The country and the city.* New York: Oxford University Pres.s

———. [1976] 1983. *Keywords: A vocabulary of culture and society.* New York: Oxford University Press.

———. 1977. *Marxism and literature.* Oxford: Oxford University Press.

Wilmeth, Marlyn Walton, and J. Richard Wilmeth. 1977. Theatrical elements in Voodoo: The case for diffusion. *Journal for the Scientific Study of Religion* 16, no. 1:27–37.

Wilson, William A. 1973. Herder, folklore, and romantic nationalism. *Journal of Popular Culture* 6:818–35.

Wise, Gene. 1979. "Paradigm Dramas" in American Studies: A cultural and institutional history of the Movement. *American Quarterly* 31:293–337.

Woodson, Carter G. [1936] 1968. *The African background outlined or handbook for the study of the Negro.* New York: Negro Universities Press. Original publication, Washington, D.C.: Association for the Study of Negro Life and History.

Wright, Irene. 1910. *Cuba.* New York: Macmillan.

Wurdemann, J. G. F. 1844. *Notes on Cuba: Containing an account of its discovery and early history; a description of the face of the country, its population, resources, and wealth; its institutions, and the manners and customs of its inhabitants, with directions to travellers visiting the island.* Boston: James Munroe.

Zuesse, Evan. 1979. *Ritual cosmos: The sanctification of life in African religions.* Athens, Ohio: Ohio University Press.

INDEX